# Anaïs

by the same author

# Anaïs

## The Erotic Life of Anaïs Nin

## NOËL RILEY FITCH

LITTLE, BROWN AND COMPANY

BOSTON    NEW YORK    TORONTO    LONDON

First Edition

*Library of Congress Cataloging-in-Publication Data*

Fitch, Noël Riley.
  Anaïs : the erotic life of Anaïs Nin / Noël Riley Fitch — 1st ed.
    p.    cm.
  Includes bibliographical references and index.
  ISBN 0-316-28428-9
  1. Nin, Anaïs. 1903–1977. 2. Authors, American — 20th
century — Biography. 3. Women and literature — United States
— History — 20th century. 4. Erotic literature, American —
Women authors — History and criticism. 5. Women authors,
American — Sexual behavior.
  I. Title.
PS3527.I865Z628   1993
818'.5209 — dc20
[B]                                                93-7029

10  9  8  7  6  5  4  3  2  1

MV-NY

*Published simultaneously in Canada*
*by Little, Brown & Company (Canada) Limited*

Printed in the United States of America

For
Albert Sonnenfeld,
with whom I share passion and literature

"There was once a woman who had one hundred faces. She showed one face to each person, and so it took one hundred men to write her biography."
—Anaïs Nin, 20 April 1931,
*The Early Diary of Anaïs Nin,* Volume Four

"The final belief is to believe in a fiction, which you know to be a fiction, there being nothing else."
—Wallace Stevens, *Opus Posthumous*

# Contents

# Anaïs

# Introduction

"I am a writer. I would rather have been a courtesan."

—*Anaïs Nin, 1946*[1]

ANAÏS, Ah·nah·ees. Her name has inspired numerous legends of love and literature and a perfume by the French house of Cacharel.[2] Famous for her erotica and her passionate affair with Henry Miller, Anaïs Nin (1903– 1977) was an artist of life. And of her life she made a book, a diary of some 35,000 pages in 150 volumes, from which she spun poetic novels and short stories. "Like Oscar Wilde," she said, "I put only my art into my work and my genius into my life. . . . I play a thousand roles."[3]

The title of her first novel, *The House of Incest,* and scenes in four pieces of fiction say it all.[4] Senor Joaquin Nin y Castellanos, a distinguished Spanish composer and concert pianist, seduced his daughter. This fact is impossible to prove conclusively, but it is borne out by her subsequent behavior, which fits the classical patterns of a child who has been seduced.[5] She only remembered that he was sadistically cruel to his children, that he told her she was ugly, and that the only affection she received from him before he deserted the family when she was ten was when she posed naked for his photographs: "He always wanted me naked. All admiration came by way of the camera." She learned to seek approval in a sexual way. She sat for "countless pictures" in a prefiguring of the literary disrobing in her diary. In her first childhood diary she pasted one of the nude photographs, apparently unaware that the photograph revealed unusual behavior on her father's part.

In a fragmentary entry in a later diary she writes: "Guilt about exposing the father. Secrets. Need of disguises. Fear of consequences."[6]

When her Don Juan father deserted the family to live with a young woman in France, her mother took the three small children from Barcelona to New York City. On board ship the eleven-year-old Anaïs began her diary as a letter to convince—to charm and seduce—her father to rejoin them. This was always her explanation for the journal, and it has become legend.[7] But she was also creating for herself, in words, a "good girl," one worthy of love, to replace the bad girl who had been rejected by Papa.[8] She was rehabilitating herself in her own eyes, first as a devout Catholic girl, then as a devoted young wife. This portrait, in large part a fictive construct, was her reality: "Nothing exists until it is on paper," she was fond of saying. After rejecting Catholicism, marrying, and returning to France, where she had been born, she was again seduced by her father, this time knowingly sleeping with him at the age of thirty, in July 1933 in Valescure-St.-Raphaël. This time, she left him.

The pattern of seduction seems evident from her life and art, even without her verbal clues.[9] She exhibited both of the extreme responses to abuse. At first, like Emily Dickinson and Virginia Woolf, she hid from it, wounded; then she acted out her secret. She seduced the major father figures in her life, from her husband's professor John Erskine to her two analysts in Paris, Drs. René Allendy and Otto Rank, and Edmund Wilson, at the time the leading New York literary critic. She not only became the bad girl her father desired, she became his double, a Donna Juana. Yet instead of confronting and devouring life, she contained, and obliquely seduced it. Afraid of losing control again, she manipulated people and events in her diary and life. She only partially acknowledged this controlling instinct when she referred in a favorable way to "my obsession with preserving, portraying, recording."[10] When she was thirteen she told her father, "I am nothing but dust. . . . I want to spread myself on a lot of paper, turn into lots of sentences, lots of words so that I won't be walked on."[11]

She wrote in silence and exile, and certainly not without cunning.[12] Her first diary, considerably expurgated, was not published until she was sixty-three years old, and it made literary history both for the genre of autobiography and for the women's movement. Henry Miller, who had read the unexpurgated diary in the 1930s, claimed it would (when fully published) take its place "beside the revelations of St. Augustine, Petronius, Abelard, Rousseau, Proust."[13] Fifty years later, Kate Millett called Nin "a mother to us all" for this "first real portrait of the artist as a woman."[14]

Why does a writer who kept a diary all her life need a biographer? *Because her diary is itself a work of fiction,* an act of self-invention. Untrue confessions. The thirteen volumes so far published are reworked and self-censored versions of a work almost twice that length. Though she claimed that the diary was "untranscribed,"[15] she rewrote, retyped, edited, added dialogue, suppressed key events and people, occasionally reordered the sequence of events, superimposed later judgments on earlier experience, omitted her husband (the man who paid for all this courageous independence), and transformed her life into an art form. In short, her diary is not to be trusted. When Maxwell Geismar, critic and friend, wrote to tell her that her "*real* diaries were a remarkable literary achievement," she put his words on a published volume of what he called her "doctored diaries" without asking; after she died, he called her the "best known diarist since Samuel Pepys" but charged her with being "evasive and mendacious in her literary expression."[16] Her own editor admits, in the introduction to the first published diary, that "Miss Nin's truth . . . is psychological."

The artist, said Stendhal, uses words "to hide and camouflage." So did Anaïs Nin hide from her reader behind a million words, enticing, yet camouflaging herself with a labyrinth of mirrors. A literary striptease. Not unlike the Truth or Dare of American pop icon Madonna, another lapsed Catholic girl. While asserting that the ultimate dare is to tell the truth, they both conceal themselves. One behind the camera, the other behind her expurgated diary.[17]

A lot of people love to hate Anaïs Nin. Much like her first liberator, D. H. Lawrence, she inspires extremes of attack and adoration. Adored by those whose lives have been transformed by her diary, disdained by those who have read only a volume of her erotica—admitted hack work—and pronounce her a bad writer. Is she a saint or sinner? "Madonna of St. Clitoris," as one friend asked, or "Venus with an over-bite"?[18] Her appearance was exotic, her costume always impeccable. One friend described her as embodying a "touch of the geisha, a touch of the governess, and a touch of the Gish sisters."[19] Just the kind of femininity to have raised Simone de Beauvoir's hackles.[20] Gore Vidal, her Judas, wrote delicious, malicious parodies of her and said she "gave self-love a bad name," but he never got over her, writing her into five of his novels.[21] Yet "poets are always Narcissi," said A. W. Schlegel. "Love for oneself is always the beginning of a novelistic life," added Thomas Mann, "for only when one's ego has become a task to be assumed, does writing have any meaning." For every acquaintance who called her calculating, dishonest, humorless, and narcissistic, there are two who testify to her charm, wit, and unselfishness. She belongs, all camps agree, to the dreamers and idealists who take Life and Art and Self seriously.

Even those who knew her best describe her in conflicting terms. Her friend Marguerite Young acknowledged Anaïs's nymphomania, but added, "I think of her as one of the world's great innocents."[22] Lawrence Durrell called her a "diva" with a "shy, virginal side."[23] Though Henry Miller said she "was forever ethereal, forever guileless, forever innocent," he added that she was a "very adept, adroit prevaricator" and "a very ambivalent creature."[24] In her first novel, Nin acknowledges her dual nature: "I would reveal innocence and duplicity, generosity and calculation, fear and cowardice and courage. I want to tell the whole truth, but . . . I would have to write four pages at once. . . ."[25]

She was like Marcel Duchamp's *Nude Descending a Staircase,* a multitude of woman-images. She played many roles and cultivated mystery with veils and mirrors: "I always play roles to appear more powerful, more impressive than I feel."[26]

She was in fact a complex and neurotic artist, in part because she was so long alienated from her own anger and pain. She worked her neuroses out through her art, and it was one of her greatest achievements. "To conceive a fuller life out of deprivation is not an easy task," says a German psychologist.[27] From a shy, hurt girl, she became a courtesan in Paris, then goddess to a group of gay artists in New York, and ended as a guru for the women's movement in Los Angeles. Her art moved from neurosis, in *The House of Incest,* to liberation, in *Seduction of the Minotaur.*

Eventually rejecting the father figures, she sought the intimate and artistic company of a number of young men. "Father betrayed me and I split . . . into a million small relationships," she admitted.[28] Her sexual activity in the 1930s and 1940s was prodigious, and her fear of losing approval, of being rejected, was obsessive.[29] She loved her father's Don Juan game even more than the physical possession itself.[30] During the last twenty-five years of her life she divided her time between two husbands, flying from coast to coast every four to eight weeks. And all the while she was writing, shoring up her reality with words, revealing herself yet hiding in the words. These words were a defense against unconscious knowledge. In her fifty-fourth year she named the key to her behavior:

> Every act related to my writing was connected in me with an act of charm, seduction of my father. . . . Every act from selling a book, accepting a dollar, involving others, was charged with direct sexual associations: courting the world. . . . In my dreams at night I did not achieve a work of art and present the world with it, but I lay naked in bed (with an invisible lover) and all the world could see me.[31]

Art and psychoanalysis in part redeemed her destructive beginning. Psychoanalysis became her religion, for it gave her knowledge, which gave her control of her life. Of course, no life or body of work can be explained by a childhood trauma alone. But in the life and work of Nin it is an essential key to understanding. Initially she turned to art to create a girl and a world in which she could live.[32] She viewed the nature of reality as shifting, complex, and subjective. Self-knowledge and art were the keys to imposing meaning on this reality.

"My writing is *me*," she told Edmund Wilson (and her future biographers), "and my life and writing are one whole, integrated and indivisible unit."[33] Just as she had turned inward in her childhood diary, so her fiction turned to psychological reality, not the "realism" of the traditional novel. She began her fiction with the dream, she said, and often quoted Jung's dictum "Proceed from the dream outward." Yet all her fiction is foreshadowed in her diary, and all her characters are "real." The fiction and all but the last diaries lack historical and cultural context, though they give a full portrait of a woman's interior life.

Though she credited such European influences as Lawrence, Proust, and Dostoyevsky, she is linked as well with her adopted country. Like Thoreau, Emerson, and Whitman, she sought the ideal, questioned material reality, and searched for self. They gave her the American narrative of self-discovery, self-invention, and rebirth. She was an American Eve after the Fall: she never had a clear national identity, and her own history was but buried memory. D. H. Lawrence, subject of her first book, saw that this innocent homelessness is "the true myth of America. She starts old, old, wrinkled and writing in an old skin. And there is a gradual sloughing off of the old skin, towards a new youth. It is the myth of America."[34]

She saw in the world symbols of her internal geography. A child of the Romantic movement, she moved to Paris naive and idealistic, sexually frustrated in an unconsummated marriage, and repressing the memory of her father's seduction. In Paris in the 1930s she fell in love with Henry and June Miller, became sexually compulsive, lived on a houseboat to entertain her lovers, and began her lifelong engagement with psychoanalysis. When she returned to New York City during the war, she was more Henry James's Madame Merle than innocent Isabel Archer, and her lyrical novels were completely out of step with the politically engaged literature of the 1940s.[35] Yet she refused to write according to prevailing trends, refused with the same determination that she used to slowly build her way out of childhood pain. She marched to the beat of her own drummer.

What do women want? Freud asked. His onetime disciple Otto Rank: How do we know the true self of woman unless she keeps a diary for herself? His patient Anaïs Nin kept the lengthiest and most complete record of any developing artistic consciousness. For this reason she has been called by

some the "most important psychologist of women."[36] Her best diaries, from
1914 through about 1939, form a woman's bildungsroman, for it is closer to
an autobiography than to a diary: a diary tries to achieve the illusion of
something approaching immediate, uncensored spontaneity and an audience
of one; the autobiography, on the other hand, is consciously as well as
unconsciously self-censored, edited, and cognizant of the reader's gaze. Her
journal began as her own creation, herself the only audience (she called it
her "shadow," her "mirror," her "confidant," and her "cave"); it was a mirror
reflecting the ideal (she thought it "made the ideal real") and holding off
further painful rejection.[37] Thus it was, initially, more psychologically than
historically true, and more typical of women's than men's diaries, concen-
trating as it does on the private experience rather than public deeds.[38]

After meeting Miller, she felt the tension between her impulse to record
her life as she saw it and her impulse to have it published. The conscious
alterations of the diary increased. Her breaking up and rearranging and
rewriting were not unlike the secondary elaboration or revision of psychoanalysis. Both helped to give or impose meaning on her life and consequently confuse the distinction between fiction and reality.[39] The final volume of her diary was put together by her executor from her letters, travel
writing, character sketches, and reviews; and the public, thinking it her
work, called it self-serving.

An American Proust, Nin has sometimes been called, though self-censorship kept the full fifty-year diary from public view. The childhood diaries are
now available in full, but the complete adult diaries will only eventually
come to us, piecemeal, with separate publication of the expurgated portions
(*Henry and June*, 1986, and *Incest*, 1992, are the first two volumes of this
material to appear). She also wrote more than nine books of poetic fiction
in which she focuses on psychological reality. At its best the fiction is
brilliantly dreamlike, at its worst it is purple sentiment. Her early work
(particularly *House of Incest*—the article was dropped from the title after the
first edition—and *Under a Glass Bell*) is her best, coming out of her neurosis
and edited by her lover Henry Miller. Her "fiction is among the most
neglected substantial literature of the century," claims Benjamin Franklin V,
her bibliographer.[40]

Her place in women's culture and literature has not been fully appreciated, in part because academic feminists are embarrassed by her delicate
feminine personae.[41] She insisted on defining herself as the Ideal Woman
Writer and identified what she saw as the differences between men's and
women's writing. She posited the theory of the unique gift of the woman
artist: in addition to her reason and logic, she has intuition and a genius for
the personal. She is subjective, multitudinous, and unconscious.[42]

Nin's diaries were required reading for millions of introspective young women. Though she became the High Priestess of diary writing and the patron saint of those who seek their own path, who hand-set or pay a vanity press to publish their books and wait for the fame they deserve, she sought in vain to win what Maxine Kumin has called a "vertical audience"—the acceptance of her literary peers. She endured years of critical rejection in part because she persisted in her own fictional voice and technique and in part because her decision to self-censor chopped up her diary and cut her out of her rightful place in literary circles.[43]

There are certain individuals, says the psychoanalyst Erik Erikson, who while resolving their own personal problems serve as paradigms for a large group of people. Nin influenced Henry Miller, Otto Rank, Edmund Wilson, Robert Duncan, Gore Vidal, James Herlihy, Marguerite Young, Henry Jaglom, and Judy Chicago, and her artistic and cultural associations ranged broadly from Paris and New York City to San Francisco and Los Angeles. No woman has left such an extensive record of the inner life of the artist. And no writer has told "the story of woman's sexuality more honestly" than Nin, says Erica Jong.[44] Nin's place in literary history lies in the genre of autobiography, in women's studies, and in explaining the transition between Gertrude Stein and the Beat poets. She is a key figure in illuminating the Age of Aquarius, and the continuing presence she exerts over us tells us something about ourselves: youthful diaries by countless others. A dozen parodies, including Gore Vidal's *Two Sisters* (1970) and *Live from Golgatha* (1992) and Darwin Porter's 346-page novel *Venus* (1982). Six books of criticism. Two dozen university dissertations. A French perfume. A legend.

# CHAPTER ONE

# 1914–1918

# Too Much Reality

"Does anyone know who I am?"
—*Anaïs Nin*, House of Incest[1]

"I create myself."
—*Anaïs Nin*, Incest[2]

H IGH WINDS roil the waters of New York Bay as sheets of rain wash the decks of the *Montserrat*. The ship has been waiting in the harbor since two in the afternoon for the fog to clear before docking. Lightning cuts through the gray sky and seems to strike the murky sea. The Spanish passengers cross themselves and mumble prayers as they huddle in groups in the lounge of the ship.

The sun sets at 7:03 P.M. this Tuesday 11 August 1914 on a world that is dark and stormy. The *New York Times* of the morning had told of French troops facing the Germans in Belgium, of fighting in Alsace, of transports full of refugees fleeing France, and of American writer Owen Wister escaping a German cruiser aboard the *Monnetonka*. Only the ships from Spain and Portugal are still carrying away refugees. The violent thunder and lightning that shakes the Spanish passengers of the *Montserrat* seems an ominous parallel to this political weather.[3]

On deck as the ship finally docks is a tall eleven-year-old girl with a round face and very large eyes that cannot hide her fear. Amid the wicker trunks and bird cages, Anaïs holds her youngest brother's violin case in both arms, shivers in the evening air, and thinks of herself and her family as emigrant artists washed ashore, having lost everything.[4] She stands with her mother, Rosa Culmell de Nin, and her two brothers, Thorvald, who is nine years old, and little Joaquin, named for his father, who will turn six in three weeks. Missing from this scene is the core of Anaïs's heart and family, her father, Joaquin Nin, who had abandoned them in France, near the Spanish border.

She slowly and reluctantly descends from the ship, a steamer named for a mountain northwest of Barcelona, as if it were the last bit of Spain she would see, and thinks of her paternal grandmother, Angela Castellanos de Nin, near whom Anaïs and her family had been living for a year in Barcelona. Awaiting them on the dock is a small contingent of her mother's large Culmell family—Aunt Juana Culmell, Anaïs's godmother, and three Culmell male cousins, undoubtedly brought to help carry the luggage. While her mother and aunt tearfully embrace, Anaïs and her cousins eye one another. Soon Uncle Gilbert Chase (married to Edelmira Culmell) arrives to take Rosa and little Joaquin to his home in Kew Gardens, Queens; separated again from family, Anaïs goes with Thorvald to the apartment of Antolina Culmell de Cardenas, another aunt, in Manhattan.

"Germany Forces French Army Back in Alsace," reads the newspaper Wednesday morning as the clan gathers in domestic safety at the Chase home to plan the relocation of Rosa's little family. The children, including Anaïs, play on the porch and front yard and yell to one another in Spanish, for Anaïs does not know English. She is surrounded by this large extended family of devout Catholic tradition. Her mother is one of seven Culmell siblings, living in New York or Havana.[5] Despite this large maternal Cuban family, Anaïs feels estranged. She is a little girl who has been hurt, the memory of which she suppresses by focusing on the sorrow of her separation from her grandma Nin in Barcelona and her papa, Joaquin, in France, and her fear of this big ugly city. In her diary she draws a little girl dwarfed by tall buildings that lean toward one another, their tops overlapping and closing off the sky and sun. She sees herself as powerless and alone.

She had found solace the day she left Spain for America. Anaïs the writer had been born on the *Montserrat* as it left the Barcelona harbor 25 July 1914. The diary she began that day in phonetic French (for she had never gone to school in France)—and would keep for fifty years—was a matter of survival. Damaged by her father, who had told her she was ugly, beaten her, adored her with his camera lens, and then abandoned the family in 1913, Anaïs needed to create herself as a good girl.[6] To escape things that are painful, said one of her adult friends, "we must reinvent ourselves."[7] The diary would give her character and personality; it would give shape to the fictive person or creation which we, her readers, have come to know as Anaïs Nin. Not that she knew this at eleven, having repressed much of her recent past: "I was eleven years old when I walked into the labyrinth of my diary."[8]

After stops in Valencia, Málaga, and Cádiz, the ship sailed toward New York for thirteen days, during which she turned to writing in little notebooks, recording her impressions, introducing each member of her family, including her father, writing poetry, and describing sites. Her first language was Spanish, but French was the language her Spanish father chose to speak in his professional concert life.[9]

Though she later claimed that she had begun her diary as a letter to her father to tempt him back to the family, the diary itself demonstrates that it was more than this. It put order into her life, gave form to her thoughts and feelings, and became the friend who would accept and remain with her. She used it to nourish her hurt inner child. As a journal keeper, she was a "fabricator" rather than, as was Virginia Woolf, a "searcher"; Anaïs tried on attitudes, applied "experimental touches of clay, paint, and plaster in the work of constructing a satisfactory persona for a self."[10] Each day she gave birth to the girl she wished to be, the good girl.[11] "We write to create a world that is truer than the one before us," she would acknowledge years later. "I am guilty of fabricating a world in which I can live," she will admit when she is forty-three.[12]

All artists make of the chaos about them an order which is their own. Anaïs's chaos—life in at least six countries (with four languages), abuse, and abandonment—is shaped by her diary. She will become addicted to order and control as well as to change, which tests control. Childhood trauma is not the only key to a life or body of work, but these are inevitably entwined for Anaïs, determining both her genre (the diary) and her persistence in fulfilling her goal as an artist.

Thus, she became the author of her own life, the young girl who gave birth to herself. The diary was the perfect means, for, as Freud said, anyone who undertakes autobiography "binds himself to lying, to concealment, to flummery." The diary, recent scholars have emphasized, also enhances the sense of self and breaks the dependence of daughters on families.[13] This hybrid, somewhere between history and fiction, would be the perfect form in which to fabricate a life. And Anaïs's "false self," if successfully realized, would hide the True Self, protecting it from harm.[14] Not surprisingly, many of her first adult stories would begin, "I am an orphan." Usually her protagonist faces great obstacles alone, sailing surrealistically in a boat in a garden—the situation in "Waste of Timelessness" and "Winter of Artifice." This self-creation was more than an artist's desire to create her life; it was her means of survival in a world of conflict and disruption.[15]

One of the first examples of altering the truth for her diary is Anaïs's entry for 13 August 1914: "hurrah for God who has sent us to this earthly Paradise." Later she faces her true feelings and rewrites the experience of the ship moving slowly toward the city as if in "fear" and the buildings hiding "flowers, birds, fields, liberty." The city is superficial, ugly, she adds, like a "prison" or "hell." She confesses her hatred of New York and asks the diary not to tell. For years she longs instead for her father, for the artistic life he lives, and for the life of Europe, and in particular their home just outside Brussels.[16]

On board ship she had been embroidering a Spanish shawl, speaking Spanish to her shipmates, and writing her diary in French. Six months after her arrival, a gentleman at a French cultural gathering tells her that a man who knows two languages is two men. She is already studying French and English. She will be three people.

The persona she cultivates most insistently in her first five years in America is her "French" self. She was born outside Paris when her father was studying music there, and her maternal grandfather was of Danish and French descent. Though she had lived only in Belgium and Spain in the four years before coming to New York, she writes her diary in ungrammatical and misspelled French even after learning English. Her mother had taught her what French Anaïs knew. Within five months of her arrival she declares that she hates "school and everything American." Almost three years later she still insists, "I am French!" All her reading and writing outside the classroom are in French; she is reading Victor Hugo, George Sand, Alexander Dumas, and Alphonse Daudet. Nearly five years later, after taking French classes regularly, she believes she is dreaming in French and "becoming a Parisienne!"[17]

Certainly news of the German wartime oppression of the French fuels her sense of French patriotism, but studying French also keeps her close to her father, who is living and performing in France. She writes to him in French because he cannot speak English. The language also keeps her two brothers from being able to read her diary over her shoulder and sets her apart from her Manhattan classmates. On at least one occasion she believes that her popularity is based on the image she has as a foreigner. She clings to her accent, while her brothers lose theirs. Her English, like her French, is touched by other languages: she flattens her *t*'s the way middle-European speakers do and gutturalizes her *r*'s in the French manner (except at the beginning of syllables, when she pronounces the *r* as a *w*).[18] By the time she is sixteen, the image has become an affectation and the neighbor boys yell *au revoir* as she passes their yards in her white beret. She is nicknamed "White Cap," and the girls shun her.

Rosa enrolls her children in parochial school in New York City to learn

English. It will be the fourth language Anaïs has studied. The schoolchildren laugh when Anaïs speaks each new English word. Soon she hates the smell of the chalk, her yellow desk in the third row, the ugliness of the blackboard, and the "brutality" of the teachers. No wonder she prefers her private French class and confession in the French chapel. She tries to convince some of her classmates of the superiority of France. When they pledge allegiance to the American flag, she proudly exempts herself.

## Dieu, France, Papa

Anaïs belongs in church, where she prays fervently to the Virgin, gives her allegiance to God's Holy Church, nurtures the presence of Jesus in her heart, and longs for sainthood. She is particularly transported during communion, when she partakes of the Body of Christ, for then she feels closest to her father. She imagines him beside her. "Dieu, France, Papa," she whispers—God, France, Daddy.[19]

Though the family weekends include many cousins and aunts at the Chase home in Kew Gardens, she is happiest with her immediate family. She is the typical bossy older sister, her protection resented by Thorvald and welcomed by Joaquinito. It will later hurt their Latin pride that they will never grow taller than her five feet seven inches.[20] "Even as children, she would upstage us all," her youngest brother would remember.[21] Her play with her brothers is creative. They hide under the dining room table where the fringes of the long green cloth hang low, providing security against playful attack. They are Indians in their teepee, looking out for the hostile white men from the dangerous world.

Her closest friend continues to be her diary, to which she turns each day. She calls it her "only friend," her "silent friend," her "inseparable companion" and "mate" for life. Perhaps most important, it is her "mirror."[22] As a creation of her own imagination and control, the diary will not betray her.[23] When she says that her "genuine self" is in the diary, and fears that if the diary burns she will cease to exist, she reveals what recent psychologists call a small "dislocation of the self" from the person writing to the one on the page (a subject and object confusion).[24]

A girl's self-image emerges from the admiration of her father and the example of her mother. Daily Anaïs is reminded by the numerous photographs pasted into each new journal of the one she wishes to please. Yet she has been told by her papa that she is skinny and ugly after early attacks of typhoid and scarlet fever. Her mama tells her she is frail, calls her "dainty little doll from Saint Cloud,"[25] and will not let her play hard. Anaïs prays that she will look like her godmother, Juana Culmell, who is tall, thin, and ash blond, and lives by the sea in Havana without a husband. Once Anaïs had cried when she discovered that the new doll this aunt had brought with her on a visit to Brussels had brown, not blond, curly hair. When Anaïs looks in the mirror she sees a broad forehead of pale apricot skin, brown hair, prominent almond-shaped, brown-green eyes, and a long, slender nose. Her mouth seems pursed over her large set of teeth. The eyes dominate her face and captivate those who meet her. If she smiles broadly, which she rarely does for photographs, the skin above her mouth wrinkles. She has an 1830s face.[26] She is tall—rapidly approaching five feet five inches—but slender as a reed. She will always appear younger and shorter than she is. When she is fourteen she rides the train at Far Rockaway on a children's (twelve-and-under) fare. She thinks of herself as an asparagus stalk and is painfully shy. When she lowers her eyelids, her long black lashes seem to rest on her cheeks. She does not feel at home in her body any more than she does in America. Yet as she moves shyly and gracefully, raising and then lowering her head demurely, one can see an emerging swan.[27]

While her brothers roughhouse outside with firends, Anaïs sits in the window writing and dreaming. The specter that dominates her diary for five years is her missing father. She had loved him when she fell in love with the ship's captain on the voyage to America, and she will continue to love him by falling in love with other men who play the piano or write books or behave as Don Juans.[28] Anaïs pastes a photograph of her father in her diary and writes under it that this is the face of the greatest pianist in the world. One of his formal photographs is signed to his three children, with a signature that reads "J. J. Nin." As inaccessible as God. Father Nin gets mixed up in her prayers to the Holy Father during Mass: "*Au moment de la communion il me semble plutôt embrasser Papa et le recevoir que de recevoir le Bon Dieu* [At the moment of Communion, it seems more as though I am kissing and hugging Daddy, rather than receiving the body of Christ]."[29]

He becomes connected with dreams and reveries, in contrast to the harsh world of her surroundings. He becomes connected with a lost paradise of music, books, art, and travel—a towering ideal. Abused children often idealize their abusers, make excuses for them, even protect them—all behavior that stands in the way of knowledge and anger.[30] He becomes her ideal of the Artist, and she identifies herself with him. Because he is gone, she blames herself for his absence. Because he does not seem to love her, she covets his love more than any other's. She longs for his validation. She longs for him to come and kiss her, put his arms around her. She wants her parents reunited, and transcribes in her diary words from the nuns on Holy Matrimony. Her mother never speaks of official separation or divorce. She is Catholic. Each Christmas Anaïs expects him to come, writes long letters to beseech his return, waits for word of his arrival, and is devastated when he does not appear. Christmas becomes connected with abandonment, not hope.

Her mother does not explain his absence. Her only hint comes when the children do something wrong and she tells them they are like their father, selfish and vain. Soon Anaïs includes her mother in the blame for her father's absence. When her mother says she looks like her father or acts like him, she further identifies herself with him. Unconsciously displacing her mother, she writes long, confiding letters to him (he returns them with the French corrected).

"I do not remember . . . I do not remember . . . I do not remember," she will write in her first novel.[31] Where is the beginning of pain or of memory? The extent to which she can take herself out of her present pain suggests the extent of her pain. Yet her mother's criticisms will slowly help to peel away the memories of her father and the pain he caused her, the quarrels of her parents and their separation. In her story "Stella" years later, she captures the loss of memory that comes to a victim of trauma, who can only "remember" by means of the photographs shown to her by her mother.[32] Pieces of her father's story will crop up in adult analysis and fiction for forty years. Lillian, her protagonist in *Seduction of the Minotaur,* is a "transparent" child whose father wants a boy and spanks his children in the attic—the only time he talks to or touches them. As an adult woman, Lillian finds herself aroused while viewing a pornographic film in which a child's panties are pulled down for a spanking. "Pain had become inextricably mixed with joy at his presence," she realizes, and suddenly understands her quest for pain mixed with pleasure, and why Jay (a character based on Anaïs's onetime lover Henry Miller) satisfies her and Larry (based on Anaïs's husband, Hugo Guiler) does not.[33]

But at this time she does not yet remember the severe beatings that her father had given her, or that he did not want a girl, or his critical displeasure with everything she did. "I never remember a compliment or a caress from him," she would say later.[34] Innocently she had pasted in her first diary, between 31 July and 1 August 1914, a large photograph of herself from the lower abdomen up, holding a big towel up behind her naked body.[35] Only later would she remember the many nude photographs of her that her father took with his camera, the only eye of his attention. Much later, in her creation of Djuna, her strongest fictional alter ego, she presents a child with "enormous fairy-tale eyes" who is sexually violated by the watchman at the orphanage where she lives.[36]

She does not have a childhood, in part because of a loss of memory and in part because of her isolated dreaming. As Henry Miller will observe years later, she never spoke of her childhood experiences or friends, it was like a "lack or a gap."[37] The effect is like a kind of "soul murder," a term used in the nineteenth century by an author writing about Kaspar Hauser, a German boy who had spent fifteen years chained in a cellar.[38] It will become one of Anaïs's favorite stories.

All she remembers now are her "failures" in becoming ill as a child. First there was her typhoid fever in Cuba, after which her father first told her she was ugly, very ugly. Then her illness in Belgium. They had moved to Uccle, a suburb of Brussels, so that her father could be near the violinist Eugene Ysaye to rehearse for a trio (with Pablo Casals on cello). They lived there nearly three years, providing Anaïs with her strongest memories of a European home. She was nine years old and attending a German school when she became ill, was misdiagnosed, and nearly died of peritonitis after a ruptured appendix. She took three months to recover.[39]

To speed her recovery, and in time for Anaïs's tenth birthday, Rosa had taken her three children from Belgium to Arcachon, a resort on the southwest coast of France, where their father was vacationing. Les Ruines resembled a ruined castle out of Edgar Allan Poe, Anaïs would remember, a gloomy setting for the catastrophe she did not know was coming.[40] She remembers the look of displeasure on her father's face when he saw them arrive. Because Anaïs was there to recover from her appendix operation, she believed the displeasure was her fault. She always felt included in his anger and rejection. She could remember years of screaming fights, which terrorized the children. Were they quarreling over his infidelities? Over his treatment of Anaïs? She did not understand. There was fighting at the dinner table and late at night. There were angry words from another room and fearful insecurity. In her diary over the years, Anaïs would go over and over the details of her memories of Brussels and Arcachon, adding bits and pieces, changing some of the details, trying to fill out the impressions, unable to distinguish among what she remembered, what her mother had told her, and what she knew from studying photographs.

After several weeks in Arcachon, and after particularly bitter parental fighting, her father prepared to leave on what he said was another concert tour. Anaïs clung to him hysterically, her thin body trembling. "I'll be back," he promised.[41] But young Anaïs knew that he would not return. She was right.

### Rosa and Joaquin

Rose (Rosa) Culmell and Joaquin Nin had met in a music store in Havana just after the turn of the century. She and one of her sisters had gone to buy sheet music for Rosa's vocal studies when they heard piano music from the back room. It was love at first sight for Rosa; Joaquin eyed her sister. He was well-mannered, handsome, and his blue eyes never missed a young woman. He had returned to Cuba from Barcelona to avoid the military draft (another story has him fleeing the family of a very young girl pupil with whom he had fallen in love), and he was poor and shabby by Culmell standards. But Rosa saw him as an artist, invited him to her father's house, and secured his agreement to tutor her musical voice. Soon they were courting, much to the disapproval of her father, whose sense of class distinction was typical of turn-of-the-century culture. Thorvald Christensen Culmell was the consul of Denmark to Cuba.[42] Nin was poor, and there were hints that he was of Jewish lineage.[43] When Rosa defied her family and married, it was a family disgrace.[44] She was thirty years old, and he was only twenty-two. Rosa was unmarried in part because she had been the mother figure to her four sisters and two brothers when her mother had abandoned her husband and children. With Rosa's money the couple went in 1902 to Paris, where Joaquin studied piano and composition at Schola Cantorum and their daughter, Anaïs, was born.

Anaïs Nin y Culmell was born in Neuilly, a suburb of Paris, at 8:25 P.M., 21 February 1903, the year the first airplane was launched and Picasso painted his first "Blue Period" painting. She was named after her mother, paternal grandmother, and maternal aunts, according to her first published diary: Angela Anaïs Juana Antolina Rosa Edelmira Nin y Culmell. Later she changed the order: Rosa Juana Anaïs Edelmira Antolina Angela Nin. According to the town records of Neuilly-sur-Seine, however, she was born Rose Jeanne Anaïs Edelmira Antolina Nin. On 21 June of that year, while her parents were still living in rue du General-Henrion-Berthier in Neuilly, she was baptized. She could not be christened Anaïs because it was a pagan name and thus illegal in France. The confusion of names is only her first mystery.

Anaïs Nin—pronounced AH•NA•EES NEEN. After Anaitis/Anahita/ Anait, a Syrian war goddess, usually depicted with helmet, shield, and battle-ax, whose worship was introduced into Egypt in the fifteenth century B.C.[45] The Greeks identified her with Athena. Anahita was also known as the moon goddess, victim and judge.[46] Typically, Anaïs would take moon baths just inside her bedroom window during her adolescence. She embraced her unusual name, her French birth, and her birth date. She was born under the sign of Pisces, took the double fish as her symbol, and lived near or on water most of her life.

During the first ten years of her life Anaïs lived in hotels or temporary apartments while her father traveled and performed, supported, while Rosa's father still lived, largely by Culmell money. Consequently, Anaïs had very little formal schooling.[47] Her brother Thorvald was born 12 March 1905 when they were in Havana. During this period in Havana, Anaïs had a severe attack of typhoid. She lost most of her hair, prompting her father to decree her "ugly!" The family moved to St. Cloud, a suburb of Paris; then to Berlin, where her second brother, Joaquin, was born 5 September 1908; then, in 1909, to Cuba, where her father founded a concert society and a music magazine; and finally to Uccle, outside Brussels, Belgium. Here she lived from her seventh to her tenth year, surreptitiously reading in her father's study when he was gone (she wiped her feet before entering), and learning to speak French. She would also remember that her father in anger beat a cat to death and that she disappointed him by becoming ill with appendicitis and then peritonitis (after the operation).

When Joaquin Nin deserted his little family in Arcachon, he went to Brussels and took what he wished from the house. Rosa, abandoned for the second time in her life, left her children in the care of a wealthy Cuban family named Rodriguez and returned to Brussels to seal up what was left in the house. Years later Anaïs would learn that the Rodriguez family had rented the house for Joaquin Nin so that their daughter, Maria Luisa, could study music with him. Maruca, as she was called, was only about six years older than Anaïs and would eventually be Joaquin Nin's mistress.[48] Rosa, when she returned for the children, took them by train to Barcelona, where they moved in temporarily with their grandfather and grandmother Nin just east of the city.

Anaïs was suddenly thrown into the dysfunctional family from which her father had come. Her grandfather, Joaquin Marìa Nin y Tudó, was a stern retired military officer and director of the first non-Catholic school in Spain. He had reared his son with beatings. Anaïs found him tyrannical, cold, and miserly (he counted the beans they ate). Grandmother Angela was a self-sacrificing, browbeaten, but saintly woman who was always held up as a womanly ideal (later Anaïs would claim that this ideal was a "handicap" to her own personal development). Undoubtedly the home was far more oppressive for Rosa, whose independence, social class, and devout Catholicism provoked disdain from her father-in-law.[49]

Anaïs waited for her father's return, but all that arrived were letters of instruction on rearing the children. She wrote poetry, a play about a blind father and his daughter, and dreamed of opening an orphanage when she grew up.[50] When Rosa found a job teaching voice at the Granados Academy of Music, she moved the children to an apartment near the sea in Barcelona. Anaïs and Thorvald had their first Communion 31 August 1913 at their parochial school chapel. She later pasted into her diary a photograph of herself in her white dress and veil, her hands clasped together earnestly. Anaïs would remember a world of blue and white from her balcony in their apartment by the sea. She also remembered the kindly nuns at school, her Catalan studies, writing verse, the love of her grandmother, and her prayers for her father.

A visit from Anaïs's aunt Antolina in 1914 convinced Rosa Nin that New York City would be a better culture for a single mother. Schooling would be free, and her sisters could more easily help with finances.[51] The Culmell sisters had lived in New York, where Rosa was educated at the Brentwood Catholic convent during the years of the Spanish-American War in Cuba. True to the rigorous teaching of the Brentwood nuns, Anaïs's mother did not plan to divorce Joaquin, and she always wore her wedding ring. But the move to America certainly signaled her permanent separation from him.

During their first year in New York, Rosa sings in concerts and takes odd jobs performing professionally and in churches as she struggles to support her children. Her Danish ancestry asserts itself when dire need calls for hard work and self-denial, although the habits of Havana luxury and society occasionally thwart her caution. She and the children live in the apartment, at 166 West Seventy-second Street, belonging to Antolina, who is in Cuba.

## Improving on Reality

While Rosa expands her circle of Cuban musicians, Anaïs retreats into dreams and her diary, seeing the world through her own temperament. Although informed of the war by newspapers and talk in the house, it is her reading of romantic novels that fuels Anaïs's religious sentiments and patriotic furor. She transforms herself into a French girl who believes "her" country is the most beautiful and noble in the world. She longs to be Charlotte Corday (who had stabbed Marat), or Jeanne Hachette (who had beheaded the Burgundian king in 1472). Barring political martyrdom, she will be a religious saint.

The same age as Flaubert's Emma Bovary when her father took her to the convent, Anaïs sees the world in much the same romantic way. Both girls are sensually attracted to religious symbolism, mixing religion and sexuality. Both venerate Joan of Arc and fill their heads with romantic literature. The little Catholic "French" girl, concerned with her sins and imperfections, draws a "staircase" of virtues in her diary, with the failures on the left (anger, impatience, vanity) and the victories on the right (charity, sacrifice, evening prayers). Whether riding the subway with her mother, visiting Riverside Drive with her brothers, or attending the opera, her intellect is curious and piety is her guide.

The one virtue she does not practice is truthfulness. She has a vivid imagination—her brothers call her "Linotte," after *tête de Linotte* (scatterbrain or featherhead)[52]—but she also escapes by withdrawing and by lying.[53]

She tells her school friends that she traveled through Russia on a covered wagon; she sends herself flowers; she tells her aunt Anaïs that her train had been attacked by strikers and blood was shed; she tells an audience at a taped lecture late in her life that she had lived in thirteen countries by her eleventh year; lying becomes a lifetime habit that she excuses by saying that lies for the sake of a beautiful illusion do not taint the soul. They are like costumes.[54] But one of her adult friends calls her a "monstrous liar or prevaricator or fabulator" who could not tell the truth because she could not bear reality: "She had to alter reality to suit her own view of the world."[55] She admits as much: "If I had not created my whole world, I would certainly have died in other people's."[56]

The diary that gave birth to the artist and its good girl is permeated by the romantic temperament of eighteenth- and nineteenth-century romanticism, focusing on imagination, sensibility, individualism, and sentimental melancholy. Impressions are always her "measuring stick." She values the imagination over reason, as do all adolescents, perhaps, but it is a value she never abandons. Later she will say that one should either fight romanticism or become an artist and make the "imagined true." My ideas are "free, they fly away . . . and are full of illusions. . . . I love to dream. I love to leave this harsh world and soar toward the infinite where there is only sweetness." She calls it "up there," where every day is Christmas. "Up there" she can be Joan of Arc rescuing France from the evil Germans or a famous writer elected to the French Academy—both are persistent fantasies.[57]

One night when she is twelve she dreams of opening a heavy door marked "family life" and suffering a sharp pain. Drawn to another door, she finds a great light and the words "Against whom will you fight?" Against the world, she concludes. But she sees a light illuminating the word "life," then sees a dark shadow and awakens perspiring. She interprets the dream as her own struggle between dreaming and wrestling with reality. Which is better? Her soul struggles with the decision, as it will all her life. Two days later she concludes that dreams will be her guide.[58]

Anaïs's response to music illustrates a second aspect of her childhood romanticism. When her mother sings, Anaïs's tears flow and she feels her heart sobbing. Music seems to come from a deep human cry of the heart. She indulges these fits of tears and hours of sadness, savoring her emotionalism and expressing her sentimental belief that she can sympathize with the joys and sorrows of the world. Attendance at daily Mass and Catholic school reinforce the theme of suffering saints and bleeding hearts: "I wept because I had a great desire to be consumed in love for our savior. I wept because I am too small and I would like to suffer greatly, like the martyrs."[59]

She records the sensibility of a perfect little girl who wants to serve Christ

("I belong to Jesus") in conflict with the world. In her dreams of martyrdom she is glorious; she cloaks her sad indulgence in nobility. She has tears and piety, but not the humility.[60]

In keeping with the romantic temper that values the individual self as the center of all experience, her diary almost singularly focuses on her and her feelings, which she believes are unique. This focus, which will continue in the life of the diary, comes in part out of the natural narcissism of adolescence, but also from the need to record and thus create a lovable girl and woman. She documents every positive reflection of herself from any surface.

Just before her fourteenth birthday, Anaïs finds her first literary confidante in Mrs. Sarlabous, a poet and the wife of an ear, nose, and throat specialist for the Metropolitan Opera singers. They talk of books and authors—Hugo, Verne, Dumas, and Daudet—and Mrs. Sarlabous reads the poetry of Anaïs and teaches her about rhythm. When she tells Anaïs that she has a poetic soul, the little girl is thrilled. Although Mrs. Sarlabous makes only one appearance in the diary, Anaïs concludes after this meeting that she is not "crazy" as she had feared and that she can continue to think and dream. But she will keep it a secret, she concludes, after seeing a movie about a romantic girl who is mocked by others. She does not yet know that Freud had extolled the daydreaming or fantasy that gives birth to one's sense of self as a creative reflex.[61]

Her romantic temperament idealizes herself, her past, and those she loves—her mother, Joaquin's music teacher, her godmother, and her father. Idealized portraits unify her fragmented and repressed memories. Her most carefully cultivated ideal is of the man who had hurt her the most. She gives her father the most elaborate portrait—he is the most handsome, the most famous (his "name is on every tongue"), the greatest musician in the world. By leaving her he had trapped her in an insatiable desire to please him, to prove herself worthy—and him wrong in leaving her. Because he had found fault with her, she will be perfect. Because he loved beautiful girls, she felt ugly, for, as she says years later, "I lost my first beauty contest [for my father]."[62] Beauty will become "a law for her . . . a mask . . . she will wear to protect herself from the world," says a later friend.[63]

If, as Jean-Paul Sartre insisted, "Beauty is reassuring," Anaïs remains ill-assured until adulthood. Instead of seeking revenge for being treated as ugly, Anaïs allows it to brutalize her.[64] She spends her life seeking assurance and love. She is preoccupied with grooming herself and with pleasing others.[65] "She had a terrible thing about rejection," said Daisy Aldan, her friend late in life. "When she became attached to somebody, she really held on."[66] In a long passage on fear of abandonment in the novelette "Lilith," later called "Winter of Artifice," Anaïs will write the following about her alter ego:

"the smallest incident could arouse an anguish as great as that caused by death, and could reawaken the pain of separation as keenly as she had experienced it the day her father had gone away."[67]

## The Boardinghouse

On 28 April 1917, Anaïs and her two brothers are moved by Rosa into a five-story house at 158 West Seventy-fifth Street, where they will live for two years and five months. Unable to earn enough money with her concert singing, her mother has taken up another career—the buying of clothes in Manhattan stores for wealthy Cuban customers, including her sisters. She charges her purchases and adds ten percent to the cost, which she receives when the women pay. To make the house payments, she will also rent the rooms of her house to boarders. (Her wealthy sisters have made the down payment on the house, essentially setting her up in business.) They also give her the used clothing of their children, which makes Anaïs feel like an orphan.[68]

When she comes home each day from Holy Trinity School on Eighty-third Street, Anaïs is caught up in the life of the boarders, the bustle of the big house, the energy of her mother, whom she thinks has the courage of a man, and her own domestic self-sacrifice. This is the happy face of her diary. Several times in her later years, when she is more in touch with her feelings, she will admit to being humiliated by the presence of strangers in her house, burdened by her chores and her fear of poverty and being unwanted. "I was not in life," she will observe.[69]

The boarders and visitors do have a salient effect on her life, however. In addition to one member or another of the Culmell family who always seems to be staying there, there are a number of young musicians. Teresita Carreno-Blois, daughter of the great Venezuelan pianist Teresa Carreno, rents the basement; Emilia Quintaro, pianist for the Metropolitan Opera singers, comes to give Joaquin piano lessons; Michael Jovet plays the guitar, her brother, the piano, and from the top floor come the violin notes of Enric Madriguera, a nineteen-year-old prodigy who brings a gang of happy youth into the house (including his sister, who will later marry Andrés Segovia, the Spanish classical guitarist). Musical soirees fill the house. One of those who attend is her cousin Gilbert Chase, who claims this group sparked his career as a music historian.

Before Anaïs begins to fall in love with Enric Madriguera and the references to her father begin diminishing in her diary, she considers her vocation. When she wins a contest for her English composition, her vocation as a writer seems evident. And she has a vision. Once while struggling with this question of vocation (she considers music, painting, and writing), she sees a vision of a nun all in white, surrounded by light. Suddenly the nun disappears and Anaïs sees a young girl standing beside a stack of books and holding a pen in her hand. These are her choices. In either one, she senses she will be alone. Inside her diary for 5 June 1916, she draws a picture of her choice, a young girl sitting at a desk reading a book "by Anaïs." She fills numerous school notebooks with tales written in French.[70]

In the spring of 1917, two events occur that seem to raise other conflicting goals for the fourteen-year-old Anaïs—a conflict of values that embodies the larger struggle between her allegiance to her mother and her allegiance to her father. The first occurs on a swing when her brother Thorvald announces that John O'Connell, a classmate she has come to admire, wants her for his girl. Almost falling from the swing, she asks him to repeat the news three times. "Is it possible! A girl of 14? Yes, my little diary, it's true! Your crazy little confidante has found her knight, her tiny and nice little knight (American) . . . [A]nd that's all that I want." Of course she is only a little girl, and this is a school game, a bit foolish, she acknowledges, but soon she checks out a book on housekeeping from the library, makes an apron, and takes up biscuit making.[71]

Her traditional domestic calling is interrupted by a second and more powerful event when she is asked to be a dancer (playing a peasant of Lorraine) in *Jeanne d'Arc à Domrémy,* written by family friend Mrs. Polifeme, for the Union Square Theatre. Despite her fantasy and longing to go to battle for France, it is not the drama of Joan of Arc that enthralls Anaïs, but the makeup that transforms her into a beautiful dancer (perhaps greasepaint, not bacon grease, will win John O'Connell), and the hurly-burly noise of backstage with its anxiety and stage business.

When she and her godmother arrive at the theatre, she finds half-dressed vaudevillian women, disgusting smells of wine and cigarettes, and a stage and curtain that are dirty, faded, and torn. She watches a weeping actress leave the stage and just beyond the lights burst into laughter. She thinks the lesson that she learns that night is to appreciate the hard work of backstage, but in fact she absorbs a lesson in the magic of deception. It is one she has half known already. She is filled with a strange sensation, a mixture of astonishment, admiration, and confusion. The applause of the crowd feeds her neediness. She remembers the applauding hands in the darkness. The actress who is born that night will not find her place on the American stage until 1966.

Although she confuses her attraction to the stage with a vain desire for fame, it is in fact a hunger for approval and the appeal of illusion, of creating beautiful appearances. Her childhood wonder at color, movement, and lights will never leave her.[72]

The pull between reality and illusion, between the useful and imaginary, between self-sacrifice and ego satisfaction, become embodied in the struggle for her loyalty between her mother and her father. Her father represents the artist—sexual, free, and selfish (meaning destructive). Has her mother not told her she is "just like" him when she expresses vanity and dreaminess? That she is a Catalan type like her father? She adores him and wants to be an artist as well. But this desire betrays her loyalty to her mother, who has been betrayed just as she has. Her mother embodies human values of loyalty, nurturing procreation, self-sacrifice, domestic duty. Anaïs draws a picture of herself in her diary that expresses this ambivalence: she is in an apron, holding a mop, her back to the viewer; she is facing a large door, either waiting for her father or hoping to escape. Men are selfish, Rosa says; and when Anaïs feels bad, she identifies with her father (and when she feels selfish she feels bad). For years she will vacillate between taking pleasure in feeling useful in her domestic chores (fairly light, for they always have a maid) and fleeing to her books and diary, to her calling as an artist. Sometimes she enters one of the unrented rooms and indulges in "waking dreams," until her mother calls her to the reality of her chores. A family cousin remembers the philosophy of Rosa, whose mother had abandoned her seven children: "When a girl's love is not one of self-sacrifice, she is no woman . . . no, she is a monster, a coward, a super-egoist, a weakling, a fraud. . . . [She is] a bad woman!"[73]

Anaïs is learning the mother-conditioned, ambivalent bargain, that self-effacement is the means to power for women and that pulling one's punches avoids the loss of love.[74] Years later she will learn that this tension between the self-effacing muse and the creator is the central conflict for any woman artist.

The changes in Anaïs that will become prominent in her sixteenth year begin to reveal themselves before she is fifteen. The world beyond her enters the diary more frequently—news of the war ("Germans Invade Italy! Buy a Liberty Bond") and of the New York August heat wave in which two hundred die. She gives Spanish lessons to an upstairs boarder, joins the Secret Service Club at school and soon becomes its president, rereads her diaries, and pronounces judgment on her dreams. She resolves to cover up the dreams, turn them into something useful by publishing them, and cultivate popularity by earning C grades.[75] She believes that she wants her school friends' approval so that she can lead them. Even school seems tolerable, probably because she has to attend public school while the Catholic school is being rebuilt. Her teachers give her positive attention for her writing, and for the first time she enters a description of a teacher in her diary. Estelle Storms, her English teacher, stimulates her thinking and gives her confidence in herself. Next year she wins her first "publication" with a single-page school essay entitled "Why Every Home Should Own a Liberty Bond."[76]

She still gets lost in her reading, particularly when she is ill, which is frequently. She enjoys being sick in bed because she is free of responsibility and can read all day. When Joaquinito walks by her room and sees her curled up in bed with her diary and their new cat, he yells, "Miss Boring!" Thorvald says she has "stuck her nose in the book." Her mother says she has gone "away." Yet her mother notices the change. "You are becoming civilized, my daughter."[77] After reading Oliver Wendell Holmes's "The Autocrat of the Breakfast Table," Anaïs records her family breakfast conversation.

In three stories she will write about the "hurt" that drives one on "a long voyage" far from the "place of the hurt" ("The Child Born Out of the Fog") and into the "labyrinth of her diary" ("The Labyrinth" and "Through the Streets of My Own Labyrinth"). Fearful and claustrophobic, she sometimes breathes with difficulty because behind her is darkness, a "shadow left behind," the echo of a father who has left his imprint on her back, her soul.[78]

The first strong note of anger toward her father appears in her Christmas letter of 1917. She admonishes him for his "eternal painful absence" in a letter she does not send. The fourteen-year-old Anaïs has stopped dreaming of reuniting her parents. "I am becoming sensible as I get older," she assures herself as she settles at a new desk given her by her godmother.

# CHAPTER TWO

# 1919–1923

# Passion and Penitence

"My childhood was an invented one."
—*Anaïs Nin*

"Life only became real when I wrote about it."
—*Anaïs Nin*[1]

AM I BEAUTIFUL?" she asks the mirror framed in brown wood on the wall. She steps closer, in an oft-repeated ritual, the face not smiling back, for she is in a trance, afraid of frightening away the image she is trying to capture. Proof of her visibility. She will stare the same way into the faces of boys and men hoping to find her answer to the question she will ask all her life: "Am I beautiful?"[2] All girls ask the question, but the traumatized girl compulsively questions, and the artist sees potential for hundreds of masks.

### Mirrors

She studies her light blue dress with its tulle sleeves—she is slowly letting the hem down to appear older—her white silk stockings, shoes, and coral necklace. Recently she has been combing her hair up in a chignon at the back of her head. Today, on her sixteenth birthday, she has a blue ribbon tied around her hair. She longs to feel prettier, to feel "inside," where it is warm. She always feels outside of life, as though hearing music from another room.

You are the prettiest girl in the class, her friend Frances Schiff assures her. They are classmates at school, and both of them want to be writers. Though still painfully shy and hating school, Anaïs is class president (or so she later claims). Yet she feels powerless, unable to sway opinion or control events. Her anxiety and insecurity suction every compliment from a friend or relation. She studies the mirror to test the slim sixteen-year-old waist—just the age of Maruca, her father's mistress, when last she saw her about six years ago.

The year after her sixteenth birthday is critical in the development of her sexual and social identity. Hence the voluminous size of her diary, the longest of her adolescence. She needed a new volume (130–200 pages) every three months instead of the annual volumes of previous years. She turns from innocent piety and precociousness to being what one reader calls the "silliest coquette who ever doodled a boy's name on a beach with a pointed stick."[3] She refuses food—to save money for her mother's budget, or so she says. No kitchen tastes or smells permeate her diaries or her fiction. Two exceptions are burned food: the memory of a burned omelet made by her father when her mother was in the hospital giving birth to Joaquinito, and her own burning of a pan of noodles while she is busy reading. A Freudian critic suggests it was anorexia nervosa, an unconscious fear of physical and sexual maturation: "Only in the guise of a thin, girlish soubrette could Anaïs retain the slender form of the nude child whom Daddy loved to photograph."[4] Her lack of interest in food and food preparation is also a rejection of her mother and her mother's nurturing role.[5] Underlying all these possible explanations is a need for control. She keeps up what she calls a "mad correspondence" with girlfriend Frances (whom she calls "Dick"), records fewer letters to her father, drops out of school, and will develop a major infatuation for Madriguera, the young violin player. By the end of her seventeenth year, she will speak somewhat less of France, though she keeps up her French-language studies, and more about being Catalan or Cuban (depending on her preference for her father or mother at a given moment). Whatever identity she chooses, there is no question she has been "programmed by a Latin culture" (as she would express it years later).[6]

Easter Sunday after Communion. Her mother writes the letter to her teachers, as she promised she would do, withdrawing Anaïs from school. Anaïs drops out the next day, 21 April 1919, with her mother's blessing.[7] Soon Anaïs realizes that her mother expects her to work around the house and write only when the chores are done. Anaïs also helps her mother shop and pack boxes for Cuban clients, works in the garden, and mends her brothers' socks. This last chore is mentioned so many times in the diary that it becomes a metaphor for her self-sacrificing good-girl self. When Anaïs does do chores, she vacillates between feelings of martyrdom and elation, singing and dancing, pretending that the kitchen is a theatre.

Anaïs and her mother talk about the day when Anaïs will be eighteen and go to Cuba for a husband. That staying in school might have enhanced her skills as a writer seems not to occur to Anaïs. She will read every book from the library, she determines. The remainder of her life she will stand proudly an autodidact. Her greatest insult will be to call someone, especially one who has betrayed or criticized her, an "intellectual." Lacking the rigorous analytical skills of formal education, however, she will remain vulnerable to criticism and to lapses in full artistic mastery.

Enrique (Enric) Madriguera and his family rent the top floor of Rosa's house at just the time that Anaïs concludes that boys are like princes looking for princesses. Enric's daily practice makes her heart race. He is an artist like her father and a Catalan! Whereas once she would dress up and dance alone in her room before the mirror, now she frequently attends dances (it is the only exercise she gets) and practices the skills of the shy coquette, her head bowed slightly and angled to the side. Girls her age call her the "biggest flirt." She vows never to cut her hair, records every compliment in her diary, and insists to the good-girl diary that the compliments are not true. Her brothers call her a princess. "Love me, someone!" her heart cries out. She writes about finding "my Shadow," the boy who will fill her "empty space."

She is preoccupied with clothes and fashion. Her mother's occupation as a clothes buyer for wealthy women explains in part the beginning of this lifelong interest. Seduction and the trying on of various identities are also factors. In her diary she expertly draws the various styles of the day. She carefully cultivates the Parisian look, wearing a cape and a white beret (the cape makes her feel powerful, she observes). A "vanity case" carries her cosmetics. She buys clothes and remakes hats, listing her purchases in her journal, sometimes spending a hundred dollars at a time (when her mother can afford it). There are white satin shoes with Louis XV heels, a black velvet beret, even ermine. "I dress up to cover my vulnerability," she will later admit; clothes are "a pose in the world."[8]

It is a warm July day in 1919 when the train arrives at Lake Placid, New York, carrying Anaïs and several cousins and aunts. They will be here for a three-week vacation. Her mother stays in the city to buy fall clothing and linen for her Cuban clients, and Anaïs leaves her with regret. She has also torn herself from Enric, who is off to Spain for the summer. Just before she left, she let Enric kiss her (melodramatically she calls it an "awakening" and a "let[ting] down" of her "hair" and a "fatal transformation"—for she links kissing with a sacrifice of her virginity). She carries him, her knight and prince, in her heart while rowing by moonlight, taking long hikes, and dancing and flirting with her cousin Eduardo Sanchez. Eduardo is a handsome young boy her own age and temperament who arouses her physical longing. While she and Eduardo are listening to Schubert's *Unfinished Symphony*, she experiences what she believes is intense sexual hunger, for she calls this her first pangs of love. Her blood seems thin and her body feels fragile.[9] She is so stirred by this experience—and by her homesickness for her mother—that she calls for Rosa to come get her. This Lake Placid holiday is a "moral awakening. My character actually changed," says the naive sixteen-year-old girl, who concludes that it is because she has learned how much she loves her mother and home.

Coming home renews the conflict between her loyalty to her father and her loyalty to her mother, a tension that becomes articulated in the competing desires to be an artist and to be domestic. To be an artist is a masculine and egotistical calling (how else to explain her father's absence except as a reflection of his devotion to art?). Thus family and children become the province of the feminine. Sometimes she feels like two people. Especially when she has to take on domestic chores when her mother is in Cuba finding new clients and when her mother moves the family out to Long Island for the summer.

Rosa Nin and her sisters buy a little house in Edgemere, Long Island, near Far Rockaway. Eduardo and Thorvald go to the beach and play with their friends. But Anaïs feels distanced from the city, and her mother goes off each day with a briefcase to work in her office and to check on the running of her house and boarders on Seventy-fifth Street. Anaïs dreams of being a bluestocking, someone "out of place in a home."[10] At night when each family member is working, practicing, talking somewhere in the house, she feels what she thinks is a domestic bliss. Certainly it is a sense of security and order. Her love and loyalty are to her mother, but in the future Anaïs will accuse her of an engulfing domination.[11] Her occasional resistance to housework she blames on her impractical and selfish "Nin" nature. Occasionally the tension gives her sharp pains in her side, but her doctor says it is only worry.

She swings between belief and despair. In diary and dreams, she creates idealistic portraits of God, mother, godmother, father, self. One day she cannot pray and her heart feels closed; the next day her heart melts and she feels spiritually transformed. Her worship of her godmother is followed by disillusionment and rejection. The complications of her large Cuban family lead to quarrels and collapsing sand castles, falling altars, and crumbling pedestals—to use her adolescent imagery. Taking care of her two brothers makes her feel like a "poet who had the bad idea of getting married and is attacked by a great big, very cumbersome family."[12]

A letter arrives from her father early in November of 1919. She is already concerned about her mother's financial worries and ill in bed. As she reads the letter, she cannot reconcile it with her idealized view of her father. She asks her mother to lie down near her and talk to her about the innuendos in the letter. Thorvald and Joaquinito have also received letters from their father claiming that he has "never done anything wrong."[13] He suggests to Anaïs that there are things that he wants to tell her but cannot or should not. She asks her mother what he means, and Rosa suggests he wants to tell his daughter bad things about her mother. He has great skills in lying, she adds.

Surprised at her mother's bitterness, Anaïs is distressed by this ugly image of her father. Rosa had earlier given broad hints concerning her husband— hints that Anaïs, with her romantic illusions, was never ready to hear. But Rosa apparently did not openly explain the separation, and Anaïs's idealism had grown each time she received a letter from her father talking about the many people in Europe who adore him. Now Rosa informs Anaïs that her father gave up all his rights over his children when he "deserted" them. Anaïs is surprised, having come to believe that *they* had deserted *him*. Rosa also tells her of having been locked up in a room so that he could beat the children; though Anaïs nods her head, she seems not to remember and does not ask for more information. As if to shake her daughter's idealism, Rosa declares that her father will never come to America; he has never loved his family; there will never be a reunion. Your hopes are romantic and useless idealism, her mother tells her. Heartbroken, Anaïs cries for hours.

You are just a sentimentalist, whispers her cousin Charles (Carlos de Cardenas) the next day. It is intermission at a Molière play in Manhattan, and she lets a "furtive tear" escape her eye. Read Dumas's *Ascanio*, she tells him, by way of explaining her position. Read more Bulwer-Lytton, he answers as they leave the theatre. Expose your sentimental ideas to the "X rays of logic," he adds. He sounds like one of her mother's friends who calls Anaïs a little old lady and accuses her of false modesty and coquettishness. Each is a major (though futile) voice for realism in her adolescence. She records but does not internalize their contrary views. "I am a visionary," she concludes, a girl "entirely" made up of dreams.[14] She believes that the reason for her shattered dreams is that she expects too much of Life. The reality of her father's brutality is only seen in the context of a temporary assault on her idealism. Her Christmas letter to "Dearest" father is only slightly subdued in its loving enthusiasm and worship, reminding him that three children will be dreaming of his "dear presence" around the Christmas tree. The false sentiment—for Joaquinito does not even remember his father and the boys do not talk of him—reveals her persistent clinging to an ideal. She patches her castles in the air and does not think unhappy thoughts.

## Richmond Hill

The family moves to Richmond Hill, in Queens, in early November 1919. It is a palace in fairyland, she believes, and to keep up the illusion she refers always to the town as Kew Gardens (a wealthier, adjacent neighborhood). She includes a long description of her room in the Christmas letter to her father. The suburban neighborhood offers playing fields for the children, but the strain of juggling servants and renters for three houses (the sisters Culmell still rent houses on Eighty-sixth and on Seventy-fifth) takes its toll on Rosa. The recession of 1919 means that some of Rosa's Cuban customers delay paying their bills (for purchases overdue on Rosa's charge accounts), and occasionally a room goes unrented. Anaïs tries to help by doing some of the shopping and handling the bills, thinking that she is playing the role of a logical father. When the finances are particularly strained, she blames her mother for driving away her father (despite the fact that her mother's money had supported him).[15]

The house at 620 Audley in Richmond Hill is her last adolescent home, and her room the expression of her being. She begins here a lifelong practice of designing her physical space to express her dreams and her ideal self. This little room is on the second floor and her window gives onto a high porch, where she can pretend that the sky is her roof and the treetops her walls. She begins taking moon baths, lying naked on the floor by her window. On pale blue walls hang sketches of Mark Twain, Robert Louis Stevenson, "The Ideal Woman," and "Young Girl." She also wants drawings of Walter Scott and Shelley, whose worlds occupy much of her thoughts. The most important image, other than the one reflected in her three-sided vanity mirror, is a drawing by some unknown author, entitled "Love Locked Out." In it a child waits in front of a heavy closed door. Every night before going to sleep, Anaïs glances at the drawing on the wall, illuminated by a shaft of moonlight, thinking that love awaits beyond that door. Her last thoughts cultivate sadness—and hope. Ah, the sweetness of what she calls "spiritual suffering."[16]

In this blue room are books, including all the English and American Romantics, for reading takes her into what she calls trances. There is also a bird cage; increasingly she refers to herself as Miss Linotte, for she feels like a bird, small and fragile; she also sometimes feels like a leaf, light and windblown. The color and objects of her dreamy room set her apart from her hardworking, stout mother and her rambunctious brothers.

Thorvald (Tor) is a thoroughly American Boy Scout, rough-hewn, full of teasing and practical jokes (he puts little dead mice in Anaïs's shoes). He is fourteen years old when they move to Richmond Hill. Anaïs thinks of him—and his boyfriends—at last wearing long pants, as more civilized now. They will make willing dance partners. Though he has studied violin, Thorvald's interests are mathematics—he is studying to be an engineer—and baseball. Thorvald and Joaquin were only eight and five when their father left, and they are growing fast—and out of her influence.

Joaquinito is "a linotte in masculine form," says his sister proudly.[17] He has her artistic nature. They write an opera together, for he is a serious piano student. Though he has "magical" hands and can write poetry that moves her, he is a mischievous boy, once sent home briefly from school for mocking the janitor's Italian accent. "A mountain of whims and selfishness," she describes him on his eleventh birthday. He will carry both his father's name and his profession; but his loyalty will remain with his mother. Neither boy seems as affected by or obsessed with their father as Anaïs is. They tease her about her diary and now, as later, will call it fiction based on fact.

The children publish a neighborhood "newspaper," which they call "The Icicle Chronicle" or "Frolic Weekly." The boys play hard outside while she prefers reading novels and writing lengthy letters to friends. Like Emily Dickinson, she prefers to keep those she loves at a distance and write letters. Both fear what they each call "fulfillment."[18] She feels great joy when she has a letter in her pocket to be answered. She never seems to run or shout. On a few occasions she goes sledding with Thorvald before retreating into her reading and world of dream. At seventeen years the Anaïs of her diary is a melancholic romantic, moved always to tears by her mother's singing, by Joaquinito's piano playing, by Tennyson, or for no known reason.[19]

"I created you," she writes, sitting in front of her three mirrors. Rereading the journal, she imagines this image coming alive, just as did Pygmalion's statue, and declares that she will "love you so much." So, undoubtedly, would her father, for the image reflects her "best self."[20]

Anaïs takes the train to the city three times in March to meet Marcus Anderson, her new boyfriend, whose acquaintance she made at the party of a friend. She attends the opera (hearing Caruso for the first time) and two plays. It is Marcus's Easter vacation from school, where she has been writing to him all winter, presenting her sensitivity in long letters to him, for he has introduced her to the works of the French Romantic poet Alfred de Musset. Marcus declares his love and grows in her esteem as the letters increase. Unlike Enric Madriguera, who is older, less sincere, and more physically demanding—later she will say he was "too human in his longings"[21]—Marcus will be her Prince Charming. This romance and the Easter theatre season change her mind about New York City, which she decides she loves. On 4 June she takes a three-hour train trip to visit Marcus's Berkshire

School declamation contest (he wins first prize for his poem "Tennyson" and second prize for his declamation); but amid his wealthy family she feels estranged by her poverty and "the whole army of my Spanish ancestors."[22]

This spring and summer of 1920 are full of sexual titillation (expressed only in words of romance or as a "tingling" of the blood). Marcus writes that he loves his Sweet Princess. And she engages in a flurry of flirtation with boys named Jack, Jim, Edward, Macaya, and Homer. She wants to be seventeen forever. But in July she drops Marcus when he dares to ask for a good-bye kiss after she has said she does not love him. She expresses profound disillusionment when the ideal prince becomes a hungry boy. The pattern of her behavior with Enric and now Marcus is overt neediness and habitual flirtation (she decides her coquettishness is "natural" and cannot be helped), until the physical assertion of the boys' needs (and perhaps her own) frighten her from any intimate touch. Her mother "fought" in her, Anaïs will say years later, "the kind of woman who had displaced her."[23]

Eduardo Sanchez, the cousin who had emerged from the pack of cousins on their Lake Placid vacation, is another pen pal. He has now replaced her girlfriend Frances as her poetic confidant. He also writes poetry and keeps a diary. His French is weak—he confuses *cousin* with *cousine*—so their common bond is English. Eduardo is a beautiful boy, sensitive and attuned to the idealism of Anaïs. He will become her "perfect" friend and companion, for she senses in him a passive love that will make no physical demands.[24] When he visits New York, he asks her if she is a suffragette, an idea she rejects heatedly, asserting that "a woman's place is in the home." He breathes a sigh of relief. When he returns to Cuba, where his father is a rich cattle-breeder, she writes fifteen-page letters to him. With him she can remain her ideal domestic self.

The tension between her idealism and her hormones, between romantic dreams and physical acts, threatens to unbalance her. It is the tightrope she walks between self-worth and the image reflected in her father's disapproving eyes. The diaries of her mid- and late teens contain many references to being bad ("wicked" is the word she uses most frequently) and being good. She seems conscious of this split at one point when, while wondering about the "thrill" that Marcus gives her, she says he thrills Anaïs Nin—not Linotte.[25] Linotte is now the ideal fictive construct she portrays with her pen, Anaïs Nin is the one whose blood "tingles."

At seventeen, Linotte says she would rather be good than pretty. Almost every month she vows to be "good" and "useful," to help her mother, to serve others with a sense of duty instilled in her by her church, family, and culture. This is the girl that will model herself after her mother. The diary of Linotte, therefore, is a consoling fiction. That is why she calls it her "old friend" and "anchor" as well as her "cave" and "shell."

I want to be bad, Anaïs tells her diary during a rare confession. To be bad is to be worldly and selfish—"to paint my face, to dress like an actress, to be a coquette, to tell everyone the truth about my 'niceness.'"[26] When she gets cross or selfish or moody, she adopts the Oh-Lord-I-am-not-worthy tone of voice, says one acquaintance, the Lord being "her father the perfectionist who drives nails into her own flesh."[27] Just before her nineteenth birthday she admits that the diary would not exist if she were perfect, "for you have really grown out of my efforts and battles and imperfections."[28]

*The Delineator* has accepted two poems by Anaïs for publication, and she feels at the beginning of a career. She takes the train into Manhattan in the summer of 1920 to meet the verse editor of this monthly magazine for young girls. Her feelings are mixed as she watches the houses out the train window. Carefully she presents the serious and practical self to her diary. When dreams of literary fame seem in conflict with her obligations to her mother, she rationalizes them as a means to make money for the family. After sewing and working on the bills for her mother, Anaïs longs to write in order to discover the "source of the voice" that calls her.[29] One day at a Macy's book sale, she thumbs the Thackeray, Hawthorne, Dickens, and Emerson volumes longingly, then buys a "useful" cookbook.

She is living "the life of Miss Anaïs Nin, not Linotte" when she goes to the movies and dances with Waldo Sanford, her most recent beau, when she catches her own reflection in the shop windows and notices the boys' glances in her direction, and when she concentrates on her tasks at home. Sometimes she feels very "wicked" and worries about her "double person." Linotte the dreamer and artist should be hidden. Only to Frances Schiff does she sign both names, "Anaïs and Linotte." Miss Nin is the "sensible side of me," the obedient daughter and housekeeper, she tells her girlfriend; Linotte the "verse scribbler" and tragedienne.[30]

After reading Plato and Aristotle this summer, she tries to enroll in a philosophy course at Columbia University. Professor Glass suggests that she try a private secondary school because she will not be able to keep up with the students. Devastated, she returns home to her mirror and recognizes that her scrubbed face, beret, and white collar indeed make her look like a schoolgirl. The French schoolgirl appearance that she had long cultivated to give her distinction and attention in school—and certainly her failure to finish high school—now have led to rejection at Columbia. Determinedly, she studies two hours a day with plans to assault the university again at the winter term. "We are studying and discovering things, you and I," she informs her diary. Again, like Emily Dickinson, she reads and studies alone, playing mistress of "the great, still house." Hurt, she retires deeper into the shelter of her "shell," her "prison," her "pretty little room."[31]

From a business acquaintance of her mother's, Anaïs borrows Henry Murger's *Scènes de la vie de bohème*, which quite shocks her. The love affairs of the bohemian artists of nineteenth-century Paris fill her with wonderment and "faint disenchantment," particularly the way love is portrayed. She feels that she has suddenly awakened into the twentieth century, when in fact she is shocked by the nineteenth century. She is a romantic convent girl of seventeen (only occasionally doubting her faith during Mass), while in Paris a new generation of artists, including Ezra Pound and James Joyce (who arrive this summer of 1920) are creating a modern world. Love is freer and more diversified than this young reader of Murger yet dreams.

## Cousin Eduardo

Eduardo is her only real love. For him her French diary dies. On 9 June 1920 she begins writing in English. "Mon Journal" becomes "My Diary," and they exchange diaries. Theirs seems like the perfect relationship until his letters from Havana stop and she hears he has recently been in New York City on holiday and not come to see her. She dreams about him and waits for "real life" to find her. Neighborhood dances only fan the "great tempest roaring" inside of her. She puts Murger aside and reads three volumes of the journal of Eugénie de Guérin, which she holds next to her heart, thrilled by the "purity and womanliness" of this young French girl. Envying Eugénie's piety, Anaïs concludes that she may not be worthy of God's continual presence.

Though she does not share her mother's interest in the democratic presidential candidate or women's suffrage, she does share her mother's interest in the music season. Concerts bring back the glamour and prestige of the family's European years. Visiting musicians bring news of her father. The visit of violinist Juan Manén, a former friend of her father's, sparks her desire to recall her early life, and she questions her mother. The first year of her parents' married life, she learns, was spent in the rue du Four in Paris, near St.-Germain-des-Pres, in what she mistakenly thinks is the midst of the Latin Quarter of "poets and madmen." Certainly this is why she was "born" to be a poet. She also learns that her father wanted a boy when she was born; Thorvald must have been his favorite, then, she concludes. Scattered through this long recounting of their lives are references to the "gaps" in her memory and her difficulty in recalling her father ("Somehow here my memory fails me").[32] Now she thinks she remembers the violent quarrels, fearing for her mother's life, falling to her knees to beg her father not to leave; she thinks she remembers her father's fear of germs, his vegetarianism and filtered water, his cruel beatings, his killing of a cat in anger, the lifting of her dress for a spanking. She also now remembers trying to run away when they lived in Belgium. Yet when one of the visiting musicians says she looks like her father, she longs to become him and concludes that all her life "has been one great longing" for the man as she had wanted him to be, her "dearly beloved Shadow."[33]

In the 1950s in *A Spy in the House of Love,* Anaïs will create Sabina, a woman protagonist shattered by some "shock" from a cruel father. The more he beats her the more she creates the gold dust of illusion or make-believe. Sabina remembers feeling humiliated when petted by her father's mistresses and angry at her mother for allowing this to happen. She will become a mistress and assume her father's role as a seducer in order not to be betrayed, yet she calls out for someone to hold her so that she "will not continue to race from one love to another."[34]

In her mother's musical world Anaïs feels closer to her father and the glamorous European life, but the wealthy Sanchez family of her mother's sister Anaïs Sanchez does not approve of the "old life" of Rosa's association with artists. Though it is her Sanchez cousins who give Anaïs her hand-me-down dresses and Aunt Anaïs who contributes to the purchase of a squirrel coat for her namesake this winter, the young Anaïs resents their judgment and prefers to feel "elevated" in the presence of her mother's musician friends. She makes an exception for Eduardo Sanchez, who has a poetic nature like her own.

During dances at the Kew Garden Club with Thorvald, she flirts with the boys, while her other self longs to go home. The house is always filled with young men these days, either Thorvald's friends or the friends of Enric, who is again renting a room. She records every compliment, assured that many bold boys are trying to kiss her. She describes her outside self as consisting of Eduardo in the morning, Jack all afternoon, and Miguel Jorrin (the younger brother of her uncle Enrique's wife, Julia) and Enric all evening. They are all "victims" of her charms. Because she worships genius—and indirectly her father—she wants to marry an artist. She is "bursting" with love.

Just before her eighteenth birthday, 21 February 1921, her loyalty to her father is further weakened. He demands a divorce from Rosa, and his mother, Anaïs's own beloved grandmother Angela, seems to side with him. When Rosa is informed by legal document that she must return to Europe and contest the decree or grant him a divorce, the entire family is upset. Rosa consults a lawyer, but does not technically refuse to return. She wants to set conditions to protect her family. Angry with her father, Anaïs confesses that she loves him only because he is her father. He will not have her admiration, but she continues to send him letters. She has not yet won his approval.

Anaïs tries again to enroll at Columbia University. This time, she tells her diary, she is successful, except in her effort to take philosophy and psychology. She believes it is because she is too young, but her lack of a secondary degree continues to be an obstacle. She enrolls in English composition and French, but focuses on collecting male admirers.[35] No. 1, No. 2, No. 3, she calls them, as they line up to carry her books and accompany her to the subway. Occasionally she thinks of Enric, who leaves for Europe in what she thinks is great sexual frustration. But classes are tiring, the routine suffocating, the commitment to homework a tyranny against contemplation and diary writing.

"Do you read much Stevenson?" asks her English teacher, who thinks her compositions old-fashioned in style. In fact, she has recently discovered the wit of George Meredith's *The Egoist,* which affects her like a "bombshell." It is not the satiric English novel that challenges her romantic view, but the comments of the teacher (writing nowadays is "terse, direct, plain," it is explained). I must conquer the influence of romanticism and poetry, she determines. For the second time in a year (the first was after her reading of Murger), she awakens to acknowledge that she has been "traveling in old worlds of chivalry, elegance, elaborate speech, formality and pomp."[36] Just as she promises an end to romanticism, the spring of her nineteenth year brings her more of the same.

Eduardo arrives for the Easter week holiday, and this time she has his full attention. They read their diaries to each other, sit by the fire, take long walks in the nearby woods, share secrets and jokes. He gives her her first red rose. She is madly in love, though she calls it "like" and speaks in terms of ideals and dreams. Eduardo is handsome in a beautiful way and confident to the point of strutting. Her greatest satisfaction comes when he tells her that she inspires him and offers him intellectual companionship. Her heart almost suffocates her; it "leaps up" and "aches" when he looks at her; she dreams of him, and has to turn away from the "light in his eyes."[37] When a friend of her mother's tells her the next month that intimacy between cousins is "not right," Anaïs says the woman misunderstands; theirs is a "hunger of the spirit," and she intends to inspire him.[38]

The day before Eduardo leaves, he walks with Anaïs and Miguel Jorrín through the woods just a few blocks from her house. The buds of the trees and bushes are swelling with new life, and the warm air is beginning to heat the earth. Each man praises her, calling her Mimi de Bohème, until she is fairly floating, with only her tiptoes touching the ground. She is supremely happy in the company of admiring men. She feels an "invisible chain" linking her to all the admiring men in her life—Charles, Enric, Miguel, Eduardo, and . . . "Mr. Guiler," the latter an older boy she has recently met.[39]

She had met Hugo Guiler a month before when she was invited to a dance at his home in Forest Hills. The invitation from his sister Edith is an honor, for the Guilers are members of the country club and live in the wealthiest suburb in the area. Hugo dances the first and last dance with Anaïs, confiding to her that he too writes poetry. Despite the fact that she had said she would not meet her true love at a dance—for she is not her real self at dances—he will, in fact, become her "Shadow," her "Mysterious Stranger." And she will be, he says years later, his "deer eyed girl in the fairytale, the woman in the doorway. I danced all night with her."[40]

In the nearly four months before her next meeting with Hugo Guiler, she nurtures her love for Eduardo with lengthy letters about their readings. She takes long walks in the woods with a new appreciation for nature (she is reading Emerson's essays), and flirts at every dance, collecting admirers. One minute she longs for solitude, the next she buys a new blue dress and counts the number of boys who cut in while she dances. She wants to arouse their chivalry and honor, she believes. Yet she weeps for shame and visits her parish priest, Father McLaughlin, for weekly study of Christian theology and vows to be loyal to the church unto death. At the brink of womanhood, she is expectant, trembling, and perplexed.

The most popular book in the spring of 1921 is Sinclair Lewis's *Main Street,* and she reluctantly puts down Emerson to pick up the choice of the American public. Shocked by the vulgarity of the plain prose and its lack of idealism, she wonders if she will ever find a readership of her own. Nine years later, when Lewis visits the cafés of Montparnasse, the expatriate writers in Paris will snub him for similar, though less sentimental reasons.

Sitting on the screened porch of her house, Anaïs thinks about her own writing style and the importance of where she is writing. She has temporarily abandoned the "blue nest" of her room upstairs to sit here halfway outdoors. The worn chipped paint of the porch reveals the natural wood and feels homey; the screen protects her from mosquitoes and outside intruders. But it is the wide-limbed trees surrounding the three-story wooden house and lining the road that seem to nestle her securely and protectively. Similarly, her perceptions and self are harbored within the diary held on her lap. The book serves as a room of her own, a laboratory of her soul, a preserver of self. This day, 18 May 1921, she starts a new life: no more classes; she will read and learn on her own. She will enter in daily pursuit of her calling ("I have ink in my blood") and a devotion to being "useful." Perhaps she can earn money by posing for an artist, as a young painter at Columbia has suggested. She also assesses her writing: her fastidious avoidance of colloquialisms and contractions, her unfortunate tendency to moralize (adults seem to hate this, she notes), and what she calls her "tedious, stilted, voluminous" style.[41]

She finds guidance in Emerson's *Essays*, particularly "Essay on Self-Reliance." Following Emerson, she asks herself questions on the meaning and purpose of life (Mother always offered the "blessed resignation" of the church). Following Thoreau's *Walden*, where she marks each page, she decides to live on the porch nearer to nature, to be more practical, and to hike in the woods every morning. On one of her walks, she picks up three maple leaves and glues them into the diary. She moves through the woods as two young girls: one intent on keeping out the world, the other hoping someone will find his way into her lonely life.[42] Reading Carlyle's *On Heroes, Hero-worship, and the Heroic in History* she determines to combine passion and reflection, to be less self-absorbed, and to reflect on the "Divine Idea" that underlies Appearances. Her diary of this period in the early 1920s is one of the best documents ever written of a youthful girl's developing consciousness and artistry.

These intellectual concepts, along with her Catholic piety, help her poeticize her sexual longings and need for love, which for now are focused on Eduardo. His letters from Cuba have virtually ceased. When he eventually explains that his family has forbidden him to see her, she assumes it is because of her poverty. She is the penniless daughter of a musician. Humiliation is added to the worry caused by Rosa's periodic financial crises. She consoles herself with a new dress, dances with local fraternity boys, and entertains Thorvald's boyfriends: "with my accent, my peculiar inflections, my gestures, I turned commonplace phrases into things that made them laugh."[43]

Later Anaïs learns that their parents have intervened to break off her relationship with Eduardo, though she does not understand yet the incest taboo that is threatened. Nor does she comprehend Barnabe Sanchez's displeasure with Anaïs's poetic influence on his son. Rosa had gone alone to Eduardo's hotel before he left for Cuba and returned with a new diary inscribed from him to his "Lost Princess." He pledges his devotion and a return when his wings are no longer pinned. Anaïs fears he might try to kill himself, as one of their uncles had done when forced to marry against his will. She is moved by the beauty of their forced separation.

She will use the interference of an authority figure in several of her later works of fiction. In "The Sealed Room" portion of *Children of the Albatross*, written twenty-five years later, Michel is the twin with whom Djuna (age sixteen) dances "a deft dance of unpossession." But they are kept apart by a watchman who is the lover of the directress of the orphanage where Djuna lives. He demands that Djuna submit to him before she can meet her boyfriend. This and other novels reflect several tensions of her adolescent years: the feeling of abandonment—her protagonists are frequently orphans; the abuse and authority of an older male figure (the watchman); and being kept from intimacy with a youthful (often homosexual) male twin.

## Hugo Guiler

Anaïs does not wait long. Just when she concludes that all boys are "young, inexperienced, ignorant, [and] vacillating," Hugo Guiler reappears in her life. While his parents are in Europe, he is visiting his aunt and uncle Parker, who live just three doors down the street. He carries a copy of Emerson in his pocket, expresses devotion to Stevenson, and keeps a journal. Fate is at work! It seems to her that "all the things I loved in Eduardo had come back to me in someone else, in an older person [he is twenty-three], and mixed with still more seriousness and *wisdom*."[44]

Hugh Parker Guiler (he is called Hugo to distinguish him from his father, Hugh) was born 15 February 1898 in Boston of Scotch-Irish descent. Because his family moved to San Juan, Puerto Rico, soon after his birth, Hugo liked to claim he also had Spanish blood and that Guiler was a corruption of the Spanish name Aguilera.[45] Yet his parents had a different view of Catholic Puerto Rico and sent him to be educated in Edinburgh from age six through fourteen. His relatives were stern, and every time he did something "natural" he got punished for it, he said later to describe his Scottish moral upbringing.[46] He is tall, with a strong jaw and wide forehead, and he speaks with a slight British accent. Only his eyes reveal his vulnerability. He appears to fit her ideal of the suitor with a man's body and a poet's heart. Several days go by before she describes him in her diary, for her heart feels like a "great white room" that has been "carefully prepared for a visitor."[47] Will it be Authorship or Wifehood, she wonders, hoping she can be both writer and woman by juggling both pens and needles.

His effect on her is to make her feel healthier and more active. The dance invitations multiply, she plays tennis (Hugo's starring sport at boy's school) and loves their long walks in the woods. He encourages her to read more of Carlyle and Emerson, though she explains that her preference for escapist reading is due to her having had a frail and sickly childhood with too many days spent in bed. He introduces her to the works of John Erskine, his English professor at Columbia University and his "source of moral strength."

Guiler's maturity and his active life in business keep him apart from her often. He had begun working for National City Bank of New York after his 29 October 1919 graduation from Columbia. His busy life away from her only increases her admiration and longing. She idealizes him—his unselfishness, brilliance, humility—and concludes that while Eduardo is her equal, Hugo is the finest of her friends. By November he is incomparable. She shares one of her diaries with him, and he shares his theories of life, summed up in Longfellow's "Psalm of Life": "Life is real, life is earnest." Her interest in Hugo helps to distract her when her mother forbids her to answer Eduardo's letters to his goddess, his angel, his Mimi. Anaïs bows her head submissively. Yet she waits long days to hear from Hugo and does not always see him on weekends, and then not alone.

She characterizes herself in the diary as laboring for "others" around the house and choking on the dishwater, the smell of kitchen soap, and the dust. Then back she goes to alternating between frivolous dancing and hours of reading and introspection. If only her diary could absorb color, she thinks. She hangs rose-colored cloth on the lights in her bedroom and renews her commitment to continue her writing career, for she is reading the diary of Marie Bashkirtsev, which speaks her own heart. The neurotic, intellectual, and melodramatic Bashkirtsev, a Russian painter, had kept a diary until her death by consumption at twenty-three years of age in Paris.[48] For Anaïs, she will set a standard of the diary as a work of art.

When the girls next door, Martha and Wilhelmina Forgie, give a party and include Hugo and his sister Edith, but not herself, she is crushed. They must be jealous about her friendship with Hugo and see her as a young foreign intruder. They must think me a "dangerous foreign seductress" behind my angelical face, thinks Anaïs. While the party goes on, she writes in her diary, assuring herself that she should be flattered by their jealousy. She calls to have Hugo come by the next day to pick up a book of poetry.

While Hugo works, takes singing and guitar lessons and a business course at City College, and plays tennis and golf, Anaïs writes for hours in her diary, expressing her thirst for life and love. If only she were a man she would be Don Juan and take what she wanted. When she tries to work in her mother's office, she becomes fatigued and returns to sewing. Is he cold-blooded, she wonders when Hugo does not call. Is it his Scottish blood? Is he too English? He has told her that he is his own master. She has never been treated this way before. But when the telephone does ring, she "melts" at the sound of his voice.

Among their "perfect" dates are three. They are sitting in a theatre in Manhattan on the evening of 5 October 1921 waiting for the opening curtain of a musical called *Blossom Time*. Hugo expresses admiration for her dress and suggests she should dance professionally—he is not the first to have noticed her liquidity of movement. At eleven-thirty they go dancing in Greenwich Village, where as the only couple on the floor, they improvise. By

2 A.M. they are walking home, she under the spell of his "magnetism"; though he had gripped her hand on the dance floor, sending a shock through her body, he makes no other physical demands. The second date is two days later, when, upon the invitation of her mother, he accompanies them to a play and lecture by Gustavo Galarraga, a Cuban poet. In the dimly lighted box, she notices him gently stroking her silver gray coat on the back of her chair. How manly, unwavering, and absolute he seems. Later she watches him play tennis at the Forest Hills Club tournament. When she hears Schubert's *Unfinished Symphony* with him—the piece that had first aroused her at Lake Placid—she knows she is in love. The third perfect date, not mentioned in her diary for several years, is a train trip to Long Island—Hugo in golf suit and she wearing a hat with dangling cherries—when he gives her her first "true" kiss. When she looks at his legs in golf stockings, she senses a physical stirring in herself.[49]

Her love for Hugo and her dreams of the future provoke many lengthy passages in her diary about women and their contradictory beliefs about submission and intelligence. In her public demeanor she has found her place in shy "womanliness." Only by being reserved, she thinks, has she won the devotion of Eduardo, Enric, Marcus, and Hugo. This outer behavior will not change, but the inner girl is divided. It is a "constant battle" between the Anglo-Saxon and the Spanish blood. Though she admires the virtues of spiritual purity and usefulness, her heart wants to be Donna Juana, seductive. In the latter mood she poses before her mirror in exotic clothes and jewelry until her eye catches the bookshelf. Suddenly the little philosopher, as her mother calls her, plunges into thoughts about ideals. Should she dance seductively for Hugo or engage him in deep discussion? Should she submit or demand mental and educational equality? But does not a woman cease to be a woman when she steps out of the home? "I will not always be eighteen," she assures herself.[50]

Where Anaïs wants to "live," she thinks, is in the world of feeling and thought; the ideal, not the real; the spiritual, not the physical. She claims it is her artistic nature, her ancestry: "I am the least American of the three of us," she tells her father in a twenty-six-page letter; "my heart beats only for poetry and beauty, the great, sublime and spiritual things." Hugo has told her that they know four languages—the fourth being poetry.

She is, in fact, afraid of the physical and appears to disdain it. The strong grasp of Hugo's hand had frightened her. The priest's sermon on sin and hell is a "cruel shock." In what is by now a rare discussion of religion in her diary, she recalls a week of mission services that she and her mother attend in November. At first guilty about her rebellious thoughts concerning religion, she is swept up by a sermon on Christ's sacrifice and murmurs repeatedly, "I believe." Kneeling, she realizes how deeply Catholicism has rooted itself in her. Sleeping, she dreams of incense, candlelight, and organ music. But the second night, during a sermon on sin and hell, she responds with cold reason, welcoming a sense of disappointment and despair into her heart.

She can almost feel herself maturing and her writing skills improving as she fills her notebooks this fall and winter, writing on every paper and envelope in her mother's office and in the kitchen and while riding in trains and streetcars. A friend of her mother's notes that she is less dreamy and irresponsible these days. Perhaps she is maturing out of her idealism, she speculates.

When Eduardo visits in January, she makes the inevitable comparisons between Hugo, who seems so "present . . . real," and Eduardo, who has the fragrance of "old books, old heroisms."[51] The contest between her poetic Cuban cousin and the "English" boy down the street has tipped in favor of the latter, the banker, whose power is based on his age and his unavailability. She is always on her tiptoes, trying to stand as tall as he. Eduardo, who is younger, is most like her, and she loves him for her own reflection in him. He loves for the same reason, and when he says her name, it is the name of his mother and his sister as well.[52] During a performance of *Madame Butterfly*, they gaze longingly into each other's eyes and promise to continue their correspondence. Theirs is the cause of Friendship, and she will be his teacher and inspiration. When he echoes her beliefs she is thrilled with her influence.

## Modeling

Anaïs's nineteenth birthday comes amid her first job, a short-lived (perhaps eight-month) career modeling for artists, illustrators, and photographers. Encouraged by the remark of a young painter in her mother's studio—he said she had a face like a Persian princess—she registers as a model with the Art Worker's Club for Women. Though she had earned a dollar for a poem earlier, she earns her second dollar with her looks, not her pen. This job, which will move her away from her mother and initiate her into the real world of seduction and deceit, begins a year of great change that will ultimately take her to Cuba and betrothal to Hugo.

The average American in 1922 considers the word "model" a euphemism for "prostitute." Yet in the world of the Nin family, where artists are revered, the role of the model is understood, and there is no evidence that her mother objects to her daughter's employment. But Anaïs is aware enough of the American view of models to fear what she calls the Anglo-Saxon prejudices of the Guiler family. Anaïs idealizes her role as representing beauty. When she begins what she calls her first novel later this year, her character Aline is a young model in New York City who inspires artists to great success.[53] All their paintings are masterpieces, and even a rough and misogynist painter named Sterling is inspired by her innocence.

Anaïs begins by modeling for the Review of Models at the Art Worker's Club, to which her mother's friend Mrs. Norman belongs. Later she models costumes at Lincoln Arcade near Columbus Circle. She poses in a "Watteau" costume, and the painting appears on the cover of the *Saturday Evening Post* 8 July 1922. She loves most of the assignments, which allow her to play a different role with each costume. She is excited to be a part of the world of art, though a passive part, "touching the hem of Art's garment." And she is earning money for her mother and brothers. The long hours of posing are no bother, for she can dream to her heart's content. Most importantly, she can see her reflection in the artists' gazes. For a young woman fond of studying her visage and form in the mirror, she revels in the observations about her. "How the artists gathered around me!" she exclaims.[54]

Her Catholic innocence leads to some unexpected and upsetting encounters: a little cautionary introduction to larceny and lechery. In February a Mr. Brown (who had painted the *Post* cover) tries to kiss her and get her to dance with him. When other artists remark on her virginity, she does not understand. Often during the rest period a painter puts on the phonograph and asks her to dance. One day in March she is posing for a painter who sings bawdy songs and chews tobacco while he paints; she is posing near his soiled, unmade bed, and he makes snide remarks about being able to tell that she is a virgin. She never returns. When Luis Mora, who is drawing subway advertisements from her poses, tries to touch her, she slaps him and runs out without her money. Another time she is cheated by an artist, and she often has to struggle when she refuses to pose naked. She cannot tell the painters why, for fear they will laugh at her. She is revolted by sex. She shivers from fatigue. Yet she suggests new poses, seeks new costumes, and wins more work, even from the painters with "bad reputations," in order to earn more money. Though she has always told her mother everything, she does not share these shocking encounters that unveil "sin and misery" to her. She weeps and suffers humiliation, which is not recorded in her diary. On the contrary, she will use the hurtful experience in her art and portray chiefly its glamour and color.[55] Only in an unpublished early version of one of her stories will she capture the fear she experienced and describe it in her protagonist, a young model who is groped by the artists for whom she poses.[56]

Her private view of the art world changes from a sense of its wonder and charms to a sense of its threatening reality. Previously she has filled her diary with abstractions and theories, and now she thinks she knows about "throbbing life" and can write more knowledgeably. Now she believes she is really living. She is writing less, seeing Hugo less, and even flirting with some of his friends, including an Irish boy named Edward King and a Russian boy named Boris Hoppe. Unlike the frequently absent Hugo, Boris Hoppe is sexually aggressive. After taking her to a masquerade dance to which Hugo has declined an invitation, Boris walks her through the woods near her home and kisses her passionately. The kisses feel good, though she fears she will get pregnant (she calls it "fecundate"). No passionate kisses are mentioned in the diary, and only later does she mention Boris's heated attention in the first version of her "Father Story," written in November 1935.[57]

After despairing, then rejoicing, at each disappearance and return of Hugo, she pours out her heart to him one day in June as they walk in the woods. Later, at the Atlantic shore, they kiss. She has figured out that kissing does not make babies, but it is certainly a step away from engagement. As the kisses continue, she is aroused; but when he begins to push her bathing suit aside, she squeals in fright. He withdraws in shame, as he had during his Edinburgh days when his aunt caught him and his brother examining themselves. He assures Anaïs that he loves her. Though he is not ready for a full commitment, he begs her to wait for him. In the last page of her diary, she writes, "This is no longer *my* Diary!"[58] When she asks her mother about sex—for she wonders about the wetness of her bathing suit—her mother says it is like a man urinating, and not beautiful.

"Journal of a Fiancée," she writes on a new diary book that will contain her June 1922 to January 1923 experience. Hugo's picture is pasted inside the front cover. Her informal engagement to Hugo follows a spring of his inattention, stemming in part from his family's disapproval (they have "[f]rigid English hearts," she observes).[59] Because she has previously accepted a summer job in Woodstock, New York, where many of the artists from the city migrate in the summers, she reluctantly leaves Hugo. She is to spend the summer posing for Gerald Leake, who assumes she will be living with him and sharing his bed. She is unaware when she accepts the job to pose and have "freedom unbounded" that she will be thrown upon her own resources and deprived of her mother's counsel. When she walks to the swimming pool in her bathing suit and black stockings, others are swimming nude. When she takes a ride with Leake, he fakes a breakdown of his car and offers her a bed in the grass. She walks the eight miles back. Perhaps the coquette has given signals, but the results shock the good girl, who sends for her mother.

Unexpectedly, Rosa's three-day visit precipitates their first quarrel. Anaïs does not tell her about Gerald Leake but about her desire to live her life with Hugo. Upset, Rosa asks for allegiance from her children. Anaïs has never thought of these conflicting loyalties. For the first time, she realizes that Rosa wants to continue to direct her life. Suddenly she collapses in tears in her mother's arms, guilty for wanting to leave her mother, longing to have a private life with Hugo, and angry at the injustice of these conflicts. "What a child you are," says her mother.

She writes to Hugo, hoping that he will call her back and deliver her from her anguish. While waiting for a response, she spends long hours walking and writing. Modeling assignments fall off after the word about her is passed among the painters. Though lonely and homesick, she finds pleasure in the individuality of the vacationers and disregard of conventions at Woodstock. During her walks, she weaves flowers in her hair.

Hugo does not call her back. His letters are forwarded to Richmond Hill, where she returns on her own. His nonresponse causes her to throw herself on the bed and sob at his seeming lack of love. He encourages her career ambitions at the exact moment when she wants to put love first and find protection. She is fleeing to her mother's house, and he is sending her a copy of Ibsen's A Doll's House. It will take her three months to figure out that he is just repeating to her what she has said to him; he is upholding her own ideal of an independent career. It will take her several years more to figure out that he is as afraid of intimacy as she.

She has brought her pure heart and body back to Hugo, but her rites of passage have just begun. She has to deal with their growing physical desires. Her own are expressed in terms of confusion and turmoil. His are perhaps more directly expressed, for she writes that they discuss everything and have some differences concerning "ideals of conduct," specifically when they reach the point at which they have to decide upon "an Act."[60]

When she secures a job modeling at a clothing shop, both customers and management seem to lick their lips in her presence. While she is on the phone to Hugo one day, a salesman slips up behind her and slides his hand into her dress to feel her breast. She kicks him hard in the shin. The groping of the men around her—perhaps even the tension of her personal life— builds her fear and anger to a fever pitch. In mid-July she is suffering from the ugliness of life and those "things" she had never known about before, which tear away her innocence about "evil and baseness." In early August she has lost the will to live amid "a terrifying darkness." Soon she works herself into a "volcanic anger . . . against . . . the *animal* in life."[61] Finally, she is fired by her boss when she refuses to go to dinner with the clients.

Only Hugo's love rescues her from a world of "sin and license and immorality." Just when her mood seems up—at a point when Hugo is her haven—she learns that his family is sending him to Europe for three months. She believes, or tells her diary, that the trip is for his health—"He has had a breakdown and his health is seriously impaired." In fact, his Protestant family does not approve of this Catholic girlfriend. They send Hugo to be with his grandmother for three months to get him away from Anaïs, who is foreign and from the wrong side of the tracks.[62] His mid-September sailing will precipitate a sexual crisis for her.

She reads again *The Woman Question,* by Thomas Robert Smith, which Hugo had given her in July. The book had initially shocked and challenged her "unrestrained maidenliness" with its talk of sex. She wants the physical to be spiritualized, and certainly not talked about; Hugo seems too physical, she too spiritual. The night before he leaves, she realizes that he wants more from her physically, and she apparently yields more than she wants, for she blames him for thinking only of himself and leaving her in "agony." Just when his love should have been the most inspired, he had wanted to touch her body. She took refuge in her mother's arms: "Had it not been for her that night, I would have died."[63]

Hugo calls twice before sailing 13 September 1922, but she does not reveal her crushing disappointment at what she sees as his selfishness. How can she have loved him more than herself if he is so selfish? Four days after Hugo sails, she answers her father's request that his children visit him in Europe. She refuses. Fueled by the seeming desertion of her young love, she strikes out at her father.

When she sits at the desk in her bedroom to pen yet another letter to her lost father, she has angry fire in her breast, not longing. She will not come to Europe to be with him! She refuses his request in the name of Justice— that is, justice for her mother, who has struggled to support her children. Their childhood has been darkened by him. Her sense of injustice swells her prose, and she describes Thorvald sacrificing a career in engineering and herself working in a department store. With little money they must struggle to help support the family that he, their father, created and abandoned. Their sacrifices have been many, she tells him, and it is his fault: "we are paying the price of the obligation you ran away from."[64]

She also begins to withdraw her allegiance from the Catholic church. Though she will later claim she left the church at sixteen, when God did not answer her prayers for a Christmas reunion with her father, it is in fact several years later that she makes the break.[65] Though for years she continues to attend Mass occasionally and to kneel in prayer to please her mother, she stops believing.[66] In part it is an intellectual decision, after months of study and reading for Father McLaughlin. In part she rejects religion because God resembles a disappointing father. If some women fall in love with God because they are in love with their fathers, Anaïs Nin pointedly rejects God the Father. A third factor is that she lacks a religious sense, as Henry Miller will later tell her. Her "religious" sense is psychological and aesthetic, not mystical and metaphysical. The diary records no metaphysical struggle but simply a statement of unbelief.

## A Cuban Marriage

Anaïs herself will make the sacrifice for family when her aunt Antolina arrives to take her to Cuba for the social season. Rosa had asked in January if Anaïs could come, hoping that in Cuba Anaïs will attract and marry a millionaire. But Anaïs thinks it is she who devises a "great plan" to fulfill her mother's dreams.[67] She will not immediately divulge her plan to her diary, but clearly she intends to sacrifice herself in a marriage to a rich Cuban. She sees her decision as noble, but when her relatives say that the only solution to Rosa's difficulties is Anaïs's marriage to money, it sounds base to her. She longs for Hugo, whom she will always love, and asks Eduardo to continue writing to her because she is spiritually lonely. On 7 October 1922 she boards the train for Florida and a boat to Cuba, certain that her primary love is to her mother.

Anaïs's response to Havana follows a pattern of ecstatic enthusiasm ("whatever is Spanish in me has now come to the surface"), to disillusionment ("dirt and laziness . . . vulgar ornamentations and the primitive barbaric traits"). "Less tradition and more cleanliness" is needed. Her diary entries are sparse, her social life active. Anaïs lives at Finca La Generala, Luyanó, Havana, the ranch of her aunt Antolina, widow of General de Cárdenas and mother of Antolina, Carlos, and Rafael (Felo). She is surrounded by luxury, servants, a country club and tennis club. She pastes into her diary a photograph of herself in a riding habit, standing next to her horse. Her name is in the society pages of the newspaper.

She is swept up in the "dazzling splendor" of the wealthy social life of Havana. The pictures of these fall and winter months show her posing in photographs and society news pictures. To her diary she expresses pious thoughts, prayer, and spiritual thirst—especially during a lavish Christmas party that lasts until 3 A.M.[68] Yet her social calendar is full of activities with her cousins and young suitors. Her best friend is Tana de Gamez, a dark and exotic young woman, who falls in love with Anaïs.[69]

Hugo writes poetic letters, confessing that he loves her with all of his nature, a veiled apology for frightening her by seeming to want more than a final kiss. Though she returns his love, dramatically she says that she cannot marry him; nevertheless, his love gives her the strength to face her great sacrifice for her mother. This sacrifice she makes her central melodrama: "to be separated materially will only emphasize the pain of the spiritual loneliness we are condemned to suffer without each other."[70] But selflessness has a short shelf life.

In the last long diary entry of the year (25 November 1922), Anaïs describes herself as a "coquette on the road to perdition." Even while writing love letters to Hugo, she flirts outrageously with others and has been aroused by a young man named Ramiro Collazo. She allows three young men, including a cousin, to kiss her—a liberty she considers grave and keeps from her diary. "I have deceived them all," she later confesses.[71]

The Latin eagerness of the young men arouses her fear of intimacy and makes her long for her cooler Scottish beau. She writes to ask Hugo to come to her in Havana, if he really wants her. She enjoys the power and control of playing with the other young men's feelings, and they assure her of her beauty. But it is make-believe for her, a means of losing herself in a "labyrinth of personalities." Final thoughts of her mother's happiness are set aside when in a letter from Hugo during the first week of December 1922, he proposes marriage. He has rushed to comfort and shelter her—or so she will portray it in a fictionalized version written thirty years later.[72] She responds with a cable promising to marry him, temporarily justifying for herself that this move will lead to a greater happiness for her mother.[73]

From December 1922 through February 1923, when she stands "unwaveringly, in expectation" of Hugo's arrival in Havana, Anaïs is alternatively (if not at once) ecstatic with love, full of questionings about her decision, and wracked with guilt about failing her mother. All the while she plays the indefatigable society girl, listing at the end of her present diary a "Calendar of Frivolities or Journal of a Society Girl." By all rights, she confesses, she should be keeping three or four diaries at once. But to the one diary, she conveys her thoughts and actions in ever more abstract and vague language. She is writing now not as a dreaming girl but as a wife-to-be, "preparing to enter the Kingdom of Kingdoms and to fulfill [my] earthly mission."[74]

Hugo arrives the third week of February. He had written his parents for money to come home from Scotland and is stopping in Havana on his way. Wavering and indecisive about most things, he has finally acted in time. He arrives with his tall, military bearing, appearing as her protector. Public notice of their intentions is placed in four Cuban newspapers and pasted into her diary. The notices mention the expected arrival in Havana of the "distinguished Rosita Culmell," but her mother does not come. The betrothed file for a joint Cuban passport.

Anaïs marries Hugo Guiler on 3 March 1923, just twelve days after her twentieth birthday. Tana, Aunt Antolina, and Aunt Juana and several cousins attend. Anaïs wears a black dress with white fur and a white hat with a long veil. Her godmother has given her silk things to wear underneath. It is a simple, civil ceremony in Havana. No picture of the event has ever been published. They will present their parents with a fait accompli. Hugo gives her a gold ring after they sign the book. At the dock, where friends see them off, Anaïs weeps at the absence of her mother.[75]

# CHAPTER THREE

## 1923–1927

# Portrait of a Wife

"Before marriage she thought of herself in love; but since the happiness that should have followed failed to come, she must, she thought, have been mistaken."
—*Gustave Flaubert,* Madame Bovary

"I pulled the fine web toward me with all the wisdom my love could teach me."
—*Anaïs Nin, 1923*[1]

$A$S THE MARCH WINDS shake the windowpanes, Anaïs Nin Guiler embraces her new husband before their three-mirrored reflection in her blue virginal room. They are in Richmond Hill, far from the heat of Havana and their hasty marriage and from the unreality of their voyage to St. Augustine, Florida, where they honeymooned briefly before returning to New York. Behind them in the dusk of Anaïs's guilty imagination stands her weeping mother.[2]

### An Ominous Cloud

In choosing to marry the non-Catholic Hugo, Anaïs believes that she has acted rebelliously. If she had betrayed her mother during those adolescent years when she wrote to her father in Europe, casting herself in his artistic image, certainly now, with her unconsecrated marriage, she has broken her mother's heart. Yet she and Hugo have moved back to Richmond Hill to live in the very shadow of her mother's grief, which looms "immense and terrifying." Anaïs listens to Rosa's murmuring and feels alternately overwhelmed, angry, and guilty. She also feels resentment over what she perceives as her mother's fear of losing control. She calls this struggle their "Calvary."

She spends more and more time with her mother to reassure her of her love, and appeals to Aunt Antolina to intervene. Anaïs and Hugo talk about asking the National City Bank for a transfer to Paris. For her part, after many tears over her daughter's marriage, Rosa goes to Cuba for four months and begins focusing her energies on Joaquin and his musical studies. By December of 1923, Anaïs and Hugo have moved into their own home—a one-story bungalow with a tiny garden at 620 Audley Street at Curzon Place, in Queens. Anaïs determines to live her life differently from her mother: she will mold her marriage to suit her art, will make of her life her art, and certainly never have children. Marriage and children, like beauty, do not last.

She has not considered the effect on Hugo's family of *his* marriage to a Catholic. His family had sent him to Europe when he fell in love, and was bitterly opposed to his sudden morganatic marriage to the daughter of a divorced Catholic woman.[3] Hugo will not see his parents for a year, and then only his mother, briefly. In a single reference in her journal, Anaïs exults in having his entire heart; his estrangement (she calls it detachment) from his family makes her feel more secure and allows her to love him as a mother and sister as well as wife. Six years later she will credit him with great courage in having defied his parents to marry her, but she will qualify her praise by referring to the slowness of his decision, his wavering character.[4]

Looming behind the haunting image of her tear-stained mother's face is a more ominous cloud, mentioned but not identified in the diary. In fact, Anaïs temporarily stops writing her diary because she cannot mention conjugal sex or deal with her apprehensions about the subject. The only indication of a problem may be found, more than a year after her marriage, in a reference to Hugo, "whose delicacy and sensitiveness every day keep me from the things I had feared in life."[5] Her fear is of having sex. They have not consummated their marriage.

Hugo's inexperience and lack of libido come in part from his youth in Scotland. Years later he will tell Anaïs about the punishment from his aunt, who discovered him and his brother examining each other's genitals, and his sense of physical shame and guilt. Though more worldly than Anaïs about sexual matters, he remembers her recoiling when he touched her bathing suit on the beach. When he sees the same look in her eyes now, he responds as he did to his aunt. She has chosen him because, unlike her father, he does not pose a challenge to her control of her own body. Intensely phobic to the point of illness during their honeymoon, they eventually fondle each other nervously.[6] The young couple is inhibited, ignorant, and frightened by sexuality.

The church-inspired fears of the young Catholic girl are greater than her husband's inhibitions. When admitting the truth to her diary years later, she will blame him for not gently persuading her away from the "virgin's natural recoil."[7] Her barrier, though, is more than a girl's sense of sin, it is a daughter's violated innocence. Her "reaction formation," says one psychoanalyst, is a "predictable result of childhood sexual experiences." That Anaïs cannot even mention her sexual fears and failures in her private diary at the time indicates the depth of her repression of these fears.[8] When she gives into despair and weeping, she says it is the spirit of the young French diarist Marie Bashkirtsev taking possession of her.[9]

Anaïs's escape mechanism is denial and the creation of a fictional happy marriage in her diary. When she finally takes up her "diary of a young wife," she fills the pages with passages of praise for Hugo. He is a loving and compliant mate, ready to meet her contradictory needs for a traditionally strong husband with whom she can play the clinging wife, and at the same time a soul mate who can join in her poetic flights. He dutifully keeps his own journal, anticipating her emotional needs with what she calls a sensitivity and delicacy akin to a woman's. She seems surprised when he sometimes does not show strength and confidence, yet she delights in having him cling to her. Wisely, he encourages her to write, for he honors her as an artist. The only hint of a contradiction between her idealized portrait of married life and the reality of inevitable disappointment is an occasional reference to a future when they may love each other less. Hiding the truth from her diary, she declares, "It is a joy to be consumed by flaming adoration."[10]

In April, when Eduardo visits from his classes at Harvard, the three of them attend a performance of Ibsen's *Peer Gynt* in Manhattan. Hugo seems to know no jealousy of her love for Eduardo; on the contrary, he seems to share her devotion to him. In September she tells her diary that she will someday write the story of a woman who can love two men simultaneously, and will show "how she can fall asleep in the arms of one and dream of the other." By December, devotion to Eduardo has evolved into a "purely mental character." Whenever she thinks too intensely of him or of her young suitors in Cuba, she transforms her emotions into literature. Her fears that Hugo does not love her will not be treated in her writing until some thirty years later, in *Seduction of the Minotaur.*[11]

Her turn to fiction results from a fear of dealing with explicit issues in her diary. The anxiety over her conjugal failure, her feelings about Eduardo, and her attraction to other men are secrets best placed in fictional form rather than in the confessional of her diary. A veiled reference to "a subject" that she has long wanted to write about but cannot because it will create "trouble" certainly refers to sex.[12]

During the summer and fall of 1923, she writes "Aline's Choice," an autobiographical fiction. Aline, an innocent and lovely model, inspires all the New York painters she sits for, even the woman-hating Sterling. Aline's role in the New York art world is essentially passive; she is a muse and object of beauty, her relationships are idealized and nonphysical. Anaïs shares her manuscript with Hugo (who corrects her spelling and split infinitives), with Hugo's former Columbia professor John Erskine (whom they both idealize), with Eduardo, and with Richard F. Maynard, a sculptor for whom she is sitting. With all these male readers, she feels quite uncomfortable in exposing her most intimate thoughts.

Like Flaubert's Emma Bovary at her marriage, Anaïs had "tried to find out what one meant exactly in life by the words *bliss, passion, ecstasy* that seemed to her so beautiful in books."[13] She seeks out Richard Maynard because he is both a painter and the author of a successful story published by *Scribner's* magazine. Ever worshipful of artists, she is shy at first, but soon establishes an emotional and intellectual dependency. As an artistic father figure, he advises her about art and life. In his diary, parts of which he shares with her, he compares her to a shining light in a transparent lantern. Her flirtation is couched in aesthetic colors of art, beauty, and mutual sympathies. He seems so gentle, she thinks, casting an uneasy eye at the portraits of many women on the wall of his studio. She asks him to paint her picture. Eventually he will also create several sculptures of her figure.

Anaïs spends 1924, which will be her last year in New York, in a flurry of domesticity, yet another means of avoiding the issue of sexuality. She decorates each room in her bungalow in a particular mood and color, lavishing care on every vase and curtain. She shops, sews, and paints with creative fervor. Her dining room is blue, the parlor green and brown with yellow and orange accents, and the bedroom rose and gray—she even paints the back of Hugo's hairbrushes. Her greatest decorative creativity, however, is reserved for the central room, where she works: it is exotic, with Moorish arches and furniture, curios, and a lantern. Each room expresses a different side of Anaïs. The artist is expressed in the writing room, where she is a poet, casting a "mist" (as she describes her writing style) around her subjects. In the bedroom, overseen by a photograph of her mother framed in black, she is the dutiful and domestic wife, submitting to the incomplete early gestures of lovemaking when Hugo visits her twin bed. Anaïs keeps separate scrapbooks where she pastes recipes and pictures of home interiors, ordering her domestic world as she orders the interior world in her diary. In home and journal she maintains control: Hugo is depicted returning each evening to smoke his pipe while Anaïs sews at his feet and their collie Laddie sleeps nearby. The scenes are a parody of a Hallmark greeting card, but they conform to her ideal of domesticity. The sexual implication of their nickname for each other—Pussy—is unintentionally ironic.

Her misty idealism and abstractions are the fabric of her early fiction. Thorvald and Hugo encourage her to be more realistic in "Aline's Choice." Her cynical cousin Eugene and Professor Erskine try to steer her away from the sentimental. She concludes that this inclination toward sentimentality is the result of an influence of English Romantic literature, and that she cannot make her writing more concrete until she herself becomes more concrete. That, of course, would bring her face to face with hurtful reality. By the end of the year she claims triumphantly (and prematurely) that Eugene, Erskine, and Hugo have rid her of her penchant for the sentimental.

She even brings her dreams to the task of caring for her mother's house during the four months that Rosa and Joaquin are in Havana. She will publish her Aline novel in order to help her mother's financial difficulties. While she and Thorvald have been trying to rent the rooms in Rosa's house, they have had trouble paying her creditors. She hates her mother's business. Anaïs's sensibilities are wounded by dealing with creditors and money worries (an attitude that will later extend itself to Hugo's banking career).

A summer holiday offers temporary escape from her mother's creditors. Anaïs and Hugo arrive in Woodstock, New York, in June 1924. They spend a two-week vacation in the very scene of her traumatic encounter with artists' sexual advances just two years before. They stay in the same room she had occupied. Here she writes the Woodstock chapters for "Aline's Choice," but in her fictional version the artists' model inspires art, not lust. Once again, Art triumphs over reality. While she writes, Hugo keeps up his diary. They talk all day and whisper into the night. Their "play[ing] at coming together" is gaining confidence.[14] This holiday is a calm before the storm.

Anaïs returns to face her final financial embarrassment when Rosa Nin, reared in a wealthy family and always impractical about financial matters, runs into serious legal straits. She had ordered a truckload of pebbles for her driveway, assuming that her sisters would pay the bill. After months of trying to collect their bill, the creditor takes her to court. Anaïs and Hugo plead with the judge to be allowed to take her to Europe, where they intend to put her into a big house and let her live the life she understands.[15] When Rosa sells her house this summer of 1924, the die is cast for Paris. Hugo will get his bank transfer, Rosa will devote her efforts to Joaquin's career, and Anaïs will prepare to leave her first real home.

It is not Anaïs's wish to go to Paris at this time. But Paris is a goal of Hugo's, and they really do have to get her mother away from her creditors. Additionally, Joaquin can study with the conservatory masters in Paris, where Hugo will support them all on his banker's earnings. Her ambivalence about leaving her home is evident in a rare example of sustained physical description of every room in her bungalow. Thoughts of Paris place her under considerable stress during the next months of selling the Nin furniture and packing boxes. Her mood swings—though she no longer records "every quiver and flutter of my inward mechanism"[16]—are evident in her first quarrels with Hugo and in a brief illness. The financial and marital stress is compounded by her knowledge that a return to Paris might mean a reunion with her father.

After ten years in America, Rosa and Joaquin sail 13 August; Thorvald leaves in October; and Anaïs and Hugo will follow in December. Her preparation for Paris is both physical and intellectual. She sells her own furniture, reads Henry James's *The Ambassadors,* and studies French with Hugo. The move will challenge her identity, for she feels American now, and she wants "to write for this country."[17]

Despite her later acknowledgment of her three European "gods of the deep" (Dostoyevsky, Proust, and Lawrence), Anaïs also belongs to the American tradition of Emerson, Thoreau, and Whitman. She seems to be Henry James's Isabel Archer, poised to test her innocence in Europe. The search for happiness, the primacy of the self, the American narrative of self-discovery and invention—are these not her hallmarks? Emerson had declared in 1841 that the novel would "give way, by and by, to diaries or autobiographies."[18] Her diary will eventually be rewritten and added to, clipped and altered, edition after edition (not unlike the process Whitman used in his epic poem, *Leaves of Grass*). Her love for transcendental things, her belief in the meaning of abstract nouns such as Beauty and Art are of the nineteenth century.[19]

Though she has become "American," she was born in France, and her heart will always leap at the name "Paris." She loves both countries, she concludes, but is probably a girl without a country (Hugo has certainly said that she is a girl without a single good language).[20] She is also a good Spanish Catholic girl anxious about the sensuality of Paris. On the way home from Woodstock, she had read Anatole France's *The Red Lily* only to be revolted by the French novel's depiction of the "lust of the flesh." She is troubled also by her prudish reaction to the novel, which reminds her of her own unconsummated marriage. But Hugo is urging her to read such worldly books. She picks up her diary to record her reaction to the French novel and to create her first record of her wedding night—an idealized and inaccurate portrait of Hugo reading poetry, then kneeling with his face in her hands before turning out the light and making delicate love to her.[21]

Paris will bring her closer to reality. It will bring her to her father, who embodies Paris ("Yes, he was Paris—intelligent, insidious, cultured Paris").[22]

She is both frightened and intrigued by Paris and her distant father. She would like to control them both. During a flurry of letters from her parents in Paris—letters initiated by her mother's angry response to receiving her divorce papers—Anaïs takes her father's side. It is the same role she played when she was eleven. Believing that she has worked for months to soften her father with letters until he stands "ready to obey my every word," she is angry that her mother has undone this power. For a time Rosa seems to her hysterical, Joaquin reasonable.

"I understand men better" than women, she concludes, and "can talk more easily to men and win their friendship."[23] Certainly she is better able to control her relations with them. Two men she is attracted to during the months before sailing are Richard Maynard and John Erskine. Both are older men, one an artist, one a writer. She poses for Maynard every week, records his opinions in her diary, and shares her writing with him. In his study she feels like a lady. Her attitude toward Professor Erskine is ambivalent because she cannot attract his attention. At a lunch with Erskine just before the Woodstock vacation, his presence so intimidates Anaïs that she can hardly eat or talk. She is tongue-tied and frustrated in his presence, especially when Hugo raves about her writing. Frightened, she refuses his "polite interest," then resents his chatter about his own writing. She will not get his full attention until later, in Paris.

At the pier 17 December 1924, Anaïs meets her mother-in-law for the first time, and they embrace with tears. The Guiler family (except for Hugo's father, who refuses reconciliation) say farewell to the young couple. At this point in her diary, Anaïs drops the diminutive "Hugo" and begins referring to her husband as Hugh, the name he shares with his father.[24] On board the S.S. *Paris* (her diary says *La France*), a newspaper man takes a photograph of Anaïs, which is captioned with the news that the Guilers are going "to spend the holidays abroad."

The trip is luxurious, the weather perfect, yet her insecurities and mood swings are apparent. The flattering glances of the men thrill her as she descends the stairs with Hugo. She feels the competitive glances of the women and realizes that she has it easier with the men (with them "you are pretty or nothing"). Sensing that she may be a Jamesian innocent, she resents the "foreignness" of the French on board and realizes that she stands out in part because of the American man "tagging" after her.[25] Hugo looks like the young T. S. Eliot, with his strong angular features, his round eyeglasses, and his hair brushed back from his high forehead. Their first encounter on board with a worldly European is with Horace, son of a Count Guicciardi. Horace will become a good friend during their first year in Paris, though his worldly talk of life, women, love, and marriage both impresses and repels Anaïs. He embodies for Anaïs the dangerous sensuality of Paris.

## Paris, Unreal City[26]

"But Paris is so dingy!" exclaims Anaïs, immediately struck by the taxi trumpets, the gray buildings, the December sky, and the shabbiness of the people on the streets.

"No, Paris is ancient!" explains Hugo.[27]

Her depression increases when she sees the cold and uncomfortable garret where her mother and brothers live and when she learns that Joaquin has been diagnosed with tuberculosis and will have to move to a warmer climate. Thorvald is completely unnerved by the entire move.

But the greatest blow is meeting her father two days before Christmas. Senor Joaquin Nin approaches his daughter with tears in his eyes and an appeal to reason in judging his divorce from her mother. Though filled with shock and conflicting emotions, Anaïs remains silent, weighing his expressions of emotion, seeing through his protestations of love. She tells herself that she has been prepared for this encounter with her father by her shipboard conversations with Horace Guicciardi: "how cold-blooded, how cynical, how utterly devoid of illusions, of delicacy, of purity, each is in his own way!"[28] By controlling her emotions, she feels she is out-acting him. She feels that she is in control of the struggle between her mother and father. Thorvald tells her later that by courting them their father is trying to protect his social standing and to humiliate their mother. Though Thorvald decides not to see their father again, Anaïs has more to settle with him. She dines with him and his fiancée, the twenty-seven-year-old heiress Maria Luisa Rodriguez, or Maruca, whom Anaïs had known as a child in Barcelona.

A peaceful walk with Hugo on Christmas morning calms her. They walk through the Tuileries, past the Louvre to the lovely Church of St.-Germain-l'Auxerrois, and lean over the rail of the Pont Neuf to stare into the water. Just then the weak sunshine briefly lifts the winter mist, and she feels the pleasure of being in Paris. A similar New Year's Eve walk on the boulevards with Hugo and Thorvald leaves her feeling indifferent to the city. Her mood is not helped by reading Anatole France's *La Rôtisserie de la Reine Pédauque,* set nearby in the rue du Bac: the novel is horrible and so is Paris.

Hugo is much more open to realistic fiction, which he has been urging her to study in order to put aside her idealism and prudery, which he derides. He is sexually starved when he arrives in Paris, hoping at last to find the sensuality and sexuality long repressed and denied.[29]

Anaïs and Hugo move 3 January 1925 into a pension at 60, rue d'Assas, just around the corner from the Luxembourg Garden and near the garret where Rosa and her sons abide. But room number twenty-seven depresses Anaïs with its damp sheets, bare light bulb, lack of heat and domestic conveniences, and ugly wallpaper. At the end of the month they will move to an apartment on the Right Bank.

During those first weeks in the sixth arrondissement on the Left Bank, Anaïs writes a flurry of letters, begins her second attempt at a novel ("The Blunderer"), and a play. She had decided the previous year that "Aline's Choice" was an early work, but not worth completing. Rosa and Joaquin go to Hendaye, a coastal town in southwest France, for his health, and Thorvald leaves for Havana to live with Aunt Antolina and cousin Carlos de Cardenas. Anaïs writes them daily letters. She addresses flirtatious and literary letters to Richard Maynard, enjoying the sharing of personal confidences. He agrees to exchange journals with her.

Her new fiction again deals with a woman who inspires artists. Rita, married to a musician named Joseph, wants to be a novelist. She leaves Joseph and longs to go to Paris with Edward, a writer who has dedicated his book to her. He wants her to marry him and forget her writing, which he calls infantile, mushy, and ridiculous. She returns to Joseph, who now says she can write all she wants, but she will settle for inspiring his opera and giving birth to their son. The unfinished novel reflects Anaïs's own struggle with the vain hope of being an independent writer and her conflicts about a woman's role. Like "Aline's Choice," this manuscript is an awkward early attempt that will never be published. Its value lies in illuminating the author's struggle to be an artist and her early resignation to the role of a muse who sets other artists "aflame."[30]

During February and March of 1925, they live at 15, avenue Hoche, in the apartment of an American named Mr. Hansen. Anaïs is isolated in the apartment, enjoying Paris only when she crosses bridges in the fog or visits the Louvre. Vulnerable and insecure, she resents the men in Hugo's office who take him away from her. She attends dinner parties with him, but is reluctant to allow him to spend time in "coarse" male companionship. She walks him back to his office at 41, boulevard Haussmann after each lunch, and encourages him to keep up with his journal. She wants him to be a writer, an artist. Unperceptive as ever, she does not see any parallel to the control she condemns in her mother. Her love, she believes, is "tyrannical because it is ideal, because I love his soul, his thoughts, because I could no more bear the sullying of his body than of his mind." Ever yielding, Hugo declines the invitations of the men in his office, and the young couple cling to each other, falling asleep to whispers of love. Anaïs is holding off the last physical intimacy.

A major theme of the early Paris diaries is her ambivalence toward the city and her fanatical hatred of its literary and cultural sensuality. A ribald farce makes her feel sullied; the rudeness of the people offends her; the novels of Anatole France shock her; she is even startled when she hears Hugo ask a friend if Anatole France has had many affairs. The greatest shock, and one she will not mention in her diary for years, is her discovery of a cache of erotica left by the owner of the apartment.

Anaïs climbs on a chair to reach the back of Mr. Hansen's closet. She has already taken down his pictures of nude women, and she now wants to reorganize the space in his bachelor apartment, for he has left many of his belongings behind. There stacked on the top shelf are French books with lurid covers and illustrated sex scenes. Secretly over the next weeks she reads the erotica in a state of shock and excitement. These paperback novels with their colored pictures introduce her to prostitution, whips, and garters. She struggles to accept or understand sensuality (which she thinks of as impure) on an intellectual level. One moment she hopes for the day when the world will choose the Good and the Beautiful, the next moment she secretly imagines herself a prostitute. She will not record this incident of finding the erotic novels until her diary of 1932.[31]

She will only admit to accepting realism when she reads the novels of Edith Wharton. With Wharton's fiction she ceases being "surprised by evil." She can believe *Glimpses of the Moon* and *The House of Mirth,* but she still cannot believe Anatole France. Also, in reading Wharton Anaïs becomes ashamed of her own novel, remembering the many words of Hugo and Professor Erskine about discipline and use of the concrete. Reading Wharton's books is her "real birthday," she notes on her twenty-second birthday.

Oblivious to her surroundings, she is reading Wharton, Madame de Stael, and Gabrielle d'Annunzio, at the very time that modernist literature is in fullest flower on the Left Bank. Though Ezra Pound has already left for Italy, James Joyce, Gertrude Stein, Ernest Hemingway, and dozens of other international avant-garde artists are making literary history in Paris. Anaïs mentions Hugo reading Joyce's *Ulysses,* which has been for sale at Sylvia Beach's Shakespeare and Company for three years. But knowing her Catholic sensibility and prudishness, he only tells her about it and does not urge her to read the Irish novel. Only once does she mention *Ulysses* this year, and then in the context of "nauseating smells and sights" on a trip to Hendaye. She is cocooned in domestic love, assuring her diary of her "perfect marriage" and her "perfect lover," and clinging fiercely to their innocence.

Yet the uneasiness of their bourgeois life is evident in her diary and fiction. Behind the descriptions of their walks in the rain and rowing in the lake in the Bois de Boulogne hover her sexual repression and her disapproval of French sensuality. When the two-room apartment feels cramped she becomes philosophical about the role of women. Because her only social life is with Hugo's business friends, she throws herself into clothes and fashion. Clothes cheer her up. Like costumes, they deny ugliness and hardship. She dresses stylishly in resewn dresses and redesigned hats. At one dinner party she is surprised to find that the wife of the host, who makes twice what Hugo earns, is dressed humbly and expresses depth of thought. Suddenly Anaïs is uncomfortable with her own elegant clothes and fashions, which she has always justified as part of her own sense of artistry.

Hugo and Anaïs think themselves bohemians, but physical discomfort soon cures their romanticism. Paris should only be seen romantically, she believes, but in every way it disappoints her—from the damp cold to the rude, pleasure-seeking people. She says she wants to hurl Emerson and Carlyle at their apathy and materialism. Once she questions if she might love Paris had she been tutored in French history. But her struggle lies deeper, in that aspect of the French reflecting her father's libertinism. She attends his concerts, but avoids contact with him, referring to him as the family's "Problem." In Horace Guicciardi, she will contend, in microcosm, with her relationship with both country and father.

Guicciardi is a garrulous, complex man, worldly and versatile, a stimulating conversationalist cynical in his remarks about women and marriage. He openly challenges her idealism and sentimentality. She, in turn, will try to change and inspire him—as she has Eduardo, Enric, Miguel, and the other men in her life. She had concluded on board ship that his cultural refinement shone like a pearl, and she desires to win him to a higher purpose. He shows Hugo and Anaïs Paris; they invite him to tea. She admires his clever phrases, his intellectual freedom, his willingness to listen to her idealism, but she disapproves of his casual relationships with women and argues for a greater delicacy in human affairs. She can easily win Frenchmen's glances, now she is after their minds. She argues books and ideas with him (they both read Dante and James Branch Cabell), hoping to win him to her noble ideas. She hopes to set him aflame with idealism—a task she now believes to be her vocation.

But there is one man she cannot intellectually seduce, cannot control. Her father is the man responsible for her need to create an illusory and beautiful world of purity. She will not be ready for this encounter until eight years from now, and then only after years of psychoanalysis. For now she tries to avoid her father, in part out of loyalty to her mother. Initially, during her first month in Paris, she had felt she was in control of the battle between her parents. She had met and judged her father and found him egotistical, hypercritical to the core, and unlovable. She determines to tell him that she does not love him but cannot, for she fears him and fears the past. She

cannot tell Hugo why she feels the way she does because Hugo is "so good";
he cannot understand her instinctive dislike—"I would not want him to
understand," she says.[32]

In March, after they attend a concert of her father's Spanish music, she
broods despondently and sifts through the old familiar torments: "I sink,
back into the brown shadows while the red fan lies hidden in tissue paper."[33]
The implication in the diary is that she does not tell him of her decision to
reject him, she just fades from his life as he does from her diary. Only a few
more mentions of her father during these Paris years are recorded—mentions
of his lack of creativity, his anger and fussiness.

On 8 April, about a month after their second wedding anniversary, Anaïs
and Hugo move to an apartment in rue Pauquet (now called rue Jean-Gi-
raudoux), then leave by train for Hendaye, on the west coast of France,
where Joaquinito is regaining his health.[34] They visit nearby San Sebastian
several months before her contemporary Ernest Hemingway visits there
from the Pamplona bullfights. Unlike Hemingway, who will trace the spiritual loss of his generation in *The Sun Also Rises,* she focuses on the "soul"
of the Basque people and attends Good Friday religious services with her
family. She still believes that her first responsibility is homemaking, for such
is her traditional concept of marriage in Latin culture. She is a wife who also
writes. This March she begins an essay on journal writing, which will be her
major creative effort during the next two years in Paris. Her diary and her
decoration of their apartment will be her best fictive creations, both the
artistic expression of what she always calls the "perfect" marriage.

## Good Wife–Bad Wife

What emerges from the diary during these years is a struggle between the
good wife and the bad wife. The first year of marriage Anaïs practiced
obedience and "little sacrifices," polished Hugo's shoes, filled his pipe, and
sat on the floor at night with her head on his knee. Though the wifely
attentions continue, the subtext of inner conflict emerges. As her father's
violation of her youthful innocence had led to the creation of a good girl in
her early diary, so the stimulus of Parisian life (with its gross sensuality, its
coarseness and sacrilege, her father's proximity, and her own sexual dissatisfaction) leads to the creation of a good wife and perfect marriage. Even
Hugo's job and attendant associations are a threat to her security. Though
she expresses pride in his work, she fights the hold his bank job has on him.
In the name of saving his artistic soul and their life together, she urges him
not to become just a "providing machine." Yet he is the sole provider for her
family, and she sleeps late mornings for her health and is served breakfast
by the Irish maid. She spends her time in thought and writing—a higher

calling than bank work, she reminds Hugo. She will have to do the thinking for them, he confesses. What emerges is a pattern of analysis, sharing, confession, and contrition. She relives events in her diary, expresses concern about neglects or slights, then discusses or reads them to Hugo. Occasionally she brings him to tears of contrition. After such confidences and confessions she always feels closer to him. The closer they get, the less they see of Paris and Parisians. The isolation is broken when they settle into a permanent apartment.

I am essentially a Producer—an Actor—she decides a year after moving into her dream apartment, a studio for artists at 11 bis, rue Schoelcher (a Left Bank street once home to Picasso and later to Simone de Beauvoir). Beginning in the late summer of 1925 she throws herself into sewing and decorating this ground-floor apartment whose two large windows look out on the wall of the Montparnasse Cemetery (her mother and brother live in the facing studio). She buys furniture and rugs, has bookshelves made, drapes shawls and hangs Oriental lamps, creates each room as if it were a stage setting from Rubáiyát, makes social plans for dinners and musicales, becomes obsessed by beautiful baubles, and has clothes and accessories made in matching colors. She invents a form for her life, a reality with which she can live, and she rewrites and types her diary very much the way she decorates her house.

The idealism and Puritanism of the good wife is buttressed by her perfectly decorated apartment. In their brief trips to the Loire Valley she waxes eloquent about chivalrous and legendary France, makes lists of what she will accomplish, seeks only beauty around her, and attends Mass. Yet something else is going on as indicated in the repeated expressions of her desire to be "good," meaning unselfish, polite, unambitious, cheerful, nonargumentative. She must never contradict Hugo, must never express her hatred of Paris, she insists, then adds that she would really love to run away. She will confine her outbursts to the diary, which will also serve as a reminder to be good. Once she admits that her "very real self is not wifely" but "wayward . . . active and hungry," and controlled only by love. What "takes room" and makes her "bad" is the self, with its will and its need for definition and freedom. Her moodiness, restlessness (Hugo calls her dissatisfaction "a kind of madness"), egotism, and imagination are all bad. Sometimes she thinks about the boys she could have married. If good is selflessness, bad is selfishness; if good lies in the purity of English ideals, bad is Latin. Increasingly she thinks of locking up her diary.

When John Erskine returns to Paris with his wife and children at the end of 1925, Anaïs determines that she will win his attention for Hugo's sake. Her idealization of Erskine nearly paralyzes her movements when the family arrives for a Sunday-afternoon visit, but she succeeds in articulating the ideas she has rehearsed for him. They return for Christmas Day, and they all visit Chartres during the first week of January, when for the first time she has private moments to talk to this father figure her husband so admires. He comes to dinner a week later and she hangs on his every word, watching his face, "trembling with joy" when he praises her. He has lit a fire that will later turn passionate. But most important, he offers her two things: praise for her essay on journal writing, which renews her confidence, and an introduction to Mme Hélène Boussinescq, who will introduce her to early modern literature.

Though Anaïs initially sees Mme Boussinescq as a middle-aged, assertive, and disagreeable woman, she learns to admire her knowledge as a French teacher of English literature and to value her instruction. Boussinescq, a Huguenot and socialist from the south of France, is amused by the naïveté and American provincialism of Anaïs, but soon recognizes her eager mind and sound, though unschooled, literary judgment. Even an autodidact needs an occasional mentor, and Anaïs asks if they could meet regularly for guidance in reading and writing. Madame Boussinescq is a friend and translator of Sherwood Anderson's work and does not fully appreciate the novels of John Erskine—a judgment that eventually will affect the attitude of Anaïs—but she does introduce the Guilers to modern literature, even if the discussions of Waldo Frank, Thomas Mann, Heinrich Mann, and Jules Romains are often over Anaïs's head. Soon she is reading L'Europe and Le Figaro litteraire and checking books out of the American Library. Boussinescq, who introduces her to Léon Bazalgette, the translator of Whitman, is certainly a catalyst in Anaïs's introduction to the literary world. Anaïs affirms a preference for the biographies of intelligent women, and both she and Hugo find their worldview echoed in Miguel de Unamuno's The Tragic Sense of Life. They are thrilled to learn that they live in the neighborhood of important artists, including the American sculptors Janet Scudder and Jo Davidson and writers Christopher Morley and Edith Wharton.

What Anaïs does not know during her studies with Boussinescq (the family now calls her "Boussie") is that they are a generation too late. Anaïs could have crossed paths in Paris with Pablo Picasso, James Joyce, Gertrude Stein, Ernest Hemingway, F. Scott Fitzgerald, Djuna Barnes (the avant-garde novelist Anaïs will later try to seek out), and Jean Rhys. But Anaïs has not yet heard of most of these writers, nor is she yet ready for the avant-garde: she finds the early moderns occasionally difficult and discordant.[35] However, within the year she will read Manhattan Transfer, by John Dos Passos, and be pleased by its powerful (though ugly) portrayal of life. Had she walked past the Dôme café in Montparnasse, just two bus stops from her apartment, she might have seen Dos Passos. But she has often been told that there are only fakes on the café terraces.

The security of her beautiful studio, her growing knowledge of world literature, and the praise of her writing by John Erskine signal a new self-assurance for Anaïs on her twenty-third birthday in 1926. She has made a friend of Katrine Coolidge Perkins, the wife of James H. Perkins, the manager of First National Bank (later called City Bank) and the man who made the bank international.[36] Compliments from the men at Hugo's bank convince her that her force of personality is in the power of her "prettiness." She begins talking on social occasions and shines on the dance floor. Horace Guicciardi tells her that he now finds her interesting because she giggles less and has a lower-pitched voice than before. Once, he confesses, he had not liked her "cuteness" and the habit she had of pressing her lips into a pout. She herself believes that her eyes are no longer set in frightened or "owl like fixity" at the world. Yet all this effort to look pretty distracts her from her writing. She doubts her vocation as writer. Her writing, the good wife says, is second to Hugo and a convenient occupation, for it does not interfere with his comfort.

Anaïs and Hugo sublet their apartment for a month and take a train to Italy in the spring of 1926. They spend a month traveling in Tuscany. The public kissing, streetwalkers, the theatre remind her of the hated sensuality of Paris. Coming out of a French play, she remarks, "Is there anything closer to the animal than the French?"[37] But Italy gives her a great feeling of freedom, and she realizes that France has been crucifying her creativity. While Hugo has succeeded in Paris, where the French are weak in business, she has been undermined by the monster called "Literary Tradition." Their last stop in Italy is the Aurora Hotel in Fiesole, above Florence, where despite the rain and idle café-sitting she delights in the country. She and Hugo decide to go back to New York City, where at least there is a secrecy about sex and evil. Their present forays into sexual intimacy are either too disappointing, painful, or infrequent to merit mention in any of her diaries.

When they discover the "High Place" in their Paris apartment in May, they decide not to return to New York. Their concierge offers them the use of the maid's room with a balcony, traditionally the top half floor of Parisian apartment buildings, as extra quarters. There they discover a quiet world, a high perspective on Paris, where Anaïs thinks she can write her books.[38] From the balcony they can look down into the cemetery and in the distance to the north can see the top of Montmartre and the Sacré Coeur. The discovery of the maid's room encourages their isolation. They move their bed up there and Hugo exercises on the balcony each morning. But she still is bothered by her "badness," what Hugo calls her madness, and seriously flirts with Horace, questions her literary calling (she calls her second novel unfinished and useless), corresponds with her early beaux (Eduardo and Eugene), and changes her hairstyle. Only the visit of the Guiler family in July returns her to her wifely dinners and entertainment. Proudly she shows them her decorations, her studio, her dinner table—a living expression of what she calls her ideals. She appears to win them over with her social graces and shopping skills.

At twenty-three Anaïs is not a modern woman. There are no cocktails, bobbed hair, smoking, or dancing the Charleston for her. She belongs in a different century, as others frequently tell her. She chooses longer dresses, antique jewelry, pulls her long hair in a rolled wedge in the back of her head and holds it with a Spanish comb. Her new hairstyle involves a minor cutting of only the front hair, which is parted in the middle and brought straight down the side of the face with a curl against each cheek. She feels more mature and classical in this character, for she is a woman who loves Oriental veils and costumes. She wants to be a tropical flower, her mother tells her mockingly, when she will not go out on the cold winter days. She would rather collapse on a couch amid colorful pillows, weep at concerts, and believe that life is a play in which the stage needs to be elaborately arranged.

She confuses reality with realism, ideals with fantasy. In an ugly and hurtful world she must make a life in which she can live. Her need to control, to arrange the furniture on the stage and shut out competing elements, leads her to choose the beautiful and declare it the real. Her imagination (in life and diary) transforms events, parties, conversations into the best light: she declares she has a gift for finding the best word in every conversation; with her taste and manners she could have been a marquise; she settles all family quarrels; her husband agrees with her in everything. The diary persona is both a lovable and good young wife and a defense. If reality is not lovely, she transforms it (she tells one man her husband is of French descent and the vice president of National City Bank, but later says that she has supported herself in Paris by dancing and her own wits).[39] She pulls the thread of Ariadne and hears "the empty wooden spool knock against the floors of different houses," as she says of a character years later in *Children of the Albatross* (1947).[40]

She also confuses the senses with sexuality. At a party when each guest is choosing touch or smell as their primary sense, Anaïs chooses sight (to which Hugo agrees). Though she flirts with men, including Enric Madriguera, who visits this October, and dresses for dramatic attention, she does this in service to her ideal, she believes. Her fear of sexuality continues to lie behind her tirades against the sexual aspects of French life. She refuses for now to read Freud or Proust (she had read him once and never again) and abhors Stendhal. Though she acknowledges that her senses seem to be coming to life in the third year of her marriage to Hugo, she casts this erotic awakening among her sins. When Hugo looks at photographs of women and wants to play with her body, she becomes fearful and confused; she goes as far as she can in becoming "physically sensuous" by dancing seductively for him in the evenings. Her refusal to allow Hugo to experiment sexually is followed immediately by a reaction: she develops tonsillitis and then influenza. Then she is distracted by the return of her mother and Joaquin, followed by visiting aunts, "idle" Cubans, and musical Spaniards. But her uneasiness about Hugo's emphasis on the body remains. Anaïs wants only what she calls a "poetry" of sex.[41] She needs to poeticize and purify the physical, in contrast to her father. She does not think she is puritanical, just a lover of beauty.

She will capture in her fiction years later the sexual inexperience and coldness of these early years of marriage. In "Lilith," an erotic story in *Delta of Venus* (not published until after her death), her protagonist is dry and "sexually cold, and her husband half knew it, in spite of her pretenses." Her temper and stormy scenes are "a symbol of the tension which did not take place between them sexually." Her husband "did not know the preludes to sensual desire, did not know any of the stimulants that certain jungle natures require, and so . . . he retired behind this wall of objective understanding."[42]

These struggles with reality, sensuality, and sexuality are perhaps naive, often noble, and heartbreaking. And they are directly related to her writing. After reading her essay on journal writing, Hugo tells her that she cannot write objectively. The minute she leaves the personal (concrete experience), her writing becomes "deadened," he says.[43] Recalling the small honors of her school years, the publication of two poems, and the encouragement of Hugo, Maynard, and Erskine (who originally suggested she write about journal keeping), she wonders if she has not been deceived into believing that she can write. And yet she knows that she has a rich inner life, understands human nature, and feels isolated from the world—certainly she is an artist. She has begun several other novels and abandoned them. The best writing, she accurately concludes, is in her journal, where she is more direct, less studied, and deals with experience. The diary of this period contains ample evidence of her hours of introspection and study, her articulate expression of events, her imagination. Carrying the dead weight of her essay with her to the top floor of her apartment building, to the "High Place," she feels less discouraged. Even the best essay, however, will never "make up for unattractiveness."[44]

As she approaches her twenty-fourth birthday, she knows that she is "too Latin" not to admire the authority and rule of Hugo as he rings the bell for the maid, Clementine, at the dinner table. Anaïs makes her life one with his and believes that they share every opinion, habit, and social preference. She is so dependent on him that when he goes golfing or away on bank business she cries and, in order to control her feelings, goes to three movies to fill up the time until his return. That she will begin to make a life for herself years later reflects her own strength of will. When a letter from Mrs. Erskine (John Erskine had just published another novel, *Galahad*) informs her that they will return in the fall of 1927, Anaïs fairly pants in anticipation. Will she be ready for him? she wonders.

The struggle between her life with Hugo and a Catholic dedication to monogamy, on the one hand, and, on the other, the honoring of her own intellectual growth and exceptional talent—is the theme of her journal. In this theme lie her links to the feminist movement. One critic, who says Nin's "Diary of a Wife," with its "rising consciousness of a young woman," makes a "compelling case history for the rise of feminism," believes it is the closest of all Nin's diaries to the autobiographical genre and the best of too few female bildungsroman.[45]

In her New Year's List of Accomplishments, Anaïs lists seventy-five books read and three hundred pages of her journal recopied and revised. She is still reading and marking books for discussion with Boussie. After a discussion of Erskine's *Galahad*, including a perceptive analysis by Boussie of Guinevere's beauty, new dresses, and manipulation of men, Anaïs feels that Boussie is mocking her coquetry. Then she glances at the plain clothes and appearance of her friend and vows to continue unashamedly her own devotion to beauty.

Then suddenly life changes. Though Paris has been her "Calvary," Anaïs and Hugo decide he should stay with the bank. The bank officers hear of his plans to return to New York and raise his salary by seventy-five percent, including a paid yearly return visit to New York City. Soon Joaquin has a baby grand piano and Anaïs fills her life with new gothic furniture, a series of maids, numerous plays, new books and films, visits to the beauty salon, massages, dressmakers, a visit to a spa in the Pyrenees, dance classes, and two weeks of art classes (she is more interested in the story behind the face of the nude model than the artwork). Her life is filled also with family, the move of cousin Gilbert Chase to Paris (he stays in the maid's room), the numerous young male friends of Joaquin, and the return visit and flirtation (followed by remorse) with Enric.

Anaïs and Hugo sail on the S.S. *Mauritania* for a month's visit to New York. It is the summer of 1927, less than three years after their coming to Paris. They read Will Durant's *Story of Philosophy* on the ship, enjoy the luxury of the dining rooms and the bite of the salty wind, as Anaïs studies the profiles of people who walk back and forth on the deck. As they sail into New York harbor that sweltering hot June day, she recalls the anxiety of their arrival in New York as a newly married couple more than four years earlier. Eduardo meets them at the dock and remarks on her new "steadiness" and lovely clothes. Perhaps it is the new clothes she has designed and had professionally made, and perhaps it is her education with Boussie. She begins smoking the day she arrives and during the entire visit relishes playing the Parisienne. She feels foreign and is critical of small things in Americans and America. Only American theatre, which is less cynical, does she find preferable to the French. Anaïs and Hugo attend nearly a dozen plays.

They stay in the studio of Richard Maynard when they are not with the Guilers in Forest Hills, and meet several times with Eugene and other Culmell relatives, her "New Family" (her name for the Guilers), Frances Schiff (her grade-school classmate who is now a reporter for the *Tribune*), and Professor Erskine. Anaïs meets secretly with Enric. While posing for a new portrait by Maynard, she describes life in Paris with such imagination that she falls in love with this fictive Paris and looks forward to her return. She is filled with nostalgia when the Maynards drive her and Hugo to visit the former Nin and Guiler homes in Richmond Hill.

Only two negative notes mar the visit: the Guilers prefer that Hugo's two sisters not spend much time with the Catholic Nin cousins until they are older (unknown to Anaïs at the time, Hugo has agreed to his father's request that he leave the Catholic church). Second, after all the compliments on her clothes (she records each one), she is upset that so little attention is paid to her ideas and opinions. That people will not be able to look past her cosmeticized face and designer clothes to see the intelligence and artistry of her mind will be a lifelong problem, but she will never cease to pay homage to beauty, both physical and intellectual.[46] She accepts Maynard's compliment that she is an "artist in living."

Their only serious grief occurs on board the return ship when they discover that her cosmetic case with their two diaries has been lost. Grief and seasickness are short-lived, and Anaïs reconstructs from memory her diary (begun at the spa in the Pyrenees) and makes fresh plans for Paris, a smaller and softer city than New York, and a city that she no longer sees as her Calvary. The most vital coming event is the fall arrival of John Erskine, whom they had visited in New York. His life had seemed so energetic and beautiful. Anaïs has become "utterly convinced of his greatness."[47] Perhaps she anticipates her seduction.

# CHAPTER FOUR

## 1927–1931

# Intimate Betrayal

"[An] artist . . . is born with a mania to complete himself, to create himself. He is so multiple and amorphous that his central self is constantly falling apart and is only recomposed by his work."

—*Anaïs Nin,* Ladders to Fire

"I feel like a well-appointed laboratory of the soul . . . in which none of the vitally fecund and destructive, explosive experiments has yet begun."

—*Anaïs Nin, 1931*[1]

SENOR PACO MIRALLES, teacher of professional dancers, follows Anaïs into the dressing room and, in what seems a continuation of the dance, drops to one knee gallantly. She places a hand on his head, as if to acknowledge his tribute, and he moves his arm around her puffy nylon skirt, which swells and rises like a flower.[2] He leans forward and places his lips on the tightly bound mound of her panties. His kiss that October day marks the loosening of her inhibitions that began with a decision she made upon returning to Paris in August of 1927.

Soon after her arrival, Anaïs Nin sat alone in the dining room of the Bon Marché amid all the other shoppers who had come to this grand Left Bank department store. She remained after lunch with her notebook. There she acknowledged her final acceptance of Paris, and a growing sense of some warm awakening within her, a sense of her physical body—she calls it the Devil in her. No one can deny she has struggled for two and a half years against what she calls "European tolerance" and "satanic flexibility," and the French lack of "conscience, scruples, and humility."[3] But as Henry James observed fifty-two years before, it is one's second trip to Paris that fatally ensnares the American.[4] She is only twenty-four years old, still a young wife and repressed Catholic girl, though no longer technically a virgin. This scene prefigures the dichotomy of her life in the coming fall and winter: to be preoccupied by the domestic pieties and verities, yet enflamed by her senses, by her own physicality and incipient rebellion. The trip to New York has given her a new perspective on Paris and on Europe: like Henry James's Daisy Miller, she will yield to the blandishments of continental sensuality.

While Hugo works his long hours at the National City Bank, Anaïs lives the life of a pampered bourgeois wife, with new maid, hairdresser, seamstress, hat maker, and afternoon naps, which she considers absolutely necessary for her health. She works to control all aspects of her life. She shops, sews, writes letters, reads, keeps her journal, and studies to make herself attractive and her marriage secure. What would she be without Hugo? she asks. She notices that he is growing more virile, worldly, and aristocratic, and resents the sacrifice of their precious hours together to his job. But there are material compensations, of course. Most notable this summer is a new car, a black Citroën with dark red leather. Though she thinks that the driving lessons may force her to lose some of her timidity, they never succeed in making her a confident or competent driver.

She also becomes more daring in her dress and appearance. She lightens her hair and studies her wardrobe, reads a book on the history of costume, and creates clothes as costumes in the drama of her life. She understands that her role is "purely decorative," is flattered when someone compares her to the portraits of Mme Récamier, the celebrated nineteenth-century French beauty, and notes when some of the men do not listen to what she says but just stare. This staring no longer disturbs her as it once did. She takes pride in what she calls the "standard of superficial beauty . . . in decorating, dressing" that she sets. When she appears in October at a private dinner party at Durand's restaurant in a tight-fitting blue velvet dress with enormous medieval slit sleeves, tight waist, velvet turban, and matching velvet coat trimmed with squirrel, she concludes that she has achieved the "highest mark in dressing." This superficial life of dancing, beautiful clothes, and flirting has, she confesses, come to "dominate" her life. But it does give her the assurance that she needs; she concludes that it gives her "spiritual and intellectual independence."[5] Hugo, in turn, is immensely proud, confidant that his professional standing is owed in part to his elegant wife.

She nourishes her inner development by continuing her journal, planning to turn it into a kind of novel to be read by others. Because she needs an audience for her writing, she adds more vignettes to her entries. She continues her discussions with Hélène Boussinescq. Together they read of Sherwood Anderson, whose *Dark Laughter* (a 1925 novel contrasting unrepressed Negroes to sterile Caucasians) had recently been parodied by Ernest Hemingway in his *Torrents of Spring*. As far as Anaïs is concerned, Anderson has liberated her feelings and dreams from "timidity and self-consciousness"—just as dancing has liberated her body and John Erskine her mind.[6]

By December she is very restless and dreams that her hungry ego is everywhere, boundless, dazzling, and feverish. Forsaking the spiritual for the physical, she is reading books on human sexuality, studying and performing dances, and including more of the visual, such as photographs, in her diaries. The diaries related to transitional periods in her life are given different names ("John," "Writing and Dancing," "The Woman Who Died"). She also writes long descriptions of homes and places; and she mentions social and political events: the anti-American demonstrations that follow the Sacco and Vanzetti execution and the American Legion parade (which makes her hate Americans).

Together she and Hugo, who have been married over four years, read the *Kamasutra,* an eighth-century Hindu manual on sexuality with diagrams of positions for intercourse. Without using sexual words, Anaïs talks about the *Kamasutra* in terms of the "art of love," "feelings," "instincts," and "emotions." The book may have been introduced to her by a doctor, for she will admit years later that she had gone to a doctor because she thought that something was "wrong" with her sexually.[7] Hugo, who may very well have been the one to introduce the book to his wife, assures her that this knowledge should be for everyone. Yes, she agrees, it should not be left only in the hands of the "devils" who would distort it. The following month they read another book that she identifies only as a book on Oriental love. Whether they try other means to improve their sex life is not known, but in "Lilith," an erotic story she will write two decades later, Lilith's husband gives her pills containing Spanish fly to overcome her dry tightness.[8] The Guilers have not reached what Anaïs claims is a loving sexual relationship, but at least they are now talking about the subject that has hung ominously over their marriage for more than four years.

After dropping out of sketching class at the Académie de la Grand Chaumière ("The Great Dustiness," she calls it) because the nudity bothered her and the "brutal curiosity" in the men's eyes enveloped her, she has begun Spanish dancing classes with Senor Paco Miralles. She now has castanets and dresses, and, from Hugo this Christmas, a black mantilla and comb. Despite her stage fright, she is performing the tango and Sevillana for family and friends. These sensuous dances—always controlled by tradition and costume—are an ideal expression for her ego, for the artist in her, and for her emerging sexuality.

## Spanish Rhythms

In a little bakery near the intersection of rue de Liège and rue de Clichy (north of the St. Lazare train station), Anaïs has her coffee and brioche before dance class. She routinely takes the number sixty-eight bus from boulevard Raspail, a bus full of what she calls special people—headed for the Apollo and the Casino de Paris on the boulevard de Clichy, not far from where the prostitutes walk the streets. Her desire for the stage, with its bright lights, dark applauding audience, cheap dreams, and heavy makeup, is quickened as she finishes her coffee. Shopkeepers at the jewelry-repair shop, the bookstore, and the art store occasionally ask her if she is from the Casino. She loves this corner of the world. Its artificial scenery and bright lights burn away the cold, sad streets of Paris.

She is having coffee with Paco Miralles once a week after class, and with every expression of her admiration for his dedicated teaching, he grows more gallant. He directs her with his hands. When he touches her waist or her leg, she feels the warm touch of a magician or sculptor and obeys. She feels that she is "melting" into the Universal Woman—at least into the desirable coquette. When he asks her to go away and perform with him, to dance in all the cities of Europe, she cannot answer except finally to say that she is not strong enough. She is frightened. Though she had been physically aroused by his kiss on her panties, she feels more pity than passion for the man. Perhaps she is unable to achieve intimacy with anyone, she fears. When he had left after the kiss to pay the pianist, Anaïs had dressed, trembling and flushed. She will use the incident twenty years later for Djuna, her alter ego in *Children of the Albatross,* but in her diary for December 1927 she mentions only a "mental" release with Moralles in which she stops running away from his wandering hands. "Today I stay. I feel all life running through my body. . . . It bites me, soils me, bleeds me."[9] Whether she yields to Miralles physically or mentally or both—though the shocking kiss is probably the limit of their sexual contact—some barrier of fear has fallen. She wonders if she is bad. Later, walking down boulevard du Montparnasse, closer to home, she wonders what would happen if she suddenly said and did exactly what she wants to say and do. She will take that chance with another Spanish man.

Gustavo Morales is a young Cuban composer whom the Guilers met in September, a brilliant talker and mimic. In the Spanish manner, like her father, he wears powder, lipstick, and nail polish. She had been immediately attracted to him and wrote a long profile in her journal. Now he is returning from Spain, where he produces ballets, songs, operas, novels, and plays. In anticipation of the arrival of Morales 24 January 1928, Anaïs is feverish with excitement. She thinks she sees in him the same qualities she has found in Hugo: softness and strength, humor and romanticism. When he becomes too critical or frank, her defense is to flirt. She turns hot, then cold in his presence. Perhaps he will be the friend for whom she hungers. But soon he leaves again for Spain.

Since her return from New York, Anaïs has been in considerable turmoil. Her sexual hunger increases, she fears her inflammable nature, and her Catholic puritanism is at war with her Latin sensuality—a sensuality she confines to lush colors, sensuous fabrics, and beautiful movements. With all her self-examination—and certainly no woman has ever looked longer and deeper into her inner self—she has yet to acknowledge the pain inflicted by her father or the sexual dysfunction of her marriage. The image she projects and will perpetuate years later is the portrait of a free woman designing her own life and world into something beautiful.[10] But in fact she is on the edge psychologically, most certainly neurotic. "*Je ne suis pas heureuse ici* [I am not happy here]," she repeats, echoing Mélisande's words to Golaud in *Pélleas et Mélisande*.[11] She splits her personality by beginning a diary within her diary, calling it the diary of "Imagy," probably a derivation of the word "imaginary." In "Imagy" she expresses her "transformations," or the bad girl–bad wife. Here is where she records Miralles's adoring looks and kisses, which remind her of the way Enric used to look at her. To control what she calls her fever and hunger, she throws herself into dancing and social life.

Miralles is the dominant artistic director who controls her body. When she overhears him tell a friend of her father's that he has asked Anaïs to perform with him, she suddenly imagines the look on her father's face when he hears this news. She basks in Miralles's admiration and deliberately fuels his admiration with her coquetry. Yet she pities him because his students take advantage of him, just as she pities her father when she glimpses him, caught with his mother-in-law in a corner at a concert reception.

She is also performing with Hugo, who takes dancing lessons to please her. Their social life revolves around music, theatre, and the Spanish friends of Joaquinito and her mother. They even invite some of the bankers to their musical evenings in the rue Schoelcher. Hugo's performance with Anaïs of a Spanish dance astonishes them all. Her dancing seems to satisfy both the fire in her body and her need of an audience for her self-expression. She requires adulation, she admits, and looks for it on the stage and at parties. At a banquet in March, she wears a draped gold-lamé dress and gold-lamé turban that turn every man's head. Every compliment is recorded in her journal. Yet she frequently is critical in her diary of her face and hair and small breasts.

Although the music of her beloved brother Joaquinito, playing from the facing apartment, alternately stirs and soothes her, her frustration with the family (her mother's domination and the Guilers' refusal to meet her family) is evident in her smoking, her fatigue and insomnia, her flirtations and feverish dancing, and sometimes in her prudish overreaction, as when Miralles sees her in her slip in the dressing room.

When Hugo, after five years of marriage, mentions the possibility of having a baby, she is reluctant and convinces him that they are too young and free to be responsible parents. Yet he is thirty years old and has a good-paying job. Her excuses are numerous: they are lovers, not responsible parents; she is too busy with dancing; and she still does not feel free from her own mother. She is also too easily fatigued. Perhaps the most important excuse is that she is determined to remain what she calls the "Other Woman." She will not be abandoned like her mother, but one of the women her father always sought (later she will use the word "mistress"). Certainly she is not psychologically ready for motherhood, for she is still split into two women: one pure and loyal, the other (whom she describes in far greater detail) impure and restless.

By spring she is openly discussing in her diary her sexual frustration and her desire for a "friend"—she cannot bring herself to say "lover." Gustavo Morales is in Spain, Eduardo Sanchez and John Erskine are in America. Why cannot Hugo be enough? But the spring sap is warming in her body like rising music. Her flirtations excite her as much as they do the men. After the weeping and the loss of sleep, she concludes that her flirting takes nothing from Hugo, who seems not to notice, and it excites her for his evening return. Can being "bad" make her a better wife? Have these years of loyalty been foolish? Finally, she decides to live no longer only for him. Wherever this decision leads her—and it will be a year before she even considers an affair—she will do nothing to hurt him (though she believes he would forgive her anyway).

During a ten-day vacation with Hugo in Montana-Vermala, Switzerland, in April 1928, she finally reads Proust seriously and concludes that she has a "Proust-like mentality." She explains to Hugo that she is abandoning English literature and the ideal of "a spotless, detached, inhuman" self because character is less important than understanding and accepting life. Understanding, intelligence, and curiosity are what French literature embodies, she adds, and these conflict with goodness. This change of values may lay to rest the good wife–bad wife battle she has been waging, she thinks. Ever trustful and believing, Hugo affirms her decision, yet asks that she declare the supremacy of their love. Their love will be their religion, he hopes. "As long as I respect our love, then," she promises.[12]

Her sense of herself as a writer has been affected by these internal conflicts. At the beginning of their vacation, she concludes that she loves writing above everything else. Then she confesses to Hugo that it would be greater to become a woman than a writer. She may not write anything other than her journal until her "hunger" is satisfied and her "fever for living . . . abated."[13] For months now she has been writing weekly if not daily in her journal and frequently reworking portions of it into small stories. These fragmentary pieces are written in the first person and are a mixture of reality and fantasy. Her goal has been to have some writing ready for Erskine. She writes to John ("Cher Ami," signed "Anaïs"—the year before her letters were to "Dr. Erskine" from "Anaïs Guiler") that she is sizzling and fermenting in Switzerland and has written seven short stories for his "verdict."[14] When she examines her fugitive pieces, she concludes that she is not an inspired artist but an elf who haunts all the arts and is haunted by them.[15]

Her dabbling in several arts—music, writing, interior decoration, dress design, modeling, dancing, social entertaining—has enabled the Guilers to enter the musical and literary coteries of Paris. Her Paris, however, is the Paris of *Une Semaine de Paris* and *Guide des Concerts,* which lists the piano concerts of Joaquinito and his friends. Their social life, other than the obligatory bank associations, is Cuban and Spanish. If this limits her Parisian experience, it at least makes this second sojourn in Paris more pleasurable for her. When she encounters a critical, analytical Frenchman, she reacts harshly. She does not love France any more than she ever did, but the Spanish in Paris have made her love Spain the more. Her knowledge of French and American literature is becoming less influenced by Boussie, who accompanies Hugo and Anaïs to concerts and attends their parties, because Anaïs believes she has learned all she can from her friend. She can now read on her own the journals of Tolstoy ("boring") and Katherine Mansfield ("sensitive, penetrating") and the fiction of Proust and Gide.

Yet she is not ready for the newest literature, as a visit to a poetry conference at the Vieux Colombier Theatre with Boussie illustrates. Clearly the event is a surrealist occasion, though Anaïs does not use the word, for the "program" begins with actor Henry Verneuil reading Apollinaire, which is interrupted by a rebuttal reading from some man in the audience, followed by hisses and applause. The man runs to the stage and slaps Verneuil's face. Soon many are on the stage exchanging blows. When the police arrive, some participants demand to be jailed. To the experienced in the audience, this is just another staged surrealist happening. Yet Anaïs is "struck by Verneuil's helplessness" and by Boussie's "nonchalance and indifference and amusement."[16]

## Transitions

During the first really warm days of spring, she is feeling eager, womanly, and filled with Proust. She needs friends: Horace Guicciardi, their friend from the first ship passage, has left her sphere of influence; she longs to see Enric and Eduardo; she craves the friendship of Gustavo Morales, the Cuban composer; and awaits impatiently the arrival of Erskine. An unexpected telegram interrupts her spring longings and takes Hugo and Anaïs to New York for a month.

Hugo's father died at the end of April, just ten days before he was to visit them in Paris. Hugo is devastated and sobs so violently that Anaïs is frightened. The impression this makes on her remains with her as a fear of ever hurting him again. It is expressed later in her novel *A Spy in the House of Love*, in Sabina's keeping from her husband, Alan, the knowledge of her sexual liaisons:

> At the thought of confession, of confiding in him, she was almost asleep when out of the darkness the image of Alan appeared vividly and he was sobbing, sobbing desperately as he had at his father's death. . . . I must always be on guard, to protect his happiness, always on guard to protect my guardian angel. . . .[17]

They sail for New York. Her hours in Forest Hills with Mrs. Guiler are filled with mutual distrust, and Anaïs leaves every day for a few hours with her friends. Each encounter reveals and provokes more changes in her. She becomes the dark and exotic "French" woman who (according to her diary) stirs desires for freedom in Hugo's friend Edward Graves. When she shares typewritten portions from her journal with the Maynards, they accuse her of cheating by not including personal revelations such as her parents' quarrels. With Erskine she still feels young and intimidated (she is twenty years younger), but she is able to tell him that Eve in his novel *Adam and Eve* is an American, not a universal woman. Anaïs heeds the promise of fidelity she has made to Hugo and twice resists calling Enric Madriguera.

Two lunches in New York with her cousin Eduardo, however, prove astonishing and life changing. He informs her that he is homosexual and that he is being psychoanalyzed. Though uncomprehending, she is shocked nevertheless. He has long aroused her sexually, but he had been unhappy and confused by his excessively "ethereal love" for her. When he explains his daily visits to the analyst, the couch, his revelations, she listens intently. She has never heard of psychoanalysis until this day. As usual, Hugo knows more about homosexuality and psychoanalysis. Yet they both do some reading in a psychology book before the second lunch with Eduardo. Though Anaïs thinks she knows something about homosexuality from her reading of Proust and Gide, she wonders if perhaps she could have made Eduardo a man if she had followed through on their first attraction.

She is sitting on a deck chair 23 May, a blanket wrapped around her legs, and despite the vibrations of the second-class deck of the S.S. *Mauritania*, writing in her journal. Suddenly she realizes that her journal is her own psychoanalysis. She achieves from it what others do from psychoanalysis: self-knowledge and confession. She also has a new, intense desire to return to Paris since she has learned that Mr. Guiler had cut out of his will any heirs who married outside the Protestant faith. Hugo will not soon be retiring from banking, it would appear.

Though the remaining months of the summer of 1928 in Paris are filled with Nin, Culmell, and Guiler family visits, including one from her brother Thorvald, her unfulfilled desire does not abate. The weeks seem lifeless, despite attentions from Gustavo Morales and Paco Miralles. She keeps up her "Imagy" diary of sensuality, her weekly coffee meetings with Miralles after class, and her café meetings with Gustavo, who has returned from Spain. He looks so Spanish that she invites him for dinner, allowing him to read some typewritten pages of her diary. My greatest saint is Mary Magdalene, he announces, because she was capable of passion. Challenged, Anaïs retorts that she too is capable of complete passion, but the hot blush on her face testifies otherwise.

By mid-September, Anaïs finds herself caught in a comical situation; Gustavo, she notices, seems more attracted to Hugo, and she is jealous. She will always prefer to have her friends uniquely hers. Morales is also interested in Joaquin, which upsets Rosa. But Anaïs does not seem fully aware that the matter might be a sexual attraction. During the last three months of 1928 she wins Gustavo's friendship and gains the confidence of Erskine.

## John Erskine

John and Pauline Erskine have returned to Paris with their two children, Graham and Anna (both taller than Anaïs). Anaïs shops and looks for an apartment with Pauline this October. When she can she listens to the sound of John's typewriter as though it were a musical signal of his genius. Since his Columbia University days, Hugo has revered John as a father figure; Anaïs shares this admiration and, as with her own father, makes Erskine a patriarchal figure who inspires both fear and desire. He is a stocky, middle-aged man, usually photographed wearing glasses and a hat, not handsome, but with the look of authority. His musical talent (within a decade he will become director of The Juilliard School of Music in New York City) and his fame as a novelist certainly add to the appeal of this seemingly proper Anglo-Saxon professor. Every casual word of encouragement from him fuels Anaïs's womanly and authorial desires. When Pauline confides that he is restless for more experience and romance, Anaïs spends a sleepless night thinking of his sad eyes, her own deprivation, and the possibility that she could give him such experience. She could inspire him!

To overcome her fear of the Erskines, she exaggerates her French behavior and in conversation insists on the priority of the physical in any love relationship. Erskine assumes she is experienced and can be confided in. Eager to talk to someone about his affair with an American woman, he shows her a photograph of the woman, Lilith. In turn, Anaïs confides in him her flirtation with Gustavo. She envies Lilith, but notes in her diary that the woman is over forty and not entirely beautiful. When Lilith comes to Paris in December, Anaïs offers to give him an alibi if he wants to be with his mistress.

The journal entries alternate between John and Gustavo. Her imagination runs riot this fall and winter, and she feels the need of a fictional disguise as she begins a new journal. She has found a nonthreatening partner for her imaginary lovemaking in Gustavo, who meets with her over café crèmes, flirts with her, touches her knee but not her lips (the touch makes blood rush to her face), then returns alone to his apartment and creates an imaginary short story about the consummation of their flirtation, which he shows to her at their next café meeting. They record their conversations in journal and fiction, and return for more.

Images of burning flesh, leaping blood, and waves of sensuousness flow cloyingly through her journal after each meeting with Gustavo. Enough of chastity, she declares, while doing nothing to carry out the proclamation. Once she was all thought and idealism, just standing on the shore of life; now she will ride the "waves."[18] When she and Hugo perform a Spanish dance at the staid Cuban embassy, she is in a fever imagining the desires of the men whose glances caress her body. Yet she is only skimming the surface of sensuality, collecting romantic experiences for her writing, while avoiding "complications," a word she uses frequently to mean physical surrender. She needs intense experiences to inspire her, she concludes, because she is weak from rewriting and polishing her work—I really don't *work*, she confesses, I create! She abandons her efforts on yet another unnamed novel because it is terrible.

The year 1928 ends with two visits to the Riviera. In Monte Carlo, the luxury, sun, and service allow hours of daydreaming described in poetic, almost Technicolor passages in her journal. She longs for Gustavo to see the purple, blue, yellow, and red colors of the bay and the city. She feels clothed in the colors of the sea and intoxicated by the light. She, like her writing, seems to "flow" in this climate. Reading Colette, she is shaken like a "powerful wind" by the French novelist and her descriptive style. She concludes that they both are best at writing about themselves—and they both have pointed chins and are as independent and saucy as a cat. Though Colette is more human, frank, outspoken, and full of mockery, Anaïs hopes to rival her. In an honest contrast of herself and Colette, Anaïs says that Colette likes women, she men, and admits that she herself is still shy and sentimental and has a tendency to assume intellectual poses and to moralize.[19]

Half assuming that a second trip to Monte Carlo and Nice will cure her of Gustavo, she and Hugo spend Christmas week in the Hôtel Eden, Cap-d'Ail, where the weather is now cold and gray. They become ill with colds. Orgies of reading combined with unbridled coquetry prove dangerous. After deliberately drinking an entire bottle of champagne in order to help herself face a party of bankers, she makes the mistake of tempting an American man, a forty-eight-year-old lawyer from New York who is a connoisseur of women. He takes three consecutive evenings of seductive behavior seriously and suggests that he cancel a trip and meet her in Paris. She is frightened by his behavior, which she sees as a bad omen for the new year. She awakens to 1929 with a hangover, but with material for a short story entitled "Fear of Nice."[20]

Hugo by contrast is rewarded with yet another promotion. He is now submanager of the branch office. Just six months before this he had been promoted from credits to trust officer. His success comes from long hours, tennis playing, their entertaining, and his "French" wife, she believes. He is not brilliant, and certainly not a high-powered businessman like his brother, Johnnie, or her brother Thorvald; she insists he is an artist of banking. When his hours are long or he talks on too much about the office, she is bored, looking elsewhere for creative or erotic stimulation. Afterward she praises him and his attentiveness (on weekends), his understanding of her, and his "unbelievably fine" character. She also evaluates herself a "perfect wife for five years."[21] She worries that her need for passion is impure, a need that reflects both the frustration of a nonorgasmic woman and the compulsion to control her own and others' lives. She believes that she has the mystic ability to inspire others: Gilbert Chase (her cousin) writes his novel warmed by her belief in him; Gustavo rushes home from their meetings to write his stories; Miralles teaches with new vigor; Richard Maynard courageously pursues her religion of self-development. To be a muse almost justifies her existence, she concludes.

Alarmed about her frequent meetings with Gustavo Morales, members of the family confront her individually—Joaquin, Gilbert, Rosa, even Thorvald, on a six-month visit from Havana.[22] Joaquin puts on airs of piety; her mother weeps at the possibility that her daughter's flirtation may threaten Hugo's reputation and dignity. Hugo says nothing, but shows his disapproval. Anaïs has been reading biographies of Mme Récamier and Mme de Staël and understands, as her family does not, that she needs special friends to stir her creativity and intellect. With Gustavo she has what she calls a bohemian connection. Yet, in response to the family pressure, she reluctantly reduces her meetings with him to only three times a week, at the Dôme, La Rotonde, or the café at the Hôtel Lutetia. Occasionally, if he seems particularly anxious to see her, she invites him to the apartment. As she sees Gustavo less, she seeks admiration and flattery elsewhere. She poses for artists who admire her at parties, until her family confronts her to protest such libertine waste of time.

Her passion for Gustavo ultimately fades when she awakens to his weakness of character: he has no discipline or dignity when he takes money from Hugo that she had requested on his behalf. She is humiliated for him. For a moment she considers herself as little different from Gustavo, cared for by the generous Hugo, but she rejects the parallel when she recalls her own hard work as a model and writer. She continues to meet with Gustavo, gives him an electric heater, pays for the coffee, and helps him plan his ballet. But her passion evaporates. One day she lets him wait fifteen minutes in the bitter cold.

Hugo's financial success takes them from their studio apartment at 11 bis, rue Schoelcher to 47, boulevard Suchet, a spacious apartment near the Bois de Boulogne, close to their friend the Peruvian poet Armand Godoy. While waiting for the flat to be refurbished (and partitioned for Rosa and Joaquin to have separate quarters), Anaïs and Hugo remain on the Left Bank at 13, square du Port Royal, where she builds a miniature cardboard stage design of their luxurious Right Bank apartment. "Her play was now her very life," she writes in one of her short stories, "her house, carefully arranged as an absolutely fitting background to her imaginative costumes."[23] She is suddenly taken with Oriental and Byzantine designs for her clothes and apartment. She is enamored of people with royal titles, flattered to be painted by Princess Natasha Troubetskoi, a Russian émigré painter and decorator who uses Anaïs for illustrations (and will later paint a large canvas of her). Only great living women (or biographies of great older women) can inspire her. Ordinary women dislike her, she concludes, because she is "stagey" and painted and likes to please. Her reflection in the mirror sustains her as she practices hip movements for her dances.

The stories she is writing, like her journal, are composed with an eye to winning the approval of John Erskine, who had earlier wounded her with his remark that her writing had not yet coagulated. She is seeing him chiefly *en famille* in the winter of 1929, but he brings his Lilith to see Anaïs before the two of them leave for New York in February. Anaïs is delighted to be his confidante, but feels sympathy for his wife, Pauline, and the children. She has not forgotten her own parents' quarrels over her father's unfaithfulness.

During John Erskine's absence she continues to appreciate the passionate friendship of Gustavo, who claims his admiration for her holds him back from consummating their union. Her spring plans rest on the return of John and a visit to St.-Paul-de-Vence with Hugo, who denies her nothing. Hugo finally reads Proust to please her, speaks of his desire to write poetry, and pledges anew that she can have whatever freedom she desires: she should never get old with regrets. She will do the living for them both, she concludes. These silent agreements of their marriage will be fictionalized more than thirty years later in her novel *Seduction of the Minotaur*: Lillian will "change and move" for them both while Larry maintains a world in which Lillian is the only inhabitant; she "breathes" for Larry, who has abdicated from life, appearing "only when summoned."[24]

She records his declaration of her freedom in her diary and will seek to redeem that promise for the next fifty years. When Hugo expresses his own desire to be an artist, she doubts him. Though convinced herself that she could live in poverty with him if he were an artist, she is assured by his need for luxury, comfort, power, and privacy. He pleases her by insisting that she have a car to avoid public transportation.

When she hears that Erskine's return to Paris is delayed by Lilith and bad weather, Anaïs throws her book into the corner of the room. She is reading Madam Aurel's *Le Couple* on the art of adultery and taking lessons from the behavior of Erskine. She proposes to herself another solution to adultery: she will only be adulterous in her imagination, make a written study of Hugo's virtues in her diary and wait until he makes himself great in her eyes. Within a month her plan will fail.

By the middle of April, John has rejoined his family in Paris and the two families are planning a trip to Beaune, the wine center of Burgundy. There John introduces them to fine wines, to the museum and Hospice of Beaune, and the story of his military service there during the war, for which he earned the Legion of Honor. His ideas, the church bells, the red wine, the "fever" in her blood, and the look in his eyes give her no peace. "I was hungry, and here was fullness," she notes.[25] She steals several moments alone with him, tells her journal of their ideal communion, and maneuvers to get him to carry her to the backseat of the car (by stubbornly refusing to move herself from the front).

When the car drops the Guilers at their door in Paris, John asks when he can come to hear the new passages of her diary. He arrives the next day, when Hugo is at work, and they speak of pagan living and of restraint. When she confesses that she is "hungry," he says they share this longing, unlike most other people. She reads the passages about her stay in Nice, which he pronounces vivid. When she tells Hugo two days later how impressed John had been with her writing, she declares it a turning point in her life.

She sings all day, weeps at night when Joaquin plays his own composition, and feels physically numb. One night when the Guilers and Erskines are out on the town, John appears to warn her against her passion. He speaks of his new novel about a woman writer who returns to her husband because she can no longer write about her experiences and has become an insincere writer. Anaïs is upset by this plot outline, yet remains convinced that together she and John could have an extraordinary union. When he tells her—during a five-hour talk on 7 May—that he avoids seductions by considering the consequences, she persists, convinced that he is also in profound sexual upheaval. She is enflamed when his arm rests on her theatre seat. Why not, in fact, do what they have already done in their fantasies? she wonders.

She is in a constant fever these days—agitated by John Erskine, by reading Léon Pierre-Quint on Proust, by seeing Ibsen's *The Wild Duck*, by Gustavo's plans for a new ballet (she will star in it and finance it), even by her walk along the high gray wall of Prison de la Santé, in the rue Jean Dolent, near her home. But she veritably bursts into flame when John kisses her. The bold gesture happens spontaneously after several afternoons of personal and intellectual exchange in May. The very air of the room seems to her thick with her desire and anticipation, and his tongue in her mouth feels like the ultimate penetration. But he is uneasy about being with Hugo's wife and claims he loves both Lilith and Anaïs. For days afterward Anaïs thinks of little other than this kiss.

During a formal dinner a week later at the elegant Lapérouse restaurant on quai des Grands Augustins, he grips her arm knowingly and asks for a ride home, during which he presses her knee with his hand and invites himself in, where he stays until 2:30 A.M. Her description of the evening is full of girlish romantic phrases: "taut with desire," "would explode," "fever . . . melting into one another," and "his eyes devoured me."[26] All this passionate exchange of looks occurs while Hugo is off getting drinks in the other room.

When the doorbell rings the next morning, Anaïs knows it is he. John draws her to the divan for repeated kisses. He rubs his hands over her breasts and between her thighs, then asks her to change her clothes so that he may kiss her bare breasts. She remembers reading in one of his novels that one had the right to see the body one loves, and she returns wrapped only in her Spanish shawl. He carries her to the divan and lies, probably fully clothed, beside her. The kissing and caressing continue. Despite being "bathed in the moisture" of her own desire (as she describes it in her diary), he is unable to penetrate her entirely (her word is "powerless," his might have been "sexual fiasco"). He blames it on too much love, thoughts of his friendship with Hugo, and too much thinking about passion. Still awed by his maturity and greatness, she is understanding: it probably is not the moment or right mood; she begs him not to feel bad. It could have been the interference of clothing, the reader might conclude, for he asks her to open her shawl so that he may see her body. She complies bashfully. You have the body of a dancer, he whispers. "You are like a little faun—so sensitive, so little, so fine, darling little pagan."[27] When she returns fully clothed, he asks her in a fatherly way if she will not experiment with love anymore. After him how could she play with mediocrity? she assures him.

The night before the Erskines leave for the United States, they dine and dance with Anaïs and Hugo at a Paris nightclub. On the dance floor, John, casting his failure as noble abnegation, tells his little fawn with the sensitive breasts that he has paid her the ultimate compliment in not forgetting himself. Then he whispers something about her having the power to drive many men to excess.

His temporary impotence in fact empowers her. She knows that his lover, Lilith, with her humor and maturity, gives him stability, and that she herself is but a passing little flirtation. Yet he informs Anaïs that she has taken over his libido, even without physical consummation. This news assuages her feelings of guilt toward Hugo, and to compensate she increases her acts of devotion. She will write a novel about a woman artist who loves men—a creator of lives. Power lies in knowing how to use both truth and fiction, as Ibsen's The Wild Duck has taught her, and perhaps lies can be transformed into good.

As Anaïs walks down the boulevard du Montparnasse on the last day of June 1929, the sun is shining in her face and her black cape is floating behind her. Desire makes her body ache. She misses John Erskine. She hopes to pull Hugo from the mediocrity of his career as a banker to a life full of beauty and intensity. She alternates between guilt and exaltation—her secret makes her feel strong. By the end of the month, when John sends a book, not a letter, when Rosa and Joaquin are in Hendaye, and she has to spend five days in London pleasing Hugo's family on the occasion of his brother, Johnnie's, wedding, she is desperate for intensity, for "white heat." She even entertains thoughts of having a child.

She is sitting in the fashionable Cercle du Bois tennis club when she sees before her a little girl, "wide-eyed . . . her arms wide, her yellow dress fluttering." Sensing a struggle, a demand, from the child, she resists:

> I must be beaten, I thought sadly, for I am beginning to want to pass my life on to another. . . . I will never give myself entirely to anything. I will never escape from myself, neither by love, by maturity, by art. My "I" is like the God of the weak faithful who see Him everywhere, always, and can never escape the vision that haunts them.[28]

In the interim between John's leaving for New York in mid-1929 and the arrival of Eduardo from New York a year later, Anaïs fills her time designing another stage set—at boulevard Suchet—for her life. She writes nearly a dozen short stories. Ignorant of the economic depression that looms—Hugo spends three thousand dollars preparing seven rooms, which includes an apartment for Joaquin and Rosa—they move on 17 July 1929. As she looks out over the trees in the Bois de Boulogne, she assures herself that at twenty Proust had written stories that were just as sentimental as her "Aline." She will give herself until her thirtieth year.

Turning inward to regain tranquillity and self-assurance after John's departure, her mind plays over ideas, music, and the people she sees in shops—from these she will create her stories. Assurance also comes from outward control, perfection, and beauty. She fills separate scrapbooks with carefully cut-out photographs for home decoration, pictures of dance costumes, dress designs, literary articles, Oriental fantasies, travel tips, and portraits of her by other artists. Everything gets sorted, filed, glued, and arranged by her sense of minute orderliness, her need to control every aspect of her life.[29]

Because she feels she is at once Christian, Jew, and Oriental, Anaïs designs her apartment in the Byzantine manner (Hindu lamps, arched doorways, Moroccan furniture, turquoise blue, Veronese green and gold)—a setting that affects her writing, her clothes (costumes, she calls them), and her exotic dancing. The visiting Guilers are stunned by the rooms and by watching Hugo and Anaïs dance for them in the Chinese lacquer red room. She applies the same care to her appearance as she does to the design of a dressing table with three mirrors. Several men, she claims, bring their women to her to learn about appearance and manners. From a taxi on the avenue des Champs-Elysées, she looks out at the shops with a feeling of poise and worldly power. She is no longer the poor daughter of divorced parents, resewing hand-me-down dresses from her wealthy Cuban cousins; now her mail is brought on a silver tray by the maid, and she has purchased an 18,000-franc ($720) fur coat.

One day while walking down a Right Bank boulevard, she catches a glimpse of her wide eyes and confident walk and her cape sailing in the wind, and she writes that John Erskine does not know what he is missing. She waits a long time for his first letter (he clearly wants to forget their sexual encounter), answering him with carefully crafted and embellished letters that she slips under the desk blotter when Hugo enters. She sends John books. She carefully interprets every phrase of his formal responses. At times she believes her love for him is a thing of the past; at others she insists she will win him back by having him know her better. This struggle will continue for nearly two years. She cannot accept the fact that he can walk away unscarred. It shakes her self-confidence. She needs to commune with a mind older and bigger than her own, she insists. She demands total love—to be first in the eyes of any admirer. She admits to having carefully nurtured a cult of individuality, the self she began creating when her father abandoned her.

To try to forget John she makes Hugo her religion: disciplined by her Roman Catholic training, when she was young she broke her ties to the church and made beauty and love her devotion. "I need love more than food," she will later tell a friend.[30] She strives for absolute conjugal love for Hugo. Two weeks in September at the Palace Hotel in Caux overlooking Lake Geneva brings a semblance of marital harmony and a burst of creativity. Yet she also sends a discreet letter to John. A short story, ironically entitled "Faithfulness," depicts her inner struggle: Mr. Bellows suddenly declares to a surprised and disbelieving Aline that she does not love her husband: "I admire your courage, you dear, lovely, spirited young thing. You don't want to say anything, and yet things are much easier to face if you can talk about them."[31]

The short stories from this period, all culled from her journal, are sentimental and her characterization weak. She is trying to develop her craft, but hating the rewriting process. She writes fast, in English, with occasional Spanish constructions and with a sprinkling of French words. Only at the end of her life will she agree to have sixteen of these stories published as examples of her early craft, in a book entitled *Waste of Timelessness and Other Early Stories*. Her ambition at this time is to write about spiritual values or intangible truths. The reality of her sexual desires does not seem to interest her. This style, as amorphous as it seems in her early work, will not substantially change. She will always try to capture the imagination and inner life of her characters.

The domestic harmony of the Oriental palace on boulevard Suchet is disrupted this November 1929. Each evening Rosa and Joaquin, now back from the southwest of France, sit with Anaïs and Hugo around the fireplace, reading, writing, and listening to the strains of Andrés Segovia's guitar on the phonograph. One evening Hugo brings home news of the economic crash of the stock market. He shares his worries about their diminishing savings and the possible loss of his capital. At first Anaïs seems detached, philosophical, and counsels other values. She offers the consolations of her inner world, which, she tells him, his hard work has given her the time to build. She would willingly return to public transportation and give up parasitic friends (who always cost Hugo money). Hugo goes as far as to consider a loan from his mother and the possibility that they will have to sell the Paris apartment and move to the country. As the crisis and these nightly discussions continue, there are also quarrels: ever the dreamer, she hates talk of money and has been naively encouraging him for years to stand by her side as a fellow artist. When she realizes that he can only be a banker, that he lacks imagination, she is overwhelmed by unhappiness and despair.

### A Lawrentian Awakening

It is Christmastime 1929 and Hugo is in London for the funeral of his uncle George. During several weeks of intense study—she calls herself an intellectual tapeworm—she discovers the worlds of Aldous Huxley's *Point Counter Point,* which she finds too cerebral, and D. H. Lawrence's *Women in Love.* Lawrence's world thrills her with its focus on feelings, sensations, and the spirit (her first reaction is to see the sexuality only as a metaphor for the spiritual). Both men know more than John Erskine, she realizes. Though she thinks Lawrence's fiction dangerous, she continues to read his novels with a sense of astonishment: she has never known sexual passion!

Lawrence's descriptions of man's "blood-consciousness" within a matrix of nature and woman awaken Anaïs. She does not have a passionate love for Hugo. He is distant and malleable; in short, weak. What she had so needed in her arduous search for her own individuality she now sees as somewhat contemptible in a man who does not have a mind of his own and is so easily influenced by others. She says nothing about her disillusionment. Only in her short story "Tishnar," in which a woman is trapped on a bus that does not stop, does she express her frustration and fear: "We make this trip only once. . . . Didn't you see the sign in front?" says the conductor.[32] For this young Catholic wife, her early marriage seems like a one-way bus trip with no transfer.

After a two-week family vacation in the south (the stock market offered an illusionary reprieve), during which time Hugo heeds her nagging to write, she tries unsuccessfully to see him with new eyes and undergoes a tremendous psychosomatic crisis. She suffers six days of neuralgia; just before her twenty-seventh birthday she thinks she has developed heart trouble. She thinks about death. Medical tests diagnose her problems as acute depression and pernicious anemia, not heart trouble. The symptoms are evident to the reader of her diary, though not always to her. Her continued reading of Lawrence inflames her restlessness. She continues to be driven by the demonic urge for passion. She masturbates, then feels guilty. When a sixty-year-old acquaintance urges her to go out and have an affair, Anaïs takes fright and rationalizes that she will play fair with Hugo (and be as unlike her father as possible). She weeps for hours on end. She deludes herself into believing it is because Hugo corrects her writing (he mangles and kills it, she says), making her lose confidence. Perhaps, too, it is because she has lost John's affection. Or it might be the sudden financial shortfall. She knows that her brother Joaquin would tell her she needs religion.

But what she needs, she realizes, is passion; what she needs is to "bury John." As therapy she seeks work. This spring of 1930 she poses for various painters, including Princess Natasha Troubetskoi; she dances on the stage; and she cultivates her writing, surviving on liver extract, coffee, and sedatives. Occasionally she faints. Natasha warns her that if she does not eat and stop dance practice, she will become so light she will float to the ceiling. Once she thinks she sees her father in the audience, a wishful but revealing apparition. Though the petty jealousies of the dance world hurt her, she feels at home on the stage, assured, a new woman. She has a gift for posing, and prefers the artificial world, which she can control. Through costumes and makeup she believes she has begun a career as "Anita Aguilera," dancer.

The death of D. H. Lawrence comes as a blow. In her desk drawer is a letter to him and a review she has written of his works. Now she will never communicate her appreciation to him. Within a month she determines to write an essay on his work, which has not been sufficiently appreciated. In Lawrence's women characters she finds herself. On rereading some of her own stories she is amazed to find his spirit. In a blaze of inspiration, she is suddenly writing her own short stories and taking notes on Lawrence.

On a return trip with Hugo to Caux (Montreux, Switzerland), she takes along her Lawrence books. She wants to share her Lawrentian awakening with Hugo, who reads the novels and shares her enthusiasm. Like many urban married couples, they are always physically closer on vacation. But this two-week April trip is characterized instead by cold snow and hours of writing, and after Hugo returns to Paris, she stays on. She rewrites the story entitled "Anita" and meets two important women: Eugénie Kazimir, a sixty-year-old artist who is independent—a miracle of fulfillment without the help of men (Anaïs has now met her first lesbian); and a woman called Kay, with whom Anaïs has an "almost man-to-man friendship." Kay, a writer of concrete stories, reads her "Anita," which she praises, talks to her about the need for a dramatic climax in her fiction, and sends her work to her own agent. Anaïs has abandoned dancing and taken the pen name Melisendra (Mélisande in French)—revealingly the name of the virginal wife who has an affair in Debussy's *Pelléas et Mélisande*.[33] Though her first stories are rejected, her agent expresses enthusiasm for a second group Anaïs mails him. She returns to Paris both physically and spiritually as if from the mountaintop, feeling strong and "almost loving" herself.[34]

"Anita," later retitled "She," then "A Slippery Floor," is the story of a "quiet and mousy" half-Spanish dancer at a music hall. She appears in a "ballet" portion of a program performing Spanish dances with castanets, her hair curled beside her ear and held in place by Gomina pomade. Amid the "cheap dreams of heavy makeup, dazzling spot lights, a dark audience applauding her," she becomes a "new woman." One day her mother, who had abandoned her when Anita was four, returns to her life. By transforming the story of her own tragic abandonment, Anaïs is able to displace her own internal conflict about fidelity and sexual freedom. Anita's unfaithful mother lies shamelessly, loves "white heat living," and advocates following one's impulses. Anita herself counsels fidelity and self-control. When her mother's boyfriend falls in love with Anita, she resists, "denying herself a happiness that would hurt another."[35]

After another month (July 1930) in Caux, where Anaïs works on an essay on Lawrence ("Sex and Mysticism") and a long short story ("The Woman No Man Can Hold"), Hugo and Anaïs return to Paris to find Eduardo Sanchez. In the two days she has with him before he leaves for Hendaye (where Rosa and Joaquin are holidaying), she shares some of her frustrations. Even the awareness that she and Hugo will have to sublet their Oriental apartment and move out of Paris does not dampen her excitement with Eduardo. She and Eduardo sit long hours at a café, talk about Lawrence, and feel that they should have become lovers years before. Even as she leaves him at the train for Hendaye, jealously knowing that he will probably love Joaquin,[36] she thinks that Eduardo will help to "cure" her of John. That night, sensing her excitement, Hugo holds her in bed and whispers that he understands he can never satisfy all her needs.

Elena, the protagonist in an erotic story she will write a decade later, is reading *Lady Chatterley's Lover* for the first time. Elena is riding on a train to Montreux to await her husband, Alan, who is but "a shadow of herself . . . who echoed her moods." While she is reading Lawrence's novel, she realizes "that she had never known the sensations described." She has discovered the "nature of her hunger, expectations, and quest." But Alan never seeks to understand her transformation.[37]

## A New House and Publisher

Louveciennes is a small village, near the Paris suburb of St.-Cloud, set amid a forest, with a lovely stone church, tiny square, and old castle. It reminds Anaïs of the little town in which Flaubert's Madame Bovary lived and died. The town, built in the fourth century by the Romans, is west of Paris, a half hour from the Gare St. Lazare by train. On 17 August 1930, when their housing agent drives Hugo and Anaïs to see the house behind a heavy metal gate at 2 bis, rue Monbuisson, they sign a lease. It is an old building on a hill from which one can see Paris, and the street is lined by limestone walls. Their home is attached to a manor house (Villa des Filleuls) and has small rooms, thick walls, a rather dilapidated interior, and a big overgrown garden.[38] It has outdoor space and offers possibilities for a creative decorator. Most importantly, they will be saving nearly 25,000 francs ($1,000) a year in rent alone. Anaïs weeps at the loss of her spacious apartment, her elegant setting, her designer gowns and perfume.

Anaïs sits at the Dôme with Eduardo, who has now moved into an apartment in Paris, sipping espresso and playing at being bohemian. They have been planning and painting the rooms at Louveciennes, attending the theatre while Hugo golfs or dines with his banker boss, watching Luis Buñuel's surrealist film *Un Chien Andalou,* and continuing their talk about Lawrence. Eduardo feels like her twin; she could trust him with any confidence. Eduardo confesses that he is obsessed by her (it is like loving himself, he says). We are joined mentally, they agree, like twins. Joaquin and Hugo are jealous. She thinks people around Eduardo and her sense that they are bound together. As they look across at the Rotonde and the busy intersection with boulevard Raspail, Eduardo speaks of his homosexuality, which he thinks is an immature form of love. He has just broken up with a lover and hopes to move on to what he calls normal love. (By October he concludes this cannot be merely a mental decision.) But he fears that he and his cousin Anaïs will only be like brother and sister; he will lose her again. Several times, she confesses in her diary, they come close to physical intimacy. Their psychological closeness occasionally borders on becoming compulsive and controlling. The tension drives her to a closer analysis of male-female relations, and that reflection makes her more independent.

A story entitled "Our Minds Are Engaged" narrates Eduardo's return and their renewed connection through Lawrence. "What he desired was wholeness and normalcy, through the love of woman," says the narrator in this poetic story.[39] In "Elena," written a decade later, cousins Elena and Miguel, who first met during a large family holiday and are reunited in Paris, paint her country house, he fondling her while she is on the ladder above him. But his paralysis comes when he speaks her name, for it is the name of his mother and his sister. Into the story Anaïs puts her childhood desire for Eduardo, her unawareness of his homosexuality, their frustrated adult desires during the preparation of Louveciennes, and their honesty with each other.[40]

She and Eduardo also talk a great deal about psychoanalysis. He has let her read the journal of his analysis, and they discuss Freud and Jung. Psychology discovers motives, he tells her. She cannot know herself without them. Yet she senses that her diary *is* her analysis. It is a journal of consciousness, while Proust's work is a journal of memories.

Meanwhile she has sent her article on Lawrence to *The Canadian Forum: A Monthly Journal of Literature and Public Affairs,* which accepts it for publication (without pay) in October 1930. "D. H. Lawrence Mystic of Sex" is her first adult publication.[41] She asks Hugo to send a copy to John, who much to her surprise, responds with enthusiasm, prophesying that she will become a real modern novelist and should begin signing her own name to her stories. Though Eduardo has told her that her best writing is in the diary, she continues writing short stories.

One day while riding the metro and buses on errands, she thinks through a new mystical story about a woman who sails away on a boat that had been abandoned in a garden (later called "Waste of Timelessness").[42] Her fiction frequently uses water and boats—the Piscean symbol of her astrological sign (Eduardo first told her). During this fall and winter of 1930 she submits a number of manuscripts to various publications and people: Janet Flanner, the Paris correspondent for *The New Yorker,* returns them unread; Sylvia Beach, still busy with James Joyce at her Shakespeare and Company bookstore, tells her five times that she has no time to read the stories; H. L. Mencken, at *American Mercury,* does not respond. Boussie likes "The Woman No Man Can Hold" and translates it into French. One publisher, recommended by Beach, does express some curiosity.

In September Anaïs goes to see Edward Titus at the Sign of the Black Manikin bookshop at 4, rue Delambre, located behind the Dôme café, where she and Joaquin often meet. At his bookshop, supported by the cosmetics profits of his estranged wife, Helena Rubinstein, Titus has been publishing contemporary books and selling rare volumes. Just the year before, when Sylvia Beach had refused to help Lawrence, Titus had issued a Paris edition of *Lady Chatterley's Lover* for the author. Titus had recently taken over the defunct *This Quarter*, a little magazine once edited by the late Ernest Walsh and Ethel Moorhead. He is busy preparing the second issue, but is curious to meet a woman who has written about Lawrence. Though he does not accept any of her stories, he proposes that a young graduate of Columbia University help her edit the fiction. He tells her she has promise and should eliminate her numerous adjectives and poor transitions. Her manuscripts of this year prove his judgment of her writing correct.[43]

Her writing does not cease while she creates another artificial environment. Building a home is building the arena of the self, and Louveciennes will be her greatest effort at creating a magical place; she continues the painting, bookcase building, and decorating long after they move in. She moves also from the predominant turquoise of the boulevard Suchet apartment to more coral, a warmer color for a house with small rooms and no central heating. Visitors describe the decor as apricot and peach blossom; one calls the house a jewel box. Anaïs sees to every detail, from the fireplace in the library to the right of the front door, to Joaquin's bookcases in his studio in the attic (Rosa and Joaquin occupy a separate wing, and the servants' quarters are upstairs).[44] The fireplace, in blue Moroccan mosaics, is purchased at the Arts Décoratifs design center and is her favorite piece of furniture.

One of the best descriptions of the house will be given by Alfred Perlès, a frequent visitor in the 1930s. His description is of a house with a distinctly Spanish flavor:

> . . . warm mahogany paneling, stained-glass windows as in Granada, Moorish lanterns, low couches with silk cushions, inlaid tables, mosaic patterns in tone and glass, Turkish coffee in hammered coffee trays, bittersweet Spanish liqueurs. In a darkened corner, incense was burning.[45]

In her own fictional treatment of the house, it is a metaphor for her compartmentalized life, each room distinctly different. Djuna, protagonist of her novel *Children of the Albatross* (1947), lives in a house that speaks for her. It is

> divided into many cells. . . . The room of the heart in Chinese lacquer red, the room of the mind in pale green or the brown of philosophy, the room of the body in shell rose, the attic of mem-

ory with closets full of the musk of the past. . . . Every room . . .
a range of moods—lacquer red for vehemence, gray for confidences. . . .[46]

In her own writing room she hangs pictures of Lawrence, Joaquin, Hugo,
Eduardo, and John. The gravel parking area in the front and the garden in
the back are guarded by Banquo, their new Alsatian dog (named either from
Hugo's Scottish ancestry or the obvious—though unacknowledged—Guiler
parallels to the Macbeths). Ruby, the Pomeranian, has the run of the house.
Anaïs's mother, Rosa, whom Anaïs describes as suffering with "contradictis,"
keeps the two maids stirred up with her demands and histrionic scenes.
Aside from her occasional anger at her domineering mother, Anaïs believes
she is going to be happy at Louveciennes. One of its greatest advantages is
the silence it provides for writing, and she will feverishly write journal and
stories until attacked again by neuritis.

Despite her sense of herself as an artist, she concludes that she will not
make money at writing. She talks to Hugo about getting a job, for she feels
in some way a "parasite" for not earning money. She would really love to work
for one of the bookstores or little magazines, though they would not pay well.
Hugo discourages the idea with the excuse that she is responsible for their
cultural and intellectual development, their only "real riches." Every night
he comes home to her new ideas, to suggestions for books to read, to hear
her read her latest story. As long as he can, he will support her and her
family.

Her riches for the year 1931 begin with Lawrence and *transition* magazine. She discovers Eugène Jolas's avant-garde journal dedicated to the world
of dreams during a visit to Brentano's bookstore in Paris. The little magazine
contains all the new artists, including installments of James Joyce's latest
novel, *Work in Progress* (ultimately published as *Finnegans Wake*). As she
reads three substantial issues of avant-garde stories, poems, reviews, and
essays, she feels a kinship with modernism and knows she has found a
literary family. She reads little Joyce, she admits later, but responds to
everything Jolas writes.

*transition* (1927–38) celebrates the "new magic," and among the twelve
tenets of its June 1929 "Proclamation" are the following, which affirm Anaïs's
own long-held beliefs:

- The Imagination in search of a fabulous world is autonomous and
  unconfined.
- Narrative is not mere anecdote, but the projection of a metamorphosis of reality.

- The literary creator has the right to disintegrate the primal matter of words imposed on him by text-books and dictionaries.
- He has the right to use words of his own fashioning and to disregard existing grammatical and syntactical laws.[47]

Though she admits several years later that she found his style to be "full of myth and fog,"[48] Jolas and his night world send her finally to the works of "murky Freud" and to Jung. She reads the works of the great psychoanalysts with discrimination and judgment, seeking all the while affirmation and confirmation of her own beliefs. "Freud gave [her] the imprimatur of science . . . that Lawrence cast in terms of religion," says one critic. "Imagine Emma Bovary reading Lawrence and Freud."[49]

Dropping off another story at Titus's office in the rue Delambre, she happens to mention that she has written a Lawrence manuscript. When he expresses interest in reading and possibly publishing it, she makes the excuse that it needs revision. She has written only scattered pages beyond the essay that had already been published. She promises to give it to him in two weeks and returns to Louveciennes for a fortnight of concentrated writing. Eduardo comes to talk ideas with her, and Hugo reads and marks up her writing each evening. "D. H. Lawrence: A Study in Understanding," she calls her twenty-two-thousand-word manuscript. The intensity of her work, submitted on schedule, leaves her so elated that she talks about writing further studies on writers. Just before her twenty-eighth birthday, Titus informs her he will probably publish a limited edition of her book. Later that month they talk about her securing American and English publication rights; he calls her "honey girl," for he cannot get over the fact that this quiet and demure little girl would or could write such a book about Lawrence. He also makes seductive proposals when they later meet at the Dôme.[50]

## Spring Fever

Every spring her sap begins to rise, but never does it flow as freely as this year. She tests her sexual attraction by flirting with strangers in cafés, with a businessman brought home by Hugo, or with one of his bank colleagues. A dinner with Eduardo in a Russian restaurant leaves them both excited; talk about their sexual frustrations and psychological ideas makes her keenly aware of his body, but she claims to be excited by the ideas, denying the arousal is sexual. Only now does she begin to view food and eating as sensual. After reading a eulogy of the English novelist Dorothy Richardson, she considers for the first time that the possibility of love between two women might be "another voyage" for her. (Indeed in Barcelona this summer she finds herself strongly attracted to a woman she calls "Mrs. E.") She analyzes her sexual history by stating that she had absolutely no sexual consciousness before the age of nineteen. She does not question why this aspect of her nature is so repressed. She considers that her "awakening," an overstatement for the loss of virginity, occurred two years after her marriage.[51]

Her internal temperature rises during a trip south this July. She stops in the heat of St.-Jean-de-Luz, a tiny fishing village near Hendaye, on her way to meet Hugo in Barcelona. From there they will go to Mallorca. In her darkened room, escaping from the summer humidity, she examines her own body and masturbates compulsively (she calls it a "strong crisis of narcissism").[52] It leaves her with guilt and depression.[53] Once in Mallorca, she convinces her diary that she feels she has had a good sex life with Hugo ever since she asked him to treat her like a mistress, and that they share dreams and fantasies, even the "demonic." Yet she still thinks about having a "voracious" lover, and she still longs for John Erskine.

It is more than the spring sap that first stirs her sexual self-awareness and experimentation in 1931. Anaïs has embarked on a serious reading of psychology in the works of Jung (*Psychology of the Unconscious*), Freud (*Beyond the Pleasure Principle*), Adler (*Science of Living*), and Herman Alexander Keyserling, who explains the ideas of other philosophers to her. For now psychology, philosophy, and criticism interest her more then fiction. In April she began writing a study of the psychoanalysis of the creative artist as seen by Jung. In the garden in July she announces to Eduardo that she plans to be a psychoanalyst.

The years of reading Lawrence, *transition,* the poetry of Rimbaud (read aloud with Boussie in the garden), and the psychoanalysts, and the seventeen years spent analyzing her own consciousness in her diary will culminate this spring and summer in remarkable new insights and a new stylistic and daring evolution in her writing. Her journal contains flowing passages of prose that range from vivid imagery to occasional mushy abstractions. She tries a Lawrentian story of an orgy in the Bois, after which a deer leads her protagonist out of the woods ("I put certain ethical restrictions on Paganism," she says of her story).[54] Some of her best work is captured in twenty-five small prose poems composed in the spirit of *transition.* Written in a trance, with unconscious freedom, and without the self-conscious simulated spontaneity of surrealism, these pieces are the beginning of what will be her first novel (and second book), *The House of Incest.*

Her second diary for 1931 is filled with deeper self-knowledge. She observes that the desire for concealment of her true self lies behind her practice of creating illusions and lies, which she calls "embroidery." She details the lies she has told Eduardo, most of which have to do with her sexual experiences, and concludes that the strength of her imagination and her wide reading have enabled her to make what she imagines sound real. It amuses her and Eduardo and does no harm. She has, after all, a hundred faces.[55]

Her most important self-analysis is done during the vacation weeks on Mallorca, where she concludes that her anxiety, fainting, and heart trouble are caused by sexual tension (or by the lack of sexual fulfillment). She has been too ideally loved (by a repressed Scot named Guiler, an impotent professor, and several homosexual admirers). She resolves to capitulate in her struggle against sexual emancipation, which she has covered up through compulsive work and orderliness. When she learns that John Erskine will not be visiting Paris in the summer, she is surprised at her feelings of devastation. She would like to test her need and undo her dependency by seeing him once more, but understands that she still needs some "big, mature friend . . . something . . . bigger" to fill her "unfillable craving."[56] The archetypal Father image lurks in the shadows, unnamed.

She draws several other analytical conclusions. In striving for perfection, she inevitably fails and then feels inferior; she uses lying and flight to avoid quarrels and "scenes"; her restlessness, pity, flamboyant dressing, and individuality reveal her to be a vestigial romanticist. Finally, she turns to Hugo for an analysis of his fears and intense sexual nervousness. He discusses with her for the first time his repressed sexual history, becoming her first "case." In her diary she begins to record details of the initial year of their marriage and admits that there was no coitus. Freud has taught her to think scientifically; psychoanalysis has been a life-changing revelation. But she acknowledges that she has not put everything in her journal, for as Freud says, there are some things that are unbearable for the ego. Finally, in the last observation of a summer of self-analysis, she wonders if her longing for John and her "horrible and endless intellectual and physical starvation" are the result of not having had a father.[57]

Anaïs is sick for five straight days. They are on another bank leave to the States, aboard the S.S. *Lafayette* sailing for New York. After two years of struggling with her longing for John, she comes close to a nervous breakdown and one night considers jumping overboard. During their first two meetings in New York with John and Lilith, Anaïs can hardly maintain her control, particularly when he squeezes her arm. She shakes when she tries to light her own cigarette. She has trouble reconciling the real middle-aged and stout professor before her with her long-cherished fantasy. When he greets her one day in the hotel lobby and kisses her firmly, she trembles visibly and gives away her arousal. All month, as he attacks modernity, Joyce,

Lawrence, and homosexuality, and as he criticizes her "Woman No Man Can Hold" for lack of action, she successfully fights to get over her obsession. John is in the midst of leaving both his wife and his mistress, Lilith, but Anaïs no longer wants him. Just before Anaïs and Hugo leave, she tells Erskine a lie: she has recently begun an affair with Aldous Huxley. It makes her feel better, and it fills the space Erskine has occupied. The lie certainly captures his interest: he becomes much more attentive, places his hand on her knee, and suggests that she leave Hugo to live with Aldous. Anaïs secretly laughs at Erskine and concludes that most people like to be lied to, for a lie "heightens" life.[58]

During her visits with the Guiler family and her school friend Frances Schiff, her analytical powers are in full gear. She observes how much she enjoys contact with the luxury at the Barbizon Plaza, the rides in a Rolls Royce, the caviar and champagne. Still she is unsure of her real worth outside the realm of her rich imaginative life. Sometimes she wonders if she exists other than in her diary. She has always been a quiet and watchful woman, listening and learning in any social group, obtaining confidences because she is attentive and quiet. Hugo also has been observant and questions her about her new knowledge; she confesses her obsession with John for the last two years. But she leaves out any reference to their abortive physical encounter. It was only a kiss, she says. For two days they talk together to heal the breach.

On the ship back to France she tells Hugo the entire story, describing John's finger play and his sudden failure of arousal. She was prepared to go through with it, she adds quietly. Hugo responds, according to her diary, with great pity and then sexual passion. As if to test him further, she gives him her diary to read. Then comes the pain and sleeplessness, his demands to hear the story over and over again, followed by their fervent lovemaking. Hugo is tormented; she is relieved. They talk about the history of their difficult sexual adjustment, their repressions and the possibility of future infidelities. And finally Hugo gets angry and jealous. For weeks afterward they have desperate quarrels followed by passionate reconciliations. Later she will observe that she learns by this experience that love gets raised to passion through jealousy.[59]

As she approaches the coast of France, she feels energetic, decisive, and renewed. It is more than a relief to have unburdened herself to Hugo and to have rid herself of the obsession with John, though these account in part for her ecstasy. She feels that she is beginning a new chapter in her life, and she determines to begin copying her earliest diaries. She will close no more doors in her life. She even dreams of giving milk from her breasts to Hugo, and in waking hours thinks of having a baby.[60] She will tell Eduardo that her "only stability" is in "multiple fulfillment in various directions," in Lawrence's "mindless sensuality." I am "determined to have it when it comes my way," she will confide in him. She is no nurturing earth mother, but a virgin-whore. He will respond by telling her that she needs an older lover, some strong man to lead her sexually.[61]

As her ship docks in France, an unsuccessful Brooklyn writer named Henry Miller is in Paris, at his lowest ebb financially and spiritually. Had he been able to raise the cash, he would have been traveling in the opposite direction from the Guilers' ship. Instead he waits for news of another vessel that will be carrying his wife, June, to France.

# CHAPTER FIVE

# 1931–1933

# A Literary Passion and a Passion for Literature

"I . . . a sperm-filled woman, am walking down the street loaded with the phrases Henry has given me. . . ."
—*Anaïs Nin, 26 November 1932*[1]

"If we ever tie up I think there will be a comet let loose in the world."
—*Henry Miller, 14 October 1932*[2]

LAWRENCE DRAKE, assistant to the publisher Edward Titus, has the best kissing technique of anyone Anaïs Nin has ever met. He kisses her, pressing his swollen sex against her. She answers each kiss, feeling drunk under his experienced mouth. He nibbles her ear lobes and pushes her onto the couch. She feels his intensity pointing at her like a sword between her legs, she confides to her diary later, using metaphor and clothing to protect her from the reality. Aroused but frightened, she wriggles free, stammering something about not being able to do it without love, and leaves his apartment. She describes this scene in her diary that night, but it will be suppressed for fifty-five years.[3]

Anaïs has gone to Drake's apartment—not to a café or Titus's office just steps from Café du Dôme—to go over the proofs of her Lawrence manuscript. When Drake calls her a romantic, she responds angrily that she is sick of her romanticism! Reading all the signals—her worldly appearance, her interest in D. H. Lawrence's blood-consciousness—he expresses interest in her. Their work continues in a cloud of wine and physical anticipation, for she finds him most attractive: Spanish looking, "raw, easily hurt," with "sensual nostrils and mouth." She likes his fierceness when he holds her, his impetuosity.

She flees, feeling like an "over intense and ridiculous little woman."[4] Her hands are cold and sweaty. She has recoiled, she thinks, from the new experience of kissing a mustache. Then she fears he will think her a tease. But there is something that holds her back, she thinks, something as yet unstirred. His first name seems an omen. She loses her way on the metro getting home.

She returns to Lawrence Drake, but not before reading his novel and analyzing—in un-Lawrentian fashion—his capacity for imagination and feeling. There are two ways she is aroused, by kisses and by imagination, and his imagination is as deft as his kisses. (She forgets the third, alcohol.) She is coy, avoiding his kiss, then submitting to it. They continue drinking while pretending to concentrate on her manuscript. Finally, she allows herself to be placed on the couch, yet lies very still. She lets him inhale her perfume, pleased that they share a sense of smell, but then panics again, trying to deter him with "woman's trouble." He declares that there are other, less routine, ways. She is confused about the situation. He unbuttons his fly and tells her to get on her knees, which she does. When he offers his penis to her mouth, she stumbles to her feet as if whipped. He is furious at her horror and rejection.

"I told you we have different ways of doing things. I warned you I was inexperienced."

"I never believed it. I don't believe it. . . . You are playing a trick on me."[5]

While he lectures her on sexual practices, she thinks about what she calls the "true" sensuality that she and Hugo have, which is devoid of "techniques." Though angry, shocked, and repulsed at this exposure to oral-genital sex, she also admits to herself that she has deliberately aroused him. She allows him to masturbate between her legs out of "pity for his ridiculous, humiliating physical necessity."[6]

In the train home she contemplates, with some gratitude, the new experience he has revealed to her. Yet the physical images of his penis, his wet handkerchief, and the towel he offered her are burned in her memory. Eduardo has warned her about "abnormal" practices and "exoticism."[7] Now she knows.

When Anaïs had stepped onto French soil the previous month, she thought that she was cured of extramarital sexual longings. She thought she had been purged by her disappointment in Erskine in New York, by her confession to Hugo on the ship, and by her return to her Louveciennes home. There she read psychoanalysis, much to her Catholic mother's dismay, and felt strong, healthy, and energetic. But the energy was sexual, and it revealed itself in erotic "dreams of orgies."[8] She even imagined herself the love object of Eduardo's and Joaquin's sexual passions. She was puzzled and called Eduardo, who came for six hours of amateur psychoanalysis with her. She sees herself as a "virgin-prostitute"—she cannot say whore—and her dreams are warnings that she desires participation, not passivity or analysis, merely the psychological study of life. She intends to fulfill "every impulse," she told him just weeks before fleeing Lawrence Drake. Eduardo was stirred by her deep sexual longings. Using Lawrentian terms, she vowed "absolute obedience to all my impulses," to blood-consciousness, not to head-consciousness. Erroneously she claims now to understand Lawrence's "mindless sensuality."[9]

But it is more than this vow to Eduardo that brought her to Drake's couch. She has been sharing her dreams with Hugo, even encouraging his own expression. Eventually he shares his own need of orgies and further fulfillment. Initially crushed, she allows herself to be reassured of his faithfulness and offers him temporary freedom, which he wisely rejects. The issue is raised, nevertheless. During the day she copies out her earliest diaries; at night there are scenes of jealousy, quarrels and reconciliation. His jealousy about the Erskine incident in her diary and her obvious sexual frustration are buffeting their marriage as the quarreling and lovemaking become more physically aggressive.[10]

In keeping with their sustained analysis of each other and perhaps a desire to ignite their lovemaking, she tells her husband part of the story of her encounter with Lawrence Drake, leaving out her own role (she is distilling the "meaning" for him, she reasons). Hugo accepts the incident as finished, and they make love—without the "twists" and "aftertaste," she notes. Lying in each other's arms, she assures herself that their sensuality involves the "whole being"; he concludes that after seven years of marriage they are having a "mature honeymoon." Though she describes their simultaneous crying, kissing, and lovemaking, her behavior reveals the frustration and hysteria of a nonorgasmic woman.[11]

All this Sturm und Drang, her awakening by reading D. H. Lawrence, and her introduction to the realities of sex by Drake prepare her for the influence of a lunch guest they had entertained several days before, on 31 November 1931.[12] He had been brought by her lawyer friend Richard Osborn, who works with Hugo at the bank and advises Anaïs on the copyright of her Lawrence book. Osborn had shown her Lawrence manuscript to his friend Henry Miller,[13] and Miller's film review of Luis Buñuel's *L'Age d'Or* to her. At dinner at the Guilers' on 30 November—Anaïs calls it a "sizzling evening"—Osborn had regaled them with stories of his friend, the writer Henry, whom he was to bring the next day.

## The Tropic of Henry Miller

In the moments before "delicacy and violence" meet, Anaïs stands at the door and watches the lean, partly bald Miller stride up to the front steps of Louveciennes. He looks like a Buddhist monk with rosy skin, she thinks. He has come for a free meal and out of curiosity about the woman who had written about Lawrence; he stays for the stimulating conversation and for the pleasurable comfort of the gracious and exotic house.[14] She has heard numerous stories of this intense Brooklyn writer from Osborn, who shared his apartment for a time with Miller. Now they all—including Rosa and Joaquin—drink wine, talk books, argue ideas. Anaïs feels warm, dizzy, and happy. Before the afternoon is over she and Miller promise to give each other their autobiographical writings—she to him the diary and he to her the opening pages of what will be *Tropic of Cancer*, begun this fall.[15]

"I am singing, singing, . . . I've met Henry Miller," she writes in her diary that night. She responds to Miller's sexuality where others would see a short, balding man with a Brooklyn accent. She describes his blue almond-shaped eyes as cool and observant, his mouth as emotional and vulnerable, his laughter as contagious, and his voice as caressing and warm like a Negro voice that has a way of trailing off when he is thinking. He ends all his phrases in a kind of hum, she writes of his fictional counterpart, "as if he put his foot on the pedal of his voice and created an echo."[16] He is spontaneity incarnate, she concludes.[17]

This momentous meeting of two writers changes both their personal and professional lives. "[F]rom Louveciennes dates the most important epoch of my life," Miller writes in her diary one day.[18] Superficially they appear to be opposites—she the delicate European diarist whose reality is psychological, he the rough Brooklyn boy whose reality is the street and bed. She probes dreams and the unconscious; he catalogs his physical world. But both are playing roles: he is the hobo artist of Montparnasse—he has already written his own description under Wambly Bald's name for an article (14 October 1931) in the Paris edition of the *Chicago Tribune*[19]; she plays the prim wife of a banker.[20] They see beneath each other's role: he sees the imagination and intensity beneath her lowered head and pursed lips; she sees the wounded rebel, the gentle romantic beneath his blunt realism.

They are actually much alike. Both unrecognized writers, desperately devoted to their work, with strong egos that understand the necessity of the selfish writer (Anaïs sees this as a masculine trait) who must discard and hurt others.[21] One critic calls them two mythomaniacs who saw themselves as figures in an epic drama.[22] They are imaginative, love good talk, and write voluminously; each will write a "letter" to the world: his multiple-page letters will become part of his self-referential, anecdotal fiction; her diary will only begin to be published fifty-two years after it began. And each is fastidious (in contrast to his literary persona), curious, intellectually insatiable. They are both autodidacts. Each seeks both a student and teacher in the other. Norman Mailer tries to explain their attraction as a kinship between a motherless Miller and a fatherless Nin.[23]

He comes for long discussions—and stays for dinner when Hugo returns home. She points to the empty room above the garage and suggests that he could fix it up as a work studio for himself. They meet at cafés such as the Vikings on rue Vavin in Montparnasse. Every meeting seems a holiday to her. She is fascinated by his roughness, spontaneity, and experience as well as his anger and his ability to characterize people. She admits to her diary that she is "absorbed" by Henry and describes and analyzes him, comparing him to a magician, a painter, a hobo. These pages are some of her best writing; they capture Henry better than anyone else will. To her hobo friend she lends a set of Proust and gives train tickets. Soon they are drawing parallels between Proust's Albertine (in *La Prisonnière*) and Henry's favorite topic of conversation, June, his wife, who has arrived in Paris from New York City.[24]

Henry talks every day about June and her pathological lies, her possible drug use, her bisexuality, her wanton ways. He does not know where she got the money to buy his ticket to Paris in 1930, but he has his suspicions. He is obsessed, haunted by the woman for whom he left his wife and baby. Anaïs is drawn into his investigation: together they psychoanalyze June as Henry portrays her. June sometimes falls asleep with her shoes on in unmade beds. When she gets any money she buys delicacies such as strawberries in winter, caviar, and bath salts. Anaïs wonders why June hides for safety in a labyrinth of lies. Soon June becomes mythic in her mind.[25] As for Henry, he carries a manuscript novel around with him called *Crazy Cock*, the story of June and her lesbian friend Jean. Though Anaïs thinks it a heartless characterization of a woman, she believes it is a "ferocious and resplendent book."[26]

Anaïs is still working with Drake, whom she has succeeded in getting to back away, when she meets Miller and becomes absorbed in his needs. He interests her, but not physically, she insists, still afraid of masculinity (her opposite). Hugo, who admires Henry and gives him money, worries that she will be lost to him if she falls in love with Henry's mind. She assures him she can separate her mind from her body. It is Miller's work—his essay on Luis Buñuel's *L'Age d'Or* and Josef von Sternberg's *The Blue Angel*—to which she is devoted. Besides, they have both listened to his talk about whores and have decided—Hugo insists—to say no to such fascinations, to drunkenness and orgies. As Hugo goes off to Holland on business, Anaïs assures her idealized husband that she will never again run into "a blank wall" as she did with Erskine. But perfection is stasis; so is faithfulness. She has made her unsatisfactory bargain: Hugo gives Anaïs his faithfulness; she gives him her imagination. They deal in different values, and she has the temperament of a writer and experimenter. She does not collide physically with Henry for nearly four months. But within days she runs pell-mell into that blank wall.

## June Mansfield

When June (Edith Smith) Mansfield walks toward Anaïs from the dark garden of Louveciennes into the lighted doorway of the Guiler house, Anaïs is bewitched. She describes it later as drowning in June's image of female excitement. With her striking features, June fits the childhood image of female beauty that Anaïs still holds in her imagination. This night of 30 December, June seems the most beautiful woman on earth, with her burning dark eyes and heavy makeup on her whitened face. Red velvet dress (with a hole in it) and heavy cape, dramatic, nervous gestures—she smokes endlessly—all make her fantastic and bizarre. Her color, brilliance, and strangeness make Henry fade into the background. Anaïs is overwhelmed. Here is a woman with beauty—the pale blonde type—a superb actress. Suddenly Anaïs feels like a man, drawn to June's face and body. At the end of the evening, as the Millers are moving away just at the edge of the darkness of the front yard, June strikes a pose for the Guilers and Anaïs wants to run out and kiss her, embrace her, confess, "[Y]ou carry away a part of me. . . . I am not different from you. . . . You are the woman I want to be!"[27]

To her enthusiasm, Hugo adds a temperate note about June's "falsity" and "posturing"—a critical judgment Anaïs will pass off as her own when her diary is published thirty-five years later. In her sleep that night she dreams of June as "very small and frail" and insatiably craving admiration. Next day she concludes that they share the same fantasies, the same madness, and have paid "with our souls" for "taking fantasies seriously . . . for wearing masks and disguises." In her first fictional portrait of June, Anaïs says that to love her (first she calls her "Alraune," then "Joanna") is "merely to love myself, the desired, unrealized, half of myself"—hence the origin of her later theme in *House of Incest*.[28] In a novel (*Ladders to Fire*, 1946), she compares this "craving" to become each other to "touching a mirror." June is her "shadow self," says Nin critic Nancy Scholar, who notes that they share a lack of confidence, the hunger for admiration, and a penchant for lies and dramatization.[29]

Anaïs wants more; an invitation is immediately followed by a second dinner. June walks out of the dark more beautiful than before, more at ease. When Anaïs follows her up the stairs to leave her coat in the bedroom, June turns to pose in the light, against the turquoise wall. Anaïs senses more danger in the blond hair piled casually on June's head, the pallid face and sly smile and dimple, than she does in the lusty laughter of Henry in the other room. Later, posed in a high-backed chair, her silver earrings catching the light, June reveals her anger toward Henry. Henry and June talk with volatility about their quarrels, the virtual state of war between them. Hugo laughs away the tension, diffuses the bomb. Anaïs is ashamed of his conventionality and optimism, his fear of strong emotions.[30]

When they drive to the Grand Guignol after dinner, the women sit together, whispering in mutual understanding, plotting almost conspiratorially against Henry, who has mistakenly represented each to the other. June speaks of her friend Jean, the beautiful sculptor and poet, a woman with supple hands and tapered fingers. And Anaïs feels a pang of jealousy.

In the dark theatre she studies June's huntress profile, notices her indifference to the melodrama on stage, and thinks that June's life must be more interesting, immediate, and real than her own. They whisper together, and at intermission walk out for a smoke together. (Hugo and Henry do not want to smoke). As the women walk up the aisle, Anaïs notices the male glances toward their blond and brunette features, basking in the stir they create.

"You are the only woman who ever answered the demands of my imagination, the fantasies I had about what a woman should be," Anaïs says.

"It is a good thing I am going away. You would soon unmask me," whispers June. "I am powerless before a woman. I do not know how to deal with a woman."[31]

Anaïs, remembering Jean, does not believe her, but accepts June's compliments on her grace: "You glide when you walk," June confides. They speak of their favorite colors: Anaïs, red; June, purple; Anaïs, gold; June, black. But beyond the woman talk is a strong attraction that intensifies during the last acts, as they leave arms and hands entwined, and over coffee at a café afterward. Ignoring Henry and Hugo, Anaïs notices that in the café light she sees "ashes under the skin" of June's face, senses death and disintegration, and wants to embrace and follow her there—to lose herself in June, who emanates a "strange, manlike strength." "Will you have lunch with me before you leave?" she asks June.

That night Anaïs lectures Hugo on his conventional behavior, his fear of emotion in stopping the quarrel at dinner. June is aggressive and masculine and has coarse hands, he notes; Anaïs, recalling her arousal at June's touch, disagrees. He has hated her from the first moment, she charges. Yes, he agrees, admitting his jealousy, but he explains in a conciliatory tone that Anaïs's true strength lies in her soft, indirect, delicate womanliness.

This tender womanly side he wants is the woman/mother that Anaïs believes is at war with the artist/masculine side she must embrace in her June self. June is the "stronger, harder me," she concludes. "I love her . . . for her hardness, her cruelty, her egoism, her perverseness, her demoniac destructiveness. She would crush me to ashes without hesitation. She is a personality created to the limit. I worship her courage to hurt, and I am willing to be sacrificed to it."[32]

For four weeks Anaïs courts June: they meet at the American Express office, go to lunch, embrace in taxis. And June lives in Anaïs's fiction as a major character. June, who in turn will woo Anaïs as she has Jean, may also be embracing the woman to whom Henry is attracted. Anaïs undoubtedly is using June: June is the femme fatale, the mistress her own father always pursued, the mistress she had longed to be. Here is the dance-hall stripper who prances onto the stage of music halls and the mistress who glows from within in the tapestried bedchamber with the soft light of centuries of pleasure,[33] in short, the whore goddess. She pastes June's picture into the front of her current diary, and just below the title "Mon Journal and Note Book," she writes "June."[34]

June becomes her Dionysian muse. One writer says that June is "Anaïs's *fleur du mal*, flower of evil,"[35] both the dark lady and the harsh, cruel artist (recalling the Jungian dual archetypes). Yet Anaïs believes she is superior to June, who is incapable of channeling her "lies" into art. Soon Anaïs feels her own voice growing heavier, deeper, her face less smiling and compliant, her walk more assertive. She wants to protect June—then laughs at her naive thought. She wants to grasp her and take her to a hotel room and "realize her dream and mine."[36]

In her diary and later in diary passages she alters for her fiction, Anaïs recreates June and their meetings at the American Express office: she is almost ill with joy and anticipation. June strides up late, resplendent in the crowd. At lunch Anaïs cannot eat. In a taxi June presses Anaïs's hand to her breast. June wants the red dress that Anaïs wore the first night they met. Anaïs gives her the dress, perfume, and shoes.

June has never before desired a woman that Henry has liked, and he is jealous. Hugo calls June's stories cheap when Anaïs repeats them. He considers this a phase, a passionate curiosity or intellectual adventure—outside

the security of their love. Anaïs readily agrees. Eduardo, the "demonic analyst," delves deeper, questioning her motives, charging her with debasing
herself with low-class friendships, reminding her that she was first humiliated by her father, who beat her. Or she may be reacting to her experience
with Drake. No, he assures her, she is not a lesbian because she does not
hate men. One is astounded by this faulty logic from a homosexual man who
is now dating a woman named Jean. That night Anaïs dreams of Eduardo,
not June.[37]

June is invited to lunch at Louveciennes so that Anaïs can end her
suspense, confront her with the lesbian question ("Have you faced your
impulses in your own mind?"). When June answers quietly that she has, and
moves tenderly and nervously to comment on Anaïs's clothes and feet, Anaïs
is ashamed of her cruelty. Soon they are in her bedroom, June trying on her
sandals and cape. Each keeps apart, trembling, not speaking of the subject
between them. Later Anaïs walks back from the train station in a daze.[38]

The next day they are exultant, both talking at once in the women's room
of the American Express as Anaïs unwraps her gifts for June ("I wanted to
call you last night"; "I wanted to send you a telegram"). Each has feared
disappointing the other. At lunch Anaïs feels strong. "Let's be overwhelmed,
it is so lovely. I love you, June." She gives her coral earrings and a turquoise
ring (gifts from Hugo)—"It was blood I wanted to lay at June's feet"—and
insists on taking her to a shoe store to buy fancy sandals like her own. She
holds June's hand, defying the disdain of the saleswoman. When they walk
the streets arm in arm, hands clasped, Anaïs is so ecstatic she cannot talk.
At the station, their bodies press together and their faces almost touch.
Anaïs longs to kiss her but does not. After June leaves on the train for Paris,
Anaïs all but faints from the intensity of her desire.[39]

Anaïs is frightened by her own incandescence; Henry is uneasy; Hugo is
sad. She turns away from Hugo's boring talk of trusts and bonds and from
Henry's harsh earthy facts to a fantasy world with June. She sympathizes
with June's pain at Henry's "ugly" portrait of her in his manuscript (*Crazy
Cock*). The women talk of Henry's future and exchange gifts. When Anaïs
returns wearing June's silver bracelet with a cat's-eye stone, Hugo hates it
and teasingly tries to take it from her arm. She allows him to crush her hands
in pain, and assures her diary that their union is not the war between the
Millers. But she believes that her intense feelings for June are shattering her.

The two women lunch in a softly lighted place, Anaïs whispering that the
bracelet clutches her wrist like fingers, locking her in "barbaric slavery." June
drinks too much champagne, talks of hashish and another woman, and
wants Anaïs's cape to enclose her body. Though Anaïs is wary, she believes
they share this multiplicity of selves. When they walk to the steamship

company for June's ticket back to New York, Anaïs jealously watches June (who does not have enough money) lean seductively over the counter to bargain for her ticket. Soon she has the promise of Anaïs's month's allowance. Yet when the agent asks June to meet him for cocktails, she agrees. Her excuse, when Anaïs expresses irritation, is that the man will be useful in moving her up to first class. Blind with jealousy and anger, Anaïs weeps. June soothes her by placing Anaïs's hand against her warm breast, naked under her dress. She is a gold digger, thinks Anaïs, and all the softness of her ample breast cannot ease the pain. At home she sinks heavily into Hugo's arms, assuring him that she has come back to him.[40]

Soon she is waiting again at the American Express for a farewell meeting with June. It is four in the afternoon and the fat man at the door says her friend bade him farewell that morning. Anaïs fights faintness, swears she will forgive everything if she can only see June once more. Finally June strides up in black turban and velvet dress, cape, and plumed hat. She is carrying Count Bruga, a marionette in a black velvet jacket and with violet hair that she had introduced to Anaïs the day before. For this last meeting they indulge their passion for costumes and fantasy. At a Russian restaurant they have champagne and caviar. Anaïs burns under June's glances, excited by the Russian music. "I want a fiery life," June declares, and Anaïs sees her as the essence of candles, incense, flambés, fine liqueurs, exotic foods. We both seek exaltation and the madness of Rimbaud, she thinks.[41]

Yet their brief courtship is over, for June is returning to New York City. Anaïs puts her in a taxi and stands by in torment before confessing that she wants to kiss her. She will remember that June had first expressed her desire to hold and caress her as well. They kiss through the open window.

June has not escaped the acquisitive pens of two writers, both of whom see in her what they need or want to be. She frustrates Henry's simple categorizing of all "cunts." She expresses Anaïs's desire to live unconsciously and instinctively, though Anaïs adds that she also wants to live with compassion and conscience. No sooner has June left Paris than Anaïs invites Henry to Louveciennes, ostensibly to make peace but in fact to talk of June. They walk in the woods. Henry weeps. Anaïs expresses their mutual loss and obsession. That night they write at length, Anaïs in her diary, Henry in a letter to her. He admits he is aroused by her.

They spend many months in reciprocal analysis of June in talk and letters. Anaïs soothes Henry's questions about lesbianism with talk of "refuge," "harmony," "self-love," and "death"—in short, denying it.[42] Their desire to understand June is both personal and artistic. They each create a fictional June in their pages—"Mona" for Henry and "Alraune," then "Joanna," for Anaïs. Their fantasies of her enrich their art. They exchange manuscripts and analyze each other's analyses, which only feeds their mutual obsession. Subtly Anaïs shifts toward Henry, as his desire for her grows.

Henry spends January of 1932 in Dijon teaching English at the Lycée Carnot—it is Hugo who introduced him to an administrator of the French school system who had offered him the job. The Sunday after Henry leaves, Anaïs and Hugo are walking in the woods near Louveciennes with their dogs when they discover large rabbit holes in the ground. When the dogs sniff the earth, Hugo encourages them to dig into the holes, to go after the rabbit. Anaïs becomes hysterical. For weeks she has been tired, pacing the floors, unable to work, feeling trapped, caged behind the big rusty gates, hemmed in by her mother's disapproving looks from the upper window each time she leaves for Paris. Now she feels like the rabbits in their tunnels, trapped by the dogs. She begins screaming at Hugo.

Eduardo tells her to get help, perhaps through psychoanalysis. No, she will do it herself. She leaves almost immediately with her dog Ruby for Switzerland, to rest, to get over June, and to assure herself of the importance of Hugo in her life.[43] She promises Hugo she will not paint her face or nails, but she finds it still possible to flirt with an Italian man on the train. The cold mountain air and cleanliness of Calvinist Switzerland (she calls it "the place of frozen instincts")[44] give her perspective. She writes to Hugo at home, assuring him that her talk of living out all her instincts was "only steam," and to Miller in Dijon, confessing that she is "a bit sick of all this Russian wallowing in pain."[45] Hugo's letters are supportive, though while she is gone he has found the black underwear she bought with June and has found and read her journal on John Erskine.

Henry sends an avalanche of mail from his uncomfortable boys' school in cold and foggy Dijon. He writes long passionate letters, which he destroys.[46] Because he is, in the words of his first major biographer, "neurotically afraid of starving to death," he dreams of the comfort of her money and connections.[47] She sends him money and letters, thinks of him most of the day, but concludes that she will never let him touch her. She remains true to June, at least in her diary, and determines not to "tear her to pieces as Henry has done. I will love her. I will enrich her. I will immortalize her."[48]

A 29 January letter from Henry detailing his Dijon surroundings with images of death, the penitentiary, the morgue, and Edgar Allan Poe's fiction, and informing her that he has just learned he will not be compensated beyond room and board, prompts her to write to her "Dostoevsky in Siberia" to resign and "come home" to Louveciennes, at least temporarily.[49] By this time she needs to be rescued herself. With a "sudden and terrifying need" for Hugo, she telephones and he comes to take her home. She is feeling possessed—the title of her present journal volume—so she begins another diary for her good-wife thoughts.[50]

Before Miller returns to Paris, he and Anaïs exchange numerous ideas about their reading of Dostoyevsky and Proust and exchange manuscripts— her "John novel" (a reworking of her diary passages about her relationship with John Erskine) and his manuscript ("Molock, or the Gentile World") about his first marriage, to pianist Beatrice Sylvas Wickens (both manuscripts will remain unpublished). Each offers to help the other—he with her poor English and odd twists on the language, she with cutting down the length of *Crazy Cock*. They learn much about each other's earlier loves, for he is always frank about his lusts (she warns him to "beware just a little of your hypersexuality!").[51] Anaïs has sent him books, money, and her typewriter (which arrives after he leaves).[52] In short, they stimulate and strengthen each other.

In their written discussion of June, Anaïs insists that they had both "lost" their minds to her, but only she as a woman truly understands June's mystery. Yet she allies herself with Miller in having the capacity to "come up for air, for understanding." In her diary she describes June as her muse, alter ego, and awakener; Anaïs and Miller are "[o]nly the creators. [June] *is*."[53] Anaïs is preparing for a fuller emancipation.

During the weeks after her return from Switzerland and Henry's return from Dijon, she poses for a Russian painter in Montparnasse and attempts to return to the household roles of wife, daughter, and sister. Her mother, however, finally decides to find a separate house for herself and Joaquin because she so disapproves of Anaïs's writing, particularly her "dirty book" on Lawrence. She fears her daughter's influence on her younger son. Years later, Anaïs will tell friends that she herself had initiated the move.

Marriage is difficult for Anaïs. She is determined that the unbearable conflict between her "madness" and her loyal devotion to Hugo will be accommodated. She will love him in her own way and seek to grow in other directions as she does so. She believes that she is gifted with being able to live "many lives fully." After being "sundered in two by Henry and June," it is impossible for her to "grow in only one direction." She is beginning to live what Sybille Bedford Huxley called "the aristocratic view of sex," which separates marriage from passion.[54]

Freed by a job offer from the Paris edition of the *Chicago Tribune*, Henry arrives by train in Montparnasse, drops his bag at Hôtel Central, 1, bis avenue du Maine, and meets Anaïs and Hugo at a restaurant. When she sees him approach their table, she knows she is happy. After the weight and lashing of his letters, his approach to her is quiet. He comes upon her "softly," and she succumbs to his gentle way with women. She has papered the walls of her writing room with the sheets full of lists he sent her—lists of words, friends, mistresses, unwritten novels, places he has visited and wishes to visit—perhaps hoping that he will move into her attic room.

They meet daily in Montparnasse and continue analyzing June. As Henry slowly tears bits of the story of June and Anaïs from her, she compares his actions to those of Proust, who takes pleasure in being near Albertine's girlfriend, who might tell him of Albertine. Though she tires of what she calls his "shit, cunt, prick, bastard, crotch, bitch" realism, she sees beyond that man who, his journalist friend Wambly Bald says, "stands for shit" to the lusty imagist and poet.[55] She sees underneath the raw language a romantic.

Toward the end of February 1932, not long after her twenty-ninth birthday, she assesses her sexual nature and experience. The assessment is precipitated by what she calls a harrowing day with Eduardo, her "analyst." He was the first boy she loved, though his homosexuality brought her pain (she could not have loved him otherwise). After a series of weak, "overfine" men, and Hugo's bewildering moral fear ("frightened love"),[56] she then loved the manly Erskine, who lacks the imagination and understanding she needs. Hugo's strength has come too late. Courting June brought her the "joy of masculine direction"—but lesbian love seems to have no life. She has acted like a man, she mistakenly concludes, ignoring the other explanation implied in her earlier selection of weak men: she fears the masculine figure who had abused her.[57]

While sitting peacefully by the fire with Hugo the next night, she begins weeping. She feels torn into a man-woman and is desperate to be rescued. Only the "animal strength" of brutal realists like Henry (she thinks) can satisfy women; but she fears his love. Seeing her weep, Hugo holds her in his loving arms. He is the most mature of them all, she thinks, recalling the list she has made in her diary of all the things Hugo has done for her: taught her English, cured her of Victorianism, corrected and rewritten her Lawrence book, given Gustavo a thousand francs, forgiven her infatuation of Erskine, allowed her to dye her hair, never opposed her taste in plays and books, and a dozen other virtues.[58]

Increasingly she uses the studio of her friend Princess Natasha Troubetskoi as a mail drop and (soon) a trysting place. (She writes to June that she rents a tiny studio in Paris where she can spend a few hours a day to dream of her.) By the last days of February she is meeting Miller in the late afternoon of each day at Café de la Rotonde, at the corner of boulevard du Montparnasse and boulevard Raspail.

## A Passionate Union

"Henry is the only man who plucked the fruit at the right moment."
                                        —Anaïs Nin[59]

Sitting at the Rotonde one afternoon in early March, she is hypnotized by Henry's rich mind as he talks in his steady hoarse voice punctuated by hums. His bare forehead above the wire-rimmed glasses seems about to burst. He is speaking of a letter he has destroyed, a letter to her. She knows it speaks of love, for the warmth between them is palpable—she tastes it in her mouth, feels it in her loins. This is the love she has dreamed of. When she does not answer, he lifts his hand to touch hers, and without looking at him she withdraws her hand. She is frightened. I have read his notes with eagerness and horror, she thinks; the ferocity and debauchery. If only his love would die. She both desires and fears his manhood. The moment has come to yield to sexuality, she thinks, but she cannot bring herself to do it yet.

Next afternoon in Chez les Vikings, taverne scandinave, a large, darker, hence more discreet, place around the corner at 29, rue Vavin, she reads him what she has written the night before in her diary. She reads about feeling pursued by his "aggressive manhood" and tasting his "violence with my mouth, with my womb." When she reads the words about feeling "crushed" to the earth with "the man over me," his hand trembles, and she is moved.[60] You can only write with that intensity because you have not experienced it, he says. Your true nature comes out when you dance, he tells her, not when you sit like a lovely princess in a tall armchair. You have not lived, he repeats. She leans over the glasses, feeling the anticipation that lies between them, then extricates herself, still fearful of his manhood.

At home she thinks about the power she is exercising on his imagination, the power of romanticism that outlives realism. Longing outlives fulfillment, and she determines to sit eternally in the tall black armchair. She will remain "the one woman you will never have," she writes him 2 March 1932. They will "only write and talk and swell the sails," she adds in her purple ink— distilled Andalusian blood, she calls it.[61]

He has remained at their table at the Vikings, moving over to sit in the chair she vacates and lifting her glass with the lipstick smear to his lips. "I tell you what you already know," he writes, "I love you. . . . I am in a fever. I could scarcely talk to you because I was continually on the point of getting up and throwing my arms around you. . . . I am plunging . . . there is no holding back."[62] He continues to write on the stationery of the Vikings, revealing his plan to take her to his room, number 40, at the nearby Hôtel

Central. To show her his watercolors. Will she lead him somewhere else less sordid, "so that I may put my arms around you?"

She reads the letter ten or fifteen times, possessed. Hugo has warned her of getting trapped by the sparks she ignites in others. He has told her before that she has to devour people in order to know that she has their love.

In the darkness of the Vikings, Henry hands her a second love letter. Though she has worn her black lace underwear, the old fear of reality and her conditioned Catholic prudery still restrain her. He cries out for her to be real. When he says, "Only whores can appreciate me!" she protests, and he leans over to engulf her in a passionate kiss. "Come to my room," he states without question.

Her long journey ends that 8 March with a brief walk to his hotel room. "And I thought we were in love with each other's writing!" she exclaims laughingly. As they cross Montparnasse and walk around the Dôme and up rue Delambre, then a street of whores, she feels his body against hers, but not the pavement beneath her feet. She does not see the worn carpet or the small seedy room; she only feels his gentle hands and penetration. "You expected—more brutality?" he asks, watching her lying beneath his coat on the bed. Years later, in a fictional telling of this moment, she will admit that she had expected a violent intimacy like her father had given her.[63]

Only then does she see June's face looking at them from the frame on the mantelpiece. The confusion of her thoughts are soon dissipated by his experienced hand, and once again her body follows his instructing words and movements. She feels "brazenly natural" in her nakedness, perhaps for the first time. Her own joy soon terrifies her. Henry celebrates by turning a somersault on the bed.[64]

That night by the fire with Hugo, she cannot conceal her joy. Hugo is aroused by her radiance and confidence. When he begins to bear down on her, she closes her legs around his back, as Miller had taught her that afternoon. Hugo is thrilled. She feels deceitful and frets that her world is collapsing. But on the contrary, her marriage is stimulated, and Hugo more attentive. At dinner or the theatre with her husband, he whispers that he feels he is out with his own mistress, knowing this pleases her. Henry's letter burns in her pocket, until she goes to the toilet to read it. When she later senses Hugo's uneasiness, she tells him half-truths. He wants to believe. He wants her as his wife at any cost. "Everything Anaïs does is right," he reads aloud from his own diary and repeats thirty years later to reporters.[65] Ironically, Henry has cured the restlessness that threatened her marriage. She will cease devouring Hugo. She will have two lovers because she is two persons.

As her behavior is freed, so is the language in her diary, which she carefully hides. She writes passionately and in detail of her sexual activity, her wish that Hugo's sex were not so large and his movement not so rough and inept. Using images of melting blood, she describes Henry's slow movements and twisting, and the unfamiliar experience of making love standing up. Henry is experienced; Hugo, in contrast, cannot arouse her and needs to use Vaseline. To expand Hugo's knowledge and incite his infidelity (in part to punish her own), she takes him to a brothel at 32, rue Blondel to watch two women demonstrate the various positions of lovemaking. She feels that she is helping Hugo liberate himself, yet she herself appears to learn for the first time about the clitoris and its oral stimulation. She has told Hugo that they demonstrate "69" ways to make love, mistaking Henry's reference to an oral-genital position. When the women ask if she wishes to be stimulated, she declines, and hastens away with Hugo, who admits he had been willing.[66]

Henry and Anaïs embark on a fever of daytime sexual and literary activities (she no longer asks Hugo if she can go out alone at night). Thirty years later, in her expurgated diary, she will present their postcoital discussions as taking place in cafés. They send love letters and notes to each other, some written moments after they part. Occasionally she records his letters ("No woman has ever granted me all the privileges I need" and "I have never loved a woman with a mind").[67] She analyzes everything and writes at length in her diary of her conversations and lovemaking with Henry. Slowly she begins writing in a language that is ever more explicit, moving away from the euphemistic nineteenth-century romantic union-of-souls language to using the words "penis" and "clitoris." But some of the Lawrentian mystical phrases and verbal excess persist.

At first she fears that Henry will caricature their moments together—hating the destructiveness of his caricatures. Yet he seems exalted, taken to new highs of philosophy, reading, planning, and writing. He leaves her one day and writes ten pages of *Tropic of Cancer*—never including her, though he admits to wanting to make one of the women in his novel Spanish. He will transpose some of their experiences into the New York 1920s in his novels *Tropic of Capricorn* and *The Rosy Crucifixion*, and he will use the name Nys (pronounced like the city, Nice) for a woman he picks up in Café Wepler in *Quiet Days in Clichy* (1940). Anaïs believes that he cannot write about her because he truly loves her.

Her cousin, to whom she has been confiding everything, is both jealous and stimulated. In the mellow light of the Vikings, Eduardo expresses his fear of being left out. She assures him that she can love Hugo, Henry, June—and him, if he wishes. He takes her literally and kisses her before they leave. "At last!" he cries in the taxi. She sees his torment, recognizes the look she has seen for thirteen years, but now sees an aggressive sexuality. He kisses her eyes and neck, begging to repeat their meeting the next day, when he returns with the same madness. With a sense of destiny and need for what she thinks are psychological resolutions, she goes with him to a hotel, closes the curtains, and ends their thirteen years of "imaginings" about each other, twice, but without poetry. The "miracle is accomplished," she records. They return to the Vikings to consume ravenously four sandwiches. "How much I owe you!" he cries. How much you owe Henry, she thinks.[68]

At the Vikings again, Edwardo asks to continue, but she refuses, saying it is tampering with the past. He is frightened and asks her why she did not wait until he was finally healed of his homosexuality. Moved by pity and his persistence, she returns to the hotel, but the experience fills her with desolation. Sensing her play-acting and dissatisfaction, he is impotent. She whispers soothing words.

## Quiet Afternoons in Clichy

She finally meets Fred Perlès, Miller's best friend—the man who found him a job at the *Herald-Tribune* and with whom he lived at Hôtel Central. She thinks that this thirty-five-year-old Austrian writer and journalist, who has known Miller since 1928, is a "soft, delicate man with poetic eyes."[69] He later extols her "languor, fragility, elegance."[70] Their introduction is necessitated by the fact that on St. Patrick's Day 1932, the men move into an apartment at 4, rue Anatole France in a northern suburb of Paris called Clichy.

Henry takes her to his bedroom before she leaves after her first visit to the apartment. Henry, who works six nights a week, is frustrated that they do not have sustained time together. Initially, Anaïs is not at ease making love with Henry when Fred is in the other room. Then the situation makes her frenzied.[71] Later Henry tells her that Fred thinks she is wonderful, the first woman of Henry's he can admire. He takes her photograph from the *Tribune* office, after Waverley Root has written his review of her Lawrence book, and hangs it on the wall at lip level, he informs her. The photo is Anaïs Nin, an unprofessional study. She hangs Miller's watercolors in her writing room, where once the photographs of John Erskine and Lawrence had hung. Their mutual declarations of love fill their letters and her diary.

On the pretext of not wanting to make love in the apartment with Perlès there, Anaïs takes Henry to the Hôtel Anjou, where she had rented a room with Eduardo. She asks for room three, and the look in Henry's eyes pleases her. He had written her before the meeting to say he was "mad about" her and wanted "to vulgarize" her "a bit." Now she has been the aggressor—only a whore goes back to the same room with a different man—and her excitement leads to hours of what she calls "coition" and he calls "fucking." They return again and again, and each time she fills her diary with accounts of her savage joy and Henry's words of love.[72]

Anaïs finally reads her journal entitled "June" to Henry when he arrives at Louveciennes upset and clutching an irrational love letter from June. As she reads her journal in a trembling voice, he seems to be torn apart by the revelation of the love story. He should have written that way about June, he insists, not as he did in *Crazy Cock*, which is superficial. Despite the beautiful June Anaïs thinks she has created in her journal, Miller insists he still hates June for duping them both. They fear her return, but assure each other they have a bond of mind and art that excludes her.

Her sexual dreams and encounters overstimulate her. After rereading Proust's *Albertine disparue*, in which Miller has marked passages that reveal June in Albertine's behavior, Anaïs experiences an erotic dream of June, on whom she performs cunnilingus. Next day she writes to June about the dream, sends her love, her Lawrence book, and her cape. June does not respond. When Eduardo again pursues her, she again yields. Afterward she returns to Hugo's arms for refuge, longing for Henry but making love to her husband without passion, assuring herself that Proust believed happiness is something without fever. She is ill with exhaustion.[73]

Anaïs finds comfort in the quiet afternoons in the kitchen in Clichy with Fred and Henry, who often eat breakfast about 2 P.M. The apartment is orderly and clean, for Henry, like Anaïs, needs order (June mocks his bourgeois cleanliness, what one friend calls his "German housekeeper cleanliness"). Unlike his fictional persona, this friend adds, Miller "was not a bohemian" but orderly and a "moralist."[74] Their two-bedroom, thin-walled home is sparse, decorated only with Henry's own watercolors and his lists on large paper tacked to the walls and books piled on the tables. The bare windows look out over a little back street of low, ugly houses. When Anaïs arrives with Spanish wine and the scent of perfume, she enlivens both men. Perlès later recalls his first impressions of her arrival: her innocent, childlike voice, large eyes that resemble menthol drops, and expressive, white hands. "I love Pieta [Anaïs] with a profound feeling of friendship, and the fact that she loves Henry does not torment me at all." Fred thinks they are opposites, yet twin stars like Castor and Pollux. After the three discuss Proust, Henry and Anaïs go to Henry's room for what she can now describe in her diary as "acute core-reaching fucking."[75]

The best and most voluminous writing by Anaïs comes during this period when she describes her afternoons at Clichy—they call it their "black-lace laboratory"—and her growing sexual and literary partnership with Henry Miller. Both imagination and body are let loose on tangible experience.[76] Yet when she is retyping this material three decades later for what will be her first published diary, she feels she must suppress, alter, change names, and create dialogue. Even with heavy self-censorship, this is her best writing and the most important period of her literary development. Her instincts to begin her diary publication with 1931 are discerning. Miller fictionalizes this period in *Quiet Days in Clichy*, changing Perlès's name to Carl ("Alf" and "Joey" in other works), and refracting Anaïs in occasional emotions and in elements of character, such as his favorite prostitute Nys. He could never pronounce her name: she was always Anne-is, to him, not Ah-nah-ees. Her presence makes these days "a stretch in Paradise" for Miller, "the busiest, richest months of my whole life." He tells one of his oldest friends:

> Can't you picture what it means to me to love a woman who is my equal in every way, who nourishes me and sustains me? If we ever tie up I think there will be a comet let loose in the world. . . . Since I know [sic] Anaïs my life in Paris has become almost a dream. I work without effort, I live a healthy, normal life. I see things. I read all I want to.[77]

Though she tells him not to leave her out of his book, he does, for out of delicacy he cannot disguise their relationship. In his book about Miller Perlès splits her into Anaïs Nin (Henry's friend) and Mlle Liane de Champsaur (Henry's sexual partner). She is, he declares, a "clairvoyant, magician, sorceress" who grasps the "essential Henry Miller in a glance."[78]

These days are fertile and feverish. Anaïs and Henry stimulate each other physically and intellectually. Books, ideas, films, cafés, their couplings—all are discussed and recorded. His voluminous letters to her are first drafts of his books. Her letters come from her daily journal and will later be fictionalized in *The House of Incest, The Winter of Artifice,* and *Ladders to Fire.* I need your letters, she says, "save me from [my] goodness." His kiss has awakened her from a hundred years of sleeping with "hallucinations hanging like curtains of spider webs over my bed." He has taught her to make love sideways, in tandem, and standing up. He is teaching her to bite and talk dirty. Occasionally she is jealous of Henry's friendly relations with whores, but his commerce is more verbal than sexual, for he fears venereal disease. Neither lover promises fidelity, but their union includes a shared passion of the mind and for the word—an element not present in their relationships with June or Hugo. She is living out her dream of being a prostitute. The arrangement is unique for Anaïs, otherwise so obsessively concerned with abandonment.

She loves his Rabelaisian joy and exaggeration, his intoxication with life, his living in the present, his "torrential writing and tropical furies." He has taken her into the "Yes-function."[79] She loves him for taking her out of solitude into pleasure, out of artifice "into the street." He loves her newly freed passion, the accent of his name on her lips, her strength and gaiety, and her quick ability to absorb the meaning of experience. Though she seems at first to be breakable, he is stimulated by her long lashes lying on her cheek when she lowers her head and by the tightness of her legs around his waist.[80]

Though she tries to maintain her family relationships, her life with her husband seems colorless. She neglects the yard and with her allowance buys books, notebooks for watercolors and writing, and food for Miller. Spoil me, he says. I am "sick of this white poverty."[81] She understands her own need to nourish and Henry's need to be protected. She gives him the "first financial security he has known."[82] Not surprisingly, her family and friends disapprove. Except for Eduardo, they do not know what she is getting from this relationship. Joaquin, Rosa, even her friend Natasha Troubetskoi, the artist for whom she is posing, thoroughly disapprove of her gifts to Henry and what they see as her being used by a bohemian (if not degenerate) writer.

Now, with our ready access to their writing, we can see the extent of their remarkable mutual enrichment of each other's intellectual and artistic capacities. They shared what Nin called the two lives that writers live: the living/tasting and the writing/reaction. They shared ideas, quotations, and books, their essays and journals. They read and criticized each other's work. They both note the "equality" of their relationship, though he is forty-two and she twenty-nine. They even talked of collaboration (he for the money, she for the publicity), but their styles were too different. She contributed condensation to his work; he encouraged realism in hers. She gave him Proust; he made her see the streets and life around her. She piqued his interest in Lawrence, and he helped her promote her book through reviews. She introduced him to the work of European artists, and he helped her shake off her Catholic schoolgirl prudery.

If Miller freed her body, Lawrence freed her thinking about instinct and sexuality. *D. H. Lawrence: An Unprofessional Study* (1932) is her own cry for "contact with the reality of sexual passion."[83] She soon has Miller reading and investigating Lawrence; his effort to interest her in Nietzsche is less successful. This April, five hundred numbered copies of her book are published by Titus's Black Manikin Press. On the paper cover, beneath her name, is testimony from the man with whom she had a most decidedly un-Lawrentian encounter: "I learned a great deal from it," wrote John Erskine. "I am amazed at the scholarly and critical reaches—which theoretically no woman should possess."

The testimony of Erskine is, in a sense, bogus, as her unpublished letters to him reveal. When John did not answer two requests from her the previous fall for a quote about her Lawrence book, she lifted a line from one of his letters to Hugo. As the book goes to press, she writes to beg his understanding, then informs him that she has immersed herself in life since last seeing him in New York.[84]

The sexist volume is turned up in the first public review of her literary career, Waverley Root's "The Femininity of D. H. Lawrence Emphasized by Woman Writer" in the Paris edition of the *Chicago Tribune*. Miller tries to warn her of Root's attitudes toward women writers. Though Root concludes that the book has "considerable value," he devotes most of his review to talking about the "limited talents of woman" and her faults being "explained by the fact of her sex": "the task of synthesis has been too much for her. Perhaps, being a woman, she saw no need of it." Anaïs can take little comfort in his intended compliment that there "must be something of the man in Miss Nin . . . for she acquits herself with credit of the male task of analysis and comprehension. . . ."[85]

She and Henry devote hours to talk about Lawrence, about Mabel Dodge Luhan's recent memoir of Lawrence (*Lorenzo in Taos*), which they hate, and about the character of June. Anaïs's perceptive analysis of June influences Henry's fictional treatment of June. His fictional June is in fact a composite of these two amateur psychologists. Anaïs is also encouraging his exploration of dreams, giving him copies of Eugene Jolas's *transition* (the expatriate magazine devoted to surrealism, dreams, and "night consciousness").

As if her obsessions with June and Henry are not enough for her family to tolerate, the publication of her study of Lawrence is the final embarrassment. The persecutions have begun, she tells Henry. Mother Rosa gives her sad, pained looks at the dinner table. Rosa continually fears her daughter's influence on her younger brother, who faithfully attends Mass with his mother. The following year, when they find an apartment in the city, the way is cleared for more frequent daytime visits by Henry.

The family concludes that Anaïs has had too much of literature. They are unaware of the changes in her writing, unaware that the language of the diary now includes words such as "penis" and "fucking." They are unaware that she fears her assertiveness might make her a lesbian. Certainly they are unaware of her voracious appetites. In her diary she reiterates all the time-honored arguments for infidelity: hers is a "more complicated morality"; she is being honest to herself; she continues to love Hugo without hypocrisy, and everything outside their love is separate from it. The more she receives love the more she has to give Hugo, yet on at least one day she has sex, sequentially, with Henry, Eduardo, and Hugo. Not unlike victims of traumatic experiences and those with multiple personality disorder, she is able to disassociate herself from her actions.[86] Even while having sex with one man, she is thinking about the previous man and how she will write the scene in her diary.

The time has come for you to be psychoanalyzed, Eduardo tells her one evening in Louveciennes when Hugo is away at a bank function. But you are my analyst, she laughingly responds. You are only postponing the real thing, he insists. She studies his green eyes as he explains her feelings toward her parents, Henry, and June. She laughs seductively and tells him he is handsome, then begins touching him. Afterward she tells him he is a bad psychoanalyst to make love to his patient. The next morning, while Eduardo watches, she leaves for a date with Miller, new curtains for the Clichy apartment in a package under her arm. Sometimes she tells Hugo that she is spending the night with Natasha.

One other afternoon in the apartment in Clichy, she gets drunk at the suggestion of Henry. They sit in the tiny kitchen with Fred, drinking, laughing and talking, nearly touching. She senses the love of both men—Henry's bawdy and demanding physicality and Fred's tender protectiveness. She allows Fred a furtive kiss and tucks his love letter into her diary. Henry offers her to Fred, who tells him he does not deserve her. Henry says she should be loved, not worshipped. Perlès has hardly left when Henry and Anaïs fall to the floor biting and digging in their frenzy. Late that night, as Hugo drives her home from the train in Louveciennes, she feels radiant and exhausted. Only knowledge can hurt him, she assures herself. Yet she is maddened and saddened by Hugo's credulity. He does not reveal any notice of her swollen lips, the rings under her eyes, her stained underwear, the washing after returning home, her new suggestion that he "come twice," her diary writing at his feet before the fire. When she realizes that he is protecting himself by refusing to register any of these signs of her adultery, she almost longs to be punished, to be relieved. And thus freed.

## Analysis: A New Religion

In April 1932 Anaïs walks through the iron gate and up three steps and rings the bell at 67, rue de l'Assomption. This three-story building, the home and office of Dr. René Allendy, is just down the street from the Notre Dame de l'Assomption church, where Rosa and Joaquin had attended Mass when they lived with the Guilers in nearby boulevard Suchet (1929–30), before Louveciennes. When Anaïs enters the dark room with its brown walls, heavy black Chinese curtains, and red carpet, she feels she has entered a tomb and shivers. She looks out the door to the greenhouse, with the sun filtering through the tropical plants surrounding a small pool with goldfish, and feels submerged. And submerged she will become—in a year of analysis with a patriarchal father figure she will eventually seduce.

She has told herself that she is coming to talk about Eduardo, who has been Allendy's patient for some time. Eduardo, who is in love with Allendy, has been sharing everything with both Allendy and his cousin. When Eduardo urged her to enter psychoanalysis, he tempted her by saying that Allendy would be a guide, a "father"; but she denied needing analysis, for an author of a book cannot be neurotic; besides, she does not have any brakes on. Though she has read psychological theory for years, when pressed by her cousin she decides it is scientific tampering. Now she is visiting his analyst only to reassure her cousin about what she is writing about him in her diary.

The discussion between Allendy and Anaïs moves from her sexual indifference to Eduardo to her pleasure with Miller, all explained confidentially by her. When he suggests that dividing up her love reveals a lack of confidence, she defensively claims never to have to lean on anyone. With that obvious fabrication, Allendy rises as if to dismiss her, commending her ability to do without his help. She bursts into tears. Soon she is talking about the indifference, coldness, and cruelty of her father.[87]

Dr. René Felix Allendy, a Breton born in Paris, is fourteen years older than Nin. His beard and tall, stocky build make him appear patriarchal. She thinks he is handsome and healthy looking and has the eyes of a seer and the mouth of a woman. He is a medical doctor with curiosity about homeopathy and astrology—the latter an interest he shares with Eduardo. Though a classical Freudian, Allendy believes that one can control one's destiny to the extent that one becomes aware of oneself (*Problem and Destiny: Study of Inner Fatality*). He is a founder (with Marie Bonaparte and René Laforgue) of the Société Française de Psychoanalyse, lecturer at the Sorbonne, and author of several books.

During the first of what will be many visits, Allendy offers her several keys to her behavior. As she had both desired and feared her father, she sought cruelty in older men (for she cannot love without pain), and yet at any sign of cruelty she is paralyzed. She also comes to realize the effect of childhood trauma on adult confidence and relationships. What she cannot accept is Allendy's belief that at the age of puberty she might have witnessed some sexual brutality that disgusted and traumatized her, at which point she sought "the ethereal." She is not ready to deal with any such reality and dismisses the conclusion as banal—though she records it in her diary.

She goes to Allendy infrequently at first—both to have time to absorb what he says and to show her independence. Her multiple lives continue, but she is aware of her internal chaos: she simulates pleasure with her husband one day, wants to be imprisoned in his arms. The next day, she craves Henry, but wants to beg June to return.

Soon after Hugo closes the rusty green gate behind him to embark on a bank business trip, she packs for three days in Clichy with Henry, walking the streets and sleeping warmly in his small bed at night. She comes to two conflicting conclusions: she will give up everything to live with him, and she promises to see that he no longer has to work for the newspaper (the latter necessitates her staying with Hugo and continuing to receive the allowance he gives her).

On the second day Perlès suggests they all go to Louveciennes, where the magic of the house and the men's admiration prompts her to bring out her journals. While Fred reads the earliest volume (in French), Henry reads the red journal about him. When he reads her entry about Fred calling her beautiful, he exclaims his disagreement. It is charm you have, at which she places her head on the floor pillow and weeps. Surprised by her reaction, he apologizes. She tells him of all the compliments she has received from painters for whom she poses, then playfully makes up with him. In the rain waiting for the train back to Clichy, their bodies are close. But later in his room, her confidence gone, she has trouble undressing in front of his gaze.

The next day she is in Allendy's office. From the daylight of rue de l'Assomption she enters the narrow corridor that leads to his dim cocooned office. As she sits in the armchair smoking, Allendy's disembodied questions come from behind her. She only hears his words and the scratch of his pencil. Most of the questions are directed at her relations with men and imply that the traditional male domination/female submission roles are the norm. The Diana complex envies man's sexual power (could this explain her love of June?). Is she ambivalent about sex because her father left her for that reason? Why has she chosen weaker men? Does she need to conquer older men? Does she want to dominate or be conquered by men—or both? Did she will John's impotence? Did she choose pain from Miller by becoming a rival of June? Does she desire punishment, humiliation, abandonment? She weeps, feels shame, and returns home to record their dialogue as she remembers it, confessing to the page that she has never yet had a real orgasm. Analysis, she concludes, is intensely painful, like "press[ing] dry fingers on the secrets of my body"—more like masturbating than fucking.[88]

She flees to Miller from analysis. He represents living reality, and he never has to understand or probe. She feels heavy with his Rabelaisian presence, swallows his laughter like bread and wine, and falls asleep in his arms. Compared to him, Hugo is a youth, her son. She is aware that Miller, more than a decade older than she, is sometimes the father figure—from his cold blue eyes (like her father's) to his directive and knowledgeable manner. His lectures and protectiveness, his care with her slender body make her feel like a child (You sleep like a doll and take up so little room in the bed, he observes). Fearing she will reveal the child in her she flees Clichy and runs home.

One effect of her analysis is an acceleration of her daily journal writing. Even after an exhausting day, she has energy to write many pages. The diary has become her opium, her disease, she concludes. Here she can hide the different pieces of truth she keeps from each man while reliving her experiences. Her secret keeping could be an indirect deflection of the larger secret she fears fully to face. Her frequent thoughts of being a prostitute echo a similar desire in sexually abused girls who confuse sex and affection/approval and may want to control and punish the abuser by using the means they have been taught.[89]

The superficial reason for her retreat into the diary, the one given by readers and critics for years, is the explanation Miller gives her after finally reading the entire red journal with his name on it. You are a narcissist, he concludes, and journal writing is a disease. But a good disease, because she has written the most interesting journal he has read. She is having her early diary retyped and has also rewritten the first pages of her "Alraune" manuscript (about June) in the surrealistic style of transition magazine, of Breton and Rimbaud.[90] The fiction is the life. But narcissism cannot explain it all, and Allendy probes for first causes.

Everything you wear, the way you walk, sit, and stand is seductive, declares Allendy, adding that only people who are unsure act that seductively. She has just admitted her lack of confidence and her fear that others will discover her fragility, her vulnerability, her small-girl breasts. Soon she reveals the source of her seductive behavior: her father was obsessed with photographing her in the nude when she was a child. She thinks of her father's eye behind his thick myopic glasses, behind the camera's eye. She has feared the exposure of the camera's eye. An exposure of what, she cannot answer. Allendy does not pursue this question as a contemporary analyst would. He sees the abuse in the desertion, and the dancing and coquettishness as a desire to win back her father. All his admiration came by way of the camera, which, she informs Allendy, was the only time they were alone together. You have wanted since childhood to seduce your father, Allendy informs her, but when you approach success, fear overtakes you. The time she thought she saw her father in the audience when she was dancing was a willing him to be there to be seduced. She quit dancing when she realized it was an act of seduction, he concludes.[91] Allendy is echoing Freud's Oedipal theory of the child's desire to seduce the parent. (Originally Freud had proposed that neurosis is caused by sexual abuse, which he defined as any sexual encounter with adults or siblings, including seeing one's parents making love.)

While Allendy probes her past, Henry confronts her present illusions, specifically what he sees as her fictional, idealistic portrayal of Hugo in her diary. It is unconvincing and undocumented by the facts. You are superior to him in every way, he points out. His phrases echo Erskine's. Miller believes she wants to escape. Her tears of guilt acknowledge this. As she portrayed or created the good little girl, then the dutiful wife, for her earlier journals, so she has been building up Hugo. She wants to believe, she wants to cling to her self-image as a good wife, and she wants to love her husband. Allendy, meantime, is suggesting that she finds vulnerability and sensitivity in Miller so that she can conquer him.

That night she studies Hugo and faces the fact that her love for him is fraternal and she dreads his passion. Louveciennes has become a golden casket. She will make a new beginning. Yet when Hugo discovers that her routine has been broken with the gardener, mason, household accounts, and dressmaker, Anaïs admits nothing and he chooses not to see the obvious. Afraid of losing him and the security he offers, she decides that hurting him would be criminal. Though she cannot break up her life, she will not stop her affair.[92]

She unbuttons her blouse and bra to show Allendy her small breasts. The incident, obviously flirtatious, grows out of a discussion of her underweight body and undeveloped breasts. To her pleasure, the doctor's assurance goes beyond medical diagnosis: "perfectly feminine . . . lovely . . . well-shaped . . . grace of movement"—she records these phrases faithfully in her diary, along with the fact that her heart had been beating fast and her face flushed. She questions her own motives.

During this visit they also speak at length about her passion (she changes the word to "love" for the published diary) for her father and conclude that she must have begun writing the diary for her father on board ship. As an eleven-year-old courtesan, she had failed to win him back. She gives Allendy her book on Lawrence; he gives her two of his books. In order to visit him more than once a week, he cuts his rate in half if she will do some library research for his manuscript entitled *Chronicles of the Plague*. So begins a professional and (as signaled by the bare breasts) erotic alliance that will blossom. Significantly each time she approaches his house with its basement kitchen, book-lined study, back- and front yards, she is reminded of her father's house in Brussels when she was eight or nine and of the house he lives in now, nearby in Passy. What she does not reveal in this description is that her father's house is in fact just moments away (around the corner from

Allendy's and up rue du Dr. Blanche to rue Henri Heine). She has already begun seducing the father figure whose books she is reading and whose research she is conducting.

Just who is effecting her "cure," she wonders—Allendy or Miller? While she begins the process of seeking the upper hand with Allendy, Henry takes her to new passionate heights. She fills the rooms of Louveciennes with Henry, thanks to the frequent absences of Hugo, who is traveling for the bank this spring. Henry wants to be her husband, to protect her; he writes love letters to the eleven-year-old child of the early diary, is jealous of the adoration of Fred, and whispers assurances that she has captured him. But when he introduces oral-genital lovemaking, her journal and everything else become secondary.

Yet she captures in poetic passages her "Heinrich's" every gesture and habit and narrates frankly each detail of their passion, using the words "honey," "swallow," "suck," and "sperm." This language, like her own nakedness, feels comfortable, and her writing is in fermentation. During their long nights in cafés or at Clichy, often with Fred, Miller keeps his roommate from seeing his vulnerability with Anaïs. Henry reads her "Alraune [June]-Mandra [Anaïs]-Rab [Henry]" manuscript (about their lovemaking), corrects her lines dispassionately and brutally, and writes what she thinks is a fantastic parody of it.[93] She reads Fred's diary and the first pages of Henry's new work, "Self-Portrait." She contrasts their writing styles: Fred is a delicate watercolor, Henry a volcano, she a flower or ripe fruit. Something great will grow from this time, she believes. When she has to pack her black valise to catch the early-morning train before Hugo's return, she is in despair. The next day she observes the beauty of Allendy's eyes as she exclaims about how fast psychoanalysis works. Afterward she tells Eduardo that their love is fraternal as she sits with him at the café, their thighs touching.

## Deceptions and Seductions

The Salle Chopin in all its white and gold splendor holds Anaïs and all her men the night of 20 May 1932. Joaquin is to perform. Their father is at the door as if receiving the guests as a sponsor, much to the dismay of Rosa. Son Joaquin sends a note instructing his father to take his seat or be thrown out. Barely smiling, he bows to his daughter, who has invited him and his wife. Also seated in the audience is Allendy, attending with his wife, Yvonne, at Anaïs's invitation. Miller is in the balcony with his friend Michael Fraenkel.

Anaïs feels weighted down by the lights, by her lamé dress with its heavy balloon sleeves, and by all the eyes focused on her. She is aware as she moves that she is playing to her audience, seducing Allendy and Eduardo and Henry as well as the handsome violinist, a Spanish painter, and her father, whose formal manner frightens the child in her. She keeps her composure, for she knows that some part of her has been kept from each of these men. She has not relinquished everything. The evening is hers, she believes. Each man responds to her power. Her father moves his seat to be in front of her. Beside her Eduardo, drugged by her words and Narcisse Noir perfume, touches her with his knee. Hugo is her protection. Allendy seems startled by her fine appearance, but his eyes are sad. (Later she says he accuses her of wanting to find his weakness and insult his plain wife.) She is pleased to have dazzled him. Henry seems timid and out of place, but later he writes a letter praising her beauty—she was the Spanish Infanta!— and confides that his friend cannot believe that such a feminine beauty could write about D. H. Lawrence. Even her "childish despair" in encountering her father cannot shake her confidence. "You need to conquer because you have been conquered," Allendy tells her later.[94]

When Henry brings his friend Fraenkel ("Boris" in *Tropic of Cancer*) to meet the Guilers, Anaïs does not like him, though he is eloquent about her house, which Henry calls "a laboratory of the soul."[95] Fraenkel is only thirty-six years old, frail and "foxy," but already dead, she thinks, "withered from within." His system of belief is based on death. He publishes books with the American poet Walter Lowenfels under the imprint Carrefour Editions. Henry has lived in both Fraenkel's and Lowenfels's apartments at one time or another. When Fraenkel speaks of Henry's sound way of sleeping, Anaïs steals a mischievous glance at her lover. During the evening she is restless and unhappy, curt with Hugo, whom she finds increasingly hard to bear. She is always comparing him to Henry, who can slip so softly and easily into her body. She takes risks, even sleeping with Henry's love letters under her pillow; Hugo refuses to hear the rustle of the paper. No wonder she thinks she is living several lives that she cannot bring together.[96]

Riding into Paris on the train, her journal open in her lap, Anaïs feels very fulfilled and alive. Even the fabric of her clothes seems to caress her skin this early June day. She has been having what she calls liberating sessions with Allendy, finally sharing her sexual secret, what she calls a partial frigidity. She asks him why she is obsessed with sexuality yet has difficulty achieving orgasm (except when masturbating, which makes her ashamed and fearful of harming herself). His answer is that she suffers from guilt; his assurance is that these problems are frequent for women. Later when she confesses that several months before a Russian doctor had told her she could not get pregnant without an operation, he concludes that she has been using her fear of pregnancy only as an excuse for not letting go.[97]

A psychoanalyst today with the same information—a description of a violent, patriarchal father, a lifetime of seductive behavior, and dreams of prostitution in a patient who is nonorgasmic, passive, masochistic yet fearful of pain, and sickened by her own sexual aggressiveness—would look for childhood sexual experience in the patient. But according to Anaïs's recounting of her sessions with Allendy, which is all the record that exists, he does not. No studies of the long-term effects of sexual violation of children existed then.[98]

Allendy attributes her femme fatale behavior and dress to a lack of confidence and a need to be loved. She comes to their sessions in drop-dead costumes. She believes her strange costumes are a means to escape into a fairy tale or a compensation for her childhood poverty; he calls them an armor to frighten people away and promises to reconcile her to her own image. He suggests that even her interest in lesbianism is a pose. These psychological insights, the primitive influence of Miller, and the use of her dressmaker's allowance for the support of Miller eventually bring about some sense of simplicity in her dress.

Allendy tells her on several occasions that Miller's bohemian world of poverty has taken her away from her father's aesthetic world of society, luxury, and security. She feels increasingly more at home with Henry, who teaches her to play, to share his lusty humor. She loses her "Seine-like rhythm" of control, repression, and isolation. He teaches her fraternity, takes her out of solitude and into the street and café. When she realizes that she has spent all night talking and arguing in Café de la Place Clichy, she is amazed at herself. Even her writing and language become more direct. Perhaps art is a reflector and stimulator of life, not an escape from or idealization of it, she thinks.

Anaïs exhibits sexually obsessive behavior, in part because Allendy is probing its sources and encouraging Anaïs to take romance less seriously. Henry has begun to speak of their possible marriage, Fred reminds her of Henry's inadequacies as a faithful potential husband, and she fears the loss of freedom and financial security she currently enjoys with Hugo. She eats frantically (putting on four pounds), masturbates frequently, and uses the f-word often in her journal ("I have only three desires now, to eat, to sleep, and to fuck. . . . I'm going to hell, to hell, to hell").[99] She becomes confused about whose body or penis she is holding. When she wants a crazier Miller, not the watercolorist, she provokes a scene of sexual failure reminiscent of John Erskine. Suddenly he seems like a husband, "little Henry," a "gentle German," weak; and she is cruel to him in front of Fraenkel. Like June, she notes, she flirts shamelessly with other men and women and "forgets" her appointments with Allendy. She has conquered or controlled Hugo, Eduardo, and now Henry.

Two events return her to passion with Henry, both triggered by jealousy and her fear of abandonment. A young underage girl named Paulette moves in with Fred, and Henry confesses to liaisons with prostitutes. Anaïs weeps dizzily, resumes passionate hotel visits with Henry, who teaches her to "69"—"like lesbians" she describes it—and to pleasure him with her hands. The minute Hugo goes out of town on bank business, Henry arrives to play husband or Anaïs packs her bag for Clichy. But she seeks revenge against Henry's unfaithfulness by giving herself twice passionately to Hugo and by planning to seduce Allendy.

At the end of June and in early July 1932, Allendy makes two remarkable conclusions. The first he had observed before—her need to be loved *exclusively*—and now he sees her jealousy directed at him. She is jealous of his other patients and dreams that he neglects them for her. Most important, he connects her fear of food and fear of sex. One day she confesses to him that she dislikes "penis sucking" and had become nauseated before her last liaison with Miller. Her unconscious resistance to oral sexuality is triggered, he says, by an incident that awakens her sense of guilt. Perhaps more accurately, the triggering event is guilt or fear of violation or abandonment by her father.

One morning she awakens with a feeling that Allendy will kiss her. At her session with him, she announces that she will not be coming back. Rather than be cured and abandoned, she will leave on her own, with the mystery intact. As she is speaking, she strikes conscious poses with her body, plays coy, then allows him to take her hand. When he asks her for a final kiss, she is happy, then disappointed in its brevity. He does not shake her foundation as Henry does. But at this visit, he seems brilliant, a giant. She now has his interest. She will be back.

Studying Lawrence, she thinks, has prepared her for Miller, the "least conquerable" man, whom she has proudly "disarmed" with her patience and gentleness. Dealing with Lawrence and Miller is like "playing" on the "same instrument." It will not last, however, because Henry is primarily physical and passion burns out (yet she frequently entertains the idea of running away with Henry). To protect herself from loss she dreams of meeting someone else, and assures herself that men who are less physical (Hugo, Eduardo, Allendy) have staying power. She fears losing both Hugo and Henry, though her frequent contrast between the sensuous Henry and the "quick, stabbing movement" of Hugo torment her. She frequently tells her diary that she "defends" June to Henry, yet she gives him a book on the symptoms of drug addiction and discusses June's behavior with him.[100]

Despite Allendy's urging simplicity and naturalness on her, her deception and seductiveness continue. While claiming to win her men with tenderness, she in fact plays by more aggressive rules—as with her gift to Henry

of the book on drug addiction. Allendy accuses her of practicing false goodness. She leads Henry to believe that she has other lovers, calling this her
feminine mystery. A little jealousy and fear keep men interested. Telling
everyone she is going on a vacation, she risks pain and mutilation to have
her nose operated on in order to transform the tip of her nose to a straight
Greek style.

When the nurse brings her some clinic stationery the morning after the
procedure, she writes in a "faltering hand" to confide in Eduardo that she
was taken to this clinic after passing out from taking cocaine. The lie is
amusing, she rationalizes, and it has a literary quality—it even echoes her
own desire for oblivion. As soon as the swelling goes down, she visits
Allendy's dark room, hoping he believes the cocaine story he most certainly
has heard from Eduardo. She appears to feel no remorse when she hears of
Eduardo's unhappiness.

Her deception and seductiveness are played out in her journal as they are
in her relations with others. She both seduces and deceives the reader. In
the middle of her cocaine hoax, she speaks of her journal as both a means
of stabilizing her madness and as a "product of my disease, perhaps an
accentuation and exaggeration of it."[101] The reader discovers the deceptions
eventually. And access to her collection of diaries will reveal that this summer's diary volume is not an "original" but a rewritten book without corrections or penmanship variation.

## The Weapons of Fear and Passion

In July 1932, on the train between Munich and Innsbruck, where Hugo will
later join her for a holiday at Hotel Achenseehof in Tyrol, Austria, Anaïs flirts
with a professor of philology. He tells her her name in Greek means "rising
high" or "ascension" or "élan," a discovery that delights her. She moves from
erotic dreams of June to leaden hours filled with rain and Hugo's talk of
family finances. As he talks she dreams of running away to Spain with Henry.
The hours of physical exercise each day, including a three-day hike to stand
for several hours on what she calls Henry's German soil, revive her. The
mountains may represent the health and natural youth and security of Hugo,
but her passionate need for Miller grows with the passing days and the thick
letters he sends. She goes down first each day to get the mail, hides her diary
in the Austrian stove, and tells Hugo (whose shadow covers the page) that
she is working on her novel when she is really answering Henry's letters.[102]

These three weeks of separation spawn a "duel" of letters that reveals the
extent of their intellectual exchange, their mutual professional assistance,
and their private passion. At his suggestion, she is reading Spengler's *The
Decline of the West* and the end of Henry's just completed novel, which he

will entitle *Tropic of Capricorn* or *I Sing the Equator.* "Give me all the criticism you can," he begs. "Magnificent," she concludes tentatively. They discuss surrealism, Lawrence, Joyce, Unamuno, and Henry's latest interests, Jung and Freud. Though he claims that Fraenkel sparked his interest, certainly her earlier interest and writing must have played a part. He reads some of her diary and rereads her Lawrence book. When he compares Lawrence's intensity of feeling to French literature, she rejects the approach; French literature, which she admires intellectually, only "stirs the tip of my hair, like a message through a telegraph wire." The expressions of their mutual love are eloquent: you "tore the veils down," she says. "You are food and drink to me," he writes, "the whole bloody machinery." And he awaits a "literary fuck fest" when she returns.[103]

The fest lasts four days and nights after she returns alone to Louveciennes. It is a marriage for both, the "apotheosis" of her life; he says he comes away with "pieces of you sticking to me."[104] But it is preceded by a scene of drama and fakery. Thinking he has betrayed her and angry that she loves him so desperately, she decides to provoke his jealousy by dressing in an elaborate *maja* costume and burning a picture of John Erskine and a fake letter from Erskine in her bedroom fireplace grate just as Miller arrives.[105] He is shocked, frightened, and aroused, and quietly denies any unfaithfulness.

What we have is life and literature combined, Henry announces. Their sex is compulsive and consuming; their talk is "big"; each wants to "leave a scar" on the world. Hers will be her diary, he says, for no one "has ever told us how and what women think."[106] She persuades Hugo to invite Henry for an overnight visit to escape the heat of Paris, an invitation he extends after reading with enthusiasm Miller's new manuscript. Privately Anaïs assures Hugo she is only interested in Henry as a writer and is surprised by her own lies and Hugo's willingness just to be loved. But Henry balks, grows sentimental, she thinks, and refuses to hurt Hugo. She dissolves in angry tears. Henry comes to Louveciennes.

After Hugo has returned from the bank in the evening, she becomes angry at both men. Following a nimble and self-assured presentation of all her ideas about psychology, Henry declares that he does not trust Allendy's ideas or Anaïs's thinking. Hugo, probably hurt by her physical rejections, quietly agrees that her "neat pattern" is too slippery. The solidarity of the "ponderous German" and the "unflashy Scotsman" outrage her, and she writes later in her diary that "Faithfulness is a joke! Wisdom is the absence of ideas!"[107]

Thus begins a tug of war between Miller and Allendy (whose wife had recently sent him to Brittany to get him away from Anaïs). Anaïs begins it, with a comment about Allendy calculated to arouse Miller's jealousy. When

Miller explains his jealousy the next morning in the garden, she realizes that she has met her match in cleverness. Two dissemblers and mythomaniacs have had their first all-out fight. As he explains himself she looks at him and wonders if he is lying to her. She can love and lie, but her lies are only costumes, she believes. Soon Henry takes her against the ivy-covered garden wall, in what could be a scene from *Lady Chatterley,* for he is the "cannibal," the "genius-monster" who can fuck her best.[108]

Later when she is recording the event and analyzing her own lies, she decides to record all the lies in which she has wrapped herself. Allendy has told her that her lies ("what my mind engenders fictionally") are so invested with her feelings that they soon fool even her. She excuses her lies as the nature of the writer and without malice; they do not "penetrate my soul," she assures herself. "I am the noblest of the hypocrites." She writes openly to Henry about her enjoyment in creating dramas. At least she no longer gives lip service to idealism, which she has replaced with relative fictions and the excuse of being true to herself. She is an artist creating "complications" and "chaos."[109]

June cables Henry that she will return to Paris in October. He and Anaïs have been writing about her, their joint creation, since she left. But now Anaïs is angered by his portrait of June and their marriage in New York City because she believes he is appropriating her own concept of June. Jealously, she determines that her manuscript, "Alraune" (which she began in the spring), will be something that he could not have written: it will be closer to the myth and poetry of June and a work in the Rimbaud style. She will capture June's dreams and fantasies surrealistically and "proceed," in Jung's words, "from the dream outward."

In a burst of lyricism she writes thirty pages—a symbolic distillation of June's consciousness, she calls it—that baffle both Hugo and Henry. The latter asks to help her revise what will become her first novel, *The House of Incest.* She is now committed to and focused on a poetic work about the twinship of love, or loving ourselves in another. Incest, she calls it, meaning self-defeating and narcissistic love. It explains her love for June and her fifteen-year relationship with Eduardo.

When Allendy returns from his August vacation, she resumes her analysis with a double purpose: to arouse Allendy and to get even with Miller. She had sent the psychoanalyst a portion of one of Miller's letters to her. Jealousy, she believes, not love, incites passion. When Henry calls and postpones a meeting and a vague plan they had about going to Spain together, she decides to give herself to Allendy. But first she invites Henry out while Hugo is away. When he arrives on his bicycle, "soft and anxious," she hands him a letter, taken from her journal, full of criticism of him and thoughts on June,

Allendy, and Hugo. She observes his silence, then his confused terror. "What do you want?" he pleads. "Nothing more than this closeness," she responds. She has whipped him into a frenzy again. He stays two days.[110]

She admits she is capricious, crediting Allendy with freeing her from her guilt. He has freed a dangerous force, which she uses on him. She looks at him with "newborn power," and they kiss upon meeting with what she believes is greater warmth. When they talk of domination, she exaggerates Henry's cruelty; Allendy is paternal, protective, and certain. She lowers her head to hide her smile, knowing it is only coquetry on her part. She provokes Miller into calling Allendy a "brutish, sensual man, lethargic, with a fund of lunaticism in the back of his eyes."[111] She provokes Allendy into suggesting that Henry is perhaps schizophrenic, perhaps homosexual. This same week she provokes Eduardo's jealousy and pain by locking eyes with a young Cuban doctor on the dance floor. She tells Allendy that she feels a kinship with her father's "volcanic life hunger," and that his analysis has lost its objectivity, is breaking down. She plans to destroy it further: Hugo, who is away for five days, has promised to begin analysis with Allendy himself. Perhaps Hugo will become more interesting, but she confesses on 20 August 1932 to finding his body and caresses "intolerable."[112] She kisses Allendy, and within an hour is in Miller's arms in Louveciennes.

Now she is feeling like a "most corrupt" woman with a Madonna face. "I will practice the most incestuous crimes with a sacred religious fervor. . . . I will swallow God and sperm." Then she lists the following sins in her diary: love for her own blood (Eduardo), her husband's spiritual father (Erskine), a woman (June), the woman's husband (Henry), and her analyst (Allendy), who is Eduardo's spiritual father and now Hugo's guide. And all her sins are committed beautifully, she adds. Now she has fully embraced the bad girl created by her father's abuse. All that remains is to consummate the ritual of sin with her father.

## An Incestuous House

Perhaps the most incestuous entanglement, before her reunion with her father, comes from Allendy's simultaneous analysis of Anaïs, Hugo, and Eduardo and his indirect analysis of Miller's dreams. Anaïs keeps up a steady dialogue with each man about the others, and Eduardo is drawing up each of their astrological signs. She admits to her diary that she has gotten Allendy to love her in order to betray him. At the next visit she evades his kiss and refuses analysis. When he holds her against his big body (not unlike John's body, she notes) and tells her it will be "pleasant," not dramatic, she hates him for it. He senses her disappointment, which keeps him off guard. She tells Eduardo the entire story. When Hugo begins to depend on Allendy and his behavior to reflect Allendy's influence on him, she is bemused. Allendy uses Hugo's jealousy (even of Allendy) to cure him of what Anaïs calls Hugo's "homosexual passivity, by which he always allowed other men to love his wife."[113] She lets Henry read Hugo's diary. She is like a devil temptress directing all their lives (an image she used to describe Allendy in her diary). She is "the dark queen of intrigue," as she says of her alter ego, Djuna, in *The Four-Chambered Heart*. She is a novelist tangling up pivotal characters in a plot, then twisting the plot again and again.

Despite her knowing attempt to seduce Allendy, it is he who violates the trust and is responsible for the flirtation.[114] According to her—and we only have her word on it—her sessions with him are implicitly sexual and tender ("I have lost a father!"), not analytical, though they talk of Hugo, Eduardo, and astrology (the latter a topic of central interest to Allendy and Joaquin). The scenes she stages for Allendy do not provoke a frenzy in him as they do with the other three men in her life. Recognizing that his love is her trophy and her hysteria is neurotic, he insists that he finish his work for her as a doctor before proceeding to an intimate physical relationship. She submits, knowing that analysis, which intends to simplify life, also makes it dramatically complicated. Then she writes the entire story of her deliberate toying with Allendy for Henry to read. Is not her game as passionate as June's dramas? Has not the novelist baffled the psychoanalyst? Has she not deceived all those who believe she is sincere? Is she not falling into June's chaos?[115]

Lies are less necessary with Henry, for their talk has always heightened, exaggerated, and colored their experience; it is the "satanic joys known to writers only." Their neuroses have created his novel and her diary. Their relationship, both human and monstrous, is "surcharged with life" and "saturated with sex."[116] They talk of marriage, wanting it but knowing it would be financially impossible. Henry writes to his longtime confidant Emil Schnellock that his "next wife is Anaïs," who is the most "courageous" woman "of any period. . . . Lawrence seems small in comparison."[117] She gives Henry Hugo's money. In café and bed, drunk and sober, they read each other's words—he, her young wife's diary (offering to type it for her); she, his love letters. It is a marriage of style. They are creators and adventurers together; their works are interrelated. His masculine style, her "enameled" style. He writes about her new work: her "language of nerves . . . larval thoughts, unconscious processes, images not entirely divorced from their dream content; it is a language of the neurotic . . . of decadence."[118] She is ecstatic. She walks the fine edge of confrontation with Hugo, making love to Miller upstairs with the aroma of Hugo's dinner cooking in the kitchen, collecting Miller's bites on her flesh to mark her betrayals. But she has sent Hugo to

Allendy for the latter's compassionate protection. Accordingly, Allendy explains to the tortured Hugo that his wife's adventures are literary, a child's playing with experience.

Anaïs has just written a note in the third week of October to explain to Henry why she is not writing anymore on the "Mona" ("Alraune") manuscript: she is too happy! The book came from her pain and madness. The telephone rings with news from Perlès: JUNE ARRIVED LAST NIGHT! Anaïs writes the words in bold print in her journal, then falls apart. She had often wished that June would die. Henry's bewildered call informing her that June is "subdued and reasonable" only adds to her pain, for he is disarmed.

As she had as a child to win her father's love, she collapses, feeling that she is going to die. Hugo and Allendy care for her with tenderness. She believes that Allendy cannot conceal his happiness that her affair with Miller might be over. He wants her to stand on her own strength, and then to love him, she assumes. A real man has protective instincts, he reminds her.

The next night June arrives in Louveciennes, and Anaïs walks through the dark town with her, listening to her defend herself against Henry, the literary monster, and begging Anaïs to save her from him. She has read all he has written about her and concludes that he has betrayed her (she wants to be an admirable mythic character). He is cruel and false, everything he accuses her of being. She speaks eloquently, without hysteria, this third member of the mythomaniacal triangle in which each seems to be finding the image of himself or herself in the other. They walk up the hill and stand under the light over the front door, where they had first seen each other, their dream illuminated as if by a stage light. "Anaïs, you are giving me life . . . what Henry has taken away." Suddenly Anaïs feels that she would do anything for June.[119]

In an emotional, if not physical, sense, Anaïs and June are lovers. The kissing and caresses are repeated in every diary and fictional account. Though Anaïs will take pains in her later years to deny publicly any lesbian activity, she was clearly experimenting with this form of love. In *Seduction of the Minotaur* (1959) she will say Sabina and Lillian had "kissed once. It was soft and lovely, but like touching your own flesh." As late as 1972 Anaïs will say that had June initiated her at the time—had June loved her enough—she might have been awakened to a sexual love of women.[120] The mythologist would note that she was kissing her mirror, and the psychologist would recognize her need to affix her mouth on any approving mouth.

At midnight, as the train rushes by them at the station, they are kissing. When June whispers, "Anaïs, I am happy with you," Anaïs feels her madness returning. There are occasional moments of eroticism during the next six weeks—moments during long talks in cafés, with knees touching under the table, feverish kissing in train stations, caresses on beds, close dancing, sad partings when June's pale and frightened face looks as if she were drowning through a rain-spattered taxi window.[121] But the true madness comes in the struggle, tears, and drunkenness of this trio, each talking, analyzing, accusing, betraying the other—until Anaïs flees to Allendy, Henry attempts to flee to London, and June finally leaves Paris and Henry.

The most stable center of this autumn is their art. During Anaïs's Austrian summer vacation, Miller had written literary agent William Aspenwall Bradley, asking him to read *Tropic of Cancer* and submit it to Jack Kahane, owner of Obelisk Press.[122] Now Kahane, who specializes in erotica and has published an edition of Lawrence's *Lady Chatterley's Lover,* enthusiastically agrees to publish it but without financing the printing costs. Anaïs has agreed to find the money. During June's litany of complaints against her husband that first night with Anaïs, she urged her not to pay for the publication of Miller's novel. But Anaïs's commitment had already been made. By way of advance publicity, Kahane (who eventually becomes Anaïs's publisher) asks for a fifty- to sixty-page brochure on Lawrence or Joyce to publish first, then changes his mind. But by then Miller is launched on a full-scale manuscript on Lawrence, with Anaïs acting as both librarian, supplying armloads of books, and editor. He is feeling "like a seer . . . a prophet," he declares amid the piles of notes around him and the lists taped to the walls. "[C]ome to Clichy . . . prepared to roll up your sleeves." She discusses the ideas and reads his pages full of quotations; speak for yourself, she cautions him wisely.[123]

Anaïs's art lay in manipulating the live tableau and in recording it in her journals—creating the characters, moving them on her stage, initially recording the scenes, then altering them for symbolic presentation in her fiction, which was rewritten many times. Thirty-three years later she will refine these journals further, even expurgating a great deal when she retypes them for publication.[124] Among the various scenes she creates this fall—with perception as well as a certain amount of self-justification—are heated embraces with June in taxis, work with Henry on his Lawrence essay, and drunken arguments in the Clichy apartment. "The drama is everything," she says, for the artist is a hero.

It is impossible to separate Anaïs's erotic pleasure from her desire to preempt June's beauty and earthiness and her role in Henry's life. In the journal version of their relations she understands each better than the other does, explains and praises one to the other, and thus gives them back to each other. She takes credit for being the indispensable "revealer" and for the relative harmony in the Millers' marriage.[125]

Henry's letters confirm the initial harmony. But there is little loving, fighting, or curiosity in his relationship with June, whose presence interferes with his writing. This obsession with his writing project sends June back into the warm, perfumed, costume- and gift-giving arms of Anaïs. They talk in cafés about Henry and dance rebelliously in a jazz club—"How quickly I slide down the slope of a snowy voice, plunge into smoky eyes, diffuse into music," Anaïs writes.[126]

Henry seems indifferent. Take June for what she is, he writes to Anaïs, but do not let her come between us. Believe in me, he repeats. He sees June only as a pathological child. Anaïs confirms his view of June's childlike dependence, praises the greatness of his art, and assures him that her relationship with June only deepens her love for him. She gives June erotic mothering, and becomes indispensable to Miller's wave of creation, winning him with art and money (her first royalty check). June, who disapproves of their "inaccurate" literary portraits of her and is jealous of Anaïs's offer to pay Kahane, certainly feels used. Week after week everything one says to the other is altered and repeated to the third member, and Anaïs and Henry mythologize each scene for their art.[127]

The dynamics of these dependencies and motivations explode in several scenes in the apartment in Clichy. Sometimes Fred, who is typing Anaïs's diary from age sixteen, gets involved in the scenes and enjoys stealing kisses from June and Anaïs. In one scene Anaïs sits on the bed "translating" and "clarifying" the two Millers to each other—her egocentricity, his dependence on criticism, his distortion of June (because of his love and hatred of his mother). Anaïs's analysis often voices June's privately given complaints. Henry complains that June will not let him alone during the most important period of his creative life. Other scenes begin with banter and teasing while they drink. On one occasion June drinks Pernod until she is white with anger, then weeps hysterically. Anaïs holds the sobbing June. Eventually June is lying in her own vomit in her black satin dress. Henry cleans up the floor while Anaïs, who seems to be presiding over the death throes of the marriage, cleans up June. Later that evening June walks her to the station and buys her some violets. As the train speeds toward Louveciennes in the dark, Anaïs throws the violets under her seat. The ugliness and emptiness of the scene, what she calls the "barbaric jungle of Clichy," make her "yearn for the ecstasies."[128]

The next day, after recording each moment of the Clichy scene and weighing each individual's charges against the other in her journal, she finds herself in rue de l'Assomption standing outside Allendy's office, where just days before June had kissed her neck. She walks up and down outside the house, as if she were walking in front of the church across the street in some soul-wrenching debate with herself. She imagines Allendy inside "bottling dramas into alchemist's bottles, distilling, annotating." When she finally walks up the stairs and into the dark confessional, she decides to give only half of herself to the scientist and healer. The other half she will give to Henry the sensualist and "crazy genius" who loves her body as well as the artist in her. That second half invents a lie for Allendy, who takes her in his arms.

I have broken with Henry, she tells Allendy, and I love you. I accept your wisdom. I desire your strength. He is overjoyed that she has abandoned the degenerate Miller. But she has pleased Allendy with a momentary lie ("I simply got ahead of myself," she rationalizes). Back in Clichy she invents yet another lie for the pleasure of the audience there: she has met with the great French man of letters, André Gide. She repeats this lie in her first published diary. This fabrication had its genesis in a mention of Gide at a dinner party the night before. When she tells Henry and Fred, she considers it a "prophetic lie, because this interview *will* take place . . . later."[129]

Whenever she goes home instead of returning to Clichy, she believes that Miller thinks she is sleeping with Allendy. The intrigue and betrayals of moving from one lover to the other in one day stimulate her. When exhausted she returns to Louveciennes to sleep, write, masturbate, and write again. One psychologist has suggested that this fragmenting of her life into different parts is a means of making her neurosis concrete so that she can control the fragments.[130] It certainly gives her the impression that she has control of her emotional existence and, as one observer notes, "diffuse[s] the risk of dependence and, therefore, the potential hurt of a rejection."[131] Another psychologist and friend suggests that her sleeping with many men while remaining seemingly virginal is clearly a "separation of sexuality from her essence," a manifestation of what can happen with childhood trauma.[132] A recent feminist heralds her "sexual freedom . . . as the true *pícara* of sex." But her behavior, her drinking, and the deterioration of her handwriting in her diary suggest that she is falling apart.[133]

Her intimate moments with June seem awkward. Once after putting June, who is ill, to bed, Anaïs lies fully clothed beside her, feeling the contour of her body. Another night, with Henry and Fred sleeping in the other room, she and June shyly acknowledge their physical intimidation and their wish to inhabit the other's body—one wanting the full and earthy physicality, the other wanting the pale and boyish build. They lie partially clothed in Miller's bed, kissing passionately. But June hesitates to remove her clothes, and awkwardness follows. Before Anaïs leaves, June asks her if she loves Allendy. The response is a long "half-truth"—a description of a lover in New York (taking facts from John Erskine's life) with natural expression of adoration (while thinking of Henry). The lie is transparent to June, who tells her husband she has pulled a "lesbian act" to discover everything about them. Henry denies it all and, when June stalks out, comes to Louveciennes for a day and two nights in Hugo's absence. Anaïs claims it is she who "pulled the lesbian act" to learn of June's feelings for him. When a guitar string snaps while she is lying on the couch with Henry, she claims to feel the sudden realization of the end of her love for Hugo. She will use the image in more than one story. Only Hugo's return puts an end to the happy scene. Henry returns to the Clichy apartment to find Anaïs's love letters to June wrapped around her gifts to June. On the back is written, "Please get a divorce immediately."[134] A week later, after Henry reads her diary amid a momentary calm in the storm over June, Anaïs feels truly married to Henry in an "absolute dissolution of myself into him."[135]

Her language and thought reach a fever pitch, sometimes brilliant and full of insight and metaphorical surprise, sometimes mad. Structure and meaning crash, as Anaïs herself explodes in hysteria or drunkenness. (Alcohol deadens her sometimes "paralyzing neuralgia.")[136] She feverishly lives, lies, loves, and writes—freed and protected by her adoring maid, Emilia, who says nothing when Anaïs locks Henry in the guestroom at night just before Hugo returns late from the office. Sometimes the risk and ethics shake Henry, who is awakened when the banker leaves the following morning. But Anaïs claims to feel no remorse: "I feel unfettered . . . [a]moral," she writes. "I have no morality." She only feels terrified that her diary may be discovered. After thirty years of "famine, dreaming, renunciation, [and] detachment," she is living in excess and joy, she says.[137]

Two additional love affairs, not mentioned in any published diary, occur this winter. Documented in original diaries thirty-seven, "La Folle Lucide," and thirty-nine, "Schizoidie and Paranoia," are serious flirtations with Ana Maria Sanchez, Eduardo's sister and Anaïs's cousin, and Ethel Guiler, Hugo's sister. As with Anaïs and June, there are expressions of love and kisses. When Allendy accuses her of debauching her cousin, Anaïs claims she wants to give Ana Maria the gift of experience as well as pain, to shake and enrich her life. Her control and power seem to be an aphrodisiac. In her thirty-ninth diary, she compiles her own "Liste d'Amoureaux," which includes June, Ana Maria, and Ethel.

### Farewell to June and Allendy

The lecture hall at the Sorbonne is cold and austere in January 1933. René Allendy is lecturing on the "Metamorphosis of Poetry" (as part of a series entitled "New Ideas") with his gray-haired wife in attendance. Anaïs, feeling feminine and "silky" dressed in fur, listens critically to his dissection of poetry. She thinks instead about her return to Allendy at the time of June's ugly exit from Paris. She had always exaggerated for him her narrative of Henry and June. But now she thinks he has not helped. Once her anchor, he now reveals his weakness. The distinguished, slightly stooped scholar at the podium had confided in her his sense of his dead father's presence in his house, and his interest in the occult and tarot cards. Yet she has also betrayed her analysis by lying to him. When he demands she break with the Millers—you are a "flower in a dung pile"—she swears she has done so. She only regrets that her lie cut her off from talking about Henry, but she cannot lose Allendy, and she enjoys the ironic humor of deceiving a professional analyst and of "having gone to Allendy to get cured of a lack of confidence in my womanly charms, and that it should be those charms he has succumbed to."[138] She also enjoys gliding between her two worlds: the café life with the sounds of Henry's talk, the street accordion wheeze, cabbage cooking in the Clichy kitchen (the earthy world of her mother); and the elegant society nights with Hugo, who is now suspicious and possessive.

As Allendy's lecture drones on—like the doctor over the cadaver of poetry, she thinks—she tells herself he is not a poet and she needs a poet, she needs literature. Like Henry, she has begun reading *Art and Artist,* by another analyst named Otto Rank, wishing she had written the book herself.[139] Soon she will leave Allendy, who has been one of her paternal, learned, idealistic heroes. He had played a key role in what she called her quest for a father or savior or God. Once he revealed his vulnerability and his need for love, her maternal instinct (which she sees as dangerous "masochism") rushed to reassure him of her affection. She felt she was taking care of him, not he her. They humorously reversed roles, with him on the patient's armchair and her diary full of analysis of his childhood. Even describing for her journal the collegial working sessions with Miller (who is feverishly writing "Self-Portrait," later to be published as *Black Spring* and dedicated to her), she uses maternal descriptive phrases and techniques of the analyst. Allendy has empowered her, she says, "to help me take care of my children." Analysis, like writing, embodies both the roles of the father (selfish, assertive) and the mother (nurturing, passive, receptive).[140]

Anaïs writes a check to help Miller from the battle zone with June. He has his bags packed for England when June returns to the apartment in Clichy and discovers the plot. What follows, according to his letter to Anaïs 18 December, are hours of humiliating harangue and threats (including one to reveal everything to Hugo). To protect Anaïs, he gives June the check, unpacks his bags, and writes with shame to tell Anaïs that her money is gone. He asks her not to give him any more money.

She insists he come to Louveciennes for a brief stay. He brings his manuscripts and books for safekeeping and she gives him her desk. In the stillness of the house, they work together on his notes—she is having them bound—with serenity and focus. Because June is still in town, Fred Perlès gives him money for a trip to England and urges him to leave immediately.

At Newhaven he is stopped by immigration authorities, who subject him to intense examination. They are suspicious of his frayed clothes, the small change in his pocket (187 francs), and his explanation for being in England (he is running away from his wife!). They jail him overnight and deport him. Overjoyed to be with his typewriter in the quiet apartment with Fred, he feels free of his fear of June. Soon he learns that June has indeed left Europe. Anaïs, who had raised the money for June's ticket and left it at the American Express office where they had so often met, will never see June again. Henry will not see her again for more than a dozen years (their Mexican divorce by proxy will come in late 1934). June had turned at the door when she left him and said, "And now you have your last chapter for your book!"[141]

Henry and Anaïs are sitting at her desk on New Year's Day 1933. Anaïs is helping Henry organize the notes (he says the notes are "being embalmed") of his three years in Paris. He is putting the finishing touches on the notebook (into which she pastes a photograph of her eyes). They are spending ten days together while Hugo is in London. She has refused the holiday hospitality of her mother. When she notes that Henry has not written of their moments together, he takes her diary and writes a long passage about the view of Paris from Louveciennes, the view of the countryside and billboard from the train window, the village tobacco shop and grocery store—all his memories of the town and house, from which he dates "the most important epoch of my life."[142] But while they are entering notes and memorabilia into the notebook, he looks around at the photographs of her husband and lovers, at the bound volume of her diary, at the neat organization of the house ("everything is categorized, labeled, filed," he notes), and thinks of all the people whom she has attracted. Is the voluminous diary not enough for her romantic "I"? "Here the eye regards the eye that regards the eye . . . ad libitum, ad infinitum," he adds to his letter.[143] When Henry has to leave and she awaits the arrival of Hugo and his sister Ethel, Anaïs yearns for "wholeness with Henry." Later she dreams of "carrying Henry's head in [her] womb."[144]

During the month of Anaïs's thirtieth birthday (February 1933), Henry and Fred give her a copy of Joyce's *Ulysses*. She is still loving both Miller and Allendy—taking her "magic chariot" taxi from Gare St. Lazare to Allendy's office, then to a café to meet Henry. For Allendy's forty-fourth birthday, she and Hugo give him a completely glass aquarium, including the fish and flora, like the one he admires in their house. His first visit to her home signals the intended end of his analysis of her, and it is the classic seduction by house. Though he had told her she had a neurotic need for gestures and approval, he is soon admiring the fire in her blue mosaic fireplace, the light reflecting on the wine bottles and peach walls, and the limo and chauffeur she spent a month's allowance on (telling him it was lent by a countess friend). The Allendys reciprocate with a dinner party for the Guilers to meet Bernard Steele, a publisher of Antonin Artaud (the French surrealist playwright) and Dr. Otto Rank. Artaud and Rank—the crazy man and the healer—will become the next two important men in Anaïs's life.[145]

She is increasingly critical of the coldness and detachment of the man she calls her "God, conscience, absolver, priest, sage." Allendy confesses little passion for women, and she laughs to think that Eduardo and Hugo have gone to him to be cured of their passivity. He now seems like a "dying man." She often analyzes her father's character after seeing Allendy, and she increasingly responds in a maternal and nurturing way to his problems. Though she credits Allendy with freeing her from guilt (her Catholic conscience), teaching her to relax her grip on life, and helping her learn to deal with her mother, she criticizes him for trying to separate her from the artist life of Miller, whom he always calls a "barbarian." Miller, in turn, refers to Allendy as "[h]ermeneutic."[146]

In an early draft of *The House of Incest*, she creates an astrologer who will help her protagonist's divided psyche; but when the three women of the novel seduce him, his coat of armor (presumably his psychological theory, his mask) breaks and he is seen as a man without sexual or healing powers.[147] Though Allendy undoubtedly forfeits his credibility and power by hugging and kissing his patient (and allowing her to gain control by believing she has seduced him), he helps her to find a pattern in her behavior of seduction and in her need to conquer (and fear of being conquered by) father figures. There are some who object to her portrait of him in her diary. Says Georges Belmont, a journalist who knew them both, "Allendy was a good and intelligent man, probably more intelligent than she; but when you read the [diary] pages about him he looks weak and dumb."[148] Certainly his portrait is colored by her self-interest. While Allendy was unprofessional in his sexual overtures to Anaïs, he believed throughout that he was acting in her best interests.

She continues her research for Allendy because it gives her a concrete association with the surrealists. He is a close friend and supporter of Antonin Artaud, who had worked with the French surrealists in the 1920s, and

Allendy's words on them are the only eloquent words she hears during his Sorbonne lecture. For a year now she has been buying and reading with Henry every little magazine that features surrealism, including *This Quarter* and *transition*. She is drawn to this artistic movement because it affirms the creative power of dreams and the imagination.

When Allendy brings Artaud to Louveciennes, the magic of the house and garden seduce him, as does Hugo, who shares his interest in astrology, horoscopes, film, and surrealism. Anaïs openly flirts with the brooding and poetic homosexual playwright, whom Allendy protects as a son, and Allendy is displeased. In a month he will lose his two "children," whom he had once compared to each other.

When Antonin Artaud meets Anaïs and Hugo Guiler in March 1933, he is thirty-six years old, an actor in film and stage, and has been in and out of hospitals for morphine addiction and mental illness. He is also the author of a manifesto entitled "Theatre of Cruelty." Having disavowed surrealism, he advocates the theatre as a place to shout out pain, disease, and violence. His first experimental theatre, at the Théâtre Alfred Jarry (1926–29), had been supported principally by the Allendys, as was his only screenplay, in 1927, parts of which were used by Luis Buñuel and Salvador Dalí for their famous surrealist film *L'Age d'Or*.

Anaïs and Hugo, eager to cultivate and support the arts, are impressed with this famous actor, poet, and director. She is particularly excited by his brooding, nervous soul and his blue, pained "visionary eyes" of a mystic. She gives him her "Alraune" and begins a correspondence, declaring that her work is in harmony with his vision of the world, to which he responds that he has difficulty reading her "refined and exquisite" English.[149] Allendy, who intuitively perceives her obsession with seduction, warns her in vain that Artaud is homosexual, a drug addict, and mentally ill.

Henry, absorbed in his own obsessions, respects hers. He is wrestling with great ideas and his Lawrence manuscript (he is in his philosophical phase), being stimulated by Michael Fraenkel's philosophy of death, toying with a new plan for a film book with Anaïs, sending her dozens of pages to read, and writing about his 6 March visit to Dr. Otto Rank. Meantime Anaïs is reading Artaud's *L'Art et la mort* (1929) and almost daily researching and translating Allendy's plague manuscript. Her love affair with Henry is a year old on 8 March, still joyous and free; he looms tall as a thinker, she informs him, and tells her diary that she wants to live with or marry him (they would forgive each other their flirtations).[150] But she is *"afraid of the wholeness* of her love" (she underlines the passage in her diary), which would burden him; thus she will "spread" herself into many "smaller loves. . . . But the axis is

Henry." She also calls him "the real king" of her harem and the "core" of her life.[151]

In contrast to Miller, Allendy seems to her to be "tortured by jealousy." She also senses Eduardo's jealousy. He becomes ill the night of Artaud's visit and demands his cousin's attention. She writes in her diary, in uncharacteristic understatement, that "it is getting more and more difficult to make four men happy."[152]

# CHAPTER SIX

# 1933–1935

# A Season in Hell

"Every act related to my writing was connected in me with . . . seduction of my father. . . . I was doomed by the enormity of my sin (the wish to charm my father), to be punished, to fail. Every act . . . involving others was charged with direct sexual associations: courting the world."

—*Anaïs Nin, 1957*[1]

ANAÏS NIN is sitting between Hugh Guiler and Henry Miller in the front row of the amphitheatre at the Sorbonne. With them, at this 6 April 1933 event in René Allendy's "New Ideas" lecture series, are several friends, including Hélène Boussinescq. Allendy himself sits behind a table with his featured speaker, Antonin Artaud, in this lecture-hall setting, with its long background of chalkboard. Allendy looks professorial and lackluster, Anaïs observes, and his introduction of Artaud at the podium is factual and gray. Artaud, on the other hand, looks the part of the driven poet-actor; his long tapered fingers make quick gestures and his long hair occasionally falls into his face.[2]

## Antonin Artaud

Artaud's subject is the theatre and the plague ("Le Théâtre et la peste"). She listens as he speaks about great art being created out of a fear of death, and she understands his intensity if not his ideas. He loses the thread of his thought, however, and begins acting out *la peste,* dying by the plague. As his body goes into contortions of pain, he screams in agony and becomes delirious. The audience gasps in shock, then breaks into laughter sprinkled with hisses. The front row holds firm as others stamp out and slam the door. Artaud's death throes subside, and he lies still on the floor until all have left but his friends and followers. Then he stands calmly, walks down to the front row, kisses the hands of the women, and suggests that they adjourn to a café. At the door of the auditorium everyone else has other commitments—including Hugo, who must take home one of their guests who does not speak French. Anaïs wants to stay with this poet whose mind fascinates her. As they walk along the boulevard St.-Michel in the dark humid night, Artaud pours out his anger at the response to his performance. His theory—which will later greatly influence the twentieth-century theatre of Jean Genet, Peter Brook, Julian Beck, Peter Weiss and others—is that theatre should disturb the audience, for theatre, like the plague, destroys the veneer of civilization and reveals the ugly realities of man's primitive state. He had wanted to give the lecture audience the experience itself, he says, turning down boulevard du Montparnasse. "They always want to hear *about*." They are dead and need awakening, he adds as they walk past the bright lights of the cafés at the corner of boulevard Raspail. By now mist covers their faces, and he runs his fingers through his damp hair.

In La Coupole, Montparnasse's huge brasserie, Artaud talks more about himself as they sit over coffee. Anaïs is quiet and in awe of the taut and obsessed Artaud. She could calm him, understand his troubled soul, she imagines. He speaks of his fifteen-year opium addiction, recites poetry, and describes her sympathetic eyes. The next day she follows up in a letter assuring him that most of those with her understood his lecture ("It shook the world"), especially the writer Henry Miller, who is writing about the "Universe of Death" and found confirmation for his own sense that death is a source for life.[3]

Anaïs is unable to separate the artist's mind from the physical man, and fills her diary with descriptions of the man Artaud, his "[b]eautifully chiseled, tormented features," his voice that always sounds as if it is going to break, and the pain of his eyes. She must improve her French to talk to him, to "penetrate his world," to "solve the enigma of Allendy." Her head is turned by the artist, she admits, for only the artist has value. He is a genius, not a madman, in her eyes.

She accelerates her correspondence with him and invites him to Louveciennes several times.[4] He sends theatre tickets to Giraudoux's *Intermezzo* and, despite his occasional silence and moodiness (always followed by a letter of apology), she is enchanted. They both "dramatize the passage of ideas through sensation," she exclaims, and they are both Libra! (In fact, she is Pisces, he Virgo.)

She shares her admiration of Artaud with Henry, for Artaud is now one of the dramatic personages in her life, as June had been. She and Henry speak of jealousy—his dalliance with whores, her obsession with June and Artaud. Unlike less worldly-wise lovers, they will not be possessive of each other.[5] Allendy, by contrast, is furious—that she ignored him at the lecture, that she sat next to Miller, and that she left with Artaud, with whom she most assuredly will toy. Do not play with Artaud! he warns.

Allendy is so whipped into a frenzy of jealousy and sexual arousal that he finally has sexual intercourse with Anaïs. After biting and pawing her at her next visit, he asks her to go to a discreet hotel near the Métro Cadet. In her diary she describes an awkward scene on their rented bed: he is soft and fleshy, and she is unaroused by his fat awkwardness, but comes to his rescue with her expert knowledge. She had wanted to "bathe in sex as Henry has done," but she has a "flabby lover." Nevertheless she agrees to meeting the following week, when he takes out a whip for gentle flagellation that smarts her but leaves him soft. She returns home with stinging flesh—at least the whip was virile.[6]

Henry, the steady artist in her life, finds the original version of her "Alraune" on his desk during the second week of April, numbers the pages (about eighty-six), rereads portions, and then types a passionate letter of criticism to her in the voice of a "Dutch uncle." She must stop writing "silly letters to Eduardo" and cultivating her "imaginings," because her manuscript needs work! It is "damned wonderful" but "damned aborted" and she needs to "manicure her tools." He will give her language lessons and they will work through each page together slowly, "lovingly, scathingly." It can be flawless—worthy of Rimbaud or Lafargue—or gibberish, depending on whether or not she will master her medium, her craft. Later, in trying to understand her enigmatic style, he concludes that she is "ingrown" and protected, "bound up . . . restricted," not the Pisces she imagines. One reason she has "lodged" herself so firmly in the diary is her fear of "testing" her "tangible self with the world." She needs to develop muscle. He asks her for the explicit; she declares she writes poetry.[7]

When three days later Perlès finishes typing another of her childhood diaries (written when she was about fourteen) and pronounces it the "worst of the lot," "sugary" and "a bit nauseating," she concludes that his jealousy has turned to hatred.[8] Though she is unable to brook criticism, she handles Henry's blunt direction because she is assured of his love and loyalty. Henry is her only staunch supporter and critic, she concludes. He works with her at whatever moment she has free at Clichy and Louveciennes. He has given one of her journals to his agent, William Aspenwall Bradley, and brought him to see her in Louveciennes. When Bradley praises her journal, she loves Henry for the selflessness of his enthusiasm. While Kahane delays the publication of *Tropic of Cancer*, she says, "[T]ell him I will go to prison with you too, nail lacquer, false curls and all" and will not publish her own work first. "You are great, great, great Henry. . . . My journal has become the journal of *you*. It's full of you—brimming full."[9]

At William Bradley's next visit to Louveciennes she speaks of Miller before turning over her childhood journals, which Bradley says he will show to the American publisher Knopf.[10] Bradley, an American literary agent who works out of his home office on the Ile St. Louis, knows that, except for Kahane, no publisher will touch Miller's novel. With Nin's work it is a matter of style, not subject matter, and he objects to her stylization and poetry in "Alraune" (*The House of Incest*). He asks her to cut down the diary in order to publish a condensed volume; write the diary for me, he suggests as a means of proposing a more familiar style. He will withhold his sharpest criticism until September.

Kahane has delayed publishing *Cancer* for several reasons. He is writing his memoirs, in which he decries traditional English publishers who abandon their authors at the first threat of censorship. Yet he too fears censorship for Miller's novel. He is also awaiting funding. His son will charge later that Miller had sent "Anaïs in person, duly perfumed, and instructed her to go the whole way if called upon to do so."[11] In fact, it is the money (which she provides), not sex, that eventually gets the novel published.

Having put off Artaud for ten days in early May—for his visits had become psychologically intense and less poetic—she invites him to Louveciennes for dinner with her and Hugo. She senses for the first time that he is sexually attracted to Hugo. She records their discussions in her diary, sends him money, and continues her correspondence. It is his pained soul, not his body, that attracts her. She invites out Artaud's publisher, Bernard Steele, who brings her a copy of Dr. Otto Rank's *Don Juan and His Double*. She is fascinated with the idea of Don Juan seducing women who represent the unattainable mother and shares the volume with Henry. She sees the parallel to her own seductions of an unobtainable father. She and Henry have been reading and discussing Rank's *Art and Artist* and the psychology of the creative personality type, she with Artaud and especially her father in mind.[12]

For both Henry and herself, she is cultivating two men of the publishing world: Bernard Steele and William Bradley. Taking a manuscript copy of *Cancer* with her and promising to stay the night, she accompanies Artaud on a trip to Steele's house in the country. During the bantering and mockery of the evening, she promises to dance for Steele. When she sees the brooding and humiliated response of Artaud, she makes excuses and leaves for Paris with him. Suspicious, he tells her that he finds her behavior inconsistent. When she protests that she really hates the flippancy of the dinner party, he charges, "I see you as a woman who plays with men. . . . I am afraid you are fickle, changeable. . . . Your life [is] so theatrical, so exteriorized—your costumes—your house." She insists all this is for herself, not for the public.[13]

With Miller, Allendy, Artaud, and others she shares the news of the impending visit this May of her father, the archetypal Don Juan figure among many others in her life. They have been corresponding since the spring, when a friend of her brother Joaquin brought the message from Nin y Castellanos that he mourns the lost contact with his children. She sends the message back that he can write her, and his theatrical and flowing letters proclaiming paternal devotion have been arriving regularly. She sends him the typed portion of her childhood diary, which narrates the pain of her loss of her father, and she declares that the diary was written for him. He sends declarations of love, emphasizing that she is his "double," in flesh and spirit. Though initially overjoyed at the prospect of meeting her lost father again, she knows he is coming at a time when she no longer needs him as a father. This ironic timing makes her dizzy. She feels as though she were "walking into a Coney Island trick house."[14]

Why would Anaïs want to establish a relationship with the author of her pain? She is thirty years old and feeling rather secure in being loved simultaneously and actively by four men. She has been in analysis for a year—though without fully dealing with the source of her previous pain. The only charge against her father in her mind is abandonment, and she recognizes her pathological fear of loss and rejection. Now it is he, who had once told her she was ugly, who seems to be reaching out with the acceptance she craves. (It has taken a lot of men to erase his remark.) Certainly she is also curious, particularly by his appeal to her as his double. "[E]very narcissist dreams of a twin," she confesses. "My evil Double!"[15] Greater still is the unacknowledged childhood sexual memory against which she is powerless. Though she will become his victim again, her diary description portrays it as a mutual seduction.

## Incest

He comes back in a gust of face powder and playacting, to which she responds in kind. During several long meetings this spring, each musters all the charm possible to win the other. At every visit he repeats the line "We do not need to lie to each other," as if to establish that the flattery and the little lies and exaggerations are the truth. She gives a perfect dinner party, she is beautiful, and her house enchanting. He brings her flowers and a Lalique vase. All the gestures of courtship. He calls her his fiancée. He even expresses jealousy of her journal, his only rival, he calls it. He invites her to the Riviera in June, where his acquaintances "will take you for my mistress. That will be beautiful. I will say, 'This is my daughter,' and they will not believe me," she records in her diary and in several versions of her fictional account of their incest.[16]

After each visit she fills her diary with description and analysis of him and their discussions of their "twinship": their petite builds, similar height, thin lips, tapered hands, fragility, artistic temperament, indifference to food. Both love music, the sea, sobriety, and have a great need for cleanliness and order (he to the point of washing his hands every ten minutes, a repetition-compulsion disorder). They have a passion for aesthetics, creation, and drama (both wear capes), and both achieve their desires through deception (she is much more critical of his superficiality—hers, she would claim, is tempered by humanity and femininity; she has never sought luxury and money). They have pride and strong wills, and each suffers, she concludes, "from romanticism, quixotism, cynicism, naïveté, cruelty, schizophrenia, multiplicity of selves, *dédoublement,* and each is bewildered as to how to make a synthesis." They pour their genius into living—their only indulgence is lovemaking—and their talent into their art. She details his selfishness—personal luxuries but no money for his mother in Barcelona, valuing his own silk shirts over the needs of his wife and children, seeing his children only as extensions of himself. But she understands that these are the prerogatives of the artist. Like her father she is artist, perfectionist, egoist. What she does not detail is that they are two wounded, neurotic children (both beaten and humiliated by their respective fathers) who seek lovers but are afraid of real intimacy. They seek and find both a parent and child in the each other.[17]

Upon careful examination, the diary does reveal tension and anger. At the first meeting she describes "unuttered accusations . . . anxieties . . . fears . . . weakness." At the second meeting, when he admires her tapered hands and reaches out, she pulls her hand away so swiftly that it hits the glass bowl with the crystal fish and crystal ship and stones, breaking it. Water runs down the mantel to the floor. She makes some psychological explanation about breaking the "artificial, contained life and letting life break through."[18] The artifice of their lives and the glass fish is obvious, but a sexual image would have described more appropriately the tension between them. Both masters of duplicity, their charms keep the trouble repressed, but she finds it difficult to look him in the eyes. He seems to her to be father, seer, and god. Again. Now that she no longer needs a father, the severe, overcritical, and violent father is gone. This "smiling, radiant, charming father was [always] for visitors. So I am a visitor now." That night both dream of their sexual union.[19]

Her identification with her father comes from a fierce need for his approval. "He was her animus, the other side of her soul," says one of her best friends in explaining Anaïs's fixation on her father, and "she sought revenge against her mother, who had always scolded her for being like her father."[20] Anaïs argues with her brother Joaquin, who takes his mother's side and will not reconcile (as his sister wishes him to) with his inhumane father. Anaïs is proud of her father, argues in his defense. She concludes that her mother's love is only biological, her father's selfishness is the domain of the creative artist—and she prefers the love of her father (who sees his children only as his creations) to her mother's possessiveness. She argues that her mother's flight to America—unfortunately, never fully explained to the children—was motivated not by love but possessiveness. When Joaquin is adamant, she wonders what her worldly, selfish father would think of this "austere" son, who cares only for music and the Catholic church? And she implies in her description of their early family scenes that her mother was to blame for the fights and that the memories of beatings may be distortions coming from her proximity to her parents' dramatic warfare.

It is important to emphasize that sexual abuse was neither in her vocabulary nor considered a major factor in the universal taboos against incest in Europe at the time. Father-daughter incest was considered very rare in practice, but typical in dreams.[21] Do not Freud's children all want to seduce their parents? How could this dapper musician with the powdered face and dyed hair, this dandy who had played with Casals and Paderewski, be guilty of such a transgression?

"Nobody," says her father as he raises his glass at her dinner party, "nobody has given me the feeling Anaïs gives me."

"And so I am loved and can love my father," she concludes. Hope has created a miracle. She has won him back. It was not her fault she was abandoned.[22]

A meeting in Vienna, Austria, just thirty-seven years before, helps to explain the conventional wisdom regarding parent-child sexual relations and why Dr. René Allendy had not focused on childhood trauma/sexual abuse in his sessions with Anaïs. On 21 April 1896, Sigmund Freud read a paper entitled "The Etiology of Hysteria" to his colleagues of the Society for Psychiatry and Neurology. He had discovered, he argued, that all hysteria is the result of childhood sexual abuse, and he used the words rage, assault, trauma, attack.[23] The testimony of his patients, and his own experience ("My own father was one of those perverts") overwhelmingly bore out this "seduction theory" (misnamed because "seduction" implies the child's complicity). The response of his audience ("icy reception from the asses," Freud described it) and his subsequent trouble making his theory work in all cases led Freud to publicly retract his seduction theory in 1905—thus shifting focus to the unconscious and paving the way for the birth of psychoanalysis.[24] A year later, he developed the theory that would actually hide the reality of child abuse for almost ninety years: his Oedipal theory, which caught the imagination of the analysts. In the Oedipal theory, hysterical children fantasize seducing and taking over one parent and eliminating the other. In short, according to Freudian thought and conventional wisdom at the time, child sexual abuse almost never happens, and neuroses originate in guilt about childhood fantasies, a child's conflicted desires for sex and murder. In order to forgive her father, Anaïs had to blame herself. Thus, if Anaïs had analyzed the direction she was taking in planning her visit to her father in the south of France, she would have accounted for her actions as her own need to seduce her father. She dismisses Allendy's warnings that her father wants to sleep with her as crude imperception. An argument with Joaquin over their father makes her acutely ill for a day.

While she is planning her reunion and feeling strengthened by her father's approval, she quarrels with the other men in her life. It begins when she and Henry forget to lock the squeaking gate at Louveciennes. Amid lovemaking and her words of commitment to Henry's financial security, Hugo returns unexpectedly and without honking the horn of his car as he usually does. Though Hugo catches a glimpse of Henry rushing from the Guiler bedroom, Anaïs explains that she was afraid with the maid away and had asked him to spend the night in the guest room. "He needed to believe, poor Hugo," she says, though his confidence would never be the same. When he leaves the next morning, she goes to the guest room.

There follows an exchange of letters, she informing Henry that there has been no big fight, and he sympathizing with her discomfort ("These must be trying days—I know from experience what the atmosphere is like afterward—the heavy, choking, smothering spell like dry electricity accumulating"). Overwhelmed by her gift of security and independence, Henry only regrets that he cannot offer her "anything." He speaks of feeling no fear of Hugo's discovery, though he himself "might have been killed"; he feels only calm, and returns about ten days later horny and in high spirits. Yet his behavior is more formal now that he has been reminded of his visitor status. He is not the husband of the house, as he had often pretended. Interpreting his behavior as indifference, and angry when he remarks that her father will "soon be disillusioned," Anaïs dismisses him in what he calls her "grand Spanish lady" manner as if he were her gardener. In an angry and hurt letter of 23 May, she accuses him of only loving her for what she can give him. She had needed him then, but he had gone back to his selfish life and returned "cold." She will ensure his security, but all the rest is "dead. You killed it."[25] She sends a telegram and money order.

His lengthy reply of 24 May is a masterpiece of clarity, reconciliation, and love that reveals the best qualities of Miller. "To gain her good graces," he later tells a friend, "[is] like climbing Mt. Fuji."[26] He calls her reaction "melodramatics," behavior unworthy of her and based on one incident, and says he imagines her after his dismissal rushing to convert everything to her diary or her "Alraune" manuscript, making "a human doormat for me—for *your* art." Yet he also apologizes for failing her, explaining what his true feelings had been when he arrived, and explaining his comments on her family—his dislike of the "brother-sister devotion" with Joaquin and his own identification with her father (for he too is estranged from his daughter by his first wife). Standing by his comments on her father, he assures her that her faith certainly will be disillusioned—"one gets only ghosts" after all these years. He believes that there is something in her life that had "invited illness," something that she cannot tell him. He refuses to feel bitter about life, for he feels happy and healthy. "You are the Holy Ghost inside me. You make my spring. You make the Gare St. Lazare and my love for Paris."[27] Their reconciliation is sweet; she comes to Clichy several days in a row, and buys a Victrola for the apartment.

Her father continues to write letters of endearment from Spain, letters with erotic undertones. His love for "all" of her—hands, voice, eyes—has made him unable to love another. He uses words such as "intimacy," "penetration," and "fusion," and decries the "false morality" that would spurn "all the forms of happiness possible to us." His intentions seem very clear. She sets her trip to visit him for the latter half of June.[28]

This period of her life, which, to quote Rimbaud, she later calls "a season in hell"—she names the diary "Incest"—is marked by two impossible and incestuous flirtations, with Artaud and her father. In the garden at Louveciennes, Artaud places his hand on her knee, and she is both startled and warmed. The question of sex hangs in the air between them, postponed by her surprised look. They speak of the jealousy of Allendy (she changes the name of Allendy to Steele when she first publishes her diary account of this garden scene). That night she dreams of making passionate love with Artaud, who pulls her away from writing in her journal. But "I sleep with everybody" in my dreams, she confesses. The men she tantalizes during the day she dreams of at night (in one dream, she mentions in passing, her father behaves amorously toward her in front of her mother).[29] Her flirtation with Artaud, the mad genius, is an aphrodisiac. She will leave Henry at Louveciennes during one of Hugo's trips to London, just to experience a tense hour of poetry and pain with Artaud. She is compulsively promiscuous, a behavior she shares with those who have suffered emotional deprivation, such as abandonment, instability in adolescence, and/or abusive fathers.[30]

Sitting at a marble table at La Coupole, she accepts Artaud's kisses, which give her no pleasure. While she assures him of her sincerity, she is aware that she is driven by "some demonic force to tantalize, to act, to give an illusion of closeness." Though she does not want the physical side of this drug-stained homosexual madman (as she sees him), she is flattered to be at the center of the mad poetic soul and considers following him into death and destruction. She enjoys the playacting and invents a story of her own madness. He is a trophy, a man who pours out poetry and raves like Hamlet. Perhaps she is a trophy for him—one that Allendy, Miller, Eduardo, perhaps Steele—would like to claim. She admits that she loves the ritual of seduction and is not interested in physical possession per se. Unlike Don Juan, she wants the souls, not the bodies, of men. She would ask more than the whores. Perhaps she loves sacrilege, as Henry once told her.[31]

On 13 June she goes to Artaud's cell-like room dressed in black, red, and silver as if she is the god Mars in his armor. She tells herself and him she wants only a meeting of the minds, but she is, indeed, there in his room. He is all "iron and white flames," accusing her of trickery, of hurting Allendy, of being a sorceress. She yields to his fierce kiss, he bites her mouth and throat and legs and breasts—but he can do no more, cursing his drug addiction and demanding that she leave. To save him from humiliation, she relieves him with her hands—later she will describe it as "the futile outpouring of honey"—and leaves the impression she is different from other women in not placing importance on sexual intercourse, even preferring to avoid the "human connection." "You are the plumed serpent," he exclaims, clutching her. When he offers to "burn everything for her," she belives that she possesses him and loves the feeling of power.[32]

She comes home to "Henry's flesh," describes the drama and poetry of her encounter to him, which excites and entertains him. The story of the plumed serpent is great, he tells her, wishing he could say things like that to her. The next day Henry writes her twenty-four pages of fantasy and love. The night Hugo is to return from another bank trip to London, she sends Henry away in order to spend the evening with Artaud, first at the same table she and Henry had shared at the Vikings, then walking along the Seine amid the students' Quatz Art Ball reveling. They kiss violently on the quays, she records in her diary, and sit late at another café. The next day she sends him two long letters addressed to Nanaqui (his childhood name), full of vague and spiritual "coalescing" imagery.[33]

Then she flees to Nice alone, leaving a note for Hugo and a telegram and check for Henry. She tells her diary why she is physically exhausted from performing on too many stages—sometimes several in a day: "[I] write about Artaud while Henry is sitting near me, [go] to meet Hugo with the bitter taste of Artaud's kisses . . . [and] go to Artaud as I went to Allendy, filled with Henry's white blood. . . . I am becoming aware that I am wreaking a kind of vengeance upon man . . . to win and abandon them."[34] She may be doing evil, but she feels no remorse. In her eyes the trip to be with her father is a flight from Hugo, her mother, Artaud, Henry—all of them. But she may also want to confront the one who won and abandoned her, the Don Juan father.

While the hot mistral blows outside, she settles in to Coirier's Grand Hotel in Valescure-St.-Raphaël,[35] to rest and write to Henry and Artaud. As she awaits her father's arrival, she pens a long letter begging Artaud to forget her, for she is indeed like the legend of Alraune, a natural force poised to destroy. She flirts and lies, she admits, then as if to illustrate this truth, she narrates her dramatic story of abandonment, saying she has not seen her father in twenty years (it has been ten), describing her frustrated love for a poet and actor when she was sixteen (not mentioning that Eduardo is her cousin) and her faithful marriage (a "physical martyrdom") until a year ago when she met Henry (she met Henry and June eighteen months before).[36]

The day of her letter to Artaud, 20 June, Miller writes to tell her she is the "whole world" to him. Though he does not want to travel, having just been on a bicycle trip to Luxembourg with Perlès, he suggests that he might come down. She has asked him to join her in Marseilles; he later suggests Carcassonne instead, then asks her how her talks with her father have evolved: "*Love*—and keep your shirt on! Let your father devour you. It will give him dyspepsia."[37]

Her father, after having sent ahead a telegram, flowers, and a half dozen special orders for the hotel, arrives pale, stiff with lumbago (he will be fifty-four the next month), and appearing cold and formal. He seems to fear intimacy, she thinks, and to be carrying some crime in his suitcase. They will have nine days together to talk, to take a car to the ocean and sit on a rock (he cannot move the next day), and to narrate their life stories to each other. His behavior is obsessive and rigid: special bed, special drinking water, room sprayed for bugs, no bread or tomatoes allowed. When the waiter spills a drop of water on the tablecloth, he winces. She concludes that he is clearly not the Don Juan who leaves the next morning after a conquest. No, he tells her, he sends red roses after the third or fourth night of a conquest when there might be danger of falling in love. His interest is control of others and of his environment. They exchange stories of their respective conquests. He tells her about his marriage to her earthy, possessive, high-tempered mother, who called his illusions lies. Anaïs returns to her room, filled with flowers (he leaves notes on her pillow at night), to record all he says with little irony or judgment. She quotes the pillow notes in letters to Henry. The theme of all their talk is their "twinship." They are amoral but devoted to inner development, he says. "You are the synthesis of all the women I have loved," he tells her. "What a pity you are my daughter!" She records: "All my own tricks and lies and deceptions are offered to me out of my father's magician's box."[38]

She has spent the day sitting on his bed talking. Nursing his lumbago, he lies flat on his back, talking about her beauty and telling her that he does not think about her the way a father should. Eventually they translate what she calls the orchestra of music between them into physical expression. When he asks for a kiss, she feels his arousal. She starts to leave twice before he uncovers himself. She lifts her satin negligee and sits on his swollen sex. His ecstasy is matched by her "desire to unite with him." In the unpublished versions of her fictional recreation of the scene she uses images of musical instruments, such as violin strings, and of flowers, such as a red pistil.[39] Long after midnight she returns to her own room, and when the door opens, the mistral wind slams the window shut with such force the window cracks. She glances toward the mosquito net over the bed and thinks of a white bridal canopy. She will use this poetic imagery of marriage when she tries to recreate the story in fiction.

Indeed, as the publication of her unexpurgated diary finally revealed in 1992, she and her father become lovers. For nine nights and days they talk. Some nights she returns to her room with a handkerchief between her legs, for he could penetrate her three and four times. His first violation and abandonment—and now his words ("You must have courage. We are living out something tremendous . . . unique")—compel her. She teaches him "fuck" in English; he teaches her *hoder* in Spanish. They boast to each other of all their conquests. During these days she is disassociated from herself, observing her actions from a distance. As always in her diary, she paints the most beautiful face on every event and portrays herself in control. Yet amid her words about her own "joy" and his being "the most virile man I have known" is a subliminal text, revealed in the use of words and phrases such as "revulsion," "guilt," "the sperm was poison," and "unnatural." She may have finally won her father's approval, but at a cost. The "joy" was probably not sexual, and she has no orgasm.[40]

When she joins Henry 2 July in Avignon (he had not liked Carcassonne) he has been there five days, bicycling to nearby villages and waiting for their first vacation together. After being with her father for nine days, she feels safe knowing that she is deceiving him by being with a man he does not like (he thinks she is on her way to London). She and Henry travel to Grenoble and then to Chamonix in the French Alps, to bicycle, sit in cafés, and make love. In a state of shock, which she calls obsession with her father (*le Roi Soleil*), she has to pretend with Henry. She becomes ill with anxiety, thinking it is her heart, and finally tells Henry everything. He expresses no jealousy. They look out on the mountains from their window and talk of buying a press for Louveciennes to publish their books. On 10 July he leaves their room at Hôtel du Fin Bec before Hugo arrives for a stay with his wife. Henry is off for more travel on his own.[41]

For the next three weeks, she and Miller keep up an almost daily correspondence while she and Hugo move to Annecy, then settle into Aix-les-Bains, where she enjoys casino gambling. Hugo showers her with gifts and keeps her active in physical walks, biking (with Henry's letter in her bicycle basket), billiards, and climbing. Despite the Guilers' low funds (Hugo takes a salary advance in Annecy), she sends checks to Henry. She also writes love letters to her father, and tells Hugo everything about her visit with her father, except the sex. Hugo does his father-in-law's horoscope ("He seeks to injure no one. . . ."), as he had done for Miller and Artaud, and writes to Senor Nin about how happy he is that Anaïs has found the father of her dreams. The Nin-Miller literary letters are full of devotion ("during the sunbath I open my legs and think of you"), full of Paris news, their reading, and his mother (whom he says he sees in other women). On the latter point she suggests that they "fuck our parents and thereby rid ourselves of them. Fucking shadows of them accomplishes nothing."[42] When she returns, she suggests, she should meet Dr. Otto Rank for a "roof-raising talk" on these matters.[43] In her diary she expresses her intention of getting "absolution for my passion for my father."[44]

On Monday evening 30 July, Henry arrives in Louveciennes with a bottle of champagne. Anaïs has arrived that day alone and again fallen in love with her beloved house. She takes charge of her "kingdom"—the mail, telephone calls, letters to Allendy, Artaud, Miller, Joaquin, and Hugo (in Geneva), as if each were the first to be contacted. People need lies, she believes, for lies give life and she is the fairy godmother of everyone's wishes. The truth will be saved for the diary (she thinks)—her evil, thus, will be posthumous, in the truth.[45]

She receives from Miller a nine-page typed letter to William Bradley dated 2 August 1933—a "bombshell" she calls it—arguing for the undiluted publication of her childhood diaries, which by the year 2000 will have "perhaps millions" of readers worldwide "when the original manuscript, with the correct names, is brought to light."[46] In an accompanying letter he tells her that her diary "must not be aborted." Believe in yourself, he exhorts, for he can see the world eventually "knocking at your door." Though she chooses not to mail the letter to Bradley (she knows it is for her) she is overwhelmed by the loyalty of her warrior with the fire-breathing nostrils and offers to go to Kahane again to try to get *Cancer* published. This very day Henry has received assurances that Kahane will publish the novel. Write on, she says. "I love you[.] I believe you are the greatest writer on earth today."[47]

"I closed the main theme of my life when I found my father again," she prematurely announces to Henry. The evidence reveals otherwise; she has just opened the door to this theme. Her diary, which reveals that all the old wounds are reopened, is filled with numerous quotations from her early diaries, lengthy memories of her relations with men, and reassessments of her parents—in favor of her father, not her puritanical mother. Later she will spend years rewriting the story of this encounter with her father and discussing it with her analysts and close friends, before burying it as a shameful secret. "She felt so guilty and terrible about this," says one of her later friends.[48]

She confesses all to Allendy and returns to analysis, but not to their affair ("I could not feed five fires. I had to let some of the men down"). She tells Eduardo "proudly" that she and her father are lovers. When she tells Artaud, he calls her love for her father an "abomination" and accuses her of "literary living" and "absolute impurity" in loving and deceiving many men. During his diatribe, she thinks he looks like an "outraged castrated monk." The affair is over.[49] Though she will continue to see her father for some months before letting go, she has been a victim to his ego twice. Like Eurydice, who died while escaping from attempted rape and then again when her husband, Orpheus, was rescuing her from Hades and disobeyed the gods by looking back, Anaïs has been sacrificed a second time.[50]

## A Life of Artifice

Nevertheless, Anaïs decides to spend the last ten days of August 1933 with her father, who has asked if she will come to Valescure in order to ride back by car with him and his wife (and mother-in-law) to Paris. She had known Maruca when they were both children in Arcachon, where her father had abandoned the family. Maruca is small, round, and friendly—a Japanese wife, as Anaïs calls her, who defers to her husband. They dine with the pianist Paderewski (during which time her father angers the Paderewski retinue by dressing formally while they are in informal Riviera clothes). During the trip, Anaïs and her father have what will be one of their last sexual encounters, furtively, in Evaux-les-Bains. His theme with Anaïs for this phase of his seduction is "live only for yourself." Sensing his competitor in Henry Miller, he warns her to give up "parasites," "Bohemians," and failures: "Let the weak ones die."[51]

This time, Anaïs sees her father with more objective eyes. In one of her letters to Henry, the gentle, wise Polish pianist Paderewski comes off better than her father in their duel of manners. She observes her father's rigid habits, his strict controls on life, and his destructive critical attitude. He sits at table criticizing every speck of dirt and observes the tics and absurdities of everyone in the room, but reaches to pet a mangy cat or overtip the waiter. When they leave the hotel in Issoire, he writes in the hotel book, *"Merde!"* "This place is full of shit!" Yet she is still ambivalent, for she tells Henry how "wonderful" it is to have a "father of stature." And she echoes his pride in his Spanish blood.[52]

This fall in Paris she frequently visits the spotless, bourgeois home of her father and stepmother at 27, rue Henri-Heine (near the home of Allendy in the sixteenth arrondissement). She does not inform her mother. Her father's Paris life seems cold, hard, and decorative—"a winter life of artifice."[53] Disharmony develops slowly: her father thinks Lawrence's work is boring, Artaud's theories shocking. When she writes to him before hearing his reply to her last letter, his sense of order is upset. He tries to bring her into his world for the new music and social season by changing her clothes and hair. When she urges him to resume his love affairs, he swears he has none since finding the apotheosis of his life in reunion with her. Angry, and perhaps insecure, she believes that he is telling her the same lies that he tells his wife. She realizes that she and her father lie to each other, but his narcissism seems stronger than hers, for he can only love someone just like himself. Once again she has lost her "guide [God] halfway up the mountain."[54]

Henry is no God either, but he can at least love his opposite, the other, tell her the truth, and give her the support and love she needs. If her father's criticism paralyzes her, Henry's lack of judgment frees her. (He does not judge her incest.[55]) Her father molds life to his will; Henry breaks all the molds—he broke her windows and let in the oxygen, she says. If her father is compulsively controlling, her lover is "Chinese," as he likes to call himself—passive, receptive, free, in tune with the karma of the Orient. She concludes that there is power in "imperfections, Dostoevski, Lawrence, and Henry."[56]

Thus the autumn of 1933 is one of the most productive for their "literary passion." She packs her bag for overnights at Clichy (leaving a note on Hugo's pillow that she is staying at the home of Caresse Crosby, an expatriate American publisher whom Anaïs has never met); or Henry comes to her home when Hugo is gone. They meet at the Trocadéro to visit the Museum of Man, talk in cafés, and read the same books. Most important, they push each other to write and read and criticize in detail one another's work. The fever of writing, reading, and thinking fills their hours together and their letters. They get drunk on talk, ideas, images. She reads several chapters that will be part of his "Self-Portrait" (*Black Spring*), a book that will be dedicated to her. She also sees his new writing on Lawrence, and his "Scenario" (he calls it "Palace of Entrails"), a film treatment of her "Alraune-June" story.

"Write your blooming head off," he tells her. "This is war." She replies, "Please read, Henry, read. I need your faith."[57] She rewrites the June story and rewrites or adapts portions of the journal with names changed, the latter for Bradley (who has asked for a fictionalized manuscript): Henry becomes Rab (for Rabelais); June becomes Alraune; Allendy becomes Auroil. She even starts a fake journal for Hugo to find, with situations reversed and seductions spurned. The latter is necessitated when she deliberately leaves the diary open and Hugo reads about an encounter with Henry in a hotel room: "I know everything," Hugo says with torment. "You only read the invented journal," she explains.[58]

Her first two novels are taking form, each based on her encounter with June and Henry (she cannot yet write about her father). Like all her fiction, these works are culled from her diary. On the first of November she moves passages around from what she called Alraune One ("The House of Incest")—the word she cannot utter against her father, she shouts in the title of her first book—and Alraune Two ("Djuna"). The first is an hallucinatory or nightmare fantasy, a prose poem, using water imagery and characters based on June, Henry, Artaud, Eduardo, Allendy, and others. For example, the passage from the diary in which she walks through the leaves with June, speaking of Henry and the death of their love, becomes the following in *The House of Incest*: "The leaf fall of her words, the stained glass hues of her moods, the rust of her voice, the smoke in her mouth, her breath on my vision like human breath blinding a mirror."[59]

She calls her writing style "symphonic writing" and could have claimed Gertrude Stein's "portraits" as precedent. The ambiguity suits her. Some readers have called it a character study, not a novel.[60] The unnamed narrator, lost in a dream world of Atlantide (Atlantis), encounters the earthy, passionate Alraune, who almost takes over the narrator until the latter finds her way back by following Ariadne's thread to her own identity. She then encounters Isolina, an idealist who lives in a house of stasis and decay because she loves her own brother, and an unnamed dancer, at first pictured without arms because she clings too desperately, then with arms when she can love without possession.[61] By recognizing that each woman is an aspect of herself, the narrator finds her multiple and imperfect self and learns the paralysis of self-love (as Anaïs had discovered in loving Eduardo, June, and her father). In the last lines she dances "towards daylight." Anaïs was indebted, says one literary critic, to Rimbaud and the Gnostic religious belief that one can achieve one's own personal liberation. This book will remain her most complex work, the best illustration of her literary beliefs in the primacy of psychological reality and the Jungian dreamworld. She will tell Lawrence Durrell that it is a woman's "Season in Hell"—after Dante and Rimbaud.[62]

The second work, entitled "Djuna," is her "human" book. Though it is about the same characters and the same themes of incest and narcissism (loving oneself in others) and repeats some of the same phrasing, it lacks the surrealism and abstraction of *The House of Incest*. Johanna (Alraune), Hans (Rab), and Djuna (Mandra)—Perlès is "André"—so closely resemble June, Henry, and Anaïs that the story will be published only once (in 1936) before being suppressed and will precipitate years of deceitful denial that her fiction is based on her diary. For "Djuna" she writes a beautiful portrait of Henry and informs him that she wants to reveal him more completely than she had Lawrence.

The character of Isolina (in *The House of Incest*), who will appear as "Jeanne" in later fiction and in the first published diary volume, is really her friend Louise de Vilmorin, a French aristocrat and novelist.[63] She was married to Henry Leigh Hunt (a client of Hugo's) when Anaïs first met her two years previously, when she told Anaïs that her love of her brothers had kept her from mature love relationships and led to her divorce. Anaïs is fascinated with the tall, blond Louise because of her wealth, the castle she lives in (Anaïs will describe it in a short story entitled "Under a Glass Bell"), and the mental torture of her life ("I love my brother," Jeanne cries in *The House of Incest*).[64] Anaïs, always attracted to women who are beautiful, strange, ethereal (says her friend Marguerite Young), will periodically write about and emulate women of aristocracy or high culture whose homes and lives she admires.

No one has yet considered (because some diary passages have never been published), that in addition to June and Louise, Ana Maria Sanchez and Ethel Guiler may also inform the portraits of Anaïs's women in *The House of Incest*. When Ethel had returned for a visit in September, she and Anaïs had renewed their declarations of jealousy of and love for each other, embracing on Ethel's bed at night. Ana Maria would never return to visit, but at the time of her wedding in Cuba the following February, she sent a letter denouncing Anaïs. Certainly these flirtations reinforced her theme of the futility of self-love.

Henry reads the portraits of himself and June, including descriptions of their lovemaking, and makes detailed marks in the margin, changing words and sentence construction, informing her where to elaborate and what to cut. Initially baffled by her *House of Incest,* he now admires it. Only a letter that details her need to study the craft of fiction and urges her to put down the diary so she can get away from psychological synthesis and hyperbole offends her (in part because he praises Kay Boyle's *Year Before Last*). She accuses him of cruelty and ridicule. In his loving Dutch-uncle voice he reminds her that she asked for the truth and he is on her side. Do not avoid the conflict by pulling back into your shell, he warns her. You will only be evading art! She goes back to work, for despite the brief quarrel with Henry, increasing frustration with her father's demands, and the news of the death of Paco Miralles (her former Spanish dancing teacher), Anaïs is happy. She hates to leave Clichy and return home, for she would love to live continuously with Henry as they work together on their books. When he suggests that they stop putting off the inevitable, she answers that marriage would mean that she could not continue to give him freedom and peace to write. She "would kill a dragon a day" for Henry, she writes 30 October. She wants to live with him, but she will not marry him: "whole love is too dangerous, too feminine."[65] What she really wants is to have him work in a room in her house. Later, when she considers getting a job, he warns her against it and offers to have her "cut [him] down to the bone" financially so that he can help her write her two books.[66]

## Otto Rank

"He said: 'With you one travels so far away from reality that it is necessary to buy a return ticket.'"
—*"The Voice"*[67]

On the train into central Paris, with her diary open in her lap, Anaïs plans the presentation and postures she will offer to the renowned analyst Otto Rank. She does not spend time assembling the truths of her life for this first visit; she rehearses her expressions and gestures, as she would prepare for a seduction. After changing to the metro at St. Lazare, she arrives at Métro La Muette, near his apartment and office in the sixteenth arrondissement. She sits on the bench in a section of the Jardins du Ranelagh, located between the metro station and the grand boulevard Suchet that runs along the east side of the Bois de Boulogne. Though this November 1933 day is cool and foggy, she takes time to weigh the question of which Anaïs will interest Rank. She has read his books on the artist, the double, and the return to the father and knows that she has much to offer him. In fact, she has lived out his writings. She has just had a brief final encounter with her father at Louveciennes.

Here she is, tortured by her sexual encounter with her father, having questioned (in August 1931) Freud's help beyond the "consciousness and knowledge" stage of neurosis, and definitely unhappy with Allendy's scientific approach.[68] She needs help in knowing how to continue creatively, she thinks, as she walks past what is now the Musée Marmottan at the beginning of rue Louis-Boilly (which is one block long and ends at boulevard Suchet). Rank's building is on the left at the corner. Just around the corner is the building where she and Hugo lived before moving to Louveciennes.

The man who meets her at the door and ushers her into his office is short ("Dr. Caligari body") with dark skin and thick glasses. She focuses on the dark fiery eyes behind his thick glasses as she takes a seat near the window that overlooks the park. Here is a man who has been legend to her. Henry had already visited him once, on 6 March. But her own visit is triggered, she thinks, by seeing Rank's birthdate and the blank place for his death date on the library cards at a psychoanalytical library. The living legend is forty-nine years old and mortal. She must see him in person, she tells herself. I am one of the artists you are writing about, Dr. Rank, she wants to tell him. And I am being torn apart by my conflicting relationships![69] She also wants the opportunity to dramatize her conflicts.

She outlines her life and work, and when she says there is more to her relationship with her father than competition with her mother, she thinks his smile is knowing. She has come assuming he will understand the artist and is delighted when he speaks of her desire to create herself (Allendy would have talked in Oedipal terms). Rank speaks in literary and mythological terms, not in the scientific theory of Allendy. They speak of the Greek legend of the abandoned daughter being found twenty years later by an unknowing father who falls in love with her (in the traditional story they recognize each other before committing incest). This legend will form the motif of their therapy to come. What she hears Rank say this day is that there is nothing wrong with her "intellectual adventures"—even the adventure of a visit to him in order to dramatize her conflicting relationships. Her "lies" and disguises are fiction and myth. She also hears him say that neurosis is not "illness" but art and imagination gone wrong, or failed. And an artist's first creation is herself, her own personality. As she prepares to leave, he notices the diary and asks her to leave it with him. Though she hesitates, seeming to be flustered that he will read her fabrications written on the train that day, she leaves it, knowing he might be shocked. She also feels a thrill at his demand for her surrender.[70]

Otto Rosenfeld, the son of a tyrannical Austrian father, had begun a journal when he was eighteen years old, the year Nin was born. Self-educated in psychology, his essay "The Artist" so impressed Freud that he hired him as a secretary, which allowed him to complete all his schooling, including the Ph.D. (he never studied medicine), and to write several books. Rank (he changed his name apparently to match Ibsen's Dr. Rank in *The Doll's House*)[71] had been like a son and heir apparent to Freud. He had been teacher, analyst, secretary of the Psychoanalytic Society of Vienna, and editor of the society's review and publishing house when he defected and moved to Paris in 1926. Just three months prior to Anaïs's visit, he wrote a colleague that his ten years of crisis separation from Freud had ended and he was learning to live more freely.[72] He was now a humanistic psychologist, rejecting the Oedipus complex for the theory of birth trauma as central to psychoneurosis and rejecting scientific positivism with its medical language for literature and the language of myth.[73] He prized individualism and creativity over any deterministic formulation or "namings" of human behavior. For Anaïs, who has been told by Allendy that her imagination is "delusion," Rank's proposed expansion and probing of her creative process, of her fantasy, is exhilarating.[74] She will be a creator in her own therapy. Years later she will say that he taught her to build a center of strength within herself, which he called a second birth: the creation of the self.

During her second session, Rank surprises her with two demands: that she cease the diary—that center, or "traffic island," from which she surveys her analysis in order to control it—and that she isolate herself from all her roles by temporarily moving out of Louveciennes. He believes in short, intensive therapy, reducing analysis to a few months, like an intense attack on an infection or an emotional shock treatment. Thus on 8 November, the diary dies, as she describes it dramatically. When she resumes the diary 20 January 1934, she tries to recreate more than three months of experience.[75]

She rents adjoining rooms at a modest hotel at 26, rue des Marronniers in Passy near Rank. Miller agrees to move to be near her. She rationalizes this cheating on her analysis by saying to herself that she is not in conflict with Henry and they will encourage each other with their writing. Neither Hugo, who consents to Rank's prescription, nor, initially, Rank himself, know about Henry's room next to hers (nor does she tell her father that she is living in his neighborhood). She misses writing in her diary in the evenings. She works on her two books until sometime in December when she starts what she calls a "sketchbook" in order to create a portrait of Rank, her muse and the man who rules her three and a half "empty" months during their analysis. When she shows him her portrait of him, he is delighted.

During the weeks of late fall and winter, she and Rank probe the artist Anaïs. She comes to trust this Viennese doctor who punctuates his sentences with "You see? You see, eh?" His spontaneity and inexhaustible enthusiasm are contagious; psychoanalysis becomes an exercise in creation.

She is learning a new order of time based on memory, not the diary calendar.[76] Writing, she concludes, will be the positive realism to offset her past pain; it will be her road to redemption.

Among the observations Rank makes are that Anaïs's personality discord comes from a deep disparity between her ideal self and her actual self, and that the diary is an attempt to create herself in the image of what her father wanted. Thinking she had disappointed him before he abandoned her, she yearns to win him back by telling him pleasing stories. When she and Rank discuss his theory of the Double—Don Quixote and Sancho Panza (she adds Henry and clownish Fred Perlès)—she realizes that her father is trying to create her in his own image, just as she was trying to replace the lost father by imitating him. Her love of June was not lesbianism, he assures her, but an acting out of her father's behavior, a Don Juan courting women.

They also speak of the mother and the confusion that exists for Anaïs between woman and mother. The nurturing, protecting, serving, self-sacrificing qualities, which she equates with woman, are in conflict with the creative, mature, and striving person, which she equates with masculinity. All her imagination and creativity have gone into playing this role in order to meet men's needs. Thus she has tried to be both her mother (and her saintly paternal grandmother Nin) as well as her talented, artistic father. She has also used her imagination to recreate what she has lost—Spain, art, Europe—in her diary. She wants to abandon the sorrow and protection and stand "without crutches."[77] Her creation, which Rank prizes most, must be free to expand on its own.

They also speak of sex. Rank separates sexual liberation from true maturity, which is deeper than the Freudian analysts would acknowledge. The simple act of sexual liberation, which is what Allendy had heralded, does not touch the deeper self, Rank tells her. Despite this deeper insight, he shares a Freudian view of father-daughter relationships and, though he is interested in her case for its incest implications, is unaware of the long-term effects of childhood sexual abuse—effects that will be largely ignored until the early 1980s.[78]

When they close up Louveciennes for the winter (the lack of central heating has made winter living there increasingly difficult), Hugo moves into a large, overly furnished but cold apartment full of ticking clocks in avenue Victor Hugo. Anaïs continues to live at rue Marronniers. Even when her analysis with Rank is over in March, she continues to spend time at rue Marronniers, where Henry remains for a while. The simplified life she has lived there has relaxed her. The life with Henry has been fruitful. Indeed, unbeknownst to her she has become pregnant, probably at the end of February. She notices changes in her body but believes she cannot conceive.

She enjoys living with Henry and working on their writing. The pace of their writing is in part set by their desire to publish and be free to live together. Miller, who has read most of her diary, strongly opposes Rank's decree against the diary. (He is not crazy about "soul doctors," anyway.[79]) Though he has often mentioned her tendency to take refuge from life in the diary (and he hates the rewrite she did for Bradley), he believes the original diary is a creative and immortal work.

She throws much of her creative energy into helping Henry on his Lawrence book, a work she says "is also my child."[80] They talk over every page. He is the one who is obsessive now, withdrawn from living and surrounded by his notebooks, lists, sketches, and schemes. She urges him to select and simplify, to live for the moment. She is growing tired of the ideas of Miller, Lawrence, even Rank, fatigued by worries about Louvecienes, Hugo's family's problems, crises with the hired help, and her father's demands for attention. The more she simplifies her life, the more repulsive and artificial her life seems. She wants to break with her father and make him suffer, but she only breaks down in sobs.

Anaïs and Henry's work with dreams increases under the influence of Rank, who has "a special analytical flair for interpreting dreams" and myth, according to Ernest Jones, Freud's biographer.[81] Henry has been collecting dreams and Anaïs has been recording hers in her diary, but Rank encourages the psychological investigations of dreams. In the spirit of adventure, Henry records his dreams and his own analysis in his "Self-Portrait" (*Black Spring*) manuscript and in 247 typed pages that he later binds under the title "Dreams, Original Versions," dedicated to Anaïs.[82] In their long discussions of using dreams and surrealism in their writing, Anaïs's poetic style prevails. She argues that there is no language in dream—referring to scenes from *Un Chien Andalou*—and thus images should run together like watercolors. The dream will be her specialty, as she proves in *The House of Incest*.

She has begun a new work during February and March that she entitles "The Double" or "Father Story" and later on "Winter of Artifice." She also begins the story that she will use to justify her incest: she will tell her close friends (who repeat it to this day) that it was Rank's idea that she sleep with her father and then abandon him. Such a story is impossible, not only because she had not met Rank when she committed incest but also because no competent analyst would do such a thing.[83] Certainly afterward he urges her to abandon her father before he abandons her. Though concurring, she cannot yet let go. She feels "compelled to act out the scene of abandonment from beginning to end," she writes in her fictional account. Because her father is curious, she takes Henry to dinner to meet him; Maruca loves Henry's naturalness. In her visits to her father's home, Anaïs keeps up the gaiety, but is increasingly revolted by this dandy and Don Juan who boasts about his success with women and their pursuit of him. Occasionally she insists on her own choices and on the truth, informing him that she prefers Dostoyevsky and Anatole France to the authors he reveres. He is hurt and offended, for he would even have her smoke his brand of cigarettes. At any sign of her contradiction, he claims that he is losing sleep and would lose his reason for living were she to reject him. She only feels "a strange joy" and a sense of the righting of an injustice. Her final dispute with her father is over his plan to take a young girl violinist to Spain for a concert, alone. She writes the scene into her "Father Story"—her jealous confrontation, his denial, her demand for truth, Maruca's defense of her husband, and her own parting tears.[84] Her final blow against her father is to tell Maruca, who will tell him, that Anaïs is trying to leave Hugo to marry Henry.

When she believes that she has finished the father story, she shows it to Henry, but reacts poorly when he suggests changes. After a night's sleep, she takes the story apart and rewrites it; she and Henry repeat the process in order to meld the real and the fantastic. He checks her craft and integrity, hones her fighting spirit, and urges her to ignore the antagonism of Bradley, Joaquin, and her friend Hélène Boussinescq. Anaïs will write a bigger book and include two June stories. She describes the writing that follows in terms of "the pain of childbirth" and yearns "to be delivered of this book."[85] She slows down only in mid-March when she becomes sick and feverish. She apparently does not know or acknowledge to herself that she is pregnant.

Henry and I "alone—against the world" she writes 28 March when she learns that Jack Kahane's business and loyalty have failed. She may not be able to build a married life with Henry, but she feels that their artistic life is wedded.[86] They revise their plans to buy and install a printing press above the garage and print their own books. Soon Henry moves from the dull Passy quarter of their love nest to Hôtel Havana near the pimps and prostitutes of Montmartre. Here he polishes his last draft of *Cancer*. They speak of a life together and the need for money.

She is getting her life in order. Able to return to Louveciennes for Easter, she sets her neglected house in order, discarding, cleaning, cooking. By 15 April, hating Hugo and feeling abandoned at losing regular consultations with Rank, Anaïs invites the Ranks and Henry for dinner. Beata Rank's coldness and cutting remarks are only partially offset by Henry's enthusiasm for the food and drink and Otto Rank's gaiety.

Kahane has again reaffirmed his commitment to publish *Cancer* if she pays for it (Obelisk Press is broke). Believing she can find another publisher, she goes to London like a midwife, carrying Henry's "Self-Portrait" (*Black Spring*) manuscript and his Lawrence work. She will help Henry and preserve their individual independence. She visits Rebecca West, who had written an elegy for D. H. Lawrence. The English novelist had written to praise Anaïs's book on Lawrence ("[Y]ou seem to have real and unmistakable genius").[87] But Anaïs stirs no interest in Henry's manuscripts. She will have to get the money to pay Kahane. Meantime, Miller fails to win the interest of Sylvia Beach ("She's got snow in her veins"), who has no money, is relieved to be finished with her own publication of Joyce's *Ulysses,* and resents being considered a publisher of erotica. Sitting at a café to keep warm, Henry cuts down his manuscript to quicken its pace, then writes to Anaïs in London that "after all the sacrifices you are making, this book has to be good!"[88]

## The Birth

She returns to the Paris spring, in physical bloom and happy herself. She is living in the moment, filling each day with friends, and walking the streets: "Henry saved me. He took me down into the streets."[89] Now her head is full of names, not ideas. Her life is full of Henry and his street smarts and humanity. She appears to have answered the question Rank had asked her that winter: Will she be a woman and enter life, or will she be an artist? Sensing her independence, Hugo turns himself over to Rank for analysis. Sensing at last that she may be pregnant, Anaïs goes to a doctor.

On 16 May 1934 she knows without a doubt that she is pregnant with Henry's child. Her surprise comes because a doctor had once told her she could not conceive. She believes she is five or six weeks along, but in fact she is really about ten weeks. Other than an occasional consideration of the possibility, she has not wished for a child. When she knows she is pregnant, she makes a point, she will tell a confidante years later, to have sex with Hugo, who treats her "like a new and precious mistress."[90] When he learns later that she is pregnant, he is delighted. When her father learns the news, he informs her that she is worth less as a woman now.[91]

"I must destroy it . . . it is a choice between the child and Henry," she asserts. "He does not want it. I can't give Hugh a child of Henry's." Furthermore, "motherhood . . . is an abnegation . . . the supreme immolation of the ego."[92] Hugo is determined that she have the child and resorts to threats and astrology, but she is resolved to have an abortion. She contacts a *sage-femme* (midwife) and begins taking various potions to end the pregnancy "naturally." No one—especially Hugo and her mother, Rosa, who is thrilled by the pregnancy—can know anything about her visits to the midwife.[93]

She leans more on Rank for steady companionship. On a Tuesday in May, when she is about three months pregnant, she decides to become an analyst. She will study with Rank and open her own office in Paris, thus becoming financially independent and expressing her talent in reading character and her desire to help. This decision will also allow her to live with Henry, the father of her child.[94] Initially, she will live in an apartment with him in Paris, returning to Louveciennes on weekends. In June she believes that she will be leaving Louveciennes perhaps for good in September. By August she secretly wishes she were going to be living alone ("because I love too many men").[95] Though he does not know about her plans with Henry, Hugo accepts her professional plans for a cheap studio in Paris and their proposed separation during the week. When Rank hears the news, he thinks she is just identifying with him, as she had with her father, and he puts her to the test. If she wants to be an analyst, she must join his summer conference for analysts beginning mid-July at the Cité Universitaire.[96]

According to Jesse Taft, an American psychologist with whom Rank had been planning this conference all spring, Rank was phasing out his writing and his analysis. The previous August, in coming out of his own spiritual crisis, he had determined to seek joy and creativity in living and in reading more Mark Twain, his favorite author. To do this he had decided to train a few people to carry on his ideas, thus withdrawing from his profession "without offending his Old Self." Anaïs was one of his last two patients. He is in a particularly vulnerable period of his life. He is bored with analysis and feels Europe threatened by war. In a lecture at the Sorbonne, he declares that psychoanalysis is a bourgeois ideology killed by the failure of democracy and individualism.[97] His last gesture is the Summer Institute.

On the very week that Anaïs decides to become an analyst, she puts on her new blue dress to visit Rank, determined that he will kiss her. When she kneels in front of him and offers her lips, he holds her tightly until she is dizzy with the ecstasy of a new love. Their affair begins 1 June 1934 amid her equal passion for Henry. Because of the treatments with the *sage-femme* she does not have intercourse, but drinks his sperm (the first time she had this experience was with Henry just days before). Rank, vulnerable in his unlived life, becomes an aggressive and passionate lover. He replaces her father, who now seems to her like a "stiff inhuman schoolteacher." Eduardo, always her confidant, says she is playing beauty to the "beast" Rank, and because she cannot have God, she "will have the analysts."[98]

Anaïs does not last the full six-week term at the Psychological Center. She is radiant and in full bloom—she uses the word a dozen times in her diary—and in a Grecian mood this summer. As the lectures drone on, she gazes out the open window into the garden; when a break is called, she exits by the window. She is unaccustomed to the discipline and bored by the intellectual tone of the classroom, having fled her last one in the first days of high school. The Cité Universitaire she describes as clean, white, and cubistic; the present and future American therapists are boring and stupid, the discussions all craft and technique, and the women saggy-breasted. Her small breasts are now full and sensitive. The midwife's potions are not working.

One exception among what she calls the "twenty withered schoolteachers" at Rank's conference is Hilaire Hiler, a thirty-five-year-old American painter and master of color from whom Henry had taken lessons the previous fall. Hiler has published several books and once owned the Jockey bar in Montparnasse. She meets him the first day and he pours out his life story, including his desire to be a psychoanalyst (because it has saved his life). He is a six-foot, sensuous man whom she describes as a dark animal with Indian and Jewish blood. Their lunches are more compelling than the lectures. Soon Hiler asks her to be his mistress, and failing that to be his analyst, or failing that at least to smoke a kef with him. But Rank, now a "stirring lover" ("lascivious, voracious") is taking her each noon to the Café du Rond Point and then to a house in rue Henri Rochefort, near Parc Monceau, for loving (sometimes they have a catered lunch and champagne in bed). She is taking his soul as well as his body, she believes.[99]

Café Zeyer, at the intersection of avenue du Maine and rue d'Alesia, becomes an important setting for her social life. Northwest of the Cité Universitaire and the Parc Montsouris, the cafés Zeyer and Alésia overlook the large place Victor Basch and the entrance to Métro Alésia, the closest station to rue Villa Seurat, where later this summer she will rent a studio. One of her first visits to the café is with Rank. She feels wonderfully "turned inside out" these summer days. She dresses in bright colors and a big floppy straw hat set at a rakish angle on her head. Hungry for life, and full of Henry and Otto, she is dwelling in the realm of pure sense. At this time in her life when she is most living in the present, she believes that she least needs psychoanalysis. In fact, she is resisting it, and begs out of classes. Though disappointed, Rank agrees to her dropping out. Because she is staying in Paris during the week, she keeps up her busy social life, even inviting members of the seminar, including Hiler, to a dinner one weekend in Louveciennes. She keeps up the diary (her kef), recopies "The Double"—her "novel of hate," a "superior drug"—and finishes translating the first volume of her childhood diary into English.[100]

As the summer progresses, she is anxious on two fronts: she is becoming increasingly frustrated at the failure of the midwife to induce an I.V.G. (*interruption volontaire de grossesse*), and her view of Rank and Miller is changing. Initially, she saw Rank as burdened by thought and Henry as a man who could delight in life's humble details. As she spends more time at Café Zeyer with Rank, she sees his "explosive" and assertive side. She sees him as caring, Henry as nonchalant. Henry wants peace and strength for his work, that is all. Rank is wooing her away from Henry and Hugo, criticizing both men (though Hugo is still his patient). She has become physically obsessed with Rank, as is her custom with a new love, and she now meets him each Friday in the borrowed studio of her friend Chana Orloff. "She is falling in love with the Voice. She felt that he was the subtle detective who made all those discoveries in her, who made her state the very nature of what hurt her. He liked the game of tracking down her most difficult thoughts."[101]

The seminar with Rank has taken her into the Montsouris quarter of Paris and, more important, into the real world of economic anxiety and historical pessimism. The heaviest blow comes with Rank's financial crisis after he stops work as an analyst. Forced by the upsurge in Freudian analysis in France, he makes plans to go to the United States to open a psychotherapy practice, for his lectures and writings are well-known there. He begs her to go with him for a few months. He tells her that she has helped to push him into life and he needs her now. He will train her, give her a job as an analyst, and pay her well. She says she will follow him anywhere.

Chana Orloff's studio is in rue Villa Seurat, an *impasse* of artists' studios in which Henry's friend Michael Fraenkel had lived at No. 18. Orloff, a former friend of the painter Amedeo Modigliani's, specializes in sculpting larger-than-life women in various stages of pregnancy. Her own son is a cripple, confined to a wheelchair. Though Anaïs finds the sculptress and her son's creaking wheelchair oppressive, and is saddened by the idea of bringing a child into such a "despairing world," she sits every afternoon for a bust to be made. (Orloff has already made a bust in wood of Rank, who occasionally drops in to share his difficult decision about emigration.) Anaïs seems most pleased by her discovery of Villa Seurat, named for the pointillist Georges Seurat (1859–1891), with its colored stucco two- and three-story buildings with skylights, windows, and balconies for artists' studios—artists including Chaim Soutine, Artaud, Salvador Dalí, and André Derain have lived in this cobblestone street with narrow sidewalks. What a perfect place for a studio for herself and Henry, who hears from Walter Lowenfels that the upper-right apartment at No. 18 (Fraenkel had lived on the ground floor, left, until July 1931) was vacant. One month before Anaïs rents the studio, Artaud leaves it.[102]

Earlier she had given Henry two vital gifts: a preface to *Tropic of Cancer* and the money to underwrite the book's publication. Although she had persuaded Hugo to pay printing costs, at the last minute he balked at assisting the "enemy" (as Henry phrased it), and she had to raise the $600 (5,000 francs) herself by borrowing it from Rank (and telling no one).[103] She and Henry collaborate on a revision of her preface, using phrases from her journal and some of his language.[104] The preface makes grand tongue-in-cheek declarations:

> In a world grown paralyzed with introspection and constipated by delicate mental meals this brutal exposure of the substantial body comes as a vitalizing current of blood. The violence and obscenity are left unadulterated, as manifestations of the mystery and pain which ever accompanies the act of creation.

Some of the later phrases are distinctly hers ("restorative value of experience," "obedience to flow," "obstetricians of culture," and "oblique symbolism of art") and some of the language is his ("putrescent cadavers," "the crazy jig and maggot dance"). Merriment hovers beneath the surface: "resurrection of the emotions" is "erection," Henry confides to friends.[105]

On 27 August she is with Henry in Louveciennes, packing books for their home together, thinking about Rank, and half wanting to live alone. But she has made her decision about the apartment and the pregnancy. Henry feels burdened by her and the pregnancy and hopes that her study of analysis will give her freedom and financial independence. In turn, the burden of Henry's needs and requests weigh too heavily on her shoulders. She worries about all the "children" she has to care for in her life (Eduardo is now living at Louveciennes). The six-month fetus in her womb weighs especially heavy.

She finally sees a friend of Otto Rank's, a doctor who tells her that the work of the midwife has done nothing. His work will take one week. Because Henry is very anxious about the abortion, she takes Rank to the empty apartment in boulevard Suchet. The next morning, after he leaves, she prepares for the arrival of the doctor. Afterward she helps him clean the instruments and blood. In the dark studio, Anaïs's hand rests on her belly. She tells the fetus there is "no father taking care of us. . . . You will be a child without a father as I was a child without a father. . . . There are no real fathers."[106] She talks for hours to the fetus, and in the most revealing words tells it that its father is an artist who is also a child and will run away just as he has left his wife and daughter. Man the artist is a child who needs all the nurturing for himself, would hate the noise and mess of a baby and flee. "You would be abandoned [as] . . . I was abandoned. . . . [It is] better to die than be abandoned."[107]

Hugo drives her to the clinic when the bleeding starts again. When Dr Endler arrives at the clinic, he feels no heartbeat. He is the German doctor who talked of the persecution of the Jews in Berlin when he inserted his instrument earlier at the apartment in boulevard Suchet, when he told her that her pelvis was too small, that it would not be easy. The nurses raise her legs (in the gesture of love, she notes) and tie her feet and legs to the table in the hope of provoking a "natural" birth. For two hours she struggles to give birth to a dead fetus too big for her pelvis, drifting in and out of consciousness. They try the next morning. Push, Dr. Endler demands angrily. After four hours she prefers death. Eventually the dead fetus emerges, the umbilical cord wrapped around its neck, and she demands to see what she will call her first dead creation.[108]

Once again Anaïs converts her life experience into writing. The following year she will write:

> The last time she had come out of the ether it was to look at her dead child, a little girl with long eyelashes and slender hands. She was dead.
>
> The little girl in her was dead too. The woman saved. And with the little girl died the need of a father.

This passage ends "Winter of Artifice," the story of her reunion with her father, in which she comes "out of the ether of the past," thus revealing the link, in her mind, between her abandonment, her incest, and her abortion—the abandoning and/or killing of two children.

Her second fictional account is the story "Birth," in which the doctor is angry and impatient and the child lying "inert at the door of the womb, blocking life" is like "a demon strangling me":

> [W]ith the tips of my fingers I drum drum drum . . . on my stomach in circles. . . . Like a savage. . . . The nurse presses her knee on my stomach. There is blood in my eyes. A tunnel. I push into this tunnel[.] I bite my lips and push. There is a fire and flesh ripping and no air. Out of the tunnel! All my blood is spilling out. . . . I feel the slipperiness, the sudden deliverance, the weight is gone.

In the fictional use of the abortion later in *Ladders to Fire*, when Lillian tells Jay she is pregnant, he looks "irritated" and suggests they find the money for an abortion. Because Jay continues to treat the pregnancy as "an intrusion," she tells the child "you ought to die because you are a child without a father. . . . Did the child hear her? At six months she had a miscarriage and lost it."

Hugo, Henry, Eduardo, and Rank are all at the hospital. Rank had rushed back from England. Hugo believes it is his; Henry, who knows it is his, is "weeping and trembling like a woman."[109] Her mother writes that she can try again to have a child.[110]

On the third day Anaïs is in pain with the milk in her breasts, but awakens the next morning feeling she has slept in God's arms. When she returns to recuperate in a detached and dreamy state in the garden at Louveciennes, beneath the falling leaves of autumn, she describes her experience in her journal, both the endless pain on the table and the religious experience of feeling penetrated by God, "melting into God." She will call her short story "Birth," not "Death." It is she who has been born. "I was born woman. To love God and to love man. . . ." Now she knows that "everything" she has done is "right."[111] She pastes a small picture of Dr. Endler on the back page of her diary.

She has had a "stillbirth," she tells her family, friends, and the public in later years. In her diary in 1958 she says, improbably, that the adhesions from her 1912 appendicitis operation "strangled my child, causing the stillbirth." And in an interview in 1971 she is quoted as implying that at her "stillbirth" she discovered that she was not able to have a baby because of surgery when she was nine years old. As years went by she confided the truth to her closest friends, until 1972 when she signed the *Ms.* magazine appeal to reverse abortion laws with the statement "I have had an abortion." The statement was signed by others, including Nora Ephron, Lee Grant, Lillian Hellman, Billie Jean King, Grace Paley, Anne Sexton, Susan Sontag, and Barbara Tuchman.[112]

## Villa Seurat

On the top-floor studio in Villa Seurat she cleans, paints, and hammers; in rue de la Tombe Issoire around the corner she finds the plumber and cleaner. This is her studio, where she plans to live with Henry during the week; she brings furniture from Louveciennes and hangs the curtains. Hugo believes that she will stay here alone. Rank, hurt, knows she is with Henry. Henry's friends (who help him move), as well as biographers and historians for the next fifty years, believe it is his home and that he lives here alone. Perlès, who is very disappointed not to be invited to move in, and Eduardo know better.[113] There is a large work and living area (hung with Henry's watercolors, lists, and charts), a bedroom, bath, and tiny kitchen furnished with discarded plates from Louveciennes. It was more like a shoe box, says a neighbor who later lived in the more commodious two-story apartment beneath. Henry's is a back apartment in this low pastel building. The studio is so light and airy that it is drafty, and Henry catches a severe cold in October.

Miller is ecstatic about his new apartment, the productivity of the past year, and his new beginning in Villa Seurat. There is no record of how he feels about the loss of his child, for he keeps silent to protect Anaïs. *Tropic of Cancer*, begun here on the ground floor in Fraenkel's studio four years before and now with her introduction, is ready at the printers. The circle seems complete to him. But Anaïs cannot share his joy with the studio, nor can she always feel love for him. She is meeting Rank at the boulevard Suchet apartment and mourning his coming departure for America. She feels empty. The tiny still girl she had demanded to see, and then looked at with hate out of her own pain, she now thinks about with loss and regret. She feels strangely detached from the present. On 23 September, she cooks dinner for Henry and then they wrap, for the post, the first copies of *Cancer*, their other baby.[114]

She is a man's woman, not a mother, she told the child in her womb, and this fall she is divided into more than three women. At Louveciennes, which she and Hugo are planning to sublet for the winter, Mrs. Guiler is served breakfast in bed by her Spanish maid, Emelia, supervises a gardener, pays domestic bills from her checkbook, translates her second childhood diary into English, and looks out the window with longing. At the Villa Seurat, Madame Henry (as one neighbor calls her) peels potatoes, wipes her hands on dish towels discarded from Louveciennes, walks to the market, and sits in cafés talking books and films. At the boulevard Suchet, with her ardent lover, Dr. Rank, Anaïs reaches what she believes is the first clitoral orgasm of her life. "He broke through the shell of my frigidity."[115] Yet she saves part of herself for several other flirtations, with a man named Turner (a business client of Hugo's), Harry Harvey (husband of critic Dorothy Dudley), and Louis Andard, a French politician and publisher. With Turner and Andard, according to portions of her diary never published, she has weekly sexual liaisons.

Rank urges her to come to New York and return to dancing; she makes plans for a rehearsal of her repertoire, but only attends one practice. As he begins to see New York as a chance for a new life, as a liberation of the Huck Finn in him, he steps up his pressure for her to come with him. He is deeply in love with her.[116] He had denied life before—for his parents, for Freud, for his wife. New York means new life and better money, and he will write a book on Mark Twain. She is necessary for his liberation (and he must get her away from Henry). He takes her with him to look at a first edition of Twain, and buys Chana Orloff's sculptured head of Anaïs for his office. Fearing the loss of Rank (as she had of her father) and the economic future, she promises to go. For his last night in France, she meets him in Rouen and gives him a ring that her father had given her. After returning to Paris she makes love to Andard.

The decision to go to New York City, the subletting of Louveciennes, the guilt and conflict over her father,[117] her abortion, and her multiple relationships have shaken Anaïs. Rosa and Joaquin have the church; Hugo and

Eduardo compose astrological charts. She tries both approaches. With embarrassment she consults a fortune-teller with dirty fingernails who stares
into her glass ball and says she sees a man on a ship going to America and
thinking of her, she sees a new career, and she sees a man with whom she
is incompatible harming her. Anaïs also visits Abbé Alterman, at the urging
of Joaquin, who believes that her religious experience in the hospital will
bring her back to the church. When she visits this brilliant converted Jew
(who had won Max Jacob and other artists to Christianity) in his monastic
room, she is dressed as Thaïs (the fourth-century courtesan who converted
to a life of Christian penitence) in a low-cut black dress.[118] She had hoped
to seduce him and deprive Joaquin of his faith, she says. It is a lengthy
dialogue, until she mentions Dr. Otto Rank. Alterman warns about black
magic and the devil's work of psychoanalysis, which leaves her convinced of
her decision to live fully and richly in the earth and its pleasures. She will
love the relative, not the absolute, and psychoanalysis will be her religion.[119]
But the "axis" of her life is love; any art will be a "by product."[120]

By mid-October the Guilers have put their home furnishings in storage,
and she feels like she has been ejected from her fairy-tale world, her source
of dreams. They move into an apartment at 41, avenue de Versailles in the
Auteuil district of Passy. Up the avenue, which runs parallel to the east bank
of the Seine, live Rosa and Joaquin, at 18 bis. As she rides the bus back and
forth between 18, Villa Seurat and 41, avenue de Versailles, she tries to sort
out her men. She still occasionally, without feeling, sees her father, who
suffers from eczema and lumbago; continues to protect Hugo from any truth
that would hurt him; and packs to join Rank, "another" father, she admits.[121]
She is trying to live in the present, but the move, Hugo's financial troubles
(his salary has been cut), and Henry's casual disregard for money depress
her. Just after leaving Henry (with two hundred francs that Hugo had given
her for new underwear) one morning, she sits at a café in rue de Rivoli and
weeps over a letter to him. Her financial pinch and what she sees as his
irresponsibility and thoughtlessness are depressing her. He gives money to
others and never hesitates to ask for more. You are a child, she charges.[122]
Nevertheless, she has offered to earn enough money in New York so that
she can bring him there.

In the weeks before she leaves for New York (Henry believes she is going
with Hugo), she and Henry see a number of other artists. Since the publication of *Tropic of Cancer*, his circle of admirers has grown. They visit
Marcel Duchamp; Dorothy Dudley; Brassaï, the Hungarian photographer
and friend of Henry's; and Blaise Cendrars (who comes to praise *Cancer* and
writes the first published review). With Duchamp they speak of the chaos
of time, the value of unfinished work, and yielding to life; this easygoing and

nonintellectual approach is Henry's genius, she concludes. Duchamp gives Anaïs a portfolio of reprints to show galleries in New York. When they visit Dorothy Dudley, the recent biographer of Theodore Dreiser, she gives Anaïs letters of introduction to Dreiser and Waldo Frank. When they visit Aleister Crowley—Henry has fallen under his psychological spell—the old man refuses to look at Anaïs, whom he accuses of being a sorceress.

Rank's letters (sent through Joaquin) are pleading for her presence in New York, she records. He reminds her that he left his London lecture to rush to her hospital bed. "I am dying now. Come to my rescue." Hugo, who is scheduled for his annual leave the first of January and will join her, gives his blessing to her study of analysis. Besides, she has explained that she is leaving for New York City to get away from Henry. Just before she leaves, Hugo finds one of Rank's letters addressed to "darling," and once again she succeeds in giving him a story he can live with, convincing him that Rank loves her but is only a father figure to her. She says all her farewells and has her ticket in hand. But listening to Florent Schmitt's *Psalms* on the radio makes her weep at the "terrible algebra" of trying "to live by her own truth."[123]

## Babylon

Anaïs sails for New York City at the end of November, leaving a web of lies in her wake. Hugo paid for the ticket believing she was fleeing from Henry. Henry bade her farewell thinking she was accompanying Hugo on official business and will be ingratiating herself with Rank so that they both may practice psychoanalysis. Rank believes she is coming to take up dance and theatre. The other men (Andard is crushed when she breaks with him) believe she is going to study psychoanalysis in New York.

She begins the trip by weeping on the train, but is soon yielding to romantic adventures on board ship.[124] It is a rough ride, but a gala social life. She is made love to and dines, dances, and gambles all night. As the ship arrives the night before Thanksgiving, a southern gentleman is whispering his love into her ear, the band is playing, and Rank waits at the pier with theatre tickets and a full social calendar. (His wife has not accompanied him to New York.) "A fine Thanksgiving for Otto," Henry writes. "I am jealous."[125]

She is soon settled into the Barbizon Plaza at the corner of Sixth Avenue and Fifty-eighth Street and inundated with clerical work. Rank's office is a three-room apartment in The Adams ("Hotel Chaotica," she soon dubs it), Fifth Avenue and Eighty-sixth. She sits outside his consulting room and makes appointments, listening to the mumbled sounds of secular confessions from the penitents in the next room. Not surprisingly, when she fictionalizes this experience with analysis and Rank, she will call it "The

Voice." Soon she is looking over the rough translations of his work, which he wants her to refine and edit.[126] Though she makes cynical remarks about Americans (their "life Principle is Surface") in a letter from the ship, she is immediately swept up in the glitter and status of New York City and Rank's famous clients and friends. "I'm in love with New York" is her litany in letters. "It matches my mood." She will later say she was "drunk on liberty." The feverish pace ("electric rhythm") of the city cures her depression. But her enthusiasm annoys Miller, who hates the city (though he has long wanted a return visit to see his friends). The city is magic with its tall buildings and a million windows, its freedom and space ("Babylonian proportions"), and the luxury of daily fresh flowers, elegant elevators, and glass chutes for the mail. She encloses a piece of cellophane in a letter to Henry and describes in rhapsodic detail her busy life, assuring him that his letters should be sent directly to the Barbizon, for they never send up the mail. Her implication: she can pick it up at the desk before Hugo sees it.[127]

Meanwhile, Henry is playing "Body and Soul" on his phonograph at Villa Seurat and thinking of her dining at the Ritz and Waldorf with Hugo. She has left checks for him, and he is mailing copies of *Tropic of Cancer* to Ezra Pound, Aldous Huxley, Katherine Anne Porter, and other writers. Flyers for *Cancer* and copies of the novel and his manuscripts are with Anaïs, along with lists of friends and places she is to visit.

When the first letter from Anaïs arrives, inside is a letter of love to Hugo. In panic, Henry draws two conclusions: first, that she is not with Hugo, as she told him—Hugo is in Paris; and second, the letter she wrote to him has reached her husband! For days he sends her letters and cables (to a friend's address); certain that Hugo will come to shoot him, he hides behind locked doors when the doorbell rings. He asks Perlès to move in for protection. He warns her to be careful, then fears for himself, then expresses relief that the truth is finally out. After three years, their Scandal is to be played out, he concludes. Disappointment follows when Eduardo, who enjoys Henry's humiliation, brings her letter to Henry, which had gone to Hugo.[128] It has no word of love.

Henry now figures out that she has staged the entire switch to reassure Hugo and to keep himself on edge. But his overwhelming feeling is despair and misery at her need to lie to him ("Must you deceive me too?") and the realization that she is truly with Rank. "I believe in you. That's just it. *We all do,*" he adds ironically, for his faith is deeply shaken. Meanwhile, her "tinsel" letters arrive (by ship, ten days after they are mailed) implying that she is with Hugo and full of what he calls "jewel dust and klieg lights." Henry is so angry he chews up the piece of cellophane.[129]

Anaïs is swept away by the bright lights and social life that Rank offers her, and he is like a young boy in love and in rebellion against his profession (he is no longer well received by the Freudian analysts in New York).[130] He gives her emotional freedom; she frees his physical self. She takes "Huck" Rank to Harlem for jazz and teaches him to dance. She asks him questions about his childhood and helps him discover and dissipate the "unused life" in himself, as Henry and June had done for her. Rank has seduced her with analysis; she has seduced him with play and physical freedom. He rules their daily work, she the nights.

Henry, once his week of terror ("refined torture") has passed, urges her to literary business with names and journals and editors. He is in literary bloom: finishing "Tailor's Shop" for *Black Spring* (which he sends to her), writing voluminous letters to promote *Cancer* (which is selling slowly), looking for translators for her earliest diaries written in French, and rewriting his film scenario (after her "Alraune"). He is also receiving numerous letters from Ezra Pound, Katherine Anne Porter, Stuart Gilbert, and others who have read his first novel.

When letters and explanations do not arrive, he fears their separation and offers to give up writing itself if it means losing her. He loves her more than he has any other. In a series of eloquent love letters this month, he encourages her to take out citizenship papers (she still has a Cuban passport with Hugo), declares his passion for her and his determination not to share her, and threatens to come to her immediately if she does not cable. In the most eloquent letter (14 December 1934), he proposes that she give up everything and live with him openly and full-time. Her unsigned letters of explanation only begin on the nineteenth of December, when she implies that her trip to New York was to earn money for him. Hugo has discovered her check writing, she says; she owes Rank for the money he loaned for the printing of *Cancer*.[131] On 20 December, the day that news of June's proxy divorce in Mexico reaches Henry, Anaïs writes that his letters have "made everything right." Though she wants to stand on her own feet, she pleads, "Oh, Henry, Henry, let's get close to each other again." She declares her love, but he thinks this all sounds like "strange new talk." There are accusations: she is losing her soul to New York glitter, always needed flattery, will not trust him as a man, an equal. He is weak and helpless (to allow Perlès and his girl to move in on his writing space)—all of which necessitates her "business" career. Yet his letters reveal his increasing distraction.[132]

When Anaïs writes to Miller on New Year's Day 1935 that she belongs to him "as nobody . . . ever [has], come and take me all back again, Henry, Henry!,"[133] Hugo is to arrive the next day and Miller to sail the day after that. Both men are arriving in fear and with suspicion, in Henry's case a month before she has planned for him to arrive. She moves with Hugo to his family home in Forest Hills, but keeps working for Rank, who is teaching in the Graduate School for Jewish Social Work and traveling to lectures in Philadelphia, Hartford, and other eastern cities. Their affair continues this month, though he sees in her Tom Sawyer's love of seeking complications and playful deceptions.

She meets Miller's ship, the *Champlain*, which arrives late in a heavy fog. He had cabled all his friends to raise the ticket money, left Perlès at Villa Seurat, and arrives determined to marry his "perfect mate." After five years of exile he is returning to a city he hates for the woman he loves. "No more double life. No more Hugo." No more "love-sick" Rank, he has declared. She is anxious, for in his last letter he declares an end to the "kingdom of fathers and mothers" and threatens to confront both Hugo and Rank. She puts him into her room at the Barbizon Plaza with the promise that on 1 February, when Hugo leaves for a three-week business trip, she will arrive with her suitcases.[134]

Her affair with Rank essentially ends before February, less because of the arrival of Hugo and Henry than because her passion has waned, she realizes that Rank is not going to turn over his practice to her, and Rank discovers that she has been lying to him about Miller and other men. He breaks off the romance and asks for his letters back, then leaves to lecture in California. The speculation that Anaïs broke up his marriage or that she overwhelmed him with her plunging necklines ("Poor Rank," Maxwell Geismar would say in 1979, "such a brilliant theoretician, such a confused and tormented man, he never had a chance")[135] gives him too little credit. He ends the romance and pursues interests outside of New York City. She will say that it was she who ended the romance and left him heartbroken. "I tempted him as a man, and when he became a man and desired me, then I was angry at him," Lilith says in "The Voice."[136]

In his absence, Anaïs answers telephones, opens mail, sees patients, and refers some to Henry. They are analysts to many "patients." As early as the previous August, Henry had told a friend he was thinking of practicing psychoanalysis in New York and could make money by working for Rank, but there is no evidence that Rank knew anything about Henry's "work."[137] By the end of February, says his first biographer, Henry is seeing four patients a day and proud of his ability to analyze the neuroses of others.[138] He may have been recording his dreams, but after only a one-hour meeting with Rank, he is not even remotely qualified to practice psychoanalysis. Anaïs is not qualified either, but she had long probed her thoughts and dreams, has a talent for asking questions, and has been analyzed by Drs. Allendy and Rank. Henry thinks she is an excellent psychoanalyst.

Henry introduces Anaïs to his friends from Brooklyn and takes her to see his "street of early sorrows." There is no evidence that either one of them contacts June. Once again Anaïs is divided between two worlds, a contrast keener in New York City than in the French capital of art. She first becomes aware of this contrast when Emil Schnellock visits her at the Barbizon Plaza in December. Emil is Henry's schoolboy friend and the one who gave him the only money he took to Paris in 1930. Emil does not like the Barbizon, and takes her instead to Greenwich Village to see the cafés and expatriate artists from Europe. She feels apologetic for staying uptown, where the bank people can call her. The Guilers are now renting an apartment for the next three months on Park Avenue and Thirty-fourth Street and being entertained in palatial apartments. Henry's artistic ways seem in stark relief to modern New York City. At the Barbizon Henry collects calls for Anaïs from various men until he moves to a cheaper room at the Roger Williams Apartments, 28 East Thirty-first Street. She journeys between the two apartments and, when Rank returns in March, to his new office on Riverside Drive.

Rank has fallen in love with California and decides to move there to start a new life. In the meantime he hires a new assistant, Estelle Buel, a multilingual American woman who had attended his summer classes in Paris in 1934. He also applies for citizenship and is dividing his practice between Philadelphia and New York. Anaïs continues to handle some of his patients and claims to be relieved not to be constantly analyzed by Rank. When he renews his request for Anaïs to collaborate on English translations of his works, she resists. She sees it as a lifetime work less preferable to analysis and an abdication of her own writing. She claims she has never given herself fully to Rank and is now disillusioned with him, as she had been with Allendy and her father when they proved vulnerable.

While the five months in New York were devoted to analysis, the writer lived on in the journal, which Rank praises as a record of woman's consciousness. He writes an introduction to her early diary, which Henry tries to get published.[139] Her present journal includes more of her outside world—descriptions of the city from Broadway to the boardwalk of Long Beach. Both the influence of Henry and the healing of the hurt child within have made the journal more her literary journal than the compulsive repository of her consciousness. When the journal of these New York months is published, however, Henry is nowhere mentioned—she is alone in New York and practicing analysis with Rank.[140]

Rank insists she finish her poetic "Alraune" (*The House of Incest*) and helps her with the conclusion. It must end with her dancing—"dancing toward daylight." He writes an introduction to the manuscript version of "Alraune" (that will be rediscovered forty years later and printed in a journal devoted to his work). In his introduction he analyzes the legend of the bad woman "re-created by a woman . . . made bad by her father. She first wants to win him back by becoming good." When this fails she becomes bad again to both please and punish him.[141] Rank believes that women possess a "real" self that is concealed in order to please man. He sees this theme in *The House of Incest.*

Except for Henry, Anaïs's literary circle in New York is scattered. Most of her literary contacts are made by a written request for a meeting, enclosing a letter of introduction from Dorothy Dudley. Her letter to Sherwood Anderson evokes no response.[142] She goes to Theodore Dreiser's room at the Hotel Ansonia for dinner, though he is a member of what she disparages as the materialist-realist literary mafia. He assumes by her presence and flirtatious manner that she will be spending the night. When she says no, thank you, to the sixty-four-year-old Dreiser, he chuckles. Later she has lunch with Rebecca West, who introduces her to several actors, including Norman Bel Geddes and Raymond Massey. After an ice-hockey game at Madison Square Garden, they go for drinks at Reuben's, where John Huston joins them. Later at a private club she flees when the verbal jockeying gets mean and hateful. Apparently only with Bel Geddes does she continue a flirtatious friendship.

She also calls on Waldo Frank, to whose work she had been introduced by Hélène Boussinescq. At first she is annoyed when Frank makes the same assumption that Dreiser had. But she does not resist long. She has dinner with the forty-six-year-old Frank, whose novel *The Death and Birth of David Markand* had been published the previous year. He looks Spanish, she thinks, and he lived in Paris during 1916 and 1917. She has long admired his introspection, poetic style, and interest in mysticism. He is also "gentle" and sensitive. Finally, when she goes to his room, he reads her his description of a Catalonian woman (from his *Virgin Spain*) and whispers to her that God has sent her to him so that he might finish his book. We only have her *Diary* as evidence of these encounters, but a recent biographer of Henry Miller describes her as being "shepherded around town by Theodore Dreiser, Waldo Frank, and Norman Bel Geddes" while "banishing" Miller to the Roger Williams Apartments.[143]

The literary world of New York City in the 1930s is characterized by its political concern. In Greenwich Village and elsewhere there are growing numbers of Europeans and returning expatriate writers. Even Waldo Frank will turn to Marxist themes in his next book. Walter Lowenfels tells Miller that his decadent bohemianism is out of fashion. Miller the anarchist and Nin the analyst are not moved by political concerns. Nevertheless Miller has more literary acceptance: Hiler, who like Lowenfels is now in New York City, introduces Henry to Nathanael West, James T. Farrell, William Saroyan, and

William Carlos Williams. He also meets e. e. cummings and Kay Boyle in the Village. But he does not find a congenial literary group and he dislikes Brooklyn, where most of his landmarks are gone. He is feeling trapped in the drabness of his past.

The Nin-Miller romance cools down some after February, when they act as analysts in Rank's absence. Henry has made Anaïs the center of his emotional life, but she is busy meeting her clients and participating in the social world of Hugo in their Park Avenue apartment. By March, when she seems to be moving away from him, Miller stands outside her door, waits for her, and writes love letters asking her, "Move into me, Anaïs, stay there. . . . You are the flame that burns within me."[144] By the end of April he finishes *Black Spring* and is bored with analysis, for he has cured no patients, though he says he has compounded cures for them from "a little measure of St. Augustine, an ounce of Emerson, a pinch of the Old Testament, a tincture of Forel and Freud, and a sprinkling of Lao-Tse."[145] But Anaïs's love seems to be withering outside the Paris atmosphere, and no formula seems to be working.

Anaïs is also tiring of analysis. Rank at first told her she works "magically," and later complimented her on keeping her interest in people.[146] She does record in her journal the joy of helping others to walk and to love. But more frequently she speaks of escaping each day into night parties, music, sleep. The six to eight patients a day exhaust her. She moves from feeling "restless and impatient" to feeling she is cracking. She begins longing for Paris. She loses sleep and weight. Her problem is that she is not objective. She takes the worries of her patients home and is haunted by them at night.

Anaïs is ready to say good-bye both to analysis and to Rank. As she will later say, "[H]is work was his seduction. It outlived the seduction." Now the work itself is finished. She says later, "[I] expected Rank to give me my liberty, by letting me inherit his work, but he did not give me that."[147] However, his gifts to her have been to give each of her gestures a sense of importance, to give her understanding, justification, absolution. He has helped her deal with her father incest, though she attached her father need to him temporarily. She has also learned a basic theory of the psychology of men and women that will appear in her fiction the remainder of her life.[148] He has helped her stop feeling guilty for being a writer, for creating. "I could not have flowered and expanded . . . but for psychoanalysis," she tells a friend. "No religion, no love, no friendship could rescue me."[149] An important lesson she learns from Rank is to view the self as process, not fixed entity, and the person as constantly becoming, re-forming, reinterpreting sensations and experiences.[150] And finally, of course, he gives her material for her writing, for she uses his physical appearance and character four years later in modeling "The Voice" (a "modern priest") in *The Winter of Artifice* and "the lie detector" (a "soul doctor") in *A Spy in the House of Love.*

She has freed him sexually (he concentrates on living and writes no books after he falls in love). But she has helped him to the point of exhaustion, she thinks. The break in their romance lessens the hold of professional psychoanalysis on her. The turning point occurs at a meeting for psychoanalysts in Long Beach, Long Island. The setting by the sea should have been lovely, but she sees the boardwalk as gritty, the sea colorless, the salt air bitter, and the convention hotel as a penitentiary. The conference itself is worse. It smacks too much of the academic world she has fled. Analysts, name tags on every chest, examine fragments, bottle and label life. Rank is the only metaphysical man in the profession, she concludes. She listens for the sound of the pulse of the sea, which lies beyond the drawn curtains, and senses that it is this oceanic life that the conventioneers are trying to bottle up. As she enters the dining room, she is caught by the ticket taker. She is not a psychoanalyst but a fraud in this world. She is a writer, and she should be in Paris writing another novel.

A few days later her ship slips out of the New York harbor in the fog. She is going back to Louveciennes, and Henry will follow in a few weeks. Sirens of the ship signal her escape. She has lived her dream and is free, a "poet still."

# CHAPTER SEVEN

## 1935–1939

# Drifting Toward War: Publishing and Politics

"Every time she was faced with a sacrifice of the self, with the demand of another, a hunger, a prayer, a need, there came this joy. It was like the joy of a prisoner who finds the bars of his cell suddenly broken down."

—*Anaïs Nin, "The Voice"*[1]

O N THE SHIP back to France for what will prove to be her last four years of residence in Paris, Anaïs suffers night- and daytime anguish. In one dream she is greeted at the pier by Dr. Endler, who wants her to return to the hospital to relive her abortion nightmare; in another she is in her father's house and the dream is all in brown, a color she hates. Though she believes that Rank has freed her of her need for a father, she has yet to resolve the conflicting identification of paternal and maternal instincts within herself. This conflict will color her view of Paris and her relations with Henry over these next years.

During the first few months in Paris she misses the masculine vitality, individual freedom, and nervous energy of New York—which had staved off her postpartum depression. By 22 June 1935, she and Hugo return to Louveciennes, which the renters have left in disrepair. Her fairy-tale house now smells like the musty past itself. Her colored bottles seem faded, light bulbs and curtain rods are missing, and the sheets smell of mildew. With the bright lights and frenetic activity of New York behind her, Louveciennes is like returning to the house of the dead, to a prison in a sleepy provincial village. It literally is returning to the dead, of course, for Anaïs is struggling with guilt about her abortion. This is revealed in her creation of a scene in which a five-month-pregnant woman throws herself to her death from the twenty-fifth floor of the Hotel Chaotica.[2] Her second struggle, over the affair and breakup with Dr. Rank, can be understood through the examination of recent studies that suggest patients who engage in sexual relations with their therapists (during *or* after therapy has ended) are more emotionally scarred than when they began treatment.[3]

Henry, who returns several weeks after Anaïs, feels only relief to be back in Paris. She is free in New York, he in Paris—where his soul, he believes, is fertilized by the fecund rot of the city's deterioration, a physical degeneration that allows his soul to expand. He is now more productive than ever, while to fight off her depression she walks the streets (a habit he has taught her) and visits friends.

## The Siana Press

She renews the dream that she and Henry had of a printing press at Louveciennes, though this time he is less interested in self-publication, and the enterprise (now publishing, not hand-printing) will be located in Villa Seurat.[4] When she, Miller, Perlès, and Fraenkel meet in Louveciennes to talk about the idea, the men seem to take control. She is especially upset at Fraenkel, whom she characterizes as a frail little man with the ego needs of a giant. Perlès names their press Siana, reversing the spelling of "Anaïs." Despite the name of the press, when Fraenkel constructs an initial list of books they will publish, he omits her name and titles. Eventually they decide to publish Miller's *Scenario* first, and then her *House of Incest,* upon which the Miller work is based. While she expects to put up some of the financing, Fraenkel will pay to print *House of Incest.*[5] (They pay for one another's books.)

Anaïs lives what she calls a divided life between the quiet and orderly Louveciennes and the gregarious world of Villa Seurat. Sometimes she feels like the "young mother of the group," a role she will struggle with for the coming decade. At others, she feels as if she makes herself "personally responsible for the fate of every human being" who comes into her life.[6] She has certainly become, in the words of one of Miller's biographers, his "shadow wife and shadow mother."[7] Momentarily she thinks that it was Lawrence and Miller who took her away from the rational role (she thinks she served as a "husband substitute" for her mother) and toward the feminine world of intuition and instinct. She engages in "ideological wrestling matches" with Henry and feels he shares her nonrational view of life and art.[8]

Anaïs returns from New York a transformed but not yet confident artist. Henry returns determined to demand recognition. His letter-writing campaign is so extensive that his young French friend the writer Raymond Queneau calls the Villa Seurat apartment *maison d'un commerce.* Miller even launches a campaign to collect money for Perlès and publishes an appeal letter, *What Are You Going to Do About Alf?,* financed by Michael Fraenkel and Eduardo Sanchez. The letter goes to T. S. Eliot, Aldous Huxley, Ezra Pound, Jean Cocteau, and numerous other writers. Perlès, who lives around the corner, in rue des Artistes, may never have received any money,[9] but Henry is trying to do for Perlès what Anaïs does privately for Henry. The letter also serves the purpose of allowing Henry to express his artistic position. If Anaïs's natural medium is the diary, his is the letter. Almost all the material of his fiction is first expressed in letters to Emil, Anaïs, and other friends.[10] His epistolary art is typed in the heat of the moment for the world to read; hers is entered in the diary by hand, then typed with additions. This August of 1935, for example, she is typing up and expanding her New York trip so that she can place the original diary in a bank safe-deposit box. She will also rework it into a fiction called "Hotel Chaotica" (later called "The Voice").

Anaïs signs a contract with Jack Kahane to publish her "Lilith" with his Obelisk Press. She continues to add to and revise this essential tale of her reunion with her father. One day while lying in the Elizabeth Arden salon, with moist cotton balls on her eyelids and half asleep, she experiences a Proustian reverie that gives her the beginning of her monologue about her father. Now with more objectivity than she had earlier when she first tried to write this story, she knows how to shape it. She tells it in the first person; only later will she change to third person and retitle it "The Winter of Artifice."

While writing the "Lilith" novelette this late summer, she is forced to deal with her "lost" memories of her father. She begins the story with Lilith waiting for the arrival of her father, whom she has not seen in twenty years, recalling his abandonment, then their reunion. (The twenty-year figure is a dramatic fiction, for Anaïs had seen her father several times when she returned to Paris a decade before.) While writing the end, a year after her own affair with her father, Anaïs turns the tables and reverses the abandonment by leaving *him,* an artistic denouement that will give readers the mistaken impression that revenge was her own motivation for entering into the incest with her father (the fiction only suggests incest through metaphor). While writing this "fiction," she speaks in the diary of the "emotional shock" that probably caused her to forget her unbearable experiences by incurring "myopia" and a state of "sleepwalking." Some portions of her life, she admits, were lived as if she were under a fog or ether. Some, she now realizes, were eclipsed altogether.[11] This passage is the closest she comes in her published lifetime diary to acknowledging the power or shock of her childhood abuse in causing her memory loss. She is "coming out of the ether of the past," she declares hopefully. She ends the work with the narrator coming out of the ether to look at her dead baby girl. "The little girl in her was dead too. The woman was saved. And with the little girl's death died the need of the father."[12]

By mid-October Anaïs and Hugo begin packing their personal effects in Louveciennes for a winter in Paris. She looks longingly at the New York tags on her luggage and tries to convince Henry to return to New York with her. Her former patients have been writing that they miss her.[13] The apartment of Louise de Vilmorin ("Jeanne" in the published diary) at 13, avenue de la Bourdonnais has its compensations: a view of the Eiffel Tower, satin sheets, a white telephone beside the bed. Anaïs is reminded that she indeed enjoys beauty and luxury.

An increasing amount of the passion of Anaïs and Henry is directed into writing, literary promotion, and social activity. With "little gift for intimacy," says one of his biographers (probably echoing Anaïs), Henry needs a "steady turnover" of friends.[14] To Anaïs, who likes her friends completely devoted, the Villa Seurat apartment seems like an open house for Henry's artist friends. True, his friends write witty prefaces for one another, share books, and argue in cafés, but Henry lives alone and works long hours. One of their friends gives Anaïs credit: "Henry Miller had a tendency to fly apart, to overextend himself. Anaïs helped him to focus. This period at the Villa Seurat was his most productive period."[15] His best years are just beginning; little wonder that he does not want to return with Anaïs to New York. His growing reputation is documented by the letters of praise from Eliot, Cendrars, Pound, Cocteau, and Huxley. Thanks in part to his self-promotion and certainly to his hard work and *her* financial support, he is becoming a celebrity. She is both jealous and proud of him. Since she and Hugo moved into town at the end of October—she carrying in her lap the fishbowl, crystals, seashells, and aquarium—she has moved often between the seventh and fourteenth arrondissements, between the bourgeois apartment of de Vilmorin and the artistic pastels of rue Villa Seurat.

The parties in Villa Seurat are sometimes memorable. Rebecca West, visiting from London, recalls (probably with poetic license) one party that she attended with Anaïs. Admiring of Anaïs's genius, she deplores Henry's obscenity and his influence on her friend; she considers Henry a "dreadful American lout," and portrays him as such:

> Henry Miller got very drunk. . . . He tried to take a bath half-dressed and Anaïs Nin and I discovered him under the water, blowing bubbles. We pulled him out, and in the course of this the rest of his clothes came off. I may say that Henry Miller without clothes was even less appealing than Henry Miller with clothes.[16]

Anaïs also will take liberties with the coloring of buildings and friends when she immortalizes these parties in the "Bread and Wafer" section of *Ladders to Fire* (1946). In the novel, a party is held on a "small street without issue lined with white cubistic villas." The description of the party is surreal or jazzlike in its technique and choreographed like a musical dance. She also uses the image of the squares in a chess game to arrange the characters at the party, including many of "Jay's [Henry's] warm winey white-trash friends."[17]

There is a kind of Dadaism at the Villa Seurat that she cannot share. Their burlesque antics and Henry's burlesque of sex alienate her. Writing about her father seems to be deeper and more serious work. Tired of the mother role, she spends more time in a cultural whirlpool of ballet, symphony, and art. But she does not stave off depression, for she does not feel she belongs in either Louise's elegant world or at the Villa Seurat. She perceives this conflict as one between her feminine self, who wants to live in harmony with and nurture the masculine world, and her masculine-creator self, who desires freedom, adventure, a world of her own. She cannot practice analysis without Rank, cannot start a publishing company because she fears Fraenkel will dominate it, cannot live alone and travel because she does not have money.

## Rhythms of New York, Labyrinths of Fez

As she and Henry walk along the Seine on a foggy night, they talk of their malaise—her need to make her own world, his depression about the world's failure to recognize his work. Their mood is echoed in the cold fog. Later she will describe their scene and their contrasting views of the world in the persons of Jay and Lillian in *Seduction of the Minotaur* (1959): "Together they would walk along the same Seine river, she would see it silky gray, sinuous and glittering, he would draw it opaque with fermented mud, and a shoal of wine bottle corks and weeds caught in the stagnant edges." Lillian says, "We do not see things as they are, we see them as we are."[18] Determined to get herself and Henry away from Paris—she says it is to follow the promise of the letters from her former "patients"—Anaïs decides to earn what money she can in New York (where analysis pays better than in Paris and where she feels freer) and convinces Henry to go with her for an extended visit. The money will give them the resources they need and Henry can again pursue arrangements for a pirated U.S. edition of his *Tropic of Cancer*.

The Christmas tree is withering in her rented apartment near the Eiffel Tower, and Rosa and Joaquin are safely away in Cuba for his concert with the Havana Philharmonic, when Anaïs sails for New York with Henry 18 January 1936 on the S.S. *Bremen*. He is reluctant, but Anaïs can hear the "new rhythm" of New York City calling her. And she has Henry to herself, away from his compatriots. She settles him into the Barbizon in time to join a family reunion (the excuse given Hugo for her trip). She attends the U.S. debut of Joaquin at Town Hall on 24 January with her mother, aunts, and cousins. The audience of Cuban artists seem like ghosts of her Richmond Hill past. She looks like "a snow queen" in her dramatic white fur cape and hat. "Dazzling," says one observer.[19]

According to Anaïs, she and Henry have again brought in (probably without declaring them) copies of *Tropic of Cancer* to be sold at the Gotham Book Mart, the avant-garde bookshop on West Forty-seventh owned by Frances Steloff. Henry spends time unsuccessfully trying to arrange for a pirated edition of his novel, and Anaïs consults a judge about the legal implications of book piracy.[20]

Once more they set themselves up as psychoanalysts by seeing old and new "patients" at the Barbizon. They visit the studio of their friend Hilaire Hiler, where Anaïs dances and pretends that the marijuana (which she does not inhale) has wildly intoxicated her. She sees the actors (Massey, Huston) and writers (the Middletons) whom she met the previous year, and visits Otto Rank for one hour (as if she were still his patient) in his Riverside Drive office. She tells him that she is still in conflict with her feminine self, and living not by analysis but by feeling. He approves. Just back from the South, he looks tanned and younger. She thinks he looks sad, but in fact he is breaking away more often for California, where he wants to settle on a new life and divorce his wife. Anaïs will never see him again, for after marrying Estelle Buel at Lake Tahoe in 1939, he dies in October of that year in New York City.[21]

A more satisfying reunion occurs with her brother Thorvald, who has been in South America for a decade, with occasional visits to Paris. They weep upon meeting and talk throughout dinner on board his ship, where he is detained for some error on his passport. Thorvald, now almost thirty-one years old, is thoroughly American, she observes, unlike the other family members. (He is proudly a businessman, disdainful of the dilettante life of his father and sister.) Anchored there on the shore of the past, she recalls their first voyage to this land, and he recalls her bossiness. She thinks he wears a mask like his father and will not show his feelings.

"Brother and sister walking through the skeleton of the monstrous ship which had taken him away and brought him back with the same diamond lodged in the breast. Bathing in the acid of the past, they bared the bones unbleached and this diamond."[22] Such is the description of their meeting as she creates it in the fictional story she is writing ("The Voice"). When he reads her account three years later, he will be angry. They have little in common, and their alienation is virtually ensured, some have said, when his father tells him about his sexual encounter with his sister.[23]

Without professional associations or credentials and with negligible clients and pay, Anaïs again suffers from too much exposure to the feelings and the illness of people around her. Analysis is sapping her energy and emotion, and she decides she has fulfilled her duty to her patients after two and a half months in New York. On 5 April, she and Henry sail for France. She anticipates Fraenkel's preparations for the publication of her poetic novella *The House of Incest: A Fantasia of Neurosis*, by their Siana Press (they will drop the subtitle).

Less than a week after her return to Paris, Anaïs and Hugo visit Morocco. "Well, Professor Hemingway, are you glad I came without my diary?" she writes Henry 17 April 1936.[24] The blue sky and purple sea of Africa, the sun and colored tiles, the music and birds—all the romance of the exotic makes her passionate. The Arabs seem a physical manifestation of her dark passions, her Cuban blood. In her daydreams, Henry visits her body. You would love it here, she writes him during a stop in Marseilles en route to the Palais Jamaï in Fez. She describes the overwhelming smells and a visit to Fatima, the queen of the prostitutes—all to Henry's delight.

Fez, or Fès, the North African Florence of centuries ago, had been French-occupied, and Anaïs connects with both the language and what she calls her Moorish blood. She and Hugo check into the Palais Jamaï, a thirteenth-century palace later immortalized (under a different name) by Paul Bowles in *The Spider's House* (1955). Bowles captures (in this and other novels) the hypnotic quality of Fez, with its maze of streets, brass shops, date palms, and exotic heat and smells. Because her hotel is on the edge of the old city, Anaïs wanders through the streets hypnotized, vaguely aware that the worries of her mind have been put to sleep.[25]

On the journey home, she carries a velvet chest that will for years hereafter hold her current diary. At Cádiz, Granada, and Seville, past sites that remind her of her flight from Spain to New York in 1914, she looks in vain for the little lost girl abandoned by her father. She writes to tell Henry, "I wanted so much to see these with *you!*"[26] His letters, using Fraenkel's return address, assure her that Perlès will be out of the apartment by her return and that Fraenkel has left suddenly for London—promises that imply they will have the studio for more intimate hours.

After her return at the end of April, she records the descriptions from her letters into the journal. Because she left analysis and introspection behind with her journal, her verbal expression had flowered in her letters. Fez is veiled and labyrinthine, she declares, "an image of one's inner cities"—the first glimmer of the title of her future novel sequence (*Cities of the Interior*).[27] All these qualities, including the circuitous and mysterious, are for Anaïs akin to the singular nature of woman (she will later associate Fez with the womb)—a view of woman and her art in marked contrast to the view of Rebecca West and Virginia Woolf, who believe that the artist should have an androgynous mind.

In Paris she rewrites a long and lovely description of visiting a bathhouse with the Moroccan women, whose "beautiful faces" rise from "mountains of flesh," where she experiences the epiphany of washing the old dead flesh from her life. This incident will later be fictionalized in "Through the Streets of My Own Labyrinth," a story in which the protagonist gives herself up to the smells, sights, and experience of the city, aware that the "little demon of depression" that has been devouring her for twenty years is stilled. The "cancer of introspection" ceases its gnawing. As Anaïs walks from the bathhouse back through the labyrinthine streets (a metaphor she will use the remainder of her life), she believes she can completely abandon herself to the beauty of the day and, she adds, to the "pleasures of multiple relationships."[28] She does not wait long.

Her return from Fez had been to a dark and unhappy Paris littered with strikes and talk of war—and to the whooping cough. Eventually she finds a new doctor, Max Jacobson, who cures her physical problems. She does not know what his various shots and vitamins are (perhaps $B_{12}$, if not amphetamines), but he seems a miracle worker. Her energy rebounds. She will not learn the truth about "Dr. Feelgood" for many years, but until then she will depend on him.

Henry is going through what he calls an "air pocket" and shares his fears and frustrations with her—as if she were his wife, she notes. But the memory of the freedom of Fez will sustain her, as will the newly arrived bundles of *The House of Incest*, her second book. Siana Editions of 18, Villa Seurat has published 249 signed and numbered copies of *The House of Incest*, the second work issued under the direction of Fraenkel and printed in Bruges. The book is beautifully printed, only about a hundred words on each of the ninety large pages, the size of European notebook paper.

When Emil Schnellock reads this novella (and a prepublication copy of *The Winter of Artifice*), he writes to Henry (who has sent the books) that Anaïs is "moving out of the circumscribed and fastidious orbit" of her bourgeois Catholic family.[29] Her publisher (Kahane published the Siana Edition books) is not as impressed with her daring: "Kahane is furious about putting Anaïs' book over on him. (Really incomprehensible rage.) I haven't told Anaïs," Henry writes three years later to a friend.[30] Kahane, always looking for an erotic book that will sell well, had tumbled for her misleading title. Just so, the public will always unjustly conclude the same, that the book is erotic because of the title. The central image of the surrealistic novella means that the lover creates the loved one by projection, making narcissistic love an act of incest. If Kahane is angry, others are pleased. Stuart Gilbert writes to praise a "clairvoyance" that in earlier times would have had her burned at the stake. Anaïs collects all responses to the book, especially this one from Gilbert, an English critic and a friend and translator of James Joyce. His response will be published as a foreword to a 1974 reissue of the book. With Fez and the publication of *The House of Incest,* she has turned a corner. The change will be expressed, typically, in the decoration of a new apartment. She and Hugo move to 30, quai de Passy (now avenue du President Kennedy), on the Seine. Their departure from the apartment of Henry Leigh Hunt and Louise de Vilmorin may have been precipitated by Louise's break with Anaïs when she recognized her portrait as Isolina in *The House of Incest.*

Ever the creator of theatrical settings for her life, Anaïs works in the medium of home decor and living tableaux, which are then again transformed and enhanced in journal and fiction. Anaïs creates a new life. She senses the temporary nature of her creation, for she watches the strikes below in the streets. As the Seine flows beneath her balcony and the dark tides threaten Europe, she clings to art. Still, she signals this new life with a tropical housewarming party in late summer. The party setting is now her modern apartment overlooking the Seine. The apartment has orange walls, a seashell clock, tropical plants, a white wool rug from Morocco, and furniture of light oak and pine—all reminding her of the sands of the beach. She hires Tahitian singers, hangs orange paper lanterns, and invites all the interesting people in her life, including Stuart Gilbert and Conrad Moricand (both influential men she wants to meet), Henry Leigh Hunt, and René Allendy, who eyes the Tahitian girls. But towering above everyone, both physically and in her eyes, is her Inca god, who whispers words of love in Spanish in her ear as they dance: Gonzalo More.

## *Gonzalo More:* Nostalgie de la Boue

Anaïs had first heard of Gonzalo and Helba More at a lunch at the apartment of Roger Klein, a French artist and neighbor of Henry's. Another guest talked at length about this poor but extraordinary Peruvian couple. As Henry had once piqued her curiosity about June, so the talk by Klein, Henry, and others stimulated her imagination about the Mores. Soon she met the pale Helga and the swarthy Gonzalo. Anaïs had once seen Helba perform the dance of a woman without arms (an image she used at the end of *The House of Incest*). It was Gonzalo—tall and "black as a Negro" with long dark curly hair, high Indian cheekbones, and carrying a guitar—who made an impression on her. On the spot she invites them to her tropical party and begins an affair with Gonzalo.

After the tropical housewarming party, it is Gonzalo's whispered words of praise for her voice and style, her vision and fragility, that she records in her diary. Her attraction to Gonzalo is physical. He is uninhibited, explosive, and virile. He looks like Othello, one of her friends notes. What she calls her Spanish blood responds to his Scottish–Peruvian Indian blood. Her imagination is also aroused by his talk of the Inca culture. They speak Spanish together (his French is bad, his English little better), and he weaves tales of myth and poetry like a chanting Indian, making her think of Inca statues, mountain lakes, the smell of incense, and mating firebirds. Like June, he talks impulsively, feverishly, and flirts with destructive, irrational powers. And the power that claims him is alcohol, as drugs had claimed June. Helba, who had given up dancing when disease destroyed her hearing, is a hypochondriac, malnourished and neglected by Gonzalo. They live impulsively and on the edge of starvation, and Anaïs is drawn toward what she sees is the irresponsibility of the "artist" once again. Through them she can live her desire to be a dark and capricious gypsy. For years to come, she will claim that she is trying to balance their forces of creation and destruction, but in the absence of any evidence of their creativity, one can only conclude that her involvement is a kind of sexual slumming, *nostalgie de la boue.*

It is 1936 and Gonzalo is political, not literary; he is a Marxist, and Spain is on the brink of war. Thus Anaïs is soon drawn into the political arena, and for the first time in her life struggles with the tension between art and politics. Humanity will be saved by politics, not art, Gonzalo insists as he talks of sacrifice, death, and Karl Marx. Though not political at heart, and distrustful of economics, she is sensitive to people's struggles and, as one friend observed, could "resonate" with others.[31] Soon she declares that Henry has destroyed her bourgeois virtues and Gonzalo her art world.

Anaïs, who loves the silent polish of New York elevators and the silky caress of French lingerie, takes off her war paint for her Inca warrior. She removes her bright fingernail polish and goes with Gonzalo to a political rally where Pablo Neruda, "fat and very pale," she notes, recites his poetry. His verses of Chilean rage are a blend of Marx and surrealism. She goes with Gonzalo to Notre-Dame, where the heavy organ music and the purple light from the stained-glass windows touch her soul again and she weeps. Soon they are embracing in the night shadows of the cathedral. For a while, the Catholic, the pagan Incan, and the Marxist worlds of Gonzalo vividly contrast in her mind with what she believes is Henry's impersonal, passive, and bloodless world. Hugo's world does not even enter the comparison.

She calls her diary "drifting" this summer of 1936 when she struggles to maintain her several worlds—political, literary, cultural, familial—fearing the loss of any element. One day she is at the Villa Seurat for the arrival of the first copy of Henry's *Black Spring*, dedicated to her. The next day she visits the damp, filthy slum cellar flat near Denfer Rochereau occupied by Gonzalo and Helba and other revolutionaries. Another day the visits of her parents almost coincide at her elevator door: her "pathological" father ("clean as a Frigidaire"), visiting from Spain, meets her mother and Joaquin from Mallorca, leaving for an Italian concert tour. Anaïs has to console her weeping mother.[32] Though Anaïs complains about her own giving and others' selfishness, she needs the approval of them all. When Jonathan Cape, the London publisher, rejects "Lilith" ("The Winter of Artifice") she doubts the importance of her work. Though she has already offered it to Kahane, she also works with Denise Clairouin, a literary agent who wants to find a publisher for her diaries. She tells people she is no longer writing except in her diary, and visits Montmartre to consult with Conrad Moricand, a forty-nine-year-old French occultist whose horoscopes she characterizes as poems.

Though Eduardo and Hugo have long practiced astrology and "done the charts" of all their family and friends, Moricand reads the heavenly planets for a living and his advanced work quickens the interest of Anaïs, who introduces him to Henry and rounds up other customers so that Moricand can pay his rent. He does Henry's horoscope and makes a believer of him. Henry and, for a time, Anaïs, find comfort in studying the cosmos. Astrology, numerology, and the occult answer their need for unity and order. (Even Freud, suffering from migraine headaches and nasal infections, took cocaine treatments at times determined by numerology.) Eventually, Anaïs will reject these "sciences" because they deny the individual will. Yet the colorful (if not fraudulent) Moricand furnishes them each with a character for their fiction. Anaïs later writes the short story "The Mohican," a portrait of Moricand, from her diary, which describes him as looking like "a white Indian."

He studies charts, maps, and mythology all day in the library, but "Out of all his researches, his calculations, he extracted nothing but the poison of fatality." An "incurable dandy, living the life of a beggar," Henry calls him in *A Devil in Paradise,* written after Moricand visits California in 1947.[33]

The immediate future for Anaïs and for all of Moricand's customers lies in the events that will ultimately drive them from Europe: the political unrest in Spain and Germany. Yet amid the talk of war, Anaïs can see from her window the French construction crews laying the foundation for the 1937 World Exposition. The Villa Seurat is also a beehive of writing and publishing, its inhabitants oblivious to political events. Only with Gonzalo is she caught up in the political present. He takes her to communist rallies to hear La Pasionaria and André Malraux and to see the waving red banners. She vibrates to the rhythm of her emotions, but is unmoved by the clichéd political rhetoric. She will walk until dawn with Gonzalo, past hobos and ragpickers, but awaken the next morning to be served breakfast in bed by Janine the maid. On the tray are letters from the cured (or "freed") of New York, her former patients whom she calls "my children."

She does not fail to note that Gonzalo's world of "action" is belied by his failure to act. He has not left for Spain yet, runs the refrain of her diary. He walks around with a bottle of red wine in his pocket, occasionally attends drawing classes, and announces that he intends to make Anaïs class-conscious. When he takes her to the ragpickers' village, she records it in vivid detail in her journal and later rewrites it as the short story "Ragtime." When a friend returns from Spain with tales of terror, she weeps hysterically. She thinks of her grandmother Nin in Barcelona. She feels she is being asked to give up her life to the cause.

Her attraction to unstable friends stems both from her power of compassion and empathy and from her attraction to the world of the spirit and the clairvoyant, occupied by poets, dreamers, and madmen. Her intimacy with Helba includes shared confidences about Gonzalo ("He is a child") in the same way she talked to June about Henry. Though Anaïs describes Helba's shabby clothes, yellowed complexion, and pathetic theatrics, she also devotes long passages in her journal to Helba's story of physical abuse by nuns, of saving Gonzalo from the opium dens of Lima, their flight to Havana and New York City, Helba's successful Broadway career with Ziegfeld, and her many illnesses. One day after Anaïs rushes her to the hospital and serves as translator, she learns that Helba's father had died insane, perhaps from syphilis, that her mother was half crazy, and that Helba herself had contracted syphilis from her husband at fourteen and had been treated with injections of mercury—hence her deafness.

Anaïs had also seen Helba in her dancing glory. In the European Edition of the *Chicago Tribune* in 1931, Wambly Bald described her dancing as "sinister, revolutionary . . . as fluent as the prose poems of Gertrude Stein."[34] Her poetry and genius left when her dancing stopped. Now she lives a prosaic and homely life, depending on Gonzalo, and both of them depending on Anaïs, who feels put upon, yet needed. When she buys a tabletop printing press—she tells each man, Henry and Gonzalo, it is for him—only the diary hears that she has a greater need for it than they.[35] (As with her gift of a typewriter to Henry, neither man seems to be keenly interested in her gift.) She turns her self-pity into art in a lovely sustained analogy of watching a fish breathe in an aquarium. She watches the breathing belly of the fish with such Zen-like intensity that she fails to breathe for herself.

By the following year she finds the political ideologues stagnant and destructive, and the Mores unaesthetic. Gonzalo and Helba dress, indeed blow their noses, in rags because they cannot bring themselves to launder the growing pile of dirty clothes. Gonzalo, who mangles his native Spanish and knows little French, sleeps until noon, gets drunk in the Dôme café, and ignores his work. Anaïs may be attracted to destructive people, she observes, but she does not yield to their ways. She rolls up her sleeves and goes to work printing his political posters on the press she bought him. She could have printed a book in the months he has spent doing almost nothing for the Spanish Republican cause. Because her efforts are for an individual (Gonzalo), not a cause, she can move freely from the communists in rue de Lille, to a dirty movie theatre in Alesia with Henry, to tea with her stylish friends or coffee at the Deux Magots with André Breton. One friend, who knows only a few of her roles, calls her a chameleon. Sometimes she thinks she cannot stop living to write; she only has time to fill up her diary.

The anarchists also appear petty and paranoid. Jealous friends of Gonzalo will begin a whispering campaign at the Spanish embassy charging that Gonzalo is a fascist spy receiving money and a printing press from the daughter of an aristocrat. After testimony by Anaïs and Roger Klein (who had been wounded in Spain), Gonzalo is cleared of the charges but left disillusioned. Anaïs is banned from helping at the press or calling him. They continue to meet privately for sex, at first every other day, then twice a week, then once a week—as Helba's illness makes increasing demands on his time.

In the world of art and creation, she is still with Henry, who begins afresh this summer his *Tropic of Capricorn*, written, she says, "with sperm and blood." Out of their frequent talks come insights about her diary writing and her need for love and approval. Her diary answers her fear of loss and change. What is wrong with writing out of this neurosis? she asks Henry. After all, Proust wrote out of a neurotic need to remember and resuscitate the past. They read each other's manuscripts. She still admires his gargantuan appetites and manuscripts and wonders if she has "breathed meaning into the crowded streets" of his fiction. He is the only true surrealist, she concludes. When he reminds her that she was wrong to predict that women would like his fiction, she agrees that he de-poeticizes women. By the following spring she will openly attack his dehumanizing of women as only "an aperture." Gonzalo's troubadour romanticism woos her from Henry's lack of romanticism ("It is not enough just to take a woman in bed, you know," she tells Henry).[36]

At Henry's suggestion, she writes Frances Steloff at the Gotham Book Mart in New York City to promote her book, enclosing three copies of *The House of Incest* and saying she has sent subscription blanks to all her friends informing them that the book will be available at the Gotham.[37] Henry urges her to write more fiction; Gonzalo urges her to live more freely, then takes a near fatal overdose of heroin and is hospitalized. Anaïs nurses him as well as Helba, describing herself in images such as the Fates weaving cloth and sewing buttons as "the Mother of them all." To find a quiet place for herself, and a rendezvous for her liaisons, she goes shopping for one of her persistent dreams: a houseboat.

Unable to find renters for the Louveciennes house because there is no heat, Hugo allows the lease to lapse in the summer of 1936. They decide to auction the furnishings. When Anaïs arrives to find her curious neighbors gathered around her furniture and draperies, she feels violated. When they shake the drapes she thinks she hears the voices of Artaud, Allendy, Joaquin, Henry, and June. In a portion of the diary she suppresses at publication in 1967, she says: "I remembered mostly my passion for Henry, our caresses, the furnace of our talks."[38] Suddenly she enters the bidding and reclaims her Arabian bed, bookcases, and desk, which she puts in storage until she can find a houseboat. The end of the Louveciennes kingdom after six years is so traumatic that she does not describe it in her journal until late in November, when she calls it a "sacrifice" made in order to meet the needs of others. Saving that rent allows the Guilers to live at the elegant edge of the Seine, Miller in the Villa Seurat, and soon herself on a houseboat. She later admits to Lawrence Durrell that giving up Louveciennes, firing her Spanish maid, and selling the car were necessitated by their growing debt and Hugo's losses on the stock market.[39]

## Pisces on the Seine

She feels pulled toward the Seine along with the windblown leaves. From the top of the stone steps she glances down at the river, then descends the quiet quay, leaving the street noise behind. Hurrying past the tramps embracing their wine bottles and a lone fisherman holding a long pole before him, she mounts the gangplank and boards the water-stained boat, surrounded by its line of clinging moss. This scene opens her short story "Houseboat."

During the third week of September 1936, Anaïs, born under the sign of the fish, takes possession of half a houseboat. She had once dreamed of a houseboat after visiting Maupassant's house in Etretat. In 1930, she had written "Waste of Timelessness," about a woman's discovery in the garden of a boat (used as a tool house) where she spends the night and dreams of sailing away from her husband. Anaïs is reenacting the short story (and her own dream), for the houseboat is an escape from her marital apartment. It is also a place to meet her new lover, Gonzalo, who has no private room of his own. He calls the boat "Nanankepichu," an Inca name meaning "not at home." Like her diary, the boat takes her out of time and space, unifying her with the flow of the water.

The houseboat is moored at the quai des Tuileries near Pont Royal, across from the Gare d'Orsay, whose enormous clock face presides over her assignations and lovemaking. She shares the boat with a one-legged alcoholic "captain" and an orphan named René who does the heavy work. She rents the wooden studio, with bedroom, built atop the lower rooms of what was once half of a coal barge. Because it has windows on three sides and a portion of the roof, she calls it a "glass studio," in the first of several fictional touches. The tar walls, green mildew, gangplank (she calls it a drawbridge), and heavy anchor chain make it her medieval castle. The Byzantine lamp casts magic patterns on the tiny bedroom walls. Her descriptions of the houseboat in her diary, and later in the story "Houseboat," emphasize romantic details: lapping water, heaving sway, creaking beams, sunlight in the window. Even the leaking roof, the mildew, and the tramps sleeping under the bridge (Moricand gives her a revolver for protection) add to the romantic adventure on this "island of joy."

"As soon as I was inside of the houseboat, I no longer knew the name of the river or the city. . . . Every time I inserted the key in the lock, I felt this snapping of cords, this lifting of anchor, this fever of departure."[40] She admits to her diary in October that she creates an "illusory paradise . . . by selecting only the high moments" for both her life and her diary, thus holding off mundane reality. She will live by her own "selections," choosing the dream over reality without question. "Facts are destructive," she had said years before.[41] Even the imagery suggests she would prefer to stay inside Plato's cave, looking at illusory shadows:

> At night I closed the windows which overlooked the Quays. As I leaned over I could see dark shadows walking by, men with their

collars turned up and their caps pushed over their eyes. . . . The street lamps high above threw no light on the trees and bushes along the big wall. It was only when the window rustled that the shadows which seemed to be one shadow split into two swiftly and then, in silence, melted into one again.[42]

"We [her several selves] are on the ship of our dreams, alone," she says at the end of September. "Three lives. Three homes. Three loves."[43] This floating world is not bound to the earth of the husband who pays the rent on the boat or on the chairs she rents when Gonzalo invites Pablo Neruda (nicknamed "Yogurt," for his sallow color) and his fellow Latin communists to a political planning session on board. "I have no use for capitalism," she writes to a friend. Yet her banker husband's money pays the anarchist's rent.[44]

No theorist, Gonzalo is anti-intellectual, anti-cultural, and opposed to analysis. He reads little. All he and Anaïs seem to have in common is sex and their Spanish blood and language, something she is rediscovering. His dark irrational nature touches that same vein in Anaïs that June tapped. He is the swarthy man, "baked *à point* . . . born of the potter's third lot," she will say, capturing their racial difference for her short story "The Child Born Out of the Fog."[45] She is imaginatively engaged by his Marxism, though she feels it is naive and utopian, for she believes no system can change human nature. He is a political anarchist, she a "spiritual" anarchist. Certainly another reason for her involvement with the Mores is her need to nurture; she believes that they would starve without her. She briefly considers breaking into her father's closed house (he has now moved to Spain) for their use.

If she sees a light in the bedroom of the houseboat, she tosses a stone onto the roof so that Gonzalo will come to lead her from the dark street to warm safety. He unties her shoes, rolls her stockings down, and kisses her feet before taking her on the floor or the bed, rocking the boat with his kisses. "In the dark they gave each other their many selves, avoiding only the more recent ones," she says in one of her novels. They rock the boat so fervently one night that the little red lantern falls on the floor and the glass breaks.[46] Though she usually leaves in time to catch the last bus around midnight, this night she sleeps until five-thirty, untangles her body from Gonzalo's arms, and reaches her room at home by 6 A.M. without being discovered. Descriptions of such scenes fill each diary volume.

Anaïs, like Miller, transforms everything and everybody into art. There are long passages on Gonzalo's Peruvian childhood in the diary, passages she will later use for a novel (*The Four-Chambered Heart*) about herself, Gonzalo, Helba, and life on the houseboat. After a meal at Helba's apartment, at which Helba wears a brooch without any stones remaining in it, Anaïs reads her description of the occasion to Henry. Later when he recalls the empty-brooch image, she asks him not to "steal it," for she needs it for her Helba portrait. He assures her he will not, yet he writes down the image.

Henry remains her only literary soul mate, "sly, humorous . . . mellow," in comparison to Gonzalo's political fanaticism. Lao-tse Miller, she calls him. He is the only one who is interested in her writing.[47] Occasionally, if not frequently, Henry and others visit the boat for lovemaking. In an erotic story she writes several years later, a character named Mandra (as in mandrake) lives on a houseboat and makes love to many different visitors, including an anonymous Arab.[48] Anaïs is living in several worlds and in several languages because she needs "abundance," she says. She keeps the traffic moving in part to remain "Anaïs Nin" and not "amalgamate" herself into any one person's orbit.[49]

The ecstasy of her life on the boat and her engagement in Gonzalo's political realities stimulates her writing, specifically the creative portion of her diary—from vivid descriptions of poverty to poetic images of the flowing river. She is also copying her diary for the agent Denise Clairouin, reading Pierre-Jean Jouve's poetic-psychological novels, and reviewing the manu-script of Henry's *Tropic of Capricorn*. The novel finally provokes an outcry from Anaïs against Henry's "great anonymous, depersonalized fucking world. Instead of investing each woman with a different face," she complains, "you take pleasure in reducing all women to a biological sameness."[50]

In the same letter she accuses him of living in a crowd. His celebrity and growing circle of friends do, however, bring new associations for Anaïs. Henry takes her to supper at the apartment of Betty Ryan, then a twenty-one-year-old American painting student who is living on the ground floor at 18, Villa Seurat (the painter Chaïm Soutine lives opposite her). "She had a delicate frame and large, liquidy eyes," says a friend who remembers the dust of her white face powder on her gray flannel suit and silk shirt; "she was a poor little rich girl" who had lived freely for several years and possessed a "poetic way of narrating a story."[51] Betty is a good friend of the local artists, and her stories about Greece provoke Henry's interest. At first Betty does not know about the "arrangement" between Henry and Anaïs, but she soon begins to figure it out. She remembers this supper and Anaïs, who is eleven years older than she, as very glamorous the evening they met:

> [Anaïs] was wearing a black lace dress with flounced skirt and long fuzzy black eyelashes. Her voice was thin and monotone. Her conversation was documented and analytical. Her person

was resplendent, captivating. Yet, as she talked on, I caught a callow note which made me feel oddly old, more experienced in the way the world is than she. As I knew Anaïs better, I noticed that she was always alarmingly lucid. She planned and she achieved. She husbanded time. I doubt if she indulged . . . in lost hours. . . .

Henry also takes Anaïs to meet Hans Reichel, a German painter who is giving him art lessons in his nearby studio. She is quite taken with Reichel's work and thinks she grasps the eye motif in his paintings. When she and Henry are walking back to No. 18 afterward, he tells her that she will describe the studio in her diary and he wants to read what she writes. She later transforms her diary portrait into "The Eye's Journey" for her short-story collection *Under a Glass Bell*. This verbal portrait of Reichel's paintings is surrealistic and full of floating eyes, unlike the more naturalistic verbal portraits she does of others to whom Henry introduces her.

Having heard from Anaïs about the paintings of Reichel, Hugo rings the bell at Betty Ryan's studio one day in October 1936 to see the Reichel exhibit on her walls. As per instruction, before answering the door, she taps on the heat pipe to notify Anaïs and Henry, who lower their voices in the apartment above. It is Anaïs's weekly overnight at the Villa Seurat, and Betty can always hear them reading their manuscripts to each other through the paper-thin walls. After Hugo views the Reichel paintings, he invites Betty for a drink at Café Zeyer without a word about the Villa Seurat "arrangement." Betty is fascinated by the intrigue:

> I saw her life as an embroidery of secrets, a series of separate elaborated patterns without connecting thread. In fact it came to light that Anaïs was expert at stitching and by her needle helped to fund the various isolated pockets of her Paris existence. She would copy for her own use a dress created by a prestigious Paris couturier like Patou and charge Patou prices to household accounts, an aid in meeting Miller's rent, the cost of piano lessons for her younger brother Joaquin, rent for her mother who was lodged in a dismal, diminutive apartment with a good address.[52]

When Anaïs is not around, Betty Ryan is sexually involved with Henry (as she had been with Soutine)—a fact she will acknowledge only years later. Though she believes that Henry will eventually marry her, he may be keeping her on his second string.[53] She now remembers Henry telling her about his debt to Anaïs: "I shall stand by Anaïs until she is on her own feet. I am deeply in debt to her. I feel bound hand and foot."[54] Whatever his intentions, she was well liked by his circle: "We were all in love with her though she was *untouchable*," says Perlès mistakenly. She had the face and bearing of a Madonna.[55]

Soon Hugo is taking weekly painting lessons with Reichel. His interest in art began, he later explained, when he watched the smoke smudges appear on a piece of paper he moved around over a candle flame. He moved from "candle drawing" to charcoal drawing, and now painting. But his black-and-white drawings will eventually lead him to an engraving career.[56]

Many of Henry's friends become carefully drawn portraits in her diary this winter. She is trying to move away from the diary pulse-taking, for she has concluded (temporarily) that the diary is a feminine activity. Stuart Gilbert and Denise Clairouin, who read some of the diaries, tell her that she will probably not get them published: too natural, too naked, they explain (and their predictions will hold true for thirty years). She draws character sketches of Conrad Moricand and Jean Carteret, the latter an astrologer with pale, penetrating eyes. The artists' characters, studios, and party conversations come alive in her hands.

"She collects numerous 'children,' Carteret, Moricand, Gonzalo and Helba," giving away her "vital power," says Sharon Spencer, a friend of Nin's later years.[57] She collects many wounded people, including a troubled Brazilian painter whom she counsels for several months before urging her to go to Carl Jung.[58] So fascinated is she by interesting and troubled people, all of whom seem to need her, that she is blinded by their eccentricities. Carteret, whose portrait becomes the short story "The All-Seeing," is a "wretched charlatan," declares Henry, who cannot understand how Anaïs could be taken in by him. Later she admits to Henry that she does not dare to "see the other side" of people or she cannot love them. She fears betrayal in herself as well as others.[59] Ironically, her fear of rejection leads her to dismiss people suddenly and cruelly. "She was one of those hot-blooded vendetta-loving Spanish women with the memory of a baby elephant," says David Gascoyne, the British poet, who took part of her manuscript to England while he continued typing it for her, not understanding that she would be upset. He also says that she was theatrical and picturesque "in the Moorish decor with which she surrounds herself, the 'barbaric' jewelry, the incense-burning, the glass tree, the other exotic stage properties that she required in order to convince herself that she is leading an intensely interesting 'inner life.'"[60]

A mutual friend of Carteret's and Anaïs's, and one as interested in astrology as they, remembers Anaïs's desire to please in astrological terms: "For me, Anaïs was a Libra, always trying to please and to charm . . . sometimes aggressively so. She was most generous and giving of herself, but if one tried

to get hold of her or be aggressive, watch out!" One day in the late 1950s
the three of them were to dine in Paris and the two French friends asked
Anaïs to chose the restaurant. "She could only ask what we wanted. She wa
tortured because she did not know what she wanted. She could only
please."[61]

## Woman as Artist

During one of her overnights with Henry, in March of 1937, the lamplight
and stove are hot with light and warmth. He paints watercolors and she
writes to Lawrence Durrell, a young man who has just turned twenty-five
and will become the closest to being an adopted child of their own. She
writes in superlatives about the manuscript for Durrell's novel *The Black
Book.*[62] Durrell sends his only copy of the manuscript to Henry, saying, "I
you think it stinks, throw it into the Seine."[63] Anaïs writes back that she
would throw her own book into the Seine first. They have not yet met thi
young Anglo-Irish-Indian writer living in Corfu, but Henry has corresponded
with him for more than a year since receiving a fan letter about *Tropic o
Cancer.* She and Durrell have been corresponding since January, in response
to Henry's exchange of their work. Her letters are full of enough superlatives
to make the most eager author blush. He has high praise for *The House o
Incest,* calling it "iridescent," and "insightful and poetic." When he calls the
title "silly," she agrees and suggests she is going to change it. She copies hi
letters of praise ("MARVELOUS. ABSOLUTELY MARVELOUS") into he
diary. Though he has reservations about her "organic form"—his euphemism
for formlessness—she seems not to grasp his implication. Her letters to
Durrell over these nine months before he comes to Paris are filled with artfu
and thoughtful ideas about writing (writing for her is akin to swimming with
fins, she says). His wit and admiration for her work seem to inspire fine and
insightful writing from her.[64]

Her art and love life flourish in Hugo's absence. When Hugo takes an
administrative position in the London office of City Bank and Farmers Trust
she does not consider moving to England. He will come for weekends at th
quai de Passy apartment. He sometimes seems to thrive on her coldness
she observes. Respectfully, she has always given him a reasonable excuse fo
her own absences—a trip to the country home of Caresse Crosby, a part
out of town for Kay Boyle (though Anaïs has not met either writer). Hugo
wants to believe. Determined not to lose her, he reluctantly lives with he
freedom. She needs it for her art. He is proud to have an artistic wife, and
he is generous with her allowance.

"Life is a dance," she writes in January; "Life comes to a climax, a
orgasm," she writes in February; in March her days "burst almost from

fullness and richness." Even in August she is calling for heavy objects on her head and feet to keep her from leaving the ground and floating away.[65] Though she is happy and protected (some of Henry's friends never meet her) as she moves among her three homes and loves, she is never in the center of any literary coterie.[66] Yet this spring she meets several leading literary lions, including Stuart Gilbert and Eugene Jolas—both closely linked to James Joyce. The Gilberts entertain the Guilers in their apartment on Ile St. Louis; he tells her that she writes emotionally about herself, but with irony and humor about others. Eugene Jolas, the multinational editor of *transition* magazine, whose pages she and Henry have been devouring, comes to visit her and talk to her about his "language of the night." In 1939 he will publish a fragment of her *House of Incest* in his *transition*.

The words of her several men—Miller, Gilbert, and Durrell—make her more conscious of writing as a woman. Durrell tells her she has a sensibility different from male writers. She concludes that she writes from a real womb, and man fabricates his womb. Her "feminine" diary differs from "masculine alchemy." The weakness of Henry's realism is a fear of the extraordinary, the mysterious, the marvelous. The weakness of psychoanalysis is that it fails to account for the creative end of escape and of neurosis. The weakness of surrealism is that it is rational and calculated, a product of the mind, and she wants dreams, poetry, fantasy. Sitting in a café, she swallows its noises and records that she feels "divorced from man's world of ideas."[67] She is womb; she swims in nature. When Durrell writes that she is "the submarine superwoman," she agrees, adding that because she had tried to "think like a man," it took her "many years to recover [her] fins" and her "swimming strides."[68]

The snags in the current ahead are her own personal needs, which dissipate her creative energies. She senses her own lurking anxieties arising like the floodwaters of the Seine: her fear of the "monster" (loss of love), debts that necessitate visits to the pawnshop, and the irrational behavior of several of her unstable friends. One day in the spring of 1937, when the river is swollen and threatening, she lowers herself from the wall by rope ladder, dropping the current volume of her diary into the bottom of the rowboat that is to take her to the houseboat. The diary is soaked, the houseboat a mess, and water is seeping through the floor. She awakens the morning of 4 March realizing that she has already spent her month's allowance on her "orphans." She is still feeding Gonzalo and Helba and paying Henry's rent, though he has now received his first royalty payment for *Cancer*. By summer she concludes that she is trying to support too many "children" because she is a Pisces, "the giver," and charity gives her pleasure. "Because the father failed you. . . . You cannot depend on others. You prefer to be depended on," says The Voice to Lilith in *The Winter of Artifice*.[69] The nurturing mother role also secures love and keeps at bay the monster of abandonment.

Despite the distractions, she writes voluminously in the diary, going through a new volume (300–368 pages each) every two or three months. The diary has become a different medium: once a disease and her only means of communication, it is now a receptacle of her "abundance" in describing others. The outside world has crowded out some of the introspection. Because Faber and Faber inform Denise Clairouin this summer that they cannot "shape" the diary "into book form," Anaïs continues to cull short stories and "novels" from her diary descriptions. She is writing the best short stories of her life and seriously evaluating the differences between the diary and fiction.

The diary is more truthful, she believes, because it records changing and conflicting aspects and moods, whereas fiction selects details for a theme. Thus, she wonders if in her fiction she has been unfair to her father in her focus on one aspect of their relationship. Though it is common for an abused child to question her own charges against her father, this moment of doubt serves to reveal a basic difference in her two genres: the diary is "closer to the truth"; the novel is "an act of injustice." She will call her diary "sinicuik," a Mexican drug which helps recall the past.

Yet the diary is also ordered. In a later argument with Miller and Durrell about distance and objectivity as opposed to the immediate "faithfulness" of the diary, she fails (and they fail) to account for her talent for immediately distancing herself in her writing. Since the age of eleven she has cultivated the selecting and ordering of her daily experience. Today's careful reader of her diary can see the selecting and highlighting as she records.

Following this brief questioning of her fairness to her father, she explains an aspect of her character that comes in part from her abandonment: "I have a growing obsession with order," she admits, then describes the order of her papers, medicines, and clothes.[70] Her incomplete explanation of this obsession is that order helps her to think clearly, it makes her serene. She does not acknowledge her fear of losing control of her life.

She sits before her desk with a very large bound volume of blank pages— a new diary from Henry. As she touches the first blank page, she realizes she can leave it open on the desk now that Hugo has been transferred to London. This new diary volume has a large canvas as befits her broad life, running between Villa Seurat, "the Shangri-la of literature," and *Nanan-kepichu*, the Indian drug of poetry. On these pages she will record a kiss in a taxi, the abrupt cessation of an intense moment, the sound of a taxi door closing, the look of the pimp at a café table, and her sensation of feeling like a prostitute awaiting the brutality of a man. She thinks of the masculine thrusts of Henry and Gonzalo and of feminine clitoral stimulations. She is seeking depth and intimacy and "some impossible communion." Is she living too intensely? with too many fusions? she wonders. She has accused Henry of being unable to live except impersonally and in groups; yet she needs many loves. "What is it that annihilates the loneliness?" she asks revealingly. She cannot find in one person what she calls her fusion or "penetration of the soul."[71]

Her dissimilar worlds occasionally threaten to bump into one another, especially after July when the owner sells the houseboat and she is forced to give it up after less than ten months' residence. One day in the Bois, her father's elegantly dressed mother-in-law chooses not to recognize Anaïs, who is sitting with the shabbily dressed Helba. Earlier, when Gonzalo's drawings were to be shown in a gallery in rue de Seine, Anaïs begged her mother for a suit that the violinist David Nixon had donated to Rosa's Red Cross clothing drive for Franco's Spain. Anaïs is standing outside the gallery with Gonzalo, when Rosa approaches with Nixon. Gonzalo flees, for Nixon would have recognized his suit, and the Catholic Rosa would have smelled a Republican.

Anaïs believes that she has rescued Gonzalo from his hobo existence and restored his pride and masculinity by setting him up with the printing press in a tiny office in rue de Lille where another radical group dedicated to "Peace and Democracy" is housed. She foresees his independence and leadership, and he informs her that she is like the sixteenth-century virgin he has always loved. With printing orders coming in and Helba's health improving, Anaïs can again turn to her own work. Sometime later Helba confides in her that Gonzalo has neither bought paper nor learned how to run the press.

Despite the depletion of her energies by the Mores, it appears that her counterpoint of lovers (and the diversity of their worlds) stimulates her creativity in the latter half of this decade. The number of excellent short stories—specifically "Birth" and "Houseboat"—and the volume of her diaries certainly suggest this.

## Three Musketeers

At the Gare de Lyon train station on a foggy morning, Anaïs and Hugo meet the train carrying Larry and Nancy Durrell. Anaïs is carrying a copy of Otto Rank's *Art and Artist* as a welcoming gift.[72] They all like each other immediately. Anaïs feels she has known Durrell forever. She describes his short, stocky body as soft and ferocious and his attitude as half laughing boy, half cautious old man; he is as athletic as a fawn, and poetic.

He thinks she is "thrilling" and dramatic; she had helped Henry type Durrell's *Black Book* and wants to collaborate with Henry in getting it published. She is nine years older than he and seems so much more experienced. "I was an embryo," he will say years later. "I was a virgin. I didn't know how to write. I didn't know how to think. I didn't know how to make love."[73]

> Anaïs was very industrious and pious, but she had a sense of mischief—the best women do. She was a diva and came from a family of divas. They were all stars. Her father and brother were great pianists. They had a personal style that goes with grand presentation. She really had no right to get married. She belonged in a studio.[74]

He treats her as he would an older sister, and she compares him to her brother Joaquin. "We used to compare our semi-incestuous relationship with Stendal's Sanseverina [who half loved and promoted her young nephew]" he says.[75] He likes Hugo, whom he describes as a shy person who looks like an Esquire Man. "Hugo was cultivated, rather a tender, gentle man . . . who looked like Gary Cooper." Soon Durrell concludes that Anaïs remains married to the man who, Henry says, is "without ecstasy," because she needs his protection and because he will never contradict her.[76]

Durrell is thrilled to be visiting the Villa Seurat (he and Nancy stay briefly in Betty Ryan's apartment while she is in Capri), which he had imagined as being like the Walt Disney Studio, with Henry sitting amid a hundred typewriters. Their discussions are a turning point in Anaïs's evolution as an artist. They discuss the creative process and the delicate differences between the male and female artist. In response to these discussions, Anaïs articulates a view of herself as an artist that will inform all her later work.

When Henry and Larry tell her to "break the cord" and leap out of the womb and into objectivity and distance, she calls them "impersonal" and out of touch with nature and the human experience. Henry says the artist should wait outside an experience before writing; Larry insists that the artist must "rewrite Hamlet" before indulging in formlessness and personality. When they accuse her of the "personification of ideas," she claims Proust does this as well, and that they cheat by intellectualizing and universalizing their own feelings. In other words, their impersonal pose merely masks the personal. When they say "I am God" in order to create, she assumes they really mean "I am not a woman."[77]

She argues for replacing the world of phalluses with the womb and life flow. Creation should be like creating children, and her art will come from flesh and blood, from her womb. We are "bound" and "interdependent," she insists, and the impersonal means loneliness. She calls impersonality the English "snow disease."[78]

Her views foreshadow many opinions of fifty years later about how women learn and relate. She holds her ground in their discussions until they finally affirm that she is a real artist—at least a real woman artist. Larry tells her not to allow them to run over her. She has no intention of doing so. In an echo of Virginia Woolf, she writes that the woman artist must separate herself from the myths that man has made of and for the woman.

Arguing with Henry and Larry helps her to reconcile in part her own struggle with the differences between male and female, between creative and nurturing. What emerges in her position is a call for the "wholeness" of the artist, by which she means a recognition of the artist's feminine, intuitive side. She points out the discrepancies in their distant god/male artist assumptions. She sees that Henry is useless with his hands, impractical, occasionally paralyzed by phobias, escapes into sleep, and is given to dissipating his talents with tomfoolery and slapstick. Gonzalo would throw down his life for an idea but is unable to act. When he tries to he is messy and destructive. When André Breton, the leader of the French surrealists, comes to visit her, she is enormously disappointed in his lack of adventure and the contrivance of his technique: it is all intellectual, timid, sterile ideas (not sensations); it is pontificating, not listening. She will not be called a disciple of surrealism, or wish she were a man.

Anaïs works on her story entitled "Chaotica" (later "The Voice") from October 1937 to March of 1938. With Otto Rank as her model, she writes about a "modern priest . . . a substitute for God, for the confessor of old . . . listening to the unfaithful lying on the divan." This "soul detective" is short, dark-skinned, round-faced, with a heavy cigar and a serious face—every detail matches Rank. He is counseling four troubled people: Djuna, Lillian, Mischa, and Lilith, yet he himself is in need of help. He talks of giving up his analytical practice to "begin a new life." The story opens with a description of Hotel Chaotica, a "Babel tower" of "voices of the world," a "convent of adulteries" and confessions (called "concerts"). Into the stories of the four analysands, all crippled and sexually dysfunctional, she places elements of the stories of herself, her two brothers, and those she has counseled.[79]

Anaïs's short story entitled "The Paper Womb" (later published as "The Labyrinth") appears in the December 1937/January 1938 issue of *The Booster*, called the "Special Peace and Dismemberment Number with Jitterbug-Shag Requiem." Her story appears alongside Henry's "The Enormous Womb" (an echo of *The Enormous Room*, by e. e. cummings), Larry's "Down the Styx in an Air-Conditioned Canoe," and Dylan Thomas's "Prologue to an Adventure." Her story begins, "I was eleven years old when I walked into the labyrinth of my diary." The "carpet of pages" and "stairway of words" have no numbers, for she intends to insert later the "much" that is "left out" of her "confessions." Though a psychological study, rather than a narrative, the piece is full of visual surrealistic imagery. The prevailing impression is claustrophobic.

Fred had highjacked *The Booster*, whose is title reminiscent of Sinclair Lewis's *Babbitt* (1922), from the American Country Club of Paris. He is given free reign as editor of the house publication as long as he publishes the club's golf scores and social notes. With the encouragement of Henry, who with Larry Durrell serves as literary editor, Fred turns it into the "house organ" of the Villa Seurat. Nancy Myers Durrell is art editor. Michael Fraenkel is in charge of the department of metaphysics and metempsychosis. Hilaire Hiler is travel editor. Bill Saroyan lends his name to the staff roster. And so it goes. Not surprisingly the American Country Club withdraws its support after the second issue appears, for it contains Durrell's story of a man swallowed by the vagina of a beautiful girl.

This issue of *The Booster* is the fourth and last issue edited by Fred Perlès before he changes its name to *Delta* and Durrell assumes financial responsibility for it in April 1938. Though Anaïs is listed as society editor, she thinks little of the silly endeavor, which reminds her of "Henry's atmosphere of begging, stealing, cajoling, school-boy pranks, slap-stick humor, burlesque."[80] By the time her story appears in the journal, she has disassociated herself from the editorial board. Miller will claim that during the nearly two years that the Durrells were in and out of Paris, Anaïs never participated in their "riotous soirées," for she was not a drinker and "loathed vulgarity and boisterousness."[81]

Beyond the warm and playful world of Villa Seurat, clashing armies threaten Europe. Gonzalo brings news of this world to the life and diary of Anaïs. Though she cannot believe in his communist cure for world problems, he sensitizes her to the suffering around her. In a socially conscious entry in the diary she speaks of going to a movie with Fred and Henry and viewing a scene in which police shoot demonstrators. She is pained—"profoundly disturbed," she says at one point—but believes that injustice and cruelty are "inherent in man" and to focus on the individual struggle, as she does, is to understand the universal struggle. She is destined to live the "drama of feeling and imagination," not the "dramas of Spain"—the first indeed underlines the second. She chooses both the personal and the longer view: she is recording a "thousand years of womanhood . . . a thousand women." It would be too simple to lose herself in the world drama of men's wars.[82]

She reworks "Chaotica" ("The Voice"), which will be published in *The*

*Winter of Artifice,* hoping to submit it to T. S. Eliot at *The Criterion.* (Eventually part of it appears as "Mischa and the Analyst" in *Seven,* a London journal.) She also rewrites the diary volume (the forty-fifth volume!) about New York with Henry, her last visit with Rank, and the trip to Fez, adding material in a process she compares to putting "closed [flower] buds in water." She shifts metaphors to describe the "bonfire of words" that flows out on the page, making her feel that she is sitting on the "tip of minarets."[83]

During this period from August 1937 to May 1938, the Durrells, when they are not spending extended periods at his family home in England, escape what he calls the Dôme café circus to have coffee and long intimate talks at the Guiler apartment. They sit on pillows on the floor until all is dark around them and the lights of Paris flicker beyond the balcony. She shows him her diary, into which she has pasted his letters, and he is flattered as well as relieved when he sees what she is writing about him. She says he "danced around" with pleasure, yet on second thought, later this fall, he asks her not to write about him.

Durrell could be the literary child of Henry and me, she notes. He likes Henry's hardness, but can empathize with her. (Durrell said as much, in an interview just four months before he died: "I was really invented by them in some way because I was so young. . . . They gave birth to me.") When they meet, he is twenty-five, Anaïs is thirty-four, and Henry is forty-five, though Anaïs thinks that Durrell seems older than Henry. He is at least grateful that she does not treat him as a youth. For a while she appropriates the Durrells, for Henry is absorbed in writing *Tropic of Capricorn*—"writing like a maniac about sex," as she puts it. Because she does not have an affair with Durrell (he had too much respect for Henry), they probably (he believes) have a closer relationship. "I was very young and I wanted to learn as much as I could . . . I did not present any problem. I did not have any fixed views on things."[84]

Sometimes, of course, they are all together, calling themselves the "Three Musketeers of La Coupole." At the Villa Seurat with Nancy, it is four, with her cooking. The Durrells stay in rented apartments, or at the Guilers (for Hugo is in London at the First National Bank office), or at the apartment of Rosa and Joaquin when they are away. The latter arrangement, at the insistence of Anaïs, is clandestine.[85] The Three Musketeers write about one anothers' works: Henry publishes his essay on Anaïs's diary ("Un Etre Etoilique") in the October 1937 issue of T. S. Eliot's *Criterion.* It is an essay that Durrell said was the "best description of her and her spiritually that has ever been written. . . . He paid her back the best way he could."[86] Anaïs's essay (in French) extolling Henry's *Black Spring* is published in the November 1937 issue of *The Booster,* edited by her.[87] They both praise Durrell's

*Black Book,* which will be published by Kahane's Obelisk Press. Henry's *Scenario,* based on *The House of Incest,* is printed in the fall, prompting Anaïs to predict, accurately as it turns out, that more people would read this parody pastiche than the original. She collects two hundred francs from Stuart Gilbert with the plan to publish books by the Musketeers.[88] Henry collects subscriptions (the first from André Maurois) to get her diaries (by now fifty-four volumes) published, but nothing comes of it. They are one for all and all for one ("we would have gone through fire for each other!" said Durrell), though they could not have been more different in style, philosophy, and art. The only things they seem to share beyond their fondness for each other are a sense of revolt against the traditional literary establishment and the prophecy of a new world: Henry called it "China," Anaïs called it "self," and Durrell called it the "Heraldic Universe." According to one critic, their means of attaining the new world also differed: Anaïs would destroy time through "dreamlike autoanalysis"; Henry, through Rabelaisian accounts of street life; and Larry, through "reconstruction in language of metaphysical speculation and sexual curiosity."[89]

When Henry suggests that Anaïs edit one of the last volumes of *The Booster* on "women's writing," she knows few women writers to call on, and the issue produced turns on the theme of the womb, with work by the Musketeers. There had long been an outstanding group of women on the Left Bank, but Anaïs had never sought them out. Edith Wharton, who had just turned seventy-five and was now living in the country, was certainly too daunting. Natalie Barney also belonged to another generation, and there is almost no evidence that Anaïs was involved in the salons of either Barney or Gertrude Stein, though one friend claims to have seen Nin at a Stein gathering.[90] Surprisingly, Anaïs is not included in the readings by the Friends of Shakespeare and Company (organized by Gide), though Sylvia Beach must have known she spoke French. She had once met Kay Boyle, who published in *transition* and was only a year older than she, but found Boyle "glossy and impersonal." Jean Rhys, the English novelist, had returned home. Anaïs had seen Nancy Cunard, the English heiress who had owned Hours Press in the 1920s, but described her as "skeletonic," with "over-ripe wrinkled olive skin. I could not imagine her in bed." She nevertheless admired Cunard for her fight for blacks, but did not pursue her acquaintance. Nor did she visit Colette, whose writing she loved. She tried only to contact Djuna Barnes, the New York writer whose *Nightwood* is the "most beautiful thing I have read about women, and women in love."[91] Barnes refused to acknowledge the letter, lending weight to Anaïs's sense of feeling excluded from women's literary avant-garde circles. She never forgets her ignored fan letter.

She does work with two women. Dorothy Norman, visiting from New York, accepts "Birth" and "Woman in Creation" for her *Twice a Year* periodical ("Birth" appeared in the fall issue of 1938). And Denise Clairouin remains her agent and friend, succeeding at the end of the year in getting Maxwell Perkins at Scribner's to read the early diaries. When he asks for an abridgment, Anaïs attempts once again unsuccessfully to cut the diaries. Among the other women she mentions are Renati Bugatti, a musician who terrifies men but exhilarates her, and Lila Ranson, a writer who ushers Anaïs into her bedroom to meet her female lover, "a replica of June." Anaïs is intrigued by their caresses and declarations of love for each other and stays all afternoon, fascinated and unnerved by the scene. She leaves with a better understanding of Don Juan's desire for the newness of love, she claims in her diary. Finally, there is Helba, whom Anaïs sets up in a new and airy apartment that quickly becomes a cluttered mess.

## Rumors of War

Early in 1938 Anaïs is sitting in the Café Flore waiting for Gonzalo. The Flore, just a few steps from place St.-Germain-des-Pres, was once the hangout of André Breton and his surrealist colleagues and will become in the 1940s the office and clubhouse of Simone de Beauvoir, Jean-Paul Sartre, and the existentialists. Anaïs is reading a newspaper with news of the Spanish Civil War and imagining some violent end to Gonzalo, whose arrival at the café is long overdue. She and his wife, Helba, often think Gonzalo's life is endangered (Helba had once tried to stab Anaïs with a hat pin for inspiring him to dangerous grandstanding). Anaïs feels very alone in a dark world. Artaud has just been locked up in the insane asylum of St.-Anne, and Henry is out of touch in his own moment of delirium, writing *Tropic of Capricorn*. When the news finally arrives at midnight that Gonzalo is ill in bed, she leaves the café with a sense of relief, walks past the Deux Magots and across the cobblestone plaza, where a burning car symbolizes the general madness of the times. Inside the Church of St.-Germain, she pauses briefly in a habit of gratitude for Gonzalo's safety. As she leaves, the firemen are extinguishing the car fire.

Several times she meets friends, with or without Gonzalo, at the Flore this winter. She talks to Jean Carteret, who is being analyzed by Allendy, and to Conrad Moricand about astrology and madness—the Left Bank is abuzz with news of Artaud's incarceration. Both Moricand, who is writing a book about madness, and Carteret continue to read the stars and to construct horoscopes. Her own neurosis, Anaïs concludes, is her obsessive need to abandon herself and identify with others, to whom she gives everything she has.

Hans Reichel and Betty Ryan make their way across Paris from the Villa Seurat to have Sunday supper with Anaïs and Hugo, home from London for the weekend. (Reichel insists on walking the entire distance, more than three miles.) Anaïs has prepared a simple meal, which is served on a red metal folding table surrounded by four matching folding chairs. Betty is surprised by the seeming impermanence of the decor and furnishings in the simple apartment, which seems to have "no hospitable comfort, no illusion of solidity or permanence." (Some of their furniture is probably decorating Hugo's London apartment.) After dinner, while Reichel gives his opinions of Hugo's drawings, Betty is introduced to Anaïs's private room, painted white: "Against one wall stood a tall richly carved headboard of a bed in dark heavy wood, Spanish in style. Heavy hangings covered the window which faced the Seine. Beneath the window a very low table supported a typewriter. The room was dimly lit."[92] The headboard, rescued from the auction and formerly in her houseboat, is a vestigial remnant of a time of greater stability in Louveciennes.

In early spring of 1938, Anaïs finds another houseboat to rent. *La Belle Aurore,* owned by Michel Simon, an actor known for his depiction of life on a barge in the classic film *L'Atalante.* His boat has steam heat and a bathroom and is docked at quai des Tuileries.[93] She has no sooner settled on board when news reaches her of Hitler's march into Austria and the Anschluss. Her boat soon becomes what she calls Noah's Ark amid the deluge of politics. When Gonzalo melodramatically waves a gun in the air and talks of killing himself and Anaïs and Helba, Anaïs talks him out of it. She sees herself as the great comforter to a diseased world; she has created her own world, she believes, which will be a refuge for others—a creative world to balance the destructive one. Gonzalo denounces this idea as bourgeois individualism, but nevertheless seeks refuge on Noah's Ark. Durrell also remembers "those strange evenings on *La Belle Aurore* with Moricand the astrologer."[94]

She also gets involved in mediating her father's divorce when Maruca (her stepmother) decides to divorce her philandering husband. Anaïs even goes to Caux, Switzerland, at Maruca's request, to tell her father (who is threatening suicide) that Maruca will never reconcile and that he must get on with his life. Until he does so, Maruca offers him a modest income. Reading Anaïs's description of her father's predicament, the reader is struck with Joaquin Nin's blind selfishness: only worried about who will now take care of him and whether he will get to keep the maid, he is puzzled about why Maruca has changed, why she is divorcing him.

The reader is also struck by the parallel situation between father and daughter: years of unfaithfulness, almost flaunting one's affairs to court discovery; a "collector's need" of charm, conquest, and power; seduction under the pretense of altruism. That Anaïs is aware of the painful parallel is evident in her description of his infidelities: *his* do not come from "a love need" or a "real hunger," nor from "a natural, a primitive, warm-blooded impulse" (as presumably hers do). When Maruca rails against the selfishness and hypocrisy, Anaïs suggests that "perhaps he did this to protect you from pain"—the reason she would continue to give for deceiving Hugo. Her own anxieties are aroused by watching her father's abandonment. Though she invites him to stay on the boat when he returns to Paris, she does not respond to his suggestion that she throw out her "protégés" and "take care" of him. He spends only one night on the boat before fleeing to Switzerland; the shadows and movement of the boat frighten him, and he sees the dirt, not the "fairy tale" of her ark. Just when Anaïs accompanies her father for a last look at his rue de l'Assomption home (and the luxurious life formerly provided by his wife's money), Paris experiences a mild earthquake. She imagines the earth he stands on opening up and "swallow[ing] the colorful ballet of his lies."[95] She will use her father's divorce, the isolation of his love ("you killed my love too"), and the earthquake in the "Stella" portion of *Winter of Artifice* (1961).[96]

Reluctantly, Anaïs and Henry say good-bye to Lawrence and Nancy Durrell who, after eight months shuttling between Paris and London, return to Corfu. With Hugo in London, Anaïs divides her time between the houseboat and Villa Seurat. In a letter to Durrell, whose *Black Book* has just been published by their Seurat Series (Kahane is official publisher/distributor), she informs him that she and Henry have carried his best books from his apartment (after the Durrells had skipped out on the rent), and brags that she is a "satisfied woman"—in a world "crowded with edible men." She thanks him for his faith in her. "Outside of Henry nobody else notices what I do."[97]

With Europe on the brink of a war, the French authorities make all the houseboats move out of the city to ensure the security of arriving foreign dignitaries. Her boat is towed as far downriver as Neuilly, where she was born. Not only does this return symbolize a regression, but also this is where her father is now living in a "clinically clean" apartment. While in Neuilly she visits her father, who declares that he should have found a woman like her with whom he can have a "genuine exchange of feelings." She abandons her leaky boat there.[98]

Fearing the imminent outbreak of war, Henry stops revising *Capricorn* and leaves for the south of France. "I'm a Chinaman at heart, not a European," he says, trying to explain his political indifference.[99] They have talked about her joining him, for Hugo is in London and Rosa and Joaquin have left for the United States, where he will teach at the Middlebury Music Center at Middlebury College.[100] Many people are packing and fleeing, and Henry awaits her arrival; but she must stay, she says with some self-pity, to care for those who need her: Gonzalo, shunned by the communists for being undisciplined and undependable, needs new glasses (which he immediately drops and breaks); Helba needs an operation and a safer place to live; and Moricand needs a meal a day. She feels loved to the extent that many people need her, but occasionally, as now, she feels trapped.

After she had fearfully counted the days before war, the sudden reprieve given by the Munich Pact brings both intense relief and disillusionment. Henry returns to Paris convinced that the "German bastards" will not be stopped and determined to return to the U.S. He and Anaïs stare at each other "like two ghosts." She is disappointed with his flight and certain that the threat of war is not truly over. Paris seems to be like a cemetery. Villa Seurat looks dilapidated. Gonzalo behaves fanatically, burning some of her books on the quay to protest what he thinks is her dependence on literature. For Henry, "Paris is irredeemably altered"; he keeps his bags packed. Only the presence of Anaïs, the coming publication of *Tropic of Capricorn,* and the return of the Durrells will keep him in Paris about eight more months.

The Durrells leave Corfu and return for a second period of commuting between Paris and London, from December 1938 to May 1939. During this period they are more often in London, where Hugo entertains them and occasionally lends them his apartment when he visits Paris. The Durrells are paying for the publication of Anaïs's three pieces of recent writings under the title *The Winter of Artifice,* which will appear in 1939. It will be the third volume of the Seurat Series from Kahane's Obelisk Press (Miller's *Max and the White Phagocytes* and Durrell's *Black Book* appear in 1938).

When he goes to London for a visit, Henry takes her *Winter* manuscript to Larry to read and mark, for she has asked for criticism, which she cannot, when it comes, accept. Larry thinks her manuscript needs major surgery, which he attempts to perform. After declaring that he does not understand her style, she writes to apologize for overreacting and admits, in an unpublished letter, that she has a handicap with language—Henry has told her she is tone-deaf—and an inability to accept criticism.[101] Henry returns more mystical and withdrawn from life, just as she feels more active. Yet she cannot become engaged in any narrow ideological system, like Gonzalo's communism, for they address only the "crust" of life. She feels her strength comes from her inner life—the eternal world of illusion, ecstasy, and poetry.

Like her contemporary sister writers Djuna Barnes (*Nightwood,* 1936) and Jean Rhys (*Good Morning, Midnight,* 1930), Anaïs resists the call to political involvement in her writing. The times seem to demand social relevance in literature, but the fiction of these three women focuses on the self and personal and female experience, which may explain why their works will be ignored for nearly half a century.[102] Anaïs continues writing about herself, for like Barnes's fiction her own art is in part a defense against childhood betrayal. Their "allusive writing," to use the words of one critic concerning Barnes, "creates art as a form of defense against, or therapeutic transcendence of, a body and self defiled and betrayed by trusted . . . others."[103]

By January 1939, she is helping Henry correct proofs for *Tropic of Capricorn* and planning her own story about the removal of her houseboat (she thinks she will write a lengthy modern *Odyssey*). Her best writing is in the houseboat story, she believes, because she is following instinct and sensation (the true surrealism) and is finding symbol. To commemorate her thirty-sixth birthday the next month, Henry begins a diary tribute with watercolors and drawings he will bind the following year for her. "To Heaven Beyond Heaven," he entitles it. "For all the Seraphita who fail to find their Shangri-la here on earth."[104] It is both a lengthy tribute and a revealing appellation, for Balzac's hero/heroine Séraphitus/Séraphita, in his novel by that name, combines androgyny with Swedenborgean mysticism. Miller's tribute also includes a critique of her style, which he describes as the "cerebral atonalities of the Hindu ragas . . . [a] Hispano-Suiza"—a superluxurious, ornate automobile—"style," which unfortunately makes her sound "tone deaf." He lectures her on mastering English first.[105] On the same day that he begins this diary, he writes to commemorate her generous nature and her great diary, with its "protean metamorphoses of your unions and separations." Buried in the letter is the remark, "You have chosen not to create but to record creation."[106] Both her life and her diary are, in fact, artistic creations. "The men always believe in my disguises," she writes, sitting over coffee at a café and feeling her body alive under her fur coat, a coat containing all the many women that she is.

Because Hugo must remain at his job in London, where he continues to rent an apartment, they give up the expensive flat on quai de Passy and she moves into an apartment closer to Henry, near the Closerie des Lilas. For her final year in Paris she lives at 12, rue Cassini, a short street off avenue Denfert-Rochereau, between a maternity hospital and the Observatory. She lives in one large room, with the bed in an alcove and a kitchen and bath combined. She tells Henry she is living next door to where Balzac wrote *Séraphita*.

One foggy winter day, she and Henry are sitting in a café correcting proofs of *The Winter of Artifice*. This is her third book, made up of three short novellas: "Djuna" (the Henry and June story), "Lilith" (the father story, later called "Winter of Artifice"), and "The Voice" (the Rank story, originally called "Chaotica"). They work on her writing techniques and she discovers levels of new meaning. Their literary passion has burned for seven years. Both sought in others—June and Gonzalo—darker encounters with evil. Both were deceived. June is now transformed into Henry's art in *Tropic of Capricorn*; Gonzalo, bound to his vagabond life and his sorrow for fallen Spain, has disappointed her. Rather than she being able to fire him with new life, each failure of his only exacerbates what Dr. Jacobson calls her persistent anemia. She wonders why she, who controls all details, persists in linking herself to two destructive, undisciplined children. What she thinks is being "enslaved" to love is also her need to have these others act out the rebellious chaos within herself. Though she has been critical of Henry's friends (chiefly Fred) because they are not his equals, she does not apply the same criteria to herself.

## Farewells

Her father, who has always been her biggest disappointment, collapses at his last concert in Paris. He is preparing to move to Cuba and is appearing for probably the thousandth time on a stage in Paris. Anaïs is in the front row. Suddenly his arms drop to his side and his head falls to the keyboard. For a moment she sees him dead, alone on the stage with his piano. She accompanies his unconscious body to his home. What the doctors call a stroke she believes is "an overwhelming, crushing realization of his solitude, anguish, [and] the death of a life he loved."[107] Self-worship has left him with nothing. He even has to sell many of his music books before he sails for Havana. As if to allay any guilt, she says in her diary that she never told him directly that her love for him was dead; she let him know "gently and quietly" that she could not return his "total love." To her mother, she writes that "M Nin" is sailing, knowing that "his children do not love him."[108] She has pity but no love or guilt, she claims. Yet when he comes for a final visit, she lights the small lamps and perfumes her apartment. Later he writes to tell her that upon leaving her home he had fainted in her courtyard.

When the time does arrive for his ship to sail, she weeps with pain, knowing she may never see him again. When he had talked of going, she remained detached and neutral, silent about his staying in Paris, keeping in check the words about her dead love. But his limp body at the piano momentarily revived her love, a love she has not been able to transcend entirely. She both loves and hates him. By the time he gets to Cuba, her story of him, "Lilith" in *Winter*—ending, "And with the little girl died the need of a father"—will be in print.

As the refugees from Spain slip into Paris this spring of 1939, Anaïs helps to find them apartments. She sees in them the plight of her own grandmother Nin, about whom she cannot get news from Barcelona. Though the law forbids assisting in their shelter, she works with Gonzalo finding rooms, cooking big pots of soup, and spending hours at the Cuban consulate trying to get them passports. Helba stages theatrics to keep the attention of her husband and Anaïs. She even drinks petrol, and they have to rush her to the hospital.

Hours with Henry, by contrast, are peaceful, for he is mellowing into what she calls his "Chinese reincarnation," reading Zen Buddhism and handprinting small books for his friends. He seems to leave Hitler to astrological fate: Moricand brings him a horoscope on Hitler that predicts death or disappearance, and the men sit up all one night waiting for Hitler to die.[109]

Hugo and Anaïs spend Easter holiday in Nice, where she recovers from her second aesthetic surgery (the first straightened her nose). At first she writes her mother that she is having the space between her front teeth filled in, then she admits to having her teeth realigned to diminish the buckedteeth appearance. She is delighted by her new smile and the inexpensive seaside amenities, and decides to come back here for the summer. She does not seem to be worried by the three American cruisers anchored off the coast of Villefranche waiting to rescue Americans.[110]

The Three Musketeers part in May when the Durrells leave for Corfu, the same month that England and France sign their alliance to rearm against Germany and Italy. Anaïs will not see Larry again for sixteen years. She and Henry plan to go to the south of France for a lengthy stay, perhaps before going to America, though Henry wants to visit Greece first. She will return to St.-Tropez for the summer (rather than join Hugo in London). Their friends and family are now scattered: Fred Perlès is already in England, Hugo and his entire family are also there, and Eduardo Sanchez is in Kent. Rosa and Joaquin are in Vermont.

After four years and nine months at the Villa Seurat, Henry leaves for good, selling or giving away some of his possessions, storing others and his manuscripts at Louveciennes, and sending a large shipment of *Cancer* and *Black Spring* to the Gotham Book Mart to finance a month in the south of France. He writes a final will, which he sends to a Baltimore lawyer friend (and a copy to another friend), leaving everything to Anaïs:

> I owe a lot to France. . . . [B]ut I must add in the interest of truth
> that I owe nearly everything to one person: Anaïs Nin. . . . [H]ad
> I not met her I would never have accomplished the little that I

did. I would have starved to death. . . . [I]t was *A woman*, Anaïs
Nin, by whom I was rescued and pressured and encouraged and
inspired.[111]

He also predicts that her diary in a hundred years "will be the greatest single
item in the literary history of our time."

By the end of May, Anaïs is in St.-Tropez for the best vacation of her life,
having breakfasts in a café, spending the day in her swimsuit, and enjoying
the warm deserted beaches before the summer season. Hugo stays a week
before returning to England, then Gonzalo and Helba arrive. They ride
bicycles, cook lunch behind the beach among the pine trees, sunbathe
during the day, and dance in the village at night. Gonzalo and Anaïs continue
their affair. Jean Carteret comes down and sleeps on the beach, and Horace
Guicciardi and his wife are in nearby St.-Maxime. Hugo will eventually visit
again from London, and Henry will come from Paris, where he is stuck until
7 June awaiting the check from the Gotham and new eyeglasses.

By the time the first copies of the blue-bound *Winter of Artifice* arrive
from Kahane, Henry is in the Dordogne visiting all the sites he has wanted
to see before leaving France. They will meet in mid-July at Aix-en-Provence
or Marseilles before Miller sails to Greece and the Durrells. He hopes that
she will go with him. The Durrells expect not only Henry, but Anaïs and
Eduardo.

Henry and Anaïs meet in a hotel near the train station in Marseilles 12
July, for his boat is to sail on Bastille Day 1939. On the thirteenth they send
a postcard to Emil Schnellock from Aix-en-Provence announcing that their
two books are now published.[112] Like so many books of high modernism
(including James Joyce's *Finnegans Wake*), *The Winter of Artifice* and *Tropic
of Capricorn* are marginalized by the coming war (and, in Miller's case, by
censorship).

Aix is hot and full of holiday anticipation when Anaïs and Henry meet
for what will prove to be their last "literary fuck fest." As they have for seven
and a half years, they take their pleasure amid plans to promote their novels.
It would be easy for her to join him on the ship (escaping as her grandmother
had once done), and for them to sail away from a crumbling world. She
promises to join him, but not to divorce or remarry, for she has always
understood that Henry is not husband material.[113] She believes she never
should have married the first time.[114] In a move as fateful as that November
day in 1931 when Henry walked into the house in Louveciennes and into
her life, he sails away. She takes the train back to St.-Tropez for six more
weeks of holiday.

The war clouds are more visible from St.-Tropez. The yachts all seem to disappear overnight. The train carrying her and Hugo back to Paris is filled with soldiers. To forestall any family war, Anaïs writes to her mother, knowing that *The Winter of Artifice* may soon be appearing in America. As she had when *The House of Incest* was published, she asks her mother not to read the book. Though her mother would have known otherwise had she read it, Anaïs tells her that the book is "about psychoanalysis and the confessions I heard, so you see I am still sowing my modern oats, but I am at bottom the same old Fifille as you know who loves you."[115]

She is in London with Hugo on 1 September 1939 when Germany invades Poland. Two days later France and Britain declare war, and on the same day Jack Kahane dies suddenly. Miller's and Nin's Paris publishing connections—William Bradley had died in January—are now severed. Fred Perlès joins the British Army, she learns from Henry, who is concerned about one of his manuscripts in Kahane's safe. He asks her to take his manuscripts and books if she leaves for the U.S., for his will leaves everything to her. She and Henry had been planning to get their books to Steloff at the Gotham. She writes again to Steloff, enclosing an essay on Cocteau for Steloff's *We Moderns* and requesting that the second payment for her essay be sent to Henry Miller, who needs the money.[116] She waits in long lines to renew her expired passport and secures a visa for France.[117]

By the end of September she leaves Hugo and the London air raids to return to her apartment in rue Cassini, thinking seriously of going to New York City alone. She senses the world's schizophrenia, the madness of doing her eyelashes while listening to the news of suffering on the radio. She seeks light and noise in cafés, but cannot separate herself from thoughts of death. Even the places seem dead, the houses are corpses—Louveciennes, Villa Seurat. She has returned to Paris, where her diaries are locked in the bank vault, to see to Henry's manuscript and to care for her orphans—two of whom (Gonzalo and Helba) return to Paris from St.-Tropez. While she tries to study Marx and see the future through Gonzalo's eyes, Henry is in Corfu feeling at one with nature, "a real Chinaman," growing a beard, painting watercolors, going naked under the blue sky and blazing sun.[118] Hugo is made managing director of the newly merged City Bank and Farmers Trust in London.[119]

She sits in the Brasserie Lipp having one of several farewell dinners with Moricand, who has lied about his age to sign on with the French Foreign Legion in order to die in a style and elegance that his life could not match. She shows him some of Henry's letters about sun, nakedness, and simplicity in Greece, and Moricand is shocked by Henry's detachment. Caught up temporarily in the political turmoil, she too judges Henry harshly and admires Gonzalo and Moricand. Before spring, Moricand ignobly collapses and is discharged from the legion for being overage.

Perhaps to justify remaining in Paris and wasting her resources on weak and dependent people, she is harshly critical of Henry's Adamic Grecian life and his study of yoga.[120] At the same time she romanticizes Gonzalo's studio as a scene from "Dostoevsky's revolutionary days": the dark studio is illuminated only by a bulb covered by a blue paper; liniment for Helba's pleurisy is heating on the stove; their worn clothes are falling from open trunks. She copies a passage from a book on the Russian Revolution about the closeness of the Bolsheviks to mother earth. She romantically overexaggerates her sacrifices: "I turned a bohemian and a bum into a man who is fulfilling his first ambition, his youthful desire to save the Indians of Peru from oppression and near-slavery."[121] Gonzalo never makes it to Peru or to the battlefield of Spain, using his ill wife, as always, as his excuse.

Only Hugo does not fail her. As Jean Carteret had said, he is the "diamond" man. "Hugo's kindness and sacrifice are super human," she writes her mother in October. "At a time of crisis I realize my choosing him was the most intelligent thing I did in all my life. There isn't another like him."[122] She cannot leave him, even though the citizens of Paris are preparing for war by painting the café windows blue and covering the shop windows with green cellophane, and an 11 P.M. curfew has been instituted for all business. When she asks him to secure an appointment with the New York branch of the bank, he agrees to do so, but claims he cannot leave just yet, because he is about the only man in his London bank not conscripted.

Anaïs packs her books and household goods for storage with a friend in Louveciennes. Helba will go with her to New York, and Gonzalo, so the grandiose plan goes, will fight for Marxism and claim some family inheritance in Peru. Though she claims in her diary that she has "loved and lived to the full," Anaïs becomes overwhelmed one day while caring for Helba. She is sitting in the dirty studio, heating liniment every twenty minutes for Helba's pleurisy and listening to her litany of complaints, when she breaks into tears.

She leaves without Gonzalo and Helba, presumably because their papers are not in order. She has to leave most of her diaries in the bank vault, but she takes two briefcases, which include letters and the last four years of her diary. "I knew it was the end of our romantic life," she writes at the end of her diary for this year. Hugo joins her for the train to Portugal, then they take a hydroplane to the Azores, where they are surprised by the lovely pastel-colored houses.

She carries with her her secret contraband, the diary, fearing that the customs officials will read it at the border. She also carries letters. Moricand's letters remind her of the world of stylized culture and discipline that she is leaving—the formal and sterile grace that denies life. Durrell's letters talk of the sun-baked Henry and of the place she has in Durrell's imagination. He will always associate Paris with her: "There is a little leafy square opposite the Closerie des Lilas, where sometimes I wait for you to pass in your cloak, going homeward." The success of the Three Musketeers, he adds, has been "swallowed suddenly in the blackout and the alarms."[123]

After refueling, the hydroplane struggles through choppy seas at night before flying toward Bermuda. She feels torn away from the dark war-obsessed continent, from what Auden called the "haunted wood" of Europe.[124] She is flying above the earth and water toward yet another refuge.

# CHAPTER EIGHT

## 1939–1944

# Village Life:
# Starting Over

"The first person I gave myself to, my father, betrayed me, so I split. Ultimate giving is fatal. I split, split, split, into a million small relationships. And I seek split beings. Divided beings."

*—Anaïs Nin*[1]

THE WOUNDED CHILD who had sailed reluctantly into New York harbor in 1914 with her mother and two younger brothers had only her diary as armor. When she is cast back to these shores as a refugee a second time at the end of 1939, she is armed with three publications: a study of D. H. Lawrence, a prose poem (*The House of Incest*), and a collection of fiction (*The Winter of Artifice*). Her diary has grown to sixty volumes. After fifteen years in Paris, she is still seeking public approval, an American audience, and acclaim as a writer. She will make America her last home, first in New York City and then Los Angeles, but it will take nearly three years for any publisher to pay attention, and fame will come only with the Aquarian generation some twenty-five years later.

Upon arrival during the Christmas season, she is reminded of the bustle and glamour of those winter months with Rank five years earlier when she was wrapped in fur in a New York taxi and shopped along the snowy streets. This time she is shopping with her mother, who comes down from Massachusetts, where she lives with Joaquin, now a teacher of music at William

College. On Anaïs's first encounter with New York, she had been but a child, sponsored by her mother. On her most recent visits to New York, she had been studying psychoanalysis with Rank, then seeing some of her own patients and looking for publishers with Miller. This final return finds her in full maturity as an artist. She immediately seeks a literary base and a home for her books at the Gotham Book Mart.

Frances Steloff's Gotham Book Mart, located since 1923 at 51 West Forty-seventh Street in the midtown jewelry district, is as much the meeting place and distribution center for literary New York that Sylvia Beach's Shakespeare and Company has been on the Left Bank of Paris. Because Steloff stocks the literary reviews and books by the small English-language presses of both continents, writers congregate here, borrow money, collect mail, and celebrate the publication of their books. Because Steloff was well known for often lending money to writers, Miller had begun his appeals for help before leaving France. He and Anaïs began sending copies of their books to her. In fact, the previous 4 May, Steloff held a "Finnegans Wake" for the publication of Joyce's last novel.

Upon entering the long and crowded bookshop, Anaïs studies the photographs of Joyce, Lawrence, Pound, and other great writers on the walls, longing to join the pantheon. The store will be chief distributor for the books she has brought from Paris and for all her forthcoming books. Here she will meet James Agee, Paul Rosenfeld, Glenway Wescott, and numerous others. The shop seems like a private library to Anaïs. Though Steloff admits later in life to having read only a few pages of Anaïs's work (and to never finishing a book by Henry Miller), Anaïs knows that she has a trusted friend in Steloff. Both writers ask for money and depend on her goodwill for years to come.[2]

When Anaïs arrives at the Park Avenue apartment of Dorothy Norman, she is aware of how far it is from the George Washington, the hotel where she and Hugo live near Lexington and Twenty-third, to this grand apartment. Norman had arranged with Steloff to have Anaïs's books sold at the shop and had published Anaïs's "Birth" in her *Twice a Year* in 1938.[3] Thus, it is quite natural that this should be one of Anaïs's first social and cultural contacts. Norman invites Hugo and Anaïs often to dinners on Park Avenue and occasionally to her summer homes in East Hampton and Woods Hole, introducing Anaïs to many people, including her friend Alfred Stieglitz, the photographer. Anaïs frequently accepts her hospitality and is excited by the promise of publication for more of her work, but writes harshly of Norman in her diary: her parties are impersonal, insubstantial, and cold; Norman is unhappy, rigid, and provincial. Mrs. Norman has no inkling of Anaïs's true feelings, but the diary entries reveal more about the latter's sense of alienation at the time than they do about the former.

Anaïs is a minor player in Norman's vast artistic and political arena, which includes everyone from the mayor to Reinhold Niebuhr and Nehru. When she finally meets the two Paris writers she has published in her journal, Norman thinks Henry Miller looks like a "modest . . . serious, conventional preacher" and Anaïs like a prude:

> "[T]here is something of the nun about the way she looks. Her gray coat with its simple rounded collar, her almost poke-bonnet gray hat, suggest a professional Puritan. But her small mouth is carefully painted; her exaggerated innocent mascaraed eyes stare at me ecstatically."[4]

Though it will be a few years before Anaïs can become friends with strong, creative women, her own harsh judgment of Mrs. Norman certainly comes in part from her initial response to New York City and its luxury. Paris, when she left it, looked like "stain-glass windows all wet and alive with candlelight." The flight from Europe she describes in images of wrenching, snapping, and tearing.[5] Though initially New York City's skyscrapers shone "like Christmas trees," she soon notes that the luxury is blinding, the city lacks depth and feeling, and the people have no appreciation of myth.[6]

One woman she does like is Caresse Crosby, whom she meets in January at a party given by Yves Tanguy, the American painter born and educated in France who was associated with the surrealist movement and had been analyzed by Allendy. Crosby is a blue blood—she was born a Jacob and ultimately married into the Peabody, then Morgan families—but she associates only with avant-garde artists.[7]

Anaïs rushes out of the elevator, looking very worried and approaching the first guest she sees to ask where Mrs. Crosby is. She follows the nod of the head and, breathlessly, confesses quietly to Caresse Crosby that for years, whenever she had spent a week away from her husband in Paris, she had said that she was visiting the Crosby's famous salon outside the city. Please keep my secret, she begs, for my husband is coming up on the next elevator. Crosby takes a close look at the "small dark woman looking very distraught," smiles, and nods at her new friend with instant rapport.[8]

Caresse swept into every gathering trailing her own legend behind her. She and her husband, Harry, had owned the Black Sun Press and published Lawrence, Hart Crane, Pound, Faulkner, Hemingway, Stuart Gilbert, and a fragment from Joyce's *Work in Progress*. Crosby finds Anaïs a poised and lovely woman who carefully cultivates mystery and secrecy. It is important to Anaïs that they have several experiences in common: Paris, Lawrence, book printing, and charismatic personalities (Caresse is more flamboyant) that draw many admirers. Caresse's love affair with a black man takes her often to Harlem for jazz, and soon Anaïs is accompanying her. Anaïs admires her "flowing youthfulness" and her role as "pollen carrier"; she is saying YES to life.[9]

## Woodstock and Robert Duncan

The day after Christmas 1939, Anaïs and Hugo Guiler travel up the Hudson River for a weekend visit to Woodstock, where they meet her first American publishers. The Cooneys—Blanche and Jimmy (James Peter, an Irishman with a red mustache)—own a hand press and periodical called *The Phoenix*, where the first work of Anaïs's to be published in the U.S. (a piece called "Orchestra," culled from *The Winter of Artifice*) appeared the previous year. The youthful Cooneys are anxious to meet the Spanish princess, Miller's lover, the "fabled Etre Etoilique" (their Lawrentian journal had also published Miller's essay on Anaïs). Blanche Cooney sees Anaïs as warm and loving, with "no hint of incense," composed and attentive, and lovely in purple wool. Her description of Hugo is just as interesting:

> A tall lean Scotsman, gentle, handsome, he deferred to Anaïs, his adored one, his indulged one. No whim, no quirk, no passion or bizarre appetite would he deny her: Yes to a houseboat on the Seine. Yes to the Miller connection, to a fling with a woman, an English poet, a Peruvian Indian. Yes.[10]

Blanche thinks him a paradox, modest yet quick to laugh, a banker yet interested in studying engraving. Those who know him better at this time talk about the extent of his denial of his wife's behavior.

With her introduction to the Cooneys, Anaïs finds another literary circle initially cultivated by Miller. Though they are now "militantly pacifist" (Miller is no longer on their masthead), Anaïs meets through the Cooneys a number of people, including Kenneth Rexroth, with whom she will connect in New York and later in the San Francisco–Berkeley–Big Sur area.

The most important meeting of these early years in New York takes place this weekend in Woodstock, at the Maverick Lunar Colony—as friends called the Cooney group.[11] Anaïs meets Robert Symmes, the adopted son of Californians and recently arrived from Berkeley. Symmes, who will change his name to Duncan in 1943, reads his poetry to the group.[12] Uneasy because he is an admirer of Anaïs's fiction, he talks obsessively, not intimately. One friend calls him an "irascible . . . grandiloquent bear."[13] Anaïs describes him in her diary as "a strikingly beautiful boy, who look[s] about seventeen" (he is twenty).[14] When she learns that he keeps a diary, she asks him to call on her in New York.

Anaïs soon meets Duncan at a restaurant with a painter (and Berkeley friend) named Virginia Admiral. He praises Anaïs's work ("My *Shaman* is an emanation of a cosmic myth world awakened by your *House of Incest*").[15] Blanche Cooney, just a year older than Duncan, describes her "androgynous friend" Duncan, whom she loves as a friend, as "[D]ark, slim, his right eye off center" but with a beautiful "faun look." In Woodstock, he takes over hanging clothes on the line for Blanche while she nurses her infant son; in New York with Anaïs he is a more sensual, artistic companion.[16] Before long she and Duncan are sharing their diary descriptions of each other; he writes that she is "delicate" with "tiny bones" and feet of "cool pewter." When she reads his poems, she suggests that he could use more "transmutation" and less of the prosaic and obscene.[17] Though she objects to some of his "ugly" realism, she senses a kindred soul, he a teacher and guide.

Anaïs calls Robert Duncan and Virginia Admiral "children." At Berkeley they had published a mimeographed literary magazine together and with their friends (including Pauline Kael) had discussed radical politics. Duncan likes to surround himself with bright and attractive women, and Virginia is intelligent and has a scholarship with the great art teacher Hans Hofman. She and Duncan are frequent visitors to the Guiler apartment. She lives with two women friends in a cold, bare loft on Fourteenth Street that they consider glamorous with its floor-to-ceiling windows overlooking Union Square.[18] "When I first met Anaïs," writes Admiral,

> she was having problems with the person typing her journals (at ten cents a page, sometimes margin-to-margin, on rice paper with a carbon in French, but not a bad price at the time). I said I would type some of them for nothing since I wanted to read them anyway. Later, when I ran out of money she paid me, also Robert and Janet [Thurman, one of her roommates]. One night a week I would stay up and type one of the journals, making ten dollars, which was enough for me to live on. . . . The early journals were rather heartrending, but when she seduced John Erskine it seemed unduly unkind. At night, the journals that were not out being read or typed were locked in a huge safe in the Guiler apartment, presumably to keep them from Hugo's eyes.[19]

What is beginning in Anaïs's association with Duncan is a move away from the father figures of the 1930s, in relation to whom she played the seductive-daughter role to male analysts and writers, and gravitation toward the young gay writers and poets of the 1940s to whom she plays the seductive goddess and poet. They will become her comrades and muses. They do not threaten her sexuality or autonomy, and they provide a much needed psychic boost. This shift in roles will coincide with the gradual disappearance of Miller. Robert Duncan—"monkey" or "twin," she calls him—is the first of what one Jungian critic calls her "animus figures," her "supreme muse" being Proust.[20] He wants to free her from the prison of her house of incest: "My poor Anaïs who stares out from her intricate prisons with wide eyes; they open wider—they are startled—the soul inside is a child weeping because it is so helpless to love—her anguish because she cannot become real, free without destroying, without murdering."[21]

Duncan does help to free her, she admits in her letters to him, and she is genuinely enchanted by him—though she alters her letters revealing this enchantment when she prints them in her published diary.[22]

Feeling like a foreigner, Anaïs gravitates toward the young and unknown, such as Duncan (whose fame as a poet will emerge after the war); toward foreigners such as Yves Tanguy (their talk of Paris makes them behave like exiled White Russians, she scolds); and to blacks and Haitians she meets through Caresse Crosby. In short, to outsiders.

Henry Miller, the consummate outsider, finally returns via ship to Boston from Corfu and Greece, feeling that the "curtain is rising."[23] He will describe it later in *The Air-Conditioned Nightmare* as a "terror" akin to that of a slave having escaped again only to be brought back in chains. When he arrives in New York City, Anaïs is sick with the flu and cannot greet him. He waits with disappointment at the dock, but is soon settled at the Royalton and caught up in a family crisis in Brooklyn. His father's illness rouses Miller's pity in a way that Anaïs has never seen, and she hopes he at last understands her long-held sense of responsibility for family.

Hugo, who has to return to the bank in London for part of February and March, continues to believe that Henry is in Greece. Fred Perlès, still in the army, writes to thank Anaïs for trying to get him out of Europe, informs her that he has seen Hugo, then writes Henry that Hugo does not know that he is with Anaïs in New York. The fact that neither Anaïs nor Henry make contact with June upon their arrival lends weight to the belief that they had both used her for their own ends.[24]

Miller, who is not happy to be back in the United States, visits friends outside of New York, including Emil Schnellock in Fredericksburg, Virginia, as often as he can. Though he and Anaïs do not resume their affair in earnest, he always writes her news of films, friends, and his impressions of Americans and America. It is clear from the letters that they still link their future together, for he assumes that Anaïs will accompany him on a longer trip ("our trip") around the country.[25]

When Miller returns to New York at the end of February 1940, he stays in an apartment at Caresse Crosby's building, 137 East Fifty-fourth Street, and begins writing several pieces, including *The Colossus of Maroussi,* a book (without any sex) about his Greek experiences. ("Without Betty Ryan . . . I would never have gone to Greece," he writes.) Anaïs is writing in her diary, keeping up frequent communication with friends in Europe, and writing short fiction based on material in her diary.[26] She has no U.S. publisher for her stories or for the three books that had appeared in Europe. Miller, by contrast, has already been published by a New York press, for James Laughlin of New Directions issued *The Cosmological Eye* in 1939 (in 1941 he will publish Miller's *The Wisdom of the Heart,* which includes eighteen pieces, many already published in Europe). But Miller is obsessed with getting out of New York to experience America. He soon receives five hundred dollars from a publisher to travel the country and write a book about America. His friend Abraham Rattner, who has a studio in New York, will do the photographs for him. He is also arranging secretly to get *Tropic of Cancer* "pirated" so that he can sell it and collect the profits for himself. As usual, he meets many artists in New York (including Sherwood Anderson, John Dos Passos, Carl Van Vechten) and a well-known young poet named Kenneth Patchen, whom he (and Duncan) send to Anaïs. She writes to Duncan (when he is in Woodstock editing his *Ritual,* later called *Experimental Review*) of her admiration for Patchen's work, though she confides in her diary that she does not like the man or his poetry. (Patchen was just as uncomplimentary about her work.) He is sullen, she writes, and obviously comes to her for financial help, without making any attempt to be communicative. While Admiral and Duncan are trying to gather financial assistance for Patchen, Anaïs is trying to discourage others from helping him.[27]

With all the change in her life, Anaïs clings to the old personal ties. She finds Dr. Max Jacobson, who was her doctor in Paris. When she tries to look up Otto Rank, whom she has not seen for four years, she learns that he died the previous October. He was fifty-five years old, had been married only three months, and was about to move to California. His blood had been poisoned by the sulfur he took for a kidney infection.[28] Anaïs wonders whether she ever told him of his great influence on her life.

And finally, arriving in New York from Paris are Gonzalo and Helba More, trailing after Anaïs with their illness- and accident-prone lives. With fortunate timing, Anaïs hears of a means of making money to help the Mores and to help Miller tour America.

## House of Erotica

The erotic writing escapade begins in the spring of 1940 when Anaïs shows up at the Gotham Book Mart for what Gershon Legman thinks is a meeting with Henry Miller. Legman, a young American researcher, has asked Kenneth Patchen, whom he calls "a mean, hulking, no-talent faker," to tell Miller (whom he also dislikes) about a means to make about one hundred dollars a month (though he does not specify how). Anaïs takes charge of the meeting and the messenger.[29]

Legman is working for a pornographic publisher and bookstore owner named Jake Brussel, who is "pirating" Miller's *Tropic of Cancer* for Miller even though he thinks the book is anti-American.[30] Though the colophon on page 323 lists the place of printing as Mexico, the law will eventually track down Brussel and sentence him to ten years in jail (he served a two-year term). Legman designs the cover, which is eventually rejected as too provocative (its vaginal design artistically depicts Miller's favorite word). He is also writing dollar-a-page erotica for a private "collector" named Roy Melisander Johnson of Ardmore, Oklahoma. Legman is just twenty-three years old but already committed to a career in the study of sexuality: "I have devoted my life to the clitoris," he will repeat later in life. He is selling the erotica—through a man named "Slapsie Maxie," who takes a ten-percent cut of the action—to Barnet Ruder (until recently called "Rudolph Bernays" in references to this episode) for fifty cents a page (that is, fifty dollars for every hundred pages). Ruder, binding the book for "heavy one-handed use" (according to Legman), and mailing it to Johnson or, as some have speculated, other buyers, pockets the other fifty dollars. When Legman contacts the "collector" himself, he begins receiving the full dollar a page. But writing erotica for two years has taken its toll, making him as mentally impotent as it is presumably making the customer virile. For a while his friend Robert Sewall writes some of the erotica. Now Legman is looking for another writer, and the "collector" wants Miller. Legman admires *Tropic of Cancer,* but after reading the anti-Semitism in *Aller Retour New York* he thinks Miller is a "macho faker and pimp." Nevertheless, Legman contacts Patchen, who contacts Miller. Legman will receive twenty-five dollars for each hundred-page manuscript he can get Miller to write.

Instead of Miller that day at the Gotham, he meets an attractive thirty-seven-year-old "elegant and exotic Spanish woman." He guesses it is Miller's mistress. She has seductive ways and wears suede shoes that are tied around her ankles in a manner unfamiliar to New York. She wears a big woolen cape and is dressed "like a real *poule de luxe*":

> She had a definite air of being on the make, and judging me fast. . . . She was very dark, with enormous eyes that spoke in an unmistakable voice of suffering. Her mouth was strangely pressed

forward at the center of the lips, in a way common to Moorish and North African Negro women. No *sangre azul* there. Her nose was very pointed too, and yet she was beautiful and certainly desirable.

The clothes and the fact that she is from France, not, he claims later, he physical body, which lacks curves between her "pipe-stem arms," make he attractive to the young man. He thinks her affectation is a means of self-pro tection. She is more than a dozen years older, and he remembers later tha he "did not feel any real sexual magnetism," yet he admits to studying he nose, wondering if it matches another part of her anatomy and feeling a they talked that they "were fencing with each other phallically." Legmar thinks her well-educated, restrained, and noncommitted (except abou books and music), and he has a distinct impression that she has com "prepared to have an affair" with him if he should prove interesting. He is in his own judgment, "young and violently handsome" and "dangerous" look ing. He soon rushes out to read *The House of Incest* and *The Winter c Artifice,* both of which he thinks hostile and cruel.

When Nin and Legman talk about his design for Miller's book, a vulv above the word "Medvsa" (with a *v*), the talk turns to sexuality. He explain it by quoting the Greek courtesan in Pierre Louys's *Aphrodite,* who describe her "flower of crimson, full of honey . . . a hydra of the sea, living and soft open at night. . . . It is the human grotto. . . . It is the face of Medusa." A Anaïs gazes into his eyes, he moves directly into the reason for this tête-à tête in the Gotham alcove: the writing assignment for the Oklahoma mil lionaire. Explaining that he can no longer write to excite a man ("When h went up, I went down"), Legman gives her Ruder's name and the name c the literary agent ("Johnny Furness"—Jerry Buse), and suggests that she ca earn money as well, though no woman has ever written authentic erotic. To this challenge he adds the suggestion that she could make a valuabl contribution by telling what women really think about during sex. But cer tainly women have written erotica, she argues, naming titles such as *Fann Hill* (written by John Cleland). With each title, Legman explains it was reall written by a man. As if this were not challenge enough to take up th writing—and the young man so interested in women's sexuality—he adds glancing down at her high-heeled suede shoes, "We want to know if wome really have orgasms or if you're just faking it half the time."[31]

Their affair begins the next day, he remembers, as does her writing c erotica. In fact, she writes about their first sexual encounter. He evaluate both, advising her to be more specific in the written description. She find it difficult to include the harsh details. Privately he concludes that Anaïs is very oral, but "one of those women . . . who sometimes have a marvelous experience when you're making love to them . . . but the experience is not with you." He calls her private orgasms "negative magic," not unlike Miller's private conclusion earlier ("She surrenders to you without giving herself").[32] He realizes it is easy to have an affair with her, but the encounter is merely physical. She is collecting experience for her writing. He gives her sexual experiences for her work and supplies advice on keeping carbons of all she writes for later revision and publication. Her *Delta of Venus* (1977) and *Little Birds* (1979) are published from these carbons. In Legman's view, Nin's work contains "beautiful erotic fantasies." Later he will proudly claim a part in her erotic writing, for he believes that she is "an elegant artist of exquisite sensibility" who became famous for her books of erotica.

They argue about literature—"the arty-farty versus the earthy-folk," as he characterizes it—and he bad-mouths the French surrealists. But the event that ends their three-week affair is the publication of the Medusa edition of *Tropic of Cancer*—without her preface. "She thought I had betrayed her," remembers Legman. But the fault is with Brussel, who ran off about 1,500 copies of the novel (to pirate 200–500 for Samuel Roth, who had lent him some of the money) and ran out of paper to print the introduction.[33]

Gonzalo, another rich primary source for Anaïs's erotica material, does not betray her as she thinks Legman has, but he is consistently unreliable and irresponsible. Though they will continue to have sexual relations for seven more years, they disagree over most things, especially politics and psychology. These are major differences between them: she believes in more than material existence, the only reality in his Marxist world; he has no sympathy for psychology, which is her reality. She notes that despite his Marxist claims, he overlooks the suffering around him and does nothing to change the world, while she at least tries to heal the pain around her (her reason for continuing to put up with the Mores). Their presence in her diary for a decade deliberately defines her as a caring and self-sacrificing mother figure.[34] What she and Gonzalo have with each other is physical attraction and psychological need.

## Greenwich Village and Harlem

Against the dehumanized scale of New York City, Anaïs clings to life in Greenwich Village. Daily she scans the papers for news of the French, who are holding off the Germans behind the Maginot Line near Louveciennes. Radios and newspapers proclaim the news of Germany's march into Denmark, Norway, the Netherlands, Belgium, and France. Letters bring her news of friends in need: Moricand hungry, Jean Carteret mobilized. Later she hears that Allendy is dying in the south of France.

Greenwich Village had gone through many periods since the Dutch drove out the Indians. Thomas Paine and Edgar Allen Poe had lived there; Henry James was born there; and before and after 1920, the bohemians made the inexpensive Village famous. But the writers who made the Village so active in the early 1920s had by the 1930s moved uptown (Dreiser and Cather), to Brooklyn (Crane, Wolfe, Marianne Moore), or to Europe (Margaret Anderson, Djuna Barnes, e. e. cummings). Some, including Barnes and Cummings, have returned. The Italians, who had settled south of Washington Square generations before, are still running little coffee shops that remind Anaïs of Paris. The low houses, small shops and vegetable carts, university atmosphere, small theatres, and literary history recall an earlier Left Bank. The Italians play chess in the cafés, just as the French had in the Select in Montparnasse. She and Hugo begin looking for an apartment in or near the Village.

The cool intimacy of the Harlem clubs also appeals to Anaïs, though initially she knows only two people with any connections there: Millicent Fredericks, her maid, a Portuguese-African woman who lives in Harlem; and Caresse Crosby, whose lover owns a club there, where she takes Anaïs to dance. Anaïs prefers the jazz rhythms to the cold discussion of ideas and the New York temperament she finds at the salon of Dorothy Norman. Anaïs feels shunned for her "subjectivity" and her assumption that dreams and the unconscious breed art. She prefers to express her social conscience in help for an individual, not in group activity or cocktail talk about movements and political philosophy.

Robert Duncan and John Dudley are exceptions to the excessive rationality and detachment of the New Yorkers she meets. Caresse Crosby introduces her to Dudley, inviting Anaïs and Henry to meet a young man who she claims has come (with his friend Lafe Young) all the way from Kenosha, Wisconsin (Nin remembers it mistakenly as Des Moines, Iowa), to meet them. Dudley, a tall and handsome painter, is a teller of tall tales about his Scottish ancestors at Kenilworth Castle. Anaïs is immediately attracted to him when he performs with the musicians on the group's trip to a jazz club in Harlem. His music and drawing, his writing, his knowledge of jazz history, convince her that he is a "radiant vision of the future" who will help her reenter American life. Miller also likes him and takes the group to visit his childhood home in Brooklyn one summer night.[35]

At the invitation of Caresse Crosby, they all go to visit Hampton Manor, her home in Bowling Green, Virginia, for Caresse, according to Anaïs, loves to "encourage all forms of insemination among her friends." Artistically, racially, spiritually she is the "pollen bearer."[36] Anaïs's metaphor is apt and feeds the rumor that Crosby goes from room to room servicing her guests sexually—a rumor she confirms for an earlier period of her life when she and Harry Crosby lived outside Paris in an old mill. She is trying to recreate the Moulin, where they nurtured Hart Crane, René Crevel, D. H. Lawrence, and others, in this Virginia home, where her present husband, a Southerner, is living. She welcomes Salvador Dalí and his wife for a long visit and plans to launch his American reputation. John and Flo Dudley are there, and Anaïs and Henry probably share a bed—perhaps for the last time.[37] They all work in the morning, siesta in the afternoon, and talk (including about their erotic writing) and party at night. Anaïs writes a twelve-page erotic story called "Anita," about Anita Grey who lives on a vast property in Virginia and has a lover in Harlem; Anita and the narrator (Mandra) have lengthy undramatic discussions about the sexual prowess of black men.[38]

Miller, who stays on after she leaves, has been here before because he knows Caresse from the Paris years. He works on an introduction to *The Colossus of Maroussi,* begins *The Rosy Crucifixion* (a sequel to *Capricorn*), and continues to work on some erotica, including the story "Quiet Days in Clichy," and the essay "The World of Sex." He arranges to have the latter work published in Chicago the following year and apparently does little more writing for the "collector," for his personal and aesthetic imaginations rebel.

As is typical in her diary, Anaïs creates a romantic picture of Hampton Manor: when she arrives she sees Crosby supervising the tying up of sheaves of wheat, the sun on the dust making a halo about her large straw hat. The classical house is described as enchanted (she thinks naturally of Louveciennes), the mosses grow like carpets, the willows weep, the parquet floors shine. At night "the ponds look like Max Ernst's scenes of stagnant pools," insects gently beat the screen door, the night noises and warm earth awaken her senses.[39]

In reality, not fiction, the house is not enchanted and there is trouble in paradise: Crosby is quarreling with her husband, a mean drunk, whom she will soon divorce; the Dudleys will soon separate; the Dalís are alienating everyone (she co-opts the library for his work and they want only Spanish spoken); Anaïs and Dudley argue over the death of Europe and fondle each other furtively; the weather is blistering; the personalities of Miller and Dalí, though Miller had quoted Dalí in *Black Spring*, are "wholly antagonistic"[40] ; and there is tension in the group because, of all the guests, only Anaïs speaks English, French, and Spanish. In reality, her romantic version may be a composite of visits, for Crosby later tells her that she does not remember "you and Dudley and the Dalís [being there] all at the same time."[41] The most positive aspect of the evening dialogues is talk of Crosby's plan to rescue French artists and the group's plan to organize a printing press.

## *"Mother" and "Wife"*

By autumn of 1940 Anaïs and Hugo are settled into a fifth-floor skylight studio apartment on the edge of Greenwich Village at 215 West Thirteenth Street, where they can enjoy the local jazz, fresh pasta and cheese, and the small-town life. She creates an artistic salon atmosphere, a kind of "intimate room" like their "high place" in Paris, an ivory tower for the artist. This bright studio is three blocks north of Patchin Place, where Djuna Barnes, e. e. cummings, and others live. Anaïs buys worktables, bookcases, and unfinished furniture, puts American Indian serapes on the carpeted floor, and arranges candles in her lanterns to make lighted jewels. She covers the skylights with colored paper to create the effect of stained glass. Amid the darkness of war, of Millicent's stories of Harlem, of Gonzalo's stories of capitalistic treachery, she will "wear a mask of oxygen-giving dreams" and keep her creative cells breathing.[42] It is her intimate artistic relationship with Duncan, sixteen years her junior, that distracts her. She is delighted in what his biographer calls his fondness for hugging and kissing or, better still, curling up with her on the bed. But theirs was not a sexual union.[43]

Anaïs is making her first money with her pen, not by means of fiction or the diary but in the tradition of the many French writers who have experimented with erotica. Aside from her own curiosity about sexual practices, she has the needs of her "children" to consider—she has to get the Mores established and she wants to help Henry with the trip he is planning to take across America. Whatever harmful result the hours of writing erotica have, they force her to focus on dialogue and action as she reworks some of her short stories. While dancing in Harlem she discovers the way to divide her houseboat story; now while sitting on a park bench in Washington Square, she rewrites her portrait story of Artaud, culled from diary pieces, new information, and her imagination. In her current diary she works to get into her writing a sense of drama (as with the Hampton Manor visit) to match, she says, the verbal story-telling skills of Miller, Gonzalo, and Dudley. Her plans to publish her earlier diary are sporadic and frustrated (a condensed version of the diary is rejected by another publisher). She learns this fall that forty-five volumes of her diary, packed to be sent to her, have been lost en route. Ironically, writing in her diary on shipboard to America, she expressed the desire to have the volumes with her, for, had the ship sunk, they would have gone down with her and thus "no one would ever be hurt by the truth."

Fortunately for her peace of mind and for literature, a cable arrives in December informing her that they have been located.[44]

Henry Miller leaves on his first American Odyssey this fall after taking driving lessons from Patchen, depositing the manuscript of his Greek experience (*The Colossus of Maroussi*) with Anaïs, and arranging for her to collect the money from the sub-rosa edition of *Cancer* and send it on as he needs it.[45] He is also supplied with vitamins (he calls it medicine) by her doctor, Max Jacobson, and writes from the road that their "Martian dynamite" is making him feel "like a snorting bull."[46] Discovering America is now his goal, as he drives with Rattner in their 1932 Buick. Though she does not accompany him, as he had planned, Anaïs sends him letters and money.[47] He stops in North Carolina to visit Eduardo Sanchez, who tells Miller his astrological chart does not bode well for the trip. Miller's regular reports from the territories as well as her own sense of rejection in New York heightens Anaïs's dissatisfaction with the United States. A negative judgment of America pervades her diary in the early 1940s.

After his return in December Anaïs meets Miller frequently at a Chinese restaurant in the Village. They talk about the lack of depth and sensitivity in America, their writing, and the erotica they are turning out for the Oklahoma collector. Miller, who has lunch with Barnet Ruder several times, invents wildly pornographic plots in their conversations. Contrary to popular history, however, he only writes two pieces of about seventy pages each— "Mara-Marignan" and "Quiet Days in Clichy"—during May and June of 1940 (they were rewritten and published together under the second title in 1956).[48] Anaïs claims to have studied the *Kamasutra* in the library and writes what she thinks are exaggerated caricatures of sexual encounters. Robert Duncan offers to act out the scenes. They laugh over the plots and puzzle at the "collector's" lack of response to their work. Virginia Admiral writes a fifty-page erotic manuscript, which is rejected as too satiric. Anaïs struggles against poetic extremes. The only feedback is through Ruder's reminders to stick to story line and sex, to avoid poetry or philosophy. The contrast is considerable between the few stories she writes into her diary and the stories she changes after Ruder demands specificity. For example, "The tips of the breasts acknowledged the current of warmth" in the diary becomes "He touched her breasts" in "The Basque and Bijou."[49]

She does more than study the *Kamasutra,* however. She sorts through her own life experiences to create several long, loosely narrated pornographic manuscripts—"Artist Model," "Elena," "Maryanne," and "Marcel." She uses experiences with Hugo, Eduardo, Duncan, Miller, Gonzalo, and others as well as her experiences in Paris (Montparnasse and the houseboat), Switzerland, Woodstock, and Mallorca. Only the names are changed and, as with her earlier experiences, the sex enhanced. In "Artist Model" she turns the shame and trauma of her modeling days into pornographic scenes.[50]

Years later she distinguishes between pornography, which is animalistic and grotesque—she uses *Last Tango in Paris* as an illustration of the bestialization of sexuality—and eroticism, which arouses desire. Pornography "disparages, vulgarizes sensuality."[51] Her own erotic writing, a pioneering enterprise for women, reveals an occasional playfulness and lacks sadism or rage. It has been called everything from "arousing" and "lovely" to "musty, hot house sensuality" and "glossed with etiquette." Its literary merit is negligible. Virginia Admiral, after typing hundreds of pages of it, found it all very boring.

Both Nin and Miller need the money. Her allowance from Hugo is always spent early in the month, and then she is reduced to "borrowing, juggling, postponing, intrigue."[52] She convinces Henry, who is disappointed in a Doubleday advance of five hundred dollars for his book about America, to take the money and give her some financial relief. She claims she is exhausted ("the mother dies of exhaustion"). As she tells Henry, she has carried others' needs since childhood. At every mention of her own charity in her diary, she uses the image of "children" and "mother." Her friends frequently tell her that it is her fault that others burden her: Dudley (the young painter and teller of tall tales) expects her to find an apartment for him, Duncan asks for money, Gonzalo needs rent or a hearing aid for Helba. With her first hundred dollars from the pornography "collector" she pays Gonzalo's dentist and buys a mirror for Helba's dancing. She breaks with Dudley briefly because he sleeps in and drinks all day, expecting her to pay his expenses. And she resents the expectations of Kenneth Patchen, whom Miller has left behind for her to help. Once when she refuses to answer his ring, Patchen crawls in through the transom. He wants fifteen dollars for his gas bill. She records all these charities and impositions, which will dismay future readers of her diary; she mentions having to remake her dresses and coats (particularly when there is a society event) and speaks of "what I give up for my children." Yet it is clear that she needs the exploitation (certainly exaggerated); being needed is confused with being loved.[53] As one friend observed, she needs to have bad sons.[54] Jean Carteret told her in Paris that she was a "voluntary prisoner."[55]

Her "mothering" is vicarious, given to "divided beings," the weak, the gay, and the youthful. "You must give up everything for your writing," she tells a young cousin who is rearing three children while working as a translator. "For me, that is impossible," replies the young woman, fixing her eyes on Anaïs's concert attire—a black-lace blouse, a long tight black taffeta skirt that flares out below the knees, splashes of red in her fingernails, dangling earrings, and a flower in her hair.[56]

Her only publications in 1940 are in Dorothy Norman's *Twice a Year*, and she continues to attend Norman's formal dinner parties because she meets many important people there. Yet she feels no love or affirmation in this New York literary scene, for she cannot "bloom in the cold," as she puts it. Thus she seeks the young and inexperienced who, impressed by her European background, ask her to tell them about Picasso, Tanguy, Max Ernst, and Artaud. Her social life is among the youth, her own private world, rather than among the Europeans who have come to New York.[57]

Every morning after breakfast this winter of 1940–41, she writes erotica. In the afternoon she meets Gonzalo to experiment sexually and to listen to his *Daily Worker* theories ("Hemingway is a traitor to communism," "Psychoanalysis deflects blame from bourgeois society," et cetera). She tries in vain to explain his self-destructive behavior to him. She seeks out Gonzalo, according to a virile friend, because the other men involved in the writing project are "weak livered" guys no one would ever connect with masculine erotica. Another friend describes Gonzalo looking like a football player as he walks down the street with Anaïs.[58] Gonzalo, who shares Miller's story-telling genius, street wisdom, and gift for life, provides her with many of the story lines that she will use, including that of "The Basque and Bijou."[59]

She takes great pride in her influence over Duncan and the other young people, all in their twenties, who visit her. Her letters to Duncan are full of advice about his writing.[60] She has started an "epidemic of journals," she boasts. In this heyday of Freudianism, she competes with their analysts for influence in their lives. She records in her journal that she liberates them and arouses their passion, a claim Virginia Admiral vehemently denies.[61] They talk together about the man who will be reading this clinical sex. One observer in the Village, commenting on the erotica combine, says, "The industry roared, any number of near indigent Villagers got into the act."[62]

Of the youthful group, Robert Duncan stands "nearest" to her. She calls theirs a "barbaric friendship"; he calls them "spectral lovers." Yet he complicates their friendship by insisting that she (his feminine double) love and financially assist his friend Patchen (his masculine double)—thus enabling him to find harmony. In her diary she frequently expresses dislike for Patchen's passivity and his expectation that he will be taken care of. He gets her money anyway, through Henry. Soon she and Duncan realize that his "Patchen purgatory," as he calls it, is his own guilt burden. He shares with her a propensity to protect "children," to quest for a father, to need love each day (Duncan, who roams the New York gay bars, calls it a hunger for God). They also share a desire for tension and intensity, and even a similar vocabulary. He calls her "enchanted and enchanting," she calls him charming and seductive. His "slender Egyptian body" is firm and beautiful, and his male friends do not satisfy everything he needs. Their love is "purely fraternal," she claims. Yet it is true inversion: they each have fallen in love with themselves in the other. He has become her brother (he even looks like Joaquin) and soul mate, as Eduardo had once been.[63]

On 7 January 1941, Robert Duncan comes to the Guiler apartment for his twenty-second birthday, a birthday he shares with June Miller, Anaïs notes. With a record of *Ionization* by Edgar Varèse, which he brings, Duncan dances an abstract, stylized dance to the percussion sounds of the French-born composer's music. She loves his many poses and knows he understands her—she calls theirs a "fecund labyrinth" (her favorite expression at the time) of transformations and masquerades. His response to her helps her "sprout new leaves" after her traumatic transplantation to New York.[64] She reads his diary and knows his sexual habits. They write their diaries together, sometimes at the same table. He writes inspired descriptions of her diary, invoking Joycean imagery of flowing rivers. She recognizes in this young writer a poetic talent greater than her own. She feeds all his hungry friends, and she sends two of his poems to *Poetry* magazine, where they are published in the May 1942 issue. When her allowance is spent, she writes thirty more pages of erotica or gets help from her cousin.

Anaïs is not the only Culmell who loves Robert Duncan. During Christmas vacation 1940, Duncan and Admiral had visited Eduardo Sanchez and his sister in Asheville, North Carolina. Duncan is having an affair with Eduardo, who is madly in love. He lavishes money and gifts on him and takes the young man to the beach for a honeymoon. Duncan, who bought the Cooneys' printing press when they temporarily moved to Georgia, now informs Blanche Cooney in a letter that "Eduardo is a darling . . . a handsome Castilian knight with a grand child-like gentlemanly grace about him."[65] When the Cooneys move back to Ashfield, Massachusetts, Eduardo comes to their farm to meet them.

When Anaïs is together with Eduardo and Robert Duncan, she feels she is incestuously participating in their love affair.[66] She will use their affair in her diary, in a novel, and in her erotica. In the third volume of her diary, when she publishes it, she refers to Eduardo as "Paul," just another lover of Duncan. In a long erotic manuscript entitled "Elena," he is Miguel, the gay cousin of Elena, who, when he makes love to Donald (Duncan), is "making love to him—for her."[67] She uses the name Donald again in *A Spy in the House of Love* (1954), in which Donald is a gay youth who ridicules women's foibles ("I can only nibble at you," he tells Sabina).[68] Anaïs also uses Eduardo and Robert, as "Michael" and "Donald," in *Children of the Albatross* (1947), where she portrays the Eduardo of their youth, when he would visit her on

school holidays, and she describes his effect on Donald/Duncan, which is
to reduce the youth to the behavior of a provocative woman.

> Love flowing now between the three, shared, transmitted, conta-
> gious, as if Michael were at last free to love Djuna in the form
> of a boy, through the body of Donald to reach Djuna . . . like an
> algebra of imperfection . . . this trinity of woman sitting between
> two incomplete men. . . . "When will I stop loving these airy
> young men?" she asks.[69]

His affair with Eduardo is destructive for Duncan, who with the financial
assistance of Eduardo makes one or two visits to Dr. Ernst Schweitzer for
psychoanalysis. Duncan's friends believe that Eduardo is a Spanish macho
homosexual whose buggering borders on cruelty (Duncan prefers love affairs). Soon Duncan, tired of being brutally taken from the back and having
his masculinity ignored, flees the abusive cousins. Anaïs's feelings of guilt in
the hurt to Duncan is suggested in her erotic story "Elena," when she says
that the two cousins (Donald and Elena) have a "malicious feminine con-
spiracy to enchant and seduce and victimize Miguel."[70] Duncan also has a
malicious streak, as well as a self-righteous dedication to truth and a desire
to "save" her from her marriage so that she can live with Miller: he takes
Hugo out for lunch and tells him about his wife's many affairs. There is no
record of Hugo's response, but Anaïs undoubtedly succeeds in explaining
away the problem once again. Eduardo settles in on the Cooneys' new farm,
Morning Star, and helps out with expenses and the printing of books, including one of his own on astrology.

Miller tells her in one of his letters from the road this January that he
has stopped writing erotica and urges her to cease as well. "It's devastating.
I feel as tho' I were getting rid of an incubus."[71] Though she claims to be
doing it to earn money for him, he has cut back on his requests, except to
have her serve as his banker. In fact, she is sending him copies of her erotica
to sell to any buyer he can find. Most references to her attempts to sell her
erotica, as well as most references to Barnet Ruder, who is buying it for the
"Collector" (whose existence Miller doubts), will later be deleted from her
published diary and from the final copy of their published letters.[72]

Miller returns temporarily from his second American excursion, via New
Orleans, where he tried for Anaïs to find records on her maternal grandmother, who had abandoned her family in the previous century.[73] He finds
Anaïs depressed by the dispersion of her energies. Indeed her diary is full
of complaints about being "murdered" by her demanding children, and she
includes Miller among them: Dudley brings a young addict who later begins

calling her at four in the morning and ringing her bell at two; she notices her typewriter broken and her fountain pen missing after Patchen's climb through the transom (at first she accuses Robert, who assumes it is the work of Gonzalo). Her list of such abuses seems almost paranoid. In one of her dreams, she has no legs. The compensations are that she will not be abandoned by the needy, that Gonzalo keeps her sexually aroused and supplied with Peruvian stories for her erotica.

The return from Washington, D.C., of Caresse Crosby in the spring of 1941 enlivens Anaïs, who accompanies her friend to the opening night 24 March of Orson Welles's *Native Son,* based on Richard Wright's novel. Crosby's longtime black lover is Canada Lee, who plays Bigger Thomas. Afterward they go to Lee's club in Harlem, "The Chicken Coop." Lee is fourteen years Crosby's junior, devoted to her, and is depicted in the diary as a tender man with an "orange-toned voice." Anaïs loves the various moods of jazz, learns the names of all the great Harlem musicians, and, after Caresse leaves, begins her own affair with Lee. "I am an African," says Mamba to his lover Sabina in her *Spy in the House of Love,* and she embraces what she poetically calls "the legends of his land" when she embraces him. In this later novel, Anaïs sets Mambo's studio in Patchin Place and his nightclub in the Village, otherwise the similarities are evident. Mambo was hurt by another woman ("a woman like you," he tells Sabina), who desired him for his race, not himself. When Sabina goes to the movies with Mambo she stops in the bathroom first, then walks alone down the aisle to be certain her husband, Alan, is not in the theatre.[74] In a piece of erotica entitled "Anita," a "young prince" of Harlem is having an affair with Anita Grey (Crosby), who has a "vast property in Virginia."[75]

Anaïs is called to her mother's bedside in Williamstown, Massachusetts where she is convalescing from a fall. Her Catholic "fierceness" disappears and Anaïs is able to express her love by making her mother's bed and braiding her hair. She is now mothering the "mother lioness" herself. No long after her return to New York City, she welcomes her own "son" Duncan back from the army, soon after his discharge for declaring his sexual proclivities. She urged him three months earlier to declare his homosexuality and pacifism and be free: "Only domestic animals have guilt," she had written echoing Miller.[76]

After numerous negative reports from Middle America, Miller finally arrives on the West Coast "filled up with things to write." His long letters during the weeks of his travels continue to reinforce Anaïs's feelings of alienation from American life. He hears only "drivel." Pittsburgh is a "hell hole"; Annapolis is "sterile, puerile"; only in Hollywood does he feel that he has "begun to get something out of America." The movie stars and European émigrés delight him. Here, isolated and basking in the warm climate, "heart and soul" can flower. The Atlantic coast, he tells her, is dead.[77]

Miller and Nin have an understanding, their letters suggest, that she will join him on his travels and, if they can arrange the financing of a life together, she will leave her husband. By the time Miller reaches Arizona, he is getting anxious: "So, if you're going to join me soon I'll speed it up. . . . Then either I get enuf to send for you or I return. How's that? But let's go to Mexico then without much delay," he writes her 3 May 1941 from the Grand Canyon. "Now there are still several sources of money open—any one of them should pay your fare out," he writes 12 June from Hollywood. On 24 June he will agree to any plan, if only he knew what she wanted. She is feeling the pressure from her promises—promises perhaps given to keep from losing him to the American frontier. She responds on 15 June by picking a fight that blames him on three fronts: his desire to live in the West is "beyond any consideration for us" though she will not ask him to come back or to live in New York City; his letters are the "worst"—self-centered and expressionless regarding her ability to come to him ("Everything would be all right if you wrote the right kind of letters"); and finances are a factor ("when we planned this we were childishly ignorant of the cost"). Buried in the letter is the real problem, her "emotional attitude" about whether she "can leave and then cannot leave." She is going to Provincetown for the summer, she informs him. He replies 21 June and 9 July, affirming his love ("My whole life is made with you"), assuring her that they will not starve, for he is making some money now and can sacrifice: "You made me free, liberated—now free yourself." We are "paying dearly for our protection" by Hugo, he writes, but it is a lie that he needs her or she him. Neither can be free as long as "Hugo pulls the strings." Why should they blame each other for their "partial existence together" when he is ready to "make a break" whenever she is. Poverty is better than "the deceit and lying and illusory freedom." He awaits her counterproposal. On 12 July she brings up two new issues—his seeming ability to live without her and his refusal to return to New York. In the letters that follow, he assures her in passing of his devotion and his intention to return, but the probability of a union has faded for the last time.[78]

## Luise Rainer

The published diary of these early New York years occasionally reads like a list of parties and an exercise in name-dropping. Yet from Anaïs's encounters with celebrities there emerges a sense of herself as marginal. After encounters with Hugh and Brigitte Chisholm (she is the daughter of Coco Chanel), who have wealth and international associations, she admits to wishing she could dwell in *Vogue* or *Harper's Bazaar* for a few days. She is occasionally invited to European parties, such as one in the fall of 1941 when she joins André Breton, Yves Tanguy, Jacques Lipchitz, and Charles Henri Ford. Europe had come to New York after the war; names such as Duchamp, Matta, Léger, Schoenberg, Dalí, Chagall, Man Ray, Max Ernst, and Fritz Lang helped to make the city the artistic capital of Europe. These Paris associations strengthen her commitment to art but highlight her own failure to find an American audience. She is occasionally intimidated by the talkers, by the socially gregarious, but assures herself that she can converse through her diary.

Her limited audience is youthful, those who eagerly listen to her talk about Paris and the surrealists and read her fiction, now out of print. Duncan is particularly enchanted by her talk of the surrealists and reads a life of Dalí. Later he admits he became her "oppressive attendant," but realizes that she

> sought to propitiate [an idol of personality] each day, weaving about herself the rumors and phantasies of personality-life, claiming her glamour from the famous she had known even as she dismissed them. . . . [Yet she was only] an attendant in the wake . . . the creature of the fringe [of the European surrealists who] invaded the New York scene [at the outbreak of World War II].[79]

The parties and dances where she meets the famous sculptors (Isamu Noguchi), musicians (Edgar Varèse), filmmakers (Louis Buñuel), architects and painters (John Nelson and Frederick Kiesler) occasionally lead to visits to their apartments, but not yet to developed associations or friendships. After several lunches with Paul Rosenfeld, the literary and music critic, he introduces her personally to Sherwood Anderson, whose works she read in Paris with his translator Hélène Boussinescq. Anderson seems pleased by her flattery, but falls fast asleep for the evening. None of the connections leads to an agent or a publisher. She is only selling erotica, producing about eighty pages a week.

At a weekend party at the summer home of Dorothy Norman, in Woods Hole, Massachusetts, Anaïs spends a lot of time with Luise Rainer, the German-born stage and film actress she had briefly met at a dinner party at Norman's apartment in the city. When Anaïs first sees her enter Norman's party, she notes that Rainer is white, delicate, and floating. She, Miller, and Perlès saw Rainer in a film (perhaps *The Good Earth*) in Paris in the spring of 1938, and Miller remarked then on their similarity. He visited her in Hollywood and found her "tragic," but expresses delight when Anaïs tells im of their friendship: "My strongest impression when I met her [was] that ou were twins of some sort." Neither of them "belong in this world."[80]

The similarities are evident to anyone who studies Rainer's two Academy ward performances in *The Great Ziegfeld* and *The Good Earth*.[81] Their large, nade-up eyes (Rainer did not use makeup away from the camera); small lightly pointed chin; lidded, down-turned eyes and plucked eyebrows; eart-shaped face with lowered head; foreign accent; expressive hands; and pparent vulnerability are noticed by many friends. Unlike Anaïs, Luise eats vidly.

Anaïs was more than charmed. Rainer, who is nine years younger, seems ragile, needing protection, the "essence of femininity." And she has the bility to reveal herself, as June had. Each recognizes in the other a being eedy of approval and love, addicted to intimacy, willing to throw herself vith abandon into a friendship. They drive in Rainer's little convertible to he dunes and look out toward Europe, which Luise had left in 1935 to act n American films. Anaïs studies Luise's gestures and her ability to change noods, carry her body, act many roles, and Luise studies the same in her ew friend.

Their friendship grows in Provincetown later this summer. Inland are the tudents of the Hofmann school, in cottages on pilings overlooking the water f the bay. Among the group are Virginia Admiral and her future husband, ob De Niro (also a painter). Duncan, who writes "An Encounter" during his holiday, visits Anaïs with a young man named Tennessee Williams. Anaïs ; unimpressed with the young playwright, who never meets her eyes. She als around with Rainer (to her pleasure, someone asks if they are sisters) nd begins an affair with an opera singer, who will visit her later and ontinue the liaison in New York.[82] Someone reports her to the police when he takes off her brassiere on the beach. When she writes later to apologize or neglecting Duncan at Provincetown, she declares it is a place good only or homosexuals.[83] Yet when she writes an erotic story entitled "Life in 'rovincetown," the seaside resort seems full of heterosexual encounters for er protagonist, who enjoys a different man each night.[84]

In the fall Anaïs attends a play in New York in which Rainer is performing, nd writes long descriptions of the actress in her diary. Rainer becomes a flame" when she performs, and certainly would have been loved by Artaud. naïs envies the ease with which the actress steps out of her roles. One ight as they sit on the stairs in her apartment listening to music and talking bout Rainer's unhappy liaison with the married playwright Clifford Odets, he telephone calls from Odets ring and ring in the background. They have uickly become like confiding sisters, symbiotic, holding hands in the back f taxis, sunbathing together in their underwear, each looking for the character with whom she can identify, each finding it in the other. After Luise expresses great self-doubt, Anaïs copies her loving description of her friend from her diary and sends it to her, commanding Luise to use her as a mirror.

Far away in California, Miller is making plans to return to New York by selling some manuscripts, notebooks, and old books, trying to sell his car, and collecting royalties. We both have found "wonderful places," he writes Anaïs in reference to her talk about the sun and water of Provincetown. He now understands Otto Rank's love of California. "Next time let's find one together—yes?"[85] Then he adds, "We'll never find another city like Paris."[86] Unable to sell the Buick, he drives across the country in September.

Anaïs spends the summer and fall of 1941 playing the healer, trying to resolve Luise Rainer's neuroses, first by taking her to an analyst, then by ministering to her herself. Anaïs portrays her as demanding and cruel: at first she wants Anaïs to create a play for her (a promise Odets had failed to keep), then she says that after reading the description of June in the diary, she identifies with June and wants Anaïs to write a book in which she is depicted as June. She asks everything of Anaïs, probably courting rejection. As one of their acquaintances notes, Nin recognizes that Rainer has "negative magic" to a greater degree than she. That is why she falls madly in love with her.[87] Each woman absorbs the gestures and mannerisms of the other, wanting to be the other. Within three years Anaïs will cull from her diary a long short story about an unhappy, neurotic film star, "Stella," with hands like the baton of a conductor.

In preparation for Henry's return in early October, she renovates her working studio. He hates coming back to New York to confront his family and the past, but he must see Anaïs and meet his publisher, who rejects the account of his American journey, *The Air-Conditioned Nightmare*. He will stay until the spring of 1942.

Anaïs's friendship with several artists in Greenwich Village finally begins developing this fall, particularly her relations with Noguchi and Varèse, who live nearby. The visit to each artist's studio or apartment merits a detailed portrait in her diary that captures the character of the inhabitant. For example, she describes the phonograph in Varèse's studio as always turned to the highest volume and his music stand and walls as covered with music fragments that he rearranges and glues together. The frequent appearance of the names of these two artists suggests an intimacy that was not there. Edgar Varèse, according to a mutual friend, "disliked her intensely."[88]

She and Hugo meet Stanley William Hayter, the world-famous engraver recently arrived from France. He works with the techniques of William Blake and is rapidly becoming the father of graphic arts in America. Anaïs describes him as "like a stretched bow or a coiled spring." Hugo, who is now

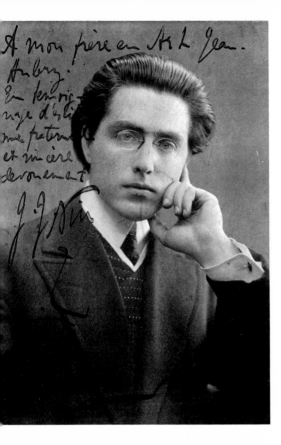

Joaquin Nin y Castellanos, age twenty-nine, in 1908. His daughter, Anaïs, was already five years old. She was to treat her adult relationship with him in her novelette "Winter of Artifice" and in the unexpurgated diaries published as *Incest*.

A page from Nin's diary for 3 August 1914, into which she pasted a photograph of her mother, Rosa Culmell de Nin, "Singer and tender loving Mother."

*Above:* The home of Nin's aunt and uncle Edelmira (Culmell) and Gilbert P. Chase, in Kew Gardens, Queens, where Anaïs spent her first two weeks in America in August 1914.

*Above:* The first home of Anaïs and Hugo Guiler. After their wedding in Havana in March 1923, they moved into this mission-style bungalow, located at 8400 114th Street, Richmond Hill, Queens. They lived here until they moved to Paris the following year.

*Left:* John Erskine, Professor of English at Columbia University and the hero of his student Hugo Guiler, who graduated from the university in 1919. Anaïs had a brief adulterous affair with Erskine in Paris in 1929.

…he Guilers' Louveciennes home, behind a …sty gate at 2 bis, rue Monbuisson. Anaïs and …ugo lived in this house, which she called her …boratory of the soul," from fall 1930 to fall …936. Louveciennes is near Versailles, a half …ur's train ride from Paris.

Henry Miller and his bicycle, his favorite form of transportation, in Paris, about 1932. He occasionally rode to Louveciennes for what he called literary "fuck fests." The affair lasted nearly a decade, and he frequently appears as "Jay" in Nin's fiction.

June Miller, Henry's second wife and the "Mona" of his *Tropic of Cancer,* who met Anaïs at Louveciennes. She is "Sabina" in Nin's novels *Ladders to Fire* and *A Spy in the House of Love.*

Antonin Artaud, French madman, homosexual, playwright, and actor. His purported affair with Nin was short-lived. Her short story "Je suis le plus malade des Surrealistes" is based on her diary portrait of Artaud.

*Below:* La Coupole brasserie, which opened in Montparnasse in December 1927. Nin and Artaud came here after his Sorbonne lecture. Nin, Miller, and Durrell called themselves the "Three Musketeers of La Coupole."

Dr. Otto Rank, standing behind his mentor Dr. Sigmund Freud, 1922. After he broke with Freud, Rank moved to Paris in 1926, where he became Nin's psychoanalyst later in 1933 (after her incestuous affair with h[er] father). Her analysis with Rank led to an affair with him the following summer. Nin['s] story "The Voice" is based on her work wi[th] Rank in New York in the winter of 1934–[5].

*Clockwise from above:* (1) The Villa Seurat, where at No. 18 (right, with curved windows) Nin rented a top-rear studio for Miller. Miller moved in September 1934, when his *Tropic of Cancer* was published in Paris, and remained for five years. This small dead-end street is named for one of the many artists who lived here.

(2) The young British novelist Lawrence Durrell joined the Villa Seurat group in the fall of 1937 and collaborated with Nin, Miller, and Alfred Perlès on *The Booster.*

(3) Alfred Perlès shared an apartment in the Paris suburb of Clichy with Miller, who called him Fred, or Joey. Perlès confessed his love for Nin in a letter that she kept folded into her diary. In his *My Friend Henry Miller* he protects Nin by calling her, when he describes her life with Miller, "Mlle Liane de Champsaur."

(4) *Left to right:* David Edgar, his wife, Henry Miller, Michael Fraenkel, his mistress Joyce, and Alfred Perlès in the garden of the Guiler house in Louveciennes. Edgar wrote for *The Booster,* and Fraenkel was an American book dealer and writer who owned No. 18 Villa Seurat. This group met with Nin in June 1935 to plan their Siana series publishing venture.

*Philip R. Nurenberg Collection, Los Angeles*

*Above*: Salvador and Gala Dalí, Henry Miller (*standing*), and Barnet Ruder at Hampton Manor, the Virginia home of Caresse Crosby, in 1940. In the *Diary* Nin describes her own visit here and her meeting with Dalí, whose films she and Miller admired. Ruder, a New York bookseller, commissioned Miller and Nin to write erotica for private collectors.

*Left*: Caresse Crosby in 1929, the year that her husband, Harry, died. Nin, who did not meet Crosby until 1940 in New York City, would accompany her to the nightspots of Harlem. Both had affairs with black club owner and actor Canada Lee.

Eduardo Sanchez, the beloved cousin of Anaïs, at James and Blanche Cooney's Morning Star Farm in Massachusetts in the 1940s. He appears in Nin's fiction, including the story "Our Minds Are Engaged," the novel *Children of the Albatross*, and the erotica.

Robert Duncan, a young homosexual poet, met Nin at the Cooneys' farm at Christmas 1939. They had an intense friendship, sharing their diaries and collaborating on the writing of erotica, until his unhappy affair with Eduardo Sanchez. She portrays him in *Children of the Albatross.*

*Left:* Edmund Wilson, dean of American critics. Wilson's *New Yorker* review of Nin's story collection *Under a Glass Bell,* published by her own Gemor Press, brought critical attention to her work. They had a brief affair afterward.

*Below:* Luise Rainer, film actress, and Clifford Odets, playwright, in Hollywood, 1936. Nin met Rainer in the early 1940s and used Rainer and Odets as models for "Stella" and "Bruno" in the story "Stella" (*Winter of Artifice*).

Gore Vidal, at twenty-one, in April 1947. Vidal worked as an editor at E. P. Dutton and secured for Nin her first commercial publishing contracts, for *Ladders to Fire* and *Children of the Albatross*. Another intense friendship that soured. He created several satirical portraits of her in his fiction.

*Left:* James Leo Herlihy, best known for his novel *Midnight Cowboy,* in 1958. Nin met Herlihy at Black Mountain College in the late 1940s, and they remained devoted friends in New York City and Los Angeles until her death.

*Below:* Anne and Maxwell Geismar, 1964. Nin cultivated the approval of Geismar, a prominent American Marxist critic, who gave her a positive review in *The Nation* in 1954. The Geismars and Guilers socialized in the 1950s and 1960s. In his memoirs he accuses her diaries of being "abstracted and doctored."

*Courtesy of Anne Geismar*

Lawrence Durrell (*left*) and Dr. Jean Fanchette in Paris at a party Fanchette gave for the British novelist in June 1959. They were celebrating an issue of Fanchette's *Two Cities* devoted to the work of Durrell. Nin served for a while as New York editor for the bilingual review.

Daisy Aldan, poet and editor, in New York City, 1964. Aldan and Nin gave readings together in New York and Los Angeles and remained close friends for almost two decades. Many of Aldan's early poems dealt with her friendship with Nin.

George Leite (*left*), Nin, and Gilbert Neiman in San Francisco in the late 1940s. She lived here with Rupert Pole while he attended Berkeley in 1948–49, and signed books at this party at Daliel's Bookstore and Art Gallery, owned by Leite. Neiman was the writer and translator who offered Miller his first home in Los Angeles.

*Courtesy of Nancy Leite*

Renate Druks, Ronnie Knox (Renate's young husband), and Nin on the California coast near Pacific Palisades in the 1950s. Druks is the heroine of Nin's *Collages*.

*Courtesy of Renate Druks*

Nin, Renate Druks, and Joan Houseman preparing for the unveiling of Druks's painting of Nin as Pisces. One of several performance-art events of the early 1960s, this one reenacted the painting by means of veils, with Nin wrapped in "the ticker tape of her unconscious," and including dead fish, gunshots, and beautiful women rising from the dead.

*Courtesy of Renate Druks*

Hank Hinton

"Anaïs Nin and Gore Vidal, Circa 1945" illustrated Vidal's 26 September, 1971, *Los Angeles Times* review of Nin's fourth published diary volume.

Nin on the lecture circuit in September 1971, the year she gave commencement addresses at Reed and Bennington colleges. She gave fifty-six lectures or readings between September 1972 and May 1973 alone, and it was not uncommon for her to address a thousand people at her college and university appearances.

*Christian DuBois Larson*

*Below:* Nin and Rupert Pole, holding their poodle Piccola, at their home in the Silver Lake district of Los Angeles, 1963. The house, completed in 1961, was designed by Pole's half brother, Eric Wright, grandson of Frank Lloyd Wright.

Christian DuBois Larson

Nin at her typewriter in her Silver Lake home, 1963, with Rupert's reflected presence in the window.

*Above:* Nin with Richard R. Centing (*left*) and Benjamin Franklin V, editors of the quarterly *Under the Sign of Pisces: Anaïs Nin and Her Circle,* at the Evanston, Illinois, home of Durrett Wagner, editor at Swallow Press, 23 January 1972.

*Right:* Nin's husband, Ian Hugo, engraver and filmmaker, in Buffalo in 1975. Hugh (Hugo) Parker Guiler changed his name in the late 1940s when he left banking for copper engraving.

*Below:* Bicoastal husbands: Ian Hugo and Rupert Pole met for the first time at a lawn party in Connecticut, 23 May 1980, after the death of Anaïs Nin. Hugo died in 1985.

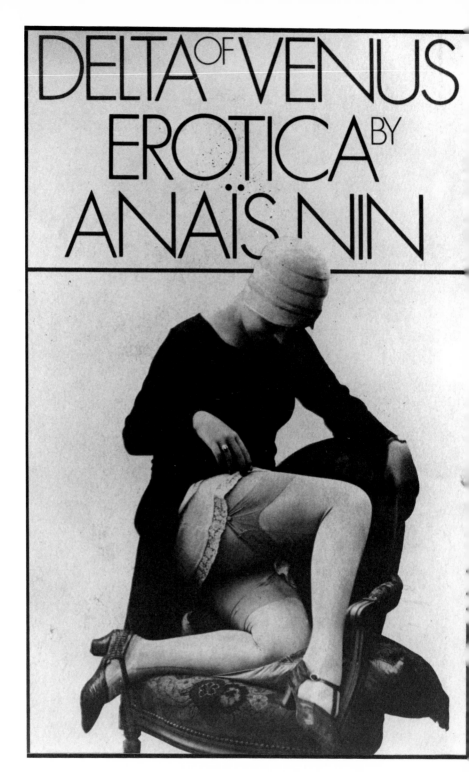

# DELTA OF VENUS EROTICA BY ANAÏS NIN

Cover of Nin's first collection of erotica, published posthumously in 1977. It was an immediate bestseller—her first.

permanently established in the New York office of his bank, admires Hayter a great deal and begins studying engraving with Hayter at the New School, what his students call Atelier 17.[89]

Hugo Guiler has a poetic and artistic bent and is a banker only in manners and modesty.[90] With friends their own age, Hugo and Anaïs appear to be a devoted couple. But her young friends are not to engage him in conversation or they risk being rebuffed by Anaïs, who desires their full attention.[91] As "Linda" says of her husband, in an erotic story by Anaïs, he "closed his eyes over her young admirers. He did not believe that she took them seriously."[92]

After polishing several of her short stories about Paris subjects, Anaïs begins thinking of her stories as a book: not merely a sketchbook, but a tapestry. Her short narrative portrait of Artaud is published by Duncan's *Experimental Review*. Seven pages of her first childhood diary, which she has translated, is published in Norman's *Twice a Year*. She imagines with delight her brother Joaquin reading her childhood description of him; but her joy is dampened when someone at the *Saturday Review of Literature* says her diary has "no universal quality"[93] and when her brother Thorvald insists he be kept out of her diary. "Whatever praise I seek is to balance the first twenty years of no-praise,"[94] she says after this unhappy brief encounter with Thorvald, who had come to New York for medical treatment.

Praise comes only from her young circle, which now includes George Barker, an Anglo-Irish poet with a sensuous mouth and a Roman nose. Barker has already published seven books of poetry in London and one in New York and is a major poet in the generation of Dylan Thomas and David Gascoyne. She soon begins an affair with Barker. He praises *The House of Incest* as her best work, assuring her it deserves to be placed beside Djuna Barnes's *Nightwood* as prose poetry. (Duncan praises both *The House of Incest* and the poetry of Barker, with whom he had briefly fallen in love, as major influences on his own style.) She covets such praise, but realizes that writing fulfills a need greater than worldly fame: it heightens life around her, leads her into life (Henry had appeared after her Lawrence book), and blasts her out of isolation. Her father had blown up the bridge between herself and other human beings and made her timid, she believes. Writing rebuilds the human tie.[95]

Her writing also plays a central role in controlling her neurosis (she calls it her "demon"). When Luise Rainer's erratic behavior becomes oppressive, Anaïs realizes how much she has learned from psychoanalysis and how much healthier than Rainer she is. Her own demon is locked in her diary, and only when she hears a fire engine does she fear the diary volumes will burn and release the demon. She has also locked up her anger, for she expresses anger only in her diary, where she rails against Patchen, Mrs. Norman, Duncan, and others. In their presence she is cordial, attending Norman's dinner parties, taking Patchen's manuscript to Maxwell Perkins at Scribner's, introducing him to an agent, and even giving him fifty dollars.

Her break with Robert Duncan occurs after an intense year of togetherness. He is increasingly disenchanted with her, and she believes he has broken Eduardo's heart by leaving him to sleep with a woman who later becomes his wife. (Duncan will be the fourth husband of his dear friend Marjorie McKee.) Though Anaïs later understands that it was an honest act of courage on Duncan's part, his move away from his journal and from his dependency on her also causes a strain. He returns to his beloved Berkeley only in part because of Eduardo's abuse and Anaïs's "revolting" portrayal of him in her diary. He accuses her of portraying him as a "whorish caricature," a "female impersonator, not only a rival but a cheat at that . . . a faggot." Her portrayal reminds him of the "small-town bigotry" of his boyhood Bakersfield, California. He calls her "Anus Ninny."[96]

Despite Miller's warning not to sell herself, the erotica enterprise continues and she describes herself as the madam of a literary house of prostitution-writing. She even writes an erotic story ("Maryanne") about a poet who lives on a houseboat in Paris and has a group of young people writing porn.[97] Anaïs supplies the paper and carbon, collects the writing of her young protégés, and sends her part-time maid to deliver the pages to Barnet Ruder, thus protecting the anonymity of Crosby, Duncan, Virginia Admiral, James Cooney, Janet Thurman (former roommate of Admiral's and McKee's), Bernie Wolfe (boyfriend of Thurman), George Barker (who writes eighty-five pages of erotica at a feverish pitch, saying he prefers it to begging to keep himself in drink), and others, including a well-known editor named Harvey Breit.

Harvey Breit takes Anaïs to a gala, end-of-the year holiday party attended by Alexander Calder and Fernand Léger (the latter is guest of honor). Breit, described in Anaïs's diary as a tanned, handsome poet with a husky voice, is a reviewer and assistant editor of the *New York Times Book Review* from 1940 to 1965.[98] She is a decade younger than Breit, with whom she has been having an affair for several months. Some of his young friends, who do not know Anaïs is married, believe that she is living with Breit. Before the evening is over, Harvey goes home with a young woman friend named Bita, who remembers years later that Breit "was a crazy poet," and when he left the party with her, Anaïs "created a scene."[99]

Anaïs is able to keep her lovers from running into each other by having a separate ring for each. She and Hugo live on the fifth floor of a building without an elevator, which means that the downstairs bell is a means of controlling traffic. "Knowing Anaïs was like reading a detective novel," says Virginia Admiral, citing the "elaborate deceptions, the complicated doorbell system," and "the problem of what this one knew and that one was not supposed to know."[100]

When the "collector" offers double pay for pornography by Miller, they write fake Miller (perhaps at Miller's suggestion, for he does not want to get involved). Crosby offers (maybe with the aid of Anaïs) to write more fake Miller, entitles her two-hundred-page manuscript (in three parts) "Opus Pistorium," and shows it to him. The collector loves this "real" Miller. Miller later denied authoring this manuscript on many occasions when contacted by collectors: "I abhor . . . 'smut for smut's sake'. . . I don't have a left and right hand—in writing," he informs one such collector. Later Gershon Legman will claim that he and Sewall, gifted at parody, wrote the last portion of the *Opus Pistorum* manuscript themselves and published it over Miller's name.[101] Both collectors and publishers since have found it convenient to believe that Miller is the author.

"I gather poets around me and we all write beautiful erotica," Anaïs notes in her diary. The writing "becomes a road to sainthood rather than to debauchery." Young Bernie Wolfe will portray the scene differently when he writes his *Memoirs of a Not Altogether Shy Pornographer* thirty years later.[102] It tries their patience and suppresses their libidos. Their serious writing style often spills into the erotica. Barker, who has already published four books of poetry, finds that his surreal poetic style creeps into his erotic short stories. Anaïs writes what one critic calls "diaphanous erotica."[103] In a short piece about a father whipping his three children, she betrays her own pain: the violence of his blows "awakened pleasure as well as pain," the blows being so close to the area of her sexual pleasure. She writes ten or fifteen pages a day, even during the air raids and sirens after Japan attacks Pearl Harbor. To affirm life and art amid the despair of war, she says, she gets her typewriter cleaned. More important, she plans to print her own books.

## A Printing Press of Her Own

Her frustration in being rejected by publishers (one asks if she would write a book like *The Good Earth*, with a beginning, middle, and end) and the growing volume of her fiction serve as catalysts for buying a press. She can use the income from a press, which would also employ Gonzalo. Henry, with all his publications by other small presses, she observes, has only seen a thousand dollars in royalties this year.

For months she has been assessing the American scene, which seems, like New York City, hostile and materialistic, diseased and decadent, and she hopes to return to France.[104] Miller writes her from Hollywood that she is right to evaluate America and her "literary situation," but wrong to be hyper-sensitive about others' reactions or reviews. She must, he insists, concentrate on her diary, which is "more important than all my work put together," and publish it perhaps piecemeal in Mexico with his help. Only the "esteem of one's equals" matters.[105] But she needs greater recognition than he can give her and thus rails against mediocrity, the disappearance of poetry from America, and the danger of the poet stepping out of the realm of "the marvelous" and "the dream" in order to "preach."[106] Such remarks allude to the chief ideological literary institution of the late 1930s and 1940s, the *Partisan Review*, located east of the Village at 45 Astor Place.

The *Partisan Review*, founded in 1934 by the New York John Reed Club, specifically Philip Rahv and William Phillips, as a forum for Marxist views, had by 1937 become Trotskyist. When Anaïs meets the editors at a party in January, she finds them cold, rigid, intellectual, and without humor. The staff includes Dwight Macdonald, F. W. Dupee, Mary McCarthy, and Delmore Schwartz (the latter will serve as editor from 1943 to 1955). They publish work by James T. Farrell and other politically engaged writers. When Simone de Beauvoir, a French writer herself politically active, visits the U.S. five years later, she observes that for the French to appreciate the American literature that they do (i.e., Faulkner) is "to insult the intelligentsia of the U.S.A."[107] Certainly Anaïs's writing, which is closer to visionary poetry and European surrealism, is anathema. In her own words, she is compressing her writing, using "a roller to squeeze out all superfluous matter," whereas the current style of realism is to include even "the amount of rent paid by each character."[108]

Consequently, she feels outside all the leading literary circles and alien-ated even from the writers who were in Paris, including the women, such as Kay Boyle and Djuna Barnes. Though they certainly met on at least one occasion (Anaïs remembers a café meeting in Paris), Boyle will not remem-ber meeting Anaïs.[109] Djuna Barnes refuses her friendship. Barnes is se-cluded in Patchin Place, about four blocks from the Guilers, and avoids Anaïs and others. Barnes's first biographer claims that she "had contempt for" Anaïs, a view confirmed by others, who claim Barnes crossed the street when she saw Anaïs coming.[110] She expresses irritation that Anaïs uses the name Djuna in several of her novels, beginning with *The Winter of Artifice*. In response, Anaïs claims she discovered the name in an anthology of Welsh names.[111] Ironically, because Anaïs speaks so frequently of Barnes, and cred-its the influence of *Nightwood* on her work, years later the *Times* of London will mistakenly call Anaïs "an intimate of Djuna Barnes."

All these factors prompt Anaïs to establish a printing press of her own. Dorothy Norman refuses her request for a two-hundred-dollar loan, but

Frances Steloff can lend seventy-five, and another friend lends a hundred. In December she and Gonzalo find a loft at 44 MacDougal Street and she studies library books about operating a press. Gonzalo buys the type and print trays. She takes possession of the skylight attic on the top floor of an old four-story house (since demolished). The rent is thirty-five dollars a month, and the room includes a tiny kitchenette, a fireplace, and a couch and desk. The uneven floor is painted black, the walls yellow, the slanted ceiling dirty white. Gonzalo hangs his drawings on the walls. They remind her of the houseboat on the Seine. The neighborhood, south of Houston between Prince and King streets, is like Montmartre, she exclaims romantically for her diary.[112]

She has finally found a focus for her life, she believes. She will eat, sleep, and dream the printing press. Like Virginia Woolf she will print her own books. She and her friends will set the type and Gonzalo will run the press. Though her youthful friends disappear at the suggestion of manual labor, Eduardo soon joins her and Gonzalo. On the day after Christmas, the day of his fiftieth birthday, Miller puts the final words to his manuscript. The decade with Anaïs is coming to an end. Soon, when spring has come and gone, he will leave the city to return to his new life in California.

Working eight hours a day, she and Gonzalo begin setting type by trial and error, making mistakes, resetting each word and line. While the headlines outside scream bold black news of wars on two continents, Anaïs is setting the words of *Winter of Artifice* (in this incarnation printed without the article). It is dirty, hard work—particularly hard work for Gonzalo, who has to pedal the press, which operates like a sewing machine. She describes his heroic battles with the primitive technology, using epic imagery of the centaur. She loves the physicality of printing. Even the floorboards groan under the heavy weight of the machine. The productive energy of the day and the physical fatigue she experiences each evening are a relief from psychological sparring: Helba's hysterical scenes, Dudley's breakdown (and his wife's attempted suicide), Dorothy Norman's second refusal to loan money. When Duncan prepares to return to Berkeley, she asks him if Hugo can buy the Cooneys' press from him, but nothing comes of the offer. These "child prodigies of intelligence" treat each other so brutally that she longs for the French code of irony, understatement, and silence (the code she and Hugo purport to live by).[113]

Hugo's copper engravings are to be printed in the book, over his artistic name, Ian Hugo. He has now dropped his last name and will henceforth be known as an artist, not a banker. His engraving teacher, William Hayter, comes to the studio to show them how to print the engravings. Gonzalo has to clean the plate after each print—more than five hundred times. Hugo's flowing images are juxtaposed against the newspaper photographs of the Polish war dead. Jimmy Cooney, who has set type for his own magazine, also comes by one day to give them some of his knowledge of printing. Eduardo, who divides his time between the Cooney farm in Ashfield, Massachusetts, and an apartment on West Sixty-ninth, helps when he can. He eventually hand-sets his own type for *The Round—An Introduction*, an account of his spiritual odyssey, on Cooney's press. Because he asks not be included in Anaïs's diary of this period, he will not receive credit for his support of the press. On Anaïs's thirty-ninth birthday, 21 February 1942, she and Gonzalo set the first two pages for a five-hundred-copy edition. By 4 March they are on page forty-four.

She lives for hours with the alphabet and dirty fingers. Picking up letters and setting them next to each other to form words, she begins to rethink her words and her story. She cuts words, molds the stories into better focus—it is like film editing, she thinks. She also sees the characters and situations in the fiction differently. She drops the opening "Djuna" story that had appeared in the 1939 Obelisk Press edition in Paris, for it reveals more than she wishes to reveal about the June-Henry-Anaïs triangle. The two remaining sections are revised, and continue evolving as she sets each word. "Winter of Artifice," which had been called "Lilith" in 1939 and before that the "Father Story" or "The Double," she begins seeing differently: the first-person Stella, who had told the story of reunion with her cold, superficial, egotistical father, is now described in the third person: "I am waiting for him" becomes "She is waiting for him." She relives the reunion with her father in her diary at night as well, remembering that this "no praise man" had created in her "such a need of approval!" As she sets the story she tells herself that she is "erecting the last monument to his failure as a father." "The Voice" remains as the last piece in the collection, but with alterations of language and tone. The Voice or psychoanalyst (Rank) in his Hotel Chaotica high above New York listens and reacts to his four clients. Anaïs finds that her views of Rank and her attitude toward her own father have changed in the three years since she first published these stories. She understands more as she relives it, and she questions the novel genre that fixes reality statically in time.[114]

As she picks up the letter *H* from the alphabet box, she thinks of Henry, who has already completed four hundred pages of *The Rosy Crucifixion*, "writing like a fountain." They are both carried away by their work, both out of step with those artists politically engaged with the nightmare of history. Safe in her "private shelter" in the Village, she is very aware of the bombarding of Paris. She reprimands Miller when he says he is indifferent to the war.

By 5 May 1942, she and Gonzalo have finished setting the last word and printed the cover. The bindery delivers the books ten days later.

The Gotham Book Mart's publication party for *Winter of Artifice* gives Anaïs some of the approval she needs. A growing group of admirers attends. She records every word of praise in her diary. One name on her list of those who express interest is Eduard Roditi, who will describe her as a "rather elegant society woman who displayed intellectual pretensions."[115] She also does not know that James Laughlin of New Directions has confided to the poet Kenneth Rexroth that the ink control of the book is poor: "Unlike the squid which she is said to resemble in bed, as printer she cannot make it flow."[116]

It is Hugo's day as well, and his engravings win the approval of other artists. Eduardo is there also. The typesetter of the book, Gonzalo, will only stand on the sidewalk and glance in the window, like the little match girl.

Anaïs's approval from her peers is short-lived. Earlier, when James Laughlin had asked her to name her own reviewer for his *New Directions*, she had chosen William Carlos Williams.[117] But when the review appears, she disapproves of the title "Men Have No Tenderness" and of Williams's biographical focus. She tries to tell him before publication that he misinterprets the work. He tells Laughlin privately that he has rewritten the review four times.[118] Though Miller informs her it is a good review, she cannot see or understand Williams's praise for her lack of wordiness, for her assurance, and for her "authentic female approach to the arts."[119] Frustrated at the lack of understanding between them, he refers to her ("A. N.") at the end of the second book of his epic poem *Patterson* as an example of the cleavage between the sexes; and he tells literary critic Kenneth Burke that "some day there will be no more committee meetings, Anaïs Nin, or Karl Shapiro."[120]

Two other mixed reviews, in the *New York Herald Tribune Books* and *The Nation*—the latter by Paul Rosenfeld, whose friendship she has cultivated—connect the book to her diary and life. She believes Rosenfeld is "totally inaccurate."[121] Though Miller thinks these reviews are also good, Anaïs cannot handle the slightest criticism. Hereafter she resolves to respond to reviews and to try to have her fiction studied as fiction and not as biography.[122]

By June, Miller is back in Los Angeles, staying as a guest in the home of Margaret and Gilbert Neiman in Beverly Glen, where he has been joined by John Dudley, now separated from his wife. The two men share expenses and paint together, Dudley giving Miller lessons. Miller has now written ten books, most of which have been issued from little presses and for which he has received almost nothing. It seems evident to him that Anaïs will never leave her husband, and during his last weeks in New York he had fallen passionately in love with a woman named Laure, who will follow him to Los Angeles in May. Though the affair does not last, he stays in California because the room is free and he loves the city for its European air, the aroma of colonial Spain, and its warmth and promise. "Everything seems brand-new."[123] Here he rediscovers that he is as American as Walt Whitman. He fears that he has asked too much of Anaïs, yet he will continue to dream of winning her back.[124]

She has found a rhythm for her life that is rewarding. In the humidity and tar fumes of a New York July, she and Gonzalo begin printing a book of poems by Hugh Chisholm, whose book, *Several Have Lived*, includes illustrations by exiled surrealist André Masson. Perhaps to avoid the stigma of self-publication and to pay Gonzalo homage, she gives the press a name that echoes Gonzalo's name: Gemor Press.[125] The logo of Gemor Press includes the initials GM, AN, and ES (with the AN raised to the line above the others) to represent Gonzalo, Anaïs, and Eduardo. She considers reprinting Djuna Barnes's *Nightwood*, and Steloff suggests she reprint Durrell's *Black Book* and her own Lawrence book, but the money is not available. To meet expenses they print stationery to order. In August of 1942 she returns to Provincetown, recreating the St.-Tropez days with Gonzalo and Helba. She plunges beneath the seawater as the air force planes fly above, and she thinks she hears the depth charges pound into the sea.

Many of the same revelers are there, including Tennessee Williams, Bob De Niro, and his wife, Virginia Admiral. Robert Duncan is not among them. In May he will marry Marjorie McKee, about the time that their mutual friend is starting her own family: standing with the couple as a witness will be Virginia Admiral, by this time six months pregnant with her son, the future actor Robert De Niro. Though the elder De Niro has listened to her stories of Paris cafés and artists, he does not much care for Anaïs.[126]

She had thought that the press would solve her economic problems. But *Winter of Artifice* sells slowly, and her strained finances keep her from printing more books. Miller has still not found work in scriptwriting in Hollywood; she still occasionally sends him pocket money earned by the erotica, hoping that *he* can be more supportive of *her* for a change. They write each other long and frequent letters. He writes about meeting some of the many artists who are in Los Angeles (Erich Maria Remarque, Igor Stravinsky, Man Ray), but holds many in disdain for selling out: Faulkner is working at this time at Warner Studios. Discouraged, Miller wonders if it is his "destiny . . . not to earn money."[127] In her diary Anaïs expresses the same no-talent-for-making-money lament—for herself, not to mention her "protégés" Gonzalo and Miller.[128] When Henry senses her disappointment in him and her sense of self-sacrifice for him, he insists that she not send him any more money. She must not feel responsible for him. He makes no demands, places no blame. The fact is he blames himself, the "something lacking in me," and questions his role as a writer.[129] Once more he will express his long desire for a life with her: "Always I have the forlorn wish that there might be a way of living here with you. It's terrible to think that you have the right place and the right person, but can never bring them together."[130]

## Physical Breakdown

Anaïs sends an accusatory letter to Miller out of a sense of fatigue, guilt, and resentment. She resents him both for being a burden and for demanding that she not consider him a burden. Because she fears losing him if he no longer needs her, she blames herself for "failing" him. She has worked so hard, and yet is thrown into depression by the reviews and low sales, coupled with another rejection, from Houghton Mifflin. She is left with no money to continue publishing. All this while Miller has achieved some kind of harmonious Buddhist existence ("earning a living is not *living*," as he puts it).[131] Feeling humiliated, feeling that she has irresponsibly played the bohemian printer, she determines she will take a job. But she does not need to—she has a husband, Miller replies. If she is saying this for him, forget it; he will return and take a job himself to support her printing press. You must print your *own* work, he insists. But he recognizes it is anguish and lack of confidence he is hearing.[132] Eventually Anaïs realizes she is having a breakdown, then assures him she feels better. She is suffering her old problem with psychosomatic fatigue: anemia and self-doubt are weakening her.[133]

In her weakened state, Anaïs makes several new female friends whose stories she recreates in her diary. The first will remain her friend for life: Frances Fox Robinson (later Brown, then Field) is a beautiful and ethereal artist who grew up in poverty and has been bedridden with tuberculosis. Anaïs meets Frances through Blanche Cooney.[134] Frances's illnesses are as numerous as Helba's, but the two women respond in opposite ways. Frances is gentle and sensitive, and Anaïs loves her instantly. She is also attracted to what one mutual friend called Frances's "incredible sense of grandeur" and her "numerous lovers (one rented a Rolls-Royce to make love to her in the backseat)."[135] Frances tells stories of her poverty-stricken childhood on the lower East Side and talks of dreams and of Jungian psychoanalysis (for she is in analysis with Dr. Martha Jaeger). Talk of racial memory reminds Anaïs of the time she lost her identity in Fez. Once again, Anaïs throws herself into a relationship obsessively: "We had the most miraculous understanding of each other's lives," she exclaims. They "exchange lives" and share dreams. Soon they are going everywhere together, then reviewing their activities.[136]

When Anaïs tells Miller that she is thinking of going back to the practice of analysis, he writes to encourage her. Don't do it because you think you like to aid the weak and ill, he warns. You will be doing it to treat yourself.[137]

Her friend Moira, also in analysis with Dr. Jaeger, is a voluptuous Persian artist who reads Tarot cards and studies dreams. Anaïs is fascinated with her because she lacks the Christian concern with self-sacrifice and self-effacement. Anaïs exploits Moira's capacity for destruction (a "masculine" quality she herself wishes to have) in her short story "Hejda," and begins to change her view of woman in the process. Moira is an important friend during a period in which Anaïs struggles with the definition of gender. Her friendship with Moira, of which little is recorded or known, also leads to Anaïs's reworking of her Fez trip into a story entitled "Labyrinth."

Two arduous printing commissions for Caresse Crosby follow in early 1943 and increase the psychological pressure on Anaïs. The first is for one hundred copies of Sharon Vail's *Four Poems.* Vail is the daughter of Kay Boyle and Laurence Vail, two of the better known American artists in Paris in the 1920s, and the book is a Christmas gift from mother to daughter. Crosby does all the publisher's selection and editing, and Boyle never knows exactly who the printer is.[138] The second printing job is 610 copies of an enlarged, translated issue of the Black Sun edition of Paul Eluard's *Misfortunes of the Immortals,* translated by Hugh Chisholm with drawings by the surrealist Max Ernst. Anaïs meets Ernst and his wife, Peggy Guggenheim, and takes a strong dislike to them, to surrealists in general, and to the publisher's lack of creativity in printing (the book had to be exactly like the original). She feels that her creativity is bottled up and that her diary is now filled only with passages from books she has read, stories of the lives of Frances and Moira, and pasted-in letters from Miller.

The fatigue and depression finally break her and she collapses into exhaustion and weeping. She telephones Martha Jaeger for an appointment. Symptomatically, she gets lost and confused trying to find her way by subway to the appointment. After walking through the cold wind, she finally finds the building, on Haven Avenue, near the Hudson River. The street name and location by the water seem a good omen.

When she sees Jaeger's lovely compassionate face, Anaïs yields as would a child to tears and confession. She feels absolved of her cares and is so relaxed that she falls asleep on the subway home. Psychoanalysis cleanses her as Catholicism once had. She soon recognizes that this crisis is different from her last: this is not a crisis of the father, but of the mother. And she has turned, by coincidence, to a mother figure for understanding, to an analyst who knits as they talk. During Anaïs's many visits, she and Jaeger speak of the mothering burden, of the equation of love with abnegation and self-effacement. One day when Jaeger uses the word "masochism," Anaïs gathers up dramatic examples of starving while others eat, having no fountain pen or records while Miller and Gonzalo do. Her sacrifice and others' selfishness reach epic proportion: Miller took her typewriter, she wrote by hand; Gonzalo buys books, but hers come infested from the public library! She understands now that her father is the manifestation of ego, her mother the "sacrificed woman." She and Jaeger speak of the conflict in women between selfishness and individuality. While identifying with her quixotic father, she has been acting like her mother.[139]

Anaïs also discovers the writing of Isak Dinesen (the Danish writer Karen Blixen) and recommends her books to Henry. She and Dinesen share more than Danish blood: both had philandering fathers who left them at age ten and had an overwhelming influence on their imaginations; both have suffered from anorexia (Dinesen's is lifelong; she will starve to death); and each "insisted on creating herself as an aesthetic object."[140] Anaïs's rebellious anger at being abandoned is more suppressed than Dinesen's, though they both cultivate the masquerade of the dramatic and theatrical.

An early 1943 letter from Miller: You are the famous Pellegrina Leoni in Isak Dinesen's "The Dreamers," he writes. No man knows Anaïs better than Miller, who sends her an analysis of herself and of the character. He pinpoints the very issues she is dealing with in the sessions with Jaeger. Pellegrina has "a strange assumption that the ability to spread beauty and Happiness is supremely hers." But gifted people with prophetic powers must try not to "bequeath them to others," he warns. She pastes the long letter in her diary and confirms his insight by return mail.[141] She constructs a Jungian analysis of *Winter of Artifice* for her diary, applying its principle to understanding those around her. She is restless and anxious while going through this microscopic analysis of the damage done to her by the war between her parents. The critical silence that follows the publication of *Winter of Artifice* (she had expected many reviews) gives her both the incentive and the opportunity to listen to her inner needs.

Out of the analysis come some strong attacks directed at Miller: New Year's Day he responds to her "crucifixion theme" that charges him with sucking her "very blood": "You are mistaken if you think that is what nourished me." A month later he replies sadly to her charge that his philosophy had a disastrous effect on her. Her great "life's problem," he adds, is her need to give and to bind people to her by creating obligation. She must accept responsibility for her own selfish "sacrifices," he implies, and solve her needs herself.[142] What she has concluded with Jaeger is that she feels guilt for creating because it may threaten her femininity and cause others to stop loving her. She also feels guilt for exposing and potentially hurting, in her diary, those she loves; thus her turn to fiction to protect the truth. Over the weeks of analysis she concludes that she has been subjugating her own nature, concealing her own abilities, and placing the needs of others ahead of her own work. In their sessions, she and Jaeger are going far beyond the therapies of Allendy and Rank in attempting to create a new psychology of women.[143]

## Under a Glass Bell

The signs of healing are evident in 1943. When on her fortieth birthday she receives a hundred-dollar birthday check from Miller, who is at last doing better financially, she buys paper to print the short stories she had written in Paris and since.[144] She also takes up the piano again, gives a "resurrection" party for her friends, and finishes printing the book for Crosby. She and Gonzalo print a flyer announcing publication of a collection of her short stories, to be called *Under a Glass Bell*. She resumes her social life, which includes literary salons, regular meetings at the Bistro café on Eighth Street, and spending part of the summer at Crosby's invitation in Southampton, where she says she is gathering strength for the printing of her book. All this social activity revolves around her love for Frances Robinson, who is, she says, "good for the altitudes," and her new affair with Albert Mangones, a twenty-six-year-old architect born in Haiti to a Spanish mother and an African father and educated in France. From a spring "Haitian" party she gives for Mangones, Richard Wright, and Canada Lee, to New Year's Eve dancing at the Savoy in Harlem, she writes about blacks in her diary and in her erotica and basks in the freedom, naturalness, and sensuality of this world.[145]

Charles Duits, a Belgian poet, is also close to Anaïs and to the circle of Haitian dancers. He too goes to Crosby's July Southampton vacation gathering, where he stands out like a pale *poète maudit* amid the suntanned sea bathers. He sleeps all day and seems to Anaïs the "palest flame" of all the poets she has known. Her attraction to his almost disembodied poetic artistry is just as strong as her excitement over the sensuous voodoo dances of the Haitians, in particular the dancing of Josephine Premice.

Josephine is the daughter of Lucas Premice, a political refugee from Haiti who lives in Brooklyn. Anaïs meets Lucas and his two daughters, Josephine and Adele, at a Canada Lee party. She is attracted to their sensual enjoyment of life. Josephine, a tall and beautiful girl of nearly fifteen years, is studying dance, which will be her career on two continents. She becomes one of Anaïs's "children," even helping her set type for the Gemor Press. Josephine thinks Anaïs is startling, whether she wears all purple (including dress, lipstick, and fingernail polish) or all black.

With her alabaster skin and her eyes rimmed with khol, Anaïs is appreciated by the Haitian community. Young Josephine thinks she is Princess of the Underground. In fact, Anaïs is no longer a princess, but a diva. "She moved across a room in a grand manner, with theatrical flamboyance," says one observer.[146] She has transformed herself from a Jamesian Isabel Archer in Paris to James's Madame Merle in New York City. No longer the virgin American wife, she is the epitome of European decadence, and attracted to youth and innocence.

Printing begins in October of 1943 for three hundred copies of the short-story collection *Under a Glass Bell*, with seventeen engravings by Ian Hugo. Anaïs writes Crosby that she is setting thirty-three lines, or one page, a day.[147] Again, she relives the stories and the scene of their writing as she sets each letter and word, binds each paragraph and page, and considers how she has related dream and action in her fictional world.[148] At the end of the year, she and Gonzalo reach page sixty-four, which includes her foreword announcing her "cure" from romanticism, which she later repudiates. She notes further that the stories, written earlier in Paris, reflect her "romanticism, mysticism and neurosis" before the Spanish War—suggesting that the war was a watershed in her aesthetic development toward more action and realism.[149]

The printing is completed in February 1944 and at the bindery about the same time that Miller leaves for Monterey to visit Jean Varda, the painter who will later befriend Anaïs. Because Varda gives him free lodging, Miller will stay in northern California for several years. "All my strength comes from the example you set," he writes in his birthday letter to Anaïs, congratulating her on the new book and promising to send more money—soon twenty of his books will be available in England, France, and the U.S. Twenty-five years later, when she publishes the third volume of her diary, she quotes this letter from Henry at the end, right before the best review of *Under a Glass Bell*, suggesting that the finale of her life with Miller coincides with her first important critically acclaimed work. When Durrell writes for news of her, Miller says they have "parted" and it is a "big loss" for him.[150]

*Under a Glass Bell* is launched at an exhibition of Hugo's engravings on 6 March 1944 at the Wakefield Gallery. Hugo wants no mention of his marital or business life, she confides to Crosby, he just wants to be "Ian Hugo, engraver." The decision is probably Anaïs's, however. While signing books and looking for reviews, which are mixed in their response to the book, she is planning to borrow money for a better press and location so that Gonzalo (who is still her lover) will be able to stand on his own feet at last.

She and Hugo will be free of the Mores. In urging Caresse Crosby to come help her promote the book, she says, You are the sun woman, I the moon woman "who is a little weary of obscurity."[151]

While she is having a society photograph taken for a review of her fourth book in *Town and Country*, Anaïs receives a copy of *The New Yorker* with a review of *Under a Glass Bell* by Edmund Wilson. A review by the dean of American critics has the potential of changing her professional career dramatically, and it will directly lead to her first book contract from a trade press. Wilson calls hers "a special world, a world of feminine perception and fancy." Though he notes passages that "suffer a little from an hallucinatory vein of writing which the Surrealists have overdone," he singles out "The Mouse," "Ragtime," and "Birth" as "beautiful little pieces." He concludes that "Miss Nin is a very good artist, as perhaps none of the literary Surrealists is."[152] Soon Mr. Edmund Wilson will appreciate more than her literary artistry.

Anaïs experiences a great joy this spring—thanks to this wonderful review by Wilson, thanks to her Haitian friends and her "oracle analyst," and thanks perhaps in small part to the fact that Miller and she have set each other free. She may not have cured herself of the "drugs of romanticism [neuroses]," as she claims, but she believes she has recaptured "the sources of joy." She begins another novel.[153]

# CHAPTER NINE

# 1944–1947

# This Hunger for Acceptance

"All around me I find that one love is not enough, two are not enough."
—*Anaïs Nin, September 1945*

"I am Circe, Bill."
—*Anaïs Nin to William Burford*[1]

THE GALLERY is in a gingerbread house with bay windows on a chained-off cul-de-sac called G Place in Washington, D.C. General Ulysses Grant had once hitched his horse to the post in front. The first two floors of the house hold Caresse Crosby's G Place Gallery. On the upper two floors she lives with a young painter named David Porter. Anaïs is here to help hang the copper engravings of Ian Hugo (no longer to be known as her husband, Hugh Guiler, she warns Caresse) and to exhibit her book *Under a Glass Bell,* which has almost sold out—three hundred copies in three weeks. Henry Miller, whose watercolors are also on display, later calls his exhibit "a complete flop."[2]

Anaïs believes that she is moving toward heightened visibility and critical acceptance following Edmund Wilson's *New Yorker* review of *Under a Glass Bell.* Her confidence is high, for she believes that her fiction is "preparing a world" for those who are shipwrecked in ideologies.[3] Though her confidence will ebb several times during the years in New York, she seeks acceptance determinedly, both in the literary world and among her coterie of young men. As Gore Vidal, one of her young followers at this time, will later note, the theme of the diary of this period is her "formidable will to power."[4]

## Fathers and Sons

What is it that attracts me to the young? she asks herself in 1944. She believes that it is their spontaneity and their status as outsiders. They surround her with their beauty, but do not compete with hers, even when she dims the lights at their arrival. Their youthful malleability (she always needs pliable lovers) matches her need for control and her desire to adjust to change (the girl and artist had learned to create amid chaos). A German psychologist suggests that what appears to be a life of "disloyalty, treachery, and escapism" may be an "understandable" means of "dealing courageously with diversity and change."[5] These youths, to whom she gives off her queen bee's pheromone, worship her as they will Judy Garland and Barbra Streisand.

Her concurrent lovers Gonzalo and Henry have let her down. When Miller, who seems isolated in his meditative world on an ocean cliff at Big Sur on the Pacific, comes east to see his ill mother, he does not even visit Anaïs, fearing further reproach. Instead of interpreting their separation as a desertion, she wonders, "Did my faith in Henry make him strong enough to go on without me?"[6] He believes that it is *she* who is weak: in a letter to a young disciple, Bern Porter (whom he is sending to meet Anaïs), Miller says she is the best woman he has known, but that she is poisoned by self-doubt and must be handled very carefully.[7] Though Miller will soon marry a young woman named Janinà Martha Lepska, he by no means abandons his literary support of Anaïs: his *Sunday after the War*, published this year by New Directions, carries two essays of praise for her diary: "Letter to William Bradley, Literary Agent, August 2, 1933" and "Letter to Anaïs Regarding One of Her Books." Gonzalo, on the other hand, remains her bad-boy lover, avoiding hard work and coming in late, until Anaïs rebels and stays away while the printing work backs up. She describes the burden of her own labor and the sacrifices she makes (she buys her black velvet opera cape in a thrift shop). Her emotional and physical involvements are now with very young men, some of them sent by Miller.

"I believe th[at] young America has chosen you and me to follow. Yin and Yang!" she tells Miller.[8] They acknowledge to each other that they now have cult followings. Harry Herschkowitz, another devotee of Miller's, arrives in New York from Big Sur obsessed with the Henry, June, and Anaïs story, having read "Djuna" in the original (1939) edition of *The Winter of Artifice*. Neurotic and obsessive, he is certain of Anaïs's love for him (he pronounces her name "Anis," as does Henry). At least this is her published diary version. In fact, they become lovers, and she writes to former neighbor Henrietta Weigel in Reno that she will keep him around for her. In the meantime, she is attempting to treat him as more than a passing lover.[9] When he becomes possessive and physically demanding, she breaks it off. She tells a friend that he had become psychotic, identified with Artaud, and brought a gun to her apartment, threatening to kill himself.[10] Not waiting for her neighbor's return from Reno, she turns him over to another friend in New York City.[11]

There is a nineteen-year-old Latin American navy man named Pablo Mendez (aka Paul Runyon) whom she takes in for dinner because he has fallen in love with *Under a Glass Bell*. "I am drunk on your stories," he says on the telephone. There is Bern Porter, who will soon be publishing Miller's work in Berkeley, and with whom Anaïs has a brief affair that he will never forget. And there is a Columbia University freshman named Herbert Gold, who found himself "ensorcelled" by "a magic lady of intergalactic class, uttering hypnotic soft fragments" at a Greenwich Village poetry reading.[12] She struggles with her own mothering or "savior" complex in dealing with these young admirers—an issue that she has discussed often with Jaeger, who herself has to resist that role with Anaïs, Frances (Robinson) Brown, and their friends. For example, when Anaïs refuses to join a new group-therapy discussion, Jaeger banishes her for a time from analysis.[13]

"I am rich indeed with young men's dreams and worship," she declares.[14] For the first time she acknowledges that the world they create around her protects her from the intellectual world of Edmund Wilson and the editors of the *Partisan Review*. She cultivates Wilson's fatherly approval, nevertheless, and her letters are deferential. He turns to her for sympathy over lunch before leaving to cover the war in France. She helps him buy a uniform and sleeping bag for his trip and listens as he narrates troubles with his wife, Mary McCarthy, hinting that they might separate.[15] Wilson is only eight years older than she—there are twice that many years between her and some of her young men—but Wilson represents the authority of literature and politics, and "man and authority together [are] stronger than one's capacity for mastering them," as her narrator will say in *Children of the Albatross*, her novel about this period in her life. They make her, like her protagonist, feel powerless: "There was a little cell of [Djuna's] being in which she still existed as a child, which only activated with a subtle anger in the presence of the father, for in relation to him she . . . was rendered small again and returned to her former state of helplessness and dependence."[16]

When she meets C. L. (Lanny) Baldwin at the Gotham Book Mart, she already knows him to be married and the father of two young children. But he admires *Under a Glass Bell* and asks her to dinner. Over a French meal and wine, he reads her his surrealistic poetry and she woos him with her eyes. Despite his business suit, he begins to behave like "a true southern poet." She is attracted to his "moss-green eyes" and looks at his tight shirt collar as a challenge.[17] Their affair lasts many months before he returns to hearth and home.

Since early in 1943 she has often been seen in the company of the Belgian poet Charles Duits. He is part of the circle that attends Haitian dances, Caresse Crosby's summer parties in Southampton, and the artistic poetry readings and dances in the Village. Pale-skinned and with curly blond hair, Duits talks in poetic abstractions and he and Anaïs speak French together. He reads his poetry to her and spends time in her studio. Duits, and often Baldwin, are at all the parties Anaïs attends.

Martha Jaeger and her husband are also part of Anaïs's social circle. Because she helps Anaïs and the other women achieve "freedom," they try to help her with her hair and diet (Anaïs describes her as "fat, full-bosomed, fleshy") and console her about her unfaithful husband. She certainly reminds Anaïs of her mother, and Anaïs is critical of her for being too analytical, for not being sensuous and creative, not fitting into the artistic crowd. They treat Jaeger with "deference, like an oracle and a wise advisor," but, as Anaïs explains, "we pride ourselves in not even looking like wives, but more like mistresses. The *femme fatale* is our ideal in appearance!"[18]

## Hugo and the Gemor Press

With several hundred dollars borrowed from friends and with Herculean physical labor, Anaïs, Eduardo, and Gonzalo have moved the printing and engraving presses from MacDougal Street to a little green house at 17 East Thirteenth Street in the spring of 1944. Now the large front window displays their books, and the Gemor Press seems in high gear. She tells Caresse that she has moved the press to larger quarters and turned it over to Gonzalo, who reprints eight hundred copies of *Under a Glass Bell*. She will again devote herself to writing.[19] They reduce the number of engravings from seventeen to nine, and use Linotype instead of hand-setting. In her diary she gives a rosy picture of Gonzalo's transformation under this responsibility and of the amount of work that pours into their business, no longer intended to be just a vanity press. But instead of writing her diary or fiction, she works sometimes eight hours a day at the press, and eventually Gonzalo's poor business judgment and irresponsibility strain their relationship and threaten their business. She confesses in letters to Crosby and Miller that she is "always on the point of losing the press."[20]

Her debts are resolved by a thousand-dollar check from Miller. He has been given a monthly allotment by a benefactor/patron, which he shares with her. She is to publish her diary, he generously insists.[21] He is content to live in the "paradise" of Big Sur, where he purchases a small cottage, hauls water up the hillside, and hopes to rival Rimbaud. In her diary, she characterizes his letters as sad and full of guilt, yet what has changed is that he no longer writes her in the buoyant mode of a lover. His generosity in giving away his money soon leads to a rift with his benefactor. Anaïs condemns some of his gifts to others and writes to tell him that she had been ready to set her diary to print when the news that he would need his money back came and she stopped the press.[22]

In a radio interview several weeks later, she says confidently that she does not need to worry about "living expenses" or making money on the Gemor Press because she is supported by her husband. She repeats the Miller belief that a writer should not have to earn a living by writing. The interview is the last in a series on dependent women developing an art or craft to enrich and beautify life.[23] Miller's check had repaid the debt of moving and buying another press; Hugo paid for rent at their apartment and the press.

She and Hugo consider their plans for the future during the summer of 1944. France has been liberated and they seriously contemplate returning to Europe, in part because they spend several long weekends with restless Europeans at her friend Moira's house in Amagansett, Long Island. Anaïs tells both Miller and Steloff that she and Hugo will be returning to Paris to print books and engravings and perhaps open a bookshop on the Seine. After a five-year "eclipse" in this American "concentration camp," she is eager to return to Paris.[24] They also decide that Hugo will retire from the bank, the name "Guiler" (the businessman) will be "dead," and henceforth (she informs Miller) they will live a life of denial and poverty.[25] This romantic notion of a life of only art will become reality in 1949, when Hugo retires at fifty-one years of age.[26]

Hugo leaves every morning for the bank, where he is addressed as Hugh Guiler, assistant vice-president specializing in estate planning, retirement, and insurance.[27] She tells Lawrence Durrell that Hugo is much changed, out of his shell, and a good engraver with a "delicate imagination."[28] Yet the delicacy of his engravings leads one of their friends, a literary critic, to comment on his repression. He is "charming and funny," adds the friend, but "repressed," or "just a bore."[29] He is an engraver who, during the next two years, is also thinking about making films and about vacationing in Mexico at the end of the year to regain his health (Anaïs's letters suggest he is often ill). The "birth" of Ian Hugo (thanks in part to the printing press) encourages her to view the marriage as an artistic and professional union.[30]

Though she seems to vacillate between publishing her diary and continuing to write and publish her fiction, she has actually made an important decision. While she, Gonzalo, and Hugo (Eduardo is working more on the Cooney press) will continue to print other people's books, she will convert her diary into a long novel that dramatizes the "conflicts of women," their psychology, language, and development. She will portray various women who embody aspects of Woman. The development of the novel will be, like her own development, from "subjectivity and neurosis to objectivity, expansion, fulfillment."[31]

In June she begins "This Hunger," which is to be part of what she calls her "Proustian novel."[32] She has already written "Hejda," a "caricature" of an Arabian woman, which Miller finds is pitiful and ridiculous. In October she writes "Stella," a composite of Luise Rainer and some events from her own life, about an unhappy, neurotic film star. Each one of her friends, including Frances Robinson Brown, will be portrayed in her fiction. The preface announces that the stories deal with the "aspect of destruction in women." With Hugo's help at the press, she plans to print *This Hunger* (including "Hejda," "Stella," and "Lillian and Djuna"), the first part of the envisioned long novel, as soon as they raise the money the next spring. They sell portfolios of colored woodcuts by Hugo to get the needed money.[33]

In the early months of 1945 Anaïs has days of "feverish inspiration" in writing the lives of her women. She explores her dreams with Frances Brown, studies the reality of her female friends (such as Brown and Luise Rainer) to describe her fictive women, but has to pull from sections of her diary and her own experiences to give the characterizations internal shape. The portraits are composites, she claims.[34] By spring she divides them into Djuna (perception), Stella (blind suffering), Sabina (freedom), and Lillian (liberation in aggression). She does not see these as separate women. Nor does she see the various intimate affairs she is juggling as a splitting or "separation" of herself. Her multiple characters, like her affairs, are "symphonic, a vast gathering together."[35] There are elements of all these characters in her, though Djuna has her "enormous fairy tale eyes," delicate femininity, desire to be a mistress, and psychic understanding of (and need for) others. Stella is Luise Rainer, Sabina is June Miller, Hejda is Moira (a woman with "oriental obliqueness and new freedom"), and Lillian is in part Louise de Vilmorin. Both Lillian and Djuna have an "unsatisfied hunger for life" and desire to ascend "ladders to fire." When Lanny Baldwin or Frances Brown suggest that she write more realistically, she asserts that she is writing "beyond the facts," skipping the obvious, which she calls "Dreiserism," in order to give the "emotional relativity" of truth. Her approach is a kind of "emotional algebra." Perhaps the reason she never learns the names of birds is so that she might discover the bird of paradise, she explains. She deliberately leaves out the "upholstery" of facts for the greater truth.[36]

After trying to get publicity articles in *Harper's, Time, Life,* and *The New Yorker,* Anaïs secures a feature article in *Town and Country.* The magazine takes photographs of her posed as her fictional women Lillian, Djuna, Stella, and Hejda. The article seems to be good publicity for her work when it appears in January of 1945, but there are unforeseen problems when she uses the photographs later. The photograph of her as Lillian, with severe hair and black tuxedo and bow tie (à la Marlene Dietrich), when it is used in connection with two later books, give rise to the rumor that she is a lesbian—a rumor that distresses her. Also, the glamorous photographs, her marriage to a banker, and the fact that she is surrounded by playful homosexual men in part keep the literary establishment from taking her seriously.[37]

## Children of the Albatross

With all her young men she plays Don Juan or "Donna Juana," as she likes to call it. She reels them in with her books and marvels that she can "keep everyone in a state of romance."[38] A college student named William Pinckard, who has heard of her from Miller and Miller's friend Wallace Fowlie, writes with praise for *Under a Glass Bell*. He is a student of Fowlie's at Yale, and is inspired by stories of Miller's and Anaïs's artistic struggles and their financial support of each other. He wants to become a millionaire (his father owns an oil company) in order to provide funds for a publishing company to issue her diary. She sends him *Winter of Artifice,* and in the spring he shows up at her door.

Fowlie, an assistant professor of French literature with a doctorate from Harvard, eventually comes at Miller's urging to meet Anaïs. She is worried about his Catholicism, as is Miller, who writes several times to assure Fowlie that he must be very delicate with her. "She will lose her fear of religion one day. . . ."[39] Fowlie remembers sitting on the floor of her apartment and being struck by her youthful beauty, skillful makeup, and unique accent (neither French nor Spanish). She speaks of all the young men she is helping and praises Fowlie's book *Age of Surrealism.*[40]

When Pinckard (she will call him "Leonard W." in her published diary) rings her doorbell in March of 1945, she takes him into her house and heart. He is immature and impressionable, tall, thin, and delicate; he brings his stories and watercolors and talks about his cold mother. With his intense blue eyes he hypnotizes Pablo Mendez (the young navy man), and soon Anaïs has parties including Luise Rainer, Frances Brown, Duits (the Belgian poet), and Baldwin, among others, with Pinckard providing the means of entertainment with his hypnotism. He watches the Haitian dancing of Josephine Premice, listens to Anaïs read her latest writings, and knows that he has found a spiritual home. She, in turn, believes she has found the "nearest" of her "sons" in this "Neptunian" youth. In her eyes, he has a "curious luminosity."[41] She sends his poems to periodicals such as *Poetry* magazine of London.[42]

In the two months he has before having to report to the army, Pinckard wants to leave his parents and live with his spiritual family. Frances and her husband, Tom Brown, give him a room; Anaïs feeds him and gives him pocket money. He and Pablo create a tapestry that hangs over the Guiler bed; Pablo dyes the hair of his hamster blue; Pinckard pastes a mirror or "third eye" between Nin's eyes and hangs a metal bird from the ceiling of her studio. She takes them to the concerts of her brother Joaquin, still teaching at Williams College; and, dressed in Pablo's navy suit and beret, she takes them to find a houseboat for Pablo in Pelham Bay. Pablo, Duits, Luise Rainer, and the others read, dance with, hypnotize one another, and repaint the window frames of her studio.

When she is with Baldwin, they speak of her manuscript *This Hunger* (which he is reading and editing) and of his "emotional imprisonment." She is convinced that she is liberating him: sad and "dead" with his family, he is "reprieve[d]" with her. She wants him to ride the tide of his emotions, as she believes she does. She considers divorcing Hugo and marrying Baldwin. Altogether, the spring is joyous. She believes that she is "living out what other people only dream about, talk about, analyze."[43] She writes to tell Miller that she is "more like you in mood now than I was before." And her life is like it was in the artistic community at the Villa Seurat. Her young friends are living out her stories. They will even follow her to Paris, she adds hopefully.[44] She is not discouraged when Bill Pinckard's father complains to Yale authorities that Professor Fowlie and his artistic friends have corrupted his son. When detectives come to her house, she asks Tom Brown to talk to Mr. Pinckard, and the crisis is resolved. Bill remains in the comfort of her presence until he has to leave for Fort Dix (where he faints at his induction).

Her need to project part of herself onto others, she realizes, illustrates Rank's theory of the double. She attends a lecture by Dr. Esther Harding on this subject and reads Harding's book *The Way of All Women*. Hereafter Anaïs explains this need to live out the lives of others—even destructive lives such as those of Helba and Gonzalo—as the need to have others live out her darker self or alter ego. She does not connect this persistent behavior to any desperate need for love and acceptance, or to the fear of rejection.

During the summer of 1945, Anaïs walks back and forth on Thirteenth Street between her studio at 215 West, where she is writing *This Hunger* (later a part of *Ladders to Fire*) and entertaining her young men, and 17 East, where she labors on the press. She walks with joy in her heart, feeling pleasure in the sun's rays, the flavor of coffee, the birds on the fire escape. She is surrounded by her followers and living "blindly,"[45] as she describes it. "[Her lovers] are forever waiting a few streets away . . . priests of her cult," says Gore Vidal.[46]

She confides in Miller that she is considering remarriage and she has found her next husband. She has escaped by a "hair's breath" marrying "an American poet." The next husband "will be a European I know now. At 32," she tells Miller, "this man [possibly Duits or Baldwin] is actually like a boy of 17. Imagine me spending the rest of my life here."[47]

In June she composes forty handwritten prefaces to five colored wood-cuts by Ian Hugo, hoping that the sale of these portfolios will pay for the printing of *This Hunger*, which she calls volume one of her continuous novel. Though her diary indicates that the folio paid for the paper and materials to print her book, an unpublished cost estimate drawn up by Gonzalo reveals that the first edition would cost thirteen hundred dollars. And the unpub-lished correspondence with Lanny Baldwin, who remains her lover, reveals that he lent her some of the money. His own book, *Quinquivara*, with Hugo's engravings and her preface, is printed in three hundred copies by Gemor Press. His poems are more explicit and original than her preface, which includes, among its better sentences, the following: "There is a vital sense of motion and impetus which gives a changeful, ever renewed flavour to evanescent moods. . . ."

"New York City was a city of the young just after the war," says Anaïs's former neighbor Eugene Walter. "The bright artists from all over America came here and she was a Circe figure for them; she charmed them."[48] The city was particularly an oasis of freedom for the homosexuals, though "most of us, including Gore, were closeting it, faking it," says one of her circle.[49] "Geniuses ran loose in the Village," says Harold Norse in his *Memoirs of a Bastard Angel*, "but few made it to fame and fortune." Among this bright, young group is Marshall Barer, a young man from Florida who is studying commercial art but wishing for a career in show business. Later he will write *Once Upon a Mattress* (and marry his composer, Mary Rogers), but at this time he is only twenty-two and susceptible to Anaïs's charms. She thinks he is "another beautiful young man"; he thinks she is a "goddess," a queen (not a "fag hag," he emphasizes), and he identifies with her glamour. He believes that she is probably highly sexed, but covers the sexuality with a lot of poetry. Though they never talk about his homosexuality, she seduces him gently, then introduces him to Eduardo, with whom he also has an affair. She teaches him, with a more felicitous result than in her treatment of Duncan, that he can love a woman.[50]

Her studio is taken over by what she calls her "household of adolescents"—Pablo Mendez, Charles Duits, Josephine Premice, Marshall Barer, David Moore, and Lanny Baldwin (though the group wants to vote out the latter two, who are too pedantic and conventional—meaning older). She also believes that Baldwin is too afraid of "our world" and too concerned with safety.[51] He is unable to let himself "flow," in part because he is torn over his marriage. Gone from the group is Bill Pinckard ("Leonard" in the *Diary*), away at basic training, who receives letters of encouragement from the den mother of this brood of cubs: "Permit yourself to flow and overflow," she advises. He writes, to "Wafer," his declarations of love. With her letters of wisdom to Bill, she begins, after reading Rilke's *Letters to a Young Poet,* a practice of recording her letters to the young in her diary.

In August 1945 the United States drops its two atomic bombs on Japan, forcing the surrender. Feeling a need for art and affirmation in the midst of such world "savagery," Anaïs begins to print *This Hunger* and continues writing her stories of women ("distilling the diary," she calls it). She is progressing creatively until set back by rejection from her young lover Lanny Baldwin. After weeks of ambivalence, he leaves her to return to his wife and young children. Wounded, she strikes back, accusing him of being guilt-ridden and naive in believing that there has to be a choice (between wife and mistress) in what is clearly an opportunity for his growth. He is one of Lawrence's "rosy young men full of ashes" who enjoy "men in skirts," her derisive term for American women. She suggests that he go for analysis to Mrs. Jaeger (because she is born under the same sign as he and will understand him). She tells him to read Philip Wylie's *Generation of Vipers* (an attack on American Momism).[52]

Baldwin responds that she is a kind of "dog in the manger" with men, wanting them all to sit at her feet and devote themselves only to her with absolute obedience, while she takes a harem for herself. He does not call this freedom.[53] Does she, he asks, want him to be free also? If not, then their affair must be over. The defensiveness of her response reveals the extent of her sense of rejection: she claims to have loved more than other women; it was she who made Miller a great writer and set many passionate young men to creating books and poems, paintings and music. In comparison to them, he is like a continent priest. She gave him up long ago when she discovered that he was dead. (She suggests he read her diary for the proof.) And finally, how can she be jealous of American women, who have been losing their men to her since her arrival in America?[54] The next day she fires several more volleys: she is really in love with Bill (a man even younger than Baldwin); Henry (regretting his present marriage) has just written to tell her that no woman ever made him feel as she did. Men have been coming to her to be *"freed"* (she underlines the word) and to be reborn strong and creative. Baldwin is just like her father, she adds, unable to give love and understanding. In a final attack on his manhood, she reminds him of an incident of his impotence and effeminate weeping. Again, she urges him to read her diary for confirmation of her feelings. Her diary, she maintains, is her historical record of truth. A later generation of readers recognize that a diary is another form of fiction.

A restrained, polite correspondence resumes a couple of months later in part because she still owes him money from the press. Certainly he understands—and numerous letters to others on behalf of her acolytes proves—that she does much to promote their work, though Gore Vidal will call it her "fantasy that she is Joan of Arc forever putting Dauphins on the throne."[55]

Basically what attracts her to the young is what she finds in Bill Pinckard: innocence, an innocence she takes delight in corrupting. The intuitive and immature Bill seems to be the embodiment of Kaspar Hauser, the fictional eponymous dreamer of one of her favorite novels, by Viennese novelist Jakob Wassermann. Hauser, imprisoned since childhood, seeks to find his beautiful mother to protect his innocence from the cruel world. Because the mother cannot "transgress the barrier of age," he dies unprotected. The image of Kaspar Hauser runs throughout Anaïs's diaries of this period.[56] Not surprisingly, Wallace Fowlie writes to Miller that she is a femme fatale for Bill and for the other young men.[57]

David Moore, the most recent recruit to her circle, is a thin young Irishman with black wavy hair who came to her the previous spring in search of Miller. He had recently left his wife and decides he does not like women, though Anaïs senses his desire for her. They have long talks, and she sees herself as his muse. He is a "continuation" of Bill, Pablo, Marshall, and Charles, even of her cousin Eduardo.[58] Though he may be "too mental"— certainly the others in the group think so—she admires his intelligence. She admires the same trait in Marshall Barer. The "adolescents" hang out in her studio, take her to plays, share all her "lyrical" evenings, and confess that they love her. It is Barer with whom she celebrates with a night on the town in September when she finishes printing the 184th (and last) page of the deluxe edition of *This Hunger*.

Anaïs is surrounded by her beautiful boys, including David Moore, Marshall Barer, and Pablo Mendez, as she arrives at a party in the studio of Maya Deren, the avant-garde filmmaker she had met at Amagansett the previous August. Haitian masks glare from the walls and jazz charges the youthful and energetic crowd. Her entrance has been as dramatic as the decor. Anaïs feels safer with these young men. They do not try to possess or seize her, as the fathers do. They are like her younger brothers, with whom she had a closer bond than with her parents. She recognizes that because she did not receive enough parental loving she seeks "the child in others" to receive what she lacked. They create a childlike world of play and imagination, the true world of the artist, she believes. Their play and satire drive away the academicians and mature artists. Many years later one of the legion pens a satiric poem in which he describes her giving suckle to all the men in her life. The men are "in diapers and typewriters" kneeling before her to drink from her maternal breasts.[59]

They are her young poets—Charles Duits the most cultured and intelligent, Pablo Mendez "a carnival of gay affection." They demand that she be their "legendary woman" who creates with "veils and myths." As she is writing the second portion of her next novel, she muses that these brilliant, "magical," gay young men are like the symbolic wafer that nourishes the artist—but not the woman.[60] Hence she says the story of Kaspar Hauser is "more beautiful than that of Christ" because it is "the story of innocence, of a dreamer destroyed by the world."[61]

## Edmund Wilson

To nourish the woman she looks in part to Edmund Wilson, who returns from the war this fall to announce the end of his marriage to Mary McCarthy. Anaïs begins a brief affair with this literary father figure, who had given her her first critical public acclaim: she goes to dinner with Wilson and to his apartment in a cul-de-sac off Eighty-sixth Street between York and East End Avenue. She describes it in her diary. His house, books, and prints remind her of her father's bourgeois world in Passy. He seems fervent and lustful, but his strength and self-assuredness remind her of her father, and she feels overwhelmed, terrified, helpless. Later, apparently, he will speak to her of marriage.[62] Secretly she would like to warn him that if he tastes of her flesh she will poison him with her "luminosity," for she is a child of "the albatross" and "unpossessable." He praises her insights in *Winter of Artifice* (Lillian reminds him of Mary McCarthy), but criticizes her lack of form and realism in *This Hunger*.[63] After some talk of his embattled marriage, he asks,

"You are a friend of man's, aren't you? You don't demolish him?"

"If you demolish a man, you lose a lover," she responds coyly.

"I hear you are surrounded by very young men."

She responds affirmatively, contrasting in her mind's eye the thin, unassured Pinckard and the arrogant, traditional Wilson. She makes excuses and almost runs home. When she comes down with a cold the next day, he sends flowers and a set of Jane Austen (a possible guide for her writing), then climbs the five flights to tell her that he has reread *Winter of Artifice* and "the father is right."

"You imagine we have the same problem?" she asks.

"I would love to be married to you, and I would teach you to write."[64]

Suddenly he becomes her overcritical father, in his full tyranny, activating her childhood humiliation and anger. She strikes back at him in her diary. Always afraid of confrontation, she cannot directly argue back (arguments precipitate abandonment). She will eventually get even by abandoning her father.

She physically and metaphorically carries around her book *This Hunger* as she tries to cope with the conflicts between her needs and her responsibilities. Gonzalo gives all his profits from the printing to a "salesman" who takes three hundred dollars for a new press and disappears. Gonzalo, whom she had thought of as an advanced modern printer, is an amateur who only uses one type (sans serif), says Marshall Barer, a commercial artist who will soon work for *Esquire*. She has stopped seeing Helba, whom she despises. She is depressed as well by the "insubstantiality" of her adolescents, her failure to find "deep love" and loyalty (she tells Durrell she is looking for "the One"), and a "suicidal depression" over public review of her book.[65]

But she continues to see Wilson, who is writing a review of her novel. She resents his power, his authority ("Father, man, critic, enemy of the artist"), and sees him in colors of brown, a solid Dutch burgher. He criticizes her for surrounding herself with a cult of gay young men. Still he admires her as a woman, and this gives her some power over him (she interprets it as "reconciliation" with her father). She does not look forward to her visits to his drab house, becoming increasingly hostile toward authority and what she calls the "world of reality" in literature and life. She does not trust him to read her diary.[66]

In his 10 November 1945 review in *The New Yorker*, Wilson praises her originality and unique feminine point of view. But she must have felt the fatherly rejection as well: "There is not much expert craftsmanship," he says of *This Hunger*, noting her repetitions, blurring of climaxes, and the dim outlines of the characters. Despite these weaknesses he calls for a commercial publisher for her next book, and hopes that her intelligence and talent will produce a better book next time. Thus spoke the "dictator," she says, on his high *New Yorker* "throne," his review "weighted down by conventionalities."[67] When he hears that Anaïs complains, Wilson writes in his journal that "continued complaining and having to be comforted" is typical of women writers such as Elinor Wylie, Louise Bogan, and Anaïs Nin.[68]

Anaïs's response is to undergo the kind of self-doubt that her character Stella, the actress, exhibits. One day while walking down Eighteenth Street in her high heels, which make her taller than her five feet seven inches, dressed in black and weighing 113 pounds, she feels overwhelmed by the immensity of the trucks, the huge garage doors, and the giant buildings. She feels small, helpless, afraid, a child with no density or weight. Suddenly she realizes that she shares this vulnerability and powerlessness with her "transparent adolescents." She fears the heavy, joyless, prosaic Wilson.[69]

She also responds in her diary by defending her fictional subject matter and style. She is hurt by the call to "reality" and the charge that she dwells on neurotic people while the world is in crisis. Hers is a visionary writing that transcends class, history, time, and race, in order to reach the human drama behind these things, she declares. She will delve deeper and deeper into the unconscious until she reaches the "collective unconscious of woman." In real life she "never argues" when she is with Wilson, but waits until she reaches for the diary to defend herself against him, the "enemy."[70] With Jaeger she also examines her vulnerability and shyness, and its basis in her fear of not being loved. She also seeks out Maya Deren, the filmmaker, who is a confident artist, able to explain and defend her own work.

She has seen Maya Deren's experimental, surrealist films, watched her making a film in August at the beach in Amagansett, and visited her studio (where Deren lives and works with her husband, Alexander Hammid) with Pablo, David, and Marshall, who share her admiration for the filmmaker. Deren is a Russian Jew with wild curly hair, pale-blue eyes, and what Anaïs calls a round, primitive face. Anaïs thinks her own strong, square face is "like a Botticelli."[71] When Deren asks her to act in one of her films, Anaïs is delighted. She, Pablo, Marshall, and a couple of others dance around a maypole in Central Park early one morning for Deren's camera. Anaïs admires Deren's fighting spirit, especially her willingness to confront a public audience with her work.[72] She is an inspiration for Anaïs when Kimon Friar, program director for the Poetry Center of the Ninety-second Street Y, asks her for a poetry reading in a joint appearance with Parker Tyler.

She is terrified to appear before her first large public audience, though Frances Brown accompanies her. She reads "Ragtime" and a portion of *This Hunger,* hears the applause, signs books, and escapes, elated. They go directly to Deren's studio, where Anaïs dances wildly with Pablo. She has faced her fear of punishment and rejection, and she has won, she believes. As they leave the studio, Marshall grabs her hand and suggests that they run fast so as not to see the city's ugliness.[73]

She begins a new volume of her diary that she entitles "The Transparent Children," referring to the young men who surround her, starved for love and uncritical acceptance. Though Wilson mocks them and Frances tells her she is wasting her time, she continues to believe that they understand her better than all the others. Though they play on the rim of her life, as she puts it, she prefers their mocking company to that of Wilson—it is "impossible to gain understanding from the father, from the church . . . from leaders." They protect her from the hurt that a father can inflict. Unwilling to continue to relive endlessly the father-daughter drama, she finally breaks with Wilson.[74]

## Gore Vidal

With the approach of winter 1945, at a lecture at the Ninety-second Street Y, she meets another young man. This one has the capacity to hurt her. Warrant Officer Gore Vidal is twenty years old but "no dream-laden adolescent," unless one counts his plan to be president of the United States and a poet-king like Richard II. (Vidal later proclaims his egotism when he calls himself and Anaïs the "two narcissi of the Forties."[75]) Her first reaction to Vidal is that he is "luminous and manly," clear-sighted and close to the earth, in contrast to the "nebulous" Bill.[76]

When Vidal comes for his first visit to the studio, he walks into a "wake" for one of the young painters, "lost" because he is marrying a millionaire. Vidal's wealth and social standing set him immediately apart from the other adolescents. He has the self-assurance that comes from having lived with his grandfather, Senator Thomas Gore (of Oklahoma), graduated from St. Alban's School in Washington, D.C., and toured England and Europe. The other youngsters think him arrogant and boastful. He comes into the city from his military base on Sundays, and sometimes calls to say that "Troubadour Vidal" (as she calls him) is coming on Wednesday and she should get rid of all the children.[77]

At the time she meets Vidal, Anaïs has just had several contacts with publishers, who (taking up Wilson's hint) express interest in her next novel. But she is suspicious of the other publishers (Random House, Harper's, Viking). Pascal Covici of Viking will give her a contract if she agrees, in her words, "to change from a wafer into bread"). She is also shaken by Isaac Rosenfeld's review, "Psychoanalysis as Literature," in *The New Republic,* in which he says that her characters are "personifications of neurotic anxiety" and her psychoanalytical style "inadequate." He also protests her fear of men and her female aggression—a charge repeated in a review the following month in *The Nation,* where Diana Trilling speaks of sexual "chauvinism" and self-pity. When Vidal begins work as the youngest editor at E. P. Dutton, he expresses active interest in her new novel. She is excited to be offered and to sign a thousand-dollar contract with Dutton. She is able to send Miller congratulations on the birth of his baby and news of her first commercial contract.[78]

In the five years she has been in New York City, Anaïs has developed a reputation for her dramatic persona. She succeeds in her roles in part because she embodies beauty. Leo Lerman (who will soon begin an eminent career with Conde Nast publications) had told her that she looked "like Shelley, transparent" in Maya Deren's last film. Her persona is also connected to what Wilson, in *The New Yorker*, called her "special cult," the magic circle. In private they play charades and stage theatre acts; Vidal does imitations of Roosevelt and Churchill; Josephine Premice dances with all the young men; Leo Lerman and Truman Capote call to tell her they are reading *Under a Glass Bell* to each other; and they all act in Deren's films. Marshall Barer buys her a flapper costume for a Leo Lerman party to which she has been invited, and they fight over her refusal to wear it. It makes her look homely, she insists, recalling her father's remark that she was ugly. When someone brings Truman Capote to one of her parties, where he meets Gore Vidal, he drawls, "Well, how does it feel to be an *enfant terrible?*" Thus begins an unusual friendship and rivalry that will become a "bloodthirsty battle of wits."[79] Vidal lashes out, exclaiming that Capote gives homosexuals a bad name (as he will say that Anaïs gives self-love a bad name). Her only rival for all this youthful adoration is Maya Deren.[80] No wonder a reviewer in the *Chicago Sun* describes her as "a Franco-Spanish American exotic . . . doyenne of the Village experimental writers."[81]

Increasingly, she punctuates her calendar by Vidal's visits. They talk for hours, discussing among other things, she claims, his sexual ambivalence. He brings her a novel he has written, *Williwaw*, to be published by Dutton; and she writes letters to editors and literary friends, calling their attention to his forthcoming book. Anaïs and Gore are both lonely children who have been "badly loved," she observes, listening to the tale of Vidal's abandonment by his mother (Nina Gore) when she divorced his father and married Hugh D. Auchincloss (who was later to marry the mother of Jacqueline and Lee Bouvier). Anaïs believes that she is the first woman whom Vidal trusts, and is proud to have influence where his mother failed. He wants his mother dead, she records in her diary. "We met just at the right moment," she claims he says. Though he will dispute many of her memories, he admits thinking then that she was "marvelous."[82]

By the beginning of 1946, Vidal completes his army service and, like Odysseus with the suitors, has "dispersed the group" around her. Their hours together lead them, Vidal will have us believe from his later fictional portraits of them (specifically in *Two Sisters*), to an intimate relationship. But their different approaches to life and letters are soon apparent.[83] It is Anglophobe meets Francophobe, or "Jack London meets Elinor Glyn," as Vidal later explains it. *Williwaw* is written in the style of Hemingway realism, what Vidal calls the "American tradition of straight narrative," and Anaïs does not like it.[84] But she tells him he has much more imagination and intuition than he is using. Eventually, she gets him to stop writing poetry, where he allows his imagination to overflow, and his fiction improves immeasurably:

> She was the first to point out to me the terrible inadequacy of my Crane-Hemingway style. What sense of language that I had went into bad poetry. So I stopped the poetry. When this happened, the prose was considerably enriched. . . . So Anaïs was the spur. . . . [B]ut [I] didn't much like her writing. Years later, reading her journals, I was horrified to discover that she felt the same about me.[85]

During the first four months of 1946 she writes to meet the deadline at Dutton to complete *Ladders to Fire,* which is comprised of two sections: "This Hunger" and "Bread and the Wafer." The novel is dedicated to Vidal, with whom she considers living as a "writing" companion, if not as lover. Though the novel is in part a reworking of the Henry-June-Anaïs subject of her earlier work, it also includes the activities of the intervening years. The character Djuna, the woman of psyche with "enormous fairy tale eyes," is surrounded by young men.

A party in February at Maya Deren's apartment has the feel of a party in an African tent. Primitive ornaments adorn the walls, with furs and drums on the furniture. She dances with Paul Mathiesen, a tall bisexual eighteen-year-old blond youth from California, as if in a spell. He is a recent graduate of Hollywood High School who has just passed his union test for stage design in New York. Within weeks Paul has taken the place of Bill Pinckard, who, even after daily letters, returns distant and perhaps brutalized by the army, and plans to go to Japan. They are all acting in Deren's film *Ritual in Transfigured Time.*

Paul looks at Djuna "with his long blue eyes" and touches every part of her body. He pauses "at the last mystery of the body," then takes her finally in a "big wave of fire." When she arises and moves to the table, she begins opening each tulip in the vase, "opening them, petal by petal . . . tenderly," as if they were his manhood, until he shouts for her to stop. She realizes then that she has "opened him to love too soon."[86] The scene is in the novel she will write next year, using all her transparent children, including Paul Mathiesen. Paul is her new love, and he is attracted to her, but he thinks she reminds him of the Beverly Hills girls he has known: nose jobs, heavy makeup, and hearts of stone. She, on the contrary, thinks he is a "sexual angel." From his body, she thinks, "come waves of young, playful sensuality." Later he will recognize himself in Gore Vidal's *Two Sisters* as the blond, Nordic Eric, the young man seduced by Marietta.[87] He will also recognize himself, rightly, as Paul in *Children of the Albatross,* where his and Anaïs's sexual encounter and her opening of the tulip petals is graphically depicted. The fictional character of Paul, who has never known a woman sexually, also bears many resemblances to Bill Pinckard. Once when Mathiesen (who has known women sexually before Anaïs) was intimate with Anaïs, he confessed that his stepfather had been his lover at one time. She responds with keen interest and begins to tell him something about her father, then stops.[88]

Though Paul believes that Gore is interested in his friendship, it is an older man who sweeps him away. When Paul brings his paintings and writings for her to store (he is accompanying the man to the Yucatán), Gonzalo jealously destroys a self-portrait of Mathiesen as a faun. After nine years with Gonzalo, whom Vidal calls her "life-force companion,"[89] Anaïs has been able neither to reform him nor to break off their physical relationship. As ever he is drowning in debts and irresponsibility. She confides in Durrell that her long-term relationship with Gonzalo is violent and parasitic, that she wants to rebel. She is trying to extricate herself from their mutual dependency, she adds, for her focus is now on a "constellation of relationships."[90]

The writing of *Ladders to Fire*, the culmination of her psychoanalysis with Jaeger, and Hugo's absence (he is in Mexico making a film) lead to an intense period of analytical detachment in her views of her relations with the many men in her life. She works with analyst Clement Staff, to whom she will dedicate her next novel.[91] She is able to understand more clearly than ever her problems with her father and Edmund Wilson, as well as her attraction to homosexual men. "These men whose femininity makes them passive and elusive arouse me to distraction," she had told her diary years before in Paris.[92] In *Children of the Albatross* her narrator says, "I want to stay . . . forever not with man the father but with man the son, carving, painting, dancing, dreaming, always beginning. . . ."[93] In her diary entries and her novel, she examines her neurosis therapeutically.

Her insights develop: she is still struggling with the shadow of her father, Joaquin Nin. "A shock" threw her into her "interior" world (her words get no more explicit than this). Fearing that "[u]ltimate giving is fatal," she "split into a million small relationships." Thus, she now realizes, she learned from her father to depersonalize Man as a potential abuser who will dominate and betray. She learned with men to use her "charm to enslave and abandon [them] first." But she is still caught in the "labyrinth" of her neurosis after her recent struggle with Wilson. She feels safer in the homosexual world ("they keep Man away"), but the gays do not give her the sexual intimacy she wants.[94]

"My first love was homosexual," she observes, referring to Eduardo. She enjoys their communal living, and finds attractive the incestuous feeling of "family kinship." Words such as "childlike" and "childishness" describe homosexuality for her. In her experience, it is connected to twinship, the double, and narcissism. She claims to disapprove of their promiscuity because it separates sex from love. Not once does she admit this separation in her own life. Though some homosexual men like Eduardo and Pablo romanticize women, others fear and hate women—and it is this latter attitude she finds childish and perverse, the "opposite of innocence." She concludes with Freud that homosexuality is for most young men "a stage of immaturity" or a "pause in adolescence."[95] It is difficult in her life as well as her fiction to determine whether she has a genuine empathy for homosexuals or whether she is exploring her gift for personal analysis.

She plans to begin her own life by finding a separate apartment; "I do want to make a new life," she tells Miller, who sends her a thousand dollars in April. She may divorce and remarry: "My work is here and possibly a remarriage—but twice I couldn't make up my mind to marry men of 20 or 30."[96] She has already sent for all her goods in storage in Paris, but she waits until July to tell Miller that the press has been essentially shut down and she will not publish the diary.[97] She and Miller correspond often this spring and summer, and their letters reflect, as always, their reading, philosophy, and personal life. He invites her to visit this fall, for she is planning a lecture tour. Miller, who is finding the meaning of "home" in Big Sur, offers her the following advice, probably directed at her reluctance to leave Hugo: "The *human* instinct to spare the other person his agony . . . is a fallacious instinct. . . . The temptation to be good, to do good . . . is the last ruse, I feel, of the ego."[98]

By May she rethinks her decision and informs him that she is lonely, despite her "worshippers." She will return to Paris, if she can get some more money from their Paris publisher (Kahane's son, Girodias). She is also vacillating about Vidal, who may not be the partner she desires, for he seems to need others. But by summer, after writing her lecture speech for the fall tour, she plans to go to East Hampton with Vidal. Nobody is more surprised about her lecture-circuit plans than Miller, Perlès, and Durrell, who marvel that with her shyness and the timbre of her voice she can handle this challenge.

When *Ritual in Transfigured Time* is ready, Anaïs claims that she, Vidal, and the others are disillusioned with the result, which shows the flaws of everyone except Deren, whose features are softened. In fact, only Anaïs complains; indeed, Marshall Barer believes that "Maya made Anaïs look quite wonderful."[99] Though Anaïs tries to stop the film, she and the others have signed a release, and no appeal to friendship will move Deren to change a scene. Anaïs now sees Deren as a competitor and her hope for immortality on film is mixed with embarrassment, for the signs of age are apparent. The contemporary viewer of the finished fifteen-minute black-and-white film, which features Deren, Premice, Nin, and Mathiesen, sees no evidence of unattractive angles. What dates Anaïs, who is twice the age of most of the cast, is her slightly awkward dancing and her coifed forties hairstyle (the hair of the other women is wild and free).[100]

Vidal has rented a room in a neighboring cottage for Anaïs, who tells her friends not to mention to a soul that she is in the Hamptons. Yet several people spot Anaïs and Gore riding bicycles. And though they meet often, and she has other friends nearby, she does not like the resort. It seems clear from her description in her diary that she is depressed by a sense of being an outsider. She mentions the "monotony and uniformity" of East Hampton, but it is Vidal's wealth, social confidence, and class privileges that leave her cold. She returns to the city unrenewed. The appearance of her "Stella" in *Harper's Bazaar* (summer 1946) gives her an illusion of success, but it is a "gesture of fashion" and thus ephemeral, she concludes.[101]

One unhappy turn of events that she watches taking place over the summer is the developing correspondence between Vidal and Miller. She had written her former companion in June about her "loyal son." Though Miller is beleaguered by fan mail and unsolicited manuscripts, she knows that he will be willing to send a "line" of blessing and encouragement to her Gore Vidal ("whatever child I have always chooses you for the male"). Vidal is made up of equal parts of them both, she adds.[102] By fall she jealously mocks Miller for beginning "an absolutely unnecessary" correspondence with Vidal. All she wants from him is a line—he did not even have to read Vidal's book. "[M]ost of these people" are "merely interested in boasting" about their correspondence "with a famous man." Why would he have started such an exchange with Vidal? she asks, then answers that it must give him "a feeling of contact. . . . You can't live without it!" The irrationality of her response probably reveals some jealousy of Miller and the extent of her sense of abandonment by Vidal, who is finding an easy recognition elsewhere and making plans to go in April to Guatemala, where he has bought a house (a former monastery).

Hugo introduces Anaïs to Eugene Walter, a young man whose marionette theatrical creation (with script by Charles Henri Ford) he much admires. Hugo wants to do a film with the marionettes, but when Anaïs sees Walter's script, she wants to use real actors, including herself as the seductress. She decides that the story will be set at the shore and she will be gazing into a mirror and catching the gaze of a young man who stands looking at her from behind. Walter is fascinated. *The Dangerous Telescope* is filmed on Sundays, and Anaïs takes charge. Walter finds her oppressive during the filming ("She was pushy and directive. . . . I did not like her") and only later, when they socialize as neighbors (he lives at 31 West Ninth Street) does he learn to enjoy her company and discover her humor. Soon he realizes that the role she cast herself in parallels her life: "She loved to take over young men, who did not know what hit them. She was not mother or mistress; she was the European mystic muse, and they fell; many were intense relationships. . . . Yet she never gave herself. She was a virgin to the end of her days."[103]

He shares her sense of drama, her witty satire of others less fashionably dressed. He gives her a surprise party on her next birthday, and places a paper crown on her head at the signing party for *Ladders to Fire*. The *Virginia Kirkus Service* (a review for libraries) declares it "mystical erotica" that public libraries should "pass . . . firmly by."[104]

Gotham Book Mart hosts her book party in its new quarters at 51–41 West Forty-seventh Street. Three hundred people attend to celebrate her first commercial publication. All the praise she receives here and in the next two days at other book signings convinces her that there is a larger audience than her publisher believes. Then the *New York Times Book Review*, in an article entitled "Surrealist Soap Opera," dismisses her book as "a pastiche of contemporary preciousness" in which pale, weak, young men revolve around women who endlessly seek their "independence and self-creation."[105]

Her mood changes abruptly with the first review. Publication by a national company is certainly a mixed blessing, for it subjects her to acute pain. In November come two negative and patronizing reviews in the *Saturday Review* and the book section of the *Chicago Sun* ("somnambulistic prose") and a halfhearted review by Edmund Wilson in *The New Yorker* ("perceptive and disarming" but amorphous). Only her final review, in the *San Francisco Chronicle*, is good ("a good writer who combines the impressionism of Virginia Woolf with an intellectual searching").[106] She writes a two-page accusatory letter to Wilson saying that his remarks in *The New Yorker* should make him hang his head.[107]

Then Leo Lerman tells her to lie low and hide after exposing such a sensational story of women loving each other. But it is not lesbian love, she declares vehemently. Both *House of Incest* and *Ladders to Fire* suggest an elusive lesbianism, but as one critic claims, it is not homosexual but "omnisexual," for the gender roles are unstable and all relationships in the novels are sexually charged.[108] Lerman's remark—and his later publication of a tiny photograph of Anaïs with a veil (suggesting she has yet to be discovered)—lead to a falling out that lasts for years.[109]

Walking home one day at the frantic five-o'clock rush hour, she is suddenly overwhelmed with anguish and loneliness and has to stop, for she thinks she will choke. Though she has a multiple-book contract with Dutton and is surrounded by adoring young fans, she still feels rootless and unloved. She suffers from the misunderstanding of critics (and some friends) and from her failure to find someone to whom she can completely and openly bond in love. The press is sold and Gonzalo is slowly fading from her life, Vidal's letters from Guatemala lack warmth, and she feels herself at an impasse.

Only the young understand and respond, she notes. Her former lover Lanny Baldwin sends a letter of encouragement after the *Times* review (the following month she will send another payment on his loan to the press). And she meets, through Kimon Friar, two young poets attending Amherst, where Friar teaches (after one year he will be dismissed for his relationship with the first young man): James Merrill, a son of the Wall Street family and recently released from the army, and William Burford, a son of a Texas oil baron. Merrill, a rationalist and devotee of Proust who had published his first collection of poetry at twenty-five, is unimpressed with her; Burford finds her "fascinating" and "fiercely ambitious." "I am Circe, Bill," she says.[110]

Her first extravagant letter to Burford is ten pages long, and soon he is going to New York to her salon, longing for the intellectual stimulation of a Madame de Staël. She calls him "Kendall" in the diary, after Kendall oil because she knows his family is in petroleum. He remembers the Thirteenth Street apartment with its thick panes of glass that look like a skylight, painted with the signs of the zodiac. "Unlike a French salon, there was no discussion of ideas," he says.

> She was more a psychoanalytic hostess asking probing questions about our personal lives. Anaïs gave people the *illusion* of the French salon but had no real connection with it; she was not of its lineage. Not once did she talk about history or politics. FEEL-ING was all. [She was interested] only in the creation of a certain feeling, a flow, as we might call it.[111]

Burford walks through the Village with her, buys fur-lined boots for her, and pays for Nijinsky's *Diary*, which she finds in the window of a rare bookstore and insists that he read as one of the crucial documents of the time. She had given the same book to Henry Miller with the same instructions (Miller later made reference in a chapbook to this diary and to Nijinsky's "triumph" over homosexuality).[112] Anaïs may, indeed, share Miller's view of homosexuality.

Merrill, who is more sophisticated about literature and about the homosexual world than Burford, sees less of Anaïs. He visits the apartment on a few occasions, including one day when they smear egg whites on their faces to look drawn and white-faced like Proust. But he finds that she "takes up too much emotional oxygen."

She also meets Anatole Broyard, who will later become a major *New York Times* reviewer and mention her occasionally (and unfavorably) in print over the years. Like Burford and others, Broyard could never get over the inaccuracies in her diary accounts—"My God, what a liar."[113]

At the beginning of winter she tours several campus communities, reading her work and lecturing. Professor Carlton Lake and his wife entertain her at Harvard, where James Johnson Sweeney introduces her;[114] she records "Ragtime" at Boston University; Professor Herbert West entertains her at Dartmouth and reports that she held four hundred spellbound by reading her diary; at Goddard College she just misses Maya Deren, who has been showing her films; and at her second reading at Amherst she becomes intoxicated by talk and champagne with James Merrill and William Burford. They giggle and exchange repartee and literary observations, until suddenly they smell smoke and call the fire department, only to learn that it is two smoking pork chops from another floor. Anaïs's description in her diary makes it a lively (and more dramatic) story of rescue by the fire department.

This reading tour is her first experience as a public literary figure. The painfully shy wife from Paris has learned "to parry attacks, to resist intellectualizations, to avoid irrelevant questions," as she calls it. She returns exhausted.[115]

Though he personally finds her predatory and flirtatious, Professor Lake and his wife entertain Anaïs for two nights in Cambridge. He understands her appeal for the audiences. Despite having the "funny, chirpy voice . . . of an old lady," she captures the overflow Cambridge audience of one thousand—a number that necessitated a change of venue. Years later, neither he nor Broyard would recognize the details of her portrayal of her trip to Boston or her meetings with them in New York City. Professor Lake remembers nothing of the shared confidences and secrets that she records in her diary.[116]

Both Lake and Merrill assess the meaning of her popularity on the lecture circuit in 1946 and 1947. According to Professor Lake, just after a depressing war, the young were trying to recapture the Paris years of the surrealists. She could talk about those French years with an impressionistic sensitivity. For the student, she represents Henry Miller, the underground, and Paris. Merrill believes that the Wilson review had put her on the map, and surrealism, which was "in the air," gave her "a great deal of cachet." But he also credits her with helping to transplant to America "some of the French psychological skills and Proustian self-analysis."[117]

In her lectures of 1946 she talks about her creative process being spontaneous and free-associative, her subject matter being the highest moments of illumination, and the difference between realism and reality, between inner truth and outer fact. "Realism and Reality" is the lecture that will evolve through the years. All her observations explain and defend her art, which is the antithesis of the cult of craft and cunning.[118] The words of her lectures and writing are multisyllabic. She favors the following: "labyrinth," "fecundate," "illuminations," "ensorcelled." Years later Gore Vidal will mock her use of this last word in his memoir/novel *Two Sisters:*

> It is no accident that her favorite adjective is *ensorcelled.* She cannot write a book without it. . . . Marietta [Nin] reads everything written about her from Kyoto to Spokane, book reviewers have been astonished to receive long letters from Marietta analyzing what they have said of her and though no praise has ever been quite sufficient. . . . Marietta is a master of "ensorcelling" those who write book chat for the press, turning to them that legendary Aphrodite face.[119]

Anaïs sits opposite Vidal in the elegant Ritz bar one night soon after his return from Antigua, in Guatemala. She has read the manuscript of his new novel, *The City and the Pillar,* and has expressed her disappointment in a letter. After some talk about his new home in Central America and her possible visit, she pulls the letter she has written before the meeting from her purse and hands it to him to read. She watches his shocked response to her charge that he has "destroyed" the myths by which she lives: romanticism, beauty, magic, and illusion. He is a "cynic" with an "ugly vision" of people, who separates sex from love in his sympathetic portrait of homosexuality. The romantic Jim Willard of the novel is destroyed by his partner, Bob, who sees their union as a mere physical encounter. She is most disappointed that Gore seems to have different values than she, and thus has eluded her influence. Alas, she has failed to heal him, to cast her "glow" on him. How had she missed seeing "his cynical vision"? Though she continues to dine with him at their favorite restaurants, their relationship changes: "He could not be the son of my writing, the heir, the one whose writing I could love."[120] And, finally, she is none too happy with a character named Maria Verlaine, a femme fatale clearly modeled on herself, who goes with Jim and Bob to Mexico in a ménage à trois.

Several events trigger a newly critical view of homosexuality, including her realization that Vidal is no longer ambivalent about his sexuality. Though she has long privately sought the homosexual world, when she is publicly linked with it she is dismayed. The rumor that she is a lesbian surfaces after the republication of the photograph in which she poses as her character

"Lillian" in a tuxedo and with short hair. She feels "typed" and "damned." In her diary at the end of 1946, she states emphatically that she has never had a lesbian relationship—"that was an unfulfilled part of my life."[121] She may be surrounded by homosexuals, she acknowledges, but her first novel had only "implied woman's love to woman."

She continues nurturing her magic circle, but her criticism of its members is more evident in her diary. For example, she remarks that the work of Burford, Gore, and Pinckard is characterized by "paralysis, inability to love, linked to noncreation," though she had earlier told Durrell that Burford was the Rimbaud of America.[122] On her forty-fourth birthday, she puts on her Spanish dance costume and, with Pablo, travels through a snowstorm to a Haitian carnival where she dances with black heterosexual men whose bodies are "alive" and strong, "exuding power and passion."[123]

Yet her life, until May, is still in the world of young homosexuals, whose psyches, she believes, are "as crippled as" hers was by her "father's desertion"—they all have great needs for assurance and supportive maternal maturity. She claims that Vidal writes from Antigua that his "attachment" to her "grows more poignant, more vast, more hopeless with each day—what can one do with beauty? It is there, it hurts."[124] When Pablo boards a Danish freighter to sail around the world, the largest photograph on his shaving mirror is of her in her "Sabina" pose. She is invited to a birthday party that Merrill gives for himself. All come as their favorite characters, including Merrill as Proust (intoning Edith Sitwell's "Facade" while standing on the table) and Burford as Nijinsky in the faun costume of L'Après-midi d'un Faune. Anaïs comes as herself, in black cape.[125] But Burford disappoints; he writes a critical letter instead of slowly withdrawing from her circle. Disillusioned, Burford concludes that "she walked a line between exaggerated parody of herself and a wonderful sense of herself, but for me she overstepped the bounds. She added to my life, but she took a lot away." He takes all her letters to him to a cold potato field and burns them. "The act of a late-adolescent kid," he now says.[126]

What she does like about her circle is their artistic youthfulness and their hunger for her presence and her work. She is also thrown into the company of youth because barriers exist between herself and established American writers. These barriers from older writers consist of the importance in their lives of alcohol (James Agee), their preference for plainspoken women, their politics (James Baldwin), and the fact that Anaïs is not a native. She especially regrets that Martha Graham and Isak Dinesen (like Djuna Barnes earlier and Jane Bowles and Leslie Blanche later) ignore her approaches.

After the "Lillian" photograph appears on the cover of her *Realism and Reality* (1946) chapbook, which has a purple cover and purple ink and is

published by Oscar Baradinsky, rumors about her being lesbian again provoke her anger. She unsuccessfully tries to get Frances Steloff to stop selling
the pamphlets at the Gotham. Baradinsky's Alicat Book Shop Press publishes two Nin chapbooks, *Realism and Reality* and *On Writing* (1947), published earlier in the year by Daniel Oliver at Dartmouth (in an edition of
150 copies). When Barandinsky prints a thousand copies of *On Writing*,
with William Burford's "The Art of Anaïs Nin" included, he asks Gonzalo to
print it. Oscar and his wife, Florenz, live and run their large bookstore in
Yonkers, visit the Guiler apartment, and introduce Anaïs to their circle of
literary and political radicals. Florenz is dramatic and wears long black
fingernails and dresses like a vampire. She is also interested in lesbianism,
says one young member of their group, who confirms that Anaïs was known
as an analyst who also flirted with lesbianism.[127]

When Richard Wright, author of *Black Boy* (1945) and a friend of the
Baradinskys', comes to Anaïs's house for dinner, he seems suspicious and
reserved. But his talk of going to France to get away from discrimination and
to live free in order to write strikes a spark in Anaïs. Once again she decides
she needs to get away. She speaks in letters to several friends of Europe and
either California or Mexico as her next abode. The sound of New York
foghorns depresses her for they remind her of a frustrated desire to travel.
This state of mind prepares her to meet the man who will sweep her away.

In San Francisco several of her friends and lovers are publishing *Circle,*
a periodical started by George Leite, whom she has never met. The magazine, with Bern Porter assisting, publishes Duncan's "The Year as Catches,"
Patchen's "Sleeper Awake on the Precipice," and Miller's book reviews. She
submits her short story "Hejda," which is accepted for publication. Robert
Duncan is not pleased with her literary presence and tells friends that she
is an "unwelcome poetic bedfellow in *Circle.*"[128]

She begins suggesting to new acquaintances that they take her to the
West Coast. At one of several parties at Hazel Guggenheim's (Hugo handled
her financial estate), Anaïs meets Walter Calkins, who is working under the
stage name of Guy Blake for the Broadway production of *Lady Windermere's
Fan.* He is not yet twenty-five years old, Kansas-born and San Francisco–
reared. They begin having assignations at her apartment while Hugo is at
work. "She was coy and playful with me, but there was only one purpose in
my being there," he remembers. "I never thought of her as being intellectual,
for we never talked about art or ideas." One day when the front door opens,
he jumps to dress, but she seems unworried, as if she has an understanding
with her husband or deliberately wants to provoke a scene. At their next
meeting, she asks Calkins if he will drive her to Cuernavaca, Mexico. "I

sensed that this would be a mistake for me, and declined. I guess in today's terms I was her boy toy."[129]

The manuscript for *Children of the Albatross*, her second volume in the Proustian mode, is completed in March 1947, long before the contractual date of delivery.[130] Vidal intervenes with Dutton and the book is quickly put into production. It consists of two parts: "The Sealed Room" and "The Café." The first is the story of Djuna, the dancer who is deserted by her father and reared in an orphanage where the watchman sexually abuses her. By making the watchman, not the father, her abuser, Anaïs may be keeping locked her own final "sealed room." As a result of the watchman's abuse, Djuna prefers the company of adolescent boys:

> They treat me as one of their own, because I believe what they believe, I feel as they do. I hate the father, authority, men of power, men of wealth, all tyranny, all authority, all crystal-lizations. . . . I want to stay in this room forever not with man the father but with man the son . . . [loving those who] flow . . . feel . . . [and] melt.[131]

All the "reality" of Anaïs's inner life, if not the physical "realism" of the facts, is in this novel, including portraits of Michael, the twin (based on her relationship with Eduardo); Donald, based on Robert Duncan; and two seventeen-year-old boys—Paul and Lawrence (the latter based on Bill Pinckard, who sends a gift to Anaïs after reading his portrait). Setting the novel in Paris will do nothing to disguise the characters for future readers of her published diary and erotica.

The second section of the novel, entitled "The Café," brings the characters together in a place of Oriental rhythms. The chief characters are Lillian (bread/devotion), Sabina (fire/consumption), Djuna (light/reflection), and the hedonistic natural man, Jay (Miller). Only the friends who find details of their lives and relationships in the characters of her novel realize how thoroughly Anaïs has mined her diary for her fiction.

## Rupert Pole

In spring of 1947, Anaïs gets into an elevator with a handsome young man about twenty-eight years of age. As they rise toward the party of Hazel Guggenheim on an upper floor, they look with interest and admiration at each other. It is love at first sight, he will always say. When they realize that they are going to the same party, Anaïs introduces herself to Rupert Pole. They spend the evening talking together, and he is certain that all the other men in the room are jealous. He gets the distinct impression that she is divorced. She speaks of leaving for France, or maybe leaving the U.S. and returning in order to begin the naturalization process. The young Californian informs her that she cannot leave without seeing all the country. The actor son of two actors, Pole has decided to leave acting (he has concluded a run as Tonio in Webster's *The Duchess of Malfi* on Broadway) and printmaking. The United States is not New York City, he asserts. Miller had probably made the same point, but it is Pole who is convincing, and in a matter of weeks she leaves with him for the West Coast.[132]

In his Model A Ford with the top down, Rupert wearing a beret and Anaïs dressed in purple, they emerge from the Holland Tunnel to a great sense of freedom and space. She feels as if she had been enclosed in a tunnel called New York City and has now reached "open freedom." They do not turn back for fear of turning to salt, he says later. She has left Hugo with the explanation that she is accompanying a friend headed for Las Vegas and a divorce. And she is escaping from Gonzalo for good. She is going with the "flow," acting out her persistent theme in *Children of the Albatross*. Two years before, she told her diary that she had "to live passionately and blindly, to take risks."[133] Now she is going with her new lover, a tall and open-faced lad from Los Angeles who is smitten.

The Ford chugs south with a rhythm that brings her close to the land, from the monuments of Washington, D.C., to the mountains of Virginia and the moss and dew of the Deep South. She is particularly captivated by New Orleans, where they visit Gore Vidal. The city reminds her of Mediterranean and Barcelonese experiences, and of her maternal grandmother, Anaïs Vaurigaud de Culmell, who in the previous century had left seven children with her husband to run away with her lover to this city. The granddaughter Anaïs stops with Rupert at Shadows-on-the-Teche to sign the plantation door of Weeks Hall. Just below the signature of John Dos Passos, Anaïs writes, "A wonderful story teller" and the two lovers place their names.[134]

Anaïs is also captivated by the Southwest of Santa Fe and Taos, where she visits Frieda, the widow of D. H. Lawrence. Anaïs's romanticism is inevitably disappointed by this "tiny old lady" and Lawrence's "sunless" and faded paintings. Hurrying on, she expresses reluctance to remain with the "past of my literary loves."[135]

In Los Angeles, Rupert's mother, Helen, and stepfather, Lloyd Wright, win her heart. Wright, son of the famed architect Frank Lloyd Wright, becomes her artist-hero, and the Wright home at 858 North Doheny represents a world of ideal beauty. She has found a new family in the Wrights, though she does not know that they initially dislike her because she is so much older than their son (it will be years before Rupert himself knows the year of her birth). Rupert William Pole was born the year before Anaïs dropped out of Wadleigh High School and Hugh Parker Guiler graduated from Columbia University.

Rupert is in Los Angeles to enroll in forestry at UCLA; while in Washington, D.C., he had investigated jobs with the Interior Department (for conservation work, he was told to get a degree in forestry) and the State Department (he decided against working for John Foster Dulles).[136] He had graduated in music and math from Harvard in June 1940, but now wants to work outdoors in nature.

Later Anaïs flies to Mexico with the announced intention of reentering the U.S. under declaration of intent to become a permanent citizen, but in fact her marriage to Hugo, an American citizen, qualifies her for citizenship upon request. If she had not come West, she realizes, she would not have wanted to become a permanent resident of the United States. And if she had not found the climate too cold in Guadalajara and reboarded the plane for Acapulco, she would not have found her tropical paradise. When the plane lands on the beach at the little fishing port of Acapulco, the tropical tenderness dissolves her, as she explains it. She can feel New York City toxins being cleared from her body, and in their place emerges a keener taste for nature. Maybe she is only selecting a new cast for the "same drama," but she is hoping for the birth of a "new woman."[137] She has taken the first step toward dividing her life between two coasts.

# CHAPTER TEN

## 1947–1955

# Changing and Turning:
# Beginning the Bicoastal Life

"Tropic, from the Greek, signified change and turning. So she changed and turned, and was metamorphosed by the light and caressing heat into a spool of silk."
—*Anaïs Nin,* Seduction of the Minotaur[1]

"I only need to continue my personal life, so beautiful and in full bloom, and to do my major work, which is the diary."
—*Anaïs Nin, 1955*[2]

WITH MEMORIES of warm guavas and iguanas beckoning her, Anaïs devotes the fall of 1947 to getting out of New York City and back to the West, to Los Angeles and the healing sun of Acapulco. She tells her friends that she is now a nomad, her permanent address the Maxwell Book Shop on Christopher Street: her new joy and freedom in life is without guilt.[3] She writes Henry Miller in June that she is "trying to live alone . . . [and] stand on my own feet."[4] He encourages her to free herself, pledges to send her money when his French royalties arrive, and offers tips on where to secure lecture commitments to get her back to California and Mexico.[5] She is at a turning point after nearly eight years in New York seeking literary acceptance. She is correcting proof for the second volume of her multivolume novel to be published by E. P. Dutton. She has a new lover, Rupert Pole, waiting for her in Los Angeles, where he is taking botany and economics courses at UCLA. And she has discovered the freedom and healing nature of the Pacific Coast.

She hopes to devote herself to the continuing novel. In contrast, the diary, now seventy-five handwritten volumes long, is interrupted by her impending travels between New York and Los Angeles, San Francisco, and Mexico. She writes less and less, eventually keeping the diary on loose paper, in accordion files, undated to protect her travel secrets from Hugo. When she types them later, she will add, elaborate, explain, and alter. Now, more than ever, her diary is a revised and self-censored autobiography rather than a diary.[6]

## Seeking Nature

She packs her bags in the fall of 1947 for the promotion of *Children of the Albatross* and a lecture series that will eventually take her west. After a reading at Black Mountain College in North Carolina, she returns to New York for the book launching at Gotham Book Mart on 3 November. At this time she picks up a $250 advance from Dutton for a third book: *Under a Glass Bell and Other Stories* (to be published the next year, the fourth printing for some of the stories). She then gives readings in Vermont (Bennington College), Washington D.C. (School of Creative Arts), Chicago, San Francisco, and Berkeley.[7] She will be back in Acapulco by December.

En route news reaches her of the critical reception of her new novel. There are only five very mixed reviews (Wilson had already written his last review of her work). Though each expresses criticism of her weak plot and characterization (a "dance of generalities and types," says the *New York Times Book Review*), there is praise: the *Saturday Review* likes the lushness and symbolism of her language; *The New Yorker*, her "incandescent metaphor and image"; and the *Houston Post*, her "gift of literature" in a style "exquisitely fashioned."[8] Perhaps more than most authors, she sees only the negatives, which hurt her deeply and lead her to believe that she is misunderstood by the entire literary establishment.

The short trip from San Francisco to Big Sur is dramatic and foggy. Paul Mathiesen, her "Nordic Danish fairy-tale boy" whom she had known and loved in New York, is visiting San Francisco when she arrives for a visit, and she asks him to take her to see Henry Miller. She is in San Francisco to make contacts with former friends and lovers and with literary friends of Miller's. There is a certain symmetry in returning to Miller at this point in her life, but she soon realizes that she should not have come. Lepska Miller seems quiet and tense and talks little to Anaïs, who wonders if the Millers are having marital problems. Paul is also uneasy because he feels that he is being used: Henry, with his young wife in a see-through blouse, and Anaïs, with a young man half her age, are both preening. Too much separates the former Tristan and Isolde of Louveciennes, and Anaïs stays only briefly. Henceforth she will see Miller from afar, she says; the intimate complicity of fifteen years is over.[9]

Acapulco offers Anaïs the warm breeze of forgetfulness and the melliflu-ous language of her youth, bringing together her Cuban blood and her experiences in Barcelona and Havana. The resort town and El Mirador Hotel seem to exist only in the present. The heat of the sun dissolves thought and memory. Words are weightless, she says, half of them carried away by the sea. She is in "full possession of her body," she thinks, aroused by the smell of honeysuckle, the rhythms of guitars, the taste of mango and papayas, the jazz at Club La Perla.[10]

Her first friend in Acapulco is a Dr. Hernandez, who has studied medi-cine in France, published a book of poetry, and, though generally contemp-tuous of tourists, enjoys talking to her. He serves the natives with compas-sion, but refuses to give drugs to those who pressure him. She will create his "fictional" portrait in a later novel. Among the wisdom in his doctor's bag is the belief that we live experience over and over until it is understood and changed. That truth appeals to Anaïs, who entertains many visitors from her past, including an unnamed friend who will not take off his clothes and swim nude with her.[11]

To reconvene her coterie of transparent young men, she sends for them. Hurry here before everyone leaves, she insists, always demanding absolute loyalty. When Paul Mathiesen arrives and meets everyone on the terrace, she introduces him as the man who has driven five days to see her. Yet when he is exhausted and wants to go to bed, she refuses to leave her friends after one dance. Rather than go to bed, he goes bodysurfing instead and nearly drowns. She visits him the next day, and he knows that she has been with another. Soon Paul hears the rumor that his near drowning was really a suicide attempt over Anaïs, and he is angry.[12] Another young man who comes because her postcard says she is feeling "spiritually alone" is Bill Burford (the "Kendall" of her published diary). When he arrives at the El Mirador Hotel, she has decamped. He drives back to his family's home in Texas. Once again, she had asked for a futile sacrifice.[13]

To escape the moral censure of the hotel when she invites lovers and guests, Anaïs has signed a lease to buy a small stucco cottage opening on to the sea from a cliff. She sends a round-trip plane ticket to Rupert Pole, whose mother warns him against interrupting his studies (he has enrolled for twenty-two units at UCLA), though her displeasure may also be disap-proval of Anaïs. Taking his books along, Rupert comes for the Christmas holiday.[14]

Despite her romantic notions of natural life, the scorpions and rats in her little house and the noise of a neighbor's rooster bother her, and she moves back to the hotel. Pole, who loves to sleep under the stars, tries to teach her to love the simple existence in nature. To be sure, by the end of her vacation, Mexico has "loosened chains . . . dissolved poisons . . . healed . . . wounds." Her writing about this second trip to Mexico, which lasts through January of 1948, is sprinkled with the word "joy." The healing sands of Mexico will provide the setting of her continuous novel's ultimate volume, *Seduction of the Minotaur.*[15]

She lands at Idlewild in February 1948 during a downpour. The sullen anger of taxi drivers and shopkeepers makes for a harsh return. Dutton grudgingly agrees to give her another $250 advance (travel and multiple lodgings are proving expensive). The city, its people, the reality of her accumulated bills only make Mexican life seem more joyously reckless. Her friends, after hearing her story of the Mexican practice of a birthday serenade, sing outside her window on her forty-fifth birthday.

Her neighbor Eugene Walter, the witty young painter who had worked with Hugo on *The Dangerous Telescope,* attends Anaïs's surprise birthday party and, until he leaves for Paris in 1951, introduces her to all his friends. Though he enjoys her company, he concludes that she is "totally illiterate and not cultured" because she does not know the French writers he thinks are important. They both love exaggeration and acting superior by laughing at the improper grooming of others. "She did not have a fan, but oh her manner! . . . She had that manner with everyone, male, female, young, and old." When he introduces a young (unnamed) man to her, "she suddenly became a different person than the woman I had seen an hour before. She was about twenty different people. A different person with everyone she met. The youth falls in love with her. Their affair lasted about six months. Then there was someone else."[16]

Walter also remembers, as do others, that she had a file cabinet labeled "lies." Several who saw this file assumed she had to keep track of her numerous lies. But the label, like the bogus Paris diary she kept for Hugo in the 1930s, could also have been for her husband's eyes. She protects Hugo, whom Walter later observes on the arm of a woman when Anaïs leaves for California.[17] Hugo seems quietly to accommodate her growing interest in California and her absences, assuming that her artistic life is flourishing.

By spring 1948 she is headed back west to Rupert Pole, who is visiting his father in Colorado. When she meets the British actor Reginald Pole in Denver, where he is directing his own play (*Malice Toward None*), she thinks she sees him as the father she would like to have had (though he is only a decade older than she). Years later, when the diary of this period (1947–55) is published, many readers will assume that the photograph of Reginald Pole is of one of the men who had been her lover. But her lover, identified only as an "escort" in another photograph in the same volume, is Rupert, Reginald's son.

Reginald is tall, ruggedly handsome, a charmer, with many talents that include acting, composing, writing and directing. And, like Anaïs, he is international: born to English parents in Japan, educated at Cambridge University in England, trained at the Globe Theatre, and a friend of the poet Rupert Brooke, for whom he named his son. He tells swashbuckling tales. His former wife (and Rupert's mother), Helen Taggart, has for some time been married to Lloyd Wright. Helen, who is gentle and feminine, also has a son with Wright, named Eric. Each member of Rupert's family merits lengthy characterization in Anaïs's diary, for it is evident that she is attracted to this artistic and educated group, to which we must add Beatrice Wood, Reginald's former lover and still close friend, an artist who had studied in Paris in the second decade of the century and had love affairs with Marcel Duchamp and Henri-Pierre Rouché.[18] Rupert combines the openness of the West, which he loves, with the education and cultivation of the East, Harvard, and his English-born father.

From Denver, Rupert goes to a fire-fighting camp in Frazier, Colorado, and Anaïs flies to Houston for a reading and book signing. Hugo joins her there from New York City and drives her to Los Angeles, where he has a gallery exhibit of his engravings.[19] She is having her mail sent to the Satyr Book Shop at 6278 Hollywood Boulevard. The logistics of keeping her lives separated is time-consuming and alternately exciting and emotionally draining.

## Becoming Transcontinental

Her California life seems to come into being as the trips to the West Coast accumulate and as her commitment to Rupert grows. At the beginning of her bicoastal life she discovers the pleasure of the exit, for, as Emily Dickinson expresses in her poetry, going "is a Drama /Staying cannot confer."

Anaïs stops dating her diary when she begins commuting between two coasts and two men. She compares her movements to the swinging of the trapeze artist.[20] She flies from one coast to another, from one man to another, from one group of friends to another, embracing a different aspect of her personality in each setting.[21]

New York City means life with Hugo; he is her financial base, after all. Whether she is there on Thirteenth Street or visiting with her devoutly Roman Catholic mother and brother, the East Coast for her is the scene of the "parental" life, of oppressive "work and duties," the city of her publishers but also of Village social life.[22]

San Francisco is an arty town in which she has a growing number of New York expatriate friends. "Art was boiling over" in the city, which was rapidly becoming a major center of poetry performance.[23] Robert Duncan is a poet in the grand manner now and living here in a permanent relationship with a young male painter named Jess Collins, but Robert and Anaïs no longer associate with each other. She meets Miller's friend Jean "Janko" Varda, the artist-hero who knew Picasso, Braque, and Miró; and George Leite, editor of *Circle,* with whom Bern Porter is working. She sees Josephine Premice dancing at the Fax nightclub.[24] Here she can work and not "dissolve" into nature as she does in subtropical Los Angeles. One of her close friends is Ruth Witt-Diamant, a teacher at San Francisco State College, who will found the Poetry Center there in 1954. Ruth is one of the few who knows of Anaïs's dual life. Obligingly she writes the same letter and Christmas greeting to each of the abodes.[25]

But it is in Los Angeles where Anaïs will spend an increasing amount of time each year over the next twenty-nine years. Surrounded by snowcapped mountains and ocean islands, it is the city closest in atmosphere to the Orient, to Mexico, and to her Cuban memories. The West, she says later, is truly the heart of human America, lacking the "industrial dehumanization" she loathes.[26] She likes Los Angeles's openness to innovation and its "style of harmony with nature."[27]

She likens Nathanael West's Hollywood (where Rupert lives), to a grade-B film with its world of illusion, gaudy billboards, boardinghouses, eccentric dress, and European émigrés.[28] Paul Mathiesen, now returned to his hometown, introduces her to two talented young filmmakers who become her friends, Kenneth Anger and Curtis Harrington. Anger, whose film work will later be praised by Fellini, she had liked because she thought he had Cuban blood when they met in San Francisco (yet he makes violent and sadistic films that revolt her). Harrington makes surrealistic films closer to her fiction, for they make use of dreams, mysteries, and magic. Paul Mathiesen completes this trio of young film students. He and Anger were lovers briefly when they were in high school.

She adores Venice, the refuge of poor artists, and Venice Beach with its carnival atmosphere, white sand, and the pull of the sea. The amusement park frightens her; she loves more secluded spots where she can sunbathe in the nude on a large rock. Though she writes every day in Rupert's apartment, she often goes to the beach with Anger, Harrington, and Mathiesen, where they tell her about what they have just learned of film history in their UCLA film classes.

She loves the caressing climate, the bleached white houses and suntans of the Angelenos, the skyline of palm trees and billboards: it is a pastel city of leisure, where people ride around in convertibles or with surfboards on the roofs of their cars. Less "toxic" than New York City, the Los Angeles of the early 1950s, before Disneyland and Universal Studios tours, is still close to nature and thus not as obsessed with ambition or time. Anaïs is ready for this world. She awakens each morning to the singing of birds, walks down the hill for breakfast at Musso and Frank's, and, after writing, indulges her body shamelessly in the pursuit of sun and water and the men she loves.

She has found a man with whom she can have both a passion and domesticity. She writes an imprisoned pen pal of Henry Miller's that she is also in a prison with someone (Hugo) she should not have married, that until recently she had always had destructive passions from which she had narrowly escaped, and that her most recent flight from prison (Rupert) has lasted longer than any others.[29] Rupert is the ballast, holding her steady and on course, though she occasionally fears losing him to a younger woman.[30]

She and Rupert have a growing circle of friends, including Rupert's father, Reginald Pole, who lives in Los Angeles and introduces her to everyone from Charlie Chaplin to Cornelia Runyon; but she also sees his dissipation, his "abnormal preoccupation with his body," and his dependence on women to take care of him. His "incurable illness of the soul" reminds her of Hermann Hesse's *Steppenwolf*, which she reads. Reginald's self-destructiveness reminds her of Helba's, and she refuses to be pulled into his all-night talking and inactivity. She confides in a friend that he is a psychotic of the Elizabethan manner.[31]

Rupert's stepfather, Lloyd Wright, better fits her need for the artist-father, though his failure to understand her writing is disappointing. She warms to the family life of the Wrights and shares their appreciation of music. They hold weekly chamber music events, in which Rupert plays the viola. The Wrights (Lloyd had designed two shells for the Hollywood Bowl, in 1924–25 and 1928) embody a world of music and architecture that delight her.

During the summer of 1948 Anaïs visits Mexico in order to break her rent-to-buy agreement for the tiny cliff house in Acapulco. She seeks the help of Thorvald, who comes from his home in Lomas, near Guadalajara, Mexico, to help his sister. Thorvald Nin lives and operates a plywood business, has business connections in the country, and though he disapproves of his sister, comes to her aid. At Hugo's urging, she tries to get her family in Mexico to invest in stock, which Hugo is selling as a private broker.[32]

She flies to Antigua, Guatemala, to spend two weeks with Gore Vidal.[33] His house at the foot of the volcano had once been a monastery, and it has a bell tower and chapel. She is fascinated by the market and the quiet Indians; it is a world seemingly closer to Tibet than to Mexico. She assumed, by his invitation, that they would have a private interlude, but she finds a group of homosexual visitors. Feeling threatened, she dreams of vultures in the courtyard. She tells a friend later that on this visit Vidal, ever the mythmaker, suggests she be artificially inseminated with his seed, a suggestion that cools her already flickering ardor.[34] In her published diary she expresses only a longing to flee back to Acapulco because she is no longer the commanding influence in Vidal's life. "His interest is like Miller's: to meet everybody, to win the world," she had earlier noted. His wit still entertains her, but she is uncomfortable with his cynicism and sarcasm.[35]

Vidal secretly blames her for the poor showing of his novel *In a Yellow Wood*, published the year before. He tells a reviewer years later that the novel was "in limbo" because of the effect of meeting and being "ensorcelled" by Anaïs Nin.[36] In this novel Vidal creates the first of a series of dark-haired and alluring women characters based on Anaïs, women with foreign accents, numerous lovers, often diary-keepers, who are divorced or married to men who complacently overlook their indiscretions. His second novel, *The City and the Pillar,* will appear later this year, and the third, *The Judgment of Paris,* in 1952. His most recent caricature of her is in *Live from Golgotha* (1992), where Priscilla of Corinth helps many young men "to flow" and dances "aglow with fulfilled self-love" while her diary ("often made up") is read aloud by an actor.[37] One reviewer, in *The New Yorker,* wondered "why such a bright fellow should repeat himself so often," but the portraits of Anaïs, though increasingly harsh, testify to her impact on Vidal's life and art.[38]

In turn, Anaïs will use her visit to Guatemala in *Solar Barque* (1950). Lillian visits Michael Lomax, who appears to be a fool living among the dead in a Mexican town without wind, in a house that was once a convent attached to a church. When he takes her to a festival "for men only," she insists on dancing in the street and is passed from man to man. The dancers grow ever more ardent, Michael more angry and frustrated. "All I ask, since I can't keep you here," he says later, "is that in your next incarnation you be born a boy, and then I will love you."[39]

During her vacation she continues to write the third volume of her Proustian novel. *The Four-Chambered Heart* focuses on Gonzalo, whom she calls Rango. Working on this novel brings back the past, a kind of "residue" that clouds her mood. Consequently, she analyzes the relationship between her fiction, her diary, and her life. Life is to be lived in the sacred present, then "preserved faithfully" in the diary. In fiction, which is not tied to verifiable facts, the experience takes on a new life in the continuum of time. Fiction seeks a pattern and thus "restores the meaning." Fiction is "an act of embalming."[40]

Back in Hollywood one day, Anaïs and Curtis Harrington stop at a news-stand on Las Palmas and he picks up the latest issue of *Partisan Review*, which he reads regularly. She looks through the review section and finds her name and a review of *Under a Glass Bell and Other Stories*, reads the review, and covers her face with her hands in despair and tears. Elizabeth Hardwick claims that no other writer "more passionately embraced thin air." Her "egotism, piety, boastfulness—annihilates what was meant to be joyful. . . ." And in a final vitriolic blow, she says that Nin "seems old-fashioned . . . vague, dreamy, mercilessly pretentious; the sickly child of distinguished parents—the avant garde of the twenties—and unfortunately a great bore. . . ."[41] Of the six reviews of her short fiction this year, none is encouraging. Anaïs copies the Hardwick review into her diary to illustrate the degree of hatred and insult to which she is subjected.

## Pisces by the Bay

After a year of preparation courses at UCLA, Rupert Pole enrolls in California's only school of forestry, at Berkeley. Anaïs spends most of the academic months from 1948 to 1950 with him in nearby San Francisco. Initially they live in a Japanese tea house she has rented in Sutro Heights. Poetic filmmaker James Broughton's Centaur Press publishes a small run of *House of Incest*. "Because her printer-lover Gonzalo in New York had become incorrigibly alcoholic and indifferent sexually," says Broughton, "Anaïs gave us the font of sans serif type that he had used to print her *House of Incest*."

> She gave breathy readings from that book in our press room and became for a time our svelte good fairy bringing a certain tone to our inky basement. . . . Flirtatious, calculating and humorless she palpitated with sensitivity and ambition in a most beguiling way. . . . Anaïs lived in such a network of impulses and deceptions that one never knew whether to believe her.[42]

Later Broughton also plans to print the first volume of her diary in English, but he and his partner, Kermit Sheets, soon realize that would represent more time and money than they can afford. Anaïs tells Miller that she is now leading a secluded life and scrimping, but Ruth Witt-Diamant (her new friend at San Francisco State College) draws her into parties and readings, and Broughton, impressed with her fancy apartment (and its mirrored bedroom) on Buena Vista Heights, concludes that she is a queen bee who collects "beautiful young men for her drones."[43]

When cool weather in the damp garden had threatened her health, she and Rupert abandoned the "tea house" for the apartment Broughton visits, at 258 Roosevelt Way. There she finishes *The Four-Chambered Heart* early in the year and works on retyping her diary. She wants the diary to be a flow of her consciousness in the mode of James Joyce. She probes her writing and her memory ("To write is to descend, to excavate, to go underground"), records her dreams (often laced with her fears), and feels "anchorless, uprooted."[44] When her furniture finally arrives from Paris, she realizes it does not belong in her new life. She gives her carved, inlaid Moroccan bedstead to Broughton. What had illuminated Louveciennes and the houseboat on the Seine looks dead in the white, modern apartment of San Francisco. The past is only good for fiction, she concludes, while waiting for a verdict from Dutton on her Gonzalo story. Parents also belong to the past—at least their power does. The time has come, at age forty-six, when she wants to "revoke their imprint" on her life and accept part of the responsibility for her own life and beliefs.[45]

I am in love with the American West, she writes Lanny Baldwin, a former lover, on 15 April 1949. With Rupert she has entered into a good relationship, but Baldwin must not tell Hugo, who has not yet found anyone to console him (the false implication is that they have divorced). To illustrate how peaceful and domesticated she has become ("living only for One, for our home and writing"), she describes the change in her life: sleeping outdoors, skiing and wearing jeans and walking boots![46] Another young friend of this period describes the domestic scene with Pole as traditional and her life in New York as liberated. Perhaps she was (at least temporarily), like her literary creation Sabina, "exhausted by her flight from one man to another."

Rupert is always supportive and positive about her work and about life. His love is total, undivided, and certainly helps her accept Dutton's rejection of *The Four-Chambered Heart*. Back in New York this summer of 1949 (while Rupert is fighting fires) she signs with another publisher for the Gonzalo novel. William Kennedy is her editor at Duell, Sloan and Pearce. With *Ladders to Fire*, which weaves together the lives of Sabina, Lillian, and Djuna, and *Children of the Albatross*, the story of all Djuna's transparent children, and now *The Four-Chambered Heart*, patterns of characters and symbols have emerged. The dominant symbol is the labyrinth, indicating the detours of the characters' spiritual and psychological journeys. The ocean or flow of the river Seine is a second symbol, signifying the unconscious.[47]

She is now busy writing the fourth novel of her Proustian series, or "continuous novel." The new work will be called *A Spy in the House of Love* and covers: promiscuity in New York in the 1940s, including an affair with

Canada Lee (called Mamba in the novel); her affair with an opera singer (she calls him Philip); and the one-night stand with a young aviator (called John) in Provincetown. Alan is the husband to whom Sabina always returns. She is sexually addicted, obsessively looking for the one who can unify her multiple selves, who can reach the "core, where she felt a constant unsureness."[48] As she writes, Anaïs reintegrates youthful memories: learning to use kohl on her eyes from Moroccan women, Henry Miller (called Jay, a lover from Paris), and Otto Rank (as the Lie Detector, a character who shadows Sabina, recording her sins in a notebook).

Anaïs thinks she is creating the story of a free "Donna Juana," but the sleepless nights and the need for a confessor reveal the guilt and anxiety of the character who feels like Duchamp's nude descending the stairs: numerous outlines of the same woman. Sabina needs both freedom and expiation.

Anaïs takes her manuscript with her when she flies to Acapulco this summer to meet Hugo, who is making what will be his first successful art film (Ai-Ye). Though there are rumors that he has been fired, the official story is that he has asked the City Bank and Farmers Trust to send him back to Europe to finish his professional career with them (twenty-five years of foreign service allows retirement at fifty-five). When they refuse, he resigns without his pension, so the story goes, at the age of fifty-one. He abandons both banking and engraving for filmmaking and personal investment counseling as a stockbroker. He takes brief and informal instruction in filmmaking and purchases an old car and a used camera.[49]

While visiting Anaïs in San Francisco, Hugo had met with the Art in Cinema group, which includes James Broughton, whom he asked to accompany him to Mexico for filming. The two men travel extensively, filming Ai-Ye before Anaïs joins them in Acapulco at the El Mirador Hotel. They film a glamorous scene with Anaïs rocking in a hammock, which Hugo double exposes with a scene of flowing water so that she appears to be underwater. The film will eventually be titled Bells of Atlantis (1952). At night the three hang around the bar, where, according to Broughton, "Anaïs would ask Hugo to proposition [for her] whichever young man in the bar caught her fancy. Being the most generous cuckold I have ever known, Hugo did her bidding without protest and withdrew into the background of her flirtations."[50] Hugo truly adored her, Broughton adds.

It is not as a cuckold that Anaïs portrays Hugo in a letter to a confidante: Hugo has been in analysis and is obsessed with self-assertion, she tells her friend. His new career makes him happy. She tells the same confidante that she is meeting Rupert in Laredo—"tell no one" is her customary phrase.[51] "She enjoyed it both ways," concludes Broughton: "her meal ticket and her romances."[52]

She and Rupert spend a Sunday with Jean (Janko) Varda on his houseboat in San Francisco bay in early fall. She had met Varda by mail through Miller (Varda had introduced Miller to Big Sur) and had visited him on her first trip to the San Francisco Bay Area. She shares his artistic approach in viewing beauty as an escape from realism, and she admires the Oriental quality of his collages, one of which, *Women Reconstructing the World*, she hangs on her wall. In the coming years she will often mention Varda's life as the ideal life of the artist: he lives free, wears blue jeans, creates his own vision, reduces his needs to a minimum, and teaches only enough to keep food on his table. His home is now a ferryboat moored in Sausalito. He tells Anaïs that in a former life she had been a high priestess in Eleusis. She characterizes him as a "poet" and "sublime ragpicker," a reference to her short story about the ragpickers of Paris. She will use his visual technique of collecting fragments and remnants in her last book, *Collages*.[53]

Anaïs also shares the artistic perspectives of Louis and Bebe Barron, two friends she meets in San Francisco. They are skillful musicians, devoted to music as well as literature. At their request she reads her *House of Incest* and several stories from *Under a Glass Bell* for their Sound Portraits series (they had already recorded Miller and Aldous Huxley). One of the records is made with Josephine Premice thumping drums as Anaïs reads. Bebe remembers recording at the apartment of Anaïs and Rupert, where Anaïs cooked shish kebabs in a wood-burning fireplace. Though they eventually go broke with their audio series, the Barrons will record their electronic music for two of Hugo's films.

Varda, the Barrons, various young poets, bookstore owners, and publishers become Anaïs's social and professional circle in San Francisco. Kenneth Rexroth claims to have refused invitations to come to dinner ("No baby, you're not gonna get me in that diary!").[54] Bern Porter, who now has a Sunday radio program, interviews Anaïs on radio and considers publishing her diary but lacks the financial means. According to Porter, he and Anaïs continue their occasional physical encounters.[55] Porter, though he is not a part of the Leite group, assists George Leite's *Circle* magazine group, which is known for its espousal of anarchy, pacifism, marijuana, and free-love practices. Lawrence Ferlinghetti calls it "the Berkeley Renaissance."[56]

George Leite is not the first swarthy political radical (he is half Portuguese) Anaïs has known. As Miriam Patchen apparently told James Laughlin of New Directions, "[A] Stalinist American [Peruvian] Indian who used to go over to sleep with AN always left a copy of *New Masses* on the bed table for the next comer. . . . Ah, politics."[57] Unlike Gonzalo, Leite is a productive radical who also owns Daliel's Bookstore, named for his son. He and Nancy Leite are good friends of the Millers in Big Sur, where they had originally published *Circle.* Naturally, they had published Miller's work in several of their ten issues of *Circle,* and Leite had published Miller's *Varda the Master Builder.* They knew all about Anaïs. When she comes to read at Daliel's Bookstore, Leite, who is willing to try anything and practices a creative marriage, expects that Anaïs will smoke marijuana and sleep with them both. Nancy, a beautiful, blond woman half the age of Anaïs, is not interested: "Anaïs was of a piece, theatrical . . . but the touch of her skin seemed old." Anaïs does not stay the night.[58] She will insist it was she who demurred.

In the late 1940s when Louis and Bebe Barron leave San Francisco, where they know Anaïs and Rupert, for 9 West Eighth in Greenwich Village, they inevitably meet Hugo, who lives nearby with Anaïs when she returns periodically to New York. On one of their nights out with Louis and Bebe, Anaïs and Hugo go to a ballroom in Harlem. They are the only whites there. Bebe soon spots Anaïs dancing with a young black man of about eighteen; when she looks up again she sees them kissing as they move dramatically across the dance floor in tight embrace. Then they disappear. Later, when the three of them leave without Anaïs because she has not returned, nothing is said. Bebe wonders if this has happened often and why Hugo appears to be without jealousy. One answer could lie in the confidence that Anaïs shares with Caresse Crosby: Hugo has mistresses of his own.[59]

Joaquin Nin y Castellanos, Anaïs's father, dies in Cuba, the country of his birth, during the first week of October 1949. The only photographs on the walls of his room are of himself. Her brother Joaquin sends the telegram and the explanatory letters that follow. Anaïs is torn by her father's death because of the unfinished business between them. She imagines him asleep, as she had seen him the night he fainted after his concert in Paris. She has not seen him since. She feels anger—and "no memory of tenderness or care." She recalls the naked photograph in her first diary and her mother's explanation that his admiration was aesthetic. She also feels a certain guilt: perhaps she should have overlooked his selfishness and devoted her life to him; she should have forgiven him.

In her diary analysis of her deep sorrow, she does not mention or relive the violent beatings, nor does she imply any sexual motive in his picture taking. "Aesthetic" admiration is what she calls his photographic sessions, echoing her mother, the only time she received his undivided attention. But she acknowledges that the "Photographer God and Critic" is the source of her coquettishness, her need to please, and her promiscuity.

She meets James Leo Herlihy at the Satyr Book Shop at 6278 Hollywood Boulevard soon after she and Rupert return to Los Angeles from his Berkeley graduation. Herlihy was a student at Black Mountain College in North Carolina when she read there. Since that fall of 1947, they have been corresponding and she reading his stories. Now he is working where she picks up her mail. Between 1950 and 1952 she visits his Hollywood apartment and attends his play at the Pasadena Playhouse. Initially, he is one of her gay young men with writing talent; but he will go on to greater fame than his mentor when his novel *Midnight Cowboy* is filmed and receives several Oscars. Their friendship will endure longer than that of any of her other spiritual sons. "She could have run for President and been elected," he says. "How could you not like someone who loved you that much and was that open to you?" he asks. He thinks she is "dreamlike" and "elusive," with "a very highly developed sense of the *other*"; she loves his "laughing Irish eyes" and "Irish gift of tongue," though he is German.[60]

*The Four-Chambered Heart* is published and she is back in New York City for a couple of book parties early in 1950. *Library Journal* has already declared her writing fascinating and this novel more unified than the previous two. Among the earliest of the eleven reviews she receives this year is one by Hayden Carruth, who declares it "some of the finest writing of our time." They become friends. Though the reviews that follow take her work more seriously than before, some are harsh. Keith Kay in the *San Francisco Chronicle* says Nin's novels are "little more than 200-page soap operas," which should probably be called "detergent" rather than soap, given the pretentiousness of the prose.[61] Though more widely reviewed than any of her other works, this rather plotless story of the relationship of Rango, the macho guitar-playing Guatemalan, his mistress, Djuna, and his sickly wife does not find many readers. Despite William Kennedy's promises of promotional publicity, he soon leaves Duell, Sloan and Pearce for another publishing house, and by year's end the novel quickly sinks, Anaïs observes, using one of her many ship images.

Increasingly depressed by her literary career, which she characterizes in a letter to Ruth Witt-Diamant as full of "mirages," she leaves "treacherous" New York City to meet Rupert, "the little one," in Washington for the third anniversary of their first trip to the West.[62] Her diary almost succumbs to too much traveling. Her writing energy is given over to letters, to finishing *A Spy in the House of Love*, and to retyping her earlier diary. The current diary consequently becomes more of a notebook, including character sketches and notes for lectures. Her mood is unstable; she is restless and frustrated. She has an admiring group of friends and lovers, but she cannot seem to win public and critical approval. When her friend Wallace Fowlie writes a book on surrealism and does not refer to her, she complains bitterly.

The happiest event of 1950 had occurred during Rupert's last semester at Berkeley: the dual Cuban passport of Anaïs and Hugh Guiler is retired and Anaïs Nin, permanent address 258 Roosevelt Way, San Francisco, secures her first passport. After years of delay, and at Rupert's urging, she has become a citizen of the United States. For Rupert, who believes she is divorced and is concerned about their future, it seems another step toward marriage.[63] For Anaïs the passport, which she applies for without claiming her marriage to American citizen Guiler, symbolizes her freedom from Hugo.

## East Coast/West Coast

Anaïs is engaged in a series of plans for making money to finance what she calls her trapeze act, shuttling from coast to coast. She writes and sells erotica, sells her fiction manuscripts and Miller's incunabula. Her friend Leo Lerman calls her "complicated and self-driven," and her efforts toward fundraising and promotion illustrate this as well as her need for funds.[64] In 1949 she had sold several Miller items, including a hand-bound copy of a first edition of *Tropic of Cancer,* telling the book dealer that she was trying to finance the publication of her first diary. She has not made as much as fifty dollars a month on the five books she has published to date, she informs him.[65] In 1952 she will appeal to Kathryn Winslow, who owns a gallery and bookstore called M: The Studio for Henry Miller, in Chicago, to find a buyer for her fiction manuscripts. Winslow sells the manuscripts (including some of Miller's that Anaïs owns) to Northwestern, which pays about fifty dollars for each manuscript—and sixty for *A Spy in the House of Love* in 1954.[66] Her third plan is less successful: she writes to English and American reviews offering to write a regular column and sends short fiction for publication. Last, she returns to the ready market for erotica by selling "Life in Provincetown," which includes the story of a little girl who has been taught by her father to masturbate him, and "Marcel." These two stories are bound together as a volume entitled *Auletris*—four typed copies of this book are issued in 1950 by Press of the Sunken Eye in Carmel, California. She also sells to a book dealer some of the carbons of her 1940s erotica, which the Kinsey Institute in Indiana purchases.[67] She expresses dismay when the library purchases the manuscripts, perhaps naively assuming that they would remain in private hands.

The trapeze performance of flying or driving from one coast and man to the other every two or three months is subtly punishing on her body and psyche, even though she has her luggage shipped door to door. Transcontinental flying is also costly. The plane trip takes eleven hours. The strain of deception—a lifetime habit as we have seen, but now carried out on a grand scale—takes its toll on her during 1950 and 1951. A couple of times she tells a doctor that she has pain in her abdomen, but the doctor finds nothing. She makes herself indispensable to her men, and needs to know that she is indispensable to them (she confides in one friend that Rupert clings to her "for his life"). Yet she can never share her own fear that she might lose Hugo or Rupert, for that would add a burden which could threaten the bond. She is the receptacle of all their lies, her own included. Each man, she believes, wants a mistress, not a wife, and wants this mistress without the conscious knowledge that she flies from him to another.[68] Rupert continues to believe that she is divorced from Hugo. Hugo, accepting of her many men, does not know she has a steady West Coast "husband."

The pattern continues: first she is with Hugo, showing his first film (*Ai-Ye*, a twenty-two-minute colored impressionistic film) and acting in his second film, called *Bells of Atlantis* at its completion in 1952. Then she is with Rupert in his forester's cabin in Big Tujunga in the Angeles Forest above Los Angeles, where she entertains Christopher Isherwood, visiting from Malibu, or Herlihy, who comes by bus and taxi to bring her a mobile of angels. Then she is in Berkeley helping her mother and brother settle into life on the West Coast, where Joaquin has become Chairman of the Department of Music at the University of California, Berkeley. Then she is back with Rupert living in a trailer in Big Tujunga, where he fights fires. She makes her travel plans according to the "fire season." Meanwhile Hugo, traveling with his films, buys her a Chrysler so she can drive herself around, though she never learns to master it and stories of her uncertain driving abound among their friends. "Like everything else she did, she approached this activity intuitively," claims James Broughton, who says she did not stop at red lights or shift gears.[69] Juggling the deceptions gets comically precarious when they are all in the same town, as is the case in October when Hugo comes to Los Angeles to show his films at the L.A. County Museum. She handles such complications by using post-office mail drops and keeping different sets of friends on each coast.[70]

Lies. They once attracted attention and prevented rejection, boredom, and capture. "I have never found a way to get what I wanted except by lies," says Sabina in *A Spy in the House of Love*. "[I]f I told the truth I would be . . . alone." (Sabina tells her husband she is an actress who has to be out of town playing roles, when she is nearby in a hotel with a man. The real drama is in the role she is playing for her husband.) Anaïs reveals her own motives in the fictional character she is now creating, a woman who can no longer keep track of whom she has loved, betrayed, or married. Little wonder she keeps a file of "lies." But in the novel, Sabina says she lies to avoid capture, for when someone seems to listen too closely to what she says, she changes the story to elude detection. "I feel safest of all when no one knows where I am."[71]

"I would see Rupert and Anaïs, then get on a plane to New York City and she would answer the phone at Hugo's," says Curtis Harrington, who is flattered that he is never pledged to secrecy. Trust and discretion are assumed in his case, though "I never knew when I met her friends which man I should mention," he says. Harrington meets Gore Vidal at a party the Guilers give for him soon after Harrington finishes film school at UCLA and is in New York City for half a year before going to Europe. When he sees Hugo's *Ai-Ye,* he concludes that Hugo is "a talented amateur, interesting and accomplished, but an amateur." His view will not change. "You look so lovely this evening, Anaïs," remarks Harrington when the three of them attend the opera. He remembers her saying, "Oh, thank you, Curtis. That kind of compliment means much more to me than compliments about my works."[72]

Another filmmaker who sees Hugo's film is Amos Vogel, who founded Cinema 16 in 1947, the largest film society in the country. Featuring short and art films, he premiered all the important people, including Maya Deren. Hugo has his second film, *Bells of Atlantis,* which Vogel thinks is his best, shown at Cinema 16. Vogel sees Anaïs rarely except at parties at the Barrons (who had introduced them) or once when he goes to the apartment and she answers the door wearing an apron with a cigarette dangling from her mouth and a frying pan in one hand. He cannot reconcile the domestic scene any more than he can the Guiler partnership. Though neither Vogel nor Jonas Mekas, the founder of Anthology Film Archives, thinks that Hugo makes a unique contribution to film, Vogel likes his quiet, controlled, and formal friend, whom he never feels he knows. He thinks Hugo's copper artwork might be more valuable than his filmmaking.[73]

From her forest service trailer, Anaïs writes to her friend Ruth Witt-Diamant in San Francisco that this is her first year of happiness.[74] Personally, perhaps, but professionally she is facing her greatest defeat to date. When Kennedy left Duell, Sloan and Pearce, she lost her publisher for *A Spy in the House of Love* and spends the next year peddling the manuscript to nearly a dozen publishing companies, facing one rejection after another. Back in New York City, amid the rejections, she feels "exiled, alone, cut off."[75]

I am forty-eight and not selling, she tells a friend in February 1951. If she does not have readers, she certainly has friends who buoy her. She is having great fun with Maxwell Geismar and his wife, Anne, whom she and Hugo meet when Anaïs writes a letter critical of Geismar's review of a Tennessee Williams play. The Geismars live up the Hudson River in Harrison, but come in to the theatre to meet the Guilers. Their friendship is instant, and Anaïs soon confides in them her affairs with Rupert Pole, Edmund Wilson (Anaïs calls him "a red-eyed rabbit who devours her young"), and Henry Miller (she tells them that he was impotent much of the time).[76]

She also values the friendship of Peggy Glanville-Hicks, who restores her "spiritual pride" when she is "lost in a maze of humiliations."[77] Anaïs meets Glanville-Hicks, music critic of the *Herald-Tribune,* after her lecture on the obstacles against professional women's achievement. In Peggy, Anaïs hears a feminist voice that understands her plight, and she sends her all her books. Their friendship strengthens when Glanville-Hicks has surgery, and Anaïs and another friend (Sylvia Spencer) take round-the-clock care of her for four days. Though Anaïs and Peggy disagree on psychoanalysis, they both side with the mystics over the scientists of the world. As they are sitting around Peggy's kitchen during her recovery, she explains that one of her caged birds, the lapwing bird, erases its tracks with its tail wing as it walks. A perfect metaphor for Anaïs.[78]

Her invisible trail leads to the seaport of Mazatlán and Lake Pátzcuaro in western Mexico in the spring and then to a house with Rupert on the outskirts of Los Angeles. For several years, on the western swing of her trapeze act, she lives with Rupert at 2219 Santa Anita Avenue, at a federal ranger station in the San Gabriel Mountains, which are crowned by the nearly six-thousand-foot Mount Wilson. Here Rupert's crew cuts down trees in the winter and fights forest fires in the summer.[79] The powerful presence of nature makes Anaïs's life here at the base of the dry, rugged, unadorned mountain terrain of the Angeles National Forest seem a world apart from the intrigue and vanities of New York City, where she attends the ballet and theatre. When they settle into this house, Helen Wright openly wonders when Anaïs will marry her son.[80]

About this time Anaïs also finds a haven in New York. For several reasons—she mentions that her anger against publishers is "corroding" her—she seeks out Dr. Inge Bogner, a Bavarian psychoanalyst and physician who fled to New York during the war. She likes the diminutive Dr. Bogner. She chooses a woman analyst because she cannot resist seducing male analysts, she later says. And she turns once again to analysis because her life lacks control, cohesion, and synthesis, in part because she is finding it difficult to live with "dualities." They discuss her need to disguise herself, her reliance on others' approval, her need for economic independence, and her pattern of vicariously living out aspects of herself in others—sexual emancipation with Miller, anger with Gonzalo, vulnerability with Bill Pinckard. Both Bogner and Glanville-Hicks reinforce a feminist perspective that allows Anaïs to begin to seek strong women as friends.

Bogner, who sits in her big leather chair with her legs crossed at the ankles and knits the entire session, takes no notes or recordings and practices nonconfrontational or nondirective analysis. Occasionally she inserts clarifying questions. One of her patients thinks she rarely talks, another says she is positive and supportive—a cheerleader. At least two things are surprising about her work. First, she seems to view her patients as friends, inviting them to her home for dinner with her husband, a German-American Liederkranz singer (some reports say a cruel and alcoholic man). Second, she keeps these "friends" in analysis for decades (Hugo for forty-one years.).[81]

Anaïs's returns to New York and to Hugo always take her back to Bogner, for the publishers' letters this year are mounting into a tidal wave of rejection: Pellegrini and Cudahy (insulting), Farrar and Straus (a "Tiffany jewel, but not for everyone"), Pascal Covici at Viking (romantic fantasy is not for him), and Putnam's Sons ("vivid and extraordinary, but almost pornographic"). Despite what seems to be the unanimous disapproval of *A Spy in the House of Love,* she tells a friend that she thinks this story of Sabina is her best one. The novella is certainly more ambitious and experimental than her others, for she arranges the scenes spatially rather than chronologically and uses an imaginary character called the Lie Detector (she had used the name before for Rank) to express the guilt that Sabina experiences during her numerous love affairs in New York City, Long Island, and Provincetown. This is her best dramatization of the divided neurotic self or multiple existence. "The War Among the Selves," one critic calls it.[82] One can also see the guilt she feels in her betrayal of Hugo (called Alan in the novel) throughout their marriage.

In the isolation of nature in Sierra Madre, where she can hear the distant train whistles and the wail of wild coyotes at night, or in Acapulco, where the days are like "gentle ovens," her mind can be quiet. The timeless present of the El Mirador Hotel is a "detoxicating cure" for New York City.[83] But the rejection slips pursue her there and back to her home in the mountains of Los Angeles, where she is surrounded by men who give their lives to saving trees from burning. New American Library objects to the Lie Detector in her novel. Houghton Mifflin, Doubleday, Scribner's, Bobbs-Merrill, and Hiram Haydn turn her down. No one wants this third volume of her exploration of contemporary neurosis. Suddenly she looks for neurosis in the simple firemen of Sierra Madre. She also considers abdicating from fiction.

On her way back to New York for the winter, she stops in Oakland to stay with her mother, who has recently had a stroke. Anaïs continues the mothering of her gay admirers once back in New York. When Herlihy calls from his family home in Detroit, needing to be rescued from his family, upon whom he is financially dependent, she instructs the twenty-six-year-old writer to come to New York immediately. Her friends help him find and decorate an apartment. Eventually one of his plays is produced off-Broadway. He is a part of her world of gay friends and their parties. She listens to their stories of rejection. One drunk homosexual informs her that he really hates women, but loves her ("the essence of femininity") and will love her forever. It is the manner in which she gives him her undivided attention. Yes, she thinks, she does feel "such sympathy for the unloved."[84]

She too is an outcast, after all, rejected now by Harper's ("poetry, not prose") and Macmillan ("too esoteric"). The Guggenheim Foundation turns down her request for a grant. Again she considers a complete abdication of writing, except for the "secret womb" of her diary. More frequently she speaks of her life as artist as having been better in Paris.[85] Little wonder that she cannot deal with the comments of James Merrill about her recent books. Merrill has returned from Europe at twenty-six and a half years of age, forgetting "the kind of person she is." He invites her for tea after reading the novels she has given him, "forgetting her age and temperament":

> I treated her as an equal and started telling her the things in the books I did not like. Suddenly she was on her feet and looking at me in utter horror. She grabbed her books into her arms and fled. Two weeks later I saw her in the local post office in the Village and she was addressing and stamping two hundred enve-lopes. "Let me go to the window and come back and help you," I said. When I returned, she had taken everything and left. She had taken my remarks as betrayal and destruction.[86]

Yet she offered criticism to other writers. Paul Bowles tells the story of his wife, Jane Bowles, receiving an eight-page letter from Anaïs criticizing Jane's novel *Two Serious Ladies,* which the author laughed off. Later, walking on Eighth Street, the Bowleses encountered Anaïs, whom Paul did not know. "She bore down on us," he says, and took Jane aside for a forty-minute talk while he waited impatiently in the snow. When his wife returned, and he asked, "Who was that woman?," she informed him it was Nin and said, "She just wanted me to know what a terrible writer I am."[87]

Her own rejections fuel Anaïs's discussions with Dr. Bogner and cause her to evaluate, at least to justify, for herself her writing style. Only "poetry and metaphor" come close to expressing how we "experience things deep down," she believes, and only she has clothed the "deep meanings" in poetry. Like Miller, she is one of the "aviators of language."[88] Her conviction gives her courage.

### Herlihy and Geismar

The telephone rings one night at 35 West Ninth Street and three people pick up extensions. Herlihy, who is sleeping in the living room, Hugo, who is in leg traction after kicking too high in dance class, and Anaïs, who has hurried home to nurse him. Rupert is on the telephone. He has been to a party in Hollywood where someone tells him that Anaïs is with her husband in New York and gives him the telephone number (he only had the number of Daisy Aldan, where he thinks she stays). When Anaïs says she will handle the matter, Hugo and Herlihy hang up. Later she goes to Hugo and explains that the call is from a man who had escaped from a mental institution and is following her. Herlihy marvels at her extraordinary stories and the complacency of Hugo. During the months that Herlihy stays in the apartment to help, Hugo never confides in him. Rupert, who later comes to New York and checks into a Fifth Avenue hotel just a couple blocks away, believes that she is nursing her former husband.[89]

Anaïs evidently tires of her nursing role, for when the Geismars come to visit, she dresses herself up in a rented nurse's uniform to illustrate the role that she is playing with begrudging humor. They are amused by the joke and understand that she hates the experience. Another time, during the period when the Geismars are heavily involved, if not obsessed, with the Adlai Stevenson presidential campaign, Anaïs has a table display of Stevenson material standing in the hallway when they arrive for a visit. "She had no political interest and never read history or social criticism," says Anne Geismar. "She was reactionary and conservative from our perspective. She was against Castro."[90]

Her political differences with Herlihy are less important because of his youth and his creative imagination. Always perceptive in characterizing the most important people of her life, she describes Herlihy using words such as "agility," "talent," "nimbleness," "dexterity." He is an "aerialist," spiritually, emotionally, and physically. She contrasts his elegant body and movement to the slang of his speech. Son of a cop and a show girl, he came from a tough neighborhood and quickly learned the street smarts of New York (which he will capture in *Midnight Cowboy*). Yet he turns his speech into a kind of swift jazz, a streamlined style. He admires her enormously, and she responds with joy that she can "incite" him to write. "His enthusiasm sustains me," she explains; "he has the power of levitation."[91] One critic believes that their sharing of diaries is reminiscent of the Miller-Nin-Durrell sharing of diaries in Paris in the 1930s.[92] It is certainly healthier and less claustrophobic than her diary exchange with Robert Duncan.

Her friendship with Maxwell and Anne Geismar is different, both personally and professionally. It is in part a strain because they are the brilliant and ironic type she fears in New Yorkers. But Max is an important critic, and she is looking for a replacement for Edmund Wilson. And their company is stimulating; the couples often meet at Charles, a restaurant on Sixth Avenue (Anaïs could not cook well, in Anne Geismar's opinion) or visit jazz clubs such as the Blue Note. Maxwell finds Anaïs fascinating, and considers

Hugo "limited intellectually or repressed or armored in temperament," but charming. "We were a nice pleasant family and life was ordinary in Harrison," says his wife. "Anaïs was unusual." Anne likes but does not approve of Anaïs.

> She bought hard rubber washers at a hardware store to use in the pay phones to call Rupert without having to pay money. Anaïs had a physical presence in a room, even though she was not beautiful. She had a beautiful figure, lovely neck and shoulders, and dressed beautifully. Her voice was high and thin, and she smoked and loved her steak very rare. She only sipped wine. We had fun together, but she could be devouring and ruthless.[93]

Anaïs soon discovers that Max is a Marxist critic, one of those left-wing intellectuals connected with *The Nation*. He views literature historically, while she believes the artist must plumb the depths of her own unconscious. Though Anaïs believes the artist is a prophet and Max believes the artist a political creature, he gives her some qualified praise. Privately, he finds her talented, but her work empty. "Max was kind to her, and he could be savage; but she wanted unlimited praise," says Anne Geismar. "She could get very upset." They agree to disagree on almost everything.

When she talks about her diary, he asks to see it and she brings up several volumes, typed and bound. The Geismars keep the diaries in their cellar (they must be hidden, Anaïs insists), and with Anaïs's permission contact Herman Alexander, who finds a Swedish publisher for the volumes. Just when the arrangement seems complete, she backs out of it, fearing that Hugo will read them. Geismar believes they are a "remarkable literary achievement":

> What is fine really is not so much the purely physical descriptions but of course the descriptions of the emotional states that comprise the flux of love; these are absolutely brilliant. That is to say, both the description of the illusion or the exaltation, and then the accurate illumination of them, and why you originally left them. . . . This is literature of the first order.[94]

Much to his dismay, she will use his praise for her unpublished diary when the heavily edited diary is published. He will wait until after her death to condemn the expurgated diary ("sanitized . . . fleshless . . . idealized abstractions") and tell about their friendship in his memoirs.[95]

A friendship that Anaïs covets is with Martha Graham, whose petite gracefulness and "tragic intensity" she admires and with whom she identifies. Though they meet at Dorothy Norman's house and she sends Graham all her books and a letter, the dancer—like Djuna Barnes—never responds. I could have "helped her, loved her," Anaïs laments.[96] Yet she herself needs protection and strength these days, when she is feeling so vulnerable and insecure.

Anaïs is walking down Thompson Street in the Village one day with books in her arms. Several copies of *The Four-Chambered Heart* rest against her cape. She encounters Judith Malina, as she often does, and stops to explain her mission: "I am going to Ted's bookshop. He has not sold my last two books in months, but I am going to try and get him to take one more." Judith does not think this one-woman promotion department unusual. She and her husband, Julian Beck, started their Living Theatre when they were only nineteen, and she believes Anaïs is both practical and visionary, necessary qualities for any underground artist. She views Anaïs's self-promotion as indicative of an ideal working relationship between writer, bookseller, and reader. Judith admires Anaïs, and reads every one of her books, attends all the book signings, and keeps her own diary. But she believes that the elder woman's "clothing code and armored manner cut her off from the youth movement, which will later discover her."

Anaïs signs on as a sponsor for the Living Theatre and gives all her used clothing to the group. It does not seem to bother her that the pre-Beat women wear her elegant clothes with bare feet or army jackets. "After taking in her red and black checked wool dress with a high collar," says the petite Malina, "I wore it for years, beginning when I was rehearsing at the Cherry Lane Theatre. The whole theater group was garbed in Anaïs's last season."[97] Anaïs admires Julian Beck, whose paintings hang in Peggy Guggenheim's gallery, and she attends with Hugo all the performances of their Living Theatre. But after an evening's performance of Gertrude Stein's *Ladies Voices*, Picasso's *Desire Trapped by the Tail,* and Eliot's *Sweeney Agonistes,* Anaïs withdraws her support. In a letter dated 17 January 1952, she politely takes her name from the list of sponsors because she does not believe in Stein, Rexroth, Goodman, or Eliot—especially the latter, who is not a poet; he is dead, she declares to Julian.[98] The meetings at book signings and parties in the Village are a little strained after this, but Judith and Anaïs remain friends.

Though she can say no to Julian Beck and Judith Malina of the Living Theatre, she cannot say no to her agent. Max Pfeffer is European, aggressive, and authoritarian—so like her father. Thinking at first that he will protect her, she now realizes that he is wrong for her work. But she is paralyzed to change, fearing his anger, fearing his disappointment—as she had her father's. Eventually her friends force her decision, and she hires René de Chochor, a Frenchman and the partner of Tom Brown (husband of her friend Frances). But Chochor, like Geismar, suggests she take out the Lie Detector and change the end of *Spy* (perhaps have Sabina return to her husband). She is shocked at their opposition, but Chochor insists that Sabina's guilt should be internalized. She rewrites the novella, but then balks. The Lie Detector is a necessary part of her "vision." Sabina's return to her husband would sacrifice her new integrity. And changing the novella would sacrifice her own integrity. She would rather forgo publication and the money.

Anaïs herself is dealing with the question of returning to her husband this spring and summer. In early April she rushes back to New York when Hugo contracts bronchitis. After his recovery, she flies to Miami and drives back to Los Angeles with Rupert. Then Hugo slips a disk (she tells Miller it is a ruptured disk), and she again has to leave Rupert to nurse Hugo. She confides in Ruth Witt-Diamant that when Hugo is well again she intends to separate from him.[99] In the novel Anaïs is writing at this time, Sabina's husband is described as a waiting, compliant protector, a passive reflector, and all-forgiving. Djuna tells Sabina that he is an idealized "fantasy-father . . . invented by a needy child." In an early unpublished version of the novel, Alan the husband tells Sabina (divided among five or six men) that he is the father she never had. In the final version of the novel Sabina dares to tell him he is "like a father" to her. Presumably, one can, indeed must, desert but never divorce the father.[100]

The weight of guilt and the fear of hurting Hugo is taking its toll, as is the critical rejection of her work. In 1951, 1952, and 1953 no review or article about her work appears except for a brief biography in a collection about contemporary American novelists. "I have been left out of every journal, anthology, and poetry review," she laments more than once. "The world is silent."[101]

She derives some comfort from studying the Varda collage on her Los Angeles wall, taking strength from Varda's flowing, transcendent *Women Reconstructing the World*. She also finds solace in the simple life in nature in Sierra Madre. What she gains in living in Sierra Madre is an experience in community living around the pool at the neighbor's home, baby-sitting their children, changing diapers, and offering her costumes to the little girls who want to dress up. She feels close to the earth and human fraternity, and meditates on the conflict between child care and the life of the artist.

She describes her Los Angeles life during this period almost as an escape from the malice of critical rejection into the simple pleasure of the life of the foresters and visits from the little girl next door. Almost comically, their yard sprinklers will be the fountains of the Alhambra for her. Her neighbor's swimming pool will be the refreshing life force. Yet, when neighbors see her dressed in a black cape, mailing book packages at the post office, they think she looks "oddly out of place."[102]

In New York City she is sustained by Herlihy's praise for her diaries. She now measures her achievement by his response. They speak the same language, she believes, understand jazz, rhythm, improvisation.[103] By contrast, Geismar is timid, living in the past; he belongs to a movement of the 1930s she missed by being in Paris, she claims. Yet she is learning to be comfortable with the "ponderous, earth-bound men" in her life, such as Miller, Rank, and Geismar. And she is also comfortable in her relationships with women, especially Peggy Glanville-Hicks and Bebe Barron.

Through the Barrons and their Sound Portraits, Anaïs meets Joseph Campbell and his wife, Jean Erdman, a Martha Graham dancer whose posture she admires. Erdman remembers the compliment on her posture, but little else. Joseph Campbell, who taught at Sarah Lawrence College, where Max Geismar had taught until 1947, was reading only mythology and shared an interest in Haitian voodoo religion with Maya Deren.[104] Anaïs also meets Barney Rosset of Grove Press, John Cage, and others at the Barron home on Eighth Street and at the White Horse Tavern in the Village, a hangout for literati in the 1950s. Cage remembers meeting her once and associating her with the avant-garde of Breton (confessional and surrealist) while he himself preferred the Duchamp and Dada side.[105] New York also means delightful business lunches with her agent, who treats her like the Queen of Writing, she says, dramatically tossing publishers' rejection letters into the wastebasket as she watches. He is more interested in charming her than in helping her adjust her writing to the American publishing world.

Back and forth she flies in the void between New York City and Los Angeles. She kicks off her shoes, and, in the white droning time between coasts, writes letters on airline stationery to her numerous correspondents. She carries the pressures of her life with her in the pressurized cabin. "But altitude and strain wear out the heart," she admits.[106] Flying back to New York in January 1953, she feels the pain in her right side and hip so keenly she cannot sleep. Fortunately she is on a new prop jet and the flight now takes eight instead of eleven hours.

At 6 A.M. on Friday the twenty-ninth the doctors at New York University Hospital remove a tumor the size of an orange from her right ovary. She thought that they would somehow remove it through her vagina, but she awakens with constricting pain beneath the bandage over her stomach, feeling as if she has committed hara-kiri. Hugo is by her side. She accepts blood transfusions and intravenous feedings passively and sleeps under the power of the pain pills. When she can look out through the narrow barred windows of the hospital, she dreams of Mexico and plans her next trip with Rupert, a visit to the Yucatán.

Though several friends suggested before she entered the hospital that this will be one painful experience she cannot glamorize for her diary, she rises to the occasion with descriptions of wearing her red wool burnoose to the X-ray room and of the colorful presence of a patient who calls himself the king of the gypsies, whose followers camp out in the parking lot and keep vigil in the corridors. As her physical body heals slowly, she becomes more aware of the "psychic illness" of her "failure as a writer." She hibernates in weakness, a state more difficult to endure in a city "dominated by achievement, activity, and the constant game of personalities."[107]

She is still convalescing when she celebrates her fiftieth birthday in 1953 in California, examining her life for changes and writing long philosophical passages in her diary. The dry heat of the Angeles National Forest aids the healing, and by spring she is well enough to escape by car into Mexico. She and Rupert drive from Chihuahua to Veracruz to the Yucatán. And she fills her diary with vivid descriptions of the thatched houses, jungle, waterfalls, and pyramids. She could feel herself "regaining altitude."[108] In her next novel she will describe Mexico as that place she has always sought in her dreams of pushing a boat across land.

The journey has been a constructive one, for she begins her summer visit to New York City and Dr. Bogner with a certain amount of relish, attending plays, parties, and exhibitions. She is between a spring in the Yucatán and fall in Sierre Madre. Her renewed vitality is noticed by a young poet, Harold Norse, who is brought by Kimon Friar to the Guiler apartment to meet Anaïs. A friend of Allen Ginsberg's and Gore Vidal's, Norse had heard her read at the Ninety-second Street Y in the 1940s. Norse thinks she lives in "high style" with her banker husband. He describes the Guilers both dressed for cocktails:

> Tall [Norse was five five] and slender in a long black shiny gown, with fine honey hair piled on top of her head in neat buns, she looked like a Tanagra figure from classical antiquity. Her warmth came at me in waves, genteel and controlled. . . . [We gazed at each other with] the look of kindred spirits. . . . I was surprised by her thin almost childlike voice—it seemed as delicate and fragile as rare china.[109]

The Beat poets, including Norse, are attracted to Anaïs because she is an avant-garde writer with an underground following. They identify with her outlaw state and romanticize her rumored love affair with Artaud, the mad

French poet and playwright. In 1961 Ginsberg and Norse will invoke Anaïs in an outrageous and impertinent interview at a café in Paris with Paule Thevenin, the mistress-editor of the deceased poet. To all of Ginsberg's outrageous questions, she replies curtly or frostily: Artaud was abstinent. He never masturbated. He did not like men and boys and was not crazy!

> ALLEN: Did Artaud sleep with many women?
> THEVENIN (*frostily*): Certainly not!
> A: Then you were his only mistress?
> T: Yes
> A: Was he in love with Anaïs Nin?
> T: She says so.[110]

Later back in Sierra Madre, Anaïs types her diary, making frequent visits to the bank vault in Pasadena where the recent diaries are kept. She takes a one-day trip to San Francisco to get the remaining recent diaries from Ruth Witt-Diamant's cellar and visits Bekins Storage in Arcadia for the typed copies. While she is rereading and copying the diary about her Paris years with Miller—he seems so "wonderful" and "alive" (she tells him in a letter)—he is writing to her for names of cafés for his book on Moricand (*A Devil in Paradise*). She now understands the causes of the breakup of their relationship, she tells him: "Probably if I had then the sense of humor I have today and if you had *then* the qualities you have today, nothing would have broken. I have changed enormously. Have begun to open [the] diary and let it be read, to realize it's my major work."[111]

After two years of psychotherapy with Bogner and a visit to her aging mother, who lives in Berkeley with her shades drawn against the sun as if she still lives in Cuba, Anaïs assesses her own personal growth. First, she believes that though acting motherly always appeased her conscience, she is increasingly able to be herself and not what others need. Second, she realizes that she projects her own problems onto others, assigns a role to each person, and then fights that aspect of herself in them (Gonzalo's irresponsibility and violence, Miller's physical and mental promiscuity, the maternal qualities in her mother). Third, she resolves one of the central conflicts of her life: the conflict between her father, the artist who could escape the imprisonment of ordinary life by recreating and "improving" on life, and her mother, the one who seemed imprisoned in the human condition by her generosity, devotion, and sacrifice. In her fiction of this period (*A Spy in the House of Love*), she describes a mother as a "dispenser of food, of solace, soft warm and fecund," who wears "the neutral toned clothes of self-effacement, the faded garments of self-sacrifice, the external uniform of goodness."[112] She lives the domestic life of her mother, but secretly rails against it, longing for a "secret inner religion of art." She now believes she is "able to live in both worlds, the human and the imaginative."[113] Yet she leaves her mother, whom she has been caring for in Joaquin's absence, to return to care for Reginald Pole, who is ill.

## Renate Druks

Anaïs receives a telephone call from Paul Mathiesen, who is now writing for the *Los Angeles Free Press* (when he interviews Henry Miller, the old man asks Paul if he was fifteen when he met Anaïs; Mathiesen gives Miller the answer he wants to hear, yes). Mathiesen calls to invite Anaïs to meet Renate Druks, a Viennese painter, the woman with whom he is living in Malibu. She had read Anaïs's books before Mathiesen told her he knew Anaïs in New York when he was seventeen. Because Paul seems changed (he is now twenty-four), Anaïs wants to meet the woman who has evoked this transformation.

The women love each other from the first, and Renate soon becomes her best friend. They share an immigrant perspective, European culture and artistic parents, and a devotion to art with a capital *A*. They both are slim and dark, have foreign accents, and European good manners (their friends call Anaïs "the princess" and Renate "the countess"). Renate is the social center of a large group of artists, including Curtis Harrington, the young filmmaker, and Kenneth Anger, who is planning a film in which they will all act.

Paul and Renate host a masquerade party at her Sea Vista Drive home in Malibu, asking all of their circle to come as their own "madness" or fantasy.[114] Anaïs and Rupert arrive at the home Renate built (she was designer and general contractor) in 1950. Except for the incense candles, it is arranged as a jungle setting with recently cut sumac branches. Painted doors serve as tables (or beds, if needed), masks from Mexico hang from the tree branches. The walls are covered with paintings by Renate or her friend Cameron.

Anaïs has leopard-fur earrings pasted to her bare nipples, and her bare back is painted with a jungle scene. Pictures of the event do not reveal the transparent half-cut bra holding her breasts. Her head is in an open bird cage, from which she intends to have the ticker tape (of her unconscious) unroll. But the pictures of the party show the paper tape wrapped around her right arm, from which she tears off messages of her words for each encounter.[115] Rupert has his face and torso painted and genitalia drawn on his underwear. Kenneth Anger is Hecate, Samson De Brier is an Eastern potentate, and Curtis Harrington is the somnambulist from *The Cabinet of Doctor Caligari*. Renate dances until four in the morning with Anger and Paul separately. "It is so tiring to dance with your madness," she says.

The success of the party inspires Anger's film, which De Brier, who might today be called a performance artist, hosts. The filming of Anger's *Inauguration of the Pleasure Dome*[116] occurs in De Brier's rooms, painted black or red or gold, each color enhanced by the use of gels. Anger works as Maya Deren had, Anaïs observes, and he asks her to come as Astarte, the Phoenician goddess of fertility with her head in the bird cage, legs in mesh hose, and body wrapped in blue muslin. Other goddesses are Renate as Sensuous Romantic Life, her friend the model Joan Whitney as Virgin Beauty, Cameron (a painter) as Satanic Woman. De Brier is the Great Beast. Paul plays Pan and Curtis plays Cesare. Anger shoots until one o'clock in the morning, and the film, at least the 1966 recut version, looks stagy and posed.

When Renate and Paul stage another masquerade party, "A Thousand and One Nights," Nin goes as Scheherazade, De Brier reads from the *Kamasutra*, and Druks is a Persian princess. Renate's son, Peter, looks like the Little Prince from Saint-Exupéry. Only two budding designers, Rudi Gernreich and James Galanos, come in street clothes. This group loves the masquerade, which releases their inhibitions, and they stage a Roman party (which takes Druks three weeks of preparation) with "mock" orgies, readings from Pliny, and Anaïs and Rupert posing as Roman maid and soldier. This time the well-endowed Joanne Carson comes bare-breasted.

These adult masquerades exhilarate Anaïs—as costumes, role-playing, and metamorphoses have always done. The joy she takes in these many parties and physical disguises is accompanied strangely by a lessening in everyday life of her habits of pretense and role-playing. Her diary shows greater focus on description of reality. She recreates the party scenes, constructs a detailed description and analysis of Hugo's films, and records an eloquent and vivid description of a major December fire in the Angeles National Forest. The fire, which burns twelve thousand acres and threatens their house (she plans to rescue her only diaries), reveals the fury of nature. She makes coffee for the fire fighters and briefly answers the telephone at the ranger station. Her exotic accent surprises the callers. Then the January rains bring flooding and mud slides down the bare hillsides. The woman with soot in her hair at the height of the fire season and wearing wading boots to navigate raging waters during flood time is a different woman from the bourgeois gardener of Louveciennes. She discovers that she enjoys the physical danger and challenge. Even her brother Joaquin tells her that he notices the change in her.

When her red-eye flight lands in New York during a January 1954 snowstorm, she is ill with exhaustion, chills, and a low-functioning thyroid. Neither the weather nor the cold shock of reality in her analysis with Dr. Bogner discourages her. On the plane she had written a long letter to a young American Indian named Jamake Highwater (known by the adoptive name J Marks), about the heightened life one lives as a writer. She had met Highwater through Herlihy. Highwater (who will become a major historian of the American Indian) is a talented writer who asked her to read his work, to explain why one writes.

> [O]ne writes because one has to create a world in which one can live . . . an atmosphere in which [one can] breathe, reign, and re-create. . . . We also write to make our life heightened, bearable, and more infinite . . . to taste life twice. . . . It should be a necessity, as the sea needs to move. I call it breathing.[117]

But during a visit to the New York Public Library, where she observes thousands of manuscripts locked behind a heavy iron grille as if in prison, she struggles with an ethical question that haunts her. She has decided that the diary is her major work, but it has the capability of hurting many people. How could she ever publish this potentially harmful book? Maxwell Geismar will say that she "lacked . . . that final ruthlessness of a true artist to reveal the truth despite the consequences."[118] But how can she destroy the diary that has given her life? The locked room at the library looks like the tomb in which she should bury her "dangerous truths." As she looks into the grilled encasements in this mighty stone vault on Forty-second Street, she cannot imagine her diary being read in such gloomy darkness. She decides that it should be read only in full sunlight.

Yet she fears publishing the full diary to be read either in darkness or sunlight. What keeps her from publishing intimacies of her life is her Catholic sense of responsibility to family and her fear of hurting others, which would lead to abandonment. She stifles her own humanity for the temporal well-being of her family and her own security.

Though she talks about immediate publication and raises funds toward that purpose, she puts off the reality of publication into some distant future. Her most supportive private reader of the diary is still Jim Herlihy. She sees him socially and at the Satyr Book Shop in Hollywood, when she returns briefly to Los Angeles in mid-February of 1954. She also sees Highwater, who is a high school classmate of Susan Sontag's, about his writing. He is only in his early teens but is over six feet tall. He hangs out at the Coronet Theatre on La Cienega, where Anger's films are shown, and at the bookshop, reading, talking, writing, and admiring the publications of Herlihy. Orphaned and unsure of his age, he was reared by residents of Encino from whom he (as Indian and artist) feels doubly estranged. He will literally write himself into existence and become a poet and writer of fiction as well as a cultural historian; his first mentor is Anaïs; his last, Joseph Campbell. Anaïs gives him two gifts: she reinforces and approves his "otherness," and she tells him there is something of Virginia Woolf in his writing.[119]

Her bond with Herlihy is occasionally endangered by her disapproval of his James Cain/Hemingway style (she likes his more subtle, poetic writing better). When his play *Moon in Capricorn* appeared the previous winter, she thought he needed her "total admiration," but she was reluctant to give it. Aside from an occasional disagreement, however, she continues to admire his agile mind and lyrical capacity. When she is away, they correspond at length, occasionally sending each other portions of their diaries. His friendship seems to have more depth and endurance than that of the "transparent" young men, Duncan and Vidal, who have betrayed her.

After only ten days in Los Angeles, she flies on 25 February to meet Hugo in Mexico City and to drive on to Acapulco. He is working on another film. She writes vividly in her diary of the voluptuous life of eating, dancing, and swimming (the sea is "warm like a womb"). This is home, she feels, a physical existence that only the Latins and blacks have.[120]

Two rhythms welcome her back to Los Angeles in April. The first is jazz at Sardi's. While listening to Shorty Rogers's Band she feels that jazz is the music of the body, akin to the movement of passion and to the sea. The next evening she is listening to a Brahms quartet in the auditorium at California Institute of Technology, thinking of her spiritual connection to this music, which is the music of her soul. While listening to the improvisations of the jazz, she realizes that she too is withholding her theme, the diary, while playing around the outside of it with her fiction. When the musicians play Brahms, she sits and writes about a woman—a pianist with a jazz orchestra in Mexico—caught between nature and the city. This will be her next novel, using all her diaries' entries of her own Mexican experiences.

Anaïs arrives by the first week of April to join the opening of the 1954 spring season in Greenwich Village. "Spring Festival and Defoliation of Virgins," Larry Maxwell calls the celebration at his bookstore. Judith Malina records the event, believing that the behavior of the guests, with their mask-like faces ("we grimaced too much"), does not echo the spirit of the primal celebration. When it comes time to award the bridal crown, it is passed from Judith to Jean Erdman to Anaïs to Maya Deren. None have a claim to virgin status.[121]

A month later Anaïs feels deeply rejected. None of the invited critics come to her May book party for *A Spy in the House of Love* at the British Book Centre in New York City.[122] She is unprepared, even by the healing waters of Acapulco, for the pain of this critical response. It is the literary cold shoulder. Where are Edmund Wilson,[123] Wallace Fowlie, W. H. Auden, Tennessee Williams, or Truman Capote, she wonders? With the exception of Glanville-Hicks, nobody lifts a finger to support her work. On the contrary, America is trying to kill her with neglect or insult, she concludes. The first insult comes 15 May in *Saturday Review*, where Jerome Stone declares that she is trying to "illuminate the sub-cellars of the female psyche" with her dreamy style, in a book that lacks poetic imagination and psychological depth. The *Atlantic* review, by her friend Charles Rollo, is lukewarm, and criticizes Sabina's easy knowledge at the end of the book. Maxwell Geismar's review in *The Nation* is fully positive, even laudatory considering the perspective of the author and the journal. Geismar calls the novel "a perceptive story of the rewards and punishments of a woman's passions," and praises its humor and its "complete honesty reminiscent of D. H. Lawrence."[124]

Yet she feels betrayed by Geismar because, in her opinion, he does not treat the book with seriousness or understand what she was intending. Yet he calls it "the best" of her series, "a sensitive and discerning fable of a woman's life," and he makes no negative observation. He praises her for being one of the few women writers "to affirm the centrality of the biological impulses for her own sex." She talks to him on the telephone and then sends an eloquent defense of her approach to emotional reality as opposed to Marxist materialism. She had intended to explore the "motivations of Don Juanism" in a new *Madame Bovary*, and he uses, to her way of thinking, flippant expressions such as "amorous exploits." She concludes with a ringing endorsement of the greater importance of Freud over Marx. The friendship with the Geismars cools after this. Following an insulting radio interview this same month, she goes home to Greenwich Village feeling "immensely lonely in an ugly, hostile world."[125]

In Sierra Madre in early summer, she assesses the progress of her analysis and maturity, realizing that a younger Anaïs could not have survived the critical rejection of *A Spy in the House of Love*. Although she is disappointed that the novel has sold only twenty-four hundred copies in three months, her agent thinks the number respectable. She is more determined than ever to take control of her own life and find healing and wholeness, while retaining her sensibility. She can now live for months without feeling that she is being strangled by anxiety, and convinces herself she is suffering less guilt about living alternately with Hugo and Rupert. One of the reasons she abandons reading the stars, she later tells Miller (an advocate to the end), is that she wants to have a sense of directing her own destiny, of being a conqueror, not a victim of life. Thus, she tells Miller, she chooses analysis over astrology.[126]

She also reiterates her commitment to writing, defending herself as an "instrument for human consciousness" who believes her role is to say what is unsayable, to expand the reader's vision. The critics may crush her books, but they cannot stop her writing. When they give her the "solitary-cell treatment," she claims kinship with Proust, Isak Dineson, and Pierre-Jean Jouve. She sees her fiction as belonging with the poetic novels of Djuna Barnes, Anna Kavan, Isabel Bolton, and Jean Giraudoux—a group that some-day will "inherit the kingdom of Freud."[127] But the assurance in these philo-sophical and aesthetic entries in her diary is about to be sorely tested.

## Death and Birth of the Mother

In August Anaïs stops in Oakland once again to visit her mother and brother for two days. She attends Mass with them (only Rosa and Joaquin take communion), enjoys a couple of car rides (during which Rosa seems sub-dued), and goes to a movie with Joaquin. She is grateful that she had rebelled against their austerity, humility, and self-sacrifice. Before dinner, he makes her a martini (an evening habit she acquired with Rupert). The expression on Rosa's face at the martini drinking reminds Anaïs of the legacy of her parental disapproval. Their stern looks were reserved for their chil-dren, their laughter given to strangers. Once again she realizes that her mother has never approved of the woman she has become. After her brother drops her off at the airport, Anaïs boards the plane for Los Angeles and orders a martini and takes a sleeping pill; he goes home to find Rosa ill with nausea. He calls his sister later to say that their mother has had a heart attack and is hospitalized under oxygen. Rosa asks for a priest, becomes semiconscious, and dies that night. When Joaquin calls at midnight with the news, Anaïs is devastated.

Joaquin (almost forty-six years old) takes his mother's body to Cuba to be buried beside her father, Thorvald Christensen Culmell, the last name added when he adopted Cuba as his home. Anaïs does not go to her mother's funeral. When Joaquin comes to New York to visit his sister, they renew the intimacy they had shared earlier in their lives. She thinks it strange that it took the death of their mother to reestablish their childhood bond. That bond had been strained in Paris when she sought an independent life (and sexual emancipation) and Rosa disapproved of her influence on her little brother.

The death of Rosa frees Anaïs from the stigma of her mother's judgment and partially frees her from the need to rebel against her own mothering qualities. But beyond all the small regrets and guilt is the realization that she had not loved her mother enough or reconciled with her. When she next stops in San Francisco, on her way to New York again, she falls to her knees in sobs when she enters Rosa's room. Somehow she gets through the division of her mother's meager belongings and a night spent in her bed. She takes her mother's sewing machine, knitting needles, and gold thimble; and she thinks she takes on her mother's spirit. After years of rejecting Rosa and her female servitude and trying instead to be the mistress who once seduced her father, Anaïs is free to be, like her mother, a woman who cares for others. Her rebellion collapses and she feels reborn. In Anaïs's next novel, *Solar Barque*, Lillian, at her mother's death, passes into the elder woman's body for a year in a kind of possession. She is left a thimble and sewing machine as well as the moods and characteristics of her tidy, cold, and critical mother.[128]

In the months that follow, Anaïs occasionally struggles for a sense of synthesis (the dualities in her life she always ascribes to her father). She finds herself putting the house in Sierra Madre in order, throwing out items, cleaning, organizing her papers. Tidying up her earthly possessions always gives her a sense of control when outside pressures became unbearable. While watching the Army-McCarthy hearings on television, she continues to write her story of Lillian Beye. She has begun writing the episode in which Lillian returns to her home and children soon after her mother's death. Anaïs ignores her agent's suggestion that she drop the Proustian roman-fleuve and begin a separate "big" book. In fact, she discovers a title for her novel in the news of archaeologists unearthing two "ships of death" near Gaza in Egypt. The day ship and the night ship were to carry the soul of the Pharaoh to the afterlife. She will call her work *Solar Barque* (first published in 1955, then finally as a part of *Seduction of the Minotaur*, in 1959). She distills the images of the two ships to her own persistent dream of pushing a boat through the waterless city.

While Anaïs writes her novel, Renate paints her portrait. In the painting Renate captures her best friend's love of costume, her eggshell complexion and arched eyebrows, and her head in the bird cage. Anaïs loves the world of fantasy and magic that Renate and Paul create in their paintings and parties. Renate's sense of drama can match Anaïs's own, and Renate tells good stories that Anaïs repeats in her diary (and will use in her final book of fiction). Anaïs can also analyze Renate's jealousy and agony over Paul's promiscuous behavior with gay men. It seems to her that Mathiesen—like Anger, Capote, Williams, and other homosexual men—prefer the old myths and are particularly fixated on the mother. She does not want to be caught in the cycle of repetition of eternal return, she later tells Miller. She wants to live out many patterns with many people in many atmospheres.[129] Paul Mathiesen sees his breakup with Renate differently: though he and Renate were "falling apart then anyway," it was Anaïs who took Renate away from him like a rival lover.[130]

## Journeys to the Past and Future

After nearly fifteen years of exile, she returns to Paris for a visit in the fall of 1954 with Hugo, who is on financial business. René de Chochor has warned her that her Paris is dead, and the road in from the airport seems to confirm this. But the familiar assurance of a sidewalk café dispels her fears. The size of the tables, like the proportion of the city, bespeaks intimacy and humanity. The patina of centuries of living show everywhere on the fabric of the city. Even in her room at the Hôtel Crillon, that bastion of the wealthy on the place de la Concorde, she waxes romantic about the history of the furnishings. Like countless American visitors, she relishes the discomforts and imperfections of the city as intrinsically superior to unscarred America.

She is welcomed at George Whitman's Le Mistral bookshop, and notices the clientele, who seem detached from books and more interested in drugs. She takes a taxi to the graveyard of houseboats, but naturally fails to find *La Belle Aurore*. She finds the tomb of Moricand, who had died just weeks before, and makes contacts: Louise de Vilmorin at a book signing; Zadkine at his studio in rue d'Assas; Jean Carteret in the cluttered apartment described in "The All-Seeing" (his eyes no longer are); and Richard Wright, whom she had entertained in Greenwich Village. Wright seems a confirmed expatriate, feeling free of racial prejudice in Paris.

She walks the streets for hours, celebrating the Paris that she loves, which is not at all dead, she concludes. The embracing couples leaning against the walls of the bridges confirm it, as do the barges drifting down the Seine. She repeats all the old clichés as if to confirm it: the hobos beg with charm, each stone has its history, and this city is the capital of intelligence.[131]

Once back in New York City in late fall, she builds a fire in the fireplace and feeds the flames with all six hundred pages of the condensed version of the diary she had done for Denise Clairouin and Max Perkins in 1937. She will just wait to publish her "blueprint for living," her "Baedeker to freedom," until it can appear intact. The novels can be symbolic composites; the diary, she tells Geismar, "can wait for publication."[132]

She continues to lecture or read (New York City College, Brooklyn Public Library, and Pomona College during the winter of 1954–55), but does so always with fear and trembling, followed by depression. She always makes herself vulnerable to mockery, hostility, and rejection, yet afterward many seek her out with confidences. It is the critics whom she fears and loathes, and she steps up her own private countercriticism of Malcolm Cowley, Cyril

Connolly, James Laughlin, Edmund Wilson, and Max Geismar (though she works out a rapprochement with the latter). When she is particularly angry she calls them all dissectors, taxidermists, mummifiers, and embalmers (Geismar is, after all, working on a book about the genteel, nineteenth-century William Dean Howells). "I live in the future," she asserts. She is particularly sensitive to charges that she is egocentric (her mother's charge against her father) and thinks it simplistic to say that writers concerned with politics are altruistic and those concerned with the individual, selfish.

The charges of egotism and narcissism against Anaïs are in part ill-founded. She had great powers of empathy and compassion, qualities in opposition to narcissism. As one of her best critics says, "To 'overflow' with love of others is one of Nin's achievements. Her early work is a condemnation of self-love and of the incestuous loves that often torment neurotics. In *House of Incest, Under a Glass Bell,* 'Stella,' 'Winter of Artifice' and 'The Voice,' Nin exposes the crippling effects of fixation on the ego."[133]

She spends a month in New York with Hugo, often hanging out with Jim Herlihy (who is reading her new manuscript) at the White Horse Tavern—their "word jam sessions" are full of spontaneity and trust—and working with Dr. Bogner on the seeds of her repressed ("toxic") anger. Bogner, who shares her own personal secrets with Nin, believes that her patient is identifying too much with her. They talk about her fear of taking over masculine activities, as exemplified in her failure to make money, to drive a car, and to use a camera. Flying back to Los Angeles, Anaïs assesses the progress of her therapy and concludes that she does indeed feel less guilt and fear. Yet her first dream back in Sierra Madre is a dream that her mother has gone mad and committed suicide from too much servitude.

The inner music of her muse returns in the spring of 1955, and she rereads *Solar Barque* with confidence. Her confidence in the short novel is affirmed and sustained by Jim Herlihy, whom she calls her "only link to the future," her "twin in writing."[134] He has told her that if she writes nothing else in life, this book qualifies her "as a great woman and a great artist." He sends to Sierra Madre his diary description of her and asks for her diary description of him. His words more than balance the silence of the critics:

> Anaïs . . . is the strongest woman alive. If at times there are manifestations of weakness it is only because her sensibilities are greater. . . . [S]he enjoys the curse and the privilege of a kind of sainthood, sainthood being the same for high sensitivity and awareness [as for a] superhuman sort of vision. . . . Anaïs will never be a mistress of artistic forms. This flaw is the price her novels pay for the perfect integration of art and life achieved in

the diary. . . . The unity of the diary is created by the person, not
the artist. . . . The art of Anaïs Nin is the art of improvisation,
its glow and beauty the result of jazz moments in the world of
perfect vision.[135]

Students and the occasional devoted library or faculty person sustain her
less. On the trip from Greenwich Village to Sierra Madre, Hugo accompanies her as far as Northwestern University in Evanston, Illinois. She lectures
for the inauguration of her manuscript exhibit; Hugo shows his films. Felix
Pollak, the curator of the special collections at the library, is her host. The
cold academic hall, massive podium (she always steps aside to present her
full self), and campus business chatter that follow leave her unsatisfied with
the impersonal visit. Later in the spring she suffers the same sense of the
"loneliness of college life" during a visit to the University of North Carolina
in Chapel Hill, a visit arranged by the son of her cousin Gilbert Chase.

Her analysis with Dr. Bogner during 1955 is intense, for Bogner insists
that she needs independence. Though the doctor defines independence as
inner freedom, Anaïs fears the physical manifestation of freedom, which
could bring poverty. Her childhood anxiety about debts and poverty returns
and with it a reminder that lack of money means a lack of control (and the
freedom to keep moving). She and Bogner go over and over the past, her
mother's irrationality (which her daughter understands better since her
mother's death), and what Bogner diagnoses as her father's schizophrenia.

Her neurosis, as she understands it at this time, is her compulsion to
remain "mobile, fluid, to change surroundings." It is based on a fear that
putting down roots and trusting one love means entrapment and death—
"claustrophobia of the soul," she calls it. Though she swings from coast to
coast, she is not free.[136] Pole is her ballast.[137] Her life with him is domestic
and routine: the launderette, shopping at Sears, entertaining the forest
rangers. She does housework half the day, writes half the day, and goes out
for the evening. Yet in her writing she captures only the heightened moments, only transfigured experience. After about six weeks she becomes
restless, feels imprisoned and out of control. It is as if she needs the
"security" of new adjustments and change, for she has learned to cope with
change in her nomadic childhood. She plays life as a ballet, moving deftly
and lightly to avoid danger, moving seductively to win admiration, dancing
through her self-constructed minefield with her eye on the exit—still keeping the eye of the father pleased lest he abandon her. "I fear the snapping
of the cord," she had once told Durrell.[138]

Yet she sums up her analysis this year by concluding that her anger has
dissipated and that she feels "installed in the present" and no longer angry

against America. It has been a month since she suffered depression, anxiety, or anger, she testifies. She suffers less now from fear of loss of love; she feels less bitter and hurt. At last, she says somewhat prematurely, "I have overcome my neurosis."[139] When a friend of hers explains his interest in the mysticism of Gurdjieff, she expresses her disapproval. Psychoanalysis is the only way to heal the self, and then the world.[140] But when a friend named Gil Henderson suggests that she take LSD for an experiment with Dr. Oscar Janiger, she agrees to seek its visionary effects.

# CHAPTER ELEVEN

# 1955–1965

# The Diary of Others

"I have decided to retire as the major character of this diary."
—Anaïs Nin, 1963[1]

NOT LONG after Dr. Oscar Janiger gives her the blue LSD pills with a glass of water, she notices the hairs of the rug undulating. The walls liquefy and the doorknobs melt. Is she swimming or flying? When the door opens, the light from outside dazzles her eyes. She seems to have a hundred eyes to take in every sensory detail. And she can hear Balinese music vibrating through her body. Suddenly she becomes gold, with a sensation akin to an orgasm. The voyage alternates between the comic and profound as she feels the waves of gold wash over her.

Gil Henderson, a painter who has taken LSD before, stays with her (she asks him if she will return safely) to report what she says. Stanley Haggart photographs her, in a pose with her hands joined as if in prayer. As a requirement for Dr. Janiger, who comes by frequently to check on her condition, she writes a long narrative reverie while under the influence of the drug.[2] Afterward she feels burned out and exhausted for days. Later, when she analyzes her experience and the images of her voyage, she concludes that every experience and visual image has a correlation to her previous writing, especially to *House of Incest,* her first and most surrealistic work. (In fact, what she wrote during her LSD experience made use of stored images.) The chemical has not taken her to any unknown world, it has taken her to the landscape she has already visited through her art and imagination.

Anaïs confides to Dr. Janiger that the LSD trip is "extraordinary and exhilarating." What he learns from his work with her is that, unlike his other patients, she probably experienced a lesser change under the medication— "because she was already so close to her own unconscious realm, could move in and out of her inner life, and could see the world in multi-layered consciousness that supercedes time and place."[3] Betty Eisner, Ph.D., another expert on the use of LSD in psychoanalysis, reports hearing the same positive response from Anaïs.[4] Anaïs's only known negative response was a general indictment of drug usage to a friend who had a son with drug problems.[5] In her diary she says that, for herself, psychoanalysis can effect the same connection to the subconscious as drugs, and that the "dream world" (her favorite expression of the subconscious) is accessible naturally to the poet and artist.

She takes LSD for the same reason she tastes other experiences: to see if there is a world she has not yet penetrated. In the 1950s, there is a widespread belief in avant-garde circles that LSD opens a new arena of consciousness, and Janiger, a Los Angeles psychiatrist, is discreetly studying this phenomenon with a variety of people of different ages and occupations (including a writer—Anaïs—and a mystic—Alan Watts).[6] In America at large, the Eisenhower years are not years of new consciousness, and some in the nascent counterculture look to drugs with hope (and some with despair). As Allen Ginsberg later notes, some of the best minds of his generation were destroyed by drugs.

Anaïs will not try the drug again, though she participates in the "happenings" and celebrations of the flower children and tries to keep in touch with avant-garde European movements. At fifty-two she steers a middle course, closer to what the writer Betty Friedan describes as the "feminine mystique" than to liberated womanhood. During this period of her life—the decade before the first publication of her diary—she will publish two new works of long fiction. Her mood alternates between bitterness about America's rejection of her work (this winter a *Hudson Review* article by Marvin Mudrick calls her characters in *A Spy in the House of Love* "breathtakingly trite") and resignation ("It took me a lifetime to learn that happiness is in quiet things, not the peaks of ecstasy").[7] During this same decade, she also publishes one review, ten short pieces excerpted or reprinted from other works, and finds an English publisher to reprint her books.

Out of necessity, even maturity, she turns outward, travels several times to Europe, writes about others in her diary, and tries to look for the joy of life in small everyday things around her. One of her favorite pleasures, until she and Rupert give up smoking in 1959, is gold-tipped Balkan Sobranie cigarettes. Though she says she considered burning the diary, fearing it could harm others, she continues to retype it, fill it out, and update the portraits in it.[8] She speaks of developing the "characters" in her diary and subtly revises the text so that it comes closer to her expectations for the facts—a case of art transcending the truth.

Her bicoastal life continues. Mr. and Mrs. Hugh Guiler live at 35 West Ninth Street, where Mrs. Guiler dresses smartly, supervises a maid, entertains frequently, and visits bookshops, galleries, and dressmakers. "Mr. and Mrs." Rupert Pole live in rural Sierra Madre, California, until he gives up his forestry work for classroom teaching and they move to a basement apartment at 1729 N. Occidental Boulevard in 1959. Mrs. Pole does her own housework, dresses in long, loose dresses, barbecues in the backyard, occasionally baby-sits the children next door, and often visits the beach near Santa Monica canyon where her husband swims. When she is out of town seeing her publisher or lecturing in New York, her West Coast friends write to her in care of one of her New York friends. When Mrs. Guiler of New York is away in Los Angeles, where she says she can relax and write better, her East Coast friends and her husband write to her at a post office box or at the Satyr Book Shop or the London Bookshop on Hollywood Boulevard.

These two worlds differ, even down to her household pets: a cat in New York, a dog in California. She is inclined to divide the worlds into the intellectual and the physical, for her California life is informal—a "place hung between art and nature."[9] She thinks about finding a barge to live on in Los Angeles, recreating her floating Paris life. The men make a difference: Hugo, older and more international and prone to depressions (he also is in analysis with Dr. Bogner), is making art films in Greenwich Village and has returned, for financial reasons, to a banking job[10]; Rupert, a young outdoorsman, eternally optimistic, is retraining himself for classroom teaching. But the two coasts are not a struggle between the bohemian and bourgeois, for this tension exists in both places. Her friends in the film and architecture worlds of the West Coast may not match the Greenwich Village cachet of Ian Hugo's art world, but in both homes she lives amid the externals of the bourgeois wife. Though she claims to reject the furs and jewels of her Cuban relatives, she prefers financial security to bohemian independence.

At this time, only a few friends move back and forth between two coasts and know about her double life. They include Ruth Witt-Diamant, who seems more familiar with her New York life (Anaïs accuses her of trying to break up her relationship with Rupert), and Jim Herlihy, the only one who still seems to love her writing and with whom she shares her feelings of guilt and her fear of exposure. She tells him about a dream of men in a carriage trying to unveil her and about a dream of dying by injection and yelling for her mother to promise she will not read the diaries.[11] The letters to and from

Herlihy, which she enfolds in her diary, testify to his central and supportive role.

As the years go by, more and more friends are informed directly or indirectly of her bigamous secret. If one insists on seeing her on the "other" coast, she either resists or confides. If the friend persists, as one did, she says, "Anna, I want to make one thing clear; I don't want you to know my life over there because you love Hugo."[12] The friend says nothing.

When she struggles with her reasons for staying with both men in a double life, she has to admit that it is "for the sake of [economic] protection." She fears repeating the poverty, vividly remembered, of her childhood in New York. But she "pays" for her secrecy with her life, she tells her analyst, Dr. Bogner, at each visit to New York.[13] Bogner tries to synthesize the fragments brought to her.

A second reason for her dual life she confides to friends: men really want a mistress, not a wife. Had not her father left her family, drawn away by the sexual attractions of other women? She will be mistress to Hugo and to Rupert. Her leave-takings will be seductive, thus maintaining both love and sensuality. But it is a role that is strained by the process of aging, and she confides in her diary that society does not forgive aging women; she herself looks critically at Caresse Crosby, who visits Los Angeles with a wrinkled face ("a ruined mural") and bright, youthful clothes. What Anaïs does not know is that when Caresse is informed about her friend's life with Rupert, she announces half jokingly that she is leaving immediately for New York to appropriate Hugo.[14] Several years later when she anticipates visiting Caresse in Europe, Anaïs asks her friend which husband she would prefer to see.[15]

Symbolically, there is a third place where she dwells: the air. She spends a great deal of time in planes writing letters—her vast switchboard to the outside world. Both the distances and the circumstances are conducive to her writing, she records in her diary while flying to San Francisco to collect a number of her original diaries. As she classifies her life compartmentally by means of plane tickets and separate lists of friends and households, so does she shape her past by reworking the record of her life both orally with Dr. Bogner and on the typed pages of her diary.

In her analysis with Bogner in New York, Anaïs swings from feelings of being "healed" to feelings of depression as she analyzes her childhood and works to be "dispossessed" by the ghosts of her parents. She is now convinced that her father died a schizophrenic. Working through her grief for her mother, she is often early for her appointments and walks the streets near Bogner's office. Mourning for her mother even leads her to imagine she is having heart trouble, of which a doctor finds no evidence.

In Los Angeles she works on two levels of her life as she both retypes her earlier diary—she calls it "retracing steps"—and keeps up her current one, which she describes as "X-raying" or exploring her subconscious self. She names each diary volume ("Fire," "Fatamorgana," "Count Laundromat" or "Mea Culpa"). With Jim Herlihy's advice, she structures the earlier "diary" and treats it more as a novel, filling out the pictures and characterizations to make it more lifelike. She hopes to give it the "continuity and unity of a Proustian work."[16] When she is done, a copy goes to Jim, and the original is returned to one of the three metal files at Bekins Storage on Huntington Drive in Arcadia. Though in New York she criticizes the "Grecian life of California" (focusing only to its physical side), it is on the sunny West Coast where she does her best work (after making breakfast, cleaning house, running errands, and cooking lunch). She is critical of what Renate Druks calls the California concern with "maintenance" of land, house, and body (though she herself has always given the latter priority). "The world of the artist is my only native country," she would have us believe.[17]

The year 1956 is ushered in at the Holiday House, a Malibu hotel and restaurant in Italian Villa style on the coast. The hotel and restaurant are owned by the producer Dudley Murphy, a friend of Caresse Crosby's. Renate is the hostess. Anaïs dances and kisses strangers with relish this New Year's Eve. Afterward, as after her visits to Renate's Malibu home (where Renate is surrounded by her paintings of women and animals), Anaïs records the stories of Renate and her housemate, Paul Mathiesen. The union of Paul and Renate is dissolving because of his homosexual liaisons and, according to him, Renate's close friendship with Anaïs. When Renate weepingly tells her of accidently walking into an unlocked room and seeing Paul performing a homosexual act, Anaïs adds the incident to her diary (but sets it under a tree). Paul seems to Anaïs to be a "blond angel" who undressed and made love "with the choirboys." Many of Renate's stories will eventually be incorporated into Anaïs's last book of fiction, *Collages*.

"I was her analyst in Los Angeles," says Renate. Since Anaïs feels stranded in the desert in Sierra Madre, she talks on the telephone frequently to Renate, who lives more than an hour's drive away, and devours Herlihy's letters when they arrive from New York. He inspires her to continue typing the diary. You are an "angel-witch," he writes one day, inspired by her insights, her wisdom. She continues typing, with her aging cocker spaniel, Tavi, sleeping at her feet. During the spring she resumes, then stops, work on *Solar Barque,* the novella set in Mexico, but the reworking of the diary continues concurrently. The move to Hollywood from the mountains will bring her twenty minutes closer to Renate and to the neighborhood of many other friends: Joanne Carson, Curtis Harrington, and the Wrights. She now feels more a part of the artistic life of Hollywood.

New York City, where too much happens, she says, charges her batteries with its tension and stimuli. Dr. Bogner helps her synthesize the psychic fragments, and Dr. Max Jacobson—whom she portrays in her diary as an illuminated healer—gives her shots of amphetamines, what she calls her "vitamins" or "magic potion," and supposedly "cures" her anemia.[18] Jacobson, who will later lose his medical license (he was never a member of the American Medical Association) regularly gives his wealthy and celebrity patients shots of "speed"—amphetamines laced with animal cells and steroids. President Kennedy and his wife are (after the autumn of 1960) to become regular (and dependent) customers of Jacobson, who accompanies them on their triumphant European tour. "I don't care if its horse's piss. It works," Kennedy tells his aides after they have the "medication" analyzed. Truman Capote, another customer, calls it "instant euphoria." Sometime later, Jacobson's nurse, who thinks him a "butcher," will testify that he sometimes worked around the clock and that his speech was slurred—for he was his own best customer.[19]

Anaïs's New York weeks are also energized by her hours with Jim Herlihy at the Rienzi café on MacDougal Street, hours that stimulate her thinking and assure her that she belongs in the bohemian world. They talk a kind of "jazz talk," as she calls it. She renews her friendship with her dear friend Frances Brown, who had been in Europe. Frances is now married to Michael Field, the cookbook author. Anaïs also patches up her quarrel with Leo Lerman, who is a frequent guest at the Fields' parties. Louis and Bebe Barron have recorded their new electronic music for Hugo's film *Bells of Atlantis,* and for a science-fiction movie entitled *Forbidden Planet.*

The Barrons gave the most memorable parties. The Guilers' parties included "third-rate celebrities and Greenwich Village types," remembers Fabion Bowers. All were her friends; "she would have eaten his friends up if they had been invited." Bowers, a music critic who helped to publicize Japanese theatre, and his wife, Santha Rama Rau, an Indian writer, are among Anaïs's musical friends. The four attend a Ravi Shankar concert and have many dinners together at the Guiler home. It was not Anaïs, with her "pansy face" and "dark sloe eyes," that attracted him as much as did the Nin name, a golden name for him—"I knew her as Joaquin Nin's daughter." Alas, she never talked about her father, Bowers says. He tries unsuccessfully to get various magazines to publish her short stories.[20]

During the mid-1950s she contrasts her work with the work of each popular literary success. François Sagan's *Bonjour Tristesse* is "trite and superficial" when Anaïs would prefer "subtle and symbolic." Beckett's *Waiting for Godot,* brilliant but not moving, comes solely from the mind and projects helplessness. Only when she reads a fragment of a novel in progress, *Miss*

*MacIntosh, My Darling,* by Marguerite Young, does she find a spark of recognition when she sees how Young treats illusion and reality. (In order to placate the fearful reader, Young makes the dreamer, the revealer of the fantastic, mad.) Later Anaïs praises Arthur Laurents's *A Clearing in the Woods,* a play that "dramatize[s] a woman's neurosis."[21]

## Allen Ginsberg and Romain Gary

It is a Saturday night in early November 1956. Anaïs takes several friends to a home in the Hollywood hills to hear two young Beat poets give a reading. Allen Ginsberg and Gregory Corso have hitchhiked from San Francisco to Los Angeles on their way to Mexico. Ginsberg had written her to advertise their Buddhist ("I mean looney," he explains) readings as swinging and literate and to ask her to arrange the reading and to invite Aldous Huxley ("we have all used Peyote &c"), Marlon Brando, Christopher Isherwood, and James Dean (who by then was dead). They will read for free and even furnish the jug wine, he adds.[22] Lawrence Lipton (whose house in Venice is a kind of motel for poets and musicians) organizes the event. Lipton is a leader of what he calls Venice West, the southern branch of the California Beat movement—what Ferlinghetti calls the "flipsters and hipsters."[23] Anaïs brings her own friends, including Joanne Carson, the artist (called "Ingrid" in the published diary) whose breasts she envies. Ginsberg is eager that Anaïs hear his work, for he anticipates her understanding—he considers her one of the Paris surrealists. The evening enters American social history when a heckler in the audience challenges the meaning and motives of Ginsberg, who has just finished a wine-inspired reading of "Howl."[24] His purpose is "nakedness," Ginsberg answers the heckler. Inspired anew by the idea of the spiritual nakedness of the poet, he removes all his clothing and challenges the drunken heckler to do the same. The heckler leaves, and Anaïs and the others applaud loudly. Anaïs records that when Ginsberg threw off his clothes, his dirty shorts landed on Joanne, nor was he in a hurry to dress again. *He* remembers that he just dropped his clothes and put them back on promptly just as Corso began his reading. Though Ginsberg's version is less dramatic, he tells Lawrence Ferlinghetti that it is the wildest reading he has ever given. Lipton tells Kenneth Rexroth that "L.A. will never be the same again," and Anaïs records that "a new surrealism" is "born of the Brooklyn gutter and supermarkets."[25] It reminds her of Artaud's mad reading at the Sorbonne. The following year she writes an insightful essay on the Beats for her diary, linking them to Villon, Rimbaud, Artaud—and jazz.

In another literary encounter she was not as well received. Though her diary contains many references to Romain Gary, French consul in Los Angeles, and his wife, Lesley Blanch, the author of *The Wilder Shores of Love,*

Anaïs is not a part of their social circle. She meets Blanch when she goes to their house to reclaim a French translation of *Ladders to Fire,* sent by diplomatic pouch from Paris. Though coolly received, she is invited to the consul's Christmas open house and two further parties, where she meets Gregory Peck, Joseph Cotten (she prefers their wives), James Mason, and Frank Sinatra, as well as Cole Porter. She understands that Gary lives in a remote world inaccessible to her, but she tries to initiate a closer friendship. When he does not respond, she concludes that he is interested only in younger women. She gives her attention to Lesley Blanch. Increasingly as she approaches her fifty-fourth birthday and feels less like a "defeated little girl" trying to replace her mother, Anaïs identifies with the women in triangular relationships (Gary is a notorious ladies' man). She truly adores the Blanch novel, reads it several times, and gives it to many of her friends. But Blanch does not warm to her. When Anaïs and Renate later meet her at a poetry reading at the Coronet Theatre, they believe she rudely dismisses them. Remembering Rosa Nin's critical withholding of love, Anaïs wonders why her relationships always place her in a triangular formation with her parents. She feels a keen sense of failure that the Garys do not return her admiration; they are a dazzling if troubled couple (Gary later leaves his wife for Jean Seberg), and Anaïs longs to have writer friends in Los Angeles.[26]

The holiday season once again enflames Anaïs's neuroses with its heavy memories of the loss of innocence and of family hypocrisy.[27] The good news that a new (Avon) edition of *A Spy in the House of Love* has strong advance sales is overwhelmed by the bad news from her friends: a big fire in Malibu threatens Renate's house and the Eric Wright property. Paul Mathiesen grabs Renate's painting of him and escapes, leaving her to hose down the roof. Their relationship does not survive. Anaïs's New Year's party is not enlivened even when Renate brings a new lover. Also attending, coincidentally, is Paul Mathiesen.

Anaïs tells Renate that she picks flawed men, whom she inevitably abandons. With an almost comic ingenuousness Anaïs tells her it is neurotic to move from man to man. One should pick a man one can mold and educate—into an engraver, a filmmaker, a teacher, or a writer.[28] Yet she is drawn to Renate's spontaneity, to her daring acting out of her fantasies, and to her spectacular parties (Anaïs's are sparsely attended). She also admires Renate's ability to live alone.[29]

In New York she thrives on the café and theatre life of Greenwich Village, meeting at Café Figaro with Jim Herlihy (who has just sold his second play), and enjoying the protection of Drs. Jacobson and Bogner. She wishes she were not dependent on either. In 1957 she works with Bogner on several problems, especially her inability to stabilize her life and to remain faithful.

In Los Angeles she feels cut off from the avant-garde and the international scene; in New York she is cut off from nature and inner harmony. But she seems in no hurry to resolve this tension.

## Dealing with Rejection

A more serious problem, as indicated by the numerous dreams that she records in her diary, is her suppressed anger, fear, and aggression—indirectly expressed in her inability to accept criticism. The anger appears as a tiger, the helplessness as a little girl caught in a wheel (she frees her), and the abandonment as a locked door. She now concludes that her father's abandonment led to her fear of being hurt, which led to her feeling of not being loved, which led to her habit of breaking with those who criticize her (leaving them before they can leave her). At fifty-four she is still dragging around her past and treating it like a novel, a process she thinks neurotic. She justifies renewed weeks of discussions of her father with Bogner as a means of changing this neurosis. They find labels for the relationship such as fear of not being loved (hers) and Don Juanism as a childish dependency on the mother (his).

"There must be something behind this curtain," she admits, but cannot identify the block. That Bogner may have brought up sexual violation or the physical relationship between Anaïs and her father is suggested by Anaïs's comment about her childhood: "I have no memory of physical closeness to my father." She only remembers his lack of tenderness and his distance—he read during family meals—and yet she also mentions the spankings, the nude photographs, and his watching her while she slept. Even now she feels ashamed and guilty for what she believes is her desire to have him watch her.[30] He is responsible for charging all her relationships "with direct sexual associations."[31] This insight (in the fall of 1957) is followed in her diary by the confession that in her dreams she does not publish a work of art but buys a "whorish dress" and lies on a bed naked, with the world watching her.

Even the personal quality of which she is most proud comes from her father's abandonment. She has a "gift for creating intimacy" with other people, a talent developed, consciously or unconsciously, to prevent abandonment. Because she had lost her first "beauty contest" for her father's approval, she is determined to win over every new person and record every compliment from friends.[32] She can lock eyes for full and sustained contact with another person. Jim Herlihy tells her that this is the "secret of [her] seduction," and another friend says everyone wants a personal relationship with her (in explaining why few people come to her parties).

A second "gift" brought by her father's abuse is a single-minded will to survive and succeed, even to the disregard of ordinary standards of morality, a trait common both to children of family violence and to former prisoners of war, recent studies show. And how do they recover? And how does one survive? By finding "some meaning in their experience that transcends the limits of personal tragedy," says one psychiatrist.[33] That meaning for Anaïs was to be found in her writing.

In late 1957 and early 1958, she works to overcome her second major disappointment in life—America's repudiation of her writing. She always describes the rejection in conspiratorial terms and takes it personally, but she continues to try to build bridges. First she prepares a fragment of *Solar Barque* for *Eve* magazine, edited by Lawrence Lipton (the vagabond leader of Venice West). She is proud of the $310 she earns for this fragment and has great hopes of being the magazine's "roving reporter" in New York. Using her friends as material, her first piece includes references to Haiti and jazz, to Peggy Granville-Hicks, to the Barrons, Durrell, Herlihy, Julian Beck and Judith Malina (of the Living Theatre), and to historian of mythology Joseph Campbell and his wife, Jean Erdman, a dancer—all the people she believes important in New York. Unfortunately *Eve* folds in the spring of 1958 and with it a possible bridge to a wider audience.

Anaïs has high hopes for *Solar Barque,* her story of Lillian's entrance into life through nature. Joaquin expresses his enthusiasm, which encourages her. She will use the youthful drawings of Renate Druks's son (Peter Loomer) to illustrate her new novella, set in Acapulco. It is the story of Lillian, who has left her husband and children to play jazz piano with an orchestra and to regain her own perspective on life. She confronts the caged Minotaur or demon part of herself, explores her soul in talks with Dr. Hernandez (who dies before they can have a deeper talk), and renews herself with each dip into the ocean. The novelist's portrayal of Mexico is romantic (the stuffing coming from the taxi seat is described as angel hair from a Christmas tree), but the question of Lillian's returning to her husband reflects Anaïs's serious consideration of leaving Rupert for Hugo.

Anaïs also looks back to her earlier publications and begins reprinting her books, to rescue them from oblivion, she says. She issues an offset version of *House of Incest* with photomontages by Val Telberg (who has worked with Hugo). This time she does not send out press copies. The following year she offsets her "continuous novel" (*Ladders to Fire, Children of the Albatross, The Four-Chambered Heart, A Spy in the House of Love,* and *Solar Barque*) under the single title *Cities of the Interior* and wishes she could publish other writers she likes: Anna Kavan, William Goyen, Isabel Bolton, and Djuna Barnes—all names that are as yet little known in America or England. Her stationery now reads "Anaïs Nin Press, 35 West 9th Street." She even finds a distributor for her books in Tom Payne at Avon, which is reprinting her *Spy*.[34]

She also seeks new literary associations (scouting for *Eve* aids this search). She often describes her connection to the "country of art" as its jazz rhythms, which she believes express young America's rebellion against conformity and commerce. Though she cannot write in the rhythms of jazz, for she has not been born in this country, she encourages it in the young, believing it to be the equivalent of France's surrealism. She changes her mind briefly after reading Jack Kerouac's *On the Road*. Though she thinks the novel contains pure lyrical passages, its realism is too harsh. Tom Payne introduces her to Kerouac, whose first language was French. But when she cannot keep up with his drinking in the Cedar Bar, he ditches her.

Building literary bridges leads her, during a 1958 summer trip with Hugo to Europe, to a reunion with Lawrence Durrell and to a meeting with a young French writer named Jean Fanchette, who will find her a French publisher. Before Paris, Anaïs and Hugo spend a week in Brussels, where he shows his short films and she gives a reading. They attend a large dinner with Le Corbusier and Edgar Varèse. Joaquin Nin's daughter notes each luxury and titled guest ("all the talent, beauty and wit of Europe") and revealingly thinks about how thrilled her father would be with the occasion.[35]

In Paris, Anaïs visits Jean Carteret, the astrologer friend about whom she had written a story. She finally meets one of her favorite novelists, Pierre-Jean Jouve, who expresses amazement that Anaïs can publish her own work without losing public esteem. Anaïs explains the bohemian, underground tradition in American letters. It is a romantic reunion with her beloved Paris (she is so enthusiastic that she exclaims all Parisians are artists and know the meaning of life). She checks out of the luxurious Hôtel Crillon in the place de la Concorde after Hugo's departure and moves to a smaller, Left Bank hotel. Rupert soon joins her for five weeks (she confides to close friends) of touring by car: France, Spain (a visit to Joaquin, who often summers in Barcelona), and Italy.[36]

Her most important stop, the only one detailed in her diary, will be two days with Lawrence and Claude Durrell in Sommières. The Durrell daughters call the tall, lanky Rupert "the cowboy." Claude finds Anaïs hypersensitive, though Anaïs later explains that her behavior is the result of twenty years in a hostile and barbaric land. Anaïs is particularly sensitive to two things: she has been overwhelmed by Durrell's *Justine* (the first novel in his *Alexandria Quartet*), and she also feels guilty for not having helped him when he needed money during the war. She "wept" over the injustice that her own writing, which she calls the "feminine counterpart of Durrell," is rejected while *his* novel is acclaimed, a comparison that Durrell's biographer confirms: they share a tendency to shift from "stunning realism . . . into the intangible dimension of symbolism, the 'Heraldic Universe.'"[37]

When she fails to win an audience for her fiction, she believes that America rejects sensuous, sensory, poetic, lyrical, suggestive, exotic literature (she uses all these words at various times). But when the Durrell reviews appear, she cannot understand why her own work—as exotic as Durrell's perhaps, but certainly more obscure and plotless—does not garner readers. She continues to copy every article and review that affirms her belief that America alienates her artists and demands realism. Yet in a dinner earlier at the Geismars' home in New York, she rejects the works of Henry James (Geismar is writing a book about James), accusing him of writing like a woman; he is "too small" and "fussy" and indirect, "effeminate." Ironically, these same labels are later applied to her.[38]

The reunion with Durrell occurs at the same time that she is slowly regaining Henry's friendship through letters to and from Miller's new wife, Eve, who believes that she can share her love and frustrations about Henry with Anaïs. The Millers (Anaïs has never met Eve, who is thirty-five) are planning their own trip to Paris, and Eve—thinking Big Sur has been insidious and enervating for Henry—begins by establishing a connection with Anaïs. Anaïs concludes that both Eve and Claude are intellectually loving wives to her old friends.[39] She is surprised that Claude, Durrell's second wife, had expected her to be a formally dressed lady, when Anaïs remembers her Paris appearance to have been bohemian. Both reunions are tentative. Though she will tell some friends that the "old constellation" (Miller-Nin-Durrell) is being "re-formed," she will not see Durrell again until 1973 in Pasadena.

Her trip with Rupert is a means of showing him her former world as she herself revisits the scenes of her childhood and young adult travels. But Rupert remembers that it was not a happy trip from Portofino to Barcelona because he was trying to save money to build a house, his lifelong dream. The concern for finances dampens her joy. In Barcelona she finds that Joaquín summers in the house of an older woman, who, Anaïs thinks, looks just like their mother.[40] In her suitcase on the trip back to Los Angeles she has a banned copy of Nabokov's *Lolita*.

Soon Anaïs and Rupert are gazing over a brick-walled patio to the shimmering lights of Los Angeles below them. They are high in the Hollywood hills, west of Griffith Park and the Observatory, just below the O in the famous Hollywood sign. The home belongs to Aldous and Laura Huxley. Anaïs had met Laura Huxley previously, in Paris and in New York City (while working with Rank), and likes her; but she does not take to Aldous at all, and the feeling is mutual. Huxley, part of the British colony in Hollywood, knows Rupert's father, Reginald. The British novelist is intellectual, scientific, and scholarly—not a poet, as far as Anaïs is concerned. This evening, as on previous occasions with the Huxleys, the talk turns to LSD, which Aldous takes to counterbalance the loss of his sight. Among those attending the dinner party are Lesley Blanch, Dr. Betty Eisner, who works with Huxley, and Dr. Oscar Janiger, who reads Alan Watts's description of his LSD experience. When Anaïs expresses reservations about the drug, Huxley insists that she was probably given too large a dose.[41]

Anaïs wins Betty Eisner's friendship immediately: "Anaïs had remarkably ready access to her unconscious," claims Eisner. She asks Anaïs and Rupert to join a weekly group she leads (with a medical doctor) in which they use small but increasing doses of drugs such as LSD to aid psychotherapy. Rupert soon stops coming, but Anaïs continues, not as a patient or an experimenter with the drugs, but as an "explorer of the unconscious" with Eisner. Though Eisner admires Aldous, she confirms Anaïs's judgment: "he did not have access to his unconscious at all."[42]

Anaïs holds her ground with Huxley and others who disagree with her and withstands the critical reaction to her books. She is disappointed when Donald Allen's Grove Press anthology excludes her, but thinks she takes the rejection better than when Wallace Fowlie excluded her from his anthology of surrealism. To add insult to injury, Henry innocently publishes her birth date, and the Kinsey Institute publicly announces its ownership of some of her 1940s dollar-a-page erotica, which, rumors have it, comes from her diary.

But the greatest affront is a remark calling her a child of the "palace hotel life" in the preface she has asked Durrell to write for *Children of the Albatross*. (Peter Owen of the British publishing company Peter Owen Ltd., who buys the rights to *The Four-Chambered Heart* and *Children of the Albatross*, insists on the preface for the English edition.) She tells Durrell that she has to cut half the preface because it is inaccurate and lacks insight. She objects to suggestions that she came from a privileged family and that her writing is "feminine-subjective" and "iridescent."[43] She never sends him a copy of his altered essay for approval. Durrell is "staggered" by her concern over these phrases ("a storm in a tea cup") and by her alteration of his preface without his permission.[44]

## A Tale of Two Cities . . . and Two Friends

She will look to Europe for acceptance, to a new agreement with Peter Owen to have her works published in England, and to a new journal entitled *Two Cities: La Revue bilingue de Paris* published by Jean Fanchette, whom she met through Durrell when she was in Paris. Fanchette, whom Durrell thinks a "delicious Prince of Mauritius,"[45] is working on an article, "L'Art d'Anaïs Nin," and wants her contributions. Despite the failure of *Eve,* this offers a new hope for literary acceptance and travel (she always needs an excuse for her bicoastal trips).

At the urging of Lawrence Durrell, Anaïs and Jean Fanchette meet at the famous Deux Magots café. The slim, young Mauritian medical student and poet reminds her of the handsome Haitians with delicate features whom she knew in New York. He is delighted to meet Durrell's charming friend. Dr. Fanchette, who will practice obstetrics and then psychiatry in Paris until his death in 1992, thinks Anaïs is "extremely school girlish" and naive for a woman the same age as his mother. Later, in the wake of the mythologized charms of Anaïs and conjectures about their relationship, he will insist that he found her "completely unattractive sexually."[46]

His article about her, which she thinks "nearly perfect" in its understanding of her work, claims that she casts a "dazzling light" on the "alchemy of body and soul" and explores the "roots of obscure instincts." He compares her to Virginia Woolf, praises *House of Incest* as her greatest work, and calls her an original.[47] She is so excited about his essay that she has five hundred copies made and distributed ("waiting had blunted her modesty," a French woman observed).[48] Despite the demands of medical school and his young family, he will translate *Spy.* She promises to help him edit *Two Cities.* She leaves Europe full of hope for new recognition. He will be her "magic link" to France.

Early in March of 1959 Anaïs is taken to Mount Sinai Hospital in New York with double pneumonia. (Dr. Jacobson had come in the middle of the night when her fever reached 104 degrees.) In the hospital she carefully makes up her face each day—believing that the nurses appreciate her style. She tells Larry and Claude Durrell it is ten days of "jail," though her diary records many visits from friends.

She had a dream, after her return from Paris, of being on a Paris–New York flight that falls almost disastrously until righted by the pilot. Pneumonia had almost felled her. Now she will right herself by throwing her efforts into the work of *Two Cities,* penning numerous letters in the hospital to recruit contributions and subscriptions to the journal. The work allies her to a literary enterprise and gives her status and contacts. After twenty years of what she believes is vilification, she now may be appreciated.[49] She writes Anna Kavan, an English novelist whom she has not met but whose work she admires, that the United States is a "hateful" place and she hopes to return to Europe.[50] If America is to be blamed, it is for infecting her with a need for more attention, a blurring of distinction between publicity and esteem.

Volume one (April) of *Two Cities,* an "hommage" to Durrell, includes

Anaïs's "The Writer and the Symbols" and Fanchette's essay on her work; volume two (July) includes her essay "The Synthetic Alchemist." In both issues she is listed as the New York editor (there are London and Paris editors as well). These are her first original pieces of writing to appear in a journal in a decade. Thus she believes that Jean is helping to heal her. To add to this ascension, the *Village Voice* publishes an article calling her "a major figure in the avant-garde literary movement of the past twenty-five years"—and a "beautiful and vibrant blonde."[51] Her recent hair color change also lifts her spirits.

But there are rivals in the avant-garde movement, particularly Maya Deren, whom she still does not forgive (in her diary) for making her look unattractive in her film. The rivalry reemerges when they learn that their mutual friend Bebe Barron is pregnant. These "mortal enemies" suddenly compete in being maternal and solicitous. Bebe says that each believes she is the center of artistic life in the Village and probably both want babies of their own. For the sake of Bebe, Anaïs attends what Bebe calls a "remarkable" baby shower that Deren gives for all the creative women they know. Deren, a Haitian high priestess, presides over a most unusual party amid her masks. Guests sing, dance, and chant and Deren gives them what Bebe calls "stuff made with roots with magic qualities." The entire shower is "full of power; we were playing around with stuff we shouldn't have," she remembers. As a result of the plant root or of Deren's foretelling of an imminent birth or of Bebe's awe of Deren, the mother-to-be decides to "do something dramatic": she goes into labor within hours of the party—six weeks early. Several years later, after Deren's death, Anaïs writes in her diary a lengthy description of an absurd "pink" shower among voodoo masks, casting Deren as a "witch" in a "voodoo shack" who frightens Bebe, sending her into labor as she is leaving. Bebe calls the diary story inaccurate and "very unfair."[52] Once again Anaïs uses the diary to settle scores.

Contrary to the impression left by the diary, Nin and Deren remain outwardly friendly, and they both continue to be attracted to the gay world. In the mid-1950s Anaïs and Maya are even planning a film together about labyrinths, using Wall Street as a setting. One of the young artists in the group testifies that the gays "used Anaïs as bait" to attract contacts.[53] Not all gays wanted to ingratiate themselves. A young homosexual writer on the West Coast, from whom Anaïs solicited a manuscript for *Two Cities*, says that her "attraction to people of ambiguous sexuality" made him feel "precious" and resentful.[54]

Because she is uncertain of her judgment in selecting poetry for *Two Cities*, Anaïs claims that she asks the help of Serge Gavronsky and Daisy Aldan, two young teachers and poets. Gavronsky, however, was playing table tennis in France with Fanchette when *Two Cities* was conceptualized, and became an editor upon his return to New York. He claims that Anaïs put up the money to begin the magazine and that Ferlinghetti worked the West Coast (though his name does not appear on the masthead). "Anaïs was vital in founding and successfully publishing the first issue. Her friends and connections enabled us to find our first contributors, and she was instrumental in getting Miller and Shapiro to contribute," Gavronsky says.[55]

Daisy Aldan is a New York City poet and teacher whom Anaïs met several years before. Aldan had heard Anaïs talk at the Y in about 1952 and had interviewed her in the mid-fifties when she was writing a doctoral dissertation at New York University (Professor Anna Balakian was one of her advisors) on the influence of the French surrealists on American literature. Aldan, who thought Anaïs a "gorgeous creature," was quite overwhelmed by Anaïs's gracious presence and generosity in lending books and information on surrealism. Now, Anaïs seeks out this poet and editor (of *Folder* magazine), who is twenty years her junior. Soon Anaïs is visiting her from the airport on each trip to New York (she has a key to Aldan's apartment), and Aldan is the one who collects Rupert's calls when Anaïs is with Hugo.[56]

The second new, vital New York ally (after Daisy Aldan), is Marguerite Young, whom one critic will call the "artist heroine" of *Diary* volume six and whose *Miss MacIntosh, My Darling* Anaïs loves.[57] Young is one of the rare friends who declares that she neither could nor would keep a diary—"I am never introspective about myself. I delve into others." She writes about American myths, and possesses a down-to-earth sense of humor and an apartment filled with dolls. Her clothes and apartment, even her hair, are all colored in shades of red. Anaïs first reads a portion of Young's work in progress in 1959. Her genius, Anaïs says, revives the old anxiety about imaginative work being masculine (hence her fear of inventing and creating). She finds in Young a similar love of fantasy and a "feminine" connection uniting art to life. Both women are writing "epic" works, though Anaïs explores the self and Marguerite explores America. Young, a novelist and writing teacher (at the New School for Social Research), clearly inspires her to lengthy diary passages of characterization and critical appraisal. Both Aldan and Young, whom Anaïs has sought out as friends, will remain her staunchest New York supporters long after her death. These friendships with strong, talented women mark her growing confidence.

Young believes that Anaïs is "a true romantic, profound, delicate . . . one of the world's great innocents." Even after the publication of her friend's erotica, Young insists that there is no obscenity or vulgarity in her friend's nature. She is "a grand Spanish lady," a dreamer and virtuous, "selfless" in her promotion of her friends. Young is, or will soon be, privy to many of

Anaïs's secrets: she knows that the baby her friend lost was Miller's, that she has two conjugal lives, and that Hugo gives her ten thousand dollars a year (probably an inflated figure). Young admires Hugo, whom she finds "terribly elegant," but she thinks he is a father figure for Anaïs and Anaïs's brothers.[58]

If Daisy and Marguerite are literary companions and role models in New York, Renate, Anaïs's closest friend in Los Angeles, is a beacon for spontaneity and freedom. Renate is now involved in a serious relationship with a twenty-four-year-old football hero named Ronnie Knox whose ambitious agent/stepfather planned his career moves from three high schools to UCLA (he quit after playing in the Rose Bowl his first year) and a professional team. When he retires he has set a record (still unbroken) for having played for ten different football teams in as many years. But Ronnie wants to be a poet; he "escaped into my life," says Renate. Soon he is sitting with Renate and Anaïs, turning his head from one to the other as they talk of art and creativity. They both pay tribute to his physical beauty, Anaïs in her diary, Renate in photographs and paintings. Anaïs, who calls him "John" in her diary, encourages him to write about his football experiences. Renate takes him to Mexico before they settle in her house in Malibu. They keep their marriage secret, not only because of his age and fame, but because she is a little embarrassed at accepting the bourgeois institution of marriage. Such news would threaten her status as a professional bohemian.[59]

## A Problem of Commitment

Rupert and Anaïs drive through the hills that separate the downtown Los Angeles basin from the Glendale and Burbank basin to inspect a piece of property on which he plans to build a home. He had earlier purchased a lot in Malibu, where his half-brother, Eric Wright, and Renate Druks have homes, but when part of it slid into the ocean he could not get clearance to build on it.[60] The new property looks down upon little Silver Lake Reservoir and northwest toward Griffith Park. He tells her of his dream of building her a home in this spectacular natural setting.

While Rupert struggles to secure a loan[61] and then himself begins the work, using Eric Wright's plans, Anaïs confides in a few close friends that she has decided to leave Rupert and is secretly looking for a woman for him. Though she thinks the basement apartment on Effie Street she shares with Rupert is drab, she is terrified of the commitment and complications of a permanent home. Several friends are convinced that she is seriously involved with another man. She tells several friends that her years with Rupert have been happy, but she claims to have only played a role as wife. In an undated letter to Durrell, enclosing a letter to be forwarded to Miller in France, she explains that Hugo has more "depth and endurance." To Daisy she claims never to discuss literature with Rupert. To Renate she speaks of a healthy commitment to one man and the neurosis of multiple relationships. She tells Ruth Witt-Diamant that she does not know how long she can keep two people "content." She is running low on energy. Herlihy remembers that she got an ulcer from the pressure exerted by the Wright family to marry Rupert.[62]

Anaïs spends part of the summer of 1959 in Europe with Hugo, who is managing his investments (he works now in the foreign department for a New York stock brokerage firm) and making films—though her diary says she is "sent to Venice to cover fashion for magazines." No articles appear, however, though her diary contains long passages of what can be described as travel writing. Weeping on dark balconies for the beauty of Venice, rescuing a wounded pigeon from the water, she portrays herself as alone, smiling behind her veil when men kiss her hand. Occasionally these passages of purple prose overwhelm the careful descriptive details. The water, chalky colors, and romance of Venice lead her to stylistic excess. While her unnamed travel companion is filming another segment of what will be called The Gondola Eye,[63] she goes alone to Paris.

Because she and Hugo always stay at the Crillon in Paris, she writes ahead to have Jean Fanchette find a little Left Bank hotel more in keeping with her own tastes (and to await Rupert, he thinks). She writes to Durrell that she has seen Fanchette to talk at length about Two Cities.[64] One night during her visit, Fanchette picks her up at the Hotel d'Angleterre and takes her to a Chinese restaurant nearby in rue du Four. It is pouring when they emerge from the restaurant, and Anaïs's filmy Indian dress becomes soaked. He is very aware of the stares as he, a very youthful-looking twenty-seven-year-old black man, enters the hotel with this tall woman of fifty-six clad in a clinging long transparent dress, holding her wet sandals. He refuses her offer of a drink and takes the metro back to his wife and baby. At five the next morning, he remembers, she calls his apartment to declare that she is not returning to the United States. Paris is her home—the flowing Seine, the summer rain, coffee at Café Flore. He explains that she is being unreasonable, and she agrees to think about his advice. She leaves for Venice before they talk again. Years later the story will become embellished (portraying him as begging her to stay with him), much to their mutual embarrassment.[65]

She returns to her "anchor," Dr. Bogner, turns the New York editing of Two Cities over to Daisy Aldan, and accompanies Hugo's film presentations with her own readings (usually the party scene from Ladders to Fire) at the Living Theatre, at City College, at the Grolier Book Shop in Cambridge, and for Aldan's students. In her diary there is no mention of Hugo, and she always emphasizes that her lectures are not official but come from the demands of students. She abandons her plan to reprint (offset) the remainder of her books because she is both tired and financially strapped.[66] She and Bogner discuss her continuing vulnerability and her habit of breaking with people she feels are disloyal. She now struggles to keep from breaking with Fanchette and Herlihy, who, she believes, have divided loyalty—Fanchette to Durrell and Herlihy to his own style of gritty realism. The exchange of letters with Herlihy, whom she accuses of writing about "mental dwarfs," is transcribed in her diary. His responses reveal his love and diplomacy, and their letters explore such issues as the nature of fiction, the role of the artist (to "expand the world," she says), and the divergent development of their art (she is concerned with the "artist himself" and he has expanded to broader subjects, he tells her).[67]

Behind the diary is the true story: Herlihy knows that "she has trouble accommodating herself to the fame of successful men" and that "she tend[s] to break off with people . . . when success comes in." He has talked to Miller, Capote, Williams, and Durrell. When he becomes a hot property on Broadway this year, and a newspaper reporter who has interviewed Anaïs writes an article that makes her sound more like a patron than a fellow artist, she begins to cut him off. "She had a blindness and deafness in her," says Herlihy, but he loves her and insists upon a reconciliation.[68] Their friendship endures.

Her trouble with Fanchette arises from a letter that Rupert sends to her in New York, using a *Two Cities* envelope and stationery in case Hugo picks up the mail. When the letter is "returned" to Paris and Fanchette opens Rupert's steamy letter to Anaïs, he is angry that the journal should be used as a lover's mail drop (he considers himself a friend of Hugo's; Hugo visits him in Paris more often than Anaïs does). Despite the strain caused by that letter (and another) and her plan to be absent in Europe, she helps plan Fanchette's lodging for his visit in late spring to New York.[69]

Returning to Los Angeles in the winter of 1959–60, she works on rewriting her diary. She is now on volume seventy, and it is her "major work," she informs Roger Bloom, a voracious reader and articulate correspondent of Miller's incarcerated in the Missouri State Penitentiary. She cannot publish it yet because it would hurt people, she tells Bloom. She offers him her friendship, which will stimulate a decade of letters between them. She tells him that her married life has been a voluntary "symbolic imprisonment," a loss of freedom incurred to keep from harming others.[70]

She had apparently taken on a second "imprisonment" earlier, according to several of her friends who cannot establish the exact date. To preserve the happiness of the Wright/Pole family, including Rupert, who wants a wife, not a mistress,[71] Anaïs had married Rupert in a private civil ceremony. Perhaps she is referring to this decision when she informs Bloom that she has "plenty of symbolic imprisonment . . . for the sake of another person's happiness," but her reference is most likely to her lengthy marriage to Hugo. The pressure for marriage on the West Coast had been building for some time, particularly from Rupert and his mother, Helen Wright. She had told the family for years that she is divorced; it is what she has told Renate as well. She goes through with the ceremony far from Los Angeles, probably assuming that the two marriages—one in Cuba and one in Mexico (some claim Arizona)—will not catch up with her in New York City and Los Angeles. She confides in Renate only when Renate and Ronnie begin planning a trip to Europe, where Anaïs has given her names and addresses of friends who will know of her continued marriage to Hugo. Renate hears the news of her friend's bigamy with shock and concern for the legal consequences. Renate consults a lawyer, who says there is nothing to do about the situation. This narrative of the marriage, based on Renate Druks's memory, would place the ceremony in Yuma, Arizona, in 1959 or 1960. Yet there is no public record of their marriage there. According to other friends, including James Herlihy, the ceremony took place in Mexico in the mid-1950s. Whatever the details, it is clear that in trying to please everyone, Anaïs has added another major risk, the revelation of her bigamy, to any publication of her diary and consequent personal publicity.[72]

## Solar Barque

Rather than settling into domestic comfort (or entrapment) in her new home, her pace of travel accelerates. She has more opportunities to travel and gain a larger audience for her writing because Hugo is traveling internationally for his financial investment business and his filmmaking. She also will soon find a permanent publisher to reissue all her books, and new readers open up opportunities for readings and lectures. The first indication of a possible European critical reception for her work comes with an invitation to Stockholm in the spring of 1960.

She flies from Los Angeles to Paris, where she meets Billy Kluver of New York's Museum of Modern Art, and together they fly to Stockholm. (Hugo arrives later in the day from New York City.) As the plane carrying Anaïs approaches Stockholm, she is delighted by the lakes, canals, and pine-covered islands. This is the land of Ingmar Bergman films. Her Catholic Cuban blood is fascinated by what she calls the structured society with its cult of athletic nakedness (rather than erotic nakedness).

She describes in her diary her arrival, surrounded by photographers and journalists whose stories are on the front pages of newspapers the next day and who compare her glamour to that of Marlene Dietrich, another recent visitor to Stockholm. She finally savors the pleasure of fame, the flowers and telephone calls at her hotel room, numerous parties, and autograph seekers. Because of the crowds on 21 May, the Moderna Museet, located in the city's old naval base, has to move her reading and the showing of Hugo's *Bells of Atlantis* and *Melodic Inversion* (each nine minutes) to a larger lecture hall.

Nils-Hugo Geber, a painter and film researcher who meets both planes, describes that night in his own diary the picture of Anaïs in a blue velvet dress standing on a box in the large hall and "the strong northern evening light penetrat[ing] the windows."[73] Noteworthy among the parties and receptions was Geber and his wife's Sunday dinner party for Anaïs and Hugo, Kluver, and several other leading artists, including Pontus Hulton, the museum director.[74] She meets Artur Lundkvist (Sweden's most celebrated writer) and other celebrities: the nephew of Isak Dinesen, actress Ingrid Thulin, and dramatist Peter Weiss, writers and poets, and several Bergman actors. Anaïs accepts the obeisance of the Swedish intelligentsia, intrigued by "her exotic quality" and her relationship to Henry Miller, with relish, notes Kluver.[75]

Anaïs and Hugo fly to Paris, which seems to have become more worldly and somewhat gloomy, a fact made vivid by the Algerian crisis gripping the city. Amid this reality, and following her exhilaration in Sweden, she notes unhappily that in Paris she only visits celebrities rather than being one herself: she has a letter of introduction to Henri Michaux; she stops at rue de l'Odéon to see Sylvia Beach (who had been the first to translate Michaux into English in 1949); she visits with Harold Norse at the Mistral Bookstore (where she gives a reading)[76]; meets Kenneth Anger at the Deux Magots; and visits Stuart Gilbert on the Ile St.-Louis. While Gilbert speaks of his friendship with James Joyce, she imagines having once met Joyce in the same apartment. Amid the police checks, rumors of terrorists' bombs, and the grayness of the city, she returns to her old haunts, including place de Clichy, and studies the art and music scene with Hugo.

On the point of leaving the Hôtel Crillon and Paris, she learns that Gonzalo has died of throat cancer. During this European trip, Anaïs has missed both the visit to New York of Jean Fanchette and the death in Los Angeles of her "father-in-law," Reginald Pole, on 30 May.

On the way to Venice, where Hugo will finish the film segment "Etude One," they are guests in an elegant home in Florence, which inspires a short story for her diary in the manner of Pierre-Jean Jouve's poetic novels, which she admires. They stay in elegance at the Excelsior Palace Hotel on the Lido in Venice. But neither coming nor going to Venice does she detour to visit Caresse Crosby at Le Castello in Roccasinibalda, her castle outside Rome.

Hugo visits Crosby, but Anaïs makes excuses that she is exhausted and goes back to Paris to see a physician. Later she explains that it was an amoeba infection she suffered, though she may have wished Hugo to be alone with Caresse. Hugo's vivid description of his visit to Le Castello will have to suffice, she tells Caresse.[77]

Back in Los Angeles before the end of June, Anaïs helps Rupert settle into their new house by gardening and stacking wood for their fireplace, resuming the weekly musical visits to the Lloyd Wright home on Doheny Drive, and drinking martinis while looking out over Silver Lake Reservoir. They call themselves "Lord and Lady Windchime."[78] Eric Wright, Rupert's younger half-brother, has designed them a house in the Wright tradition of stone and brick, with a single slanted roof in line with the hillside. She asked that the kitchen not look like a kitchen. "She had a fetish about ugliness . . . did not like practical things," explains Rupert.[79] Later she will have the two brothers remove some of the bricks inside the sliding glass doors and build a small sandbox, where she creates a new design each day, indulging her love of imaginative play.

She brings back the past by retyping volume seventy-nine of her diary, incorporating loose pages written during her travels and passages from letters that she has kept in an expandable folder. To Herlihy (now living in Key West), she writes that she is resigned to anonymity, abandoning new writing, and abandoning composition to type her diary and live for others. The tone is adopted in part because his new novel, *All Fall Down*, is finally bringing him wide recognition. The volume of her letters increases, as she keeps in touch with Marguerite Young (they sometimes read passages from their work over the telephone to each other), Daisy Aldan, and Ruth Witt-Diamant, who visits from San Francisco. Anaïs is struggling with the "toxic burn" of bitterness, that "hemophilia of the soul,"[80] which she warns Roger Bloom (her convict correspondent) against. He had failed to win his freedom despite her several letters to his parole board, testifying as a "psychoanalyst" who had worked under Dr. Otto Rank for two years. She does win a psychic and professional victory from Ruth Witt-Diamant. When the founder of the Poetry Center at San Francisco State hears that Anaïs and Rupert have done some readings of poetic drama on a local Los Angeles public radio station, she finally asks Anaïs to give a reading at the Poetry Center. Anaïs considers it a victory long overdue.[81]

Renate is with Ronnie Knox in Barcelona and writes Anaïs long descriptions of their experiences. In Holland or Belgium they buy a boat called "Solar Barque," which they cannot manage, and when they have it transported to the south of France, it sinks. Anaïs notes and reports to her friend that young Peter Loomer (Druks), whose drawings illustrate her *Solar*

*Barque,* is seriously depressed. He is living with friends while finishing Santa Monica High School and chafing at the responsibilities and regime of "normal" family life. She calls Renate, who makes plans to hurry home to her son. What they do not know is that Peter has been experimenting with drugs.[82]

When Anaïs is back in New York for the fall and early winter of 1960, she makes plans to rent a cheaper apartment because Hugo has spent most of the last year traveling abroad. This winter and next she makes several appearances with Daisy Aldan. Anaïs reads Mallarmé's "Un Coup de Dés" and Daisy reads her own translation of the Mallarmé poem, "A Throw of the Dice." Anaïs admires Aldan's talent and integrity, writes her a recommendation for a Guggenheim Fellowship, promotes her poetry, and writes the foreword for Aldan's first major book, *The Destruction of Cathedrals,* published by Two Cities Press; in turn, Daisy praises her friend's fiction and teaches the short stories of *Under a Glass Bell* to her High School of Art and Design writing classes, even when a parent criticizes "Birth."[83]

The presence of Anaïs in Aldan's poetry of this period is pervasive. Anaïs's turquoise eyes, the sharing of their favorite flower (the white spider chrysanthemum), and their occasional quarrels are echoed throughout *The Destruction of Cathedrals,* a title perhaps suggesting the disappointment and occasional hurts Daisy feels. "I . . . fear to mistake the tenderness of your general kindness/For particular love," she writes in "Pola's Guitar." And in "Departure": "Always the walls crashed when she appeared." The note of disappointment and hurt also appears in the poetry, for occasionally Daisy is accused of spoiling everything with disharmony, when it was Anaïs who had picked the quarrel. "Let's start again," Anaïs always says after each quarrel, and Daisy stays faithful.

Anaïs and Daisy have done a three-way reading of poetry (with the Spanish read by Tana de Gamez, a Spanish novelist and Anaïs's friend in Cuba before she married Hugo) for New York radio station WBAI. Anaïs almost seems jealous when she asks repeatedly of Daisy, "Has Tana made love to you yet? Tana takes what she wants." The incident opens an unpublished story by Aldan, "N is the Sign of Pisces." The story is the closest sustained treatment of their relationship. Also clear is Aldan's implication that they loved each other as friends and did not have a physical relationship. The story ends with a quarrel, provoked, Anaïs mistakenly believes, because she will not give Daisy what she wants. I just want you to love me as a friend, Daisy finally assures her. "Thus I freed you from the steely glow of my need," she will say in "A New Poem by Daisy Aldan."[84]

The two friends occasionally discuss lesbian love. Though Anaïs says she envies Tana her earthiness and assertiveness, she denies having had a successful lesbian relationship with her old friend or with June Miller. June neither loved her enough nor had the strength to take her. Henry did! She wonders how life would have been different had she been lesbian. An acquaintance of Daisy's, an attractive novelist named Karen Kehoe, tells Daisy about her close friendship with Anaïs, whom Kehoe took into her bedroom and put her arms around; when Anaïs asks what to do next, the friend says, If you do not know, we should not proceed.[85]

## Alan Swallow

Alan Swallow, perhaps commercially her most important ally, is a Wyoming man living in Denver. Anaïs met him when she and Rupert first drove west in 1947 and stopped in Denver to meet Reginald Pole. Swallow is a poet who has been a teacher, editor, and small publisher. Now at forty-six, he has been supporting himself full-time for about six years with a press devoted to noncommercial work he admires. When Anaïs writes to suggest that he handle the distribution and perhaps the republication of her books, he expresses his admiration for her work and the belief that their collaboration is a perfect match. Her literary agent in New York handles the details of the contract, and Swallow takes over everything, including outstanding bills. It is 1961, and Anaïs has at last found a publishing home after years of wandering. He makes plans to publish *Seduction of the Minotaur*, which is an expanded *Solar Barque* (or, as some critics have referred to it, "*Solar Barque* with a long coda"), her novel set in Mexico. This work will become the last novel in her Proustian series called *Cities of the Interior*.

The coda she adds to *Solar Barque* is a retelling of the Henry-June-Anaïs story in light of the gossip and the resentments that have accumulated over the years. Jay (Henry) is a painter (working in his "Pissoir Period") who has abandoned his daughter. Fatherhood repulses him, though he lives in a "child's world" (Lillian pays his debts), doing a "Village Idiot Act" with his friend (Perlès), his Sancho Panza. Lillian (Anaïs), conditioned at the age of six or seven to equate pain with sexual pleasure, is disappointed that Jay does not make violent love. Anaïs seeks to lay to rest the "story which had filtered out" about her relationship with Sabina (June): "They kissed once." Lillian's marriage to Larry (Hugo) is based on "changelessness." In the novel, fiction has become a form of diary revision, as the diary itself has become increasingly fictionalized, a rewriting of personal history.[86]

Swallow studies all the books, many out of print, that she sends him, and determines the organizing principle of her works, an order that is still used today: the short stories in one volume (*Under a Glass Bell*), the novelettes in one volume (*Winter of Artifice*), and the novels in one quintet (*Cities of the Interior*). Thanks to him her books will remain in print and her diaries will be published. She admires his idealism and commitment, and compares his rescue of writers (he publishes Allen Tate, Yvor Winters, and Vardis Fisher) to the work of foresters who replant trees.[87]

Anaïs thinks she has another coup when two friends found a new literary journal called *The Fair Sex* in New York. The group planning the publication, to be financed in part by a handsome, young millionaire, include Jim Herlihy and Stanley Haggart. After the failure of *Eve* and her withdrawal from *Two Cities,* Anaïs thinks she will finally fulfill her fantasy of being a roving reporter and finding the two scarce commodities a woman often seeks: an income and freedom of movement. Certainly a New York "job" makes leaving Los Angeles easier. The young hopefuls buy the stationery, business cards for each member of the staff, and champagne. They have commissioned a number of articles and written several themselves (Anaïs's piece is on the Barrons' music), when they learn that the "millionaire" is really the gardener for a Phoenix millionaire. Anaïs turns disappointment into a story about the hoax that she will later use (moving the scene to Los Angeles and making Renate the editor) in her last fictional work, *Collages.* She will delay telling Rupert of the demise of her New York "job."

In her Silver Lake home overlooking the purple hills of East Hollywood, Anaïs feels close to nature. As Thoreau's bean field was central to his experience of Walden, so the house attaches her to the earth and gives her strength. She writes to a friend that the house seems to have taken root in her: the heavy protecting beams of the roof, the large stone wall of the fireplace, the glass wall facing the "lake" with its sliding doors just a couple of yards from the swimming pool, the wood and Venetian-blue-tiled kitchen on one side, the unpartitioned living and sleeping rooms, and the small writing room in the back facing the hill and the house above (where nature is less distracting). Even the hard labor of painting and planting is relieved by the afternoon hikes on the hill looking over to Griffith Park and a swim in the cool water of the pool. Only occasionally does the West Coast family intrude (they had deliberately not built a second bedroom when Reginald was living or he would have moved in). She confides in an unpublished letter to a friend that Lloyd Wright is too demanding, and that she could not live in Los Angeles all the time because Rupert is too controlling, a characteristic she blames on the strong Pole and Wright egotism.[88] When pressure builds up, she simply flies to the other coast.

In truth, it is she who must maintain control. Inventing herself, keeping strangers at bay, and living a double life help maintain this control. Some friends notice that when Anaïs is faced with circumstances over which she has no power, she seems frightened. After a lecture several years later in Michigan, as she is being driven to the home of the host for dinner, she is suddenly frightened and asks who is in the house. Just his wife and a mutual friend, the host assures her, surprised that the woman comfortable with friends or a large audience can be so ill at ease.[89] Perhaps that is why the occasional hostess or guest at a Los Angeles party scorns her shy, quiet presence and her whispered phrases that necessitate close attention and reverence: "She made everyone feel like Irish setters at a sunrise service," says one guest at a small dinner party.[90]

Occasionally her dual life is threatened when a friend innocently gives out her telephone number (she believes that each husband thinks she refuses to have a phone to allow her to concentrate on writing). Sometimes her reasons for moving from husband to husband are compromised. Such an event occurs in the summer of 1961 when Los Angeles State College (now California State University at Los Angeles) offers her a one-year visiting position at ten thousand dollars. This offer, which comes as the result of a very successful lecture, provokes a major crisis with Rupert when she turns it down. He cannot understand why this offer would not make her happy, since she could cut back on travel and stay in Los Angeles. She insists that her two "jobs" in New York are especially vital at a time when Swallow is coming out with its first Nin book and Vogue has just published one of her stories. She hurriedly writes to a friend who will be visiting Los Angeles after Anaïs has left for New York—the letter is pointedly on Fair Sex stationery—asking her to assure Rupert that her two jobs for literary publications are more important for her as a writer. Give him the personal assurance that he needs, she begs her friend. She also hints at another element in her decision: her fear of teaching, perhaps both for its demands of performance and because of her insecurity about her academic credentials.[91] She declines this job offer despite the fact that she has confided in two friends that Rupert is drowning in debt with his new house and on his teacher's salary.[92]

The 1 August issue of Vogue includes one of the several stories and character sketches on which she is always working. She cannot stop being what she has been since the age of eleven. Though she writes very little in a current "diary," she is retyping her earlier diary and writing stories. Vogue publishes "The Seal Friends"—her preference for titles was "Old Man and the Seals" or "Death of a Seal"—which with minor revisions will appear as a chapter about Renate in Collages. Her friend Renate had told her the story about a Malibu character named Cappy (Captain), who likes to sleep on the rocks near the seals. Anaïs is pleased that this is one of the first stories she has written about the West, particularly local spots like Will Rogers Beach in Pacific Palisades and Malibu.[93]

Seduction of the Minotaur, her first book from Swallow Press and her fourth book from Peter Owen of London, appears this summer with few, but

generally respectful, reviews. The *Times Literary Supplement* says she understands the human need for "wholeness and integration," *The Spectator*
speaks about her surrealism, *Time and Tide* invokes the immature expatriate
characters of Fitzgerald's *Tender Is the Night,* and Malcolm Bradbury
(*Punch*) compares her "feminine sensitivity" to Gertrude Stein and Virginia
Woolf and her setting to D. H. Lawrence's use of Mexico. The negative
notices mention dreamy atmosphere, self-consciousness (and intelligence),
and baffling flashbacks.[94] Though the critical tide is beginning to turn, she
does not perceive a change because she hoped for more reviews. She blames
what she thinks is a silent response on the problems of a small press,
claiming unjustly that Swallow books are only reviewed in college magazines.
She is also inevitably caught up in the American confusion of celebrity with
critical acceptance.

Unaware that the Swallow books will gradually attract greater critical
attention during the coming years and aware that it will be years before she
can safely publish her diaries (she gives Swallow the option for that when
the time comes), she turns to writing more objective short pieces of fiction
about others. This turning outward is indeed a sign of inner health, but her
writing suffers. And it does not seem to make her less vulnerable. The
awareness of her lack of resources, which had surfaced when the teaching
offer came, is reinforced when she is invited to the home of Jack Hirschman,
a friend who is teaching at UCLA. There she joins a typical 1960s academic
gathering of long-haired graduate students practicing formal academic criticism while squatting on the floor smoking various weeds. She feels out of
place with her personal knowledge of Artaud and her preference for his
confessional suffering; she silently blames the students for focusing only on
his madness and drug taking. She is not asked to share her personal knowledge of the man she calls her "would-be lover."[95] When Hirschman begins
assembling the texts for *The Artaud Anthology,* to be published in 1965 by
City Lights, he credits her influence.

Hirschman, a tall poet who now lives across from the City Lights Bookshop in San Francisco, does not remember sensing her unease at the Artaud
evening. He admires her (he remembers making an unsuccessful pass at her
when they met in New York in the 1950s and seeing her a decade later in a
bathing suit on Will Rogers Beach); and he admires her work (his doctoral
dissertation is on Djuna Barnes). They also share an interest in Haitian
literature. It is he, in fact, who will feel rejected about six years later when
he loses his job at UCLA for taking drugs and she drops him. But before
this they meet socially with the Barrons (now living in Los Angeles), and
Hirschman's wife, Ruth, interviews Anaïs for the radio station where she
works.[96]

## Naive Journey to Filmland

That Anaïs Nin is tempted by the Hollywood beast of celebrity and fame reveals itself in her efforts to get a film made of *A Spy in the House of Love,* the novel based on her life in New York City during the 1940s. The germ of the idea for a film may be found as early as 1957 or 1958, when William Kozlenko, a writer at MGM, expressed interest in a scenario for a film of the novel. In 1961 he introduces her to Tracy Roberts, a young film actress who resembles the youthful Anaïs. Tracy, Kozlenko, and Norman Corwin have just formed the Professional Theatre Center and think that *Spy* can be developed. Roberts is petite, dark, and has delicate features; she seems to glow inwardly when she acts, probably reminding Anaïs of Luise Rainer. Anaïs thinks she embodies elements of all her characters, Djuna, Lillian, Stella, and Sabina. Suddenly Anaïs is spending a considerable amount of her time mothering Roberts and helping her seek a script and producer. In long confessional telephone calls, the two women talk about a script and of Roberts's personal and career problems. Over a period of many months, Roberts (who wants to produce and star in the film) brings Anaïs potential scriptwriters. When film writers and studio reviewers (as do book reviewers) suggest that her characters are based on her own life, or when they moralistically judge Sabina or mention Anaïs's work in the same sentence with Gore Vidal, Anaïs reacts defensively by explaining that Sabina's story is a study of Don Juanism and the "dislocation of the personality" that makes a major contribution to woman's awareness of herself.[97]

Roberts wants to play Sabina, for both women believe that she of all Anaïs's women appeals to women. Men who talk about the character always speak of her as a vulgar nymphomaniac, but she is the character whom women write most about in their letters to her creator. Today Roberts, who owns a successful acting school in Los Angeles, has a large collage of photographs and notes, signed by Anaïs "To Tracy-Sabina," on the wall of her office. She speaks of Anaïs being one of the two major influences on her life. She remembers feeling intimidated by the seeming perfection and serenity of Anaïs, "such a delicate, spiritual creature," when she herself had not yet coordinated her own life and career.[98]

Anaïs's friend and supporter in Paris, Dr. Jean Fanchette, was more successful on her behalf. After persistent efforts with several publishers ("they started to call me Mr. Nin"), he interests André Bay of Editions Stock, who early in 1962 brings out *Ladders to Fire,* which he retitles *Les Mirroirs dans le jardin,* translated by Anne Laurel-Metzger and introduced by Bay himself.[99] He is an appropriate editor, for he is the French publisher of Katherine Mansfield, Virginia Woolf, and (later) Mary McCarthy and Kate

Millet, among other women. His introduction in her book, which will be Anaïs's introduction to the French reading public, he later explains, is also a justification of his choice. He admires her style, which is "subtly subjective, veiled by a play of mirrors and reflections which, in itself, [is] very feminine."[100]

Anaïs and Hugo go to Paris both on behalf of his film work and for her visit with her editor. They dine with the Bay family and Anne Laurel-Metzger. Bay, who intends to continue publishing Anaïs's work, considers the book "well received," with reviews in *Le Figaro* and *L'Express*. One reviewer calls her protagonist a "suffragette of love," another declares that "Nin was made to speak about women." Bay's only regret is that he does not sell many books. Anaïs has brought him one of her original childhood diaries (in French) to read, and he notices it is full of childish errors. He is interested in the diary, but chooses to read the fiction by and for itself.[101]

During her stay with Hugo at the Hôtel Crillon, they dine at the Jockey Club with some of Hugo's business associates, attend art films at Cinémathèque, and meet with agents and directors about film rights for *A Spy in the House of Love.* She meets with the filmmaker Albicocco and Marie Laforet, his wife and star of *The Girl with the Golden Eyes,* a film Anaïs saw in Los Angeles. He is a "poet of the camera," she declares to Tracy Roberts, when they speak of the possibility of Albicocco directing a film version of *Spy.* Jean Fanchette (who published volumes seven and eight of *Two Cities* the previous winter) offers his hurriedly written translation of *Spy.* They all talk seriously about making and financing the film. A novice to the film world, Anaïs is ecstatic with anticipation. As the group leaves their last dinner and Anaïs gets into the cab, Fanchette, somewhat drunk from the wine and standing with his pregnant wife, Martine, Albicocco, and Laforet, calls a final admiring farewell to her. Later she claims in her diary that he shouted (in French it was translated "screamed") that he had met her too late—"You could have been my first mistress, the mistress one never forgets." When this diary is published, Fanchette is embarrassed and denies the plausibility of such a scene.[102]

When she tells Tracy Roberts in Los Angeles that she has found funding in Paris and that Albicocco will probably want his wife in the role, Roberts fears that she has lost her film rights to the novel. Anaïs calls repeatedly to reassure her, thinking her fears are neurotic. When the film treatment arrives several months later, it is, in the words of Anaïs, "pure trash," and she feels betrayed.[103]

At the end of the year Anaïs writes to Dr. Bogner of her new confidence and assertiveness: she has convinced Roberts to drop the idea of producing, has been talking directly to many writers and producers herself, and has made Roberts raise the money for the scriptwriter's advance.[104] Other friends and acquaintances experience very aggressive behavior from her.[105] Louis Epstein, owner of Pickwick Bookstore in Los Angeles, remembers that Anaïs was "a very forward person, a very pressing person . . . [who] would demand that we keep her books in the window," making friends of one of the clerks, who then complies. The last straw comes one day when Epstein receives a large package from England, which he mistakenly signs for, even while doubting that he ordered it. Inside are fifteen copies of every Nin novel published by Peter Owen. Each clerk denies placing the order, and when Epstein writes to the publisher he is told that Miss Nin herself placed the order. "She is not our employee," he shoots back. "Where should we send the books?" When Anaïs hears from Peter Owen, she writes an angry letter from New York accusing Epstein of "restraining" the sale of her books. When she returns to Los Angeles, the calls and visits persist. Epstein insists that he owns the bookshop and places the orders. According to Epstein,

> She accused me—she has a violent temper—of everything under the sun, being unfair to her. And I just couldn't convince her that she was the one who was totally wrong, taking the liberty of ordering all those books. . . . In spite of the fact that she looks like an ethereal person, almost to be blown away, goodness, she was a hard person.[106]

Like most writers, she is competitive, occasionally spitefully competitive. Even with those she loves she can be irrational, admitting to one correspondent that the hostility and silence of American critics have taken her through various hells of neuroses.[107] When she fears that she is losing Marguerite Young's complete devotion to a favorite niece of Young's, Anaïs warns her not to trust the girl; later she accuses Young of stealing a line including the phrase "butter no parsnips" from her, until Young finds the original phrase in the Farmer's Almanac from which she borrowed it. On this occasion, as in many others, Anaïs's friends testify, she makes amends, and gives generously.

## Miller and Cancer

If she demands full loyalty, she returns it in full measure.[108] After fifteen years, Henry Miller comes back into her life. The reunion begins with a visit that Miller pays to Roger Bloom, his longtime incarcerated correspondent. They talk for hours, weep, and look at letters and photographs—including several of Anaïs, Bloom informs her. In the exchange of numerous letters, in which Bloom speaks of Henry's description of her beauty and details yet another rejection of his request for parole, Anaïs and Henry are brought together in their efforts to help Bloom, or so the published diary implies.[109] But there are more pressing reasons for this reunion.

At the American publication of *Tropic of Cancer* in 1961, Miller becomes "overnight a rich man," according to one of his recent biographers.[110] He has also become headline news by 1962 because of a series of court cases, from Brooklyn, Boston, and Chicago to Los Angeles, charging the book with obscenity (the U.S. Supreme Court will rule in his favor in June 1964). Certainly his fame can be useful to her, but her chief motivation in reentering his life stems from the fact that he has deposited his papers, including all her intimate letters to him, at the University of California at Los Angeles. To protect herself, Anaïs asks Lawrence Clark Powell, a librarian at UCLA, if she can exchange her letters from Miller for her letters to him. Henry is more than willing.

Rupert drives Anaïs due west along the route of Sunset Boulevard to the Los Angeles seaside community of Pacific Palisades. In the hills above, at 661 Las Lomas Avenue (it will be six months before Miller buys his home at 444 Ocampo Drive), the former friends and lovers meet for the first time since she and Mathiesen had stopped at Big Sur in 1947. They have an amicable and lively discussion. He is relieved at their reconciliation, and she finds him still modest, naive, and compassionate (except to his wives, she adds). A recent Miller biographer believes that Anaïs (forgetting her own refusal to leave Hugo) never forgave him for not having the courage to run away with her to Mexico in 1940.[111] Again she expresses her fears of having her letters read at UCLA, so he gives her both sides of the correspondence with all rights and royalties. This gift will more than repay the debt that he owes her. In her diary she says that Miller, who has lived his life so publicly, could not "understand my shunning publicity." But he certainly understands her fear of exposure, her need for concealment. He says during this visit that success means little: "'Success, oh Anaïs, success does not mean anything. The only thing which means anything are the few special letters one gets a year, a personal response.'"[112]

Ironically, far from "shunning publicity," she intends to publish her own diaries, and soon decides to use his letters, carefully edited (and not including her own to him), to pave the way for the diaries. Miller's *Letters to Anaïs Nin* will be published in 1965.[113] She then asks for all her letters back from Bloom.[114]

Because she is not quite reconciled with Miller, Anaïs does not attend a party to which Renate has invited him. Attending the party for the unveiling of one of Renate's paintings is Christian Larson, one of the group of artists (including Renate and Paul Mathiesen) who spends time in San Miguel de

Allende, Mexico. He had met Miller in Big Sur and knows Anaïs, whom he thinks is "all femininity and charm."[115] He will become Anaïs's official photographer the following year. Renate invites Anaïs to all her parties now and often has her young husband, Ronnie Knox, drive her to Will Rogers State Beach, near Santa Monica canyon (Rupert bodysurfs while the women talk), or to Silver Lake. One day, according to Renate, Anaïs expresses her belief that she will ultimately find acceptance: "You are young, Ronnie. You mark my words; in thirty years I will be a household word."[116] Renate believes that her friend has a "messianic" mission to give to the world and will have no peace until that is accomplished.

Renate also stages an event to unveil her painting of Anaïs that shows her wrapped in a long continuous paper tape of her diary. She is standing under an arch that seems to be floating in a lake with two fish, her sign of Pisces.[117] Both unveilings are living portrayals of the paintings themselves, which then add movement and drama, sound and light—what will be called "happenings" in the 1960s, "performance art" today. At the unveiling of the painting of Anaïs, Renate and Joan (Mrs. John) Houseman appear barefoot and dressed in white robes in front of the large draped painting that covers the wall. Anaïs appears as she does in the painting, with four-inch white bands wrapped around her body clothed in black. Rupert reads from her work. Suddenly a gunshot bursts the poetic mood, everyone screams, and stage blood appears on the white robes of the two women. They moan and, as Anaïs turns toward them, they pull bouquets of flowers from their robes. "Out of death one gives birth to beauty," Rupert reads, and the two women fall to the floor and expire in each other's arms. An enthralled audience applauds vigorously, then gapes as two large fish are carried around the room.[118]

Anaïs loves the creation of beautiful events, especially in the exposure of psychological truths. But unlike Anne Sexton, an American poet who seeks to expose her inner self through confessional poetry, Anaïs also chooses to conceal herself with veiled symbols. This choice is important, both to protect her secrets and because she believes that drama requires a certain mystery. When Oliver Evans, who has contracted to write a book-length study of her work, begins asking her questions about the autobiographical nature of her fiction, she reacts with excess. Her letter to him denies any connection between her personal life and her fiction and calls his questions a "violation." Yet in a later letter she coyly expresses surprise that he should find her mysterious, for she has "confessed indirectly so much."[119] When he becomes a college teacher nearby, they become friends, for she considers him a poet, a gourmet cook, and a friend of writers (Tennessee Williams among others) who is not tainted by the academic. Over the next three years, she will help him interpret her books and quibble over his wordings until his study is published in 1965.

The final and greatest work will be her diary, which she has learned to rewrite, condense, and edit. She claims to be after the "essence" while avoiding damage to the diary or to her loved ones. As with a plastic surgery she is planning, she will remove all wrinkles and scandal to make the diary "a monument as perfect as her face."[120] But by selecting, eliminating, and hiding she is working on a new genre that one admiring writing teacher calls the rewritten diary, "an art form in which she excels."[121] Though she tells Evans that she is on her 103d diary,[122] she is in fact no longer keeping just a formal bound diary. In what Rupert calls her "accordion folder" she keeps character sketches, such as a portrait of Marguerite Young (approaching her brilliant portrayal of Henry in the 1930s), reviews (mostly of Hugo's films), quotations from old diaries, and journals of her travels. By the mid-1960s, as she learns to make the transition from herself to others, and as she learns to edit her earlier diaries (without revealing compromising facts about her sexual life), her "current" diary dies. She later admits that she has "retired" from her own diary and is writing a "journal of others."[123]

Hugo's dwindling financial means necessitate a final move, to apartment 14B, 4 Washington Square Village, part of four enormous high-rise apartment buildings just south of Washington Square.[124] The euphemism "village" does not disguise the ugly high-rise structures. Serge Gavronsky, who attends a number of artistic gatherings there, says it looks like cheap faculty housing. But Anaïs describes the partially grassed area covering the garage between the buildings as a garden.[125] Perhaps the scrub plants looked like Japanese bonsai plants from fourteen floors up, but it is also a garden in the same way that Sabina (in Spy) calls her tenement apartment a house. Anaïs corrupts the truth to create the marvelous. For the first time she does not decorate her abode with lavish imagination. She has soft pink lights to illuminate her features, and glass screens feature Hugo's etchings. This is Hugo's apartment, but in her room she has a locked closet.[126] His copper plates hang as a group above the couch, and he makes a hole in the kitchen wall (he does most of the cooking) so that he can have a projection room for his films.[127]

On 21 February 1963, Anaïs calls Renate in desperation. "I am sixty years old!" she announces in a voice that begs for help. These two friends often give each other courage in their darker hours ("She emanated some sort of light, and when I was desperate," says Renate, "she fixed it instantly"). This time Renate comes to the rescue with the story of her cousin, who at nineteen was having an affair with the sixty-year-old Anna Magnani, the great Italian actress in Vittorio De Sica's films. When his mother found out, she demanded to know what he was "doing with that old lady." "But, Mamma," he answered, "that is no old lady, that's Anna Magnani!"[128] Anaïs laughs, cheered. She has again recently taken precautions against her aging, or at least against sagging spirits and neck wrinkles, by having her face lifted. People do not forgive a woman aging, she had written seven years earlier.[129]

Two portraits of Anaïs emerge from this period: one is private, the other public. The first reveals the informal Anaïs shopping at Hughes Market near Glendale Boulevard and Rowena Avenue in Silver Lake, dressed in long, flowing purple dresses and broad-brimmed hats. She is seen by many students from Rupert Pole's science classes at Thomas Starr King Junior High School. There are jokes around the school about the "gypsy-like" older woman he lives with, perhaps his mother.[130] The second portrait is quite different. At a writers' conference at California State University in Los Angeles, Anaïs makes a more dramatic impression. She is invited by Professor Norman Fruman, who worries about colleagues who have never heard of her. He assures them that she is "very important" (he heard that she wrote the introduction to *Tropic of Cancer*, and he has read some of her early fiction). Fearing a small crowd, he energetically rallies an audience:

> Nin showed up in a smashing outfit, the picture of sophisticated elegance, looking years and years younger than she was. . . . I introduced her in glowing terms. And then she took over. Well! What a performance! The whole audience fell in love with her, men and women alike. They were spellbound by the names she could casually drop, dazzled by her independence, the glamorous life she had led, her philosophy of life, her commitment to freedom. . . . I thought the women students were going to carry her out of the lecture room on their shoulders.[131]

While she slowly wins fans, if not readers, through personal contact, Durrell and Miller have already become well-known writers. She attends the Gotham Book Mart party with Durrell to launch the collected letters between Miller and Durrell. These New York City gatherings always remind her of her own failure to win critical acclaim, but they also allow her to make literary contacts. She draws verbal portraits of the most interesting people she meets and adds them to her numerous stories about Renate. The two friends, according to Renate, begin working on a screenplay of Renate's adventures that will absorb them for seventeen years.[132]

The commuting between husbands does not get any easier as one gets older. Bebe Barron remembers Anaïs wishing that the plane would crash so that she would not have to go through the commute again. She tells Bebe the stories that she tells Rupert and Hugo at each trip.[133] Usually the excuses involve her publications and speeches. When the first English edition (Peter Owen) of *Ladders to Fire* is published, she is encouraged that five reviews appear. But they are typically mixed and the negative comments harsh. The most amusing comment is the observation in *Punch* that her characters are "Mrs. Dalloways under mescaline." The reference to drugs anticipates her return to Los Angeles.

## Huxley, Leary, and Isherwood

The hills of Hollywood echo this summer of 1963 with news that the Mexican government has thrown out Timothy Leary, Richard Alpert, and their International Federation for Internal Freedom (an LSD colony). LSD has moved from the earlier healing experiments of Dr. Janiger, Aldous Huxley, and Betty Eisner, in Los Angeles, to Leary and Alpert's 1960–61 work at Harvard, to explode as a mass movement.[134] Anaïs meets the two Harvard experimental psychologists at one of the many parties in the home of Henry and Virginia Denison (Anaïs is studying yoga with Virginia). Alpert, who in 1967 becomes a Hindu guru, changing his name to Ram Dass, remembers falling in love with Anaïs at a Denison party attended by Rupert, the Huxleys, Gerald Herd, and a number of other people from the psychedelic scene in Los Angeles. She invites him to come the next day to swim at her house, but he does not go because of his own "life pattern" and because he knows of her relationship to Rupert. Nevertheless, the then thirty-two-year-old professor recalls being smitten:

> [A]s we talked I started to fall into her eyes and to realize that I was falling in love with this woman. When I went home with Laura Huxley, with whom I was staying, I said to Laura, "I think I'm falling in love with that woman," and she said, "You realize, of course, that she's the same age as your mother." That was so incomprehensible to me, because she was so vital, and so much, I felt, a kindred spirit chronologically as well as spiritually.[135]

Anaïs had warned Leary about taking his commune to Mexico, but he did not listen. Hallucinogenics are endemic in the arts and movie parties of Hollywood and Venice, for they seem to open what Huxley calls "the doors of perception." Anaïs and Rupert see a lot of the Denisons as well as the Barrons, now settled in Los Angeles with their baby (they arrived in time for the memorial service at Maya Deren's death). Bebe tries some LSD at the Silver Lake home and exclaims that she now understands her friend's writing. She is not the only one to say this to Anaïs, who welcomes both the increased perception as well as, initially, the psychedelic experimentation.

She also frequently meets Christopher Isherwood at these parties. Isherwood is the English novelist whose Berlin stories of the 1930s were drama-tized in *I Am a Camera,* which later became the film *Cabaret.* He has been in America since 1939 and took up Hindu religion in the 1940s. Anaïs met him in 1950 and liked his whimsy; they are nearly the same age, and she thinks he looks perpetually youthful and tanned. He is one of many emi-grants who find California life a moveable feast; he lives in the Santa Monica canyon near the beach with Donald Bachardy. Anaïs is a frequent visitor at their home in the canyon because she occasionally sits for Bachardy's draw-ings from 1962 to 1975. In 1955, when Isherwood was writing a film about the life of Buddha, he had first tried mescaline and promptly called a taxi to take him and Bachardy to church to see if God was there.[136]

Another English friend of Anaïs's whose quest is religion is Alan Watts, an Eastern mystic she met in San Francisco. He spent time with Alpert and Leary at Harvard and will write numerous books on Eastern mysticism and psychedelic drugs. He shares a ferryboat, the S.S. *Vallejo,* with Jean Varda in Sausalito. Watts is a teacher associated with the hippies of San Francisco, those barefoot youth in bell-bottomed pants and ponytails. He is also asso-ciated with the spiritual seekers near the monasteries and shamans of Big Sur and the home of the Denisons in Los Angeles.[137] When he attends Los Angeles parties during this period, he is surrounded by worshipful devotees whose silence Anaïs interprets as marijuana based. Despite her later diary observations about the failure of the drug experimenters to find their esoteric inner journeys naturally, a number of them, Isherwood, Watts, and herself, had gone through other than natural doors of perception.

Varda comes down from Sausalito with a young man in an ancient station wagon loaded with collages for an exhibition at the Burbank Art Museum several years later. They visit Silver Lake. The young man is Sid Huttner, who has been working on a film about Varda. He had met Anaïs earlier when his Documentary Film Group at the University of Chicago invited Anaïs to speak and Hugo to show his films in 1962. They now meet again at dinner parties in Silver Lake and Hollywood.[138]

She sees Huxley also, but they obviously do not communicate very well, for in her diary she reiterates her differences with him and concludes that he lacks "sensory antennae." Not knowing that he is gravely ill, she con-cludes that he gives the impression of "psychic blindness." In fact, Huxley had broken with Leary in the spring of 1962 over the growing cult of psychedelic drugs. He had once helped Leary create a psychedelic curricu-lum in 1960, when he was a lecturer at MIT and Leary and Alpert were studying the "magic mushroom" at Harvard's Center for Personality Re-search.[139] Leary was guiding sessions with Ginsberg, who was encouraging distribution of the drug to the general public. Huxley tried to dissuade them, but the movement caught fire after Leary became his own experimentee. The use of the drug would not decline until the late 1960s. Huxley's call for limiting LSD to an esoteric personal experience for the few is closer to Anaïs's belief than she knows. Huxley dies of cancer in November of 1963.

Anaïs likes Alpert, who seems to have more warmth and openness than Leary, but she notes a personality change in the tall, Irish-faced Leary, whose language becomes more free-associative. She talks to them both at parties, hears them lecture, and is critical that they do not know poetry—visionary poets like William Blake and writers, such as Michaux, who experimented with drugs. She writes an essay on substitutes for the drug (she prefers art and psychoanalysis) for a book on LSD, but the editor whom she has been helping cut her essay does not use it. Basically she is sympathetic to the new religion, though as time goes by she worries about reckless drug use. By the time the diary of this period is published in 1976, she expresses greater caution. Leary continues to look for Cosmic Answers, which by the 1990s he finds in cyberpunk and computer consciousness.[140]

She blames the pragmatism, puritanism, and materialism of America for blocking natural access to inner consciousness. The psychedelic movement, the popularity and freedom of exploring the metaphysical, the self, and mysticism are all part of a social phenomenon that changes the country. It is also creating an audience for her work.

## Collages

But the bitch goddess of commerce—or a clever agent—will be her means of sharing her esoteric vision. By the mid-1960s the plans are in high gear, first for a book of letters, exploiting her friendship with Henry Miller, next with another (and last) book of fiction, and finally with the initial publication of part of her diary. Plans for the first book begin with Miller's gift of his letters to her and the example of *Lawrence Durrell/Henry Miller: A Private Correspondence* (1963). For a couple of years she and her agent, Gunther Stuhlmann (whom she had hired in the late 1950s), diligently work to date Miller's letters to her and to edit out the private truths Anaïs wishes to protect.

She also works for many months choosing and preparing the stories she has written about other people and her own experiences over the last decade. *Collages* (1964), named after the work of the San Francisco collage-maker, Varda, whom Anaïs admires, also adapts his artistic montage technique. Except for the last story, about Judith Sand (Djuna Barnes),[141] the experiences are rewritten to be the experiences of a character named Renate, a Viennese painter who lives in Malibu. Renate Druks at first asks that her name ("use Marina instead") not be used, fearing that Peter's father will take their boy back. As publication approaches, she says, "Use my name for Peter's sake so he can read about his mommy." Varda and Nobuko Venishi, a delicate Japanese artist, also allow her to use their real names. The character of Bruce, the fictional lover of Renate, combines Paul Mathiesen and Ronnie Knox. Renate, who initially thinks that Anaïs has "glamorized" her character, now believes she "grasped the essence of my character, distilled it like perfume, and gave it to the world."[142]

The protagonists of her novels have been undergoing a continuous metamorphosis during several decades. Now Renate (*Collages*) is the woman that Lillian (*Seduction of the Minotaur*) was becoming. Anaïs's fictional self, like that of her friend Renate Druks, is a woman who knows herself and cares for others, the feminine ideal that combines both creativity and compassion—the paradox Anaïs has struggled with all her life. Through all the novels the female characters overlap and interrelate, says one of her friends, who compares the continuous novels to Julio Cortazar's *Hopscotch,* but the apotheosis is "Renate," who combines male creativity and female compassion. Anaïs and the real Renate are sometimes interchangeable; Renate points out that they give each other their own characteristics: In *Collages,* she makes Renate's eyes green when they are blue and Renate paints Anaïs with blue eyes, when they are really light green. "We mixed each other up, like a mirror image."[143] Each mythologizes the other.

When the manuscript is typed, Anaïs sends it to Daisy Aldan for her opinion. Thinking she wants a response, Daisy scribbles all over it, suggesting cuts and corrections ("This is psychology and analysis, not literature," she notes in a couple of places). But Anaïs sees betrayal, not generous assistance: "You are like all the rest," she tells Daisy, accusing her of treason. "I would be the last to betray you," says Daisy. "To hurt you would be to hurt myself." Daisy understands her friend's "need to be adored" and her "vanity, which was really insecurity." Anaïs softens, embraces her friend, and says, "Let's begin again." When Daisy receives her first copy of *Collages,* she notes that all her suggested changes have been incorporated.[144]

A similar incident had occurred a few years before when Daisy and a friend from ABC made a documentary interview (the first documentary film of Anaïs) that "horrified" Anaïs, who was unaccustomed to seeing herself under harsh lights. She was "terribly upset"; as in Maya Deren's film, she believed she was made to look bad. "It isn't that I am vain; I want it to be beautiful, for I want to leave what is beautiful." Her friend offers to destroy the film, but Anaïs reluctantly keeps it, then returns it, then asks it be returned when she cannot sleep. Finally, when Daisy realizes Anaïs is keeping the film, she asks for a pair of scissors and begins cutting it up, to the horror of an incredulous Anaïs. "Murderer. . . . How could you do such a thing." Daisy responds, "This is a gesture of my friendship."[145]

Anaïs may have integrated the artist and the woman, but she has not overcome her need for approval and her fear of betrayal. She demands full loyalty and gives it in return. After Marguerite Young's novel is published the following year, Anaïs buys up all the remaindered copies. During a lecture trip to Southern Illinois University, in Carbondale, where some of her papers will eventually reside, Professor Harry T. Moore (who had written on D. H. Lawrence and commissioned Oliver Evans to write the book on Nin for *Crosscurrents in Literature*) introduces her to the bibliophile's world of biography, history, and bibliography. He shows her the newly purchased Caresse Crosby papers. Standing before the glass cases, Anaïs is chilled by the public display of personal letters and wonders if she herself will one day be served under glass. Yet she is preparing to publish Henry's letters and wants to sell SIU her own diaries (she also tries to sell them to Northwestern, with the proviso that they be sealed until Hugo's death). What is probably bothering her the most is this confrontation with personal and public history and the possible revelations ("lies") by scholars and biographers. She realizes again that there is an "abyss" between the analytical academic world and her own "intimate knowledge of a character."[146] Soon she realizes that her diaries are her chief and only capital, and she cuts short any talk of selling them.

If the possible placement of her papers in scholarly archives leaves her with mixed feelings, her involvement with the motion-picture industry does not. She has been bitten by the film bug. She continues her work with Renate on a film treatment of *Collages* and pursues a script and producer for *Spy*. During an evening of music by a string quartet at Lloyd Wright's house (Rupert on the viola, Elmer Tolsted, a mathematics professor from Cal Tech, on the cello), she sits upstairs with Eva Wasserman, story analyst for Twentieth Century Fox. Though Wasserman likes her instantly ("She never got out of the theatricality of life") and had read *Under a Glass Bell* years before, she does not think that *Spy* is translatable to film. She struggles diplomatically not to discourage Anaïs, but does not say what she thinks, which is that the book is "not cinematic."[147]

Anaïs does interest Robert Wise, who tells her that he always wanted to make and finance an art film. Because they both admire Marguerite Duras, Anaïs contacts the novelist through her agent in Paris. Duras is interested and willing to meet Wise in Salzburg where he is filming *The Sound of Music*. But when her publisher sends Duras *Ladders* instead of *Spy*, Anaïs decides to meet Duras in Paris to explain. She is eager to put Sabina in the hands of this accomplished novelist. She and Wise go together to Salzburg with filmmaker Jerry Bick, who had introduced her to Wise. She likes the short and plain Duras, and when they return to Paris they meet at the Deux Magots (Anaïs once again staying at the nearby Hôtel d'Angleterre, around the corner from Duras's apartment). But her high hopes are dashed weeks later when an "unrecognizable" story script arrives from Duras, and Wise rejects it. Later Duras will say that she did not understand what Anaïs was talking about. When Anaïs can see the humor in the situation she admits that her own "misty writing" and Duras's "oblique style" had inevitably "produce[d] pure fog."[148]

It is a heady trip for Anaïs, who believes that she is now at last becoming recognized as a writer in France. She meets reporters and nervously sits for television and press interviews upon the publication of Stock's French edition of *Spy*. She also works on proofs of the French translation of *House of Incest*. Though she does not see Durrell, she writes to apologize for the unapproved use of one of his quotations on the cover of *Spy*, which was taken out of her diary and out of context (he was talking about "Birth").[149] She knows that he will forgive her and not give away the deception. Besides, she is excited by the press reception and the heady talk about working with Jerry Bick, who will spend several years on the *Spy* project. She accompanies Bick to visit André Malraux (Bick wants to film *La Condition Humaine*) and serves as translator. Malraux, then France's Minister of Culture, looks like a "comfortable bourgeois with thyroid eyes," she notes, not the lean antifascist speaker that she and Gonzalo heard in Paris during the Spanish war.[150]

She also meets with Paule Thevenin, who is editing Artaud's works for the French publisher Gallimard. In an April letter, Anaïs had requested the meeting, explaining that she and Artaud had been good friends and that he had intended to dedicate *Héliogabale* to her. She brings her diary profile and Artaud's letters with her, wondering if the letters and her profile can be published in France without causing any problems with his family. Her only request is that the name of Hugh Guiler be suppressed as well as any reference to physical love. Mme Thevenin (who claims to have been Artaud's only female lover) and the editor of *Tel Quel* with whom Anaïs makes contact see nothing compromising in the letters, and they realize that Anaïs is not aware that Artaud, while abhorring all physical contact, had often written to virtual strangers about intimate subjects such as the taste of a woman's mouth. When Anaïs's first diary is published, Thevenin will charge her with perpetuating "lies" and unfairly call into question the entire friendship between Artaud and Nin.[151]

After twenty April and May days in Paris, she spends months in California on several public speeches and in revising two and a half years of her diary for publication. Anaïs appears for one day of the Pacific Writers' Conference, which also features, on separate days, Christopher Isherwood, Ray Bradbury, Rod Serling, and Venice's Lawrence Lipton. At the conference, held at California State University at Los Angeles, she repeats her stories of Artaud and other friends to an appreciative audience. As she had told Thevenin, she is indeed responsible for helping to introduce Artaud to an American audience. Among the publishers at the conference, at her instigation, is Alan Swallow, who is on crutches and (unknown to Anaïs) terminally ill. With admiration she hears him speak of the publishing business without once mentioning dollars.[152]

## Fear of Radiation: Preparing the Diary

She tells Frances Steloff in May of 1964 that she is on the brink of being published by a big publisher and "discovered."[153] By fall she has one thousand pages of edited text, and she begins the long process of writing to everyone for permission to include their portraits (people object to details, but never the "essence," she claims on numerous occasions). Alan Swallow (the task is too big for him) talks to Hiram Haydn of Harcourt, Brace and World, who agrees to publish what they will call *The Diary of Anaïs Nin, Volume One (1931–1934)*. André Bay (her editor at Stock) is also reading the manuscript in Paris. It will begin with a description of Louveciennes and her meeting Miller at the end of 1931.[154] It is a useful publishing strategy to begin the series with the thirtieth volume of her written diary, depicting the most interesting and notable period of her life (*Annus Milleris,* as one critic called it).

Hugh Guiler will not appear in her published diary (she always insists that it was his decision), so it will appear that she was not married while living in Paris. Explicit sex is also excised. Her cousin Eduardo will disappear, and so do most references to her family. The narrator-diarist will truly appear alone, which is a long tradition of autobiographical narrative. "It is almost a measure of an autobiographical narrative's ambition," says Susan Sontag: "the narrator must be, or be recast as, alone, a solitary, certainly without a spouse, even when there is one; the life must be unpeopled at the center."[155] Thus, Anaïs has to place different people in a few important scenes and transplant some dialogue into other's mouths. This is indeed a fictionalized, some will say deceptive, autobiography in diary form.

For the next year she will edit and cut to less than half the size the text of several leather-bound volumes of her journals (and the editor will take out her preface to Miller's *Cancer,* which she had wanted to include). Miller makes suggestions. Her agent becomes her editor, sometimes reducing her to tears by his changes. When the volume eventually appears, her agent's introduction acknowledges "retrospective entries" and deletions and notes that "Miss Nin's truth, as we have seen, is psychological."[156]

In the meantime, two books appear this year: Swallow's reissue of her D. H. Lawrence book, and the British (Peter Owen) and U.S. (Swallow) first editions of *Collages*. Among her publications, *Collages* is one of her slightest books, yet it attracts fewer vitriolic reviews than usual. In part this reception is an indication of the gradual, if not grudging, acceptance of her work by literary critics.[157] As her last book of fiction, *Collages* forms a curious book-end with *House of Incest*, which is surrealistic and inward in contrast to *Collages*'s more realistic technique. She says it is her only book with humor. The use of fictional as well as real names of people confuses some reviewers, who assume Renate is fictional and Varda real. Leo Lerman calls it "tangential" and "refracted through prisms of gorgeous emotional (but superbly controlled) light." William Goyen, another friend, in the *New York Times* accurately describes it as a "chain of descriptive portraits revolving around Renate."[158] During 1964 and 1965 there are five British and six American reviews, hardly constituting critical acclaim; but she is included in a long entry in a French book on contemporary American writers, by Pierre Brodin, a friend whose book she in turn reviews.[159]

A review of *Collages* in the *Los Angeles Free Press* brings her a new friend, one of the first of many young women who will put her into a leadership role in the growing feminist movement. Deena Metzger, a novelist with long dark hair and lovely eyes, had seen Anaïs once, writing in the background as Rupert's musical quartet played at the Weiss house, then read Anaïs's novels with admiration. When *Collages* arrives at the underground newspaper, she is prepared to review it. She will continue to review Anaïs, whom she calls "one of the mothers of the internal life," and begin a diary of her own.[160]

While in New York again this winter nursing Hugo, who is facing a probable prostate operation, Anaïs receives a "long cry of pain" from Renate. The voice on the phone is hysterical. She has returned to the house in Malibu to find that Peter, now a twenty-one-year-old UCLA student, has taken an overdose of drugs and is dead. She is inconsolable. She, Anaïs, and their friends agonize about missing possible signals of drug addiction. They all adored Peter, and he was like a son to Anaïs, who had used his drawings in her books. Ronnie Knox stays close to Renate during the tragic aftermath of Peter's death, but the marriage will not survive. Ultimately she sells the house in Malibu, but not the land. Ronnie, who also takes Peter's death very hard, begins a nomadic life as a street poet. Every few years the *Los Angeles Times* will run a lengthy article on "whatever happened to" the golden boy of California football.[161]

Anaïs is going through her own personal crisis as the publication of her diary approaches. It is a crisis accompanied by nightmares of opening her front door and being struck with a mortal dose of atomic radiation. Fear of killing attacks against her diary are deep-seated. Some of the publishers' rejections (before Hiram Haydn of Harcourt, Brace took the book) make her realize how much more personal the diary is than the fiction, which has been treated so maliciously. Then there is family guilt: her guilt about her sexual experience (she soon justifies leaving this out in the name of mystery) and about Joaquin's challenge to some of her memories (their father also enhanced stories, he observed sternly). She has nightmares about shocking her long-deceased mother. She fears hurting her family—that old struggle "between the woman and the creator," between guilt and self-expression.[162]

Like the Catholic going to confession, she begs Dr. Bogner for absolution. How can she open herself up to the cruelty of the world? How can she willfully face rejection as she had unwillingly faced it as a child? They struggle through each nightmare, each problem, each ethical issue. The tide turns on several issues, two of which she articulates in her letters to Bogner: she is tired of secrecy, and the diaries are her best work. The problem with the first justification is that she will keep the deepest secrets out of the diary; the diary is a confessional genre, and she has a need but lacks the courage to confess fully. Unspoken is her great need for acceptance and love. She will take the risk, but hedge her bets with expurgations. Suddenly she has a great urgency to get the diary published before she dies, a prophetic urgency because she does not as yet know that she is seriously ill.

Each step toward that "radiation" exposure makes her clutch even more at her secrets. When Oliver Evans sends questions with each chapter he is writing about her fiction, she believes he is getting too close. The more he questions, the more she insists that the diary and the fiction are distinctly different. She is upset when he uses the word "lesbian," which is "not necessarily" what she meant. She tells him that she wrote "unconsciously" and all the "coincidences of images" were merely accidental.[163] Uneasy at the close examination of herself, she informs him that she does not like his traditional and rational approach. Finally she stops reading his chapters.

The publication of Miller's *Letters to Anaïs Nin*, intended to popularize her name and prepare the way for the diary, brings up even more issues. Close readers immediately perceive deletions other than her entire side of the correspondence. Expurgated are all references to their affair, anything uncomplimentary, any references that would compromise her family or their friends, and the name of the middleman who bought the erotica.[164] Thus, with publicity come the inevitable personal questions: What was the nature of her relationship with Miller? How much did he influence her? Where are her letters to him? She tells one interviewer she was too young then and her letters are "like listening"; she could not compare to him.[165] In other interviews she is afraid to give him too much credit, though he was her first supporter.

Miller himself had indeed asked for minor changes, though he does not share her great fear of exposure. She always forbade him to mention their affair, as she earlier threatened Fred Perlès when he was writing *My Friend Henry Miller*. Perlès split her character in two and transposed all her sexual and adventuresome actions onto a fictitious woman named Liane de Champsaur,[166] a name worthy of a French courtesan. Unaware of this secrecy, Georges Belmont, Miller's old friend in Paris, writes a long article on Miller, mentioning all of his women, but stopping short of mentioning Anaïs. To this day Belmont does not know why he left her name out. Upon reading the essay, Miller writes from Pacific Palisades to commend him on his handling of his friends and wives. "The one I never married and who was the best as well as the strongest (but never losing her femininity) you omitted to mention (thank god!)."[167]

The crisis of public scrutiny threatens the "protective cave" of her journal in which she has hidden (while giving the impression of revealing confession). This 1965 period, until the spring of 1966, is marked by great ambivalence. Though she claims that after years of analysis, she has put to rest her anxiety and is now relaxed, she continues to fly between the two coasts, with all the excuses, lies, and tensions this entails. She tells one young friend, who has discovered with enthusiasm that Anaïs has a husband on both coasts, that the fact has caused her a lot of pain.[168] While awaiting her own debut, she helps two of her best friends celebrate their publications: James Herlihy publishes *Midnight Cowboy*, which will be his most famous novel, and Marguerite Young publishes *Miss MacIntosh, My Darling*, the thousand-page novel on which she has worked for seventeen years.[169] Anaïs sends in her own manuscript and begins collecting photographs and permissions. Suddenly she falls ill and is immediately hospitalized in October.

On 4 November 1965 she undergoes surgery to remove her uterus at Doctors' Hospital in New York. In the haze of painkilling medicine, she dreams of flying away with Rupert to Japan.[170] After consulting her West Coast doctors when she returns to Los Angeles, she is suddenly hospitalized for a second operation early in 1966.[171] They do not tell her she has cancer. The proofs of her diary are brought to her in the hospital in order to meet the 20 April publication date. From her hospital bed she writes to tell Ruth Witt-Diamant that the diary almost comes out "too late."[172]

# CHAPTER TWELVE

## 1966–1977

# Dancing Toward Daylight

"[A]bout America and your literary problems[:] . . . You will be accepted all right, and royally, when your magnum opus appears. That is the Diary."
—*Henry Miller, 1941*[1]

$F$AME comes to Anaïs at last at the age of sixty-three—the flashbulbs and love letters, television interviews and lectures, honors. The acolytes assemble for what will be a decade of celebration. Is the war really over? she asks. "Has the sniping really stopped? I feel like a soldier on the front, amazed by the silence of the [critical] guns." She listens again and hears the sound of "opening doors."[2] April, May, and June of 1966, she says, have wiped out a lifetime of disappointment and rejection. After longing for love, it comes like "an avalanche!" The little girl who had given birth to "Anaïs Nin" when she began her diary on board the *Montserrat* in 1914, now exclaims that she has been reborn: "I am like a new woman, born with the publication of the diary."[3]

During the twelve months after the publication of Volume One (1931–34), at least thirty-six reviews appear, representing most of the major periodicals, many times more than those responding to any of her novels. None give her the merciless trashing that on occasion she had previously received. She attributes her success to "younger and more penetrating critics."[4] The reception is generally positive and, in a few instances, superlative. Robert Kirsch, who will review each diary for the *Los Angeles Times,* calls her the "best-known diarist since Pepys."[5] A majority of the reviewers are attracted by the Paris art scene of the 1930s and the famous names of Miller, Rank, and Artaud; others focus on what they call Nin's female sensibility, wounded romanticism, abandoned-child, search-for-father themes. Occasionally the charge of "narcissistic self-indulgence" resurfaces, of course, but most praise her frankness and honesty.[6] Initially, only a few reviewers complain about what she has hidden, about the missing narration of her sexual experiences, or the silliness of leaving out her husband. Privately she defends the decision as Hugo's and acknowledges to Caresse Crosby that Hugo is "the very heart of [the *Diary*], the source of it all."[7]

Leon Edel, in a perceptive review entitled "Life Without Father," focuses on Anaïs's diary keeping as "a way of giving herself concrete proof of her own existence." It is self-absorption, he says, but "in the process it becomes also an act of self-revelation—in spite of all that it attempts to conceal." Edel, the master biographer of the master novelist (Henry James), appears to be the first to understand that the "diary also became, as it were, her father" for "an earnest, papa-pleasing little girl." Yet he judges her artistry too harshly when he concludes that the diary is a "document" rather then "an act of creation" and that Nin is "an annotator rather than a creator." He also seems a bit put off by her *petite fille littéraire* persona, when he calls her "meticulous in thought and dainty in word," with a "child-like, lotus-flower essence."[8] Her friends take up the cause of refuting his questioning of her artistry. For a long time after his review appears, he receives, anonymously, pasteups of clippings about Anaïs, as if to say, "See how you got her all wrong?" He thinks that perhaps they come from her loyal friend Marguerite Young, whom he has met on occasion in the Village.[9] Even in a review that takes her work seriously, Anaïs is personally hurt by the slightest criticism. But the wounds are no longer lethal.[10]

Not all the guns are silent; nor do all her friends join the celebration. Those who knew her in the 1930s know that she disguised her vulnerability. Her first published diary presents a strong woman, just as the earliest diary presents the good girl. The few who have read the original diary know that this published volume is a partially rewritten record of only a portion of the diary. Both Miller and Durrell refuse to write a review for the *New York Times* (though Miller writes a general essay about her for the *Village Voice*).[11] When she hears about their refusal, she understands Henry's position, for he is too close to the material, but she writes to beg Durrell to mend whatever breach has occurred. He denies any breach. When he privately criticizes her omissions, she asserts that she cannot provide bedroom scenes.[12] Maxwell Geismar is also silent, and when she inquires why, he tells her she has been praised quite enough. June Miller tells Daisy Aldan that there was no sexual relationship with Anaïs. To others June complains bitterly that she will never forgive Anaïs for being unfair and inaccurate.[13]

When Jean-Paul Sartre reads the French translation the following year, he charges her with elaborating on the diary by incorporating recent portrayals and with extending "the cult of Artaud . . . in order to satisfy the ambition of the journal: to uncover the myth under the flesh of Artaud."[14] His review reflects the opinion of Mme Thevenin, Artaud's editor, who had met the playwright after the war. American specialists on Artaud, in contrast, believe Anaïs's account. Bettina Knapp, an academic who at the time is working on a critical study of Artaud, seeks out Anaïs in Greenwich Village to learn more about her experience with the Frenchman. Though busy with her book promotion and wary of academics, Anaïs agrees to a fifteen-minute meeting. Their first encounter lasts four hours and leads to a lengthy friendship. Professor Knapp is impressed with what Anaïs knows and understands about Artaud and has no doubts about the validity of the diary account.[15]

Drowning out the critical notes is a wave of personal letters and public applause. The letters are largely from young people who embrace Nin as a pioneer feminist artist. Ironically, this embrace comes from the country she has long called "gangsterland" in "the hoodlum age." After accusing America of ignoring the sensitive artist by catering to "realism" and tough-guy fiction, she is now becoming one of its cult figures. The freedom and self-expression movements of the 1960s and the boom in psychology have prepared the soil for her diary, as has the growing feminist movement. As Anaïs presents it, hers is the story of hard-won success fighting illness, abuse, and male ego. Suddenly her gift of a typewriter to Henry Miller becomes for her young readers symbolic of a life of self-sacrifice. Through it all she persists in being an artist, and now she has won the good fight. Her confessions are "breaking the silence" for young artistic women. Her audiences swell, the invitations from universities pour in. Soon she is reading at antiwar poetry readings and working for Eugene McCarthy—activities encouraged both by her youthful audience and by the political interests of Rupert Pole.

She is in Berkeley in the autumn of 1966 awaiting a book signing at Cody's Bookstore. Lawrence Ferlinghetti and several friends are in the Berkeley Rose Garden on the hill, having a "beautiful acid trip" and enjoying the psychedelic colors of the sunset. Ferlinghetti collects yellow rose petals in a large brown paper bag before they move on to Cody's. Walking up behind Anaïs as she is seated in the center of the crowd, Ferlinghetti studies her gold-lamé gown, noting that he has the correct color. He lifts the brown bag and pours all of the petals over her beautifully coiffed head, and they fall on her shoulders and the floor. "She seemed pleased, not a bit upset, and continued signing books."[16]

Before the appearance of the first diary volume, Anaïs and Gunther Stuhlmann, her editor-agent, begin preparing Volume Two (1934–39), which appears in 1967. Others follow as swiftly as possible in 1969, 1971, 1974, and 1976—this last completed as Anaïs is dying. (Rupert will put together the seventh volume after her death.) Generally speaking, both the number of pages in each of the first five diary volumes and the number of reviews for each decrease as the years go by.[17] Yet her followers increase, judging by the size of her mail and her audiences. By the time of the publication of the second diary, she tells one friend that the fanfare of reviews is shallow, for (as Miller earlier noted) personal letters have the most value.

Volume One, like all volumes of the *Diary*, is introduced by Stuhlmann, who is listed as her editor. He sets up the diary for popular success and invites an autobiographical reading, though he acknowledges that cutting and rearranging has been made for privacy and legal reasons and because of the bulk of the manuscript. The "details of the editing are skimmed over," asserts Wendy DuBow, who has studied the marketing and reception of this first volume. The introduction "sets up an unmistakable atmosphere of commercial propaganda," she adds. The extent of Stuhlmann's revision and editing is indicated by the presence of his name on the title page and cover of each diary.[18]

A great deal of time during the last decade of Anaïs Nin's life is given to the preparation of the diaries for publication, writing to get permissions (Rebecca West says no, Robert Duncan asks for changes, and Lesley Blanch calls her lawyer and agent to stop her portrait), and keeping up with her voluminous fan mail. Actually "fan" is a superficial word to designate the intensely personal and involved letters Anaïs receives in response to her diaries. These connections with others often develop into sustained friendships. They compensate for her occasional doubt or regret about her public exposure. She warns Harold Norse to consider the cost of publishing his diary.[19] She also struggles to resist bearing guilt for charges of egotism or narcissism, for she believes that she is constructing an individual creative world, as every artist must do.[20] By studying the individual psyche, she believes, one can know the world, and one should not "confuse the 'I' of Proust with narcissism"—it is the "'eye' of the microscope," truer and more honest than History.[21]

Alan Swallow dies Thanksgiving Day 1966, and she says farewell by flying to New York for a memorial service. The service is attended by his East Coast authors and friends—a rare event for a small western publisher. She comes to pay tribute to the man who has rescued her fiction and, with Harcourt, Brace and World, is publishing the first two volumes of her diary.[22] She speaks in a dark and dingy basement room of the Parish Hall of St. Mark's Church to a genuinely grieving audience (Swallow was only fifty-one). To one young man in the back row, who has reviewed books published by Swallow, she seems "unapproachable." William Claire does introduce himself after the service and speaks of his plans for a literary journal and a book about western publishing and Swallow (*Publishing in the West*). She expresses interest, and will indeed become involved in both of Claire's efforts. Today Claire remembers her as "ethereal" and "very proper," even "nun-like" and "dressed gorgeously. . . . Because my mother was French and had certain mannerisms, I told her she reminded me of my mother. This was a mistake, for she was offended."[23]

During the next few years she also takes time for travel, more often with Rupert than Hugo, and usually on a Club Méditerranée–guided tour. She has the money to visit Japan and the Orient in 1966, Tahiti in 1967, Mexico in 1968, Morocco and Greece in 1969 (she and Rupert run into Judith Malina and Julian Beck in Marrakech), and later that year she spends a week in Germany at the Frankfurt Book Fair, followed by four days in Paris for the promotion of the German and French translations of the *Diary*. Her disparaging remarks about Greece upset Durrell, Miller, Crosby, and Betty Ryan—all lovers of that country.[24] Greece and Turkey (she spends a couple days in Izmir) pale in comparison to Cambodia, Mexico, Japan, and Morocco. To her unhistoric eye (she only finds out later that Izmir had once been called Smyrna, where her beloved Varda had been born), the history of Greece and Turkey do not translate into the present. She prefers the exotic. Travel sustains one's romanticism and powers of illusions, she observes. Yet she realizes that she cannot embrace the passivity of Eastern religions, which threaten the creative will.[25]

## Japan and California

Her trip to Japan is the beginning of a love affair with that civilization's symbolism, sense of order, and delicate beauty, which she contrasts to American technology and warmongering in Vietnam.[26] She keeps a full diary of her experiences in Japan, frequently evoking LSD dreams when other metaphors fail her. She is charmed by the delicate women, traditionally dressed with hair pulled up (in a style she herself has begun to wear), and with small closed-mouth smiles and bowed heads. Afterward, the number of her friendships with Japanese women living in Los Angeles increases. For three of them she serves in 1966–67 as friend and counselor, a role she continues to play until the end of her life. Nobuko (caught in a "rigid marriage"), Mako Francis (mistakenly thinking she will find liberation in marriage to an American man), and Kazuko Sugisaki (a graduate student in literature) all ask Anaïs to tell them how she has become "free."[27] Kazuko comes to the Silver Lake house to dance, capturing the attention of Rupert and the admiration of Anaïs. Kazuko will eventually translate *Collages* and other works by Anaïs and will move into the house after Anaïs's death. Ironically, while Anaïs helps these women find their own freedom (she comes to believe that the Japanese are very repressed), she asks her friend Ruth Witt-Diamant, who is now living in Japan, to find a Japanese girl to care for Hugo. If it works out, she will encourage her to marry Hugo, for he deserves a good woman.[28] Her love for Japan eventually will become only aesthetic, for she concludes that they have no esteem for the self and little capacity for shared feelings.[29]

The fascination with Japan is just one example of her shift toward the Pacific. These become her "California Years" for several other reasons, including the New Age reception among her readers. "Until 1966, I was her closest friend in Los Angeles," says Renate Druks. "We were equals, sisters; after the first diary came out things changed and I did not see her as much. The next generation were disciples; she was their guru."[30]

Daisy Aldan notices a division among Anaïs's New York friends. Her older, usually academic, friends in the East include Anna Balakian (Professor of French and Comparative Literature at New York University and author of books on André Breton), Nona Balakian (Anna's sister), Marguerite Young, and Aldan. These friends will be the ones disappointed when Anaïs's erotica appears a decade later, for the mature and gracious woman they know seems threatened (Aldan uses the word "murdered") by the younger woman who would commit incest and write pornography. They also believe that Anaïs would not have wanted the erotic and unexpurgated writings published. (The other group of followers, says Aldan, are the youthful magic circle, a "new audience, into the explicit.")[31] The first group of friends had arranged the most important move in the wide reviewing of Volume One. Nona Balakian, a critic for the *New York Times Book Review,* read the diary manuscript ahead of time and encouraged her editor to have it reviewed. When the publication date arrived, Aldan visited Balakian, who spoke again to the editor, who placed the review on the front page. The review is positive and praises the portraits of her friends as being like characters in a novel.[32] An early review in the *Times,* as any author knows, can tilt the reception of a book.

She meets some new friends through their reviews of her diaries and her lecture appearances. In keeping with her habit of responding to all reviews (with gratitude or the reverse), she finds several friends among those who review her diaries with understanding. Chief among these is Deena Metzger, the reviewer for the *Free Press,* who had gone with Anaïs when she visited Miller to get back some of her letters. Metzger, who now practices psychotherapy on a hill above Topanga Canyon, is an initial founder of the *Free Press* and covers each diary as it is published. The *Free Press,* published by

Art Kunkin in a basement below The Fifth Estate coffee house on Sunset Boulevard near Crescent Heights, is the vanguard of the free speech and peace movements. In addition to lucid news and commentary, it reviews the avant-garde and, on a good day, has a circulation of one hundred thousand.[33]

Her network of friends on the academic lecture circuit is represented by the historian Robert Haas of the UCLA Extension program (invitations do not come from English Departments, the last critical holdout). Except for a brief falling out, when Haas naively and inconspicuously introduces Rupert as Anaïs's husband ("It was my innocence alone that upset her"), they remain friends.[34] Briefly, in 1968–69, she believes that he will help her become Artist in Residence at UCLA.[35]

Metzger, who calls the first diary volume a "great book," later spends months helping Anaïs edit a volume of essays on writing entitled *The Novel of the Future*. It appears between publication of the second and third diary volumes, the same year that Oliver Evans publishes the first book-length study of her work, entitled *Anaïs Nin*.[36] When the book of essays is published in September of 1968, according to Anaïs, 350 people attend the book-signing party at the Gotham Book Mart. Metzger becomes aware of the dual impression that Anaïs makes, both in person and in the diary, of promising so much openness and yet remaining guarded and private. And she notices the change in Anaïs: the demands of the public world and what Anaïs calls (with her unique pronunciation) the "psychophants" take her away from serious creative engagement. Yet she needs and deserves the acclaim, adds Metzger.[37]

Her best relationship is with "the young," she writes Ronnie Knox, who has asked if he can write something about her. And California, she adds, is ideal for a writer. She informs another friend that she is treated like the Beatles when she lectures. She loves the light shows, love-ins, and sit-ins of the youth, and the way they dress in tie-dyed shirts and their grandmothers' dresses (though she prefers Rudi Gernreich's designs), and their sitars and guitars. Shocked by the assassination of Martin Luther King, Jr., she and Rupert join the protest march in Pershing Square in downtown L.A. Many of her friends live in Venice during this Summer of Love in 1968, when an entire generation is "turned on, tuned in, dropping out." They listen to Bob Dylan, Joan Baez, and Leonard Cohen (as well as to the Beatles). Their resident poets are little older than they: Charles Bukowski, who grudgingly works at the Venice post office; Jack Hirschman, who lives in the last Spanish house on Quarterdeck Street and teaches at UCLA; and Harold Norse, who will return from exile in London later in the year. They often gather at the apartment of Lawrence Lipton, who will chronicle the Beats in *The Holy Barbarians*. Norse will recreate these days in Venice, and then in San Francisco, in *Memoirs of a Bastard Angel*. While the "pigs" drive their police cars by the guitar players and jugglers on Ocean Park Walk, Harold Norse works out with a then unknown Austrian named Arnold Schwarzenegger at Gold's Gym, and Deena Metzger brings Carlos Castenada to lunch at Silver Lake. Anaïs makes efforts to find publishers for both Castenada's *The Teaching of Don Juan* and the poetry of Norse, who loves visiting her house because it has a "living" room.[38]

While embracing the idealism and freedom of the 1960s youth, Anaïs repudiates their bohemian dirt and dissipation. She tends to avoid the squalor of Lipton's Venice hangout. Earlier this year, when she and Rupert are in Mexico and visit Tennessee Williams, she frankly describes his deterioration. In his puffy features, leering grin, and drugged fade-outs, she sees "all the aging, desperate women he had portrayed" in his plays.[39] As she and Rupert leave, Williams's companion apologizes by saying that Williams is addicted to drugs he is receiving by prescription from Dr. Jacobson. At last Anaïs has to acknowledge the truth about her own periodic treatments from Dr. Jacobson and the doctor's recent appearance and behavior. Her desire for his chemical boost blinded her, but she has luckily avoided any chemical dependency.

Though the balance has shifted to the West, Anaïs continues her seesaw from coast to coast and man to man; as one friend said, she was "the Remarkable Mrs. Pennypacker leading two separate existences."[40] In New York there are Hugo (who is finishing his films of Venice), her cocker spaniel, Tavi, and the *Village Voice*. In Los Angeles, there are Rupert (teaching junior-high science), a white French poodle named Piccolo, and the *Free Press*. The heavy lecture circuit fits into the travel pattern. In New York she continues analysis with Dr. Bogner, who also sees Hugo and remains friends with them both (they are free to call her anytime). Hugo is living only on commissions now (his art films never make money), and the Village for her is no longer gay, but sinister. Her life in Los Angeles is always described in aesthetic and peaceful terms. She works hard, but her "Tahitian" swimming pool smells of alyssum (she swims two or three times a day), the mockingbirds sing, she and Rupert go to the movies, and they go to the beach for sun and space. Rupert, about twenty years younger than Hugo, is interested in science, car trips, hiking in the hills, and swimming.[41] When she is in New York, she swims in the Y pool at the same time that Rupert is swimming in their Silver Lake pool.

Though Anaïs has not found a Japanese woman for Hugo, now seventy, Henry Miller hopes he has found one for himself. At seventy-five, he is madly in love with a Japanese nightclub singer named Hoki. She is twenty-eight and largely indifferent to him. Henry and Anaïs are seeing more of each other. Bob Snyder, who is making a documentary about Henry (*Henry Miller Odyssey*), films them in dialogue. Anaïs loves the film, which includes more than half an hour of Henry talking to the camera while standing in his swimming pool, his arms moving in half circles. The publication of her diaries brings letters of inquiry about Henry, and his letters to Durrell reveal his observations about her. In 1967 Durrell informs Henry that Anaïs "has come into her own in Europe," and Miller expresses surprise that she has taken on the role of public figure.[42] Though he does not think she reads well in public because she is tone-deaf ("she doesn't know where to put the stress"),[43] he is impressed with her courage: "It's strange, don't you think, to think of Anaïs meeting the world face to face, lecturing, autographing, answering questions, and with it all seemingly very much at ease. Who'd have thunk it!"[44]

Both men remember her as painfully shy and quiet. She gives all the credit for her courage to psychoanalysis: "I could not have flowered and expanded," loved or faced criticism and the camera, "but for psychoanalysis," she wrote to a young reviewer.[45] Their letters also reveal that Durrell thinks her hiding of Hugo makes her diaries less spontaneous and that someday "all will be revealed."[46] Miller also cannot understand why she denies Hugo was her husband (Miller undoubtedly assumes there has been a divorce) when he "treated her so wonderfully. . . . But talk of 'deceivers'! She takes the cake. We are lucky to be spared, eh?"[47] This view may be shared by Joaquin, who has trouble handling her fame and has asked that his name be cut from the diary, and Thorvald, who, to keep his daughter away from her aunt's influence, maintains no communication between Anaïs and his life in Loma, Mexico, and later in Florida and Texas.[48]

Geismar also thinks she has changed from "the charming, beguiling, mysterious, elusive person" he knew in the 1940s to a woman "terribly adept at self-promotion. I suppose I shouldn't have been very surprised." He publicly articulates his judgment only after her death, when he puts his finger on the irony of her diary "revelations":

> I wondered if all the praise and adulation really satisfied her.
> How could she accept a "literary achievement" based on the
> doctored "Diaries," based on abstraction and reconstruction of
> the facts she knew so well, based on evasions and distortions of
> the human material she had both lived and written about so
> differently. How could she live with herself, I wondered, when
> her real work, her real passions and love affairs were all sup-

pressed, distorted, sanitized? How could Anaïs Nin really satisfy
the artistic integrity she had based her whole life upon, and was
so constantly promoting?[49]

Indeed, she was not satisfied, nor could she trust the fame, as one young
man found out when he naively asked her whether she did not take satisfaction in the fame, after her long struggle for recognition. "No," she answered firmly, looking directly at him. Suddenly he realized that "fame had
merely raised the stakes of oblivion."[50]

## Literary Ventures

Though she insists that she prefers the present to the past, Anaïs makes
many circular journeys to the past. She is always writing about reading about
past events that she is rewriting—until the multiple mirrors confuse the
reader. Her diary repeats events and observations as she rereads, and she
researches her diary "characters" in order to flesh out and update their
portraits. On her trip to Frankfurt in October 1969, she calls it a "double
journey" as she writes about the present while flying to a book signing for a
past diary. Other visits to the past involve old friends. She says good-bye to
some friends (Eve Miller had died in the fall of 1966, Claude Durrell on
New Year's Day of 1967), continues corresponding with Roger Bloom (who
is released from prison the year her diary is published), and changes her
vision of things as she re-encounters other friends. The two woman analysts
whom she mocked during the 1934 summer of study with Rank in Paris,
she now helps to found the Otto Rank Society and journal. She writes an
introduction to *Artaud,* a book by Bettina Knapp, who had favorably reviewed Anaïs's diary in the *Village Voice* (it was so warm they might suspect
our friendship, Anaïs worried). She infrequently sees Gore Vidal, who keeps
a home in Los Angeles and remains close friends with Bebe and Louis
Barron, who adore him. On at least one occasion the five of them dine and
talk politics in Silver Lake.[51]

She continues to court Hollywood, which she tells Julio Cortazar will be
her "next seduction . . . the next labyrinth." She tells another filmmaker that
if she were born today, she would make films, for one can get into the
interior world with film.[52] She works a long time with Danièle Suissa, a
French-Canadian woman, on a film script for *Spy,* but when Jeanne Moreau
visits Los Angeles, they fail to get a contract with her. Later she visits
Moreau in Paris, still hoping that she will play Sabina. In the late 1960s, she
visits the Fifty-sixth Street New York office of the American Film Institute.
Though the receptionist is impressed by her attire, which includes a "white,
diaphanous, full-sleeved organdy blouse" and no bra ("her small breasts were

clearly visible"), David Adnapoz and his committee are not taken with the script.[53] Eventually, sometime in the mid-1970s, she grants for the symbolic one dollar all film rights to her fiction to filmmaker Henry Jaglom, knowing he will "do them right or not at all."[54] Jaglom works with Tristine Rainer, whom Anaïs met when Tristine was still a graduate teaching assistant in the UCLA Department of English. Now teaching an extension class in film and art for the university and enthusiastic about Anaïs's work, she is eager to help put the fiction on film. They work for eight months on an unsuccessful screenplay.[55]

Anaïs is involved with other literary ventures as well, including the journal called *Voyages*, published in Washington, D.C., by the poet Bill Claire from 1967 to 1973. Today, Claire says, "She was my most active advisor, sending me more material than I ever dreamed of receiving." His focus is on "unappreciated authors," and she finds at least one writer for each of his issues. With no benefit for herself, he points out, not even free postage, she gives him years of encouragement and assistance.[56]

"Did you have a nice dwive?" she says with her missing *r* as Duane Schneider and Benjamin Franklin arrive in a blinding snowstorm from Ohio. After fifteen hours of arduous driving to New York City, they are taken aback by the question. When she offers a beer ("Would you like a dwink?") and instead of pulling the tab, opens the entire top with a can opener, young Franklin concludes that the author of *Under a Glass Bell* is absolutely oblivious to the world outside or not familiar with the mundane realities of life. Certainly she is otherworldly. After several hours of talk, she walks to the door to open up a Japanese folding room divider; when the door opens in a few minutes, the two young academics only see the brown shoes walking from the door to the hall. She is keeping one reality from them, namely Hugo.[57]

She deliberately befriends these two men when she learns they are working on a book about her work that they decided to write over a game of poker at Ohio University. Franklin had first become enthusiastic about *House of Incest* when his graduate professor, Schneider—a Henry Miller enthusiast—recommended he read the novelette. Though the two collaborators read each other's work, each focuses on what he understands best: Franklin, the fiction; Schneider, the diary. Franklin also begins a bibliography of her work. Oliver Evans, whose book on Nin they consider intelligent and ground-breaking, is their major source of help and encouragement. "I do not think that she saw any of [our work] before it was published," says Schneider. Because it never occurs to them to have her approve it or to say anything other than the truth, their study will be an objective introduction to all her work. In the meantime, Schneider, who has bought a small printing press from Franklin's father, sets thirty to forty pages of the material not used by Hiram Haydn (Harcourt Brace) for the first diary volume. For a year, he spends Saturdays drinking cider, listening to opera, and setting the lines of *Unpublished Selection from the Diary* (1968). He "knew that she rewrote" the diary "but not how much" until years later.[58]

Anaïs becomes more directly involved with a newsletter devoted to her life and work. Richard Centing, a librarian at Ohio State University in Columbus who had met her two years before in New York, writes her in 1969 to ask if he can start such a newsletter.[59] She is not only enthusiastic, she gets involved at every step in its progress (encouraging Centing very soon to move away from the Miller-Durrell-Nin configuration) and tries to mold its presentation of her person and work. Twice, in fact, Centing will have to reset an edition because she insists on a change or addition. When they publish a piece on Ian Hugo's films, no mention is made that he is the husband of Anaïs Nin. (Anticipating her involvement, Schneider had refused to get involved with the newsletter.) *Under the Sign of Pisces: Anaïs Nin and Her Circle* appears quarterly for twelve years, from 1970 to 1981, coedited by Benjamin Franklin V and Richard Centing (after 1973 by Centing alone). Centing then continued the newsletter in his independent *Seahorse* (1982–83).

*Pisces* mixes scholarly bibliographies with informal documentation, reading sometimes like a graduate-school newspaper. Anaïs calls it a "Café in Space," and it includes pieces about Caresse Crosby, Djuna Barnes, Marguerite Young, Durrell, Miller, and the paintings of Renate Druks. But the newsletter's chief focus is Anaïs, for it lists her exhaustive lecture itinerary, her commencement addresses, and the college and university courses on women and literature that in the early 1970s use her books (including Yale, San Diego State, the University of California at Santa Barbara, Jersey City State College, Georgetown, Stanford, and Reed). It even announces proudly that she is cited three times in *Webster's Third New International Dictionary* ("sinuate," "untie," "Valkyrian") and has forty quotes (as compared to Virginia Woolf's thirty-two) in *The Crown Treasury of Relevant Quotations*. The café in space is an appropriate metaphor, for the newsletter links her supporters, encourages writing about her works, and helps to inform a wider circle of readers about the diaries.

Not long after New Year's Day 1970, Rupert drives Anaïs to the Kaiser Clinic, where she undergoes tests to discover why she has been bleeding. The tests reveal that she has a cancerous tumor that is inoperable—for surgery would involve a colostomy, and she refuses to be "disfigured." Thoroughly discouraged, she immediately flies to Hugo in their Washington Square Village apartment in New York City, where her private doctor assures her that the tumor has not metastasized and can be eradicated by the radiation treatments suggested at Kaiser. For three weeks, she dresses early each morning in beautiful clothes and takes a yellow cab to New York's Columbia Presbyterian Hospital to undergo six minutes of radiation bombing of her pelvic area. When the deafening noise begins, she closes her eyes and bombards her consciousness with beautiful scenes of lovemaking at the seaside in Tahiti or Acapulco. She learns of the death of Caresse Crosby during her own crisis, but is unable to go to the memorial service. "Love letters" from her readers sustain her, and as soon as she is able, she rushes back to Los Angeles to recuperate with Rupert by her swimming pool. She writes in her diary while Rupert and his quartet play each week. "Why *now*," she wonders, "when all my wishes are fulfilled?"[60] More ironic, friends and acquaintances note, is that the cancer has literally and symbolically struck her at the core of her femininity: the womb that was the source of her pleasure and from which her dead daughter was taken.[61]

Later in the year she takes what will be two of her last three trips to Europe. The first is a trip to London for the publication by Peter Owen of Volume Three (1939–44) and then to Paris for the publication by Stock of the French edition of Volume Two (1934–39). In London, she is reunited with Luise Rainer, who is featured prominently in Volume Three and is now married to a British publishing executive. When Anaïs meets the press, she asks Peter Owen to leave the room so that she can bribe the photographer to touch up his photographs of her.[62] She misses meeting Anna Kavan, one of the writers she has long praised, who dies (with a loaded syringe of heroin at her bedside) just before their meeting, to which Kavan had only grudgingly agreed.[63] She also fails to pacify angry English feminists. In both cities she is frightened by hostile critics and journalists, but in Paris she is returning to familiar haunts, including the Dôme, Closerie des Lilas, and La Coupole. The year before she had found Paris "artificial" and "heartless," but now she has a Parisian triumph, characterized by a hovering television crew from Germany, which follows her to Louveciennes (the gate is locked and the owner will not allow them in), Villa Seurat, and to the quay where her houseboat had been docked (she imagines it having been sunk by German target practice during the war). Dressed in her long cape and with her hair piled in rolls at the back of her head, she looks radiant. No one could know she is sixty-seven. She is always gracious, but still never completely comfortable in public roles. The only cloud in the sky is the news of the death of her poodle, Piccolo; but when she returns to Los Angeles, Rupert will have found a new white poodle for her.

She returns again to Paris in September of 1970, according to the *Diary*, to read and check the French translation of Volume Three (scheduled for publication the following May). Her translator needs help with lines such as "What Patchen knows about sex fits in a thimble."[64] In fact she is there in support of Hugo, who has been asked at last to present his films at film festivals in Edinburgh, London, and Paris. She joins him in Paris to speak where he is showing his films. According to Ambassador James M. Rentschler, then Deputy Cultural Attaché at the American Embassy, who arranged to have Hugo's films sent to Edinburgh by diplomatic courier, Anaïs appears at the film showing at the Cinémathèque Française, 14 September 1970, in a floor-length red silk gown looking "luminous." Rentschler had first read Nin's preface to Miller's *Tropic of Cancer* while curled up in his hammock below the deck of a navy troopship moving from the Philippine Islands to Hong Kong. He is full of admiration for this "rarefied" and "other-worldly" creature introduced by her husband. Though Hugo informs the Rentschlers that his wife believes her artistic identity would be compromised by publicity concerning their marriage, some newspaper articles about Hugo mention the marriage.[65] The *International Herald Tribune* says that, when asked about his wife, Hugo will only remark "she is highly strung." In Edinburgh, *The Scotsman* talks about the "curious double life" of the seventy-two-year-old stockbroker and filmmaker. The *Tribune* describes him as "tall . . . with the scrupulous and reticent air of a scholar," who admits to finally having gotten over the "considerable difficulty" of his "double life": "If you are dependent on your art," says Ian Hugo, "you end up by debasing it. I strive to be a pure artist. At the start, I regard the capital it takes to make a film as lost. It's the opposite principle to the one I learned as a banker."[66]

She walks through the lobby of the elegant, old Hôtel Pont Royal on the Left Bank near the Seine, where Editions Stock has been putting her up during these last two stays in Paris, and descends the narrow curved stairs to its famous but seedy literary bar. Here for decades most of France's great writers have met their Gallimard editors, just steps from the publishing office. She is meeting the man who found her first commercial publisher, a man whom she had bolstered with her faith years before when he was only twenty. She looks as lovely as she can and carries the working manuscript of her fourth diary volume, which covers the years 1944 to 1947. Gore Vidal enters the bar as if "[i]nto the time machine." When he glimpses her, he thinks she looks as beautiful as ever; he looks terrible (she later tells her diary). They are now antagonists, for he has created a parody of Anaïs in a recently published "memoir in the form of a novel," *Two Sisters*. She repeats the ritual explanation she has used so many times already: he can cut anything he wants, but if he cuts too much she will drop him from the diary.

She then tells him that Edmund Wilson has been wonderful about his portrait, only crossing out references to his former wife, Mary McCarthy.[67] Fifteen-love, my serve, thinks Vidal. She believes that he might be worried that she will deny their affair, for she has heard that he told many people she had been his mistress. But she will not include any intimacies. He is relieved that she has left out some of the "warts," and he crosses out several minor things. Then she brings up the question that has been on her mind: Why do you "spatter me with your venom?" she asks. Denying that she has read his *Two Sisters*, she repeats what she has heard; he claims that neither the character of Marietta Donegal nor the narrator's relationship to her is based on Anaïs. She takes it well, he decides, a certain indication that she had indeed not read the book.[68]

In the novel, which appeared earlier that year, Marietta Donegal has an "insatiable appetite for glory and sex," has published five volumes of her memoirs, and fixes everyone she meets "in the distorting aspic of her prose." When she was forty-seven and the narrator a "faun-faced poet" of twenty-two, they lived together for three months in 1947. Vidal mocks Donegal's "flowing abstractions" and manners, claims she is "entirely lacking in the creative imagination," and that her favorite word is "ensorcelled," a word Anaïs indeed uses in almost all her fiction. "Going to bed with her is like having a part in the chorus of some famous opera, lustily shouting 'Alleluia' every time the diva makes her entrance."[69]

A year later Vidal returns the serve she dealt him in the fourth volume of her published diary, and his volley provokes a tremor in her world. He reports on their meeting in Paris in a review of Volume Four in the *Los Angeles Times Book Review*. Unlike Miller and Durrell, who refused to review "their" period, Vidal recounts events of which he was a part. Here, for all her friends to read in the first paragraph of the front-page review, he gives her age and the title of his novel with the portrait of her (claiming disingenuously that only her philosophy went into the portrait). He says she "played at poverty" in Paris and New York and charges her with serious omissions ("she resolutely invades the privacy of others . . . [but] we never know whom she goes to bed with"). He also charges her with errors, while making several himself. His major charges against her are a contempt for intellect and manipulation of people, who exist for her "only as pairs of eyes in which to catch her own reflection." The underlying motif of her diary, he says, is "the will to power":

> She is not unlike the Feiffer heroine who wants "a strong man that I can mold." Her persistent fantasy is that she is Joan of Arc forever putting Dauphins on the throne. Unfortunately, whenever

Dauphin becomes King, she becomes regicide—that is, when she does not try to seize the throne herself—a normal human power drive, as Women's Lib has taught us, but for a Latin woman of her generation, a source of shame and guilt.

In perhaps his only charitable remark, Vidal says that she "can write very beautifully" when she is "seeing," but when she is merely "writing," her prose is "inflated" and "oracular."[70] To add insult to injury, a caricature drawing by Hank Hinton appears with the review: Anaïs and Gore are together in a four-poster bed.[71] The review casts a pall over the Gotham book party four days later. She will never forgive Vidal for his "poison pen" letter, and they continue to snipe privately at each other.[72] A similar blow, this time to her vanity, is Irving Penn's photograph for *Vogue*, which illuminates every pore, wrinkle, and gray hair.

By contrast, Professor Anna Balakian, in the *New York Times Book Review*, calls her "one of the most extraordinary and unconventional writers of this century."[73] Anaïs's supporters are legion, from those in the academic world who are writing learned books about her work to the "lame ducks," an expression that Renate and Anaïs use for those wounded folk who seek her counsel.[74] Anaïs's response to letters from troubled people who only hear the night sounds and dreams of her talks is a gentle reminder that they have caught only the ephemeral and not the substance of her talk. Her most visible following is among young women, whom she carefully cultivates. On 28 May 1971 she addresses more than a thousand people for Female Liberation of Boston in the Old Cambridge First Baptist Church.

## Celebrations with Acolytes

It is a hot and muggy day 3 June 1971 when Anaïs takes a taxi to Brooklyn. She is carrying the latest folder of her diary for deposit. On this warm day, she is dressed elegantly in black hat and dress and is well perfumed. With her is Richard Centing, who is one of several who will make this trip to her "transcendental testament entombed for preservation."[75] But this day, she dramatically unbolts, then unlocks one of the two metal filing cabinets, shows him the original first notebook volumes bound by her mother, photographs and negatives, and the love letters of Otto Rank and Henry Miller. As he glances through the material, he sees references to sexual entanglements. Her reply suggests that he is too much the detective and knows more about her than most people do. His silence and loyalty is renewed; he is honored.

Anaïs, who once wrote to Durrell that she lived intuitively and never remembered dates or ages, titles or signatures,[76] is now juggling airlines and time schedules and compiling a mailing list of a thousand. She is trapped by fame, she says, flying around the country from lecture to lecture (sixty lectures from the fall of 1972 to the spring of 1973 alone), receiving two to three hundred letters a week from readers, filing her reviews in separate boxes for each country, and collecting awards. One woman writes that she is the "poet laureate" of a "new consciousness." Another calls her "a high priestess of the feminist diary and poetry circles."[77] She is "the mother of us all, as well as goddess and elder sister," declares Kate Millett.[78] She receives France's Prix Sévigné for the first two volumes of her diaries, is awarded honorary doctorates from Philadelphia College of Art (1973) and Dartmouth College (1974), and is elected to the National Institute of Arts and Letters (1974). (The latter award she initiates herself; by contrast, when Vidal is elected, he will decline on the grounds that he is already a member of the Diner's Club.[79]) Bob Snyder is filming a documentary about her, and a young Canadian professor named Evelyn Hinz publishes the second book-length study of her work, *The Mirror and the Garden: Realism and Reality in the Writings of Anaïs Nin.*

In an era of photographs, the author's face is everywhere and becomes the icon we connect to the words. Anaïs is one of the clearest examples of the way in which books are colored by photographs and the body style of the author. With thirteen volumes of her diary in print by 1992, her face and myth will perhaps live far longer than her works. But growing fame threatens her control over the fragments of her life—the different compartments and lives she has constructed. When a reporter for the *San Francisco Examiner* asks why she has lived for twenty years in Los Angeles when her husband lives in New York, she answers that she has bronchitis in New York and is a sun and sea worshipper.[80]

While Timothy Leary is languishing in a jail in Switzerland and Julian Beck and Judith Malina are in a Brazilian jail for possession of a controlled substance, Anaïs is representing a more natural inner consciousness. The first "Celebration" for Anaïs and those of her spirit is held under the auspices of Berkeley's extension program on 3–4 December 1971. Not yet accepted by English departments of the academic world, she will come in the back door through extension programs, creative-writing programs, and women's studies programs across the country. She helps John Pearson, the program director, by inviting Harold Norse, Evelyn Hinz, Sharon Spencer, Deena Metzger, Richard Centing, and others to participate. (One friend quips that Centing was traveling so much with Anaïs that he could be called the "literary Kissinger."[81]) Bob Snyder shows a rough cut of his film. Pearson uses slides and music to illustrate passages from the first four diaries. The Pearsons, who adore Anaïs and Rupert, remain faithful friends, though John is uneasy about the young women who sit at Anaïs's feet, some with children and almost menial jobs, women who think she is self-supporting. Only later does he learn of her double life, from another participant, Sas Colby.[82] Zellerbach Auditorium is packed with twenty-five hundred "yelping and whooping" people, chiefly women, says Harold Norse, who tells *Hustler* magazine that performing to such an enthusiastic audience makes him feel like a rock star.[83] Besides Centing and Pearson, the organizer, Norse is the only other man who speaks (Anaïs always insists on including men). "I boomed into the mike and they loved it," he says today. "After my reading, Anaïs hurried to the stage and kissed me. I gave one of the readings of my life. . . . She and William Carlos Williams believed in me more than I believed in myself."[84] For two exhausting days she and others talk, sing, show films, and lecture, and young people stand in line, many of them dressed in purple (her color), to give her flowers and the volumes of their diaries. Suddenly the poet James Broughton, who had last seen Anaïs with Hugo in Acapulco, approaches the "enthroned" Anaïs: "When I . . . knelt at her feet (since there was no other way to approach her) she exclaimed, 'Oh James, I didn't think you still cared!'"[85] The success of this celebration—Centing calls it the "apotheosis of her public acceptance"—leads to another.[86]

Two French professors, Anna Balakian (NYU) and Elaine Marks (University of Massachusetts), are invited to attend the Magic Circles Celebration at the Wainright House in Rye, on Long Island Sound in New York. Because of her academic reputation and earlier critical review, Balakian has been asked to talk; Marks comes out of curiosity because several of her students are followers of Nin's work. Neither knows what to expect this weekend of 28–30 April 1972. Amid what the two women believe is "fawning" and effusive speeches of praise from various artists, Balakian (who has written a critical biography of Breton) confides to Marks (who has written a book on Colette) that her academic treatise will be completely out of place. Briefly she considers slipping away. By Sunday morning, when both of them have changed their initial impression and caught some of the groups' spirit, Balakian reads her formal paper. Long a champion of unrecognized writers, Balakian places Anaïs's writing in the context of symbolism and surrealism and praises her avant-garde fiction. The audience is rapt. Anaïs rises from her seat and rushes to embrace her. Amid joyful applause, one witness says, "This is the most religious morning I have ever had."[87]

"Furrawn" is the word the participants use to describe the weekend. It is a Welsh/Gaelic word meaning talk that leads to intimacy. Furrawn dominates the weekend gathering of thirty people, most of them sculptors, designers, painters, potters, book printers. In fact, Bill Claire, one of several men there (Hugo, whose films are shown, does not attend), brings a woman unfamiliar with Nin or with the consciousness-raising of the woman's movement who is shocked and uncomfortable with the open sharing of emotions. Claire speaks of writing poetry and editing *Voyages* while working for the government. Hinz talks of being a creative critic, Daisy Aldan speaks of printing *Folder* magazine and books, Beatrice Harris (who is studying for her final credentials as an analyst) speaks about the psychological problems of the woman artist, and Frances Steloff tells the story of the Gotham Book Mart. Others share their poetry, pottery, dress designs, books, and art; they all speak of their first meeting with Anaïs and her influence on their lives. They are all there, to use the image of one of the participants, to touch the hem of her robe. Elaine Marks, who was initially "nonplused by the cult atmosphere," remembers that the weekend was an "extraordinary event."[88] It is, Claire believes, "a unique celebration for a living writer."[89] Harms stresses the "creative inspiration" of the small-group dynamic.[90] It is also consciousness-raising as an art form. Being in the presence of thirty admirers, many of whom she has corresponded with for some time but never met, is exhausting and exhilarating for Anaïs, a "feast" of friendship and gratitude.[91]

Inspired both by the weekend that they have organized and hosted as well as by Anaïs's example of Gemor Press, Valerie Harms and Adele Aldridge found Magic Circle Press and publish their first book, a collection of speeches and photographs of the weekend.[92] Uncritical and laudatory, *Celebration with Anaïs Nin* unintentionally establishes or perpetuates some of the myths about Anaïs that persist today—all of them implied in the talks (and several stated by Anaïs herself) that weekend: that Miller opposed her diary writing; that she creatively stimulated him but not he her; that she asked him not to write about her because he did not understand women; that she had never turned against a friend, though some had turned against her; that with few exceptions her characters in the novels are not autobiographical; that she gave Henry, June, Gonzalo, and Robert Duncan her "bottom dollar"; that Miller could write nonstop when inspired, but she never had four consecutive uninterrupted days to write.[93] And two years later Bob Zaller unknowingly repeats the myth that Anaïs supported herself by dancing and modeling. Even the truth would not have dissipated the love enveloping her that Magic Circles weekend or later. The celebration itself became a work of fiction.

Also inspired by the weekend, Evelyn Hinz attends a number of Anaïs's lectures in the Northeast. Within a year she is editing tapes of the talks for a volume entitled *A Woman Speaks—Anaïs Nin*; the book takes several years to complete because the repetition of subject matter in Anaïs's speeches, seminars, and interviews forces her finally to organize the book by topic.

Hinz is also talking to her about a biography. With all the proposals for articles and books about her, Anaïs tries to exercise some control. For example, when Philip Jason of Georgetown University asks to edit some of her fiction and nonfiction for an *Anaïs Nin Reader,* with an introduction by Anna Balakian, Anaïs asks that no dates be given in the introduction, and sends reviews rather than critical studies of her work.[94]

Anaïs's ministrations to her acolytes this weekend and later are described in religious overtones of "joy" and "miracle." "She began as a courtesan and ended as a preacher," notes one admirer.[95] "I was electrified by her," says poet Harold Norse, who hears her speak. Young people write to her of being saved from suicide and being raised from the "dead." When they approach her in Los Angeles, she welcomes them to her home and pool.[96] Today their testimony of her influence remains strong.

Across the country, college halls become temples, faces uplifted as their oracle speaks of beauty, poetry, music, and the primacy of emotion. Free your own spirit, she admonishes, using the spirit house of Thailand as her metaphor. Her lecture tours are exhausting (Rupert takes a sabbatical from teaching to manage her schedule) but nourishing; she calls it "communing with the world." The painfully shy young woman of the 1930s, still suffering stage fright in the 1960s, is now aggressive in panel discussion, can face an audience of thousands without holding note cards and talk to them as if they are an audience of one.[97] In a joint appearance with Ira Progoff, another master of the diary-journal movement, she upstages him. It is less their differences in technique—he advocates the use of subject divisions in a journal and she the uninterrupted flow of the psyche—than their personal charisma that attracts the most questions and the loudest applause.[98] The young people tape her speeches, they write diaries, and they believe they can change the world: "If all of us acted in union as I act individually," she says, "there would be no war and no poverty."[99] If Sylvia Plath illuminates their nights, Anaïs guides their days. They give her standing ovations before she speaks, flutter around like moths afterward, and give her gifts. (Only at Smith College do they knit indifferently as she speaks.) When they flock around her afterward, she gives each one individual attention; she follows up with letters or postcards on her purple stationery.

She talks extemporaneously at the commencements of Hampshire College and Reed College, two avant-garde institutions whose students in part design their own graduation rituals, and at St. Clement's Church, on the West Side of Manhattan, where, after meditation led by women, communion, and dance, she speaks and reads her story "Birth." Of course, the audience and priest understand the story to be about a stillbirth, not the abortion that it was. Father Monick, who is planning a trip to Zurich to study Jungian psychology, calls her a "fragile queen" who has illuminated his life. She can feel herself becoming a symbol for the "modern romantics," as she calls them. There is at least one difference: whereas she has sought "the discipline of psychoanalysis," they want her to rescue them.[100] She asks herself one day if she has not become a guru. The shy and frightened young girl, her father's violated daughter, has become a confident woman of her own, the camera eye of her adoring exploiter replaced by the adoration of the crowd.

She has a captivating effect on people, including those skeptics who come unconvinced. In the 1970s (she had long stopped using notes), she keeps her audiences spellbound. She is poise personified, giving her full attention to every address. She knows the play of light on a surface and the making of masks and personae. To the audiences of a thousand at Northwestern 24 January 1972 and at Ohio State University 26 November 1974, she is radiant.[101] She "wail[s] to them like a guitarless Eric Clapton," writes a reporter for the *Chicago Sun-Times;* the audience sits in the "rapt silence reserved for cult idols."[102] She is best with words of inspiration and uplift, weakest in substantive content, remembers William Burford (a favorite in the 1940s), who is invited by Elliot Coleman of the Writing Seminars at Johns Hopkins to attend one of her lectures. "Elliot thought she was a genius," remembers Burford, but "afterward neither he nor I could remember what she had said."[103]

She is "masterful and mesmerizing," says Ben Franklin, who takes a van of students from Rochester, Michigan, to Evanston, Illinois, for her lecture at Northwestern. He has been assisting Centing with *Pisces* and working on a bibliography of Anaïs's work. Though the project does not interest her and she wants to forget some of her short pieces, Franklin knows that he is putting her literary work in order. He has been annoying her with his objective "intellectual" approach, his prying questions (it is he who figures out the three editors' names in "Gemor"), his positive reviews of writers of whom she does not approve, and his questioning of the authenticity of a catalog of her works compiled by a man who is publishing selections of her diary.[104] Finally, Franklin is subtly asked to withdraw from the editorial responsibility of the journal, the same year the bibliography appears. "I found my personal relationship with her was very trying," says Franklin today, though he adds that she is a "tremendously underrated artist."[105]

Confident and assured as she is, she always takes herself seriously. She tells Miller that she now has a sense of humor, and certainly she can be playful and enjoy a good joke. But not always about herself. She tells Duane

Schneider that she has humor like the Japanese, and he agrees. "She was conscious of herself. . . . She was always aware of who she was and what she wanted to be and how she wanted to be perceived. When I asked her who she was during her leisure time, when she could do what she wanted to do, she answered that even then she had a role to play, a persona, even for herself."[106]

## The Women's Movement

Perhaps the best image of Anaïs is as a gnomon, the stick in the sun dial, of the women's liberation movement. She shows her followers the course toward inner harmony. Or, as she tells Valerie Harms after the Magic Circles weekend, "I was not the heroine but merely the catalyzer."[107] Anaïs taps into the feminist movement insofar as it flows from trust in emotion and a "feminine" approach to life. One reviewer calls her the Boswell of women's inner lives, "a genteel version of Edith Piaf."[108] She defines liberation as living by one's own standards, and the means to that end is psychoanalysis. She is very American in cautioning against group thinking; she calls for individual creative will and development.

Contrary to the opinion of those who disparage the lack of substance in her work, Anaïs is taking the bold step of articulating a feminine aesthetic— honed in those verbal duels with Miller and Durrell—that would integrate woman's nature and her logos. "Feminine art," says her friend Sharon Spencer, "stresses feelings instead of thought processes . . . uses organic forms of prose," and can be practiced by men as well as women.[109]

She does agree with the political goals of the women's movement—curbing population growth, protecting the environment, ensuring the right to freedom of expression and independent livelihood—but she seems a moderating influence in refusing to exclude or blame men; mutual liberation is necessary, she intones. She hates all dogma. At times she seems old-fashioned in asserting that women are intuitive, men rational. She will often tell audiences that there are two approaches to liberation: political and psychological, and hers is the latter, "healing the inner self." The two approaches will seem at odds until Gloria Steinem's *Revolution from Within: A Book of Self-Esteem* (1992). But now, in the bra-less, no-makeup, hirsute era heralded by Germaine Greer's *The Female Eunuch* (1971), Anaïs seems oddly out of place. Yet by her own calculations, she represents at least half of the feminists, though not the radical activists. She likes men, never excludes them from her talks. Many lesbians come to believe that she may be bisexual and thus accept her. Any form of sex is acceptable, she says, echoing D. H. Lawrence; the only sin is not to love. In a letter to a French friend at the time of Nixon's reelection, she assures the friend that there is "another America" in the young, who are *absolutely* different, and I had something to do with this change."[110]

She begs women not to imitate men. Men are objective, detached, and cut off from nature; women are "fecundators" who give birth to life and relationships—though she carefully points out that woman is more than just nature or womb. It is men who should imitate women, she implies, for she applauds men who are more like women, in touch with their feminine self, "sensitive men," aware of the needs of women ("no potentates, no dictators").[111] She proudly notes that the mates of "my daughters" are "tender, loving men."[112] The same can be said of her own compliant husbands. Though her position about women may sound retrograde at a time when many women are calling for power, her call for a sensitive man heralds a new era.[113]

Like her childhood idol, the youthful European diarist Marie Bashkirtsev, Anaïs rallies middle-class feminists. But because she is such a visible spokesperson, she often encounters challenges from members of her audience. Her open love of men, her almost exclusive emphasis on inner liberation, and her feminine dress and manner—one friend suggests she would make a better "feminist for European women"[114]—certainly exacerbate potential hostility. The first outbreak occurs at the Old Cambridge First Baptist Church meeting when the shouts of several women temporarily stop the meeting.[115] At a luncheon of psychoanalysts in Chicago, many men walk out before her talk, and a newspaperman badgers her with questions. In other meetings she is challenged to be more practical and to deal with issues of childcare, salary equity, and economic and social sexism. In each case she is offended by the hostile attacks and characterizes these women who criticize her as antimale, Marxist, and violent "warriors." Henry Miller tells her it is "useless and silly" to try to defend herself or to read reviews. But Dr. Bogner helps her to prepare her responses and not to react emotionally. Commendably, she knows her limits and strengths: she keeps to her emphasis on the personal freeing of one's self. In the end, she believes, she liberates more women than do the "angry women's libbers." Yet she also acknowledges the role that radicals play in opening the way for moderates. When Anaïs calls for women's consciousness and writing, she means Djuna Barnes and Marguerite Young, not Susan Sontag, Mary McCarthy, and Simone de Beauvoir, writers who, she believes, have "masculine" minds.[116]

Perhaps she should be called a humanist rather than a feminist. Privately, she occasionally denies that she is a member of the women's liberation movement. "I am not a suffragette," she tells one male correspondent.[117] She emphatically denies it to Peter Owen, her British publisher, when the press coverage heats up in England. She tells Howard McCord, a friend and poet then teaching at Washington State University, that during her appearance on Virginia Graham's television talk show she is overwhelmed by "matriarchy." Her French publisher, André Bay, says she was "too feminine to be feminist."[118] These statements reflect both a semantic difference in terminology as well as her own ambivalence.

The center of her ambivalence, and the point on which she is most vulnerable in terms of the integrity of her beliefs in freedom and honesty, is the matter of her economic dependence. She refuses over and over again to speak of her private life, denies having a husband (let alone two), and chastises those friends and associates who dare to mention her husband publicly. The impression she leaves with all her young audiences is that she struggled alone, lived on a houseboat in Paris, designed her own clothes, and traveled the world as an independent, bohemian woman artist. Those who know the truth are uneasy. John Pearson thinks she should tell the young women, some single parents working hard to support themselves or to make it through college, that she has been supported by a husband all these years. One woman in an audience at the Library of Congress, where Anaïs is pressed on her relation to men to the point of open anger, concludes that the life of freedom is a "mirage," for "the first freedom is economic."[119]

After years of deceit, which she characterizes as hiding in the labyrinth or behind her veils, she seems not to see the irony of her position. For example, she can say that she has to go speak to groups so that they can see who is behind the words, for the young have been so long betrayed by adults and the media. She will also refuse to change an introduction for another writer's book because "I am too much a symbol of integrity and independence" to write what someone else asks. She will gently chastise Peggy Glanville-Hicks for requesting cuts in her portrait in Volume Five, but will make her own careful deletions. Ironically, the more she opens herself to her readers and audience, the more her inner self remains veiled. The more she seems to hide, the more suggestive the remaining details became. You are "a high priestess of the Eleusian mysteries in a previous life," says Jean Varda. A more skeptical English reviewer says that her greatest talent lies in "dabbing a spot of mystery behind the ears and going on to blur the edges."[120]

After years of living an unconventional and privately daring life, she finally, as Geismar points out, lacks the daring and "truthfulness of a true artist to reveal the human truth in art." As she said a decade before, she cannot pay the price: "Why, why didn't I have the ultimate courage to live beyond the reach of all laws and taboos . . . and not as I am doing, living in the wrong world for the sake of protection, as my father did, a protection for which you pay with your life."[121] The deceptions, of course, both enhance the sense of mystery surrounding her and threaten to expose her. They also ultimately exclude her from literary history. The woman was cheating the artist.

## The Power of Influence

The publication of each diary brings reverberations. Friends privately complain about her numerous "mistakes." Dorothy Norman is upset with her portrait in Volume Three. When Volume Four appears, William Burford complains about the use of his so-called letters without his permission, even if she has changed his name to "Kendall." I was protecting you, she tells him.[122] The sale of others' letters and manuscripts to libraries threatens to undo her. When her English publisher, Peter Owen, sells his records to the Humanities Research Center at the University of Texas, she is livid (his collection consists chiefly of galley proofs and business letters.)[123] The queries at lectures and interviews are also troublesome and elicit more lies: she tells one questioner that everything is in the *Diary*, another that "much" will have to wait for later publication ("mine is not a permanent evasion"), and Ruth Witt-Diamant that friends will have to "understand."[124] She tells one questioner she had had a stillbirth, yet signs the *Ms.* magazine list of women who have had abortions while telling yet another interviewer that she never could have children because of an operation at the age of nine (It wasn't by choice that I did not have a child, she says).[125] She talks fondly of the house in Louveciennes, where she employed maids, then urges Centing in *Pisces* to help "dissipate this destructive myth" that she was wealthy. Both she and her editor rework each diary, yet Anaïs rejects a French suggestion for an autobiography because she prefers the "immediate impressions" of a diary. The literary genre she has chosen threatens to blow aside the deceptive veils.

Her current "diary" since the late 1960s consists of her black briefcase full of letters. While she works on editing Volume Five—made difficult because she had stopped precise dating of entries when she began her bicoastal life—she and Rupert are invited to dine at Miller's home in Pacific Palisades, where Sunset Boulevard drops toward the sea. They are there with Robert and Allegra Snyder to see Bob Snyder's filmed work in progress, *Anaïs Nin Observed*. Henry is limping arthritically, considering and finally rejecting the idea of an operation on his hip. Neither old friend (Henry is now eighty, Anaïs sixty-eight) is completely satisfied with Snyder's film, for, as she points out, they see each other as they had been in Paris: he the indefatigable pounder of Parisian pavements, she the lithe and lively dancer.

If she has any misgivings about Snyder's film, she has only unreserved enthusiasm for a film to which she is taken by the Los Angeles president of the National Organization of Women. It is a preview of Henry Jaglom's *A*

*Safe Place* in the screening room at his office building. It is a film of the inner life of a young woman, played by Tuesday Weld. (Orson Welles plays the magician in *A Safe Place*, which also stars the young Jack Nicholson.) This young New Yorker's first film has just been panned as abstract and poetic after its screening in New York. The *Los Angeles Times* and *Free Press* are scarcely kinder.

Anaïs has tears in her eyes as she knocks softly at Jaglom's door after the film. Jaglom, a diary writer who has read her diary, is surprised to see Anaïs. She loves the film: "Now there are two Henrys in my life." The next day a copy of *Collages* arrives at his office, dedicated "To Henry Jaglom, the magician of the film." Out of the book falls her typed review of the film and the offer that he may use it in any way he wishes. Immediately he sends the enthusiastic review to the *Free Press* (which prints it) and to the *Village Voice*. Consequently, when the film opens, young women fill the theatre. "Thanks to her," says Jaglom years later,

> my entire course became clear. She saved me many years of agony in which I may have tried to find my way, my audience, my focus. With her name I got a different audience [than if it had been pitched to the *Love Story* audience]. Her name was the magic to open up the women on college campuses. She told me, basically, this is your audience. She made me realize that women and artists were the people I was most interested in, and my focus was what interested them: the inner life.[126]

Anaïs takes a sixteen-millimeter copy of the film with her to college speaking engagements, and helps launch the career of Henry Jaglom. "These women are still my audience," says Jaglom. "This is why eight films later I made *Eating* [1991]." In the friendship they had until her death, she also helps him determine his artistic philosophy. Reared with politically liberal views, he struggles with questions about whether he is making films that are politically engaged. She assures him (during a late-night call from Paris) that if his film humanizes people, he is winning a very political victory. "She had a tremendous influence on me. She gave me the strength to continue. In our art we shared the same motivation: to make people realize they were not alone." In every film since *A Safe Place*, someone is reading a book by Anaïs. "It is my signature." And his tribute.

Her influence on Hugo's films, which will never achieve widespread critical acclaim, continues: *Levitation* (1972) explores his wife's statement that the "poet teaches levitation." She also encourages little presses, such as Bill Henderson's Pushcart Press; he dedicates *The Pushcart Prize: Best of the Small Presses* (1976) to Nin, whom he cites as a founding editor (along with

Nona Balakian, Joyce Carol Oates, Buckminster Fuller, Ralph Ellison, and others). But her greatest impact, as is illustrated in Jaglom's testimony, is on the personal level. "She gave me the gift of confirming that being the artist was the right thing to be. That telling the truth was the right thing to do. And that the internal life was enough to share," says Jaglom, in words that are echoed by Jamake Highwater. "She met me at the level of my idealism, reinforced my sense of otherness, and affirmed my choice to be a writer on my own terms."[127] Another young writer, an East Indian, is so moved by her diary that he flies to Louveciennes and "at the locked gate" sits down and weeps. Just two years later, while in Dharamsala with the Dalai Lama, the young man dreams she is ill and writes to warn her of danger. The next day he reads of her death.[128] His is one of many such uncanny stories.

She feels the power of her influence and uses it to help those she admires. For example, she insists that all those in whom she believes—Marguerite Young, Sharon Spencer, Marianne Hauser, Bettina Knapp, Anna Balakian—should be on the same program or in the same magazine or book as she. Feeling confident and powerful, she seems less driven by the need to manipulate.

When she turns seventy on 21 February 1973, she feels strong and more certain of herself than she had at twenty. As a young wife she felt "so weak and so passive," and now she feels empowered. *This is the first year of her life she has earned her own living!* Emotionally and spiritually she feels youthful, full of joy. But her body is not holding up. The previous fall she looked closely in the mirror and acknowledged the inevitability of age, freckles on the skin of her hands, wrinkles on her face only temporarily held off by surgery, a body that cries with fatigue after some lectures. The "feeling and responding" leave her body "worn out." Since her radiation treatments, she has had trouble with her digestion. She eats very little. This year she decides to end her marathon lecturing, to conserve her energy by visiting only one college a month, and turns her attention to getting her affairs in order, primarily the diaries. At this point she is getting ready to give Volume Five to her editor, John Ferrone, to get the folders for the years 1955–66 (Volume Six) from the vault in Brooklyn, and to plan the publication of her childhood diaries. This concern with estate matters seems "paradoxical" to her, for she "never felt more alive."[129]

Rupert takes her to Puerto Vallarta, Mexico, and the cold margaritas, "caressing air," sun, and colors renew her love of the earth and life. Immediate life has never been more real; she no longer needs to write about it to make it real. Upon her return she takes an inventory of her 120-pound figure, still in the same size dress as when she was sixteen, her breasts pink-nippled as a young girl's. She has been with Rupert nearly twenty-five years (and Hugo fifty). "I still arouse desire and receive love letters."[130] When she visits Henry Miller in the hospital after surgery, she expresses the hope that she will not die incapacitated and in pain. Occasionally she thinks or dreams about her death. She has been bleeding lightly for months.

She continues to give an enormous amount of energy to answering letters and counseling young people who bring her gifts, cook her meals, sew her clothes, and come for individual writing instruction (she teaches for International Community College, a nonaccredited school headquartered in Westwood, California). She both gives and receives love and care. Some students help her with mail (by now all manuscripts are sent back unread). Jaglom brings many young women to her house and "everyone felt more deeply their own life and their own gift as artists and women. She had an astonishing effect . . . a pervasive humanity."[131] She continues to attract sensitive, artistic women such as Gloria Vanderbilt and Dory Previn; the latter's poetry she prefers to that of Yevtushenko, with whom she had once shared a platform. Even artist Judy Chicago, who disagrees with her on several issues, comes to dangle her feet in Anaïs's pool. "When I read the scene in A Spy in the House of Love in which the man uses her sexually and she runs after him trying to give him back his anger . . . it was breathtaking. I will never forget it," says Chicago.[132]

Inspired in part by Anaïs's views of woman's art coming from her womb, Judy Chicago establishes Womanhouse in Los Angeles (before the building for the California Institute for the Arts, where she teaches, is built) and later creates The Dinner Party, one of the most controversial (and largest) works of art to tour the country.[133] They meet in 1971 when Chicago is running the Feminist Art Program at California State University at Fresno and commuting to Los Angeles; they talk for hours about the nature of a female aesthetic ("I stopped trying to be a man and stopped being ashamed of being a woman and organized my picture plane the way I experienced it," says Chicago). Together they help in the beginning plans for International College[134]; and Anaïs encourages Chicago to write her own autobiography. Because Chicago knows that the first diary of Anaïs was published because she had known Miller and Durrell, she encourages Anaïs to stop talking about them and to talk about her own work. Her interest is in the artist Anaïs. They only disagree on what the younger woman believes is the "absolutely necessary" act of going beyond narcissism, beyond the womb-centered flower, and shutting off one's responsiveness to others in order to create. "Anaïs could not go beyond the flower," says Chicago, "but I revere her. . . . I was brightened by her creative power."[135] Chicago, soon drawn away from Anaïs by her own growing fame, dedicates Through the Flower: My Struggle as a Woman Artist (1975) to her "aesthetic mother," Anaïs.

In addition to her friendship with Judy Chicago, Anaïs is on a friendly basis with a number of people who teach at the California Institute for the Arts (Cal Arts), founded in 1970, in Glendale. Though it was founded with money from Disney, it offers an alternative education featuring the avant-garde. Anaïs feels a kinship with its resident artists, who include Deena Metzger; Dee Raven, a friend of Renate Druks's; Beatrice Manley, a dance instructor; and Manley's husband, Herbert Blau, the chief administrator.

Anaïs's involvement with International Community College, organized by a group that broke away from UCLA, began when she joined a public panel discussion at a home in Westwood. She, Chicago, Lawrence Durrell, and Buckminster Fuller were to talk about international education and the concept of a university without walls. Chicago remembers that Durrell arrived a half hour late, and in the middle of a lively panel discussion an hour later, Fuller arrived and "immediately strode to the front and launched into one of his dominating harangues, ignoring the panel." All her memories of glazed eyes and dominating male university professors eventually overwhelmed Chicago, who raised her hand, futilely, then interrupted with an impassioned statement against Fuller's behavior and for the premise that education was about sharing. After a stunned silence, a woman spoke against her attack on male authority. The young artist could see the audience converging on her. Suddenly Anaïs stood and gently reminded the audience that what they were seeing was an example of the problem they had to overcome: to bring the rational, masculine, objective approach together with the passionate, emotional, and personal. The meeting returned to dialogue. Anaïs feared that Judy would be angry at her mediation and compromise, but the young woman thought Anaïs had saved her life ("It is Anaïs's incredible grace that I remember!"). As they were leaving, Buckminster Fuller confronted Chicago: "I am not a male chauvinist. My aunt was Margaret Fuller!" "Well, something happened in the genetic line," she muttered almost silently.[136]

Though teaching is "life-giving," Anaïs seems aware that the young idealize her with "a desperation to become me."[137] She understands the young women, for she herself had once wanted desperately to be Louise de Vilmorin, and then Luise Rainer. Yet she fears the flattery of these young women and a repetition of her father's prideful telegrams about his successes in Europe.

"Ninnies," James Wolcott cynically characterizes the cult. The *Times Literary Supplement* calls them Ninophiles. And Kay Boyle was overheard to say that it would have been more difficult for Anaïs to be popular with peers.[138] Certainly there are many lost and wounded birds among her followers, and many testify to her saving and strengthening grace.[139]

Her influence on some women is not completely felicitous. With Barbara Kraft, one of her first writing students, she perhaps inadvertently plays Madame Merle to Isabel Archer. Kraft is a serious writing student in her mid-thirties, who has submitted a script on Yeats's Maud Gonne to the International Community College. Anaïs calls her and they work together for one year through the college and then on their own. When Kraft's fiction is turned down by Les Femmes Publishers and a request for nonfiction made in return, Anaïs urges her to submit her diary, which Anaïs has been reading each week. It includes material about Kraft's affairs and her unhappy marriage to William Kraft, a serious musician well-known in Los Angeles who is seventeen years older than she (Barbara Kraft is a trained musicologist). Both women are surprised when this first manuscript is accepted, but Kraft begins to worry about the effects of its revelations on her husband and their twelve-year-old daughter. She hears Anaïs encourage her to use real names, speak of honesty and freedom, and predict literary success.

When Kraft's diary, *The Restless Spirit,* appears just four months before Anaïs's death, it is the "first child" of the godmother. "There is no mask," she says of Anaïs. "Her creation of her self, or her persona, is the work of Anaïs, the artist." Anaïs's pride and Kraft's anticipation are dashed by the local hostility from her husband's influential friends in the city. "I became the scarlet woman. All my ties with the serious music world in Los Angeles, including the Los Angeles Philharmonic, for whom I had worked as a program annotator amongst other things, were severed . . . permanently," Kraft says. Though the marriage might have broken up anyway, the divorce is acrimonious. Not until a trip to New York, during which a friend of Anaïs's takes Kraft to meet Hugo and tells her that he is indeed Anaïs's husband, is Kraft suddenly shocked into a sense of betrayal, which she harbors for years, then drops. After her traumatic meeting with Hugo, she returns to Los Angeles to ask Anaïs why she had not been told. "I never told you because I did not want you to do what I had done. I wanted you to be free." When Kraft comments that Hugo reminds her of Rupert, but twenty years older, Anaïs answers, "Well, that's true." Kraft leaves feeling that Anaïs regrets having deceived her and, in a more profound way, regrets not having divorced. She assumes that Hugo does not know about Rupert, then concludes that they have all probably silently and independently agreed to continue the deception.[140] Today Kraft says, "Anaïs was pure poetry . . . otherworldly. [She was] the understanding mother whom I did not have, whom no one has in reality but for whom we all yearn. She led me down the garden path and I willingly went. I was a grown-up. I am responsible for what I did."[141]

Despite her fame and the increasing number of books and doctoral theses written about her, Anaïs cannot stop wrestling with her "demons": the double life (though Hugo, when he is not traveling, has a small circle of friends who care for him), the militant, man-hating feminists (as she sees them), the betrayal of Gore Vidal ("he thinks he's George Bernard Shaw and Somerset Maugham rolled into one"[142]), and anyone who criticizes her. She remains so vulnerable. She knows the toll these demons take on her body and health, for she informs William Burford (who questions the validity of her diary) that she will drop him or anybody else who cannot unreservedly support her at this time of her life. She chastises the founders of *Under the Sign of Pisces: Centing* for finding out negative things about her, and Benjamin Franklin for being a "negative critic." She calls Franklin an "intellectual" to his face (she could say nothing worse). Just before she dies she accuses Peter Owen of cheating her out of some of her royalties.[143] These acts reflect her pain but may also be attributable to heavy medication. Though she is thrilled that doctoral students are dealing with her work in academic terms, she lacks understanding of academic inquiry and seeks only praise and affirmation. Nancy Scholar Zee's doctoral work at Brown ("Anaïs Nin: Beyond the Mask") she labels a "cold-blooded betrayal" for calling the diary self-idealization and for connecting it directly with the fiction. Dr. Bogner tells Anaïs she is judging with the self that was "destroyed by the father" and convinces her that Zee's study is worthy and deserves a more objective reading. Every frustration exacerbates her digestive problems and her bleeding.

Fearing her cancer has returned, Hugo takes her to Columbia Presbyterian Hospital in New York for radiation treatments. After initial testing, she returns for four days to have a radium bullet inserted. During the most painful hours she thinks of Bali, where she wants to go with Rupert this summer. As soon as possible after leaving the hospital, she ships her luggage and flies to Los Angeles, where Rupert meets the plane with a wheelchair. She brushes it aside. She may die, she knows that now, but she will make the most of her life while she is still able. Rupert resigns his teaching to be with her and to help edit Volume Six, and Anaïs begins meditation and imaging with Dr. Harold Stone of the Center for Healing Arts.[144]

What remains of 1974 will be full, with the appearance of her fifth diary volume, a "casebook" of articles about her work, edited by Robert Zaller, and Jason's *Reader* with selections of her fiction; with the awarding of an honorary doctorate from Dartmouth[145]; and with a final triumphant return to Ohio State University, where *Pisces* is published. Again nearly a thousand students turn out, but she speaks little except for a question-and-answer period after the showing of Bob Snyder's *Anaïs Nin Observed*. When she accepts election into the National Institute of Arts and Letters, she makes a new friend of a young fiction writer named Alice Walker when she takes both of Walker's hands in hers. "Their touch was soothing, reassuring," says Walker, "the touch of the maternal muse made flesh."[146] She is surrounded by friends this year. Jim Herlihy has recently returned to Los Angeles and moves just over the hill from her. For the next three years he will frequently visit his "favorite woman," whom he calls "Queen of the Albatross" or "Goddess of the Moon."[147]

Even the three musketeers of La Coupole are reunited when Durrell accepts a two-month Mellon teaching grant at California Institute of Technology. Although she has long regretted that it was always Durrell and Miller first, both critically and alphabetically in every index, she obviously cared what Durrell thought. Her unpublished letters to him reveal that for three years she has been writing explanations or self-justifications of her behavior and reprimanding him for saying that Hugo and she had money.[148] But the year before she expressed her interest in reconciliation by calling him at Henry's house, where he was visiting. Now the group meets several times, and she talks to his seminar at Cal Tech. Miller confides in Fred Perlès that Anaïs is the most intelligent woman he has known and that Durrell is an incurable alcoholic.[149] When they reminisce at Henry's house or at the house Larry rents at the beach, their memories of events differ. "[I]n every individual lies a different vision of the same subject," she writes in the introduction to a friend's book of photographs.[150]

She gets her wish for a refreshing rest in Bali when a French airline pays her for articles on Mouméa and Bali, with photographs by Rupert.[151] The articles appear in *Westways,* edited by Frances Ring, whom Anaïs had met at a showing of *Anaïs Nin Observed* the year before and who had asked for an article on Los Angeles for her "Westways Women" series. Anaïs writes, during the 1970s, numerous other articles and introductions to books, including one for a reissue of one of Otto Rank's books. She writes an introduction to a new translation of Arthur Rimbaud's *Season in Hell,* by Bertrand Mathieu, who is a student of Anna Balakian's and is writing on Nin, Rimbaud, Artaud, and the myth of Eurydice.[152]

The most interesting preface she writes is to the American edition of a biography of Lou Andreas-Salomé (1861–1937), a friend of Nietzsche's, lover of Rilke's, and well-known psychoanalyst who studied with Freud. In her preface Anaïs admits her fascination with Andreas-Salomé and praises her for transcending traditions, leading a "non-married" life while married, loving "both older and younger men," influencing great men yet remaining independent, and "assert[ing] her integrity against the sentimentality and hypocritical definitions of loyalties and duties,"[153] all traits that can describe Anaïs. Lawrence Durrell is the first to notice a certain parallelism when Anaïs sends him a copy of the biography; he writes to Miller that "It was Lou who started off this whole thing in Geneva—her wicked sexy spirit—the spirit of the Great Instigators, like that of Anaïs herself! 'Les colombes inspiratrices.'"[154]

During the trip to Bali she becomes fascinated by the elaborate and joyful ceremonies of cremation for the dead: as the body burns, a white dove is freed, signaling the freeing of the soul. The symbolism appeals to her and she makes a wish—a wish that she will continue to think of her coming death "as a flight to another life, a joyous transformation, a release of our spirit so it might visit other lives."[155]

## Last Flights

Her last earthly flight, and the last time she sees Paris, is in 1974 when she and Hugo return to promote their books and films, nearly fifty years after they moved to France as newlyweds. The interest in Anaïs is probably as high as it has been or will ever be in France, where the young people are fascinated with the trio of Miller, Nin, and Durrell. André Bay, her French publisher, remembers her television interview with Bernard Pivot on *Apostrophe*, which did not go well: "She looked wonderful and did not tell me she was ill; but the interview upset her. She had no sense of humor about herself. She was also upset that Hugo let himself be known to me and others. When a reporter asked him how he felt to know that his wife had had so many lovers, Hugo said, 'Whatever Anaïs does is right.'"[156] The sudden emergence of Hugo in the press surprises her friends. "Hugo was rumoured to be there but in another hotel," writes Lawrence Durrell to Henry Miller. Durrell is also in Paris, but their schedules are too busy for them to connect except through a long telephone talk. "Anaïs was in very fine form," he informs Miller.

> I was most acidly ticked off [attacked] by Anaïs for mentioning [Hugo] as her husband in an article and had to do a public repentance with sackcloth and ashes. Now she has forgiven me but not until I "apologized formally for my mistaken views." I wonder what Rupert makes of all this mystery and whether she doesn't feel that the diaries will in the long run lose spontaneity—for obviously one day all will be revealed by an industrious sage from Garbo College. Or someone's memoirs, perhaps Hugo's? I don't know. But it is quite wonderful to see the way

she deliberately skates where the ice is thinnest! No wonder the
MLF [French women's liberation front] is proud of her![157]

Miller responds, "Yes, A.N. is indeed a puzzle!"[158]

Anaïs squeezes into Jean Fanchette's sports car and they drive back to
the Hôtel de l'Abbaye, where she has a beautiful suite paid for by Editions
Stock. She tells Jean that she has terminal cancer. He records the news and
date inside his copy of her latest diary. They talk confidentially and, though
she occasionally lies to him (she swears she did not have an affair with her
cousin Eduardo), she does talk about her dual life. According to Fanchette,
"She had made the decision three years before she died to tell Hugo the
truth. She did not tell him how long she had been with Rupert, but she told
him. She realized that she had to choose when she knew that she was going
to die." Fanchette believes that she loves Hugo as a sister would, but found
the unity she had long searched for when she met Rupert. Hugo, coming
from another hotel, joins them for lunch. Says Fanchette, "Hugo had
aged."[159]

As the airport cab carrying Hugo and Anaïs pulls up to the curb at West
Third in Greenwich Village, Anaïs catches sight of Marianne Hauser, her
neighbor and friend. While Hugo is helping her from the car, Hauser looks
around to see Anaïs in a vision of white chiffon from head to feet. Her
face is white as a Japanese mask with rice powder and she looks like she
weighs nothing. Not realizing that Anaïs is very ill, Hauser asks about her
trip. "Paris was awful, the garbage stunk"—because of a garbage strike—"it
was dreadful."[160]

In January 1975 in Los Angeles, she has surgery that temporarily spares
her life, though it leaves her mutilated by a colostomy. She is in Cedars-Sinai
Medical Center from Christmas Day 1974 until 7 March 1975. She dedicates Volume Six, published the following year, to the four doctors and two
nurses who have rescued her from the jaws of death. She resists death,
focusing on life—and facing both with courage. She writes Peter Owen in
England on 31 May to inform him that she has been in the hospital for three
months receiving chemotherapy for cancer, but is now home, walking and
swimming. She writes letters to Centing, quibbling over his Durrell feature
in Pisces (he is astonished over her present concern with trivia), and she goes
shopping for a wig with a friend.

She makes every effort to stave off death: she takes Dr. Maruyama's
cancer vaccine made in Japan, swims when she can, avoids stress, and
toward the end allows her friend Sister Corita Kent of Immaculate Heart
College to try the laying on of hands. Rupert drives her up the bumpy hill

to Ski High for psychological healing therapy with Dr. Brugh Joy, though the trip sometimes causes her bag to leak and the journey is painful. She also prepares for death. Her agent, Gunther Stuhlmann, comes out to have the will drawn up naming Rupert, himself, and Dr. Bogner as trustees of her estate. Later, when they realize that the committee approach is too complicated, the will is redrawn naming only Rupert as the trustee. In a final irony, she tells him that he will have to take care of Hugo.[161]

According to Renate Druks, Anaïs forbade Hugo to come west during the last two years of her life. "She wanted to die in peace." One of his neighbors in Greenwich Village is visiting Hugo when Hugo speaks of Anaïs being in California and ill. Hugo calls Barbara Kraft in Los Angeles to inquire about her health. She is just fine, Hugo reports back to his visitor.[162] Daisy Aldan, while visiting family in Los Angeles, comes for her final visit with Anaïs, who whispers that she is trying to establish a circle of love in an ugly world.[163]

Although Anaïs attempts to sell the Nin-Miller letters (Miller says for $100,000[164]), her major concern is her voluminous diary, which is shipped to Los Angeles in 1975 after she decides she will deposit it in a library in the West, probably UCLA. For years she has looked for a university library to buy the diaries, asking $50,000 in 1964–65 and $100,000 in 1972.[165] Harvard has not answered her letters; Howard Gotlieb of Boston University cannot raise the funds, though periodically through the years he has visited the Brooklyn vault and shared Chinese meals with her; Dartmouth raised less than half the amount she required and would not pay her annually as she requested.[166] At the suggestion of Digby Diehl (of the *Los Angeles Times*), who urged a quick decision but did not expect the full amount requested, philanthropist Joan Palevsky puts up all the money for the UCLA purchase, which for tax purposes has to be delayed until after Anaïs's death.[167] Thus the 250 volumes are kept in the vault of a bank in downtown Los Angeles. When the bank decides to close its vault after a robbery of rare coins, Rupert moves the diaries, two heavy suitcases a day, to a fireproof vault he has built in Anaïs's study. But they both think they should photocopy them.

Rupert withdraws an armload at a time from the downtown vault so that he will not be away from Anaïs too long. He takes each volume to nearby Occidental College, where he photocopies it. She is fearful of his reaction, for this is the first time that he has read the diaries. He is hurt, one of her friends says, only when reading of her decision at one time to leave him. Today he says, "When I read the diaries for the first time, I thought she was courageous to live her life as she wanted to."[168]

After the agreement is settled for the gift from Joan Palesky to UCLA to buy the Anaïs Nin archives, Rupert and Anaïs host a small party for the donor as well as Robert Haas, her friend and head of the UCLA extension program. Also there are Robert Kirsch and Digby Diehl, both of the *Los Angeles Times*. Anaïs is carefully prepared by her hairdresser Pat Paterson, who comes each week from Yuki's famous hair salon on Sunset strip to wash and set her thinning hair as she reclines on a chaise longue.[169] When she insists on a photograph of the event, Haas hurries out to get a camera from his car. Though he mistakenly thinks the camera empty, he takes several photographs of the group.[170] In the pictures, she looks unrecognizable in her emaciated state.

She and her editor are also working with Harcourt Brace to prepare her *Early Diary* for publication. Jean Sherman, an American poet who lives in France, is translating from the French the first (covering ages eleven to seventeen) of four volumes. Though Sherman has a master's degree in French from UCLA, Anaïs is convinced that she is not "literary or pretentious." Sherman works two years with typed versions, consulting photocopies of the original (written in phonetic French), then consulting Anaïs as to what she meant. When finally Rupert has to read to Anaïs each section of the eight-hundred-page "Child Diary" (an editor decides later to call the first volume *Linotte*), she says, "I cannot imagine I did not write that myself."[171]

She continues to meet several students of journal writing from the International Community College. Tristine Rainer and Nancy Jo Hoy, both with doctorates, are her teaching assistants, and each meets regularly with two or three students to carefully analyze their work and assist with rhetorical and grammatical techniques. Anaïs meets only about once a month with the group as a whole to give her impressions and inspiration. One of the young women credits Anaïs with giving them all "enough inspiration for a lifetime" and a sense of themselves as writers. "I believe that because of Anaïs I learned that the journal creates *me* as much as I create the journal," she says.[172]

By the end of the year Anaïs is back in the hospital and is keeping a diary of pain (her diary of music is written when Rupert's quartet plays each week). At home in Silver Lake, she lies on her chaise longue, looking out at the garden and pool and the lake beyond. During the weeks, off and on, that she will be in the Cedars-Sinai Medical Center, she is visited by many of her friends. Renate comes in a forced mood of uplift and humor. Some of her friends cannot come. Tracy Roberts makes several appointments and does not show up; a guilt clings to her memory for years.

The final honor Anaïs enjoys is being chosen one of the *Los Angeles Times* 1976 Women of the Year. Because she is unable to attend the award ceremony, Christopher Isherwood accepts for her in the Harry Chandler auditorium 24 March. Digby Diehl writes a full feature article about her for the newspaper. She is also honored by a special session of the Modern Language

Association dedicated to her work held the previous December. There are three such academic sessions (she was aware of the first two), planned and led by supporters. The emerging acceptance by the academy pleases her. She sends two hundred dollars to Tristine Rainer to attend the first session, knowing that a graduate student will not get university funding.

In June of 1976 she writes to Elliot Coleman, director of the writing program at Johns Hopkins, that she is unable to leave the house because a fistula developed from extensive radiation, the nurse is coming three times a day, and the doctor is threatening to hospitalize and feed her intravenously. But she is still able, she tells Coleman, to complete a few pages each day of her last diary. Only a few know that the cancer is in her throat now, and the pain is intense. When two young friends visit, she suggests that they join Rupert in the pool, where he is swimming naked. He needs to see a young body again, she says.[173]

She writes final apologetic letters to several friends about the publication of another volume. At the urging of Rupert and her editor John Ferrone, she reluctantly agrees in 1976 to allow Harcourt Brace Jovanovich to publish some of the erotica for which she was paid a dollar a page in the 1940s. The erotica will appear after her death and sell even more than any of them anticipate, and will help pay her medical expenses and support Hugo until his death. Daisy Aldan and Renate Druks remain convinced to this day that publication of the erotica, as well as the unexpurgated diaries, is in poor taste and not what Anaïs wanted.[174] Others, including Henry Miller and Rupert Pole, are convinced that she died wanting everything published. But others, remembering her abhorrence of vulgarity, which she considered the worst sin, find it ironic that her *Delta of Venus* (and later *Little Birds*) give her posthumous fame.[175]

To several young women she talks repeatedly of her concern about leaving Rupert alone. She refers to one of them pointedly as "the girl of the house who will take over for the mother." At least two of these women (Margot Duxler and Barbara Kraft) seem puzzled, then surprised at the implication of her talk. Neither is interested in taking Anaïs's place at Silver Lake.[176]

In keeping with her practice of decorating her environment, Anaïs supervises the transformation of her hospital space by draping the television, hanging plants from the ceiling, and covering the walls with photographs. When Frances Ring visits, she is moved by the "hanging things, the draperies on the window, [Anaïs's] books surrounding her." Barbara Kraft notices the books everywhere and the tiny stuffed red bird on the thermostat. Rupert brings his chamber-music group to play for her.[177] The women at Los Angeles's feminist Women's Building donate blood for her.

One day a man pushes himself into the hospital room in a wheelchair, and Anaïs looks up to see Henry Miller. Surprised and moved, she whispers, "Why, Henry, how nice of you to visit me!"

"I'm not visiting you. I'm a patient here myself," he replies.[178]

When Renate arrives the next day, she hears birds singing and inquires about the source. It is a recording of the birds in the trees of Silver Lake, and Anaïs plays it as music. She tells Renate the story of Henry's visit as they walk down the corridor, Anaïs dressed in a red velvet robe and pushing the stand that holds the intravenous bottle.

When she returns home, where she insists she wants to die, Rupert takes loving care of her. Even those of her friends who could never understand why she loved him adore Rupert for his devotion and care, for his sleeping with her until the end. He has an enlarged version of the Thailand spirit house built just outside their bedroom wall. When she is helped outside, she leans on the little house and says, "Wood is so life-giving, don't you think?" Then she looks out past the pool and the reservoir to the ocean in the distance, thinking perhaps of Lillian's dream in *Seduction of the Minotaur:*

> Some voyages have their inception in the blueprint of a dream, some in the urgency of contradicting a dream. Lillian's recurrent dream of a ship that could not reach the water, that sails laboriously, pushed by her with great effort, through city streets, had determined her course toward the sea, as if she would give this ship, once and for all, its proper sea bond.[179]

On Tuesday night 4 January, Jean Sherman brings the next translated section of the *Early Diary* and kneels down beside the bed to begin reading. Anaïs can only listen to four or five pages, and can only whisper. She wants to talk in French about whether Sherman enjoyed the translating and identified with her childhood, about Elizabeth Kübler-Ross's ideas about dealing with death, and about her own death. Says Sherman, "I reminded her of the passages in [the early diary] in which she said that if she could express what she had in her and make her dream concrete, then she would be ready to go when the time came." Anaïs moves her hands from under the covers, and, when Jean takes her hands in hers, Anaïs lifts Jean's hand and kisses it.[180]

Rupert no longer carries her to the pool. He carries her to a chair just outside the front door or to the chaise longue that looks out on the pool. Morphine lessens her memory as well as her pain. The junipers stand framing her world and the breezes ripple the pool. It is a struggle for her to let go. She is afraid of taking the death journey alone. Though most of her friends think she dies at home, in fact, when the difficult end approaches, Rupert becomes alarmed and takes her back to Cedars-Sinai Medical Center.[181]

At 11:55 P.M. on 14 January 1977, Anaïs Nin dies. In the words of Rupert, remembering the Balinese cremation, "her dove rose."

> I took her ashes aloft in a small plane over Santa Monica Bay. I had studied the navigation charts carefully. All the markings were described by ordinary fish names except one. Mermaid Cove. I told the pilot to fly there, and I let go of the blanket containing her ashes just as a ray of sunlight broke through the overcast sky.[182]

# Postscripts

## Coastal Times

The *New York Times* obituary of Anaïs Nin lists her widower as Hugh Parker Guiler, also known as the artist Ian Hugo; the *Los Angeles Times* obituary of Anaïs Nin lists her widower as Rupert William Pole.

DEAR HENRY[,]
. . . As for Anaïs, I suppose the fur will start flying now as they search for the real girl among the four or five masks she left lying about with false clues attached to them. . . . [S]he was so secretive and pudique that I know nothing about her and could not answer the smallest biographical question. . . . As things are the official statue of Anaïs will be carved by the two men who knew her best, Rupert and Hugo—and this is quite as it should be. . . .
      Love[,]
      Larry [Durrell][1]

In a call to Richard Centing to inform him of the death of Anaïs, Rupert says that Anaïs had wanted to die for some time and that she would be meeting her father again in death, not the hated father, but the "ideal" father.[2]

## Formal Memorials

On what would have been Anaïs's seventy-fourth birthday, a memorial celebration is held at the Scottish Rite Auditorium on Wilshire Boulevard in Los Angeles. Dory Previn reads her song "Morning Star, Evening Star" and Christopher Isherwood presides before eighteen hundred people. Stephen

Spender reads three poems, and John Williams's music group plays "Requiem for the Lady of the Houseboat," written for the occasion. Numerous friends, including James Herlihy, Louis and Bebe Barron, Daisy Aldan, Tristine Rainer, and Sister Corita Kent, speak of her. Rupert Pole shows slides and reads a tribute from Henry Miller:

> It is only once or so each century that our sorry sublunary world is graced by the passage of a spirit as rare and courageous as was that of Anaïs Nin. In the realm of literature, I can think of few feminine figures who could hold a candle to Anaïs for artistic inventiveness and sheer personal radiance.[3]

The following day at Snow Room, in the research library of New York University, with Sharon Spencer (perhaps the best critic of Anaïs's fiction) presiding, 150 of her friends gather around Hugo, who shows *Bells of Atlantis*. Anna Balakian speaks of Anaïs's innocence, Kate Millett heralds her as a woman artist, and other friends, including William Claire, Marguerite Young, and Frances Steloff read from her works and pay tribute. "Last was Joaquin Nin-Culmell, younger brother of Anaïs, who had to break out of a kind of envelope of grief, as he stood at the mike, faltering and going for his handkerchief, finally recovering, then giving his own birthday tribute: 'Even when we were children, she would upstage us all.'"[4]

The San Francisco tribute is held at the Poetry Center of California State University with Joaquin Nin-Culmell and Anaïs's friends in the Bay area. Ian Hugo's *Bells of Atlantis* is shown again. The Washington, D.C., celebration is held in Powell Auditorium and inaugurates a fellowship in her name in the comparative literature program of New York University. William Claire presides and Hugo shows two of his films including *Anaïs*. After Henry Miller's tribute is read, Hugo slowly stands up in the front row and announces to a surprised audience that he was and always had been her husband.[5]

## Anaïs, Anaïs

Dear Henry[,]
   . . . It will please you to know that the new Cacharel scent named after Anaïs ('Anais-anais') is a great success and when last I had the luck to take a youngling to bed in Paris that was what she smelt of. I lay there in the dark smelling it and thinking and saying never a word. . . .
                                        Larry[6]

## A Curried Shrimp Recipe

When Rupert and Kazuko Sugisaki, his companion and the Japanese translator of Anaïs's work, visit New York for the promotion of Volume Seven and *A Waste of Timelessness and Other Stories,* Hugo graciously invites the couple to lunch and serves a dish of curried shrimp, which he says was a favorite of Anaïs's. It is a recipe that Helen Wright taught her son in California.

## Erotica Forever

"UCLA announces the purchase of 200 volumes of Anaïs Nin's diary June 1977 for $100,000 from Rupert Pole, Miss Nin's husband and trustee. The gift for the purchase came from Joan Palevsky."
—*Los Angeles Times, 15 June 1977*[7]

"Anaïs has given me my life's work [editing diaries]—and I am so grateful—I would be lost now if I tried to go back to teaching."
—*Rupert Pole to Lawrence Durrell, 2 March 1977*[8]

Following the publication of two volumes of her erotica—*Delta of Venus* (1978), which in two weeks is number four on the *New York Times* bestseller list, and *Little Birds* (1979)—Rupert begins reissuing the portions that were expurgated from her published diaries. Two works consisting of most of the material expurgated in 1966 from Volume One (1931–34) eventually appear: *Henry and June,* in 1986, and *Incest,* in 1992. These "unexpurgated" books present her affairs with Henry Miller, René Allendy, Joaquin Nin, and Otto Rank. Two more works are planned from the material expurgated from Volume Two (1934–39): *Fire* (concerning Gonzalo More) and *Nearer the Moon* (including her friendship with Lawrence Durrell), all part of a series entitled "A Journal of Love." Like Anaïs, Rupert is a two-finger typist and works from the photocopied pages of her diary at the black typewriter that he bought her in 1948.

When the first of this series, *Henry and June,* is released, some of her closest friends refuse to read it, either doubtful about the fact that she had even written it or certain that she had not intended it to be published. Sales of Harcourt Brace Jovanovich books by Anaïs Nin double after the appearance of the erotica, the unexpurgated diaries, and the movie *Henry and June.*[9]

Dear Joey [Fred Perlès],
. . . How ironical that she who detested "vulgarity" should win posthumous fame by a highly erotic work. . . .
Henry[10]

Before Philip Kaufman's film *Henry and June* can be released by Universal Studios, Kaufman contests the Motion Picture Academy's X rating, which would group it with hard-core pornographic films. After considerable negotiation, the Motion Picture Academy changes its classification ratings to include a category for artistic adult erotica (to which no one under seventeen can be admitted), and the film is awarded the first NC-17 rating. Almost all her friends go to see it, and their response to the film varies extremely, though they all agree on the uncanny likeness of actress Maria de Medeiros to Anaïs. Rupert goes to the movie theatre every day the opening week.[11]

## Widowers

Rupert Pole, who continues to live in their Silver Lake home, is the heir and only executor of the Anaïs Nin Foundation.

> "After her death, I had a party here and I tried to include Hugo, who was lonely. He took me out on the terrace for a private conversation: 'Do you know anything about the will?' he asked."
> —*Marianne Hauser, 2 Washington Square Village*[12]

> "When Hugo came to Paris after Anaïs's death, we went to the same restaurant where they had eaten in 1974. 'You look tired,' I said. 'I am,' he replied. We went to his hotel and shared a bottle of champagne and he told me he knew everything all the time, 'But what I cannot understand is how could she love that bastard Miller and how could she have published *Delta of Venus?*'"
> —*Dr. Jean Fanchette*[13]

During the last month of his life, Henry Miller, deaf and nearly blind, imagines he is in Paris. He dies of cardiovascular failure 7 June 1980.

When Hugh Guiler dies 7 January 1985 near the age of eighty-seven, Rupert arranges for the cremation and, honoring Hugo's request, drops his ashes in the Santa Monica Bay, not far from where the ashes of Anaïs were scattered.

# Acknowledgments

"In general, the world has been more injured by silences, erased tapes, rewritten words, shredded documents than it has ever been damaged by revelations of the heart."

*—Erica Jong**

THE ENTIRE life of a self-confessional writer, especially a diarist, must be examined. The truth must be told even if that artist herself did not tell all the truth or tell it straight. Not surprisingly, the testimony of those who knew Anaïs Nin is as varied as the multitude of selves she herself claimed. Perhaps not a single friend or relative will recognize this full portrait. For those who would not want the truth, she left behind, as if for her own eventual biographer, some words of caution. She said that the "destructive element of truth is neutralized" by a "deep probing" of "motivation": "What is understood is not judged." I will stand behind her words.

For this reason and others—the sheer volume of her published diaries, her secrecy and duplicity, and her insistence on publicly separating her fiction from her life—no full biography has as yet been published. At her death Anaïs Nin appointed Evelyn Hinz her official biographer. In 1991 Elisabeth Barillé published a semifictionalized portrait, a brief biography in the French belletristic manner. Nin liked to say it would take one hundred biographers to tell her story.

Though the original diaries from 1914 through 1934 are now available to

---

*Jong is arguing in favor of the family of Anne Sexton, who released the tapes of her therapy to a biographer. "Anne Sexton's River of Words," 13.

scholars, the diaries from 1935 through 1939 are closed until the unexpurgated portions can be published. The biographer can decipher many clues of Nin's censored life in the 1940s from her erotica, housed at UCLA and at the Kinsey Institute. After this period less was censored. After 1964, she wrote very little in her diary. Her fiction, particularly those early manuscripts housed at Northwestern University, clearly reveals truths never destined for her diary. In her fiction, the earliest versions are the most invariably explicit and detailed. These manuscripts, together with hundreds of interviews with those involved with the subject and with those who read the diary before it was sequestered at UCLA, helped me fill in the story of Anaïs Nin. Because of the discrepancy between the world of her diary and the memories of her friends, the biographer must depend upon a montage of recollections and memories.

I wish to thank Rupert Pole for his kindness and hospitality. I relied heavily on first-person records, and therefore owe a great debt to more than two hundred friends and acquaintances of Anaïs Nin's who shared their memories, letters, personal diaries, and tapes with me. (Unfortunately, Nin's agent, Gunther Stuhlmann, denied me use of his store of Nin family photographs.)

In *Europe,* where Nin lived from 1903 to 1914 and, in Paris, from 1923 to 1939, I wish to thank Elspeth Barker, André Bay (Nin's French publisher), Georges Belmont, Jean-Yves Boulic, Georges Cleyet, Beatrice Commengé, Lawrence Durrell, Dr. Jean Fanchette, David Gascoyne, Robert Bartlett Haas, Felix Landau, Gershon Legman, Bertrand Mathieu, Einar Moos, Peter Owen (Nin's English publisher), Marguerite Rebois, James M. Rentschler, and Gore Vidal. (Mr. Vidal declined a full interview.) I am grateful to Nils-Hugo Geber for a detailed report of the Guilers' visit to Stockholm in 1960.

In the *New York City area,* where Nin lived from 1914 to 1923 and from 1940 to 1947 (and thereafter part of every year until 1975), I thank the following: Frank Alberti, Daisy Aldan, Anna Balakian, Nona Balakian, Fabion Bowers, Dolores Brandon, Andreas Brown of the Gotham Book Mart, Nina Burnelli, John Cage, Francis F. Dobo, Bita Sulzberger Dobo, Jean Erdman, Dr. Erika Freeman, Serge Gavronsky, Anne Geismar, Robert Haller of Anthology Film Archives, Valerie Harms, Hilary Harris, Erica Jong, Lillian Kiesler, Billy Kluver, Bettina L. Knapp, Jill Krementz, Jennifer Lee, Leo Lerman, Eline McNight, Judith Malina, James Merrill, Dorothy Norman, Josephine Premice, Edouard Roditi, Raymond Rosenthal, Barnet Ruder, Sharon Spencer, John Tytell, Amos Vogel, Marguerite Young, and Harriet Zinnes.

In the *Los Angeles area,* where Nin lived for much of her last thirty years:

Don Bachardy, Bebe Barron, Marshall Barer, Ray Bradbury, Betty Buchanan, Walter Calkins, Judy Chicago, Lucretia Cole, Rita Crafts, Samson De Brier, Digby Diehl, Renate Druks, Lester Ehrlichman, Eugene Epstein, Michael Hargraves, Curtis Harrington, Raven Harwood, James Leo Herlihy, Jamake Highwater, Joyce Howard, Charlotte Hyde, Henry Jaglom, Dr. Oscar Janiger, Athan Karras, Barbara Kraft, Mildred G. Kramer, Christian DuBois Larson, Timothy Leary, Paul Mathiesen, Deena Metzger, Lepska Miller Warren, John Motley, Sydney Omarr, Gloria Orenstein, Ann Quinn, Frances Ring, Tristine Rainer, Maryanne Raphael, John Rechy, Tracy Roberts, Albert Ross, Douglas Saxon, Kazuko Sugisaki, Leah Schweitzer, Cynthia Sears, Jean Sherman, Bradley Smith, Robert Snyder, Kay Stenberg, Trudi Alexy Sternlight, Seba Kolb Tomkins, Eve Wasserman, W. C. Watt, Bernadette Wehrly, Beatrice Wood, and Noel Young.

In the *San Francisco area,* where Nin lived in 1948 and 1949, my thanks to Richard Alpert (Ram Dass), Margot Duxler, Lawrence Ferlinghetti, Herbert Gold, J. A. (Jack) Hirschman, Nancy Leite, Harold Norse, and John and Liz Pearson. And at the Henry Miller Library in Big Sur, Jerry Kamstra and Stevanne Auerbach.

In *other locations* I interviewed or corresponded with Kay Boyle, James Broughton, William Burford, William F. Claire, Blanche Cooney, Polly Crosby Drysdale, Leon Edel, Judy Flander, Hugh Ford, Wallace Fowlie, Norman Fruman, Elmer Gertz, Harold B. Gotlieb, Suzette Henke, Judith Hipskind, Carlton Lake, James Laughlin, James E. Lieberman, Elaine Marks, Joyce Carol Oates, Georgianna Peacher, Bern Porter, Lawrence Clark Powell, Betty Ryan (Gordon), Bradley Smith, Studs Terkel, Eugene Walter, and George Wickes.

I am greatly indebted to the *scholars of Anaïs Nin,* whose books and articles about her journal and fiction (duly listed in the General Bibliography) have preceded mine. With the exception of Professor Evans (deceased), they were generous in their assistance: Nancy Scholar Adams, Oliver Evans, Benjamin Franklin V, Evelyn Hinz, Philip K. Jason, Bettina L. Knapp, Duane Schneider, Sharon Spencer, and Robert Zaller. Thanks also to Jean L. Sherman, who translated the early Nin diaries into English. The special Nin collections of Richard R. Centing, Sidney F. Huttner, and Jean Fanchette have proven invaluable.

Other *biographers,* my valiant colleagues in this profession, have responded readily with assistance, and in some cases have read portions of my manuscript: Dore Ashton (Noguchi), Gordon Ball (Allen Ginsberg), David Callard (Anna Kavan), Walter Clemons (Gore Vidal), Anne Conover (Caresse Crosby), Mary Dearborn (Henry Miller), David K. Dunaway (Aldous Huxley), Ekbert Faas (Robert Duncan), Bettina Knapp (Antonin Artaud),

Dr. E. James Lieberman (Otto Rank), Ian MacNiven (Lawrence Durrell), Brenda Maddox (D. H. Lawrence), and Jay Martin (Henry Miller).

My gratitude also goes to Nancy Bond, who first introduced me to adult survivors of incest and gave me psychological and analytical insights into child abuse. For consultation and insights concerning particular neurotic behavior, I am indebted to psychiatrist E. James Lieberman, M.D., of Washington, D.C., and to two psychoanalysts: Erica Freeman of New York City and William O'Neil Erwin of Los Angeles.

I wish to thank the following for their *assistance in my research:* Tom Auer, Mary Lynn Broe, Marianne Caws, Richard Centing, Lucretia Cole, Linda Collins, Wendy DuBow, Judy Flander, Colette Faus, Wendy Gimbel, Michael Hargraves, Roger Jackson, Patricia L. Kahle, Michael Neal, Bénédicte Niogret, Philip Nurenberg, Gail Riley O'Neill, Janine and Roland Plotel, Cliff J. Scheiner, Layle Silbert, Craig Peter Standish, Toby Widdicombe, and Jack Wright. And in Paris, for her skilled professional research and assistance, Karen Walker.

A special thanks to Ron Gottesman and Bob Snyder, who have given us works of art on Anaïs Nin and Henry Miller. We three, occasionally joined by Michael Hargraves, formed the Miller-Nin breakfast circle at Rae's café and offered humor, insights, and tips to each other.

Parts of this book were read in manuscript by many people, including Gwyn Erwin, who is an expert on the silent agreements within families (and author of *Silent Agreements*) and who hastened my pace by awaiting each chapter, and many of the witnesses listed above who read "their" portion of the story.

My immeasurable debt and gratitude go to Albert Sonnenfeld, my husband, who gave me humor and encouragement, helped me with translations, and read the final manuscript with the critical eye of my most skeptical reader. Whatever errors or misjudgments remain are my own, of course.

To the American University of Paris, where I teach and work each summer, my special thanks. For my undergraduate students at AUP and my nonfiction graduate students at the University of Southern California, my appreciation for what you have taught me.

All writers know the value of a good agent and a good editor. I have been blessed with both. I thank my agent, Margret McBride of San Diego, and my editor at Little, Brown, Jennifer Josephy, for their skill and enthusiasm.

I am grateful to the curators and librarians who assisted me with the following manuscript collections: The Bancroft Library, Manuscripts Division, University of California, Berkeley (including Robert E. Duncan, City Lights Books/Lawrence Ferlinghetti, and San Francisco Poetry Center/Ruth Witt-Diamant Papers); The Berg Collection, New York Public Library (Collections of Caresse Crosby, Frances Steloff and the Gotham Book Mart, and Henry Miller); Rare Books and Manuscripts Library, Columbia University (Papers of John Erskine and Otto Rank); The Harry Ransom Humanities Research Center, The University of Texas at Austin (including Henry Miller Collection; Peter Owens Papers); The Kinsey Institute for Research in Sex, Gender, and Reproduction, Indiana University (erotica, including *Delta of Venus* and *Little Birds*); The Lilly Library, Indiana University (Roger Bloom and Harold Norse Collections); Northwestern University Library, Special Collections Department, Evanston, Illinois (Anaïs Nin Collection, including her fiction manuscripts); Ohio State University, Division of Rare Books and Manuscripts and Richard R. Centing's Anaïs Nin Collection; Morris Library, Special Collections, Southern Illinois University at Carbondale (Collections of Caresse Crosby, Philip Kaplan, and Lawrence Durrell); University of California, Los Angeles, Research Library, Department of Special Collections (including Anaïs Nin, Henry Miller, and Bernard Porter Collections). Scattered letters are located in The Beinecke Rare Book and Manuscripts Library, Yale University; Mugar Memorial Library, Boston University; The Poetry/Rare Books Collection, University of Buffalo, State University of New York; Special Collections, Dartmouth College Library; Special Collections, University Library, University of Delaware; Houghton Library, Harvard University; The Milton S. Eisenhower Library, The Johns Hopkins University; Kenneth Spencer Research Library, University of Kansas Libraries; Library of Congress; The Newberry Library, Chicago; Rare Books and Manuscripts Division, New York Public Library; Manuscripts Department, Wilson Library, The University of North Carolina at Chapel Hill; Firestone Library, Princeton University; McFarlin Library, The University of Tulsa; Doheny Library, Special Collections, University of Southern California; and Special Collections/Manuscripts, Alderman Library, University of Virginia.

# Notes

Much of this book is based on interviews, library archives, unpublished materials, and the thirteen published diaries of Anaïs Nin. Because the truth concerning anything to do with Anaïs Nin is subject to debate, I have taken care to document every important detail or claim. In the notes that follow, I have used the abbreviations listed below. For full publishers' information, see the bibliographies that follow. Sources in *Anais: An International Journal* (eleven volumes, 1983–93; cited as *A 1–11*) are not listed individually in the General Bibliography.

*Persons*
AN: Anaïs Nin
LD: Lawrence Durrell
NRF: Noël Riley Fitch
HM: Henry Miller

*Books*
ALP: *A Literate Passion: Letters of AN and HM*, 1932–1953
D 1–D 7: *The Diary of Anaïs Nin*, Vols. 1–7 (1966–80)
DML: *The Durrell-Miller Letters*, 1935–1980
ED 1–ED 4: *The Early Diary of AN* (*Linotte* is cited as *ED 1*), vols. 1–4 (1978–85)
H&J: *Henry and June: From the Unexpurgated Diary of AN*
LAN: *Letters to AN*, by Henry Miller

*Libraries*
BANCROFT: The Bancroft Library, University of California, Berkeley
BERG: Berg Collection, New York Public Library
COLUMBIA: Rare Books and Manuscripts Library, Columbia University
HRHRC: The Harry Ransom Humanities Research Center, The University of Texas at Austin
KINSEY: The Kinsey Institute for Research in Sex, Gender, and Reproduction, Indiana University, Bloomington
LILLY: The Lilly Library, Indiana University, Bloomington
NORTHWESTERN: Northwestern University Library, Evanston, Illinois
OSU: Ohio State University, Columbus, Ohio
SIU: Morris Library, Southern Illinois University at Carbondale
UCLA: University of California, Los Angeles

## INTRODUCTION (*pages 3–9*)

1. AN, at about age 43, *D 4*, 178.

2. "Le Premier Parfum de Cacharel," as "Anaïs Anaïs" was first advertised in the *New York Times Magazine* 15 Mar. 1981. The very feminine layout pictures the faces of two women among soft rose petals.

3. AN, *D 4*, 176. The small childhood volumes have been bound together, making the present, renumbered, volumes fewer in number.

4. "Life in Provincetown," "The Hungarian Adventurer," and "Two Sisters" are erotic manuscripts that contain stories of children seduced by fathers or a male authority figure, AN Collection, UCLA. Portions of these manuscripts have been published in *Auletris, Delta of Venus,* and *Little Feathers* respectively. In the novel *Children of the Albatross,* Djuna, sexually abused by the watchman at her orphanage, describes "a shattering blow" to her body and "something broken inside me," 8.

5. The pioneering work of Alice Miller in Germany claims to verify trauma with the aid of "later biographical data." In talking about Freud and his Wolf-man, she could be describing AN: "One can spend all his life reenacting a severe childhood trauma (sexual abuse) in all kinds of situations and can even unconsciously lead several analysts of high repute to misuse him repeatedly for their own purposes." *Thou Shalt Not Be Aware,* 160 ff.

6. AN, *D 3*, 260. In *Seduction of the Minotaur* (111), Lillian and her brothers suffered nightly spankings in the attic from their father: "the rest of the time he did not talk to them, nor play with them nor cuddle them. . . ."

7. The "genesis" of her diary, as AN explained in *The Novel of the Future* (142), is her "desire to keep a channel of communication with the lost father."

8. In 1972 AN remembered Dr. René Allendy saying that she "was made bad by her father." When Allendy had told her in April 1923 that she had "witnessed some brutal aspect of love," she rejected the idea as banal.

9. Child abuse has not been discussed before in relation to AN's early years, though Meryle Secrest ("Economics and the Need for Revenge," *A 6*, 35) says that AN's father "seduced her mentally as surely as if he had thrown her on a bed, and did her terrible injury."

10. AN, *D 3*, 5.

11. AN letter to her father, quoted 25 Nov. 1916 in *ED 1*, 145.

12. In his *In-Discretions,* Hoshang Merchant (146) first makes this echo of James Joyce's *Portrait of the Artist as a Young Man.*

13. HM, "Un Etre Etoilique," 269.

14. "Our form is autobiography," says Kate Millett. "Anais—A Mother to Us All," *A 9*, 4.

15. AN to Krishna Baldev Vaid, "Writing and Wandering," *A 1*, 55. Many of the "original" diaries, housed at UCLA, are rewritten in the same hand and pen, without erasures or variations.

16. Geismar, "AN: An Imprecise Spy," 3.

17. "Anais wears a necklace of imaginary foreskins emblematic of make-believe conquests . . . but Anais never gets piked. She entices us to the shadowy fringes of Lesbos and then pulls down the shade. . . . It's Vassar and Radcliffe and Smith in the days of the high buttoned shoes and straw boaters; sighs, coquetry, hanky-twisting, tears on the pillow and sobbing hearts," says Dick, *HM,*155. Madonna told one interviewer that for her book *Sex* she was asked to write erotica "in the vein of AN." Jonathan Ross, "Exclusive with Madonna," BBC, 13 Oct. 1992.

18. Dick, *HM*, 122; Merchant, *In-Discretions*, 14.

19. Currie, "Anaïs Redux," 46–47.

20. "Her notion of femininity makes my hackles rise," writes de Beauvoir, *All Said and Done*, 153.

21. Vidal, *Two Sisters*, 172. "She was always on the borderline between sublime self-love and the ridiculous" (Vidal to NRF, 26 Feb. 1991). Vidal's portraits range from gentle to brutal: *In a Yellow Wood* (1947), *The City and the Pillar* (1948), *The Judgment of Paris* (1952), *Two Sisters* (1970), *Live from Golgatha* (1992).

22. Interviews with Marguerite Young, 18 Mar. and 7 May 1991.

23. Interview with Lawrence Durrell, 14 June 1990; LD to HM, 22 July [1968], *DML*, 430.

24. HM, in a letter to Fred Perlès (Joey), after AN's death, *Book of Friends*, 233, 266. HM also referred to her "inveterate lying, her chicanery, her duplicity," 265.

25. AN, *House of Incest*, 67–68.

26. AN, *Unpublished Selections*, 7.

27. Linde Salber, "Two Lives—One Experiment: Lou Andreas-Salomé and AN," *A* 9, 89. Salber also published a psychoanalytic monograph in German (*AN*).

28. AN, *D* 4, 139.

29. The "post incest patient has a tendency to confuse sex and affection or to 'sexualize' all relationships," says Meiselman, *Incest*, 348. I have interviewed more than half a dozen of AN's sexual partners and counted dozens more by reliable secondhand reports and by her own admission in published and unpublished diaries.

30. AN, "With Antonin Artaud," *A* 6, 16.

31. AN, *D* 6, 109.

32. "We write to create a world that is truer than the one before us," said AN, quoted in Highwater, *Shadow Show*, 10. Susan Henke ("AN: Bread and Wafer," 7–17) draws several comparisons between AN's diaries and Freud's *Interpretation of Dreams*: (1) both AN and Freud were "haunted by the need to gain control over personal trauma," (2) both were "victim[s] of Oedipal attachment," (3) both took refuge in father surrogates, and (4) both viewed psychoanalysis as the vehicle for self-discovery and "reclamation."

33. AN to Edmund Wilson, n.d., Edmund Wilson Collection, Beinecke Library, Yale University.

34. Lawrence, *Studies in Classic American Literature*, 54.

35. She was "the temperature taker of the mood and weather of the . . . soul," says Jean Garrigue ("The Diary of AN," 30), and a vital yet always minor strain in American literature. Though Kenneth Dick (*HM*, 138) says AN's writing fell "somewhere between the precious and the pretentious," he calls it "mood literature, like Haiku poetry, diaphanous like a Chinese painting of mist on far off mountains, vague like a shadow crossing the moors at dusk." Some told her to write about refrigerators, but she focused on reflection and relationships.

36. Bradford, "The Self," 14–25.

37. In *H&J* (113) AN calls the diary "a lie": "At the moment of writing I rush for the beauty. I disperse the rest. . . . I would like to come back like a detective, and collect what I have washed off."

38. Estelle C. Jelineck, "Discontinuity and Order: A Comparison of Women's and Men's Autobiographies" (seminar paper), quoted in Bloom and Holder, "AN's *Diary* in Context,"193. John Haffenden (*The Life of John Berryman*) compares the diaries of Berryman and AN in their scope and effect as "neurotic solutions to the problem

of living" and as self-gratifying mythoepic recreations of their adultery, 167–168, 178.

39. Daniel Stern ("The Novel of Her Life," 571) declares the diary is a novel in the form of a diary, "nothing less than a major 'fictional' construct of the modern era."

40. Some critics, such as Bettina Knapp and Sharon Spencer, prefer the surrealist and Jungian qualities of *Cities of the Interior,* AN's five-volume novel series.

41. AN was an early proponent of what is now called "essentialism," the position that women's difference from men is critical. She was "the quintessentially feminine artist," reflecting some women "back to themselves at twice their natural size, heightened into mythic propositions." Margaret Miller, "Seduction and Subversion," *A 1,* 88.

42. AN's subjective, unconscious view that we are all part of the whole is a view reinforced by recent studies such as Gilligan's *In a Different Voice,* which asserts that women are "relational" and not "autonomous."

43. AN has also been hurt by the defensive intolerance (and maudlin imitative sensibility) of those who love her most. In a 1993 assessment of AN criticism, Philip K. Jason says that it has been "cloistered in special houses where family manners required applause and assent and where a kind of incestuous siblinghood reigned." Jason, "Issues in Nin Criticism," *A 11,* 77.

44. Jong, *The Devil at Large,* 98.


## 1. TOO MUCH REALITY (*pages 10–26*)

1. AN, *House of Incest,* 26. The major sources for Chapter One are "Mon Journal," bound volumes 1–3, AN Collection 2066, box 2, UCLA, published in *Linotte,* the first volume of *The Early Diary of AN,* translated by Jean Sherman and published after AN's death. See also "The Labyrinth" in *Under a Glass Bell* and "Winter of Artifice" in the book of the same title.

2. AN, 20 Mar. 1933, *Incest: From "A Journal of Love,"* 125.

3. *New York Times* (11 Aug. 1914): 1, 2, 15; AN, *D 1,* 218; *ED 1,* 12–13, 501–2; Gilbert Culmell Chase, "From 'Kew' to Paris," *A 1,* 60.

4. All references to the thoughts of AN are taken from her diary, published and unpublished.

5. There were five Culmell sisters: Rosa, Edelmira, Antolina, Anaïs, and Juana. Their brother Thorvald was visiting with his family from Cuba, where their second brother, Enrique, also lived and where all seven siblings had been born. Several of the sisters lived in the New York area all or part of the time when they were not in Cuba, for the entire family had once sought refuge in New York during the Spanish-American War in 1898. Rosa, born 7 Dec. 1871, had been educated at the Brentwood Catholic convent in New York, where she learned English. Among them, the sisters had 17 children.

6. Dr. William O'Neill Erwin (interview 12 May 1992) says that whether or not AN was touched sexually, the experience of having her father take photographs of her in the nude is seduction, and seduction of an innocent child is abuse because it lays the foundation for later neurosis. The effect of seduction can be just as strong without physical contact as it would have been had he touched her arm or her genitals. "I believe one writes because one has to create a world in which one can live," wrote AN, *D 4,* 117.

7. Highwater, *Shadow Show,* 10.

8. AN, "The Labyrinth" in *Under a Glass Bell;* "I walked into my own book, seeking peace," *House of Incest,* 62.

9. Interview with Jean Sherman (19 Nov. 1991), who spent two years in the 1970s translating the diaries written in French (ages 11 to 17). She and AN agreed to leave out expressions such as "ha, ha," "good night," and "Dear diary," as well as some of the many expressions of Catholic piety.

10. Kathleen Leverich divides diarists into chroniclers, searchers, and fabricators. She uses Virginia Woolf as an example of the searcher, AN as an example of the fabricator. "Nin, Master of Artifice, Effect," 4.

11. In AN's only use of the "good self" and "bad self," she claims that the "incubator of fear" in her family made "goodness" a means to "attract love." *Four-Chambered Heart,* 84.

12. AN to Leo Lerman, printed in *D 4,* 177.

13. Hunter, "Inscribing the Self," 51–81; see also Carroll Smith-Rosenberg's "The New Woman as Androgyne."

14. D. W. Winnicott, President of the British Psychoanalytic Society, in *The Maturation Processes and the Facilitating Environment,* 144, 148, and *The Family and Individual Development,* 153.

15. AN later admitted to Lawrence Durrell that she was afraid of the world, AN to LD [ca. May 1938], Papers of LD, SIU.

16. AN, *ED,* 14, 502. Only recently have psychologists studied the importance of "father hunger" and the need for girls, if they are to be independent persons, to identify with a parent who goes out into the world. See, for example, Victoria Secunda's *Women and Their Fathers.*

17. *D 7,* 142; *ED 1,* 53, 66, 42, 164, 231. At various times in her life AN declared herself French or Spanish or American, though in music reference book biographies both her father and her brother called themselves Cuban.

18. A linguist friend who spoke both English and French with AN claims that her distinctive r's revealed her Spanish influence in both languages. "As a linguist, I was interested in her voice, which did not sound like a French woman speaking English." Interview with Lawrence Ferlinghetti, 1 Oct. 1992. Professor Albert Sonnenfeld, who notes the flattening of her t's, believes her accent is a Middle European phonetic mixture. He bases his analysis (9 Jan. 1993) upon the documentary of AN made by Robert Snyder in 1973.

19. AN, *ED 1,* 58.

20. Telephone interviews with Rupert Pole (16 Oct. 1992 and 19 Mar. 1993), who insists that AN was five seven and looked him in the eye. *Current Biography Yearbook* (1975), however, lists her height as five four.

21. Joaquin Nin-Culmell remembered his sister at her memorial celebration at the NYU library 22 Feb. 1977. Bernard, "A Reading and a Mourning," 32.

22. *ED 1,* 184, 40, 28, 49, 140, 109, 122. Even twenty years later she would tell Lawrence Durrell that she was only natural in her diary. AN to LD, n.d. [July 1937], Papers of LD, SIU.

23. "The isolation which strikes the neurotic at the first shock of destructive experience is not narcissism," AN declared when she was seventy. "It is a willful isolation and has nothing to do with self-love. It is a withdrawal to rescue what is left of a shattered self. In the same way, self-development and a quest for self-awareness and identity are not ego trips." AN at the Magic Circles weekend (1973). Harms, ed., 142.

24. Coleman, *Vital Lies,* 148. See also Kim Krizan, "Illusion and the Art of Survival," *A* 10 : 18–28.

25. AN, *ED 1,* 148.

26. On at least two occasions, AN describes her women characters as having an "1830's face"; e.g., Lyndall in "Fear of Nice" (*Waste of Timelessness,* 18).

27. AN, *ED 1,* 282. In a 1972 interview with AN, Betsy Brenneman ("AN," 4) describes her as "Swan-like . . . progressing by shyly lifting and then lowering her head."

28. Unpublished ms., "Father Story," Northwestern.

29. Her communion fantasy occurs when she is 11 years old, 15 Nov. 1914, first bound journal, UCLA, published in *Journal d'enfance: 1914–1919* (Paris: Stock, 1979), 61. (See also *ED 1,* 27.) Later she acknowledged a "confusion of religious ecstasy and incestuous passion." *H&J,* 245. The connection between sexuality and religiosity has long been evident, but its modern manifestation is best embodied in Flaubert's *Madame Bovary.*

30. Alice Miller, *Thou Shalt Not Be Aware,* 63.

31. AN, *House of Incest,* 17.

32. AN, "Stella" in *Winter of Artifice,* 30–31.

33. AN, *Seduction of the Minotaur,* 111–13.

34. AN, *D 1,* 76.

35. Unlike most of the pasted-in photographs and drawings in the original diary, this photograph was not reproduced in the published diary.

36. Djuna is the protagonist of *Children of the Albatross* and *Ladders to Fire.*

37. HM, *Book of Friends,* 267–68.

38. Kaspar Hauser. See Shengold, *Soul Murder.*

39. AN, *D 1,* 76; *D 6,* 154; *ED 1,* 234; *ED 3,* 147.

40. AN, *ED 1,* 181. She pasted postcards of Les Ruines in her journal. See also *D 1,* 76.

41. The scene of loss is recreated between Djuna and her father in *Children of the Albatross,* 195; see also *ED 1,* 446 and *D 1,* 217–18. Though AN would be amazed in 1932 when an analyst suggested that her father's desertion could have so brutalized her that she turned "to the ethereal," (*H&J,* 115–65), in *Winter of Artifice* (52) she says, "[t]he core of this drama is that at an early age I lost the element of joy."

42. Thorvald Christensen, father of this clan, had added the name Culmell to his name when he moved from Denmark to Cuba after stops in France, Haiti, and New Orleans. He had been a wealthy merchant and had been appointed Danish royal consul to Cuba 19 Aug. 1891. He was less fortunate with his wife, Anaïs Vaurigaud, a woman from New Orleans, who was born in Cuba. She left him and their seven children to run away with one of her many lovers. Rosa, the eldest, had reared her sisters and brothers (Anaïs, Antolina, Edelmira, Juana, Enrique, and Thorvald). With father Thorvald's death in 1907, his 22-year-old son and namesake became consul. Generally speaking, except for Rosa, the Culmell children had married well (only Edelmira had married an American, Gilbert Chase). Juana remained single. They were accustomed to money and travel, and proud of their *sangre-azul* (blue blood), and this would later have a strong influence on AN. Despite the Danish and French blood, the family was culturally and spiritually Cuban.

43. AN told several of her friends of her Jewish lineage, but Joaquin Nin-Culmell denies this lineage. Their father, Joaquin Nin (born 29 Sept. 1879), was the son of

Joaquin Maria Nin y Tudo (born in Barcelona, Spain) and Angela Castellanos de Perdomo (born in Cuba).

44. *ED 1,* 223–34; *D 1,* 103–4. Interview with Marguerite Young, 7 May 1991.

45. *New Century Cyclopedia of Names,* 1954.

46. Merchant, *AN's Texts of Pleasure,* 146.

47. Krishna Baldev Vaid, "Writing and Wandering," *A 5,* 49.

48. AN, *ED 1,* 88; *D 1,* 181, 248.

49. According to Marguerite Young (interview 7 May 1991) AN said that her grandfather Nin was cruel to Rosa and starved them because Rosa was Catholic and he was Jewish. Joaquin Nin-Culmell questions this heritage.

50. Dick, 108; see the story "Hejda" in *Under a Glass Bell.* The play (ms. UCLA) is about a blind father whose daughter has to describe the world for him. When he is cured, he is not shocked by the discrepancies between what he sees and what his daughter has described, but says he will create the world as she had described it for him.

51. *ED 2,* 89; *D 1,* 115, 201–3; *D 4,* 245. On her way from Paris to Mallorca many years later, AN realized that her "conscious life began" on that balcony in Barcelona, a "big, flat-roofed city at the foot of a mountain flanked by the sea." *ED 4,* 436.

52. Linotte (*linnet*) means songbird. When the diaries of the first four years, those written in French, were published after AN's death, the publisher entitled them *Linotte.* Contrary to current speculation that the childhood diaries sound too precocious for an 11-year-old, they are a fair translation (with spelling and grammatical corrections) by Jean Sherman of the originals.

53. Her friend James Herlihy claims AN had a talent for "passing onto other levels." (*D 4,* 76–77), and another friend tells of spending a day with her in and out of doors in 10-degree temperatures, she in a flimsy dress and cape but showing never a sign of chill. "I was freezing, but she seemed to be able to ignore her physical situation." Telephone interview with Benjamin Franklin V, 16 Nov. 1991.

54. Unpublished ms., "Father Story," Northwestern; *ED 4,* 338; Brandon, "AN." In *Winter of Artifice* (63) AN's narrator blames her lies on her father, and in *House of Incest* (40), she says, "I am enmeshed in my lies, and I want absolution. . . . I prefer fairytales . . . [T]he lies I tell [are] like costumes." See also *Incest,* 308.

55. HM (*Book of Friends,* 47) told his and AN's friend Fred Perlès that "before very long, the whole world will be made aware of her inveterate lying, her chicanery, her duplicity."

56. AN, May 1931, *ED 4,* 427.

57. AN, *ED 1,* 86, 68, 151; English, "An Interview with AN," in Zaller, ed., *A Casebook on AN,* 194.

58. Her awareness of her illusion-creating process is a sign of health and a reasonable and creative coping mechanism. Not surprisingly, she will come to specialize in the dream and psychoanalysis. But her rejection of reality all her life suggests a profound pessimism about the evil and ugliness of reality—and it is another argument for her being abused as a child.

59. AN, *ED 1,* 123.

60. AN, *ED 1,* 59, 37, 127, 27, 58.

61. Freud, "The Relation of the Poet to Daydreaming" (1908). Freud compared the imaginative writer with "one who dreams in broad daylight," 180.

62. *ED 1,* 9; *D 6,* 98.

63. Kraft, "Lux Aeterna Anaïs: A Memoir," unpublished ms., 321.

64. Eisler describes Georgia O'Keeffe's revenge against being told she was ugly with reference to Sartre's words in *O'Keeffe and Steiglitz*, 15.

65. "In the early volumes of her diary, Nin was obsessed with pleasing others, preoccupied with being loved, wanted, accepted. She preened the image of the perfect Anais for others and fled when they were taken in by the subterfuge. Feeding the perfection of the persona, her energies were expended on the role, on the appearance, which concealed the frightened self. Because of the split between real and apparent selves, the apparent self—no matter how perfect—was always experienced as insufficient." Nancy Jo Hoy, "The Poetry of Experience," *A 4,* 59.

66. Interview with Daisy Aldan, 20 Mar. 1991.

67. AN, *Winter of Artifice,* 73. Recent studies of the daughters of divorce or abandonment reveal that these individuals suffer from the following: yearning for intimacy yet fear of commitment, longing for love, debilitating fear of abandonment, chronic anxiety that others will leave them, sense of blame for their abandonment, hope for the return of the loved one, an over-bonding with the mother, early acting like a grown-up and losing out on childhood, unrealistic expectations of men, assuming of father's role and psychological characteristics, fragmentation from abuse, a tendency to throw themselves into many relationships and/or promiscuity. See Judith Wallerstein, *Second Chances.*

68. In "Stella" (*Winter of Artifice*), the protagonist is ashamed of her clothes and feels she looks like an orphan—a discomfort erased only "by becoming someone else" (32).

69. AN, *D 6,* 135, and *D 2,* 11, 8–9.

70. These tales were bound and entitled *Conte I* and *Conte II,* UCLA.

71. AN, *ED 1,* 171.

72. One friend who went Christmas shopping with AN late in life says her eye could be caught by every unusual and mysterious item. Interview with Deena Metzger, 6 Nov. 1991.

73. Chase, "AN—Rumor and Reality," 3.

74. Janeway, *Man's World, Woman's Place,* 56, 57, 83.

75. Late in life AN told a reporter that she had "the greatest gift for friendship . . . this feeling for people," which she thought she began learning in school. Chare, "Starring Herself," 11.

76. The one-page essay on liberty bonds, dated 23 Oct. 1917, is in the AN Collection, UCLA.

77. AN admits enjoying her childhood illnesses, "Journal d'une epouse: From the Diary of a Spouse, 1923–1924," *A 1,* 27, and *ED 3,* 44 (there are variations in these two accounts); *ED 1,* 183, 197.

78. AN, *Under a Glass Bell,* 87, 68.

## 2. PASSION AND PENITENCE (*pages 27–51*)

1. AN, *D 2,* 161, 310. The events of AN's life from ages 16 to 20 are detailed in *The Early Diary of AN*, vols. 1 (1914–20) and 2 (1920–23), and fictionalized in an unpublished story, "An Artist's Model," Northwestern. Her courtship is fictionalized in *Children of the Albatross*, 22–25. Her diary for 1918 has been lost (bound Diary IV, Jan. 1918–Mar. 1919).

2. AN, *D 2,* 181–82. No matter how traditional or archetypal is the image of mirrors for all authors, it is central to the life and very existence of AN.

3. Mesic, "An Appealing Chapter," 2.

4. Henke, "AN," 10.

5. Elisabeth Barillé, a French poet-novelist, calls AN anorexic and observes that in her fiction her "characters never eat" and the only smells "come from night clubs, from bedrooms, never from kitchens." *AN*, 64.

6. Tape of AN's lecture at Mills College.

7. Years later AN will say she dropped out of school in the sixth grade and never went to high school. Snyder, ed., *AN Observed*, 99. In *ED 4*, 228, she says she went to half a year of high school.

8. AN, *ED 2*, 43. See also *ED 1*, 219, 264, 355.

9. In a later work of fiction, *This Hunger*, (28), the narrator describes a hunger for human warmth and approval so profound that it thins the blood and makes the skin fragile.

10. AN, *ED 2*, 276.

11. AN, *D 1*, 69

12. AN, *ED 1*, 281.

13. AN, *ED 1*, 265.

14. AN, *ED 1*, 435. See also 258, 365–66. She declared her "noble blood" and "aristocratic" parentage (see 382, 402, 355–56).

15. AN, *D 6*, 21.

16. AN, *ED 1*, 387; *ED 2*, 189.

17. AN, *ED 1*, 275.

18. "Fulfillment itself was the danger," AN's narrator says of Lillian, the protagonist of *Seduction of the Minotaur*. *ED 1*, 418. See Dickinson's poem "I dwell in Possibility— / A fairer House than Prose—."

19. "In Richmond I was always meditating, eating my own thoughts," she says in the spring of 1928, *D 4*, 71. Original diary 7 (UCLA, box 2) has several clipped poems pasted into it and, in the back, a list of the books she has read.

20. AN, *ED 1*, 410, 472.

21. AN, *ED 2*, 386.

22. AN, *ED 1*, 480.

23. AN, *D 5*, 182.

24. AN will use Eduardo as a model for "Gerard" in *Seduction of the Minotaur*, written in the 1950s. Gerard had appealed to Lillian because of his passivity. He was safe and would not be "swept away" by life, for Lillian "fears being at the mercy of another human being" (108–9).

25. AN, *ED 1*, 488.

26. AN, *ED 2*, 460.

27. Dick, *HM*, 148.

28. AN, *ED 2*, 366.

29. AN, *ED 2*, 22.

30. AN, *ED 2*, 33–35.

31. AN, *ED 2*, 71, 101, 134.

32. AN, *ED 2*, 83; *D 2*, 180. The memory lapses, the tyrannical father, and so on are typical of the pattern that has recently been identified as associated with child abuse.

33. AN, *ED 1*, 72, 87.

34. AN, *A Spy in the House of Love,* 108–9, 133.

35. AN admitted that she studied four subjects: composition, grammar, French, "and boys." She was even distracted by her English teacher. *ED 2,* 197.

36. AN, *ED 2,* 156.

37. AN, *ED 2,* 159, 217.

38. AN, *ED 2,* 216, 219.

39. AN, *ED 2,* 162. The *La Bohème* character is Louise in Murger's novel, Mimi in Puccini's opera.

40. Rochelle Holt, "Luminescence: A Visit with Ian Hugo [Hugh Guiler]," unpublished ms., OSU; AN, *ED 2,* 188, 153.

41. AN, *ED 2,* 208.

42. AN, *Children of the Albatross,* 148.

43. AN, *ED 2,* 229.

44. AN, *ED 2,* 232.

45. The Spanish blood is not verified, according to Joaquin Nin-Culmell, "Hugo, My Brother-in-Law," *A 4,* 11.

46. Hugh Parker Guiler, "Recollections," *A 4,* 27. Hugo saw his parents only once every two years. The Guiler family was reunited in New York, where Hugo attended St. Paul's, in Garden City, and Columbia University.

47. AN, *ED 2,* 238.

48. Marie Bashkirtsev (1860–1884) was of Russian descent, began her diary at age twelve, aspired toward greatness as a painter, was described as a "beautiful hot house plant," and is buried in a $20,000 vault in the Passy Cemetery. Like AN, she was parodied and accused of self-love unbecoming of a woman.

49. AN, *H&J,* 163.

50. AN, *ED 2,* 303, 339. Years later, in the character of Djuna in *This Hunger,* AN acknowledges that she wore the "costume of utter femininity" to disguise the active, hungry lover.

51. AN, *ED 2,* 362.

52. In an erotic novel entitled *Elena,* AN will acknowledge Eduardo's psychological association of her with his mother and sister. Elena and Miguel, cousins who meet in crowded family holiday celebrations, fall in love. Elena has the same name as Miguel's mother and sister, and he thinks of them as he makes love to her. Ms., 94, UCLA.

53. "An Artist's Model" is part of a "first novel" written when AN was 19 years, old. Northwestern.

54. AN, *ED 2,* 407, 401. Interview with Betty Ryan Gordon, 6 July 1992.

55. AN describes the hard work and challenges of her modeling career in *ED 2,* 414, 416, 423; her later acknowledgment of her humiliation, her "first confrontation with the world," comes in *D 2,* 57, and *D 6,* 32.

56. In an early version of "Winter of Artifice," called "Father Story," AN's young protagonist talks about the groping artists, referring to them as "Jews," and says that for years she could not remember her modeling experience because the "intensity had been unbearable." Northwestern. Two decades after the modeling experiences, AN uses them for a long erotic story called "Artists and Models" (originally titled "Artist Model"). Box 7, folder 7, UCLA.

57. "Father Story" undergoes considerable change before being published as a fictional short story entitled "Winter of Artifice." Early versions reveal the sexual experi-

ences, later deleted, that lead up to her reunion with her father. She implies that she knew Boris before Hugo. Box 3, folder 4, part 3, Northwestern. In the early versions, Boris Hoppe's name is used. He is mentioned by name as a friend of Hugo's who attempts to make love to her in *ED 2*, 415–18.

58. The last words in the burgundy datebook given to her by Eduardo (inscribed to "My Lost Princess") declare it the diary of AN and Hugo, 16 June 1922. Box 9, diary 17, UCLA. By the next journal, "Journal d'Une Fiancée," she has moved away from daily entries.

59. AN, *ED 2*, 426. She reveals more of her sexual fears in a 1931 diary, *ED 4*, 441–44, 486.

60. AN, *ED 2*, 464.

61. AN, *ED 2*, 459, 462.

62. Telephone interview with Rupert Pole, 7 Jan. 1992.

63. AN, *ED 2*, 473–74.

64. AN, *ED 2*, 477.

65. In an interview with Priscilla English, AN said she left the church at sixteen ("*New Woman*," 29); AN, *D 6*, 215.

66. AN, *Four-Chambered Heart*, 112.

67. In a brief fictionalized portrait of AN's life, Elisabeth Barillé (44–47) suggests that Aunt Antolina, a "merry widow" with many lovers, comes to AN's rescue by taking her to Cuba and helping to arrange the marriage between Guiler and her niece.

68. AN, *ED 2*, 495, 497, 504, 519.

69. According to Daisy Aldan (interview 5 Dec. 1991), who was AN's intimate friend years later, Tana de Gamez became a novelist, worked with the resistance in the Spanish Civil War, raised money for Israel, and settled in New York as an editor. Aldan would meet de Gamez through AN in the 1950s. AN expressed envy of her Spanish friend's bawdiness: "She takes what she wants." Yet she did not win AN, Aldan was told. De Gamez claimed she attended the Guiler wedding and saw the newlyweds to their departure.

70. AN, *ED 2*, 502.

71. AN, *H&J*, 257. The months in Cuba, AN writes as the last entry of the year 1923, "did not make me five months older, but a woman." AN, *A 1*, 17. Her behavior, considered libertine for the time and place, shocked her cousins. In an unpublished early draft (1935) of her "Father Story," AN reveals her flirtatious behavior with the young Cuban men.

72. When AN fictionalizes this scene in *A Spy in the House of Love*, "Alan" (Hugo) is a protective, fatherly husband who smokes a pipe and is five years older than Sabina (AN); he "rushed to comfort and to shelter" (17).

73. Joaquin Nin-Culmell, "Hugo, My Brother-in-Law," *A 4*, 13; *ED 2*, 512, 513, 515.

74. AN, *ED 2*, 522. In *Children of the Albatross*, AN says that as other brides prepare a trousseau by sewing, she "embellished her cities of the interior" in preparation for "a great love" (17).

75. AN, "Journal d'une Epouse," *A 1*, 22; *ED 3*, 30. Telephone interview with Rupert Pole, 7 Jan. 1992.

### 3. PORTRAIT OF A WIFE (*pages 52–70*)

1. Flaubert, *Madame Bovary*, 24. AN, *ED 2*, 523. This period of AN's life (ages 20–24) is covered in six bound diaries, the first of which is called "Journal d'une Epouse,"

box 10, AN Collection, UCLA, and published with alterations and some deletions as *The Early Diary of AN*, vol. 3 (1983). Unpublished fiction reflecting the marital tensions of this period includes "Aline's Choice," the "Unfinished Novel" of Rita, and a "Play" (Northwestern). See also the erotic story called "Lilith" in *Delta of Venus*.

2. AN, "Journal d'une Espouse," *A 1* (1983), 3–41, and *ED 3*, 1–72, contain different portions and versions of her diary for these years and reveal the editorial alterations made to the diaries after her death, in 1977, when all four volumes of the early diaries were published.

3. AN, *ED 3*, 280. Rosa and Joaquin were not yet legally divorced. Two years after the wedding, Hugo's uncle George Guiler reconciled with him, expressing regret for the falling out over AN's Catholicism. *ED 4*, 27.

4. AN's credit and blame for Hugo's inaction and failure to know what he wants was made September 1929. *ED 4*, 227.

5. AN, 30 June 1924, bound diary 20 (UCLA), which includes the date for the passage published in *ED 3*, 46.

6. Telephone Interview with Rupert Pole, 7 Jan. 1992.

7. AN, *ED 4*, 447. While admitting her "virgin's natural recoil," AN describes Hugo's impotence, ill health, and weakness. In retrospect, she believed he could have gently seduced her. In "The Voice," the final portion of *Winter of Artifice*, written in the late 1930s, she describes Lilith's resistance to intercourse and her simple husband's inability to "woo her," 146. Interview with Sharon Spencer, 23 Apr. 1992. AN, "Dreams," *A 10*, 9.

8. Dr. Erika Freeman (telephone interview 26 Apr. 1992) confirms that the "reaction formation" of nonconsummation is certainly one indication of probable child molestation. Other indications include the development of escape mechanisms, obsessive organization, and a need to control. Dr. Freeman, who was a friend of AN's, was not aware until recently of the early circumstances of the Guiler marriage.

9. "I love to weep; I love to give myself up to despair; I love to be troubled and sorrowful," said Bashkirtsev, *Journal*, 29.

10. AN, *ED 3*, 8; *ED 4*, 487.

11. In *Seduction of the Minotaur*, AN explains that Lillian and Larry select each other in order to keep "their fears from overwhelming them." Larry is described as being absent from his own body because his mother did not want him, punished him for interacting with the natives of "Brazil" (Puerto Rico), punished him for examining his brother's sex, and sent him away to boarding school, 109, 132–36.

12. AN, *ED 3*, 33.

13. Flaubert, *Madame Bovary*, 24.

14. AN, *ED 4*, 447.

15. Interview with Marguerite Young, 5 Dec. 1991.

16. AN, *ED 3*, 44.

17. AN, "Journal d'une Epouse," *A 1*, 27.

18. *Journals of Ralph Waldo Emerson*, vol. 5, 516.

19. She told HM ([23 July 1932] *ALP*, 71–72) that she loved the word "transcendental," which she got from Emerson.

20. Anna Balakian (interview 9 Mar. 1991) quotes Hugo: "Anaïs does not know any language well. All her languages are incorrect." Balakian adds that precisely be-

cause "her communication is not idiomatic, her fiction is not dated . . . her most frequent words are universal."

21. The idealized portrait (*ED* 3, 45–46) of AN's wedding night is contradicted by her later reports to Rupert Pole (interview 7 Jan. 1992) and *ED* 4, 447.

22. AN, *ED* 3, 80.

23. AN, *ED* 3, 65.

24. To avoid confusion for the reader, the name Hugo is used throughout this book. Hugh Guiler will later change his name to Ian Hugo.

25. AN, *ED* 3, 78–79.

26. In his notes to "The Waste Land," T. S. Eliot credits his expression "Unreal City" to Baudelaire: "*Fourmillante cité, cité pleine de rêves.*"

27. AN, *ED* 3, 80.

28. AN, *ED* 3, 80–81.

29. AN, *ED* 4, 486. By conforming to her "ideal," Guiler becomes "gentle and colorless," she admits later, 487.

30. In March she lists those she has tried to "set . . . aflame": Eduardo Sanchez, Enric Madriguera, Miguel Jorrin, Frank Monteiro, Eugene, Francis, Richard Maynard, Ruth, and the artists for whom she posed, *ED* 3, 129.

31. Finding the erotic novels is acknowledged in her diary in May 1932, at which time she is in therapy with Dr. Allendy. "Even today I cannot enter a hotel room without feeling that first shiver of delight awakened by the books of Mr. Hansen." AN, *D* 1, 95–97.

32. AN, *ED* 3, 95.

33. AN, *ED* 3, 121. See also 148 and 185 for references to her father.

34. If Rosa, Joaquin, and AN had come full circle with their visit to Hendaye, south of Arcachon, where their father had abandoned them, AN and Hugo drew a larger circle when in July they visited her youthful abode at Uccle, a 20-mile drive from Brussels.

35. Joaquin Nin-Culmell, "Preface," *ED* 3, xiii.

36. Interview with Fabion Bowers, a friend of Katrine Coolidge Perkins's, 19 Mar. 1991. Bowers reports that she was intrigued with AN, who was the first woman she had seen wearing gold sandals in the evening.

37. AN, *ED* 3, 186.

38. Gerald Kennedy (*Imagining Paris*, 14–22) offers a thorough analysis of the importance of the "High Place" in allowing Anaïs to grasp the larger meaning of Paris and to conquer the sinister face of Paris (symbolized in her description of the gargoyles of Notre-Dame). She "articulated her displacement through a recognizable sign of place . . . [and] absorbed the topographical subtleties of Paris," says Kennedy (19, 22).

39. Dick, *HM*, 112.

40. AN, *Children of the Albatross*, 20. Djuna, her alter ego, dances a "deft dance of unpossession" with her disguises and lies.

41. AN, *ED* 3, 235.

42. AN, "Lilith" in *Delta of Venus*, 58–59.

43. AN, *ED* 3, 221.

44. AN, *ED* 3, 223.

45. Anna Balakian, "A Tale of Two People," *A* 6, 59, 65.

46. Her love of clothes and the glamour of Parisian cultural life would come back to

haunt her when both HM and LD commented on her bourgeois life. She insisted to Durrell that she had not wanted this bourgeois life but the artistic life. AN to LD, 29 Nov. 1973, SIU.

47. AN, *ED 3*, 285.

## 4. INTIMATE BETRAYAL (*pages 71–99*)

1. AN, *Ladders to Fire*, 127. AN, *D 1*, 8. The period of her life from ages 24 to 28 is described in six leather-bound volumes (nos. 25–31 of "Journal and Note Book," dating from 9 Nov. 1927 to 19 Oct. 1931), as yet uncataloged when I read them in the AN Collection, UCLA. Large portions of these journals were published as *ED 4* (1927–31). Her fictional treatment of these years is far more revealing, particularly drafts of stories in the archives of Northwestern: several versions of the unpublished "John Novel" and 25 early short stories, some of which were published after her death in *Waste of Timelessless* (1977). A fictional treatment of her marriage and other relationships is evident in erotica manuscripts such as "Lilith" and "Elena," at Kinsey and UCLA.

2. AN uses this experience with Miralles in the opening scene of her novel *Children of the Albatross* (1947), where she says that her "skirt like a full-blown flower opened to allow a kiss to be placed at the core. A kiss enclosed in the corolla of the skirt and hidden away. . . ." (7).

3. AN, *ED 4*, 2.

4. James (*Parisian Sketches*, 3) notes that the returning American is "hungrily, inevitably, fatally" and most acutely aware of Paris.

5. AN, *ED 4*, 20, 37.

6. AN, *ED 4*, 25. Probably her friend Boussie did not yet know this new generation of midwestern writers, such as Hemingway, for her protégé claimed that Armand Godoy, a Peruvian/Cuban poet now forgotten, is the "greatest poet alive" (18).

7. AN, *Incest*, 196.

8. When John Ferrone, AN's editor at Harcourt Brace, was editing "Lilith" and other erotica for *Delta of Venus*, he guessed she was paraphrasing her stories from her unexpurgated diary. Ferrone, "The Making of *Delta of Venus*" in Spencer's *Anais, Art and Artists*, 42.

9. AN, *ED 4*, 38.

10. Meryle Secrest ("Economics and the Need for Revenge," *A 6*, 33) calls AN's self-created image a "mirage" and claims she fails the first test of freedom, which is economic.

11. Joaquin Nin-Culmell, Preface, *ED 4*, xiii.

12. AN, *ED 4*, 81, 82, 84–86.

13. AN, *ED 4*, 71, 80.

14. AN to John Erskine, n.d. [Apr. 1928], Erskine Collection, Columbia.

15. AN, *ED 4*, 67. Many of these short stories will be published in *Waste of Timelessness*.

16. AN, *ED 4*, 54.

17. AN, *A Spy in the House of Love*, 26.

18. AN, *ED 4*, 137.

19. AN, *ED 4*, 141, 316. In the leather-bound "Journal and Note Book," 26, AN makes two lengthy parallel lists contrasting herself to Colette. The lists were condensed and presented in paragraph form for publication in *ED 4*, 141 (an illustration of the editorial freedoms taken by her executors).

20. In "Fear of Nice," AN makes the male protagonist afraid of a young woman's powers. This and other awkward early stories of this period were not published until 1977, in *Waste of Timelessness*.

21. AN, *ED 4*, 153, 131.

22. The infrequent visits of her brother Thorvald, 23 at this time, have little effect on her life until this year, when after several weeks in Paris and a summer visit with their mother in Hendaye, he saw their father in nearby St.-Jean-de-Luz and decided to stay with him. AN concluded that he was like their father.

23. AN, "Our Minds Are Engaged," in *Waste of Timelessness*, 44.

24. AN, *Seduction of the Minotaur*, 131, 136.

25. AN, *ED 4*, 174.

26. AN, *ED 4*, 188–89. AN pastes into her diary the brochure picture of the Lapérouse, and inside the front cover of her current diary she pastes a photograph of John Erskine.

27. AN, *ED 4*, 190.

28. AN, *ED 4*, 199.

29. Kathleen Chase, the wife of AN's cousin, describes this apartment, the concerts and opera they attend together, and Hugo's guitar accompaniment of his wife's dancing. "Being 'Family' in France," *A 1*, 63–65.

30. Leo Lerman (1967), *D 4*, 177.

31. AN, "Faithfulness," in *Waste of Timelessness*, 81.

32. AN, "Tishnar," in Ibid., 62.

33. Claude Debussy's opera *Pelléas et Mélisande* (1902), after *Tristan* and the play by Maurice Maeterlinck (1892).

34. AN, *ED 4*, 301. Upon her return from Caux, AN joins Sylvia Beach's Shakespeare and Company bookshop and lending library, a center for avant-garde writers; she checked out several books during the coming weeks, including e. e. cummings's *The Enormous Room*.

35. AN, "A Slippery Floor," in *Waste of Timelessness*, 88, 101, 104.

36. On this occasion Joaquin and Eduardo do escape Rosa and go to Granada. AN states in her diary of 12 January 1930 that she observes in Paris that the two cousins are attracted to each other and acknowledges that Eduardo talks to her about this attraction. In March she says he has proposed love to Joaquin, who rejects him. She accuses her brother of being "mother-bound" and "puritan" on several occasions. *ED 4*, 404, 407.

37. The "Elena" ms. (UCLA) is 200 pages in length and includes several pieces that were carved out for publication in *Delta of Venus*.

38. The best description of the house in Louveciennes is found in the opening passages of *D 1* (1931–34), pages written for publication in 1966. In 1989 *Anais: An International Journal* published many of AN's diary passages about Louveciennes in "A House and a Garden," *A 8*, 32–46.

39. AN, "Our Minds Are Engaged," in *Waste of Timelessness*, 45.

40. This erotic relationship between AN and Eduardo is the basis of a portion of the 200-page manuscript called "Elena" (UCLA).

41. *The Canadian Forum* (11, no. 121, 15–17) was published in Toronto. Two short pieces ("Why Every Home Should Own a Liberty Bond" and "The Password" were printed in her public school quarterly, *The Criterion*, John Jasper School, P.S. 9, 72d Street). Some adolescent poetry appeared in *The Delineator*, a magazine for young women.

42. The desire of the narrator of "Waste of Timelessness" is to escape her "usual husband" in order to "find a world which fits me and my philosophy." *Waste of Timelessness,* 1, 4.

43. The typed manuscript of "The Gypsy Feeling," written early in 1931, is full of typos, misspellings, clichéd language, dashes, and awkward descriptions of the dance, and reveals no plot or character development. In her diary of this period, AN says she wrote it with impatience and first called it "The Gypsy Dancer," AN Collection 2066, box 7, file 4, Northwestern. Published in *Waste of Timelessness,* 23–27.

44. Chase, "Being 'Family' in France," 63–66. In addition to her description of the house in Louveciennes, Chase establishes that AN and Hugo were surrounded by family who lived and visited in the house.

45. Perlès, *My Friend HM,* 107.

46. AN, *Children of the Albatross,* 18, 16.

47. The Proclamation was signed by 16 writers, including Jolas, Kay Boyle, Caresse Crosby, and Stuart Gilbert (AN will eventually meet the last three). See *In transition,* intro., NRF, 19.

48. AN to LD, n.d. [July 1937], SIU.

49. Pierpont, "Sex, Lies, and Thirty-five Thousand Pages," 75.

50. AN, *ED 4,* 395. Bern Porter to NRF, 19 Nov. 1990.

51. AN, *ED 4,* 442. This July (1931), she admits in euphemistic terms her delayed "sensual awakening" two years after her marriage in 1925.

52. AN, Journal 33, UCLA and *ED 4,* 442. In writing erotica a decade later in New York City, she includes a story about Linda's trip to Mallorca with her Spanish maid, during which time she masturbates four or five times a day. UCLA.

53. AN told her first analyst that she masturbated on vacations, including this one in St.-Jean-de-Luz, though afterward she felt ashamed and depressed because she believed the act was "wrong, morally and physically." *H&J,* 173.

54. AN, *ED 4,* 414.

55. She calls her lies "embroidery" or "fixing up things." *ED 4,* 430. She does not identify her lies to Eduardo. "[F]ew know how many women there are in me" (419, 71).

56. AN, *ED 4,* 396, 426, 437–38, 443.

57. AN, *ED 4,* 460, 441, 447.

58. AN's insight about lies (*ED 4,* 481–82) is, of course, the premise of fiction.

59. AN, *H&J,* 238.

60. "I want a baby." Unpublished portion (29 Oct. 1931) of "Journal and Note Book" 32, in which several weeks are lost between *ED 4,* published in 1985, and *D 1,* published in 1966.

61. Eduardo says he would take AN himself if he did not fear his own impotency. AN, "Breaking Through the 'Ideal' Barrier," *A 4,* 6–8.

## 5. A LITERARY PASSION (*pages 100–144*)

1. AN, "With Henry and June," *A 5,* 13. This is the Nov. 1932 portion of what will later be published as *Incest.*

2. HM to Emil Schnellock, *Letters to Emil,* 107.

3. Bound journals nos. 30–38, only about half of which were used for *The Diary of AN,* vol. 1. Other major sources for this period of AN's life (ages 28–33) are the unexpurgated portions of this diary published as *Henry and June* (1986) and (the first third of) *Incest* (1992). The correspondence to and from HM in *A Literate*

*Passion* is also a major source for this period. Her fictional accounts of the events are in several unpublished manuscript versions (at Northwestern) of "Alraune 1" (*House of Incest*) and "Alraune 2" ("Rab, Alraune, Mandra" and "Winter of Artifice"); in various versions of her "Father Story," finally published (in *The Winter of Artifice*) as "Djuna" (not republished after 1939 until *A 7*, 3–22); and in the novel *Ladders to Fire*. It is fictionally revisited in *Seduction of the Minotaur*, 95–136. From no other period of her life does she draw so much for her fictional subject matter. HM appears with various names, such as Pierre, in pieces of her erotica written in the 1940s and housed at UCLA and Kinsey.

4. AN, *H&J*, 6–7. According to the unpublished diary, this meeting occurs 9 Dec.

5. AN, *H&J*, 8–9.

6. AN, *H&J*, 10. This publication of the expurgated portion of *D 1* occurred in 1986, after the deaths of AN, Guiler, and HM.

7. AN, *H&J*, 10.

8. AN, "Breaking Through the 'Ideal' Barrier," *A 4*, 10, 4–5. This excerpt covers the unexpurgated portion for the completion of October 1931, at the end of *ED 4*.

9. AN, *H&J*, 1; *A 4*, 6–8, 10; these two sources, though both published in 1986, use different wordings and first names for Guiler, who began to use the name Ian Hugo in the 1950s.

10. AN, *H&J*, 4–5; *A 4*, 8.

11. AN, *H&J*, 10, 5; AN uses expressions such as "madness" and "hysteria" to describe her mental state at this time.

12. The date of the meeting of AN and HM is established by the original diary. Some confusion about the date of their first meeting is caused by an error on AN's part: she writes 31 "December" in her diary, though all the days surrounding it in sequence are November. Following this error, someone penciled in "October" on HM's first letter addressed to "Mr. and Mrs. Guyler," about their forthcoming meeting. This letter, like other letters through January 1932, is addressed to Mr. Guiler or Mrs. Guiler or to them both. When these letters (SIU) were later published, they were edited so as to appear to be addressed to AN (*LAN*). Others have misdated the meeting with HM as October because journal 32 begins on that date. A close examination of the original diary establishes the meeting as occurring on the last day of November 1931.

13. HM (1891–1980), the son of a Brooklyn tailor and a mother from whom he felt emotional rejection, had married twice and fathered one child, a daughter by his first wife. Though he had taken his writing seriously since 1924, he had not yet published his first book.

14. Interview with George Seldes, 23 July 1981. In a letter to AN, HM emphasizes the "peace and security" he experienced in her house, [Dec. 1931], *LAN*, 4. Later, in her novel *A Spy in the House of Love,* in which he appears as Jay (a kind of Lao-tzu), HM is described as finding an audience for his nonstop talking in Paris cafés (114).

15. Fearing the crude language might be offensive, HM would have Osborn read the manuscript first, before showing it to AN, HM to AN [Dec. 1931], *LAN*, 4.

16. AN, *Ladders to Fire*, 40, where HM is Jay. Her best fictional characterization of HM was "Hans and Johanna," originally called "Alraune," and published as a novella entitled "Djuna" in *The Winter of Artifice* (1939) but dropped from the revised edition of *Winter of Artifice* (no article) because it was too revealing. The more poetical, and thus disguised, version of the Anaïs-Henry-June story, *The House of*

*Incest,* was written at the same time in the 1930s. Long out of print, "Djuna" was reprinted in 1989 in *A* 7, 3–22.

17. Her descriptions of their first meeting, and the lunch that follows, have been rewritten, partially quoted, and vary considerably. This description of the lunch (called dinner in a rewritten version) is based on several versions: *D 1,* 8–11, 14; *H&J,* 5–6; Stuhlmann's introduction to *ALP,* x; and unpublished diary no. 30. In her unpublished "John Novel" (Northwestern) Duncan tells the protagonist he would like her to meet a man who is casual and brutal, "a torrent" who "laughs at miracles." She wants to meet him, she says.

18. *ALP,* xiii–xiv.

19. "Wambly Bald Meets Henry Miller," reprinted in Ford, ed., *The Left Bank Revisited,* 142–44.

20. Jay Martin calls them "actor and actress" in *Always Merry and Bright,* 241.

21. "Between Henry and me there is the diabolical compact of two writers who understand each other's human and literary life" and egotism, *ALP,* xv. "He is like me," AN had written in her diary soon after meeting HM.

22. Telephone interview with George Wickes, 19 Sept. 1990.

23. Mailer, *Genius and Lust,* 367.

24. June Edith Smith Miller (also known as June Mansfield) was born 7 June 1902 and had worked as a waitress and taxi dancer to support HM after their marriage, 1 June 1924, when she was 21 and he 32.

25. AN, *D 1,* 9–19.

26. AN, *H&J,* 33; *Crazy Cock* was not published until 1991. June met Jean Kronski in a Greenwich Village club, according to Dearborn (*The Happiest Man Alive,* 105), and their "relationship was passionate and intense."

27. According to Dearborn (79), June was born Juliet Edith Smerth, with "blue-black hair." AN and June meeting: *D 1,* 20–21; *H&J,* 14–15; the latter is truncated, in places rewritten, and less critical. By omitting Hugo in the first published diary, AN creates major distortions; e.g., jealous expressions of Hugo are credited to Joaquin or to her own observations; Wambly Bald, in the *Paris Tribune* (25 July 1933) called her "the girl with the golden face" (Ford, ed., *The Left Bank Revisited,* 148).

28. AN, *D 1,* 22, 140; Hans-Joanna-Djuna ms., see *A* 7, 20.

29. Scholar, *AN,* 56.

30. When preparing her diary for publication decades later, AN says it is Joaquin who prevents HM's violence from exploding. *D 1,* 22.

31. AN, *H&J,* 16–17.

32. AN, *D 1,* 28. Lori Wood argues that in re-valuing June, AN "revalored" the dark, feminine qualities of the artist as woman. "Between Creation and Destruction," *A* 8, 15–26. AN, *H&J,* 19.

33. AN, *D 1,* 26.

34. This leather-bound diary was begun 29 Oct. 1931. See also *D 1,* 26. An article on June in Wambly Bald's "La Vie de Bohème" column in the *Tribune* is also pasted into her diary, UCLA.

35. Barillé, *AN,* 89.

36. AN, *H&J,* 20; AN had first learned about lesbian love while reading Lawrence, and she recognized her first lesbian, a woman she called Mrs. E, in Barcelona a few months before (*ED 4,* 458–60).

37. AN, *D 1*, 28–29; *H&J*, 20–22.

38. AN, *H&J*, 22–23; *D 1*, 29–31.

39. This account of the relationship is AN's view (*H&J*, 23–26; *D 1*, 31–32). June later denied to several people that they had had any sexual relationship or that she had taken anything from AN (interview with Daisy Aldan, 20 Mar. 1991). She gave the coral earrings and turquoise ring back, she told Dick, *HM*, 120.

40. AN, *D 1*, 35–39; *H&J*, 26–31; June later claims that it was AN who made a pass at her (Dick, *HM*, 139).

41. AN, *D 1*, 39–40; *H&J*, 31–32.

42. AN, *D 1*, 43; *H&J*, 33.

43. AN, *H&J*, 35 (this entire episode is suppressed in the first published diary).

44. AN to HM, 3 Feb. 1932, *ALP*, 1.

45. AN, *H&J*, 35–36.

46. HM to AN, 4 Mar. 1932, *ALP*, 16. Most of the letters that they did send each other are in *LAN* and *ALP*. See HM's account of life in Dijon in the last portion of *Tropic of Cancer.*

47. Martin, *Always Merry and Bright*, 208; AN, *H&J*, 203.

48. AN, *D 1*, 40.

49. AN to HM, 3 Feb. 1932, *LAN*, 4–6; *ALP*, 1–2.

50. She is split in two, and into two diaries. The large leather diary is called "The Possessed" and begins 2 February. The other one, half its size, begins 16 February and declares that she is giving up this possession by her imagination. Clearly a neurotic splitting of personality or a decoy for a husband's eyes. UCLA.

51. AN to HM, 12 Feb. 1932, *ALP*, 4.

52. *D 1*, 50; AN told various versions of the typewriter story through the years, most portray her gift as a sacrifice, which he pawned, though the letters suggest he did not ask for the machine and in fact informed her that someone else had offered him one.

53. AN to HM, 22 Feb. and 13 Feb. 1932, *ALP*, 12, 9. AN, *H&J*, 45.

54. AN, *D 1*, 47, 51. The aristocratic view of sex separates passion and marriage—Erica Jong (quoting Bedford) to NRF, 3 June 1991. After reading *Incest* in 1993, Jong declared that AN "utterly transformed" female sexual behavior by living out all her fantasies (*Devil at Large*, 98).

55. AN, *H&J*, 49, and *D 1*, 55.

56. "I still suffered under . . . [a] 'black cloud,' this terrible religious and moral oppression," said Hugo Guiler, "Recollections," *A 4*, 27.

57. There are many variations in the wording in *D 1* and the so-called unexpurgated version in *H&J*, 50–51, and *ALP*, xvii—the latter two versions published long after her death. These variations illustrate the corruption of the original text by AN and her editors. They also reveal the artful rewriting of the diary to keep a narrative line and include more dialogue. On her fear of the masculine figure: the character The Voice in *Winter of Artifice* (151) tells Lilith that she cannot "bear to be . . . dominated."

58. AN, Journal 33, UCLA; *H&J*, 51.

59. AN, *Incest*, 129.

60. Journal 33, UCLA. AN, *H&J*, 53.

61. AN, *ALP*, 16; *H &J*, 54.

62. HM to AN, 4 Mar. 1932, *ALP*, 16–17.

63. In her final fictionalization of her affair with HM, she concludes in the 1950s that she/Lillian had expected HM/Jay to be a passionate and violent cannibal whose actions echoed his violent talk, for she had been conditioned by her father to want (and fear) violence with intimacy. AN, *Seduction of the Minotaur,* 114ff.

64. Journal 33, UCLA. The first and most detailed presentation of this incident is found in her "Alraune" manuscript, later renamed the "Djuna-Hans-Joanna" manuscript, published only once in her lifetime as "Djuna" (1936, repr. as "Hans and Joanna" in *A 7,* 3–22), where she uses phrases such as "dreams of semen" and "furnace of caresses." A later and further fictionalized version is AN, *Ladders to Fire* (1946); the unexpurgated diary account is found in *H&J,* 56–58; A letter establishes the date: AN to HM, 9 Mar. [1932], *ALP,* 21–22, 137. Gunther Stuhlmann guesses that the consummation was 8 Mar. 1932. Béatrice Commengé (*HM,* 137–38) recreates this scene from HM's point of view.

65. Interviews with Frank Alberti (19 Aug. 1990) and André Bay (9 Aug. 1990); AN, *H&J,* 59–60.

66. AN, *H&J,* 76–77,100, 133; whorehouse: *H&J,* 70–72; when she types this incident thirty years later, she says HM took her there, refers to "Henry's whores," and truncates the incident, distorting the experience. *D 1,* 58–60. The rue Blondel incident, prominent in Kaufman's film *Henry and June* (1991), was used by AN in "Erotika" (Kinsey).

67. AN, *ALP,* 22; H&J; 61; *D 1,* 60–61.

68. Journal 33, UCLA. AN, *H&J,* 73–74. The published and unpublished versions vary.

69. AN, *H&J,* 79. When rewriting her diary in the 1960s, after they had a falling out, AN called Perlès "timid, sad-eyed, a sad clown," *D 1,* 62; he later called her "ductile and malleable" in his *My Friend HM,* 37.

70. Perlès, *My Friend HM,* 5.

71. AN, *H&J,* 81; AN was in such sexual heat at the beginning of her affair with HM that she becomes aroused during a professional massage (80).

72. Journal 34, in purple leather, a gift from Eduardo, begins 18 April 1932 and is entitled "Henry"; later she adds "René Allendy" to the title.

73. AN, *H&J,* 90–92; all but the Proust quotes are omitted from *D 1,* 65, thus reversing the meaning and context of the quotations.

74. Interview with Betty Ryan Gordon, a neighbor and lifelong friend of HM's, 6 July 1992. Ryan also stresses his cleanliness: "Even if he wore the same pink shirt or green tweed jacket, he and his apartment were always clean. In his writing, his fantasy is phallic, his reality is the streets and his friends."

75. Perlès, "Pieta at Clichy," translated from Perlès's *Sentiments Limitrophes* by Frank S. Alberti, *A 5,* 15–18. Both HM and Perlès were warned by AN not to use her name in any memoirs or fiction; Perlès, *My Friend HM,* 37. Her descriptions of her Clichy visits can be found in *H&J,* 92–93, and *D 1,* 62 ff. Perlès calls her "a marvelous cook" (90) for her Spanish omelets and paella, but all other reports indicate otherwise.

76. Gore Vidal to NRF, 26 Feb. 1991.

77. HM, *Quiet Days in Clichy,* 41; HM to ES, 14 Oct. 1932, *Letters to Emil,* 107.

78. HM, *Quiet Days in Clichy,* 24, 41; Perlès, *My Friend HM,* 38, 116–17—a book almost ghostwritten by HM, says George Wickes (telephone interview 19 Sept. 1990).

79. AN, *D 1,* 8–9, 72, 73; *H&J,* 81, 204; AN to HM, [21 Mar. 1932], *ALP,* 35.

80. In *A Spy in the House of Love,* the narrator says the dropping of her eyelashes and

head, which create a gesture of apparent obedience and docility, is really "a form of absence," 94.

81. HM to AN, [3 Apr. 1932], *ALP,* 46.

82. Mary Dearborn to NRF, 10 Oct. 1992.

83. AN, *D. H. Lawrence,* 144. Gilbert (*Acts of Attention*) says that H.D., AN, Katherine Mansfield, and Mabel Dodge Luhan were "women in love" with Lawrence because he advocated flux, nature, body, and saw men as the second sex.

84. AN to John Erskine, 21 and 28 Nov. 1931 and 16 Feb. 1932, John Erskine Collection, Columbia.

85. Waverley Root is best known for his many books on food. His review, which appeared in Mar. 1932, is reprinted in *A 6,* 75–76.

86. Telephone interview with Dr. James E. Lieberman, 8 Dec. 1992.

87. Versions of this first visit vary considerably between *D 1,* 74–77 and *H&J,* 96–97, 107, 114–16; for one thing, she leaves Eduardo out, claiming that a patient named Marguerite S. introduced her to Allendy.

88. AN, *H&J,* 116, 118, 128–34; *D 1,* 81–83.

89. Meiselman, *Incest,* 232–34.

90. Alraune, the German name for the mandrake plant, is a word June loved and thus the name that AN gives her fictional character. AN, *Incest,* 31.

91. Again, there is considerable variation in the versions described in *D 1,* 86–88, and *H&J,* 138–39. In *H&J* (145), Allendy tells her she has two voices—the breathy innocent child and the deeper confident woman—but in *D 1* (91) she credits Perlès with this observation.

92. AN, *H&J,* 139–43. In 1966 she omitted most of this material and indicated that HM had questioned her about her mother and brother, not about Hugo, *D 1,* 89.

93. The "Alraune" manuscript at Northwestern is peppered with HM's line edits ("Oh gawd! . . . too victorian" and "too too too dramatic").

94. There are contradictions between the two versions of this evening presented in *D 1,* 99–101, and *H&J,* 158–61, but both portray AN as dazzling. HM's letter is probably 22 May 1932, *ALP,* 57–59.

95. HM essay written into AN's diary, *Incest,* 82.

96. *H&J,* 161–62, 168; *D I,* 101–3, 105.

97. AN, *H&J,* 171–74, 176–77; expurgated *D 1,* 109–10. Through the years she told several people about the Russian doctor's verdict.

98. AN and HM were reading and discussing Dostoyevsky's *The Brothers Karamazov* (1881) and *The Possessed* (1871), both of which present scenes of violation of children, but there were no psychoanalytical studies of the long-term effects of childhood sexual abuse until 1980, with the work of Alice Miller in Germany and a number of researchers in the U.S.

99. AN, *H&J,* 179. Her language is HM's language and the language that her father used with other Spanish men. *D 1,* 124.

100. AN, *H&J,* 199–202, 204; *D 1,* 122–23. AN copied the essay on drug addiction into the back of her diary (no. 35, UCLA).

101. AN (July 1932), *H&J,* 207–8.

102. AN to HM, 23 July and 31 July 1932, *ALP,* 70–73, 82–84; *H&J,* 208–9. "I have exhausted my scruples," she admits (211).

103. This duel of letters is in *ALP,* 69–95, and *LAN,* 53–54.

104. AN, *H&J*, 217; HM to AN, 14 Aug. 1932, *ALP*, 95–96. She calls Journal 35 (9 June 1932 to August 1933) "The Apotheosis and Downfall," UCLA.

105. In Journal 35, UCLA, there is in fact a letter (22 July 1932) from Erskine asking her to divorce Hugo and marry him when his daughter comes of age in nine months. The letter is addressed to "Lilith," the name of his former mistress, either an error or a suggestion that Anaïs is taking her place.

106. HM to AN, 14 Aug. and 16 Aug. 1932, *ALP*, 95–98.

107. AN, *H&J*, 227–29. in *D 1*, 126–28, she sets the scene in a café and gives Hugo's words to "Marguerite."

108. AN, *Ladders to Fire*, 74; *D 1*, 225, 231; *Incest*, 179.

109. AN to HM, 29 Sept. 1932, *ALP*, 111–12; AN, *H&J*, 231 and *D 1*, 127–28.

110. AN to HM, 28 Aug. 1932, *ALP*, 101–3; *H&J*, 234, 238–40.

111. AN *H&J*, 228; *D 1*, 126.

112. Journal 35, 242, UCLA. *H&J*, 232, 245.

113. AN, *Incest*, 9. The present chapter has been enhanced by the publication in 1992 of *Incest*, the unexpurgated diary of the 1932–34 period.

114. Not until 1975 were sexual malpractice cases against therapists even heard of in the U.S., and in 1992 only nine states criminalized patient-therapist sex, according to the American Psychiatric Association and the American Psychological Association. Lynn O'Shaughnessey, "A Broken Trust," 1.

115. AN to HM, 29 Sept. 1932, *ALP*, 110–12; *H&J*, 247–58, 264.

116. AN, *H&J*, 265; AN to HM, 6 Oct. [1932], *ALP*, 115.

117. HM to ES, n.d. [Oct. 1932], HM Collection, UCLA, and 14 Oct. 1931, *Letters to Emil*, 106; Martin, *Always Merry and Bright*, 263.

118. HM to AN, 13 Oct. 1932, *ALP*, 117.

119. "Djuna" manuscript on Hans and Joanna (reprinted in *A 7*, 1989), 14; *D 1*, 135, 136.

120. AN, *Seduction of the Minotaur*, 127; *D 7*, 198.

121. AN, "Djuna," 16, 21; *D 1*, 133, 137–38; *Incest*, 11.

122. Jack Kahane was an English Jew, a charming and well-dressed man who lost a fortune in England before moving to Paris, where he married a French woman and founded (in 1931) the Obelisk Press, which specialized in books that could not be published in Britain or America. See his autobiography, *Memoirs of a Booklegger*.

123. AN to HM, 8 Nov. 1932 [1933] *ALP*, 126; HM to AN, four undated October letters, LAN, 64–70; HM's Lawrence work was not published, except in various articles and collections, until *The World of Lawrence* (1980).

124. After her death her editor and executor will continue the editing, altering, and piecemeal publication of her diary in their journal *Anaïs* and in the volumes of unexpurgated diary: *Henry and June* and *Incest*.

125. AN, *D 1*, 136,143; AN to HM 25 Oct. 1932, *ALP*, 123; In "Alraune," later called "Joanna," it is she who can explain June's mind to HM (Hans), *A 7*, 13.

126. AN, *D 1*, 138, 145–46; HM to AN, 21 Oct. 1932, *ALP*, 120; *H&J*, 272.

127. AN to HM, 25 Oct. and 30 Oct. 1932, *ALP*, 123–24; *D 1*,135–36,140,145. In a selection of her dreams and their associations, AN said she gave HM her first royalty check from her Lawrence book (*A 10*, 5).

128. AN, "With Henry & June," *A 5*, 3–5; AN, "What the Writer Has Seen He Never Forgets [from unedited diary, Nov. 1932]," *A 8*, 3–8; *D 1*, 140–44, 148–49,151; *Incest*, 34–35.

129. AN, "What the Writer Has Seen," *A 8,* 7–8: At the home of René Lalou the night before, she had felt "a current between Lalou and me." With Hugo in Berlin and afternoon memories of Allendy's heavy arms around her, she suggested that she go get her brother Joaquin, knowing Lalou would join her in the taxi. He "came very near to kissing me, and I to joyous receptivity," she records. The literary talk, Lalou's familiarity with France's leading writers, and her own "electric intelligence" that evening made the lie about Gide seem plausible to her as she wrote her journal; *Incest,* 35–36.

130. Interview with Margot Duxler, 26 Apr. 1991.

131. Patricia-Pia Célérier, "The Vision of Dr. Allendy: Psychoanalysis and the Quest for an Independent Identity," *A 7,* 88.

132. Interview with Betty Eisner, 30 Sept. 1992.

133. Erica Jong, *Devil at Large,* 98. "Journal of a Possessed," no. 36, UCLA. From the neat and controlled script of 24 August 1932 to the large and irregular scribble of 23 October 1932, one can see indications of these changes in AN.

134. AN, *A 5,* 6–14 , and *A 8,* 14, and *Incest,* 39–41 contain the expurgated portions of *D 1* for November 1932. A comparison of the various publications reveals the extent to which AN went to rewrite her diary for initial publication in 1966. To protect AN, HM would always say that June's final note was written on a scrap of toilet paper.

135. AN, *Incest,* 47.

136. AN's original diary contains occasional references to drinking alcohol, sometimes to excess.

137. AN, *Incest,* 123, 25, 103, 112.

138. AN, *D 1,* 163; AN, "The Discovery of Life: Two Letters to Dr. René Allendy," *A 10,* 29–31; *Incest,* 59, 66.

139. Rank's chapter from his longer work with the same title was translated and printed by Edward Titus in *This Quarter* (December 1932), where many expatriate writers in Paris discovered it.

140. AN, *D 1,* 157–67; 170–73 for dream fantasy of her two worlds; AN to HM, 16 Jan. and 17 Jan. 1933, *ALP,* 132–33 on Hugo's jealousy and her work for Allendy.

141. HM to AN, 1 Jan. 1933, *LAN,* 70–71 abbreviated in *ALP,* 131–32; HM used this trip to England for a short story, "Via Dieppe-Newhaven," in *Max and the White Phagocytes* (1938), reprinted in *The Cosmological Eye;* AN, *D 1,* 157; *Incest,* 66–78.

142. Typescript of letter, UCLA, reprinted in *A 7,* 47–50. He also included two descriptions of Louveciennes in the "Walking Up and Down in China" chapter of *Black Spring.*

143. HM's description first appears in full in *Incest,* 80–85.

144. AN, *Incest,* 87, 90.

145. AN, *D 1,* 174–77, 183, and *Incest,* 107, 113; HM to AN, 20 Feb. 1933, *ALP,* 134.

146. HM also calls him "Popper Allendy" (to AN, 7 Feb. 1933, *LAN,* 76–77); *D 1,* 176–80, 193. AN said Allendy "has taught me to relax my grip on life, my willful grasp of it," in expurgated selections published in 1992 as "Dreams," *A 10,* 8. *Incest,* 8, 94, 102.

147. AN claims (*Incest,* 89) that Allendy feels "he has failed as an analyst" by giving in to his attraction to her before his analysis of her and Hugo had ended.

148. Interview with Georges Belmont, 11 July 1991.

149. Antonin Artaud to AN, 3 Apr. 1933, "Antonin Artaud, Letters—1933," *A 1,* 54.

150. AN to HM, 9 Mar. 1933, *ALP,* 137; AN, *Incest,* 99, 111.

151. AN, *Incest,* 115, 116, 120.

152. AN, "With Antonin Artaud," *A* 6, 5–6; *D 1,* 189–90; *Incest,* 122, 124.

## 6. A SEASON IN HELL (*pages 145–184*)

1. AN, at the age of 54, *D 6,* 109. I encountered this confirmation of my thesis after my work was well under way. When AN had this insight concerning her compulsion to seduce, she was under the analysis of Dr. Inge Bogner, a woman she worked with longer than with any other psychoanalyst. Major source material for Chapter Six, other than interviews and letters, include *The Diary of AN,* vol. 1 (using only half the material in Journals 38–41, UCLA) and *Incest* (the expurgated portions of the published diary of 1934–35), as well as the AN-HM letters in *A Literate Passion.* This period (between the ages of 30 and 32) is one of the most voluminous of AN's diary life. Fictional treatment of this period: "Winter of Artifice" (especially the early versions of "Father Story," Northwestern); "The Voice" in *Winter of Artifice;* "Birth" in *Under a Glass Bell.* The last segment of the present chapter draws on *D 2.*

2. The expurgated *D 1* entries on Artaud (191–93, 209–10, 220–22, 225–35) should be read with the following: AN, "With Antonin Artaud: From the Unedited Transcript of the Original Diary," *A 6,* 3–26; Antonin Artaud, "Letters—1933," trans. Nyuka Laurent, *A 1,* 52–59; AN, *Incest,* 118 ff.

3. HM had already become interested in the topic of death through his friendship with Michael Fraenkel (who appears as "Boris" in *Cancer*), an American writer and publisher who preached the gospel of death.

4. AN sometimes wrote daily letters. Artaud's letters to her first appeared as "Onze lettres à AN," *Tel Quel* (Winter 1965), 3–11; they were translated into English for *A 1* (1983), see note 2. Her letters to him first appear in *Incest,* 1992.

5. One key to the longevity of the AN-HM love affair was their lack of possessiveness. HM wrote a longtime correspondent (16 June 1933) that upon returning from Louveciennes, "after fucking my head off (and working hard too)," he gave AN's money to his favorite whore with a "huge rolling torso." HM, *Letters to Emil,* 132–33.

6. AN's sexual relations with Dr. Allendy, for which we have only her word, occur when her analysis is almost over and she is working on his manuscripts. She will tell Eduardo and Henry about the comic panting and satisfaction of Allendy. *Incest,* 134, 136–49.

7. HM describes her gems as "clotted, spangled phantasmagoria of neurosis." HM to AN, 10 Apr. and 20 Apr. 1933, *ALP,* 142–45, 147–48 (repeated in *Incest,* 141); AN, *D 1,* 198. Later AN told LD in an undated letter (SIU) that HM called her style "neurotic fulgurations."

8. HM to AN, 13 Apr. 1933, and AN to HM, 15 Apr. 1933, *ALP,* 145–46.

9. AN to HM, 15 Apr. and 3 May 1933, *ALP,* 146, 150.

10. AN to HM, 15 Apr., 9 May, and 15 May 1933, *ALP,* 146, 150, 152–54. Kahane believed that HM "mobilized all of AN's powers of seduction to win over Bill Bradley . . . [and] then built up on the latter's prestige to impress and convince Jack Kahane to publish *Cancer*" (Girodias, *The Frog Prince,* 117).

11. Kahane's biography is entitled *Memoirs of a Booklegger.* During World War II, his son Maurice changed his name to his French mother's name, Girodias, and took over his father's business. He published works by Beckett, Genet, Nabokov, and Kazan-

tzakis. Though Girodias praises AN's book as "a ballet on ice," he nevertheless portrays her as an international seductress and "midwife to genius" (*The Frog Prince*, 117, 208, 231, 234).

12. Although she would later say that she introduced HM to Rank (AN to Philip Jason, 10 Apr. 1972), they seem to have discovered his writing together; HM would be the first to visit the psychoanalyst.

13. Unexpurgated portion of diary concerning Artaud, *A 6*, 12–14.

14. AN, *D 1*, 181, 193, 201–3 and *Incest*, 111–12. Gustavo Duran was the friend of Joaquin's who conveyed the message from AN's father in Feb. 1933.

15. AN, *D 1*, 208; *Incest*, 155.

16. The sources for the adult incest are implied in the first published (expurgated) diary, *D 1*, 206–17; a clearer picture is found in several versions of the fictional accounts, in the AN collection at Northwestern. The story was eventually published as "The Winter of Artifice." The expurgated portions of the diary were finally published as *Incest* in October 1992 (152 ff).

17. In the published version of "Winter of Artifice" (82, 81), she says she came "looking for a father" and found a child, he came looking for a child and found a mother (when he calls her Amazon, she feels protective of him).

18. In "Winter of Artifice," both father and daughter are commenting on the youthfulness of the other when the fish bowl breaks under the pressure of her leaning body and water gushes to the floor like a fountain. Both stare at the growing pool of water. For dramatic effect, AN sets their reunion after 20, not 10, years, in both diary and fiction.

19. Both father and daughter later confess to each other that they dreamed: she of his loving caresses, he of her masturbating him with jeweled fingers. *Incest*, 157, 208.

20. Interview with Renate Druks, 12 Apr. 1991.

21. "Taboo," a Polynesian word, like "sacer" (Roman) and "Kodaush" (Hebrew), refers to universal tribal restrictions against in-group sex, including sex between people related by marriage. Dr. Otto Rank, quoting Freud, said that "dreams regularly represent . . . repressed infantile-sexual material" (235n).

22. AN, *D 1*, 206–20.

23. "I therefore put forward the thesis that at the bottom of every case of hysteria there are one or more occurrences of premature sexual experiences, occurrences which belong to the earliest years of childhood." Freud, "The Etiology of Hysteria," 203.

24. Theories vary widely about why Freud abandoned his "seduction theory." Dr. William O'Neil Erwin (telephone interview 12 May 1992) believes Freud gave up the exclusive abuse basis of hysteria/neurosis chiefly because of the results of trying to make his theory work; Peters ("Children Who Are Victims," 401) claims Freud recanted after a storm of criticism, and the result was that thereafter therapists "overlooked incidents of actual sexual victimization in children." Masson, former projects director of the Sigmund Freud Archives, has recently revealed the suppression of references in Freud's writings to his persistent acknowledgment of sexual abuse. My gratitude also to the research of Dr. Jack Wright.

25. AN to HM, 15 May and 23 May 1933, and HM to AN, 17 May 1933, *ALP*, 154–57.

26. HM, "Joey" in *Book of Friends*, 233.

27. HM to AN, May 1933, *ALP*, 157–65. HM to AN, 27 May 1933, *LAN*, 93–94.

28. AN, *D 1*, 223–34.

29. AN's dreams of this period (1932–34), including her dreams of her father, were recently printed in "Dreams," *A 10*, 3–14.

30. "The purpose of the sexual promiscuity seems to be to relive the experience with the father and hence, through the mechanism of the repetition compulsion, to work through their anxiety and at the same time achieve a restitution of the lost parent." Gordon, "Incest as Revenge," 284–92; Howard, "Incest," 223–25; Meiselman, 230–31. Some suggest that promiscuity is motivated by hostility toward the parents (e.g., Maisch, *Incest*).

31. AN, *D 1*, 223–30; *A 6*, 12–17; *Incest*, 185–86.

32. AN, "With Antonin Artaud," *A 6*, 18–20, 22 and *Incest*, 191–92—expurgated in *D 1*, 230–32. Although Artaud developed a number of fervent attachments to women and wrote passionate letters, there is no reference anywhere to other physical relationships with women. We have only the AN testimony.

33. AN, *A 6*, 17, 20–22; *D 1*, 234; *Incest*, 192–95.

34. AN, *D 1*, 230; *Incest*, 196. Later she told her father that she enjoyed the symmetry of finding two lovers in the same room, giving one the handkerchief of the other—as she had taken Henry to the hotel where she took Eduardo, and Artaud to Henry's table at the Vikings. (early ms. of the "Father Story," Northwestern).

35. Coirier's Grand Hotel closed in 1937 and the records of registration no longer exist, according to the Syndicat des Hoteliers, St.-Raphaël, 22 July 1992.

36. AN, *Incest*, 198–200.

37. HM to AN, 18, 20, and 22 June 1933, *ALP*, 167–71.

38. AN, *D 1*, 235–38, 241; *Incest*, 204–8.

39. See various versions of the "Father Story," AN Collection, Northwestern, and the recently published *Incest*, 209.

40. AN, *Incest*, 209–14, 265. "I know of no other case in which an adult woman has knowingly slept with her father," says E. James Lieberman (interview 8 Dec. 1992). Lieberman believes that AN's powers of disassociation are similar to multiple personality disorder patients.

41. Three early versions of the "Father Story" ("Winter of Artifice"), Northwestern. See also various letters between HM and AN: *ALP*, 176,178,180,182, *LAN*, 107.

42. AN, *D 1*, 191. In January 1928 she had written, "All parents are cannibals anyway, but eaters of souls instead of flesh," *ED 4*, 45.

43. AN to HM, 24 July 1933, *ALP*, 191.

44. AN, *Incest*, 221.

45. AN, *A 6*, 26; *D 1*, 241,146–47.

46. "Letter to William Bradley" was eventually published in HM's *Sunday after the War*, 276–84.

47. HM to AN, 3 Aug. 1933, and AN to HM, 6 and 8 Aug. 1933, *ALP*, 200–204.

48. When she told Renate Druks, one of her best friends in California, the story of her adult incest, AN feared losing Druks's friendship, but the friend made no judgment. Interviews with Renate Druks, 12 Apr. and 12 Dec. 1991.

49. AN, *D 1*, 242–48; *A 6*, 26; *Incest*, 234–235, 242. She wanted more than anything to have an impact on Artaud's life, and when he said he was miserable before he met her, she was overjoyed. Several Artaud scholars today argue that AN was neither a friend nor a lover of Artaud's. Colette Faus interview with Martha Robert, July 1991; Paule Thevenin quoted in Barillè, *AN*, 153.

50. I owe the use of the Eurydice image to Bertrand Mathieu, whose unpublished manuscript ("The Eurydicean Matrix: Symbolism, Rimbaud, and the Gnostic Outlook in the Writings of AN") shows that AN attempted "Orphic descents in search of her doomed Eurydice." While I focus on her double sacrifice, Mathieu

discusses the freeing of her Eurydicean self in her writing. Mathieu (*Orpheus in Brooklyn*) believes that "Miller is the younger brother to the likes of Orpheus, Dante, and Rimbaud." BM to NRF, 10 Oct. 1991.

51. AN, *D 1*, 248–50.

52. AN, *D 1*, 250–52; AN to HM, 23, 25, 26, and 27 Aug. 1933, *ALP*, 205–10.

53. Early ms. of "Winter of Artifice" ("Father Story"), 74, Northwestern.

54. AN, *D 1*, 261.

55. Telephone interview with Rupert Pole, 15 Aug. 1992. HM's reaction to her incest was to give understanding and support, despite his jealousy. He sympathized with Senor Nin, for they both had abandoned their daughters.

56. AN, *D 1*, 267.

57. HM to AN, 3 Oct. 1933, *LAN*, 121–22; AN to HM, 4 Oct. 1933, *ALP*, 212.

58. AN, *Incest*, 268. The fake diary that she wrote for Hugo is at UCLA.

59. AN, *The House of Incest*, 22. The 72-page novelette includes only 42 pages of text.

60. Evelyn Hinz believes that all Nin's novels are "character studies" because nothing "happens" in a traditional sense. Harms, ed., *Celebration of AN*, 59.

61. The various drafts of this work, called "Thousand and One Nights in Montparnasse," "The Mona Pages," and "The June Story," are at Northwestern. In all editions after the first (1936), Alraune is called Sabina and Isolina is called Jeanne.

62. Mathieu, "The Eurydicean Matrix," 13. AN, *D 1*, 289 and *D 2*, 151.

63. Because Louise de Vilmorin died before AN could secure her permission to use her name in her first diary, AN changed her name to Jeanne. De Vilmorin's novels include *The Last of the Villavides* (1938), *The Return of Erica* (1949), and *The Letter in a Taxi* (1958).

64. The de Vilmorins are "lusty decadents," AN says. Louise's mother was a drug addict and lover of many men. *Incest*, 115, 153.

65. AN, *Incest*, 279.

66. HM to AN, 6 and 12 Oct. 1933, and AN to HM, 8 Oct. 1933, *ALP*, 214–19.

67. "The Voice" in *Winter of Artifice* (164). The character The Voice is based on Dr. Otto Rank.

68. AN, *ED 4*, 372–73.

69. AN, *D 1*, 269–71; HM to AN, *LAN*, 80–86, tells of his visit to Rank; *Incest*, 290–93.

70. AN, *D 1*, 269–75, 284. Rank saw analysis as a situation in which the patient tells stories to please the analyst. He also believed that the first creative work of every artist was her own personality. See Spencer, *Collage of Dreams*, 160.

71. When Otto Rosenfeld and his brother repudiated their father, who was an alcoholic who beat their mother, they changed their names to Rank. Then they were accused of being Jewish anti-Semites. Interview with Sharon Spencer, 23 Apr. 1992.

72. Rank to Jessie Taft, 8 Aug. 1933, in Taft, *Otto Rank*, 177.

73. Rank, *The Trauma of Birth* (1924) and *Art and Artists* (1932). A chapter from the second book, translated by Titus, appeared in *This Quarter* in 1931, which is probably where HM and AN first discovered Rank. In "Validating Otto Rank's Work," Peter Orban argues that recent knowledge confirms Rank's theory that the trauma of birth is the primary biological reason for neurotic disturbance. *A 6*, 120–21.

74. See Lieberman, *Acts of Will*, 340–55; *D 1*, 278–79, 282–83. At least one HM biographer mistakenly interprets AN's interest in analysis with Allendy and Rank

as coming from her need for a confessor figure during her adultery with HM (Ferguson, *HM*, 226).

75. AN, "A House and a Garden," *A* 7, 40; *D 1*, 277, 284–85.

76. Rank had written years before that historical truth can evade psychological reality, which is in the present, feeling experience. Thus, he wants AN to live in the present. Lieberman says that her descriptions of Rank's technique reveal "profound insight" (*Acts of Will*, 333).

77. AN, *D 1*, 300.

78. Among the pioneer work was Alice Miller's *Das Drama des Bebagten Kindes* (1979), trans. as *The Drama of the Gifted Child* (1981), and *Du Sollst Nicht Merken* (1981), trans. as *Thou Shalt Not Be Aware* (1984). When asked if she owed anything to Freud, Miller said, "20 years of blindness toward the reality of child abuse."

79. HM to ES, 15 Feb. 1934, *Letters to Emil*, 145.

80. AN, "A House and a Garden [unpublished diary portions]," *A* 7, 41.

81. Quoted in Taft, *Otto Rank*, 123.

82. One of his dreams recreates the scene in which Hugo discovers AN and HM, but in the dream, Hugo gives "a harmless little crack" to AN. Winslow, *HM*, 22–23; Martin, *Always Merry and Bright*, 279–84.

83. Telephone interview with E. James Lieberman, 8 Dec. 1992.

84. AN, *D 1*, 295, 307–8, 313–14, 316–19; "Winter of Artifice" in *Winter of Artifice*, 95, 97, 105.

85. AN, *D 1*, 315.

86. AN (6 Mar. 1934), "A House and a Garden," *A* 7, 42.

87. Rebecca West is quoted in "AN," *Current Biography 1944*. West (1892–1983) had an established reputation in England as a spirited feminist, journalist, and novelist.

88. HM to AN, 26 and 28 Apr. 1934, *LAN*, 132, 134.

89. AN, *D 1*, 323.

90. AN, "A House and a Garden," *A* 7, 42. Interview with Marguerite Young, 5 Dec. 1991. Every indication among those that knew AN is that she never gave any sign that she wished to have children. Her cousin's wife remembers AN's first question upon seeing her new godchild: "Is he much trouble?" At the child's confirmation, she immediately returned the child when he fussed. Kathleen Chase, "Being 'Family' in France," *A 1*, 65.

91. AN's father's reaction to her pregnancy is found in the second unpublished version of her "Father Story," 123, Northwestern, and "The Voice" in *Winter of Artifice*, 111.

92. AN, *Incest*, 329.

93. Telephone interview with Rupert Pole, 28 Aug. 1992.

94. Although speculation about the identify of the child's father has ranged from Hugo, HM, her father, and Rank to her cousin Eduardo, she always knew that it was Henry's child. Hugo always believed it was his. Interviews with Rupert Pole (14 Feb. 1990), Marguerite Young (18 Mar. 1991), and Renate Druks (20 May 1991).

95. AN, *A* 7, 43–44.

96. Rank's Psychoanalytic Center was located at the Cité, on the ramparts at the edge of Paris, built by Rockefeller for housing foreign students.

97. Taft, *Otto Rank*, 177 ff, 185; Lieberman, *Acts of Will*, 304, 341.

98. AN, *Incest*, 357.

99. AN, *Incest*, 360–61, 364. AN, "Return to Louveciennes," *A 11*, 6.

100. AN, *D 1*, 333, 329. While translating and retyping her earliest diary, she added material: "Will anyone . . . believe and admit the possibility of this, that a woman should employ her power in the pursuit of psychological studies and researches?" *ED 2*, 511. She did not learn about psychology until almost a decade later, from Eduardo. When Knopf rejects her "Double" manuscript, she takes it with equilibrium, for Knopf compliments her work to Bradley (who thinks it is too condensed).

101. AN, *Winter of Artifice*, 148.

102. Martin, *Always Merry and Bright*, 303, 327; AN claimed she found the apartment, *D 1*, 335.

103. Hugo's refusal is established by HM to Richard Osborn, July 1934, UCLA; Martin, *Always Merry and Bright*, 302; AN to HM 19 Dec. 1934, *ALP*, 265.

104. There has been much speculation concerning the authorship of the preface of *Tropic of Cancer.* Mary Dearborn (171) mistakenly claims that HM wrote the entire essay "and had Nin sign it." Martin (302) and Ferguson (232) call it a collaboration because HM told Emil Schnellock "Anaïs and I are just struggling over a preface" (14 July 1934, *Letters to Emil*, 152); HM told Richard Osborn that he wrote a four-page preface, using some of her diary pages, n.d., HM Collection, UCLA; HM to Gerald Robitaille, Aug. 1971. In later years, HM insisted in interviews that the preface was hers. AN says (*Incest*, 347), "I awake and write a preface for Henry's book," then two weeks later (353), they "worked together" revising it.

105. Martin, *Always Merry and Bright*, 302–3.

106. AN, *D 1*, 338–39. There is no evidence that AN knew that HM's live-in love, Pauline Choutreau, had aborted her five-month-old fetus.

107. AN, *Incest*, 375.

108. Telephone interview with Rupert Pole, 20 May 1992. AN's treatment of the loss of her fetus in the first published diary (*D 1*, 337–49) makes no mention of the *sage-femme.* Early drafts of "Birth," her short story taken from her diary, are more revealing about her fear that the child's father will abandon his child. My major source on this, Rupert Pole, believes that when she saw the umbilical cord coiled around the baby's neck, she concluded it had been wise to terminate the pregnancy, for "she might have been poisoned." In the so-called unexpurgated diary, AN says, "the tumor in its head" [sic] would eventually have "infected" her (*Incest*, 381). This single reference to some abnormality, contradicted by other comments by her, suggests justification for her abortion.

109. AN, *Incest*, 383.

110. Telephone interview with Rupert Pole, 28 Aug. 1992; *Incest*, 383, 387.

111. AN, "Winter of Artifice" (119); "Birth" was first published in *Twice a Year* (Fall/Winter 1938), then in *Under a Glass Bell* (1944), 100; *Ladders to Fire* (78); *Incest*, 384–85.

112. AN, *D 6*, 154 and *D 7*, 172; *Ms.* (Spring 1972), 34–35.

113. According to Betty Ryan Gordon, Perlès was forbidden by AN to stay the night at HM's Villa Seurat studio (Ryan to NRF, 9 Feb. 1991). Betty Ryan believes that AN was very unfair in her fictional treatment of Perlès, who had a great sense of the ridiculous.

114. AN, *A 7*, 44; *D 1*, 338, 351; Jay Martin says September 1; AN's published diary suggests the third week of September.

115. AN, *Incest*, 389.

116. Rank's letters to AN, folded into diary no. 46 ("Flow"), establish this love for her (UCLA). Telephone interview with E. James Lieberman, 8 Dec. 1992.

117. In a dream this August, AN is going to visit her father with her face all prepared with paint and tattoos and held together with pins. She feels very beautiful until her return home, when she removes the pins and her face falls apart. "Dreams," *A 10,* 14.

118. Jules Massenet's opera *Thaïs* (1894) is based on the novel by Anatole France.

119. The religion of psychoanalysis holds, as does fundamentalist religion, that one has to solve the personal issue, the inner life, before one can go on to anything beyond.

120. AN, *Incest,* 395.

121. "I went to Rank to solve my conflict with my father, and only added another father to my life, and another loss," *D 1,* 354; AN, "A House and a Garden," *A 7,* 44. Rank arrived in the U.S. 18 Oct. 1934.

122. AN to HM, [Oct. 1934], *ALP,* 232. In contrast, LD will praise HM for this very lack of concern with money: HM "was concerned [only] with his soul." Film transcription, Enar Moos, 11.

123. AN, *D 1,* 359. Lieberman ("Otto Rank's Muse," *A 5,* 56) questions AN's portrait of the desperation of Rank's letters, but the letters in her diary are passionate expressions to his "Darling" or "You" (the word he cried out when she first performed fellatio). Her considerably revised first published diary suggests that her trip to New York was a professional move, but the unexpurgated diary, published 28 years later, suggests it was for love of Rank.

124. A brief description of her activities of these months in New York with Otto Rank are found in the beginning of *D 2,* 3–41, and are fictionalized (with her amours on board ship) in the adventures of Lilith and the analyst in "The Voice" (*Winter of Artifice,* 146).

125. AN to HM, 26 Nov. 1934, and HM to AN, 19 and 29 Nov. 1934, *ALP,* 233–34, 236–37, 268; *D 2,* 3, a rewritten version.

126. AN, *D 2,* 3; Lieberman, *Acts of Will,* 350 ff.

127. AN to HM, 26 Nov., 30 Nov., and 3 Dec. 1934, *ALP,* 234, 238–39; *D 2,* 46, 50, 61; AN, "Return to Louveciennes," *A 11,* 10.

128. Eduardo probably enjoyed HM's anguish, for there was no love lost between them. HM had just written to Emil Schnellock describing Eduardo as the "little fairy . . . a medieval monk" obsessed with Blake and horoscopes who lives on the first floor at Louveciennes with "a Botticelli on the toilet door and Albrecht Durer over his bedstead." HM to ES, 25 Aug. 1934, UCLA.

129. HM to AN, 7 Dec. (two letters), 8 Dec., 11 Dec. (two letters), *ALP,* 240–53.

130. See Taft (*Otto Rank,* 199) on Rank in New York and Philadelphia. Rank was eventually purged from the Freudian establishment of the American Psychoanalytical Association.

131. Two and a half years later, Jack Kahane will partially repay the money AN borrowed from Rank. Girodias, *The Frog Prince,* 202.

132. This voluminous correspondence between AN and HM is found in *ALP,* 247–290.

133. AN to HM, 1 Jan. 1935, *ALP,* 290–91.

134. HM to AN, 29 Dec. and 1 Feb. 1945, *ALP,* 281–90, 291.

135. Geismar, "AN: An Imprecise Spy," 3.

136. AN, "The Voice" in *Winter of Artifice,* 160. Lieberman confirms that Otto Rank ended the romance. Telephone interview, 8 Dec. 1992.

137. HM to Emil Schnellock, n.d. [Aug. 1934] and 25 Oct. 1934, *Letters to Emil*, 155. On Rank in U.S., see Taft (*Otto Rank*, 199 ff) and Lieberman (*Acts of Will*, 349).

138. Martin, *Always Merry and Bright*, 306–8.

139. Rank's "Preface," written late in 1934, was finally printed in *A 2*, 20–23.

140. In addition to the cultural and economic differences between AN and HM, Nancy Scholar has suggested another reason for HM's virtual absence from this segment of AN's diary: his presence "would have undercut the glamour of AN's role as analyst, in addition to making clear the emotional as well as aesthetic bonds in this relationship." *AN*, 59. Dick (*HM,*127), who is often unreliable, mistakenly claims that AN made annual three-month visits to a "Dr. Brill" in New York to earn money for support of HM.

141. Rank's introduction was printed in *Journal of Otto Rank Association* 7, no. 2 (Dec. 1972) and reprinted in *A 3*, 49–54.

142. AN to [Sherwood Anderson], n.d. [Dec. 1934], Special Collections, Newberry Library, Chicago. AN mentions Hélène Boussinescq in her letter, sent from the Barbizon Plaza Hotel.

143. Dearborn, *The Happiest Man Alive*, 180.

144. HM to AN, Mar. 1935, *ALP*, 294–98.

145. Martin, *Always Merry and Bright*, 308–9.

146. AN to HM, 7 Dec. 1934, *ALP*, 243; *D 2*, 37.

147. AN, "Return to Louveciennes," *A 11*, 6.

148. Evans, *AN*, 12–13.

149. AN to Wayne McEvilly, 1969, quoted in AN, *D 7*, 122–23.

150. Spencer, "Introduction," AN, *Cities of the Interior*, xvii.

## 7. DRIFTING TOWARD WAR (*pages 185–223*)

1. AN, "The Voice" in *The Winter of Artifice*, 163. The events of Chapter Seven are in part narrated by AN in her voluminous bound diaries nos. 41–60. Less than half this material was published in *The Diary of AN*, vol. 2 (1935–39). The fictional treatment of these events is in *The Four-Chambered Heart* and most of the short stories in *Under a Glass Bell*, including "Houseboat," "The Mouse," "The Mohican," "The Eye's Journey," and "Through the Streets of My Own Labyrinth." Persons and events of this period, between AN's thirty-second and thirty-sixth years, are reflected in numerous pieces of erotica, including "Marcel," a 93-page ms., UCLA (a portion of which was published in *Delta of Venus*, 233–50).

2. The story of the pregnant woman's suicide is included in "The Voice" in *The Winter of Artifice*, 136. Further evidence of her guilt are recollections in her diary this June of times she has "crushed" Hugo, including the day he read her "Djuna"—the June and Henry story. AN, "Return to Louveciennes," *A 11*, 4.

3. According to the American Psychiatric Association, affairs between analysts and former patients are "almost always unethical" because transference can linger for years after therapy has ended. Patients who sleep with their therapists end up more emotionally scarred than when they began treatment, says Dr. Nanette Gartrell, quoted in "Sex and Psychotherapy," 55. This journal states that "Otto Rank had a long affair with patient Anaïs Nin" (53), which is incorrect unless one calls just short of a year a lengthy time.

4. Mary Dearborn to NRF, 18 Dec. 1990.

5. AN to LD, 9 Oct. 1970, LD Papers, SIU.

6. AN, 11 July 1935, "A House and a Garden," *A* 7, 45; *D* 2, 51, 45.

7. Ferguson, *HM*, 257.

8. AN, *D* 2, 45, 48.

9. Martin, in an interview with Raymond Queneau, *Always Merry and Bright*, 311.

10. "No form, clearly, was closer to HM's imagination than the letter," says Martin, *Always Merry and Bright*, 311. About this time HM was preparing two more books using the epistolary style: *Aller Retour New York* (1935), a 147-page letter to Perlès about the artist returning to his native country, and *Hamlet* (1939), an exchange of letters among HM, Fraenkel, and Perlès, planned over drinks at Café Zeyer 1 November 1935.

11. AN, *D* 2, 57–58.

12. AN, *The Winter of Artifice*, 119; *D* 2, 62.

13. AN, "A House," *A* 7, 45. There is little record about her "patients," except for a letter from Will Slotnikoff, who had sold a book and announced his arrival in Paris in 1937, AN to LD, [Mar. 1937], "Into the Heraldic Universe: Letters to LD," *A* 5, 78.

14. Ferguson, *HM*, 257.

15. Interview with Betty Ryan (Gordon), 19 June 1992.

16. West, *The Scotsman*, Monday 18 Aug. 1980; repr. in Haynes, ed., *Homage to HM*, 129. Glendinning (*Rebecca West*, 143) says West "deplored the influence of HM" on AN. Betty Ryan (interview 15 July 1992) dismisses the West account of HM's drunkenness: "I never saw Miller drunk in my life." HM, who had an affair with Ryan, probably never showed his drinking revelry to her.

17. AN, *Ladders to Fire*, 134, 149.

18. AN, *Seduction of the Minotaur*, 124.

19. Kathleen Chase, married to AN's cousin Gilbert, "AN—Rumor and Reality," 7.

20. HM to Frank Dobo, Jan. 1936, Berg; Martin, *Always Merry and Bright*, 330–31.

21. Both Taft (*Otto Rank*, 199 ff) and Lieberman (*Act of Will*, 351, 347) portray Rank as ending his life affirmatively.

22. AN uses the meeting with her brother in "The Voice," *Winter of Artifice*, 140. Though a dandy like his father, Thorvald, first a banker, then in plywood, hated the artistic life of his father and AN. Though the family later complained about his clear-cutting of timber, he proudly remained a businessman until his retirement to Miami, then El Paso.

23. Interview with Sharon Spencer (23 Apr. 1992) and others.

24. AN to HM, 17 Apr. 1936, *ALP*, 302.

25. AN to LD, n.d. [Oct. 1937], LD Papers, SIU.

26. AN to HM, 23 Apr. 1936, *ALP*, 306.

27. The best discussion of AN's response to Fez and the female nature and expression is found in Sharon Spencer, *Collage of Dreams*, 127.

28. AN, "Through the Streets of My Own Labyrinth" in *Under a Glass Bell*, 68–69; *D* 2, 81.

29. Emil Schnellock to HM, [July 1936], UCLA. Schnellock believed the "lesbianism" would appeal to male readers.

30. HM to LD, 4 Mar. 1939, *DML*, 117.

31. Interview with Jack Hirschman, 27 Apr. 1991.

32. AN, *D* 2, 114–16.

33. AN, "The Mohican," in *Under a Glass Bell*, 43; HM, *A Devil in Paradise*, 5. HM's book is the story of his friendship with Conrad Moricand, from the day that AN brought the Frenchman to meet him in the Villa Seurat to the day HM abandoned him in Monterey after an impossible visit to Big Sur, California.

34. Wambly Bald, 13 Jan. 1931; repr. in Ford, ed., *The Left Bank Revisited*, 48.

35. AN, *D 2*, 204; AN tells LD that she is buying the press for HM ("our press"), [Mar. 1937], *A 5*, 79–80; the actions of both HM and Gonzalo reveal that their interest in the printing press was negligible.

36. AN to HM, n.d. [Mar. 1937], *ALP*, 306–9. AN, *D 2*, 97, 110–12.

37. AN to Frances Steloff, July 1936, Frances Steloff Papers, Berg.

38. AN, "A House and a Garden," *A 7*, 46.

39. AN to LD, 9 Oct. 1970, LD Papers, SIU. In answer to LD's observation that she had money, AN claimed she hated the bourgeois life and wealth.

40. AN, "Houseboat" in *Under a Glass Bell*, 20, 13; AN, *D 2*, 118, 125, 128; AN, "A House," *A 7*, 46.

41. AN, *D 2*, 118–19, 125–26, 132, 153; AN, *ED 2*, 355.

42. AN, "Houseboat" in *Under a Glass Bell*, 13.

43. AN, "A House," *A 7*, 46.

44. AN, *D 2*, 146.

45. AN, "The Child Born Out of the Fog" in *Under a Glass Bell*, 83–84.

46. The scenes with Gonzalo on the houseboat are fictionalized in the story of Djuna and Rango in *The Four-Chambered Heart*, 13, 19–21, 32.

47. AN to LD, n.d. [1938], LD Papers, SIU.

48. "Marcel" (AN Collection, box 7, UCLA) is an erotic manuscript of 23 pages and several segments and plot lines set on a houseboat on the Seine and in Montparnasse and Clichy. Mandra, Gustavo (an Argentinean), Alan (the husband), and Hans are transparently based on the events of this period in AN's life.

49. AN, *D 2*, 122, 138, 148, 132, 146, 242; Bern Porter claims to have read, at Emil Schnellock's home in Virginia, HM's letters to Schnellock concerning HM's afternoon assignations with AN on the houseboat. Porter to NRF, 17 Nov. 1990.

50. AN to HM, [Mar. 1937], *ALP*, 307.

51. Interview with Lillian Kiesler, 14 Nov. 1992. Betty was the granddaughter of Thomas Fortune Ryan, who left a multimillion-dollar estate.

52. Ryan, "Close-Up 2," 2.

53. Mathieu, *Betty Ryan, La Dame D'Andros*, 14. Interview with Erica Jong, 16 Dec. 1992. Jong, *The Devil at Large*, 122–23.

54. Ryan, "Close-Up 2," 2–3; Ryan to NRF, 29 Jan. and 13 Feb. 1991.

55. Quoted by Mathieu, *Betty Ryan*, 14.

56. Ian Hugo [Hugh Guiler], "On the Art of Engraving," *A 1*, 51.

57. Spencer, *Collage of Dreams*, 126.

58. The Brazilian painter, called "Helen R.," is unidentified, but she reminded AN of June Miller. *D 2*, 148, 167.

59. AN and HM in conversation, unpublished tape, 1968; AN, *D 5*, 185.

60. Gascoyne, *Paris Journal*, 49. Gascoyne to NRF, 26 Sept. 1992; telephone interview, 20 Oct. 1992.

61. Interview with Marguerite Rebois, 25 June 1992.

62. AN to LD 31, March [1937], and "Notes on the Black Book," LD Papers, SIU. This collection includes AN's more than 75 letters to LD, which are not always dated. Twenty-nine of her letters to LD are published as "Into the Heraldic Universe," A 5, 73–98.

63. Interview with LD, 14 June 1990.

64. Ian MacNiven, Durrell's biographer, first discussed the AN-LD friendship, quoting some of the letters, in "Criticism and Personality," A 2, 95–100. Some of her letters to him (and his to her) are in D 2, 183–184, 195, 236.

65. AN, D 2, 168, 174, 179, 219.

66. Interviews with George Belmont, 31 July 1990 and 11 July 1991.

67. "Masculine alchemy," D 2, 172; AN, Ladders to Fire, 72, uses the swallowing metaphor; "I swim in nature," D 2, 188.

68. AN to LD, Mar. 1937, "Into the Heraldic Universe," A 5, 78.

69. AN, D 2, 174, 178. 201; AN, "The Voice," in The Winter of Artifice, 145.

70. AN, D 2, 203.

71. AN, D 2, 206, 221–22.

72. LD in a transcription of Einar Moos's film Une Amitié Parisienne, 4; Wendy Beckett, "A Visit with LD," A 5, 100.

73. Moos, 5–6.

74. Interview with LD, 14 June 1990.

75. Interview with LD, 14 June 1990. The Duchess de Sanseverina is the dominant character in Stendhal's The Charterhouse of Parma (1893). Her nephew is Fabrice del Dongo.

76. Moos, 3; HM to Emil Schnellock, [Oct. 1932], quoted in Martin, Always Merry and Bright, 268; interview with LD, 14 June 1990.

77. AN, D 2, 230–34, 258.

78. AN, D 2, 226, 232–35;

79. AN, "The Voice," in The Winter of Artifice, 120–21, 125, 152, 159. AN uses the same names throughout her fiction.

80. AN, D 2, 236.

81. HM, Book of Friends, 241.

82. AN, D 2, 223, 246, 252.

83. AN, D 2, 262.

84. Interview with LD, 14 June 1990; AN, D 2, 231, 250, 253, 256.

85. Betty Ryan remembers staying in Rosa Nin's apartment with the Durrells and that they all had to remain very secretive about their abode: "It was eerily clandestine. One had to promise on oath not to speak of this haven to anybody under any circumstance anywhere." Ryan, "Close-Up," 2.

86. Interview with LD, 14 June 1990.

87. Her "Boost" was reprinted as "The Smell of the Streets" in A 5, 22–23.

88. AN to LD, July [1937], SIU.

89. In a chapter entitled "The Winter of Artifice" in his The Dandy and the Herald, Pine discusses the kinship of AN, HM, and LD in the revolt ("Heraldic saving of self") against the "Dandy" (embodied in their physical or spiritual fathers). Each prophesied a new world and tried to destroy time. LD's "gone through fire" declaration was made in a letter to Pine (30 October 1984), 8.

90. Bern Porter claims that he saw AN first at the salon of Gertrude Stein. Bern Porter to NRF, 7 Feb. 1991.

91. AN's sentimental adjective suggests she may not have understood Barnes's *Nightwood*. *D 2*, 239–40; AN later credited *Nightwood* with her decision to write poetic prose.

92. Betty Ryan (Gordon) to NRF, 20 Mar. 1991.

93. AN to LD, Mar. 1938, *A 5*, 86; in her published diary only one houseboat is mentioned, and it is called "La Belle Aurore."

94. LD to HM, [ca. Oct. 1945], *DML*, 187.

95. AN, *D 2*, 297–302.

96. AN, "Stella" in the 1942 edition of *Winter of Artifice*, 41.

97. AN to LD, [Apr. 1938 and Apr.–May 1938], *A 5*, 88–89. The Durrells had burned many of their books before leaving their apartment in rue Gazan, says Betty Ryan, 15 July 1992.

98. AN to LD, [Sept. 1938], *A 5*, 91–92; AN, "Houseboat" in *Under a Glass Bell*, 21–25; AN, *D 2*, 303–4.

99. HM to AN, 29 Sept. 1938, *LAN*, 151.

100. From 1938 to 1940 Joaquin was associated with the Middlebury Music Center group, which included Walter Piston and Ruth Morize, the director. Freeman, *The Middlebury College Foreign Language Schools*, 83, 98. Interview with Kimberly Sparks, 14 Mar. 1992.

101. AN to LD, [ca. Dec. 1938], LD Papers, SIU; Perlès [in London] to HM, n.d. [1939], UCLA. See also McNiven, "Criticism and Personality," in *A 2*, 97.

102. Benstock, *Women of the Left Bank*, 424.

103. Gentile, in *Women's Review of Books*, refers to Barnes's suffering from childhood sexual abuse. AN later wrote to both Virginia Woolf and Djuna Barnes, but neither answered her.

104. HM had been carrying around Balzac's novel *Séraphita*, given him by Moricand. When he took AN to the Balzac house to observe the manuscripts under glass, he asked her if someday people would be looking at their manuscripts and photographs. She looked just like the portrait of Séraphita, they discovered.

105. "To Heaven Beyond Heaven," an unpublished diary-letter HM, Case Ms. 30, SIU.

106. HM to AN, 21 Feb. 1939, *LAN*, 154.

107. AN, *D 2*, 323–24.

108. AN to Rosa Nin ["Mummy"], 27 Feb. 1939, "Living Through 1939," *A 3*, 79.

109. HM to AN, [Apr. 1939], *LAN*, 159; taped conversation between HM and AN recorded at his home, 22 Sept. 1968.

110. AN to Rosa Nin, 11 Apr. 1939, "Living Through 1939," *A 3*, 81–82.

111. Georges Pelorson (now Georges Belmont) read his copy of this letter (HM to Huntington Cairns, 30 April 1939) to me in Paris, 29 July 1991. In the letter HM names others who have been his friends—Perlès and LD, his "brothers," and Pelorson, Queneau, and Moricand, three Frenchmen. Cairns served as Special Counsel to the Treasury Department on censorship matters.

112. AN and HM to Emil Schnellock, 13 July 1939, HM Collection, UCLA.

113. AN to Fred Perlès, n.d. [Sept. 1939], HM Collection, HRHRC. In this letter AN says that she found she could not join HM because of legal tangles in Paris.

114. HM to AN, [9 July 1939], *ALP*, 320–21; AN to Frances Steloff, 14 July 1939, a

letter written on HM's stationery and postmarked "Marseilles." Frances Steloff Collection, Berg; AN, *D* 2, 319; Martin, *Always Merry and Bright*, 335–56.

115. AN to Rosa Nin, 19 Aug. 1939, "Living Through 1939," *A* 3, 88.

116. AN to Frances Steloff, 15 Sept. 1939, Frances Steloff Collection, Berg.

117. AN to Fred Perlès, n.d. [Sept. 1939], HRHRC.

118. HM to AN, 15 Aug. 1939, *LAN*, 181.

119. Joaquin Nin-Culmell, "Hugh, My Brother-in-Law," *A* 4, 14. Hugo came for a week to Paris and took HM's ms. of *Capricorn* back to London, AN to Fred Perlès, n.d. [Sept. 1939], HM Collection, HRHRC.

120. LD claims that the war was "too big a thing for him to swallow," AN, *D* 3, 7. Though criticizing HM's escape, AN tells her mother that she is fleeing Europe for New York, 30 Sept. 1939, "Living Through 1939," *A* 3, 93.

121. AN, *D* 2, 343, 345. A better tribute to AN was recorded in HM's last will and testimony.

122. AN to Rosa Nin, [Oct. 1939], "Living Through 1939," *A* 3, 93.

123. AN, *D* 3, 3, 7, 9.

124. W. H. Auden, "September 1, 1939," *Collected Poems*, 58.

## 8. VILLAGE LIFE (*pages 224–260*)

1. AN, *D* 4, 138. In addition to extensive personal interviews and unpublished letters, the material for Chapter Eight (covering AN's life from ages 36 to 41) is to be found in Volume Three of *The Diary of AN* (1939–44), which is the published portions of Journal nos. 60–67, UCLA. Sources from her fiction include the following: "Stella" (*Winter of Artifice*), "Hejda" (*Under a Glass Bell*), and portions of *Children of the Albatross* and *A Spy in the House of Love*. Published and unpublished erotica: "Anita," "Elena," "Maryanne," and "Life in Provincetown" in *Auletris*. "Marianne" in *Delta of Venus* is culled from the 60-page "Maryanne" ms., UCLA.

2. Rogers, *Wise Men Fish Here*, 129–30, 136; interview with Andreas Brown, 19 Feb. 1990; AN, *D* 3, 179.

3. Edited by Norman, *Twice a Year*, "A Semi-Annual Journal of Literature, the Arts, and Civil Liberties," was published in New York from 1938 to 1948, and carried the works of Stieglitz, Proust, Kafka, Saroyan, Rilke, Lorca, Patchen, Rukeyser, HM, Williams, Mann, and Wright, in addition to AN.

4. Norman, *Encounter: A Memoir*, 149, 134.

5. AN, *D* 3, 3.

6. AN, *D* 3, 12,14.

7. Crosby, born Mary Phelps Jacob, fled her Boston husband, Richard Rogers Peabody, to go to Paris with Harry Crosby, whose family tree included names such as Hamilton, Adams, and Wigglesworth as well as J. P. Morgan. Crosby gave her the name Caresse. The correspondence between AN and CC is at SIU.

8. Caresse Crosby told this story to Curtis Harrington years later in Aix-en-Provence when she was on her way from Italy to visit Dalí in Spain. Interview with Harrington, 13 Mar. 1991. The story is confirmed in an undated 1969 letter in which Crosby reminds AN that she had arrived in a flutter at the Tanguy apartment, pulled her into a bedroom, and asked her for her confidence. CC, who in 1969 had just read the portions about her that were to appear in Volume Three of the *Diary* recalls that she agreed, but cannot now remember what it was all about.

She may have been reassuring her friend of her confidence. CC to AN, n.d. [1968], Crosby Collection, SIU.

9. Crosby's "Who in the World," unpublished ms., SIU; AN, *D 3*, 15; AN to CC, 13 Aug. 1967, SIU.

10. Cooney, "The Little Magazine," 14.

11. Faas, *Young Robert Duncan*, 83. Faas calls AN's portrait of Duncan in her diary "revolting," 7.

12. Robert Duncan's first poetry was published in the Cooneys' *Phoenix*. He and others "set type, pump water, empty the buckets" on the farm. "From a Letter to Sanders Russell, May 1940" in *The Years as Catches*, 7.

13. Unpublished ms. of poet James Broughton's memoirs (*Coming Unbuttoned*), 81.

14. AN, *D 3*, 159, 16.

15. Robert Duncan, Notebook 11, quoted by Faas, *Young Robert Duncan*, 73.

16. Cooney, "The Little Magazine," 16.

17. AN to Robert Duncan, n.d. [1940], Bancroft; AN, *D 3*, 18–19.

18. Virginia Admiral to NRF, Feb. 1993. Though AN says in the diary that Virginia Admiral is a lesbian, it was her roommate Marjorie McKee who had a lesbian affair.

19. Telephone interview with Virginia Admiral, 2 Dec. 1992. Admiral to NRF, Feb. 1993.

20. Spencer, *Collage of Dreams*, 107. AN tells Duncan that his diary is a "complete emotional revelation" to her and has helped her break from the self-protection of her "house of incest."

21. Duncan, quoted by Faas, "'The Barbaric Friendship with Robert': A Biographical Palimpsest," in Hinz and Fraser, eds., *Mosaic*, 148.

22. Faas, in his biography of Duncan, traces her changes in the diary, 104–5.

23. HM to AN, 12 Jan. 1940, *ALP*, 323.

24. Fred Perlès to AN, 6 Mar. 1940, and Perlès to HM, 6 Mar. 1940, HM Collection, UCLA. Mary Dearborn to NRF, 7 Oct. 1991. In "Marcel," an erotic story, Mandra comes back to America and sees Lilith, a character with suggestions of June, but no longer loves her, UCLA. When AN meets Betty Ryan on the streets, they make an appointment to meet at Ryan's apartment, but AN never arrives (HM had undoubtedly informed AN of his affair with Ryan). Except for HM, she has fairly cut off her close Paris connections. Interview with Betty Ryan Gordon, 19 June 1992.

25. HM to AN, 11 Feb. and 19 Feb. 1940, *ALP*, 323–24. See also HM's almost daily letters to AN in *LAN*, 203 ff.

26. AN wrote or reworked short fiction such as "The Mouse," "Houseboat," and "Waste of Timelessness," *D 3*, 13, 29, 32.

27. AN, *D 3*, 31. She told an unidentified interviewer 14 July 1949 that Patchen was an egomaniac and HM was mistaken in boosting him. Telephone interview with Virginia Admiral, 2 Dec. 1992. AN denounced Patchen to his patron, Dorothy Norman, while serving on the committee to raise funds for him (Admiral to NRF, Feb. 1993).

28. According to Sharon Spencer (interview 23 Apr. 1992), Rank's daughter (Helene Swarthmore) blamed AN for breaking up her parents' marriage. Lieberman (347) says outside opinion blamed AN. HM later repeats the erroneous gossip that Rank had killed himself for AN. Lieberman (interview 8 Dec. 1992) suggests that she may have heard of his death earlier, for it was widely reported.

29. Interview with Gershon Legman, 12 June 1990. Legman, born in Scranton, PA, and

later a bibliographer for the Kinsey Institute, has lived in France for 40 years and authored various works on sexuality, including *Rationale of the Dirty Joke: An Analysis of Sexual Humor* (Grove Press, 1968).

30. Brussel published 1,000 copies sold on delivery to booksellers Frances Steloff in New York City and Ben Abramson in Chicago—profits to HM and Brussel, says Legman.

31. Interview with Gershon Legman, 12 and 13 June 1990 and 10 June 1991; GL to NRF, 2 Feb. 1990 and 3 Jan. 1991; Legman, "Erotica of HM and AN," *Pisces*, 9–18, repr. in Introduction to Kearney, *The Private Case*, 54–57; passages from *Peregrine Penis*, an unpublished autobiography; *The Horn Book* (1964), 36; Legman, "On Faking HM," unpublished ms.

32. HM to Emil Schnellock, 18 Apr. 1932: "When I penetrate her in the dark her flesh cries out in a mysterious tongue and wherever I have left bruises there is the odor of rose petals." Quoted by Gunther Stuhlmann in "What Emil Knew," *A* 8, 113.

33. Reports of the numbers of copies of *Tropic of Cancer* printed and pirated varies, according to the bibliographer of HM (Roger Jackson to NRF, 28 Nov. 1992).

34. Duane Schneider claims that in her first two published diaries AN portrays herself as "relatively flawless" and idealized, the "Great Mother," benefactress and "savior" for all around her, from the eminent analyst Otto Rank to all the young men. "AN in the Diary: The Creation and Development of a Persona," in Hinz and Fraser, eds., *Mosaic*, 12.

35. AN, *D* 3, 35–37.

36. AN, *D* 3, 38–39.

37. A recent HM biographer does not believe that they continued their physical relations (Mary Dearborn to NRF, 18 Dec. 1990). Rupert Pole (15 Aug. 1992) believes the affair was over by 1940.

38. "Anita" (AN Collection, Box 7, UCLA) has not been published in full because it is a weak and undramatic story, even among the mediocre body of the erotica, and its characters are recognizable.

39. AN, *D* 3, 38, 43.

40. HM called Dalí "hostile," HM to AN, 15 Nov. 1940, *LAN*, 210–11. Winslow, *HM*, 50; Conover on Bert Young, Crosby's husband; HM, "Letter to Lafayette," (43) on heat that summer. HM and AN had earlier met Dalí at one of his exhibitions in Paris; interview with Frank Dobo, 19 Mar. 1991. Barillé (*AN*, 174) claims that Dudley and AN were sexually involved at Hampton Manor.

41. Crosby to AN, 10 Oct. 1968, *A* 6, 55–56. Crosby, who claimed she was in Reno getting her divorce all summer, thought AN was recalling her second visit to Hampton Manor. AN so romanticized this visit that she may have placed it in 1940, during HM's first visit, when it should have been in 1941, according to the correspondence between Crosby and AN.

42. AN, *D* 3, 46–48. Their one-bedroom (with bath and kitchen) at $60 a month was across the street from where the *Dial* and the *Liberator* had once had their offices.

43. Faas, *Young Robert Duncan*, 108. Telephone interview with Virginia Admiral, 2 Dec. 1992. Admiral to NRF, Feb. 1993.

44. AN, *D* 3, 9, 20, 51, 60.

45. Martin, "HM Speech."

46. HM to AN, 5 Mar. 1941, SIU (the paragraph containing these descriptions is deleted from the published correspondence).

47. HM had been sending checks to LD, under German threat in the Mediterranean.

LD to HM, June and July, 1940, *DML*, 137–42. AN also encouraged others, including Robert Duncan, to send LD money.

48. HM's *Quiet Days in Clichy* by the Olympia Press (Paris, 1956) and Grove Press (New York, 1965). Despite the careful work of Jay Martin and bibliographers Roger Jackson (HM) and Patrick Kearny (Olympia Press) to establish the authenticity of HM erotica, rumors of more HM erotic sketches persist.

49. AN, *D* 3, 55, 57–58; *Delta of Venus*, 169; *D* 3, 59.

50. In the year of her death, these longer erotic pieces are carved up, paragraphed, and edited for *Delta of Venus* (1977) by her HBJ editor, John Ferrone. The original manuscripts are at UCLA, box 7. Several unused sections appeared later in *Little Birds* (1979).

51. AN, "Eroticism in Women," in *In Favor of the Sensitive Man*, 8.

52. AN, *D* 3, 60.

53. AN, *D* 3, 27, 29, 53, 60–61, 78, 146.

54. Interview with Gershon Legman, 13 June 1990.

55. Quoted in AN's "The All-Seeing" in *Under a Glass Bell*, 81.

56. The exchange concerning art and motherhood occurred at Joaquin's concert at the Cosmopolitan Club in Washington, D.C., 20 Mar. 1940. The young mother was married to AN's cousin Gilbert. Kathleen Chase, "AN—Rumor and Reality," 7.

57. AN, *D* 3, 66.

58. Interviews with Gershon Legman (12–13 June 1990) and Raymond Rosenthal (1 Mar. 1992).

59. AN, *D* 3, 74–75, 78. After her death, "The Basque and Bijou" was culled from the "Elena" manuscript (UCLA) and published in *Delta of Venus*, 149–87.

60. AN's correspondence with Robert Duncan is in Bancroft. The letters were written when he was in Woodstock printing his journal and helping Cooney publish the journal and books. AN told him to use magic and the primitive in his poetry, not prosaic or barbarian language.

61. Virginia Admiral (to NRF, Feb. 1993) calls AN's claims "hogwash!" AN's diary, according to Admiral, was "a collection of testimonials" and "an ongoing project in self-aggrandizement."

62. Raymond Rosenthal to NRF, 19 Mar. 1992.

63. AN, *D* 3, 82–85.

64. AN, *D* 3, 85–87.

65. Blanche Cooney, "The Little Magazine," 18–19. Cooney to NRF, 10 Sept. 1992. In a letter to Robert Duncan, AN informs him that his relationship with Virginia Admiral is not unlike the relationship that she has had since age 15 with Eduardo (AN to Duncan, n.d., Duncan Collection, Bancroft).

66. In *D* 3, 90–91.

67. "Elena" in *Delta of Venus*, 98. The original "Elena" ms., from which several stories were later carved, is nearly 200 pages long (UCLA).

68. AN, *A Spy in the House of Love*, 105.

69. AN, *Children of the Albatross*, 32–33.

70. AN, "Elena" in *Delta of Venus*, 101, 99.

71. HM to AN, [Jan. 1941], *ALP*, 325.

72. For the original correspondence between AN and HM see HM Collection, SIU. Roger Jackson, HM's bibliographer, first informed me of the virtual suppression of Barnet Ruder's name in published sources. Jackson to NRF, 3 Sept. 1991. In the

fall of 1992, a collection of 40 to 50 letters from HM to Barnet Ruder were announced for sale. In a telephone interview with me (15 Feb. 1991), Ruder denied that he knew anything about the erotica writing and cannot remember when he might have met AN.

73. AN, *D 3*, 97. In response to HM's telegraph, AN sent him the $30 to return to NYC. While in New Orleans HM had arranged to find the records of AN's great-grand-mother, who was born there of French heritage. HM to AN, [5 Feb. 1941], *ALP*, 237.

74. AN, *A Spy in the House of Love*, 60.

75. AN, "Anita" ms., box 7, folder 6, UCLA.

76. AN, *D 3*, 112, 114, 120.

77. HM to AN, [14 Feb. 1940], [3 Mar. 1941], and numerous letters after 11 May 1941 from Hollywood, *LAN*, 202, 237, 262 ff.

78. HM had two reasons for staying on the road: his mother, whom he wished to avoid, and his travel manuscript, which would be entitled *The Air-Conditioned Nightmare*. This lengthy correspondence between AN and HM is printed in *ALP*, 325–37. A key portion of one letter (HM to AN 24 June [1941]) that established their plans together was suppressed at publication, HM Collection, SIU.

79. Robert Duncan, Preface, *Caesar's Gate*, vii. AN was the "idol of personality" for "my late teens and early twenties," he says. He admits he became "an oppressive attendant" of whom she tried "to rid herself" (xxx).

80. HM to AN, [21 June 1941], *ALP*, 331.

81. Robert A. Leonard directed Rainer in *The Great Ziegfeld* (1936), with William Powell and Myrna Loy; Sydney Franklin directed Rainer and Paul Muni in *The Good Earth* (1936). Rainer was born in Vienna 12 Jan. 1912, and would make her first stage appearance in 1942.

82. AN, *D 3*, 126–34. She calls the opera singer Siegfried in her diary and Philip in *A Spy in the House of Love*, where she says she thinks of him as Tristan. In the novel all their lovemaking, even on his coat in the bottom of a boat, leaves her in a fever of unfulfillment (39).

83. AN to Robert Duncan, n.d. [1941], Bancroft. According to Virginia Admiral (to NRF, Feb. 1993), AN first visited Provincetown in 1942, after hearing about their 1941 summer. AN's letters suggest she was nearby.

84. "Life in Provincetown" is bound with "Marcel" in *Auletris* (1950).

85. HM to AN, 19 Aug. 1941, *ALP*, 341.

86. HM to AN, 25 Aug. 1941, *LAN*, 208.

87. Interview with Gershon Legman, 1990; AN, *D 3*, 137–40, 143–54, 165.

88. Interview with Lillian Kiesler, 14 Nov. 1992.

89. Philip K. Jason, "The Gemor Press," *A 2*, 26; AN, *D 3*, 125.

90. Interview with Eugene Walter, 24 May 1991. Interview with Amos Vogel, 21 Apr. 1992.

91. Telephone interview with William Burford, 28 Sept. 1991. Thinking her treatment of Hugo "abominable," young Burford engaged him in conversation, for which AN reprimanded him. He concluded that he did not understand adult relationships.

92. AN, "Linda" in *Delta of Venus*, 216.

93. AN, *D 3*, 156–67.

94. AN, *D 3*, 142.

95. AN, *D 3*, 150, 174–75, 177. For Duncan's praise of AN and Barker, see *Caesar's Gate* (xxix) and *The Years as Catches* (iii).

96. See Duncan's *Caesar's Gate* (1972), xxx, xxi, and Faas's *Young Robert Duncan* (127) and his "The Barbaric Friendship of Robert Duncan and AN," in Hinz and Fraser, eds., *Mosaic*, 141–52. The Robert Duncan Papers, Berkeley.

97. Both "Marianne" and "Manuel" in *Delta of Venus* are taken from the 60-page "Maryanne," carbon copy, UCLA.

98. Harvey Breit's papers (Northwestern) include letters from HM and William Carlos Williams, among others, but none from AN. His book reviews, from the *New York Times, Poetry,* and other journals, were collected in *The Writer Observed* in London in 1957.

99. Interview with Bita Sulzberger Dobo, 19 Mar. 1991; Dobo to NRF 24 May 1991.

100. Telephone interview with Virginia Admiral (2 Dec. 1992), who like many others did not understand the physical attraction that AN exerted on the men: "She was not sexual or sensual . . . more a bird than a sex kitten, with a coy and arch manner." Admiral to NRF, Feb. 1993.

101. Gershon Legman to NRF, 2 Feb. 1990; interview with Legman, 12–13 June 1990; Kearney, *Private Case,* 57; Martin, "HM speech"; Legman, *The Horn Book,* 36. Legman says he wrote "Sous les Toits de Paris"; Martin suggests Caresse Crosby did. Rives Childs, *Collectors Quest,* 39, 10. Somehow a copy of the fake HM manuscript called *Opus Pistorum* or *Under the Roofs of Paris* was taken to California (perhaps even by HM, who sold it piecemeal when he needed money, to Milton Luboviski). Roger Jackson to NRF, 1 Oct. 1992.

102. AN, *D 3*, 157. Bernard Wolfe's *Memoirs,* which covers these events, was published in 1972.

103. Martin, "HM Speech."

104. America is separated from its "soul," AN writes Robert Duncan, n.d. [1940], Berkeley.

105. HM to AN, [30 July 1941], ALP, 339–41.

106. AN, *D 3*, 113–14.

107. de Beauvoir, *America Day by Day,* 41.

108. AN, *D 3*, 176. Ironically, when her own editor prepared her work for publication at the end of her life, he pared her work (e.g., *Delta of Venus* and *Little Birds*) by at least a third.

109. Kay Boyle to NRF, 20 June 1991.

110. Andrew Field (*Djuna,* 223) says that Barnes "considered [AN] to be an obvious case of a little girl lost and a sticky writer." David Goscoyne to NRF, 26 Sept. 1992. Legman says that Barnes informed him that she crossed the street whenever she saw AN; Barnes told Andrew Field, her first biographer, that she never met AN, 233.

111. McBrien, "AN: An Interview," 280.

112. AN, *D 3*, 162, 179, 180. Thurema Sokol, who had collected money for AN from Gotham sales in 1938, gave her the $100 loan.

113. AN, *D 3*, 194, 187, 189. Duncan sold his press to Dave Dellinger, an antiwar activist (Blanche Cooney to NRF, 10 Sept. 1992).

114. AN, *D 3*, 192–94. Her struggle to fix reality in the novel form is illustrated by the number of versions of the "Father Story" at Northwestern.

115. "She was obviously anxious to obtain recognition as a writer in our small group of editors and contributors to *View* magazine," says Eduard Roditi (Roditi to NRF,

24 Apr. 1990). "*Sie hat sich heraufgefickt* [she fucked her way to the top]," says Roditi. Charles Henri Ford founded *View*, which published Paul Goodman, Harold Rosenberg, Paul Bowles, HM, Edith Sitwell, Man Ray, William Carlos Williams, e. e. cummings, and the art of Leger, Lipchitz, Mondrian, and Chagall.

116. James Laughlin to Kenneth Rexroth, 9 Nov. [1942], Rexroth, *Selected Letters*, 30.

117. AN had written a fan letter earlier to WCW and then a letter at the time of binding, asking if he would write a kind word in praise of the book for their publicity ("I got a letter from you once and I feel you believe in me"). She misspelled his name on both letters; n.d., Beinecke Library, Yale. Williams's review appeared in *New Directions Annual*, 1942.

118. WCW to James Laughlin, 5 June 1942, quoted in Mariani, *WCW*, 819.

119. *New Directions No. 7*, 429–36; *D 3*, 196. When he read the review in December in Los Angeles, HM thought that "on the whole it was good." Williams had paid her a "high compliment as a woman—and says almost what you yourself say—what you told Rank—about woman as creator." HM to AN, 1 Jan. 1943, *ALP*, 352–53.

120. WCW, *Patterson*, 113; WCW to Kenneth Burke, [Nov. 1945], quoted in Mariani, *WCW*, 517.

121. Gottlieb, "New Fiction in America," 14; Rosenfeld, "Refinements on a Journal," 276–77; AN, *D 3*, 204–5. HM tried to assure her that it was a "warm" review that would eventually do her good, and that she could not keep her relationship with her father secret. HM to AN, [29 Sept. 1942], *LAN*, 301.

122. Gore Vidal, "Marietta [AN] . . . reads everything written about her from Kyoto to Spokane [and] book reviewers have been astonished to receive long letters from Marietta. . . ." *Two Sisters*, 12.

123. Martin, *Always Merry and Bright*, 385–86; HM to AN, 18 June 1942, *LAN*, 296; *DML*, 151.

124. Martin, *Always Merry and Bright*, 392.

125. The *Diary* mistakenly suggests that the Gemor Press was founded in 1942 with the purchase of the press.

126. Telephone interview with Virginia Admiral, 30 Dec. 1992.

127. HM to AN, 8 Sept. 1942, *LAN*, 299.

128. AN, *D 3*, 206. Briefly, AN had thought Gonzalo would become financially self-sufficient through his printing, but this work fell through after the first check, which she had to keep and dole out to keep him from spending it in one day (199).

129. HM to AN, 9 and 19 Sept. 1942, *ALP*, 343, 344.

130. HM to AN, 19 Sept. 1942, *ALP*, 347.

131. HM to AN, [19 Sept. 1942], *ALP*, 345; *D 3*, 229.

132. HM to AN, 9 Nov. 1942, *ALP*, 351–52.

133. Franklin and Schneider (*AN*, 206) believe the contrast is related, at least unconsciously, in AN's mind: "Perhaps it is in contrast to [HM's] travels and working that Nin unconsciously senses she was overworking and broke down with uncontrollable weeping."

134. Blanche Cooney met Frances Fox in Woodstock in 1937 when Leonard Robinson brought her for a weekend. "Frances was my essential woman friend in those years. Even when she was no longer married to Lenny she came to the farm with Tom Brown. Then with Michael Field." Cooney to NRF, 15 Apr. 1991. Marguerite Young calls Frances "beautiful, strange, ethereal, and private."

135. Interview with Lillian Kiesler, 14 Nov. 1992. Kiesler believes that Frances adored AN "out of proportion."

136. AN, *D* 3, 282–83.

137. AN, *D* 3, 208, 214, 218; HM's letter is quoted on 232.

138. Kay Boyle to Caresse Crosby, 15 Sept. 1942, Crosby Collection, SIU.; Boyle to Richard Centing, 31 July 1971, Crosby Collection; Boyle to NRF 20 June 1991.

139. AN, *D* 3, 239–42, 248–49. AN's relationship with a neighbor, Henrietta Weigel, reveals both her compassion and her need during this period. AN cultivated her friendship during 1943 and 1944, expressed admiration for her writing, and sent (without her knowledge) one of Weigel's manuscripts to Dutton. Weigel, extremely shy, felt AN was trying to take over her life. When an advance arrived, Weigel ran away to Mexico (*Age of Noon* was published by Dutton in 1947). Though she did not like AN's fiction, she wrote a letter of praise (feeling like a hypocrite). The letter was printed in full twenty-five years later when AN published the diary of this period. Despite her own shyness, Weigel confided in her family, she was aware that AN "needed so much, like an actress, to be in limelight. . . . Still, I was a sort of 'Father-mother confessor' to her—for she'd reappear—sit on the floor—her head in my lap—and tell me sad sad things of herself. . . . She wanted so much to be close to me, but she never seemed *real* to me. And her super-practicality mingled with super-aestheticism was bewildering." Henrietta Weigel to Mildred and Charles Kramer [1979]; Mildred Kramer to NRF, 10 Sept. 1991. AN, *D* 3 (with HW's letter of praise) and *D* 6 contain references to HW.

140. Pelensky, *Isak Dinesen*, xxiii, 52.

141. HM's letter to AN is published in full in *D* 3, 243–46 (it is not among the HM letters to AN at SIU); AN had encouraged HM to read the story (112).

142. HM to AN, 1 Jan. [1943] and [Feb. 1943], *ALP*, 353–54, 358–59.

143. AN, *D* 3, 256–60, 263. Doris Niemayer ("How to be a Woman and/or an Artist") and Nancy Jo Hoy ("The Poetry of Experience") discuss the Jaeger analysis in *A* 6 (67–74) and *A* 4 (52–66).

144. HM planned to send her $100 a month (half his grant) if his benefactor's promise materialized [April 1944], *ALP*, 360. At HM's insistence, she considered publishing her diary and approached Steloff about selling her manuscripts to get money to publish 20 volumes of the diary.

145. AN, *D* 3, 272, 280, 282. She met Richard Wright (and Carson McCullers) at a party at the home of George Davis in Brooklyn, *D* 3, 270, 179. McCullers, like AN, was obsessed with (and rejected by), Djuna Barnes.

146. Interview with Josephine Premice, 7 Dec. 1991; LD called AN a "diva," and many of her friends described her "grand manner." Telephone interview with Jamake Highwater, 5 Feb. 1991.

147. AN to Caresse Crosby, [Fall 1943], *A* 2, 44.

148. AN, *D* 3, 300–301. "The severe test of typesetting failed to dissolve" the poetic validity of her stories, she adds.

149. Jason, "The Gemor Press," *A* 2, 30.

150. HM to LD, 7 Apr. 1944, *DML*, 162. AN lets LD believe (n.d. [mid-1946], SIU) that she broke with HM because he was self-indulgent and content to live by Hugo's money.

151. AN to CC, [Feb. 1944], *A* 6, 45.

152. Wilson, "Books—Doubt, and Dreams," 78–82; Paul Rosenfeld had mentioned the

book to Wilson, who received a copy from Steloff. Rosenfeld's review in *The New Republic* in mid-April suggests that he thought her a minor talent.

153. AN, *D 3*, 314.

## 9. THIS HUNGER FOR ACCEPTANCE (*pages 261–289*)

1. AN, *D 4*, 81. Many of the events covered in this chapter are chronicled in *The Diary of AN*, vol. 4 (1944–47), an expurgated selection from seven bound journals, nos. 68–74, portraying AN's life in part from ages 41 to 44. Portions are fictionalized in *Children of the Albatross* (where the events are set in Paris) and *A Spy in the House of Love*.

2. HM to AN, 8 June 1944, *LAN*, 331; Caresse Crosby, excerpt from "Who in the World" (unpublished ms., SIU), *A 2*, 47.

3. AN, *D 4*, 10.

4. Vidal, "Taking a Grand Tour," 1.

5. AN spent her life moving, redesigning her clothes, changing mates. She found security in flux, says Linde Salber, "Two Lives—One Experiment: Lou Andreas-Salomé and AN," trans. by Gunther Stuhlmann, *A 9*, 85.

6. AN, *D 4*, 31.

7. HM to Bern Porter, n.d. [1944] and 8 Jan. 1944, UCLA. HM says she is very susceptible to flattery and sensitive to criticism.

8. AN to HM, [Apr. 1945], *ALP*, 367.

9. AN to Henrietta Weigel, 9 July 1944, OSU. AN describes Herschkowitz as about 30 years old, intense and dark, tall, and lean.

10. Norse, *Memoirs of a Bastard Angel*, 366–67. Norse's version was apparently furnished by AN herself.

11. Interview with Mary Dearborn, 10 Nov. 1992. The Herschkowitz-Miller letters (UCLA) reveal that Harry was sexually auditioning women for Henry, even looking for Miller's long-lost daughter for a sexual union. The young man tells Miller that he would love to be a woman in order to show the great writer how much he loves him.

12. Bern Porter to NRF, lengthy 1990–92 correspondence; interview with Porter 13 Aug. 1990. Porter had published HM's *HM Miscellanea, Semblance of a Devoted Past*, and other brief works. Herbert Gold, "Running Aground," 22.

13. The relationship with Dr. Jaeger is complicated and probably unprofessional. Jaeger had made a friend of her clients, taking her own problems (an unfaithful husband) to AN, who in turn resented Jaeger's criticism that her fiction lacked warmth and humanity.

14. AN, *D 4*, 42.

15. AN, *D 4*, 32; AN to HM, [May 1945], *ALP*, 368. AN's letters to Edmund Wilson are at the Beinecke Library, Yale.

16. AN, *Children of the Albatross*, 13, 69.

17. Unpublished correspondence between C. L. Baldwin and AN, UCLA; AN, *D 4*, 32.

18. AN, *D 3*, 292, 295; *D 4*, 13, 16, 18, 69. Though critical of Jaeger, AN also suggested that psychoanalysis was like the atom, bombing personality to release new energy, and thus perhaps a cure for world strife (70–71, 78).

19. AN to Caresse Crosby, [spring 1944], *A 2*, 46.

20. AN to HM, [May 1945], *ALP,* 368; AN to Crosby [Fall 1944], *A 2,* 46–48.

21. AN, *D 4,* 16, says $1,000; HM (to AN 3 May 1944, *ALP,* 361) says he received $200 a month. The year before HM had made a public appeal that led to free lodging with the artist Varda in Monterey in 1943, then the offer of a cabin in Big Sur.

22. AN to HM, 8 June [1944] and [July 1944], *ALP,* 330, 363; *D 4,* 4.

23. Typescript of interview with Clyde Kittell and Adelaide Hawley on WEAF (NBC), dated 3 August 1944, Berg.

24. Frances Steloff to AN, 23 Sept. 1944, Berg. AN to HM, [Aug. 1944] and [Sept. 1944], *ALP,* 364–65.

25. AN to HM, [July 1944], *ALP,* 363.

26. Hugh Guiler, "Recollections," *A 4,* 28.

27. Joaquin Nin-Culmell, "Hugo, My Brother-in-Law," *A 4,* 14.

28. AN to LD, n.d. [mid-1946], SIU.

29. Geismer, "AN: An Imprecise Spy," 3. Though Geismar describes Hugo as "limited intellectually," many others describe him as quiet and dignified.

30. Philip K. Jason, "The Gemor Press," *A 2,* 25.

31. AN, *D 4,* 25.

32. Sharon Spencer, one of AN's best critics, has established the important influence of Proust: AN's diary, she says, most closely resembles Proust's *A Remembrance of Things Past.* AN makes 100 references to Proust in her first six diaries and claimed to reread the *Remembrance* of her "favorite writer" every year (*Collage of Dreams,* 142).

33. AN, *D 4,* 25, 28; AN to HM, [May 1945] and [10 June 1945], *ALP,* 367, 370.

34. AN, *D 4,* 32, 33, 36.

35. AN, *D 4,* 40–41.

36. AN, *D 4,* 55, 65, 77.

37. On AN's efforts at publicity: AN to Crosby [Feb. 1944], *A 2,* 45.

38. AN, *D 4,* 40.

39. HM to Wallace Fowlie, 2 May 1945, *Letters,* 89. HM had read Fowlie's "Narcissus" in *View* and begun a correspondence with Fowlie (Trumbull College, Yale, 1942–44).

40. Wallace Fowlie to NRF, 22 Mar. 1991.

41. AN to HM, [Apr. 1945], *ALP,* 367; *D 4,* 57, 132.

42. AN sends a poem by William Pinckard to Mr. Tambimutti, editor of *Poetry* (London) who might, HM has told her, be arranging for a small monthly stipend for Pinckard (HM to AN 21 June 1944).

43. AN, *D 4,* 54, 62.

44. AN to HM, [Apr. and May 1945], *ALP,* 366–69; *D 4,* 54, 49.

45. AN, *D 4,* 70–71.

46. In Gore Vidal's *Two Sisters,* his Marietta Donegal is a parody of AN, whose "lovers are waiting a few streets away, priests of her cult, and with the passing years no doubt well paid for their ministrations at that high and entirely public altar" (13).

47. AN to HM, 10 June 1945, *ALP,* 370. HM has offered to send her half the money he plans to make when Maurice Girodias (son of Jack Kahane) publishes his books in Paris (HM to AN, 2 July 1945, *ALP,* 371).

48. Interview with Eugene Walter, 2 Feb. 1992. New York City was "an oasis of libera-

tion," says Harold Norse, a friend of AN's, James Baldwin's, and James Merrill's (*Memoirs*, 12).

49. Interview with Marshall Barer, 30 Aug. 1991.

50. AN uses Barer's real name in her diary, though she did not ask his permission, he says; She does not hint of their affair, but she gets a number of details wrong, including his age and the name of his father (she mistakenly says he is the son of a famous rabbi). Nor did he work on the printing press. Barer makes the point that during this period there was a breakthrough in homosexual sensibility in the theatre, thanks to the work of Leonard Bernstein, Jerome Robbins, Moss Hart and Richard Avalon, and Hal Prince. Interview with Marshall Barer, 30 August 1991.

51. *D 4*, 65, 70, 72; Luise Rainer married Robert Knittel this summer and was no longer part of the circle; AN did not enjoy the formality of the ceremony (74).

52. AN to C. L. Baldwin, 23 Aug. 1945 and undated letter ("I did the weeping for both of us"), AN Collection (box 11, file 6), UCLA.

53. C. L. Baldwin to AN, Aug. 1945, UCLA.

54. AN to C. L. Baldwin, 25 Aug. 1945, UCLA.

55. Vidal, "Taking a Grand Tour," 405.

56. AN, *D 4*, 47, 64, 74, 81–82, 98, 101–2. She uses the Kaspar Hauser story in her fiction, e.g., *Children of the Albatross*, 57.

57. AN, *D 4*, 74. Professor Fowlie (b. 1908) is about five years younger than AN.

58. AN to HM, [May 1945], *ALP*, 367; *D 4*, 71–2.

59. See Malone, *Survival*.

60. AN, *D 4*, 15, 72, 81. Madonna has observed the appeal of gays for artistic women: "Actually it would be great to be both sexes," she says. "Effeminate men intrigue me more than anything in the world. I see them as my alter egos. I feel drawn to them. I think like a guy, but I'm feminine. So I relate to feminine men." Lynn Hirschberg, "The Misfit," 200.

61. AN, *D 4*, 64.

62. One biographer of Wilson's claims he "proposed to AN." Costa, *Edmund Wilson*, 141.

63. AN, *D 4*, 83–84, 142, 148. Wilson's reviews are all-important to her hope for literary acceptance. HM thought them inept reviews but generally helpful.

64. AN, *D 4*, 88–89.

65. AN, *D 4*, 88–89, 148.

66. AN, *D 4*, 90–93, 97. AN told a friend that she did not trust Wilson enough to allow him to read any of her diary. AN to Herbert Faulkner West, 26 Dec. 1946, Dartmouth.

67. Wilson, "Books—," 97–102; AN, *D 4*, 98, 101.

68. Wilson, *The Forties*, 288.

69. AN, *D 4*, 94–95, 97, 99. "[F]or years, she felt harmed and defeated at the hands of men of power, and she expected the boy, the gentle one, the trusted one, to come and deliver her from tyranny," she says of Djuna in *Children of the Albatross*.

70. AN, *D 4*, 82, 91, 97, 98.

71. Snyder, ed., *AN Observed*, 63; AN, *D 4*, 67, 75, 76.

72. AN, *D 4*, 90–92.

73. Rogers, *Wise Men Fish Here*, 125; AN, *D 4*, 96, 98.

74. AN, *D 4*, 98–101, 106, 117, 119, 137.

75. Vidal, *Two Sisters*, 173.

76. AN, *D 4*, 104–6.

77. AN, *D 4*, 105, 107, 114, 140.

78. AN to HM, [late 1945], *ALP*, 372; *D 4*, 103. See the Trilling and Rosenfeld essays in the Bibliography.

79. Clarke, *Capote*, 139. AN says that at Leo Lerman's parties and further meetings, she never spoke with Capote, for they were both shy (*D 4*, 111).

80. AN, *D 4*, 111, 117, 123, 99. Interview with Marshall Barer, 30 Aug. 1991.

81. Lex Martin, "Modern Version of Old Fable," 14.

82. Vidal and Stanton, *Views from a Window*, 117; AN, *D 4*, 106, 113, 116, 121.

83. Although "V" and "Marietta" in his satiric novel *Two Sisters* live together for three months in 1947 and the experience becomes the "central motif of one of her most Lorenzian novels" (7), the novel describes Marietta as "marvelous in the sack" but given to post-coital chatter. Vidal's biographer doubts that their relationship was physically intimate (interview with Walter Clemons, 6 Dec. 1991).

84. Kiernan, *Gore Vidal*, 3; Vidal and Stanton, *Views*, 87, 62; AN, *D 4*, 119, 115.

85. Vidal and Stanton, *Views*, 124, 177.

86. AN, *Children of the Albatross*, 53–54.

87. If Paul Mathiesen is indeed the basis of the character in Vidal's *Two Sisters*, the influence is long forgotten by Vidal, who claims not to remember him. Interview with Walter Clemons, 1 Dec. 1992. Mathiesen was born in May 1927.

88. Interviews with Paul Mathiesen, 5 and 24 Sept. 1991 and 15 May 1993.

89. Vidal, "Taking a Grand Tour," 405.

90. AN to LD, n.d. [mid-1946], SIU.

91. The 1947 dedication of *Children of the Albatross* was dropped from subsequent editions because she became disappointed in analysis with Staff. According to her friends, AN occasionally saw more than one analyst at a time.

92. AN, *Incest*, 95.

93. AN, *Children of the Albatross*, 41.

94. AN, *D 4*, 120, 139, 143, 165.

95. AN, *D 4*, 125–27, 165, 187.

96. AN to HM, [Mar. 1946], *ALP*, 373. The money from HM was half of a check from Girodias, now owner of his father's publishing company in Paris, Jack Kahane's Obelisk Press.

97. AN also informed Caresse Crosby this summer that she "no longer" wanted the diary printed, "as I'm drawing from it heavily for my serial novels." *A 2*, 48–49.

98. HM to AN, May 17, 1946, *ALP*, 376–77.

99. Interviews with Marshall Barer (30 Aug. 1991) and Paul Mathiesen (24 Sept. 1991). According to Barer, Deren was making a point about persons looking differently from afar and filmed everyone close up and exaggerated. "Anaïs tried to stop the film from being shown at the YMHA. She tried to yank it."

100. Maya Deren's *Ritual in Transfigured Time* (1945–46) is available on *Maya Deren: Collected Experimental Films*, Mystic Fire Video, 1986.

101. AN, *D 4*, 161.

102. AN to HM, [June 1946], *ALP*, 380.

103. Telephone interview with Eugene Walter, 24 May 1991.

104. Anon., 14 (15 August 1946), 396.

105. Lyons, "Surrealist Soap Opera," 16. Lyons believed AN's work was just an echo of Djuna Barnes, HM, and Edmund Wilson.

106. Smith, "Ladies in Turmoil," 13; Lex Martin, "Modern Version of Old Fable," 14; Wilson, "Books—A Note," 114; Kay, "Ladders," 16.

107. AN's undated letter to Wilson is with his papers at the Beinecke Library, Yale.

108. Dick, "AN and Gore Vidal," 157.

109. Marguerite Young (interview 5 Dec. 1991) claims that AN thought Lerman was ridiculing her socially and professionally. Lerman claims (letter to NRF, 13 Oct. 1992) that their "falling out" lasted for "some time" before they resumed their friendship.

110. AN's friendship with William Burford and James Merrill is based on interviews and letters with these men. Burford: telephone interviews, 28 Sept. and 5 Oct. 1991 and 23 Dec. 1992; Merrill: telephone interview, 27 Nov. 1991; the AN/Burford correspondence is at HRHRC.

111. William Burford to NRF, 24 Dec. 1992.

112. HM's comment on Nijinski's "triumph" over homosexuality appears in *First Impressions,* but he omits it in the reprint of the chapbook, entitled *Colossus of Maroussi.*

113. Interview with Carlton Lake, 19 Sept. 1991, and Lake to NRF, 18 Dec. 1991. Broyard ("Of Art," 39) suggests that "turning her into a vogue may be the best solution to the ungallant task of evaluating her critically."

114. As usual, she had written ahead to Gordon Cairnie of Grolier Book Shop and the head of the library to suggest they arrange a lecture at Harvard. The effort must have been unsuccessful, for she lectured at the bookstore. Cairnie Correspondence, Houghton Library, Harvard.

115. AN, *D 4,* 169–72. Her friends of earlier years are very surprised that she can appear in front of and project to an audience. Perlès to HM, 12 Jan. 1946, UCLA.

116. Interview with Carleton Lake, 19 Sept. 1991 and Lake to NRF, 18 Dec. 1991.

117. Interviews with Lake (19 Sept. 1991) and James Merrill (27 Nov. 1991).

118. AN, *D 4,* 150–55; AN's ideas are best presented in her essay "On Truth and Reality" in *The Novel of the Future.*

119. Vidal, *Two Sisters,* 3, 12.

120. AN, *D 4,* 173–75, 178.

121. AN, *D 4,* 175–76. Late in her life AN told Barbara Kraft and others that she had never had a lesbian affair. Angry letters to various news and journal publications reveal that her concern for her image remained. Centing, "AN and the Art of Photography," unpublished MLA paper, 28 Dec. 1978.

122. AN to LD, n.d. [mid-1946], SIU.

123. AN, *D 4,* 182, 184.

124. AN, *D 4,* 185, 186.

125. William Burford to NRF, 24 Dec. 1992. The Merrill party was held on the abandoned estate in Amherst of the man who wrote the Uncle Wiggly children's books.

126. Telephone interview with William Burford, 28 Sept. 1991.

127. Telephone interview with Kay Stenberg, 8 Oct. 1991. The Baradinskys' first Outcast chapbook was HM's *Obscenity and the Law of Reflection* (1945). Several other HM titles and chapbooks by LD, Fraenkel, even Ian Hugo ("New Eyes on the Art of Engraving") followed. "In fact, for a time the Alicat Book Shop Press seemed a post-war version of the Villa Seurat and Siana publications," says Philip K. Jason, "Oscar Baradinsky's 'Outcasts,'" *A 3,* 110. Maya Deren's husband, Alexander Ham-

mid, designed the Alicat logo. Outcast #14 was a reissue of Djuna Barnes's first book, *The Book of Repulsive Women.*

128. Duncan is quoted in Faas, *Young Robert Duncan,* 194.

129. Interview with Walter Calkins, 28 Aug. 1991.

130. Of the three versions of *Children of the Albatross* at HRHRC, the third version of 173 pages is corrected by William Burford, who must have helped her correct galleys. AN, who was 44 years old, changes the age of her alter ego Djuna from 30 to 27.

131. AN, *Children of the Albatross,* 65–66.

132. Telephone interviews with Rupert Pole, 14 Feb. and 17 Apr. 1990 and 25 Nov. 1992; AN, *D 4,* 196–97. Pole remembered that they both had ink on their hands and later visited each other's press (he was printing Christmas cards for a friend); he believes the party was in March and they left three weeks later for their trip west. They spent a weekend together "that lasted a lifetime," he noted.

133. AN, *D 4,* 70; AN tells HM ([June 1947], *ALP,* 385) that she cannot go to Europe with Hugo "because the bank won't pay my trip and also because as you know I am trying to live alone. So I'm finally going to Mexico July 12."

134. Interview with Nancy Scholar Adams, 31 Jan. 1992; Patricia L. Kahle to NRF, 11 Feb. 1992.

135. AN, *D 4,* 206.

136. Interview with Rupert Pole, 1 Mar. 1991.

137. AN, *D 4,* 222–23. According to Rupert Pole (telephone interview 9 Sept. 1992), plane service to Acapulco had just begun. On the plane AN had been reading about the seaport fishing village in a brochure.

## 10. CHANGING AND TURNING (*pages 290–327*)

1. AN, *Seduction of the Minotaur,* 5–6. Major sources for Chapter Ten, which covers AN's life from ages 44 to 52, are personal interviews with more than 150 persons as well as published and unpublished letters. Her recorded memories are found in *The Diary of AN,* vol. 5 (1947–55), based on 14 journals, nos. 75–88, UCLA. Chief fictional sources are *Solar Barque* (*Seduction of the Minotaur*) and *Collages.*

2. Letter to Maxwell Geismar (1955), reprinted in *D 5,* 216–17.

3. AN to Henry Rago, 11 June 1948, Lilly.

4. AN to HM, [June 1947], *ALP,* 385. AN's activities for the fall of 1947 are lost between the published *D 4* and *D 5,* which gives the illusion that she remained in Mexico from the spring of 1947 to February 1948.

5. HM to AN, 14 Sept. 1947 and 18 Sept. [1947], *ALP,* 385–88. HM's royalties had been accumulating in Paris during the war.

6. Interview with Rupert Pole, 16 Aug. 1991.

7. AN to HM, [Sept. 1947], *ALP,* 388.

8. Anon. *The Virginia Kirkus Service* 15 (15 Aug.1947), 440; Anon. "Briefly Noted—Fiction," *The New Yorker* 23 (8 Nov. 1947), 131–32; Davis, "AN's Children of Light," 36; Hart, "Analysis of the Antagonism," 21; McLaughlin, "Shadow Dance," 16–17.

9. Lepska Miller Warren to NRF, 28 Jan. 1992. Interviews with Paul Mathiesen, 5 and 24 Sept. 1991; HM to LD, [1947], *DML,* 214; LD confirms the domestic problems of the Millers in his 20 Aug. [1947] letter, 217; AN, *D 4,* 220.

10. *Diary 5* opens in Mexico. This volume, which was edited in 1971–74, is sparse and

fragmented by AN's omissions and due to her many travels. The Mexico interlude would be used for the subject matter of *Seduction of the Minotaur* (1961).

11. AN to Edwin Becker, n.d. [1947], SIU.

12. Paul Mathiesen (interview 24 Sept. 1991) had met AN in Mexico City, where they visited Gore Vidal, who was recuperating in a hospital there. When AN flew back to Acapulco, Mathiesen got lost while trying to drive his car to join her. This incident about him nearly drowning at the Miramar is rewritten as if she were not there and placed ten years later in her diary (1957), according to him.

13. Interview with William Burford, 28 Sept. 1991.

14. Interview with Rupert Pole, 17 Apr. 1990; AN, *D* 5, 15–18.

15. Interview with Paul Mathiesen, 24 Sept. 1991; AN, *D* 5, 19–22.

16. Interview with Eugene Walter, 2 Feb. 1992. Walter remembered interrupting a liaison between a pretty young blond from the New School, and Hugo, who had forgotten his appointment with Walter. Another friend remembered that Hugo preferred Balinese girls, another said Haitian. "Both of Anaïs's men [Hugo and Miller] liked exotic women," said Jean Fanchette (interview 17 July 1991).

17. Interviews with Eugene Walter (24 May 1991) and Curtis Harrington (13 Mar. 1991).

18. Beatrice Wood had love affairs with Marcel Duchamp and Henri-Pierre Roché and was a friend of Edgar Varèse's and Walter Arensberg's. AN and Rupert referred to Wood as their unofficial mother-in-law because they wished that Reginald would marry her. But Wood understood the actor's lack of discipline, his physical deterioration and growing hypochondria. She believed that she was considerably older than Anaïs, though there were only ten years between them. Interview with Beatrice Wood, 1 Sept. 1991.

19. According to Paul Mathiesen (interview 24 Sept. 1991) AN arranged the Hugo exhibit in a tiny gallery in Los Angeles and expressed jealousy when a woman became overly interested in Hugo.

20. Interview with James Leo Herlihy, 27 Nov. 1990.

21. Margot Duxler, a later friend of AN's and a psychologist, suggests that AN made concrete all the separate pains, ambivalences, and secrets of her inner life in order to control them. Interview with Duxler, 26 Apr. 1991.

22. AN to Ruth Witt-Diamant, 9 July 1949, Berg; *D* 5, 11. One of the best and most honest descriptions of AN's "tak[ing] care of two different lives" is found in her letter to Lawrence and Claude Durrell (3 Feb. 1959), SIU.

23. Poet and filmmaker James Broughton chronicles these poetic days in San Francisco in *Coming Unbuttoned*.

24. Interview with Josephine Premice, 7 Dec. 1991. Premice would also go to Paris to live before settling for five years in Rome.

25. AN to Ruth Witt-Diamant, 2 Apr. 1948, Berg.

26. AN, *D* 5, 83.

27. AN's tribute to Los Angeles: "Magic in Los Angeles."

28. HM had told AN (8 June 1941, *LAN,* 266) that the presence of all the émigrés in Los Angeles reminded him of Europe.

29. AN to Edwin Becker, n.d. [1949?], SIU.

30. "She needed him for ballast," says her friend Curtis Harrington (13 Mar. 1991 interview) of Rupert Pole. Friends note that both Hugo and Rupert were malleable and accommodating. AN, *D* 4, 34.

31. AN, *D* 4, 28–29; AN to Ruth Witt-Diamant, n.d., Bancroft; Beatrice Wood substan-

tiates AN's portrayal of Reginald Pole as erudite and charming, yet undisciplined and hypochondriac (interview 1 Sept. 1991).

32. Telephone interview with Rupert Pole, 17 Apr. 1991. Though Thorvald insisted that his sister not divorce Hugo, he himself divorced the mother of his children. When he died, in 1991, Thorvald Nin was living in El Paso, Texas, and was director general of Plywood Ponderosa de Mexico.

33. AN to HM, [summer 1948], *ALP,* 388–89.

34. Interview with Renate Druks, 12 Apr. 1991. At Vidal's home in Guatemala were Pat Crocker, who owned the house, Dan Wichonton, and Dominick Donne. Telephone interview with Walter Clemons, 1 Dec. 1992.

35. AN, *D 4,* 134, 142; Dan Wichonton and Pat Crocker were in Guatemala with Vidal. Wichonton drove back to Acapulco with AN and Rupert, says Walter Clemons, interview 6 Dec. 1991, though Rupert Pole says that he did not accompany her to visit Vidal. He was in Frazier, Colorado, working for the forest service in the summer fire season.

36. Vidal and Stanton, *Views from a Window,* 87.

37. Vidal, *Live from Golgotha,* 50, 87–88. Priscilla is a disciple of Sappho (53), a bigamist ("This is Roman high society, the fast lane . . . only little people bother to get divorced," she says, 147). Her husband, Aquila, does not want to be mentioned in her diary and "just pretended to be dim so that Priscilla would not share her secrets with him" (50).

38. Sheed, "Gore's Gospel," 130.

39. AN, *Seduction of the Minotaur* (into which *Solar Barque* was incorporated), 67.

40. AN, *D 5,* 33.

41. Interview with Curtis Harrington, 13 Mar. 1991; Hardwick, "Fiction Chronicle," 705–11.

42. Quoted from an early draft of the unpublished memoir of James Broughton, with his permission. JB to NRF, 21 July 1991. Broughton to NRF, 15 Jan. 1993.

43. AN to HM, [early 1949], *ALP,* 390; AN to C. L. Baldwin, 15 Apr. 1949, UCLA; Broughton claims in his memoirs that AN changed the date of her birth before showing him and Sheets her first diary. His observation about AN's seduction of young men is confirmed by numerous sources.

44. AN, *D 5,* 34.

45. AN, *D 5,* 40, 42. When Broughton and Sheets decided they could not publish her early diary, AN took back her Moroccan bedstead and later cut Broughton out of her diary (except for one reference to him as a mother-dominated homosexual).

46. AN letters to C. L. Baldwin, UCLA.

47. In an interview with Daisy Aldan ("AN Interviewed," 7–9) AN adds precious stones, gold ("for ecstasy, illumination"), and the ship to the list of recurring symbols in her work.

48. AN, *A Spy in the House of Love,* 32.

49. Guiler, "Recollections," *A 4,* 28. This 1986 edition of *Anais: An International Journal* devoted several articles to Guiler, who had died the year before. Fabion Bowers, through their mutual friend Mrs. Katrine Coolidge Perkins (James H. Perkins was head of First National City Bank and had opened the Paris branch), heard that Guiler was let go by the bank. Interview with Fabion Bowers, 19 Mar. 1991.

50. Broughton, typed ms. of *Coming Unbuttoned,* 12.

51. AN to Ruth Witt-Diamant, 9 July and 15 July 1949, UCLA. On 13 July, AN

complained to RWD about her friend trying "to divide Rupert and I [sic]." Nevertheless they remained good friends.

52. Broughton, ms., 12.

53. Spencer, "The Art of Ragpicking" 20–21. Franklin, "Varda," 7–8.

54. Kenneth Rexroth, in an interview with *Conjunctions* (64, OSU), adds that AN suffered from "cunto" (female macho). "How anybody could be a feminist and stand her is beyond me."

55. Bern Porter to NRF, 26 Oct. 1991; interview with Porter by Phil Nuremberg, 1980. Both Porter and a group at the Studio Bookstore on Hollywood Boulevard in Los Angeles talked about publishing AN's diary (interview with Betty Buchanan, 22 Apr. 1991).

56. Ferlinghetti and Peters, *Literary San Francisco*, 155.

57. James Laughlin to Kenneth Rexroth, [Sept. 1945], (Rexroth, *Selected Letters*, 67).

58. Interview with Nancy Leite, 29 Dec. 1991; HM's correspondence with George Leite is at HRHRC; AN's undated correspondence with Leite is at OSU.

59. Interview with Bebe Barron, 16 Apr. 1991. AN suggests such a scene later in *A Spy in the House of Love* (59) when a black dancer places his knee between her legs and holds her closely, "welding" his body to hers with an almost angry look in his eyes. In the fiction, he leaves alone after their dance. In an unpublished letter to Crosby, AN says that Hugo has mistresses, but Rupert wants to have a wife. AN to CC, n.d. [May 1958], SIU.

60. Interview with James Leo Herlihy, 27 Nov. 1990; AN, *D 5*, 53, 231; Herlihy, "The Art of Being a Person," *A 7*, 67–68.

61. Nichols, "New Books," 1818. Carruth's review appeared in the *Providence Sunday Journal*, 9; Kay's review appeared 19 Feb. in "This World," 14,16; other reviews appeared in *The New Yorker*, the *Christian Science Monitor*, *New Haven Register*, *New York Times*, *New York Herald Tribune Book Review*, *Atlantic*, and *Saturday Review*.

62. AN to Ruth Witt-Diamant, 12 and 19 Feb. 1950, Berg.

63. Telephone interview with Rupert Pole, 8 Oct. 1992. Pole says he and AN suffered long delays upon their return trips from Mexico, where her customs clearance was always delayed by her Cuban passport.

64. Leo Lerman to NRF, 13 Feb. 1992.

65. AN to Dante Thomas Zaccagnini, 2 July 1949, HRHRC. Their correspondence reveals that he paid her in San Francisco on an installment plan.

66. The correspondence between Kathryn Winslow and Felix Pollack, and later Richard Olson, reveals that later manuscripts were bought at the same rate of exchange. Northwestern.

67. AN correspondence with John Lehmann for 1953 and 1955 in HRHRC. Some of her erotica (versions of "Marcel," "The Boarding School," and "The Hungarian Adventurer" from *Delta of Venus*) was sold to the Kinsey Institute in 1949 and 1950 by one George Howard, who had worked at Ben Abramson's bookstore in Chicago (Roger Jackson to NRF, 7 Aug. and 26 Aug. 1991). Kinsey lists "Brazil Erotica" and "Marcel" as purchased in 1949; "Erotika," 1950; "Novel" and "Second Novel," 1951; and *Delta of Venus* and *Little Birds*, 1977 and 1979 respectively.

68. Interview with James Herlihy, 27 Nov. 1990. AN to Ruth Witt-Diamant, 13 July 1950, Berg.

69. Both Jack Hirschman (interview 27 Apr. 1991) and James Broughton (*Coming*

*Unbuttoned*) describe hair-raising rides with AN driving Rupert's car in San Francisco.

70. AN to Ruth Witt-Diamant, 17 Sept., 5 Oct., and 31 Oct. 1950, Berg.

71. AN, *A Spy in the House of Love*, 19, 122, 134. Anne Geismar (interview 20 Apr. 1992) believes AN lied because she was "groping for glory."

72. Interview with Curtis Harrington, 13 Mar. 1991.

73. Interviews with Amos Vogel (21 Apr. 1992) and Robert Haller (5 Dec. 1991).

74. AN to Ruth Witt-Diamant, 5 Oct. 1950, Berg. Joyce Howard, a later friend of AN's, claims AN complained about not liking the wilderness.

75. AN, *D* 5, 83.

76. Interview with Anne Geismar, 20 Apr. 1992; Maxwell Geismar, "Reminiscences of a Reluctant Radical," unpublished memoirs.

77. AN, *D* 5, 62.

78. Spencer (*Collage of Dreams*, 109) says that at this time of her life, after implementing the masculine qualities she once feared, AN begins identifying with strong women such as Glanville-Hicks, Bebe Barron, Cornelia Runyan, and Renate Druks.

79. Telephone interview with Rupert Pole, 17 Apr. 1991.

80. AN and Rupert Pole never had a common-law marriage, which in 1895 was outlawed in California. An amendment in 1969 declared that couples must have "civil license and solemnization. Consent alone does not constitute marriage" (Gail Riley O'Neill, esq.). AN's marriage to Guiler would have made any marriage to Pole null and void, of course.

81. Interviews with Gloria Orenstein and Sharon Spencer (29 Apr. 1992). Marten Sameth was younger than his wife, Inge Bogner. Wendy DuBow to NRF, 4 Dec. 1992.

82. Evans uses the phrase as the title for the eighth chapter of his *Anaïs Nin*.

83. AN, *D* 5, 73–74.

84. AN, *D* 5, 79.

85. She told HM that she thought they would all be going back to Paris, where they were "happiest." She had grown "to despise" America. AN to HM, [Summer 1952], *ALP*, 390–91.

86. Telephone interview with James Merrill, 27 Nov. 1991.

87. Bowles, *Without Stopping*, 260.

88. AN, *D* 5, 82–83, 86.

89. Interview with James Herlihy, 27 Nov. 1990. AN to RWD, n.d. [1952?], Berg.

90. Interview with Anne Geismar, 20 Apr. 1992. In Maxwell Geismar's unpublished memoirs he refers to her "remarkable political naivete," 130.

91. Herlihy is a dominating presence in her diary of these years, *D* 5, 78–79, 84, 96–97.

92. Franklin and Schneider, *AN*, 249.

93. Interview with Anne Geismar, 20 Apr. 1992.

94. AN, *D* 5, 101. The Geismars differ on the number of diaries she brought to their house: he recalls 30; she, 12.

95. Geismar, unpublished memoirs. The chapter entitled "Anaïs Nin: An Imprecise Spy in the House of Love" (in part published in 1979 by the *Los Angeles Times*) was sent to this author by Anne Geismar, who owns the ms. Geismar concludes that the Guilers cultivated an air of mystery in order to cover their own "simplicity or

shallowness." Other friends (Aldan interview, 15 Jan. 1993) testify to AN's "brilliance."

96. AN, *D* 5, 88. In an undated letter (HRHRC) to Elsa and Merle Armitage, friends of Graham, AN asks them to inquire frankly of Graham why she has never responded to the offered friendship. Graham was a very private person, says Jean Erdman, one of her dancers and a later acquaintance of AN's. Telephone interview with Erdman, 9 Sept. 1992.

97. Interview with Judith Malina, 23 Apr. 1992. Malina thinks that the dress and manners of AN were always "impeccable."

98. AN's letter to Beck and Malina (17 Jan. 1952) was read to me during an interview with Judith Malina (23 Apr. 1992) and is printed in *A* 3, 135; AN had just seen a play by Kenneth Rexroth. The correspondence between Beck, Malina, and AN at HRHRC reveals that AN continued to attend plays and promote the theatre.

99. AN to RWD, 5 Apr. and 14 May 1952, Berg; AN to HM two letters probably written in the spring (Stuhlmann says summer) 1952, *ALP,* 390–91. HM, living with Eva McClure, was soon to be divorced from Lepska. UCLA was courting both HM and AN for their manuscripts.

100. AN, *Spy,* 135. Earlier in the book (63), Sabina remembers her husband sobbing at the death of his father and vows never to hurt him. Four typed versions of the novel are at Northwestern. The production files are at OSU.

101. AN, *D* 5, 96.

102. Mildred G. Kramer to NRF, 10 Sept., 1991.

103. Several students of jazz have concluded that AN did not understand jazz intellectually or historically, only instinctively. Benjamin Franklin V, who for years had a program on jazz for National Public Radio, says AN knew only a few jazz names and little else. Telephone interview, 16 Nov. 1991.

104. Telephone interview with Jean Erdman, 9 Sept. 1992. Campbell's *Hero with a Thousand Faces* had been published in 1949.

105. Telephone interview with John Cage, 21 Mar. 1992. Cage did not connect her to her musician father or brother.

106. AN, *D* 5, 103.

107. AN, *D* 5, 107. During AN's recuperation, HM wrote from Paris that he had had a royal welcome to Paris; the city had not changed, but he was now "a different person" and homesick. HM to AN, [10 Feb. 1953], *ALP,* 393–94.

108. AN, *D* 5, 115.

109. Norse, *Memoirs of a Bastard Angel,* 232–35.

110. Norse, 369. Interview with Harold Norse, 29 Dec. 1991.

111. AN to HM, [Oct. 1953], *ALP,* 395. The editor chose to end the volume of their correspondence with this letter.

112. AN, *Spy,* 101.

113. AN, *D* 5, 130, 140.

114. Details of all these parties and the Anger film, though partially described in AN's diary, are based on several interviews with Renate Druks, Paul Mathiesen, Samson De Brier, and Curtis Harrington. Druks to NRF, 7 Mar. 1993.

115. Pictures of the party cover the front and back of *Portrait in Three Dimensions* (1979) by AN and Renate Druks.

116. Anger, *Inauguration of the Pleasure Dome,* Anger Magic Lantern Cycle, Mystic Fire Video, 1966.

117. Highwater quotes the letter in full in *Shadow Show* (18–19). When AN puts the letter in her published diary, she changes it. "She improves upon reality," says Highwater. Interview with Highwater, 29 Aug. 1992. Highwater/AN correspondence, mss. and Archives, Berg.

118. Geismar, "Reminiscences of a Reluctant Radical," ms. owned by Anne Geismar.

119. Telephone interview with Jamake Highwater, 5 Feb. 1991; Highwater to NRF, 2 Sept. 1992.

120. AN to Ruth Witt-Diamant, 4 Feb. 1954, Berg, *D* 5, 151–53.

121. Malina, *The Diaries of JM*, 318–19. Interview with Judith Malina, 23 Apr. 1992.

122. In early 1953 after numerous rejections, AN had paid for a cheap edition of the novella printed in Holland (107). Finally her publisher had sold the rights for *Spy* to the British Book Centre.

123. She sent Edmund Wilson a copy of *The Four-Chambered Heart* and *Spy*, with a letter saying that she had missed his sharp and mature critical judgment in a time when reviews are inarticulate and immature.

124. Stone, "Fiction Note," 32; Rollo, "Pot-pourri," 86; Geismar, "Temperament vs. Conscience," 75–76.

125. AN, *D* 5, 163.

126. "Miller-Nin Discussions," 1969 private tape; AN, *D* 5, 170.

127. AN, *D* 5, 166, 171, 214, 190–91. AN to Ruth Witt-Diamant [4 Feb. 1954], Berg, reprinted in *D* 5, 187.

128. AN, *Seduction of the Minotaur*, 84–85, 100 ff.

129. "Miller-Nin Discussions," 1969 private tape.

130. Interviews with Paul Mathiesen, 24 Sept. 1991 and 15 May 1993.

131. AN, *D* 5, 199–206. Apparently AN did not visit Louveciennes, which HM, on a visit the previous year, had found almost unrecognizable (214).

132. AN to Maxwell Geismar reprinted in *D* 5, 217. He will charge her later with mutilating and abstracting the diaries for publication; *D* 5, 208.

133. Spencer, *Collage of Dreams*, 165.

134. AN, *D* 5, 239, 232.

135. Herlihy's diary quoted with his permission. *D* 5, 231–32, 222–23.

136. AN, *D* 5, 233–34.

137. "She needed Rupert for ballast," says Curtis Harrington (interview 13 Mar. 1991).

138. AN to LD, n.d. [July 1937], SIU; AN informed her friend Ruth Witt-Diamant (29 May 1971) that she believed in "the couple." Interview with Margot Duxler (26 Apr. 1991).

139. AN, *D* 5, 252–53; *D* 6, xiii, 8. AN, "Comments," *A* 2, 108–9.

140. Interview with Curtis Harrington, 13 Mar. 1991.

## 11. THE DIARY OF OTHERS (*pages 328–371*)

1. AN, *The Diary of AN*, vol. 6 (1955–66), 319; Spencer, in *Collage of Dreams* (137), calls *D* 6 "The Outer Life." In addition to this sixth volume of AN's published adult diary, the major sources for this chapter are interviews with some 200 surviving friends and AN's unpublished letters. Experiences of her life from ages 52 to 63 are also fictionalized in *Collages* (1964) and in *Solar Barque* (1958).

2. Text of her report for Janiger was first published in *Two Cities* (15 July 1959) and reprinted as "The Synthetic Alchemist," *A* 10, 79–82.

3. Interview with Dr. Oscar Janiger, 14 Sept. 1992. The Janiger experiment was a one-time dosage. AN's rewritten report of her LSD experiment: *D* 5, 255–62; *D* 6, 3, 130; Snyder, ed., *AN Observed*, 92; AN, *Novel of the Future*, 32–33, 95–96.

4. Interview with Betty Eisner, 30 Sept. 1992. Eisner, who met AN several years later, says that the LSD experience "made Anaïs see what a creative drug it was."

5. Interview with Renate Druks, 19 Apr. 1991.

6. Oscar Janiger studied the effects of LSD between 1954 and 1970. Despite his work with some celebrities, such as Cary Grant and Jack Nicholson, he kept his work quiet and scientific.

7. Mudrick, "Humanity Is the Principle," 610–19. As AN's bibliographer points out, the reviewer stops just short of calling the novel inane. AN, *D* 6, 8. After the publication of *Spy* in 1955, she publishes *Solar Barque*, expanded as *Seduction of the Minotaur*, and *Collages*, her last books of fiction.

8. AN, *D* 6, 149. According to Rupert Pole (interview 8 Oct. 1992), they gave up cigarettes after he taught a science class on drugs and brought home a *Scientific American* article on the dangers of smoking.

9. AN, *D* 6, 89.

10. AN tells Myron Wood (28 Jan. 1957, Northwestern) that Hugo has gone back to the business of earning a living downtown each day and makes films on the weekends. Confirmed in interview with Amos Vogel (21 Apr. 1992). His *Melodic Inversion* (nine minutes), a Hugo-Telberg film with AN, is finished in 1958.

11. AN, *D* 6, 14, 24–25.

12. Interviews with Anna Balakian (9 Mar. 1991) and James Herlihy (27 Nov. 1990).

13. AN, *D* 6, 23.

14. Crosby visit: *D* 6, 61. Interview with Curtis Harrington, 13 Mar. 1991.

15. AN to Caresse Crosby, n.d. [May or June 1958], SIU.

16. AN, *D* 6, 66.

17. AN, *D* 6, 76, 98.

18. AN, *D* 6, 43, 83–84.

19. Reeves, *A Question of Character*, 295–96; Heymann, *A Woman Named Jackie* (308, 311) quotes nurse Ruth Mosse.

20. Fabion Bowers was "absolutely overwhelmed" by *Under a Glass Bell*, but when he met her he disliked her "high-pitched, lisping baby-like voice" with a Spanish accent. Interview with Fabion Bowers, 19 Mar. 1991.

21. AN's comparative literary judgments are in *D* 6, 27, 46, 42, 72–73.

22. Interview with Allen Ginsberg, 7 Mar. 1990. Ginsberg had AN's address from Ruth Witt-Diamant. AN's version of the Ginsberg-Corso poetry reading is in *D* 6, 63–65.

23. Ferlinghetti and Peters, *Literary San Francisco*, 157.

24. Ginsberg first read "Howl" ("I saw the best minds of my generation. . . .") 13 Oct. 1955 at Six Gallery, Union and Fillmore in San Francisco, helping to launch the local chapter of the Beat Generation, whose smell of marijuana competed with the garlic aroma in North Beach. Ferlinghetti had opened City Lights Bookstore in June 1953, the year Ginsberg arrived in the city and met Kenneth Rexroth, Robert Duncan (who was running a poetry workshop at San Francisco State College), and Ruth Witt-Diamant.

25. Maynard, *Venice West*, 57–59; AN, *D* 6, 65; Miles, *Allen Ginsberg*, 215–16; and Interview with Ginsberg, 7 Mar. 1990.

26. AN, *D* 6, 66–70, 89–91; interview with Renate Druks, 20 May 1991. In 1947 HM

had contacted Romain (Romain Kacew) Gary (1914–1980), when the latter was First Secretary of the French delegation in San Francisco, for help in getting royalty money out of France. Anne Metzger, a friend of Gary's, was AN's French translator.

27. Only in *D 7*, her last diary (164–65) does AN express her understanding that her Christmas depression is caused by the loss of innocence and awareness of hypocrisy and fraud (that is, the illusion of family harmony in Christmas celebrations).

28. Interview with Renate Druks, 12 Apr. 1991.

29. AN, *D 6*, 91–92, 93.

30. AN, *D 6*, 98–101.

31. AN, *D 6*, 109.

32. AN, *D 6*, 86, 73, 91.

33. Herman, in what has been called one of the most important psychiatric works since Freud *(Trauma and Recovery)*, says that chronic, hidden family violence is actually *more,* not *less,* traumatic than sudden violence at the hands of a stranger or an enemy during war.

34. Tom Payne, with whom she shared a love of creating and navigating the complications of life (137), introduced her to Jack Kerouac (116); she trusted him with editing 500 pages of her diary (117, 144). AN, *D 6*.

35. AN, *D 6*, 153. The strong impression during all her travels is that she has been invited to give lectures in these European cities and is traveling alone. LD's letters to Jean Fanchette confirm Hugo's presence and their lodging at the Crillon. *Two Cities,* 12 ff. The Guilers presence at the 1958 Brussels World Fair was at the invitation of Gilbert Chase, the son of AN's uncle Gilbert P. Chase and aunt Edelmira Culmell and a poet, musicologist *(America's Music,* 1955), and for many years a member of the diplomatic service. His wife, Kathleen, would write several reviews of the works of AN.

36. AN to RWD, 23 Jan. 1959, Bancroft. Interview with Marguerite Rebois, 25 June 1992.

37. AN to LD and Claude Durrell, 3 Feb. 1959, SIU; *D 6*, 103; Ian S. MacNiven, "Criticism and Personality," *A 2,* 96.

38. AN, *D 6*, 77.

39. AN to LD and Claude Durrell, 3 Feb. 1959, SIU. AN's letter, written eight months after her visit, details her two lives taking care of two men and rushing from one coast to the other.

40. Telephone interview with Rupert Pole, 16 Aug. 1991.

41. Dunaway, *Huxley in Hollywood,* 326. The Huxley's home, high among the chaparral, burned down in 1961.

42. Interview with Betty Eisner, 30 Sept. 1992. Eisner remembers her first meeting with AN as including only Huxley, AN, and herself.

43. In her diary AN reprints what she says is her letter of rebuke to LD for calling her "a child of palace hotel life." In fact, the original letter reads differently (he mentioned her "Grand Hotel childhood" and she is only amused with his fantasy). Her explanation of her childhood poverty remains essentially the same in the original letter and diary accounts. But clearly she saves her anger for the diary and forgets to mention that on her flight to Los Angeles she wrote him that she was no longer upset (she underlines this sentence) and understood his hurried approach.

44. LD to Jean Fanchette (26 Jan. 1959); MacNiven, "Criticism and Personality," *A 2*, 98; AN to LD (two letters), n.d. [Mar. 1959], SIU; *D 6*, 172–73, 182; *DML*, 335.

45. LD to Jean Fanchette, n.d. [Aug. 1966], *Letters to Jean Fanchette*, 92.

46. Interview with Jean Fanchette, 17 July 1991. Another young man she met about this time thought she was "blond, vivid, beautiful, soft-spoken, very feminine." W. C. Watt to NRF, 19 Aug. 1991.

47. "Notes pour une Préface" was published in *Two Cities* (15 Apr. 1959), 56–60; AN, *D 6*, 179–81.

48. Barillè, *AN*, 215.

49. AN to Louise Varèse is quoted in *D 6*, 189. AN had encouraged Louise Varèse (translator of Rimbaud) to translate the Fanchette article. AN believed that the Varèses are supportive. When Edgar Varèse died, the last work he was writing was music inspired by *House of Incest*.

50. AN to Anna Kavan, 9 Mar. 1957, SIU. AN's literary agent may have been also representing Kavan.

51. Fancher, "AN," 4–5.

52. Interview with Bebe Barron, 16 Apr. 1991; AN presents her version of the baby shower as a recollection in her diary of the 1963–64 period, adding gratuitous remarks about following Deren to campuses for lectures and hearing student complaints about her. *D 6*, 350–52.

53. Interviews with Athan Karras, 26 Apr. and 22 Sept. 1992. He also speaks of AN's continued sexual activity.

54. Interview with John Rechy, 16 Sept. 1992. Rechy says AN invited him to an underground reading by AN and Rupert Pole.

55. Telephone interview with Serge Gavronsky, 23 Aug. 1991.

56. Interview with Daisy Aldan, 20 Mar. 1991. Aldan, with a B.A. from Hunter and an M.A. from Brooklyn College (1948), taught at the New York High School of Art and Design from 1945 to 1973. According to Aldan (letter to NRF, 17 Dec. 1992) she collected calls from HM as well.

57. Spencer, *Collage of Dreams*, 138.

58. Interviews with Marguerite Young, 18 May and 5 Dec. 1991. Daisy Aldan insists that Hugo was not a father figure to AN. Aldan to NRF, 17 Dec. 1993. Renate Druks (to NRF, 7 Mar. 1993) says AN's allowance was $300 a month, or $3,600 a year, far less than the amount Young reports.

59. Interview with Renate Druks, 12 Apr. 1991; Bob Oates, "Poetry in Motion," 3.

60. Interview with Renate Druks, 12 Apr. 1991.

61. Rupert Pole, though he had a tenured teaching job, had trouble securing a $16,000 loan, in part because the architectural plans were avant-garde. He took a 90-day loan from a mortgage company until a bank could see the beginnings of the project. Interview with Rupert Pole, 16 Aug. 1991.

62. AN to LD, two undated letters [May 1959], SIU; interview with Aldan, 20 Mar. 1991; interview with Druks, 12 Apr. 1991; AN to RWD, n.d. [1959 or 1960], Bancroft; interview with James Herlihy, 27 Nov. 1990.

63. AN's description is found in *D 6*, 193–200; Hugo's *The Gondola Eye* incorporated segments called "Venice, Etude One," and "Etude, Number Two," totaling 16 minutes, with music by Harry Partch in an early version and David Horowitz in the final version. *A 2*, 75. Hugo layers or superimposes images of flowing water

for an impressionistic portrait of Venice. His films are in the Museum of Modern Art, NYC.

64. AN to LD, 29 July 1959, SIU. Her published diary makes no mention of a Paris visit.

65. Interview with Jean Fanchette, 17 July 1991. Secondhand stories have him begging her to stay in Paris with him. AN makes no mention of being in Paris in her published diary. He later admitted that he took for granted all the work that she did for his *Two Cities*. But Fanchette was aware that she had trouble separating fact and fiction and that she needed the approval of her writing. "The best way to be her friend was to believe in her work."

66. One of Hugo's financial deals did not materialize, she tells LD, n.d., SIU.

67. In her diary, AN reprints more of Herlihy's letters than those of any other friend.

68. Interview with James Herlihy, 27 Nov. 1990.

69. Interviews with Jean Fanchette, 17 and 31 July 1991.

70. Her letters to Roger Bloom (1960–73) are at Lilly; HM, who had written to Bloom, gave him AN's address. Bloom flatters her by confusing her with Djuna Barnes. After his release in 1966, he owned a barbershop and lived with his wife, Gertrude.

71. AN's letter to Caresse Crosby about her marriage agreement with Hugo, who has his mistresses, says that Rupert wants a wife, not a mistress. AN to CC, n.d. [May 1958], SIU. Pole will only say that he wished for legal reasons to marry Anaïs and that Hugo prevented the marriage (telephone interview 18 Jan. 1993).

72. Interview with Renate Druks, 14 Apr. 1991. Interview with James Herlihy, 27 Nov. 1992.

73. Diary of Nils-Hugo Geber. Letter to NRF, 7 Jan. 1992.

74. There is some evidence that AN had left for Europe 13 May. Nils-Hugo Geber, whose name is misspelled "Gelber" in *D 6,* and Billy Kluver declare that the diary is unreliable and inaccurate. Telephone interview with Kluver, 30 Oct. 1991; Kluver to NRF, 5 Nov. 1991. Both Geber and Kluver correct many errors.

75. Billy Kluver to NRF, 5 Nov. 1991. He recalls that during sightseeing AN was "naively enthusiastic about everything." Nils-Hugo Geber says that the trip "did not [make] her publicly visible in a permanent sense," in part because she had to compete with the shooting down of Francis Powers's spy plane, the breaking up of the Paris summit meeting, and a visit to Sweden by Marlene Dietrich. Geber to NRF, 21 Oct. 1992.

76. AN often used the Mistral Bookstore, facing the river and Notre Dame Cathedral, as a mailing address. Contrary to the published diary, George Whitman did not change the name of his shop to Shakespeare and Company until a couple of years after Sylvia Beach's death in 1962.

77. AN, *D 6,* 235–37; CC to AN, 30 May 1960, SIU (printed in *A 2,* 50–51) inquires about their arrival in Rocca; AN to CC, n.d. [1960] and n.d. [1961], give AN's explanations for the cancellation, SIU. Conover, *Caresse Crosby,* 186. AN to Harry Redl, who is staying in their apartment in New York (Lilly).

78. Rupert Pole to LD, 2 Mar. 1977, SIU.

79. Telephone interview with Rupert Pole, 9 Sept. 1992. The architect of the Silver Lake home has frequently and mistakenly been identified as Lloyd Wright and/or Frank Lloyd Wright, the father and grandfather of Eric.

80. AN, *D 6,* 260.

81. RWD to AN, 6 July and 2 Aug. 1960, Bancroft.

82. Interviews with Renate Druks, 12 Apr. and 10 May 1991.

83. Interview with Daisy Aldan, 20 Mar. 1991; *D 6*, 244, 249.

84. Daisy Aldan read AN's unpublished story "N is the sign of Pisces" to me 5 Dec. 1991. "A New Poem" appears in *The Destruction of Cathedrals,* 74.

85. Interview with Daisy Aldan, 5 Dec. 1991. Aldan strongly implies that neither she nor any other woman had a lesbian relationship with AN. Aldan to NRF, 16 Jan. 1993. Aldan's papers are at Yale.

86. AN, *Seduction of the Minotaur,* 113 ff.

87. AN, "Alan Swallow," 11–14; *D 6*, 253–56; interview with Rupert Pole, 1 Mar. 1991. Swallow sold each year about 2,000 to 4,000 copies of each of her novels (Patty Friedman's "Big Talents," 30), but Duane Schneider, who has published the Swallow books since 1979 with Ohio University Press, says only *Spy* has been a successful seller.

88. AN to RWD, n.d. [after 1 Aug.1961], Bancroft.

89. Telephone interview with Benjamin Franklin V, 16 Nov. 1991.

90. Lucretia Cole (letter to NRF, 16 Apr. 1990) says AN "spoke in a whisper and refused any subject deeper than flower-culture. She seemed to me to want everyone to love her as muses are loved. . . . She damped everyone's spirit. . . . I remember her as silent, humorless and beloved . . . seated as a Vestal Virgin on a tuffet and three pretty young women . . . composed at her feet."

91. AN to RWD, two undated letters [Aug. 1961], Bancroft.

92. AN to Larry Redl, n.d., Lilly.

93. Interview with Renate Druks, 20 May 1991; AN, *D 6*, 281; Franklin, *Bibliography,* 82; AN, *Collages,* 44–47; AN to RWD, n.d. [after 1 Aug.], Bancroft.

94. Anon., "Stuff of Dreams," 369; Hodgart, "Fire of Exile," 771; Murray, review, 915; Malcolm Bradbury, "New Novels," 953–54; AN, *D 6*, 255.

95. Interview with Jack Hirschman, 27 Apr. 1991; *D 6*, 263, 277–78; interviews with Martha Robert (by Colette Faus, July 1991) and Jean Fanchette, 30 July 1991.

96. Interview with Jack Hirschman, 27 Apr. 1991.

97. AN, *D 6*, 265–66 and 288–91 (essentially repeated passages), 279–81; interview with Tracy Roberts, 15 May 1991.

98. Interview with Tracy Roberts, 15 May 1991. Roberts owns the Tracy Roberts Actors' Studio in Los Angeles.

99. Interview with Jean Fanchette, 17 July 1991.

100. André Bay, "Letter from France—Return of the Prodigal," *A 3*, 45–46. At the same time, Bay published a French translation of Herlihy's *All Fall Down* (1960).

101. Bay, "Letter," 48; interview with André Bay, 28 July 1991.

102. Interview with Jean Fanchette, 17 July 1991; *D 6*, 292–93.

103. AN, *D 6*, 295.

104. The actress eventually borrowed the money from her brother. In the meantime AN got involved with two other men, giving one a down payment for a script, which she rejects. Roberts promises to cover the check with her own funds, but changes her mind and cancels the check. AN wrote in her diary that the "check bounced," and later promised to change this wording before publication (according to Roberts), but did not. Interview with Tracy Roberts, 15 May 1991; AN, *D 6*, 314–17.

105. Paul Mathiesen experienced her assertiveness when she asked if he would drive her to UCLA, where she expected librarian Lawrence Powell would be so excited

to see her. Because they had come without an appointment, they waited for some time until AN stormed out. "The delicate, sensitive, easily hurt first impression was deceiving," says Mathiesen (interview 5 Sept. 1991). "She was tough underneath, and could be uppity and stuck up on occasion."

106. Epstein, *The Way It Was*, 326–28, 385.

107. AN to Anna Kavan, 4 Sept. 1963, SIU.

108. Interview with Marguerite Young, 5 Dec. 1991.

109. In *D 6* (306), AN says that her and Miller's common concern for Bloom "renewed" their friendship.

110. Ferguson, *HM*, 344. Ferguson fails to mention this reunion.

111. Dearborn (*The Happiest Man Alive*, 281) says that HM never forgave her, in turn, for ridiculing Fred Perlès.

112. AN, *D 6*, 307–8.

113. HM, *LAN*, edited by Gunther Stuhlmann and published in 1965 by Putnam's Sons. It is a selected and expurgated collection of letters from 1931 to 1946; a fuller and less heavily edited collection of both of their letters (*A Literate Passion*) was published in 1987 (after Hugo Guiler's death) by Harcourt Brace Jovanovich.

114. AN asked for the letters back temporarily (*D 6* 306), though there is no evidence that she returned them. She was upset to learn that HM, when shown Bloom's scrapbook of letters, photos, and news clippings, had informed Bloom that it would be financially valuable (*D 6*, 305).

115. Interview with Renate Druks and Christian DuBois Larson, 24 Apr. 1991.

116. Interview with Renate Druks, 12 Apr. 1991. AN swims only with Rupert in their pool. In New York, she goes with Hugo to swim in Brooklyn (Richard Centing diary, 31 May 1971). In a letter to Myron Wood (17 Feb. 1958, Northwestern), AN says she is in California because she has spinal arthritis.

117. Both paintings are reproduced in a volume of AN's writing about Renate entitled *Portrait in Three Dimensions* (1979).

118. Interview with Renate Druks, 12 Apr. 1991.

119. AN, *D 6*, 299–300; Evans was asked by SIU Press to write the book after having published an essay ("AN and the Discovery of Inner Space") on AN's work. Evans calls her "a pioneer in the search for identity."

120. Barillé, *AN*, 215.

121. Tristine Rainer, a later friend of AN's and a teacher of diary writing, believes that AN invented a new art form with the rewritten diary, an art form in which she excels.

122. The confusion about the total number of diaries results from counting separately the small paper notebooks of her childhood, which were bound together in leather covers, and the occasional presence of dual diaries or the "fake" diary for Hugo. At UCLA, each bound, book-sized "diary" is counted as one number. According to Rupert Pole, the accordion folders were first used about 1964.

123. AN, *D 6*, 298, 299, 319, 320. AN claimed that meeting Mr. Pomeroy of the Kinsey Institute, which had expressed interest in buying her diary (they had some of her erotica), "incited" her to try and condense and rewrite her diary. Though Kinsey could not afford to buy, she determined to continue editing the diary for the remainder of her life (298).

124. She told Myron Wood (30 July 1962, Northwestern) that a change in Hugo's work and Wall Street "turbulence" necessitated their move about 30 Sept. 1962.

125. Interview with Marianne Hauser, 24 Apr. 1992, a practical friend and neighbor of

AN's, who called the "garden" a "yard" and hung a balloon on her balcony to signal
AN that she was done writing and free to talk.

126. Telephone interview with Rupert Pole, 28 Aug. 1992. Daisy Aldan to NRF, 16 Jan.
1993.

127. Hugo continues inviting Amos Vogel to preview each new film. Vogel (interview 21
Apr. 1992) says Hugo was very low-key. "He probably wanted me to do something,"
says Vogel, who premiered only *Bells of Atlantis* at Cinema 16. Even after the
demise of Cinema 16 in 1963, Hugo continued to invite Vogel to see his films.

128. Interview with Renate Druks, 12 Apr. 1991.

129. According to Tracy Roberts (interview 15 May 1991) and others, Rupert had made
several calls to find the right surgeon for "a friend" of theirs. Pole (telephone
interview 25 Nov. 1992) claims that the face-lift to remove neck wrinkles was
Roberts's suggestion and it was covered by insurance because AN lectured professionally. A devoted friend (5 Dec. 1991) says AN had several face-lifts and nose
jobs in Los Angeles. AN, *D 6*, 61. Barillé (*AN*, 29) identifies at least two face-lifts,
the second to raise her cheekbones and remove facial hair "so that her face became
like a bare beach under the glare of the photographer's flash."

130. Douglas Saxon to NRF, 14 July 1991.

131. Norman Fruman to NRF, 14 July 1991.

132. AN, *Collages*, 79–82; *D 6*, 324–25; interview with Renate Druks, 20 May 1991.

133. Interview with Bebe Barron, 16 Apr. 1991.

134. Leary and Alpert were codirectors of the Harvard Psychedelic Drug Research
Project. Eisner and the others were rather bitter about the exploitation of LSD,
which ruined their work for decades afterward. Interview with Betty Eisner, 30
Sept. 1992.

135. Ram Dass to NRF, 20 Nov. 1991. He adds that "I've regretted [not going to swim
at her house] at times, because she was such an extraordinary woman and I have
so much loved her writings."

136. Telephone interview with Don Bachardy, 9 Oct. 1992.

137. One of the best descriptions of the San Francisco and Los Angeles psychedelic
spiritual scene is found in Alan Watts's *In My Own Way.*

138. Sidney F. Huttner to NRF, 3 Sept. 1991. Huttner remembers the impression that
AN made at the time of her Chicago lecture when a group of them dined at a
Chinese restaurant and she made a rather sensuous remark about how litchi
expands when fondled in the mouth. The undergraduates were impressed.

139. Leary, *Flashbacks,* 55; Dunaway, *Huxley in Hollywood,* 371, 355. Neal Cassady calls
LSD (lysergic acid diethylamide) the "Rolls-Royce of dope." Leary, when he arrived
in California, called it "the right ecological niche!" and lists AN among a group
that is fabricating the future there. Among the group he lists Gary Snyder, Aldous
Huxley, Joan Didion, Thomas Pynchon, Christopher Isherwood, HM, and Will
Durrant (*Changing My Mind,* 208).

140. Rosenbaum, "Back in the High Life," 132–44, 154. Today Leary remembers little
of AN except her lovely manner and her pioneering erotica. Telephone interview
13 Mar. 1993.

141. When AN finally draws the character based on Djuna Barnes, who had ignored her
friendship, the isolated writer's manuscript begins with the very same lines as does
*Collages,* suggesting a tradition or link between AN and Barnes, if not all women
writers.

142. Interview with Renate Druks, 12 Apr. 1991.

143. Interview with Renate Druks, 20 May 1991. Apparently, AN's eyes, which had seemed brown to her in her youth, now appear green.

144. Interview with Daisy Aldan, 20 Mar. 1991.

145. Interview with Daisy Aldan, 20 Mar. 1991.

146. AN, *D 6*, 349. Apparently she brought photocopies of some diaries to the potential sale at SIU. Interviews at SIU with David Koch and David Braasch, 16–17 Oct. 1991. The offer to Northwestern was also undoubtedly a typed copy. AN to Jens Nyholm, 3 Aug. and 10 Dec. 1962, Northwestern. By 1964 she was sending laundry lists of things she wanted to sell.

147. Telephone interview with Eva Wasserman, 15 Aug. 1991.

148. Interview with Renate Druks, 20 May 1991. AN, *D 6*, 361.

149. AN to LD, [spring 1964], SIU.

150. AN, *D 6*, 358.

151. Thevenin charges that the AN portrait of Artaud is "a network of clichés" belonging to "a false legend" and containing a detail (*"la phrase littérale"*) that she herself first pointed out to AN during a 1964 meeting. "To read her, one would believe that she never knew him." The explanation lies, according to the French charge (repeated by Sartre), in the vivid imagination of a neurotic 30-year-old. But Thevenin is not a disinterested party, and she did not know Artaud in the decade that AN did. Also, Thevenin had no way of knowing the diarist's process of expanding her diary over many years with new material. There seems to be no question that AN knew Artaud and that her letters from him are genuine. *"Anaïs a péché par excès de zèle,"* says Barillé, *AN*, 1991, 154 (recent English translation, 122); Barillé quotes AN's letter to Thevenin and her own interview with Thevenin. *Tel Quel* published the Artaud letters in the Winter 1965 issue; the English translation of Artaud's letters first appeared in *A 1* (1983), 53–59; AN, *D 6*, 358 mentions the meeting with Thevenin.

152. The conference was held from 22 June to 9 July 1964. Ray Bradbury to NRF, 3 Sept. 1991. AN, "Alan Swallow," 12; AN, *D 6*, 361–62.

153. AN to Frances Steloff, 14 May 1964, Berg.

154. AN, *D 7*, 36–37; AN to Daniel Mauroc, 9 Mar. 1965, SIU.

155. Sontag, "Afterlives," 105.

156. Stuhlmann, "Introduction," *D 1*, xi. Interview with Rupert Pole, 14 Feb. 1990.

157. She tells Krishna Baldev Vaid ("Writing and Wandering," *A 5*, 55) that her novels were never understood: "They did not communicate." Marguerite Young (interview 5 Dec. 1991) believes that *Collages* is her most important fiction and a new development for her, using men and women in the manner of Robert Browning's poetic portraits.

158. Lerman, "Catch Up with . . ." 80. Goyen, "Bits and Images of Life," 24.

159. Pierre Brodin, "AN," in *Présences Contemporaines,* 105–22; Brodin is a director of a French lycée. AN's review appeared in *Books Abroad: An International Literary Quarterly* 29 (Spring 1965): 164–65. When Brodin visits New York this fall, she gives him a book party that includes Nabuko, Nona Balakian, Serge Gavronsky, and Norman Mailer, who is in his cups. AN to RWD, 17 Oct. 1964, Berg; telephone interview with Serge Gavronsky, 23 Aug. 1991.

160. Interview with Deena Metzger, 6 Nov. 1991. Metzger's first review appears 29 Apr. 1966.

161. Interview with Renate Druks, 12 Apr. 1991. Bob Oates, "Poetry in Motion," 3.

162. AN, *D 6*, 381.

163. AN, *D 6*, 377. The correspondence between AN and Oliver Evans is housed at HRHRC.

164. Roger Jackson, HM's bibliographer, recently uncovered the excision of Barnet Ruder's name as the pornography collector's middleman (in some places Stuhlmann does not use ellipses). Also cut are portions of letters that reveal her plan, with HM's help, to sell some of her diaries to the collector (see HM's letters to AN at SIU, e.g., 8 Mar. 1941).

165. Krishna Baldev Vaid, "Writing and Wandering: A Talk with AN," *A* 5, 49.

166. Perlès, *My Friend HM*, 1956. That HM's changes in the letters were minor is confirmed in AN to Peter Israel, 5 May 1965, OSU.

167. Interview with Georges Belmont, 29 July 1991; HM to GB, 16 Apr. 1965, Belmont Papers.

168. Interview with Tristine Rainer, 26 Mar. 1992. Rainer used the plot of an older husband in New York and a younger husband in California for *Having It All*, a television movie for ABC in 1984 (video, Lorimar), "but nobody recognized it as Anaïs's story," she notes.

169. Though AN says in *D 6* (390) that she wrote a review for the *Los Angeles Times*, her review appeared in *Open City* 52 (May 1–14, 1968), 5.

170. AN to RWD, 2 Dec. 1965, Berg.

171. Rupert Pole (14 Feb. 1990) says that the doctors discovered cancer of the uterus.

172. AN to RWD, 23 May 1966, Berg.


## 12. DANCING TOWARD DAYLIGHT (*pages 372–410*)

1. HM to AN, [30 July 1941], *ALP*, 339. The major sources for Chapter Twelve—the title of which is taken from the last lines of AN's *House of Incest*—covering her life from ages 63 to almost 74, are my personal interviews, AN's private letters, public documents, *Under the Sign of Pisces* (a journal devoted to her life and work), and the last diary volume, *The Diary of AN*, vol. 7 (1966–74), which she began before her death and Rupert Pole completed, using the journals she wrote during vacations, her letters, reviews, and memorabilia.

2. AN, *D* 7, 3.

3. AN, *D* 7, 35. AN to Renate Druks, 16 June 1966, UCLA.

4. AN, *D* 7, 132.

5. Kirsch's reviews are quoted in Rupert Pole's "Robert Kirsch: 1923–1980," *A 1*, 114.

6. If a narcissist is one who sees others only as extensions of oneself, AN is not guilty of the charge. She was genuinely kind and sensitive to others, says her publisher Hiram Haydn, who wondered about the near idolatry of young women for AN. Haydn, *Words and Faces*, 295.

7. AN to Caresse Crosby, 13 Aug. 1967, "Years of Friendship," *A 2*, 52.

8. Edel, "Life Without Father," 91. Edel is also the author of *The Modern Psychological Novel* (1955).

9. Leon Edel to NRF, 11 Apr. 1991.

10. AN to Harold Norse, 4 July 1967, Lilly.

11. HM, "Between Freud and HM," 5–6. HM's former secretary, Kenneth Dick, who had heard the secrets, will write: "She entices us to the shadowy fringes of Lesbos and then pulls down the shade. . . . It's Vassar and Radcliffe and Smith in the days of high buttoned shoes and straw boaters." He also complains that "Anaïs wears

a necklace of imaginary foreskins emblematic of make-believe conquests . . . but Anaïs never gets piked." Dick, *HM,* 155.

12. AN to LD, 5 Dec. 1966 and 3 Nov. 1966, SIU.

13. Interview with Daisy Aldan 20 Mar. 1991. June Miller apparently never spoke to the press. Aldan met June Miller through one of her former students, who shopped in the same supermarket as June.

14. Jean-Paul Sartre claims that AN "takes up her notes again and plunges into the works of Artaud, copies passages which she 'clarifies' in her own way. She reads *Béatrice Cenci* (written in 1935—two years after their meeting), sees *La Passion de Jeanne d'Arc* by Carl Dreyer—a film she had not yet seen at that time, in order to satisfy the ambition of the journal." Sartre, *"Un theatre de situation,"* in *Idées* (Editions Gallimard, 1973), quoted in Elisabeth Barillé's *AN,* 154.

15. Interview with Bettina Knapp, 3 Oct. 1991.

16. Telephone interview with Lawrence Ferlinghetti, 1 Oct. 1992. Fred Cody, who will admit later that he did not foresee that night her "approaching apotheosis as a goddess," remembers grabbing a broom after the reading: "I began to sweep the floor and hardly paused when I came, in the center of the gallery, to the circle of trampled rose petals." Cody (*Cody's Books,* 98–99) writes that the roses were red and the gown ivory, but history will side with the petal carrier.

17. For a listing and summary of reviews see Cutting, *AN: A Reference Guide,* listed under AN Bibliographies.

18. DuBow kindly allowed me to read her doctoral dissertation in manuscript form. Her thesis is that Stuhlmann uses excessive praise ("legendary," "monumental") and creates an atmosphere of intrigue and scandal (by denying its role) to set up a commercial market.

19. AN to Harold Norse, 28 Nov. 1971, Lilly.

20. AN to Harold Norse, 30 Aug. 1967, Lilly.

21. AN, *D* 7, 43.

22. Before his death, Swallow intended to continue the joint publication with HBJ. Swallow to John Christian, 3 Mar. 1966, HRHRC.

23. Gail Riley O'Neill interview with William F. Claire, 6 Sept. 1991.

24. Betty Ryan Gordon to NRF, 9 and 28 Feb. 1991. HM and Ryan are even more upset ("hurt and shocked") by her diary treatment of Fred Perlès in *D* 5.

25. AN, *D* 7, 185, 289.

26. AN also visited Hong Kong, Angkor Wat (Cambodia), Bangkok (Thailand), Singapore, Malaysia, and Manila (Philippines) with Rupert Pole.

27. AN, *D* 7, 37, 39, 46.

28. AN to RWD, 15 Aug. 1967, Berg.

29. AN, *D* 7, 179, 289.

30. Interview with Renate Druks, 12 Apr. 1991.

31. Interview with Daisy Aldan, 29 Mar. 1991. Aldan to NRF, 17 Dec. 1992.

32. Telephone interview with Nona Balakian, 15 Mar. 1991; interview with Daisy Aldan, 29 Mar. 1991 (the two friends' stories differ slightly); Garrigue, "The Self behind the Selves," 1.

33. The *L.A. Free Press* was funded by free thinkers, including Steve Allen. See Peck, *Uncovering the Sixties,* 21.

34. Robert Haas to NRF, 15 Apr. 1991.

35. AN to Peter Owen, 27 Feb. 1969, HRHRC.

36. Perhaps because he had so much trouble with AN, who deceived him during the writing of his book, he refused in 1975 to allow her to publish his letters calling her a great writer. Centing diary, unpublished, 5 July 1975. Quoted with his permission.

37. Interview with Deena Metzger, 6 Nov. 1991.

38. Norse, *Memoirs*, 426; interview with Deena Metzger, 6 Nov. 1991.

39. AN, *D* 7, 61.

40. William Claire to NRF, 2 Apr. 1991.

41. AN's interest in science was limited to the pioneering uses of light in art composition. She saw a light show of Lumia at UCLA in the late 1960s and met (through the music group or her lectures) a few people at Cal Tech and the Aerospace Corporation who explained how light can be manipulated to create in the eye of the viewer what the artist wants, and how the astronomer studies the stars. Telephone interview with Eugene Epstein, 4 Oct. 1991.

42. LD to HM, 19 Apr. 1967, SIU; LD and AN on tape at California Institute of Technology, Cynthia Sears.

43. HM to LD, 29 Jan. 1972, *DML*, 454.

44. HM to LD, 20 Sept. 1972, *DML*, 459.

45. AN to Wayne McEvilly, n.d., quoted in *D* 7, 122–23.

46. LD to HM, 28 Mar. 1975, *DML*, 477.

47. HM to LD, 4 Sept. 1975, *DML*, 479

48. Her celebrity drew attention away from the career of her brother Joaquin, say many (including Frances Ring, interview 19 Apr. 1991); Thorvald "was afraid his daughter would be like Anaïs." Thorvald, who made money in lumber in South America, sent a letter full of legalistic terms threatening to sue if she mentioned him or claimed to have protected him when he was young. Interview with Marguerite Young, 5 Dec. 1991.

49. Maxwell Geismar, "AN: An Imprecise Spy," 3. There are, in fact, many stories of her clever promotion, including her collaboration with Georges Cleyet, who had a radio program on KPFK in Los Angeles. Interview with Cleyet, 11 Oct. 1991.

50. Robert Zaller to NRF, 3 Dec. 1991.

51. Interview with Beatrice Barron, 16 Apr. 1991. "Anaïs and Gore seemed very close," she remembers. Rupert Pole (telephone interview 17 Apr. 1991) remembers socializing several times with Vidal, Paul Newman, and Joanne Woodward.

52. Interview with Henry Jaglom, 26 Sept. 1991.

53. Ann Quinn to NRF, 11 Sept. 1991.

54. Interview with Henry Jaglom, 26 Sept. 1991.

55. Tristine Rainer (interview 26 Mar. 1992) was most enthusiastic about the diary, which she had used in her English classes and which she considered "the ultimate example of having elevated the diary to literature" by combining the diary (written in the heat of the moment) and autobiography (written after contemplating one's life and seeing thematic images within it).

56. Gail Riley O'Neill interview with William F. Claire, 6 Sept. 1991.

57. Telephone interview with Benjamin Franklin V, 16 Nov. 1991.

58. According to Duane Schneider, AN befriended them precisely "because we were doing a book; she wanted to be our friends; she asked us not to do anything biographical and her request allowed us to focus on her works, which was our interest." Interview 14 Oct. 1991.

59. Richard Centing invited AN to appear at Oakland University in Rochester, Michigan, 23 Oct. 1968. *Under the Sign of Pisces* (a publication of OSU) had a high of 300 subscribers in 1970 and a low of 100 when it ceased publication about 12 years later. At his own expense, Centing published *Seahorse,* featuring AN and HM in 1983–84. Interview with Centing, 15 Oct. 1991.

60. AN, *D* 7, 129–32. When Pole and Stuhlmann edited the last diary after AN's death, Hugo was still living, and they use the expression "phantom lover" in the radiation treatment scenes. She believed her New York doctor (Raymond Weston) had not initially told her she had cancer, 191. Rupert Pole confirms this.

61. Dennis R. Miller, "Glimpsing a Goddess," *A* 3, 107. Miller and others have read her life as poetry and the agent of her death symbolically. One critic is reminded of Thomas Mann's novella *The Black Swan.*

62. The photographers informed Peter Owen about the bribery. Owen to NRF, 30 Sept. 1991. Interview with Peter Owen, 21 Oct. 1992. The Owen-AN correspondence is in HRHRC.

63. According to her biographer, David Callard (Callard to NRF, 11 Sept. 1991), Anna Kavan did not return AN's admiration or answer her letters and died officially of a heart attack with a loaded syringe of heroin at her bedside—after 30 years of drug use—5 Dec. 1968. AN was "Anna's most staunch admirer among literary critics," says Callard, *The Case of Anna Kavan,* 147.

64. AN, *D* 7, 155.

65. Unpublished diary of Ambassador James M. Rentschler, 14 Sept. 1970. Rentschler to NRF, 3 and 7 Sept. 1992. Karen Walker interview with James M. Rentschler, 10 Oct. 1992.

66. Walker, "A Seven-Minute Epic," n.p.; Pyle, "The Curious Double Life of Ian Hugo," n.p. Both articles were sent to me by Ambassador Rentschler.

67. AN and Edmund Wilson met at the Princeton Club, where he read the photocopied pages about him, certainly an unflattering portrait, with bemusement.

68. Vidal, "Taking a Grand Tour," 1, 5, 23.

69. Vidal, *Two Sisters,* 2, 5, 161, 198, 13; telephone interview with Paul Mathiesen, 5 Sept. 1991.

70. Vidal, "Taking a Grand Tour," 1, 5, 23.

71. Digby Diehl (telephone interview 23 Sept. 1992) says AN was very unhappy with him when he asked Vidal to write the review and used Hank Hinton's illustration, which Diehl thinks witty.

72. AN to Harold Norse, 28 Nov. 1971, Lilly; Gore Vidal to NRF, 26 Feb. 1991.

73. Balakian, "The Diary of AN," 28.

74. Interview with Renate Druks, 20 May 1991. See *D* 7, 76.

75. Centing diary, unpublished. Quoted with his permission.

76. AN to LD, n.d. [1937], SIU. Contrary to her claims to intuitive living and lack of organization, AN had long kept elaborate files on friends and reviewers.

77. Telephone interview with Eve Wasserman, 15 Aug. 1991. AN, *D* 7, 177.

78. Kate Millett, "Anais—A Mother to Us All," *A* 9, 4.

79. She had suggested to Harry T. Moore that she should be a member of the National Institute of Arts, *D* 7, 159; Vidal's response to the award in "Taking a Grand Tour," 13.

80. Drewes, "Portrait of AN," 4.

81. Telephone interview with Serge Gavronsky, 23 Aug. 1991. Rupert Pole attended the celebration but remained in the background.

82. Interview with John and Liz Pearson, 27 Apr. 1991.

83. Norse, "Never Fuck with Karma." Centing lists the attendance at 1,400; a local reporter says 2,500.

84. Interview with Harold Norse, 29 Dec. 1991.

85. James Broughton's unpublished memoirs, courtesy Broughton.

86. Centing, "AN Today," 3.

87. Interview with Anna Balakian, 9 Mar. 1991.

88. Telephone interview with Elaine Marks, 1 Apr. 1991.

89. Gail Riley O'Neill interview with William F. Claire, 6 Sept. 1991; AN, *D* 7, 227.

90. Valerie Harms to NRF, 2 Oct. 1992.

91. AN, *D* 7, 190, 198, 217. Evelyn Hinz, but not Sharon Spencer, attends the Magic Circles weekend, for AN is careful to keep separate the women who are writing about her. Valerie Harms, who issued the invitations, received the mailing list from AN.

92. Interview with Valerie Harms, 22 Apr. 1992.

93. Later Sharon Spencer deals with some of these half-truths in a fictional interview she writes for a book on HM. In it she has the interviewer asking AN, "But you gave so much! He took everything! Why did you allow that?" Spencer, "Henry's Gift," 16. In this fictional interview, AN responds, "Henry gave me the world."

94. Philip Jason to NRF, 3 Jan. 1992; AN later told him that the idea to include ephemeral material such as commencement addresses and reviews in his *Reader* was the idea of her agent, Gunther Stuhlmann, AN to Jason, 9 Oct. 1971. Jason, who met with AN at two lectures she gave (St. John's College, Annapolis, and American University, Washington, D.C.) was frustrated that she was cool to him and initially resisted because she mistakenly thought that a *Reader* would interfere with sales of the *Diary* and that she did not need to be introduced to the reading public.

95. Merchant, *In-Discretions*, 146.

96. AN, *D* 7, 200–203, 211, 221; Dennis R. Miller, "Glimpsing a Goddess," *A* 3, 103–4.

97. Numerous sources, including conversations with Georges Belmont (11 July 1991) and André Bay (9 Aug. 1990) report that in group appearances AN would try to dominate the conversation with talk of her own work. To some extent, of course, she had to fight for equal time and consideration. AN, *D* 7, 198.

98. Though AN "planned ahead to keep him from taking over" a joint appearance at the New School, says Valerie Harms who arranged the event, "more people were interested in her; he was astonished that a woman could upstage him." Interview with Valerie Harms, 22 Apr. 1992. Both Valerie Harms and Leah Schweitzer ("A Response to AN's Review," 5–8) admired AN and Progoff and used their techniques in teaching journal writing.

99. Brenneman, "AN," 5. Valerie Harms, ed., *Celebration*, 9.

100. AN, *D* 7, 225.

101. For two days before the Northwestern lecture, AN was hosted at the Drake Hotel by Swallow and interviewed on WFMT by Studs Terkel, who found her charming and her characters in *Under a Glass Bell* "waifs." She read "The Mouse," from the collection of short stories, and excerpts from the *Diary.* Telephone interview with Studs Terkel, 24 Jan. 1992. She also dined with the two editors of *Pisces,* Richard Centing and Benjamin Franklin, 22 Jan. 1972 (diary of Richard Centing). At OSU

she showed Snyder's *AN Observed* before she talked and signed autographs afterward.

102. Telander, "Understanding AN," 16. Nancy Scholar Adams (interview 31 Jan. 1992) says it was like a "feminist revival meeting."

103. Telephone interview with William Burford, 28 Sept. 1991. "She walked a line between exaggerated parody of herself and a wonderful sense of herself," he adds. "I always found her fascinating, but ephemeral. . . . She could read human beings and the inner self, but she was very restless in intellectual conversation."

104. William Young was asking $2,500 for his "complete" works. When Ben Franklin V published his critical response about the missing material, Young threatened to bring charges against him. The controversy may have jeopardized Young's plan to publish excerpts of AN's diary in *Nuances.* The correspondence ("*Nuances* File") is at OSU. At AN's bidding, Centing suggested that Franklin withdraw from the newsletter editorship.

105. Telephone interview with Benjamin Franklin V, 16 Nov. 1991. Franklin rates *House of Incest* and *Under a Glass Bell* as her best works.

106. Interview with Duane Schneider, 14 Oct. 1991.

107. AN, *D* 7, 228.

108. Amiel, "What Do You Get," 78.

109. Spencer, *Collage of Dreams,* 111.

110. AN, *D* 7, 253.

111. Brandon, (tape) "AN: Diarist, Novelist, Twentieth-Century Goddess." AN, "In Favor of the Sensitive Man," *Playgirl* (Sept. 1974), reprinted in *In Favor of the Sensitive Man and Other Essays,* 48. Most of the essays (originally reviews) in this book are about women.

112. AN, *D* 7, 282.

113. The power of this sensitive-man ideal can be measured in part by the reaction against it in the late 1980s, as illustrated by the enormous receptivity to Robert Bly's "Iron John" movement. Bly calls men back to their maleness in groups in nature, testing their physical prowess and courage. His movement may be less a reaction to the politically assertive impact of the woman's movement than a reaction to the feminization of men advocated by AN and others. Such at least is the view of one of the young male Amherst students temporarily appropriated by AN in the 1940s: "She was suffocating; she devoured; most men would have to get away after a few days. Her excessive femininity eventually drove us away." Telephone interview with William Burford, 28 Sept. 1991.

114. Interview with Barbara Kraft, 2 Jan. 1991.

115. AN, *D* 7, 180–82; Perhaps typical of the feminist attacks against her is Estelle C. Jelineck's Marxist attack on AN's costumes, individualism, and pandering to men (in a review of *Spy*), which is "anathema to me and the women's liberation movement." "AN: A Critical Evaluation," 312.

116. When Frenchman Jean Chalon, who told several people that he had had a love affair with AN, described her as the American Simone de Beauvoir, the Frenchwoman was upset. AN to Jean-Yves Boulic, n.d.

117. AN to William Young, n.d. [1970], OSU.

118. AN to Peter Owen, 17 Mar. 1971, HRHRC; AN to Howard McCord, n.d. [1967], University of Delaware; interview with André Bay, 9 Aug. 1990.

119. Maryle Secrest, "Economics and the Need for Revenge," *A* 6, 33, 35. It is Secrest's thesis that AN exploited her men in revenge against her father.

120. Less gently, Dick says AN left enough to titillate the reader: "she tippy toes through the field of phalluses and nipples that lead to the land of Lesbos and there darts around her admirers with the abandon of a drunken gypsy." Dick, *HM,* 157.

121. AN in 1955, *D* 7, 23.

122. William Burford initially denied they were his letters until she sent him photocopies, then he claimed they were emotional adolescent memorabilia written to please, with no literary merit. She informed him that he was the only one who had complained, that his portrait really represents a cycle in her life, and if he continued to question the value and validity of her diary, she would have to break off all correspondence with him. The correspondence among AN, Burford, Centing, and her editors (Hiram Haydn and John Ferrone) is in HRHRC.

123. Peter Owen Collection, HRHRC, contains galleys, letters, and production files for all of AN's English books and the letters about the sale of his papers. It reveals the extensive involvement of AN in promotion, reviews, and sales, and her anger at Owen for publishing in 1969 the fact that she was married to Ian Hugo. Gunther Stuhlmann's letters to Peter Owen are at OSU.

124. Chare, "Starring Herself," 11. AN to Ruth Witt-Diamant, n.d. [1971]. Bancroft.

125. AN, *AN: A Woman Speaks,* 258.

126. Interview with Henry Jaglom, 26 Sept. 1991.

127. Telephone interview with Jamake Highwater, 5 Feb. 1991.

128. Merchant, *In-Discretions,* 14.

129. AN, *D* 7, 244, 248, 251, 255, 270.

130. AN, *D* 7, 277.

131. Interview with Henry Jaglom, 26 Sept 1991.

132. Interview with Judy Chicago, 20 Jan. 1991.

133. In "Magic in Los Angeles," AN discusses Womanhouse (in which 15 women each created a room), Womanspace in Venice, and Women's Building.

134. In addition to AN, Ravi Shankar, Marshall McLuhan, LD, and Kenneth Rexroth took individual students from the International Community College of Los Angeles.

135. Interview with Judy Chicago, 20 Jan. 1991; Womanhouse was opened for only a month because the campus of Cal Arts, with which she was affiliated, was not yet built. "Arlene Raven—an art historian—Sheila De Bretteville, and I started the women's building," says Chicago.

136. Interview with Judy Chicago, 20 Jan. 1991.

137. AN, *D* 7, 298, 300.

138. Wolcott, "Life Among the Ninnies," 21. Kay Boyle has been quoted as saying it was no achievement to be popular with students. More difficult for AN to achieve would have been popularity with her peers. Interview with Richard Centing, 15 Oct. 1991.

139. Margot Duxler testifies (interview 26 Apr. 1991) that she was psychologically ill when she met AN at Wayne State University in 1968. After years of friendship with AN, including enjoying AN's hospitality in Silver Lake, Duxler is now a writer and psychologist in San Francisco.

140. Interview with Barbara Kraft, 2 Jan.1991. When Kraft asked AN why she was still

married to Hugo Guiler, she heard AN say something about an old marriage, how he was good to her family, and that she had not known much happiness. According to Valerie Harms (interview 22 Apr. 1992), "She used to say that she was sorry that she did not divorce Hugo." Kraft to NRF, Feb. 1993.

141. Interview with Barbara Kraft, 2 Jan. 1991. On her own after the divorce, Kraft worked as a journalist for *Time* magazine, and today has her own public relations firm. "It was innocent on my part," says Sharon Spencer about taking Kraft to the Washington Square Village apartment. Interview with Spencer, 23 Apr. 1992. (Today Rupert remembers that he warned Kraft not to publish the diary as it was.)

142. Chare, "Starring Herself," 11; AN called them the "Power men, Mailer, Vidal, Roth, hateful all. . . .": AN, *D 7*, 90; AN also called Vidal a "yellow journalist" (Centing diary, 1973).

143. Telephone interview with Benjamin Franklin V, 16 Nov. 1991. Her letter to Owen was accusatory and demanded reparation. AN to Peter Owen, 22 Aug. 1976, HRHRC. Owens replied (31 Aug. 1976) that he was shocked and hurt, owed her nothing more, and the books were selling slowly.

144. Telephone interview with Rupert Pole, 1 Mar. 1991. She turns against Stone when he tries to seduce Tristine Rainer, who was taking therapy with him at AN's recommendation. Interview with Rainer, 26 Mar. 1992.

145. AN assumed that the invitation came from the work of Barry Jones, a young teacher who had attended many of her lectures. AN, *D 7*, 323. Justice William O. Douglas, Agnes de Mille, and Eubie Blake also received doctorates at the same time as she.

146. Walker, "AN: 1903–1977," 46. Walker met AN at a party given by Jill Krementz and Kurt Vonnegut.

147. Baron, "AN and James Leo Herlihy," 3 ff.

148. The LD-AN correspondence is at SIU. She asks him to call Hugo by the name of Ian Hugo and stop referring to him as wealthy; she also tells him that she and Hugo separated in 1947, and says that Hugo had put on airs about having money by inflating their worth.

149. HM to Fred Perlès, 20 Jan. 1976, UCLA.

150. AN, *D 7*, 184.

151. Charlotte Hyde (interview 19 Nov. 1991) worked in travel promotion in Los Angeles and contacted UTA, the French airline, who provided flights and hotels. "They were delighted to have someone of her stature write." Hyde introduced AN to her neighbor Jean Sherman, who would translate the AN diaries written in French.

152. Several of Professor Balakian's students and friends, including Daisy Aldan, Sharon Spencer, and Bertrand Mathieu, wrote books on the work of AN. Mathieu's manuscript on AN has not been published; his Rimbaud translation was published in 1976.

153. AN, preface to *My Sister, My Spouse* (*In Favor of the Sensitive Man*).

154. HM to LD, 5 Apr. 1973, *DML*, 466. It is not surprising, therefore, that recently a German psychologist named Linde Salber has completed two monographs of Andreas-Salomé and AN and published an article in which she compares their physical obsessiveness, their use of art/psychoanalysis as a "framework" to explore their psychic "experimentation," their "indulg[ing] in ecstasies of the irrational," their compulsion for self-contemplation, their "almost childlike . . . curiosity," and their compulsion for change and metamorphosis. Linde Salber, "Two Lives—One Experiment: Lou Andreas-Salomé and AN," *A 9*, 78–91.

155. These words are the last words of *Diary 7*, 336.

156. Interview with André Bay, 9 Aug. 1990. Jean-Yves Boulic (interviewed by Karen Walker, 18 Oct. 1992), who met AN during this visit, says she thought Pivot's questioning too much in the confrontational American style. Boulic, who describes AN as *"sensuelle, belle, une vision, comme un reve,"* has devoted years to trying to restore AN's Louveciennes home as an historical monument.

157. LD to HM, 28 Mar. 1975, *DML,* 477.

158. HM to LD, 9 Apr. 1975, *DML,* 478.

159. Interview with Jean Fanchette, 17 July 1991. HM tells another story ("Joey" in *Book of Friends,* 460): HM says that just before she died AN wrote a letter asking Hugo's forgiveness for all her "capers," and he said he knew but always loved her. Barbara Kraft was Miller's source for this information.

160. "AN was courageous . . . and a personality in the best sense of the word," says Marianne Hauser (interview 24 Apr. 1992).

161. Details of AN's health care and death come from interviews with Rupert Pole, Renate Druks, Christian Larson; AN letters to Dr. Jean Fanchette, with his permission; Rupert Pole's letters to Rochelle Holt du Bois, SIU; the unpublished manuscript of Barbara Kraft ("Lux Aeterna Anaïs: A Memoir"); and Richard Centing's unpublished diary.

162. Interview with Eline H. McKnight, 6 Nov. 1990. Barbara Kraft to NRF, Feb. 1993.

163. Daisy Aldan to NRF, 23 Sept. 1991.

164. In a letter to Lawrence Powell (25 Nov. 1975, UCLA), HM says that he has talked to her on the telephone that morning and she is asking $100,000 for their correspondence.

165. Among the sources for these asking prices for the diaries is AN's correspondence with Northwestern, which in 1974 refused her offer to buy back her fiction manuscripts from the university for $500.

166. Sources concerning the sale of her diaries: Rupert Pole; AN to Gordon Cairnie, n.d., Harvard; Howard B. Gotlieb to NRF, 5 June 1992. Dr. Bogner was the only trustee who was available to go to the bank and sign the release forms for the shipping company.

167. Telephone interview with Digby Diehl, 23 Sept. 1992. Diehl says the cost of purchase was $200,00 to $250,00.

168. Interview with Rupert Pole, 14 Feb. 1990.

169. Telephone interviews with Eve Wasserman (15 Aug. 1991) and Rupert Pole (10 Oct. 1991). Kirsch had written the reviews of AN's diaries; Diehl wrote the feature on her choice as one of the 1976 Women of the Year by the *L.A. Times.*

170. Robert Haas to NRF, 12 Mar. 1991.

171. Interview with Jean Sherman, 19 Nov. 1991. " She was precocious," says Sherman, but "her spelling and French were poor. She wrote phonetically, for her first language was Spanish." Sherman also translated the French letters in *Henry and June* and in *Incest.* Rupert Pole to LD, 2 Mar. 1977, SIU; Diehl, "AN," 4.

172. Interview with Leah Schweitzer, 10 Oct. 1992. See also Nancy Jo Hoy, "Getting to Know AN," *A 1,* 81–85.

173. Information on the dying months of AN are from my interviews with numerous friends and from Barbara Kraft's diary, "Lux Aeterna Anaïs: A Memoir," portions of which were published in *Seahorse: The AN/HM Journal* 2 (1983). AN's correspondence with Elliot Coleman is at Johns Hopkins University.

174. Interview with Daisy Aldan, 20 Mar. 1991. Both Druks and Aldan claim that AN told them that Ferrone had talked her into publishing the erotica. That she wanted

her full diary published is substantiated by her final interview in a French Canadian journal (*Chatelaine,* May 1977), in which she says that after her death, "the
entire Journal will be published."

175. HM, *Book of Friends,* 47. An illustration of the generational differences in the
appeal of AN: Judith Malina says it is the erotica that drew her 27-year-old
daughter to AN; Nancy Friday (*Women on Top*) twice links AN's writings with
*Playgirl,* pornographic videos, and other modern stimuli.

176. Interviews with Margot Duxler (26 Apr. 1991) and Barbara Kraft (2 Jan. 1991).

177. Interview with Frances Ring, 19 Apr. 1991.

178. Interview with Renate Druks, 24 Apr. 1991. HM was in the hospital to have his
high blood pressure and arteriosclerosis monitored and treated. Mary Dearborn to
NRF, 14 June 1992.

179. AN, *Seduction of the Minotaur,* 5.

180. Unpublished typescript of Jean L. Sherman's final visit with AN. Other journal
accounts of AN's death include Metzger's *The Woman Who Slept,* 131 ff, 212–18.

181. "She died alone," one friend said with disapproval. See also Juliet Campos, "AN,"
1–5; Interview with Daisy Aldan, 20 Mar. 1991. Unpublished diary of Richard
Centing.

182. Rupert Pole is quoted by Marks, "Recollections," 59. Adding yet more to the
mythology, Pole says that when he returned home from releasing the ashes the
afternoon of 17 January he discovered that Mermaid Cove was in a direct-line
view from their home, interrupted only by a willow tree. When the willow tree
mysteriously died, he did not replace it in order to keep his view of the cove
unobstructed.

## POSTSCRIPTS (*pages 411–414*)

1. LD to HM, 28 Apr. 1977, *DML,* 484. See Erica Jong's words at the opening of the
Acknowledgments section.

2. Diary of Richard Centing, 17 Jan. 1977. LD died 7 Nov. 1990 at the age of 78 in the
south of France, where he had lived in the village of Sommières for 30 years. "After
a legal battle with the family of LD, the British literary quarterly *Granta* is about
to publish extracts from the journals of his daughter Sappho, in which she inti-
mates that she had an incestuous relationship with the writer, who died last
year. . . . Sappho Durrell committed suicide in 1985 at the age of 33 after many
years of psychiatric problems. Several months before killing herself, she gave her
journals to a London neighbor, Barbara Robson, with instructions that they be
published after she and her father were dead." *New York Times,* 14 Aug. 1991.

3. HM's tribute is in "AN," 100–101. The Los Angeles celebration was sponsored by
International Community College. Rupert Pole wrote to Rochelle Holt du Bois
[n.d., SIU] that they would have programs honoring AN all over the world on 21
Feb. "I don't know how Anaïs's spirit can be present at all—but I'm sure she will
manage it."

4. Bernard, "A Reading and a Mourning," 33.

5. Interview with William Claire, 6 Sept. 1991. Seven years later, AN's dresses were still
hanging in Hugo's closet (Introduction, *ED 4,* xv).

6. LD to HM, 10 Jan. 1979, *DML,* 504. The perfume company used a line from AN's
diary ("A silky fragment of woman") as its slogan.

7. Kilday, "UCLA Acquires AN Papers," 20.

8. AN and Rupert Pole correspondence with LD, SIU. Pole's remark is repeated in Kraft's "Lux Aeterna Anaïs: A Memoir."

9. According to Harcourt Brace Jovanovich, 200,000 copies of *D 1* had been sold by 1992.

10. HM to Fred Perlès, *Book of Friends*, 265. By contrast, HM's friend Erica Jong concludes that AN "tells the story of woman's sexuality more honestly than any writer who ever lived. . . . For all their self-boosting, her unexpurgated diaries constitute one of the landmarks of twentieth-century literature. Both as literary history and as the history of female sexuality, the diaries fulfill Henry's predictions. . . ." *The Devil at Large,* 98–99.

11. Interviews with Renate Druks (12 Apr. 1991) and Daisy Aldan (20 Mar. 1991). Almost every person interviewed for this biography had a strong opinion for or against the Kaufman film.

12. Interview with Marianne Hauser, 24 Apr. 1992.

13. Interview with Jean Fanchette, 17 July 1991.

# Anaïs Nin
# Selected Bibliography

DIARIES

*The Diary of AN.* Ed. Gunther Stuhlmann. New York: Harcourt, Brace and World.
Vol. 1: 1931–1934 (1966, copublished with Swallow Press)
Vol. 2: 1934–1939 (1967, copublished with Swallow Press)
Vol. 3: 1939–1944 (1969)
Vol. 4: 1944–1947 (1971) (Harcourt Brace Jovanovich)
Vol. 5: 1947–1955 (1974)
Vol. 6: 1955–1966 (1976)
Vol. 7: 1966–1974 (1980)

*Linotte: The Early Diary of AN, 1914–1920.* Trans. from the French by Jean L. Sherman. Preface by Joaquin Nin-Culmell. New York: Harcourt Brace Jovanovich, 1978. (*Early Diary,* Vol. 1)

*The Early Diary of AN.* Preface by Joaquin Nin-Culmell. New York: Harcourt Brace Jovanovich.
Vol. 2: 1920–1923 (1982)
Vol. 3: 1923–1927 (1983) (San Diego: Harcourt Brace Jovanovich) (*Journal of a Wife,* London, 1984)
Vol. 4: 1927–1931 (1985)

*Henry and June: From the Unexpurgated Diary of AN.* San Diego: Harcourt Brace Jovanovich, 1986.

*Incest: From "A Journal of Love," The Unexpurgated Diary of AN, 1934–1935.* San Diego: Harcourt Brace Jovanovich, 1992.

FICTION

(Two dates are given if the first is a limited/out-of-print book; most British editions are Peter Owen of London.)

*The All-Seeing.* New York: Gemor Press, 1944 (chapbook, 40 copies). Most Gemor Press editions include woodcuts by Ian Hugo.

*A Child Born Out of the Fog*. New York: Gemor Press, 1947 (pamphlet).

*Children of the Albatross*. New York: E. P. Dutton, 1947; Denver: Swallow Press, 1966. (Swallow Press books are now published by the Ohio University Press, Athens)

*Collages*. Denver: Swallow Press, 1964.

*The Four-Chambered Heart*. New York: Duell, Sloan and Pearce, 1950; Denver: Swallow Press, 1966.

*The House of Incest*. Paris: Siana Editions, 1936.

*House of Incest*. New York: Gemor Press, 1947; Denver: Swallow Press, 1958.

*Ladders to Fire*. New York: E. P. Dutton, 1946; Denver: Swallow Press, 1966.

*Seduction of the Minotaur*. Denver: Swallow Press, 1961.

*Solar Barque*. New York: Anaïs Nin, 1958. Expanded as *Seduction of the Minotaur*.

*A Spy in the House of Love*. New York: British Book Centre, 1954; Denver: Swallow Press, 1966.

*This Hunger*. New York: Gemor Press, 1945 (Part 1 of *Ladders to Fire*, 1946).

*Under a Glass Bell*. New York: Gemor Press, 1944; New York: E. P. Dutton, 1948.

*Waste of Timelessness and Other Early Stories*. Weston, Conn.: Magic Circle Press, 1977.

*The Winter of Artifice*. Paris: The Obelisk Press, 1939. First story is "Djuna."

*Winter of Artifice*. New York: Gemor Press, 1942. Rev. ed. Denver: Swallow, 1961. "Djuna" replaced by "Stella."

EROTICA

*Auletris*. Carmel, CA: Press of the Sunken Eye, 1950 (five typed, bound copies).

*Delta of Venus: Erotica*. New York: Harcourt Brace Jovanovich, 1977. Abridged as *The Illustrated Delta of Venus*. London: Allen, 1980.

*Little Birds: Erotica*. New York: Harcourt Brace Jovanovich, 1979.

*Aphrodisiac: Erotic Drawings by John Boyce for Selected Passages from the Works of AN*. Intro. by AN. New York: Crown, 1976.

COLLECTIONS

*Cities of the Interior* (including *Ladders to Fire*, *Children of the Albatross*, *The Four-Chambered Heart*, and *Seduction of the Minotaur*). Denver: Swallow, 1959. Intro. by Sharon Spencer. Preface by AN. Chicago: Swallow Press, 1974.

*The AN Reader*. Ed. Philip K. Jason. Intro. by Anna Balakian. Chicago: Swallow Press, 1973.

SELECTED NONFICTION

(Excluding excerpts and reprints of the *Diary*)

"Alan Swallow." *Denver Quarterly* 2, no. 1 (Spring 1967): 11–14. Repr. in *Publishing in the West: Alan Swallow*, 12–15. Santa Fe, NM: Lightning Tree, 1976.

"Dear Djuna Barnes (1937) with a Note (1971)." In *A Festschrift for Djuna Barnes on Her 80th Birthday*. Kent, OH: Kent State University Libraries, 1972, 16.

*D. H. Lawrence: An Unprofessional Study*. Paris: Edward W. Titus, 1932. Intro. by Harry T. Moore. Denver: Swallow Press, 1964.

*In Favor of the Sensitive Man, and Other Essays*. New York: Harcourt Brace Jovanovich, 1976.

*An Interview with AN*. Athens, OH: Duane Schneider, 1970.

"Magic in Los Angeles." *Westways* 66, no. 1 (Jan. 1974): 28–31, 63. Repr. in *A Western Harvest*, ed. Frances Ring, 47–53. Santa Barbara, CA: John Daniel, 1991.

"The Mystic of Sex" [on D.H. Lawrence]. *The Canadian Forum* (October 1930).

*The Novel of the Future.* New York: Macmillan, 1968.

*Nuances.* [Cambridge, MA]: Sans Souci Press, [1970].

*On Writing.* Hanover, NH: Daniel Oliver Associates, 1947. Rev., with an Essay on her Art by William Burford. New York: Alicat Bookshop, 1947.

*Portrait in Three Dimensions.* Colored plates by Renate Druks. Los Angeles: Concentric Circle, 1979.

Preface to Henry Miller's *Tropic of Cancer.* Paris: The Obelisk Press, 1934. Printed separately. New York: Gemor Press, 1947.

Preface. *My Sister, My Spouse: A Biography of Lou Andreas-Salomé,* by H. F. Peters. New York: Norton, 1974.

*Realism and Reality.* Yonkers, New York: Alicat Book Store, 1946. Repr. in *The White Blackbird* (chapbook).

*Unpublished Selections from the Diary.* Athens, OH: Duane Schneider, 1968.

*The White Blackbird and Other Writings.* Santa Barbara, CA: Capra Press, 1985.

*A Woman Speaks: The Lectures, Seminars and Interviews of AN.* Ed. Evelyn Hinz. Chicago: Swallow Press, 1975.

LETTERS

*A Literate Passion: Letters of AN and HM, 1932–1953.* Ed. Gunther Stuhlmann. San Diego: Harcourt Brace Jovanovich, 1987.

BIBLIOGRAPHIES

Cutting, Rose Marie. *AN: A Reference Guide.* Boston: G. K. Hall, 1978. (Fourteen supplements compiled by Richard R. Centing and published in *Under the Sign of Pisces: AN and Her Circle* 11, no. 2 (Spring 1980) and 12, no. 2 (Spring 1981) and *Seahorse: The AN/HM Journal* 1 (1982) and 2 (1983).

Franklin, Benjamin, V. *AN: A Bibliography.* Kent, OH: Kent State University Press, 1973.

———. "AN." In *Bibliography of American Fiction, 1919–1988.* Ed. Peter Matthiesen and Roger Zelazny. New York: Facts on File, 1991.

Goldsworthy, Joan. "Nin, Anaïs 1903–1977." In *Contemporary Authors.* New Revision Series, Vol. 22.

PERIODICALS DEVOTED TO AN

*Anais: An International Journal.* Ed. Gunther Stuhlmann. Becket, MA. Annual. Vols. 1–11 (1983–93).

*Seahorse: The AN/HM Journal.* Ed. Richard R. Centing. The Ohio State University Libraries. Quarterly. Vols. 1–2. (1982–83).

*Under the Sign of Pisces: AN and Her Circle.* Eds. Richard R. Centing and, until 1973, Benjamin Franklin V. Quarterly. Vols. 1–12 (1970–81).

FILMS ABOUT AN

*AN Observed: Portrait of a Woman as Artist.* Documentary film. 60 min. Directed by Robert Snyder, 1974.

*Henry and June.* Feature film, based on AN diary. Directed by Philip Kaufman, 1991.

FILMS FEATURING AN

*Ritual in Transfigured Time,* by Maya Deren, 1946.

*Inauguration of the Pleasure Dome,* by Kenneth Anger, 1950

*Bells of Atlantis,* by Ian Hugo, 1952
*Jazz of Lights,* by Ian Hugo, 1954
*Melodic Inversion,* by Ian Hugo, 1958
*Through the Magicscope,* by Ian Hugo, 1968
*Apertura,* by Ian Hugo, 1970
*The Henry Miller Odyssey,* by Robert Snyder, 1969

SELECTED SOUND RECORDINGS BY AN
*AN, Contemporary Classics.* Sound Portraits. Issued by Louis and Bebe Barron, 1949.
*AN in Recital: Diary Excerpts and Comments.* Caedmon, 1979.
*The Diary of AN, Vol. One: 1931–1934.* Spoken Arts SA995 and -996, 1968.

(Sixteen books of criticism and twenty-six dissertations devoted to the work of AN are listed in the General Bibliography.)

# General Bibliography of Works Cited

Aldan, Daisy. *The Destruction of Cathedrals and Other Poems*. New York: Two Cities, 1962.

————. "AN Interviewed." *Under the Sign of Pisces* 1, no. 2 (Spring 1970): 7–9.

Amiel, Barbara. "What Do You Get When a Class Writer Tries Pornography? Dull Pornography." *Mclean's* 90 (13 June 1977): 78.

*Anais: An International Journal*. Ed. Gunther Stuhlmann. Vols. 1–11 (1983–93). Articles from this journal are not listed individually.

Anderson, Kristine Jo. "Bilingualism in the Self-Imaging of Julien Green, AN, and Karen Blixen," Ph.D. diss., State University of New York, Binghamton, 1983.

Anon. "Barely Enough Flesh to Cover Her Soul." *The Staff* [Berkeley] (7 Jan. 1972): 6.

Anon. "Stuff of Dreams." *Times Literary Supplement* (16 June 1961): 369.

Artaud, Antonin. "Onze lettres à AN." *Tel Quel* (Winter 1965): 3–11.

Auden, W. H. *The Collected Poems*. New York: Random House, 1945.

Balakian, Anna. "The Diary of AN." *New York Times Book Review* (16 Jan. 1972): 28.

Baldanza, Frank. "AN." *Minnesota Review* 2 (Winter 1962): 263–71.

Barillé, Elisabeth. *AN: Naked under the Mask*. Trans. Elfreda Powell. London: Octopus, 1992.

Baron, Ron. "AN and James Leo Herlily: Charmed Pen Pals." *After Dark* 11, no. 7 (Nov. 1978): 3 ff.

Bashkirtseff, Marie. *The Journal of a Young Artist: 1860–1884*. Trans. Mary J. Serrans. New York: Cassell, 1889.

Benstock, Shari, ed. *The Private Self: Theory and Practice of Women's Autobiographical Writings*. Chapel Hill: University of North Carolina Press, 1988.

————. *Women of the Left Bank: Paris, 1900–1940*. Austin: University of Texas Press, 1986.

Bernard, Sidney. "A Reading and a Mourning." *New York Times Book Review* (24 Apr. 1977): 30, 32–33.

Bloom, Lynn Z., and Orlee Holder. "AN's *Diary* in Context." In Hinz and Fraser, eds., *Mosaic*, 191–202. Repr. in *Women's Autobiography: Essays in Criticism*. Ed. Estelle C. Jelineck. Bloomington: Indiana University Press, 1980.

Bowles, Paul. *Without Stopping: An Autobiography*. New York: G. P. Putnam's Sons, 1972.

Bradbury, Malcolm. "New Novels." *Punch* 240 (21 June 1961): 953–54.

Bradford, Jean. "The Self: a Mosaic, A Loving Perspective on the Diaries of AN." *Journal of Otto Rank Association* 12 (Summer 1977): 14–25.

Brandon, Dolores (producer). "AN: Diarist, Novelist, Twentieth-Century Goddess." 72-min. film, 1986.

Brennan, Karen Morley. "Hysteria and the Scene of Feminine Representation (Frida Kahlo, AN, Kathy Acker, Mexico)." Ph.D. diss., University of Arizona, 1990.

Brenneman, Betsy. "AN." *Los Angeles Reader* (12 Dec. 1972): 4–5.

Brians, Paul. "Sexuality and the Opposite Sex: Variations on a Theme by Théophile Gautier and AN." *Essays in Literature* 4 (Spring 1977): 122–37.

Broderick, Catherine. "A Comparative Thematic Study of Francois Mauriac's 'Genitrix' and AN's 'The Four-Chambered Heart.'" Ph.D. diss., Brown University, 1970.

Brodin, Pierre. *Présences contemporaines: Ecrivains Américains d'aujourd'hui*. Paris: Les Nouvelles Editions Debresse, 1964.

Broughton, James. *Coming Unbuttoned*. San Francisco: City Lights, 1993.

Brown, Harriette Grissom. "Animus and the Fiction of AN: A Feminine Interpretation of Logos." Ph.D. diss., Emory University, 1980.

Broyard, Anatole. "Of Art, Ecstacy, and Water." *New York Times* (26 Oct. 1971): 39.

Callard, D. A. *The Case of Anna Kavan: A Biography*. London: Peter Owen, 1992.

Campos, Juliet. "AN." *Under the Sign of Pisces* 8 (Fall 1977): 1–5.

Carruth, Hayden. Review of *The Four-Chambered Heart*. *Providence Sunday Journal* (19 Jan. 1950): 10.

Centing, Richard R. "AN Today." *Under the Sign of Pisces* 3 (Winter 1972): 3.

Chare, Harriet. "Starring Herself." *The Times* (London) (1 June 1970): 11.

Chase, Kathleen. "AN—Rumor and Reality: A Memoir by KC." *Under the Sign of Pisces* 6 (Fall 1975): 1–8.

Chicago, Judy. Interview with AN. "Women in the Arts [Feminism]." Pacifica Radio Archives, BC45304. 29 min., 1971.

———. *Through the Flower: My Struggle as a Woman Artist*. Garden City, New York: Doubleday, 1975.

Childs, J. Rives. *Collectors Quest: The Correspondence of HM and J. Rives Childs, 1947–1965*. Ed. R. C. Wood. Charlottesville: University Press of Virginia, 1968.

Clark, Gerald. *Capote: A Biography*, New York: Simon and Schuster, 1988.

Cody, Pat and Fred. *Cody's Books: The Life and Times of a Berkeley Bookstore, 1956–1977*. San Francisco: Chronicle, 1992.

Coleman, Daniel. *Vital Lies, Simple Truths: The Psychology of Self-Deception*. New York: Simon and Schuster, 1985.

Commengé, Beatrice. *HM: Ange, clown, voyou*. Paris: Plon, 1991.

Conover, Anne. *Caresse Crosby: From Black Sun to Roccasinibalda*. Santa Barbara, CA: Capra Press, 1990.

Cooney, Blanche. "The Little Magazine." *Margins* (Scotland) 11 (1990): 7–28.

Costa, Richard Henry. *Edmund Wilson: Our Neighbor from Talcottville*. Syracuse, New York: Syracuse University Press, 1980.

Crosby, Caresse. "Who in the World." Unpublished memoir, CC Papers, Southern Illinois University.

Croswell, Elva Leuvenia. "Woman as Artist in the Novels of Colette, AN, and Toni Morrison." Ph.D. diss., University of Southern California, 1985.

Currie, Ellen. "Anais Redux: On Rereading a Denizen of Elsewhere." Lear's (Feb. 1990): 46–47.

David, Sally. "The Female Angst: Discussion with AN, Joan Didion, Dory Previn." Los Angeles: Pacifica Tape Library BC0611A, 60 min., 1972.

Davidon, Ann Morrisett. "AN vs. Gore Vidal: Bon Mots and Billets Doux." The Village Voice (17 Jan. 1976): 80–82.

Davis, Robert Gorman. "AN's Children of Light and Movement." New York Times Book Review (23 Nov. 1947): 36.

Dearborn, Mary. The Happiest Man Alive: A Biography of HM. New York: Simon and Schuster, 1991.

de Beauvoir, Simone. All Said and Done. New York: G. P. Putnam's Sons, 1974.

———. America Day by Day. New York: Grove, 1951.

Deduck, Patricia A. Realism, Reality, and the Fictional Theory of Alain Robbe-Grillet and AN. Washington, D.C.: University Press of America, 1982.

Denby, David. "Miller's Crossing." New York (15 Oct. 1990): 66–67.

Dennison, Sally. "AN: The Book as a Work of Art." In Alternative Literary Publishing: Five Modern Histories, 119–55. Iowa City: University of Iowa Press, 1984.

De Salvo, Louise. Virginia Woolf: The Impact of Childhood Sexual Abuse on Her Life and Work. New York: Ballantine, 1989.

Dick, Bernard J. "AN and Gore Vidal: A Study in Literary Incompatibility." In Hinz and Fraser, eds., Mosaic, 153–62.

Dick, Kenneth C. HM: Colossus of One. The Netherlands: Alberts-Sittard, 1967.

Diehl, Digby. "Times Woman of the Year: AN, Feminism's Beacon." Los Angeles Times (30 Mar. 1976): 1, 4–5.

Drewes, Caroline. "Portrait of AN." San Francisco Sunday Examiner and Chronicle (2 Mar. 1972): Sunday Scene, 4.

DuBow, Wendy. "The Political Power of the Personal Word: AN's Diaries in Their 1960s and 1970s Cultural Context." Ph.D. diss., University of North Carolina, 1992.

Dunaway, David King. Huxley in Hollywood. London: Bloomsbury, 1989.

Duncan, Robert. Caesar's Gate: Poems 1949–50. San Francisco: San Dollar, 1972.

———. The Years as Catches: First Poems (1939–1946). Berkeley: Oyez, 1966.

Durrell, Lawrence. "Durrell Letters to Fanchette." Two Cities 9 (Autumn 1964): 12 ff.

Durrell, Lawrence, and Henry Miller. The Durrell-Miller Letters, 1935–1980. Ed. Ian MacNiven. New York: New Directions, 1988.

Edel, Leon. "Life Without Father." Saturday Review 49 (7 May 1966): 91.

Edkins, Carol Ann. "The Necessary Link: Meditation in the Works of AN." Ph.D. diss., University of Texas, Austin, 1980.

Eisler, Benita. O'Keeffe and Stieglitz: An American Romance. New York: Doubleday, 1991.

Emerson, Ralph Waldo. Journals of RWE. Eds. Edward Waldo Emerson and Waldo Emerson Forbes. Boston: Houghton Mifflin, 1909–1914.

English, Priscilla. "New Woman Interviews a New Woman." New Woman 1 (Dec. 1971): 26–31.

Epstein, Louis. *The Way It Was: Fifty Years in the Southern California Book Trade.* Vol. 1. Interviewed by Joel Gardner. University of California Oral History Program, 1977.

Evans, Oliver. *AN.* Carbondale: Southern Illinois University Press, 1968.

———. "AN and the Discovery of Inner Space," *Prairie Schooner* 36 (Fall 1962): 217–31.

"An Evening with AN." Los Angeles: Pacifica Tape Library BC0453.04, 29 min., 1972.

Faas, Ekbert. "The Barbaric Friendship of Robet Duncan and AN: A Biographical Palimpset." In eds., Hinz and Fraser, *Mosaic*, 141–52.

———. *Young Robert Duncan: Portrait of the Poet as Homosexual in Society.* Santa Barbara, CA: Black Sparrow, 1983.

Fancher, Edwin. "AN: Avant-Gardist with a Loyal Underground." *The Village Voice* (27 May 1959): 4–5.

Ferguson, Robert. *HM: A Life.* New York: Norton, 1991.

Ferlinghetti, Lawrence, and Nancy J. Peters. *Literary San Francisco: A Pictorial History.* San Francisco: City Lights/Harper and Row, 1980.

Field, Andrew. *Djuna: The Formidable Miss Barnes.* Austin: University of Texas Press, 1985.

Fitch, Noël Riley. "Introduction." *In transition: A Paris Anthology.* New York: Doubleday, 1990.

———. "The Literate Passion of AN and HM." In Whitney Chadwick and Isabelle de Courtivron, eds., *Significant Others.* London: Thames and Hudson, 1993.

———. *Sylvia Beach and the Lost Generation: A History of Literary Paris in the Twenties and Thirties.* New York: Norton, 1983.

Flaubert, Gustave. *Madame Bovary.* Norton Critical Edition. Trans. Paul De Man. New York: Norton, 1965.

Ford, Hugh, ed. *The Left Bank Revisited: Selections from the Paris Tribune, 1917–1923.* University Park: Pennsylvania State University Press, 1972.

———. *Published in Paris: American and British Writers, Printers, and Publishers in Paris, 1920–1939.* New York: Macmillan, 1975.

Fothergill, Robert A. *Private Chronicles: A Study of English Diaries.* New York: Oxford University Press, 1974.

Fowlie, Wallace. *Anbade: A Teacher's Notebook.* Durham, NC: Duke University Press, 1983.

———. "The Girlhood of AN." *New York Times Book Review* (13 Aug. 1978): 11.

Franklin, Benjamin, V. "AN." In Vol. 2 of *Dictionary of Literary Biography. American Novelists Since World War II.* Eds. Jeffery Helterman and Richard Layman. Detroit: Gale Research, 1978.

———. "Varda." *Under the Sign of Pisces* 2 (Spring 1971): 7–8.

Franklin, Benjamin, V, and Duane Schneider. *AN: An Introduction.* Athens, OH: Ohio University Press, 1979.

Freeman, Steven A. *The Middlebury College Foreign Language Schools 1915–1975.* Middlebury, VT: Middlebury College, 1975.

Freud, Sigmund. *The Basic Writings of SF.* Trans. A. A. Brill. New York: Modern Library, 1938.

———. "The Etiology of Hysteria." In *The Standard Edition of the Complete Psychological Works of Sigmund Freud.* Ed. and trans. James Strackey et al. Vol. 3. London: Hogarth, 1896; 1962.

————. "The Relation of the Poet to Daydreaming." In *Collected Papers*. Trans. Joan Riviere. Vol. 5. London: Hogarth, 1950.

Friday, Nancy. *Women on Top: How Real Life Has Changed Women's Sexual Fantasies.* New York: Simon and Schuster, 1991.

Friedman, Melvin J. "André Malraux and AN." *Contemporary Literature* 11 (Winter 1970): 104–13.

Friedman, Patty. "Big Talents in Small Ponds," *Small Press* 9 (Spring 1991), 30–35.

Froula, Christine. "The Daughter's Seduction: Sexual Violence and Literary Theory." In Lynda E. Boose and Betty S. Flowers, eds., *Daughters and Fathers*, 111–35. Baltimore: Johns Hopkins University Press, 1989.

Garrigue, Jean. "The Diary of AN." *New York Times Book Review* (23 Nov. 1969): 28, 30.

————. "The Self behind the Selves." *New York Times Book Review* (24 Apr. 1966): 1.

Gascoyne, David. *Paris Journal 1937–1939.* London: Enithermon, 1978.

Geismar, Maxwell. "AN: An Imprecise Spy in the House of Love." *Los Angeles Times* (13 May 1979): Section 6, 3.

————. "Reminiscences of a Reluctant Radical." Unpublished memoir.

————. "Temperament vs. Conscience." *The Nation* 179 (24 July 1954): 75–76.

Gentile, Kathy Justice. Review of *Silence and Power: A Reconsideration of Djuna Barnes.* *Women's Review of Books* 9, no. 2 (Nov. 1991): 20, 21.

Gilbert, Susan M. *Acts of Attention: The Poems of D. H. Lawrence.* Carbondale: Southern Illinois University Press, 1990.

Gilligan, Carol. *In a Different Voice: Psychological Theory and Women's Development.* Cambridge, MA: Harvard University Press, 1982.

Girodias, Maurice. *The Frog Prince: An Autobiography.* New York: Crown, 1980.

Glendinning, Victoria. *Rebecca West.* London: Macmillan, 1988.

Gold, Herbert. "Running Aground in the Delta of Venus: My Night With AN." *Image* (3 May 1992): 20–23. Repr. in *Bohemia: Where Art, Angst, Love, and Strong Coffee Meet.* New York: Simon and Schuster, 1993.

Gordon, L. "Incest as Revenge Against the Preoedipal Mother." *Psychoanalytic Review* 42 (1955): 284–92.

Gottesman, Ronald, ed. *Critical Essays on HM.* New York: G. K. Hall, 1992.

Gottlieb, Elaine S. "New Fiction in America." *New York Herald Tribune Books* (8 Nov. 1942): 14.

Goyen, William. "Bits and Images of Life." *New York Times Book Review* (29 Nov. 1964): 5, 24.

Griffin, Barbara J. "Two Experimental Writers: Djuna Barnes and AN." In Maurice Duke and Jackson R. Bryer, eds., *American Women Writers: Bibliographical Essays.* Westport, CT: Greenwood, 1983.

Groutt, Kathleen Eleanor McKenna. "A Metahealth Analysis of the Lives of Gwendolyn Brooks, Dorothy Day, Ruth Gordon, AN, Georgia O'Keeffe." Ph.D. diss., University of Maryland, College Park, 1986.

Haffenden, John. *The Life of John Berryman.* Boston: Routledge and Kegan Paul, 1982.

Hamalian, Linda. *A Life of Kenneth Rexroth.* New York: Norton, 1991.

Hardwick, Elizabeth. "Fiction Chronicle." *Partisan Review* 15 (June 1948): 705–11.

Harms, Valerie, ed. *Celebration of AN.* Riverside, CT: Magic Circle Press, 1973.

————. *Stars in My Sky: Maria Montessori, AN, Frances Steloff.* New York: Magic Circle Press, 1976.

Hart, William. "Analysis of the Antagonism Inherent in the Human Struggle." *Houston Post* (16 Nov. 1947): Section 4, 21.

Haydn, Hiram. *Words and Faces*. New York: Harcourt Brace Jovanovich, 1974.

Haynes, Jim, ed. *Homage to HM*. Paris: Handshake Editions, n.d.

Henderson, Bill, ed. *The Pushcart Prize: Best of the Small Presses*. Yonkers, NY: Pushcart Books Press, 1976.

Henke, Susan. "AN: Bread and Wafer." *Under the Sign of Pisces* 7 (Spring 1980): 7–17.

Herman, Judith Lewis. *Trauma and Recovery*. New York: Basic Books, 1992.

Heymann, C. *A Woman Named Jackie*. New York: Carol, 1989.

Highwater, Jamake. *Shadow Show: An Autobiographical Insinuation*. New York: Alfred Van Der Mark Editions, 1986.

Hilscher-Wittgenstein, Herta. *The Ineffable Frances Steloff: A Photographic Visit, with Comments by AN and HM*. Chicago: Swallow Press, 1976.

Hinz, Evelyn J. "AN." In *Encyclopedia of World Literature in the Twentieth Century*. Rev. ed. New York: Ungar, 1983.

———. *The Mirror and the Garden: Realism and Reality in the Writings of AN*. Columbus: Ohio State University Libraries, 1971; New York: Harcourt Brace Jovanovich, 1973.

Hinz, Evelyn J., and Wayne Fraser, eds. *Mosaic* 11 (Winter 1978). "The World of Anaïs Nin: Critical and Cultural Perspectives." Special issue, critical essays. Winnipeg: University of Manitoba, 1978.

Hirschberg, Lynn. "The Misfit." *Vanity Fair* (Apr. 1991): 158–69, 198, 200, 202.

Hogarth, Patricia. "Fire and Exile." *The Spectator* 206 (26 May 1961): 771.

Holder, Orlee Elaina. "AN's Fiction: Proceeding From the Dream Outward." Ph.D. diss., University of New Mexico, 1982.

Houseman, John. *Final Days*. New York: Simon and Schuster, 1983.

Howard, H. S. "Incest—The Revenging Motive." *Delaware State Medical Journal* 31 (1959): 223–25.

Hunter, Jane H. "Inscribing the Self in the Heart of the Family: Diaries and Girlhood in Late-Victorian America." *American Quarterly* 44 (Mar. 1992): 51–81.

*In transition: A Paris Anthology*. New York: Doubleday, 1990.

James, Henry. *Parisian Sketches: Letters to the New York Tribune 1875–76*. Eds. Leon Edel and Ilse Dusoir Lind. London: Rupert Hart-Davies, 1958.

Janeway, Elizabeth. *Man's World, Woman's Place: A Study in Social Mythology*. New York: William Morrow, 1971.

Jason, Philip K. *AN and Her Critics*. Columbia, SC: Camden House, 1993.

Jelineck, Estelle C. "AN: A Critical Evaluation." In Cheryl L. Brown and Karen Olson, eds., *Feminist Criticism: Essays in Theory, Poetry, and Prose*, 312–32. Metuchan, NJ: Scarecrow, 1978.

Jones, Robert Wayne. "A Study of Imagery in AN's 'Cities of the Interior.'" Ph.D. diss., Miami University, 1976.

Jong, Erica. "Anne Sexton's River of Words." *New York Times* (17 Aug. 1991): Op Ed, 13.

———. *The Devil at Large: Erica Jong on HM*. New York: Turtle Bay, 1993.

Kahane, Jack. *Memoirs of a Booklegger*. London: Michael Joseph, 1939.

Kamboureli, Smaro. "Discourse and Intercourse, Design and Desire in the Erotica of AN." *Journal of Modern Literature* 11 (Mar. 1984): 143–58.

Kaufman, J., A. L. Peck, and C. K. Tagiuri. "The Family Constellation and Overt Incestuous Relations Between Father and Daughter." *American Journal of Orthopsychiatry* 245 (1954): 266–77.

K[ay], K[eith]. Review of *The Four-Chambered Heart*. San Francisco Chronicle (19 Feb. 1950): 14, 16.

———. Review of *Ladders to Fire*. San Francisco Chronicle (8 Dec. 1946), "This World," 11.

Kearney, Patrick J., comp. *The Private Case: An Annotated Bibliography of the Private Case Erotica Collection in the British (Museum) Library.* Intro. by Gershon Legman. London: Landesman, 1981.

Kennedy, J. Gerald. *Imagining Paris: Exile, Writing, and American Identity.* New Haven, CT: Yale University Press, 1993.

Kiernan, Robert F. *Gore Vidal.* New York: Frederick Ungar, 1982.

Kilday, Gregg. "UCLA Acquires AN Papers." *Los Angeles Times* 4 (15 June 1977): 20.

Killoh, Ellen Peck. "The Woman Writer and the Element of Destruction." *College English* 34 (Oct. 1972): 31–38.

Knapp, Bettina. *AN.* New York: Frederick Ungar, 1978.

———. "The Diary as Art: AN, Thornton Wilder, Edmund Wilson." *World Literature Today: A Literary Quarterly of the University of Oklahoma* 61 (Spring 1987): 223–30.

Knox, Irene Zubiel. "The Intuitive Quest in the Novels of AN: A Reader's Guide through the 'Cities of the Interior.'" Ph.D. diss., Fordham University, 1988.

Kraft, Barbara. "Lux Aeterna Anaïs: A Memoir." Unpublished manuscript, private archive. Three portions published in *Seahorse* 2, nos. 2–4 (1983): 1–5, 1–7, 6–16.

———. *The Restless Spirit: Journal of a Gemini.* Millbrae, CA: Les Femmes, 1976.

Kuntz, Paul Grimley. "Art as Public Dream: The Practice and Theory of AN." *Journal of Aesthetics and Art Criticism* 32 (1974): 525–37.

Kurth, Peter. *American Cassandra.* Boston: Little, Brown, 1990.

Lamm, Elyse Katherine. "A Necessary Artifice: A Phenomenology of the Performing Self Explored in the Life-Text of AN." Ph.D. diss., Northwestern University, 1990.

Lawrence, D. H. *Studies in Classic American Literature.* New York: Viking, 1961.

Leary, Timothy. *Changing My Mind, Among Others.* Englewood Cliffs, NJ: Prentice-Hall, 1982.

———. *Flashbacks, An Autobiography.* Los Angeles: J. P. Tarcher, 1983.

Legman, Gershorn. *The Horn Book: Studies in Erotic Folklore and Bibliography.* London: Jonathan Cape, 1964.

———. "On Faking HM." Unpublished manuscript, 1983.

———. "Peregrine Penis." Unpublished manuscript. Portion published as "Erotica of HM and AN: Chapter from the Memoirs of G. Legman." *Under the Sign of Pisces* 12 (Spring 1981): 9–18.

Lerman, Leo. "Catch up with . . ." *Mademoiselle* 60 (Mar. 1965): 80.

Leverich, Kathleen. "Nin, Master of Artifice, Effect." *The Christian Science Monitor* (10 Sept. 1982): B4.

Lieberman, E. James. *Acts of Will: The Life and Work of Otto Rank.* New York: Free Press, 1985.

Lindfors, Viveca. *Viveca.* New York: Everest House, 1981.

Lundberg, Christine. "Narrative Voice in AN's 'Cities.'" Ph.D. diss., Northwestern University, 1982.

Lyons, Herbert. "Surrealist Soap Opera." *New York Times Book Review* (20 Oct. 1946): 16.

McBrien, William. "AN: An Interview." *Twentieth Century Literature* 20 (Oct. 1974): 277–90.

McEvilly, Wayne. "The Bread of Tradition: Reflections on the Diary of AN." *Prairie Schooner* 45 (1971): 161–67.

McLaughlin, Richard. "Shadow Dance." *Saturday Review* 30 (20 Dec. 1947): 16–17.

McMath, Whitney Vickers. "Feminine Identity in AN's 'Cities.'" Ph.D. diss., University of Tennessee, 1978.

Madden, Deanna Kay. "Laboratory of the Soul: The Influence of Psychoanalysis on the Work of AN." Ph.D. diss., University of Miami, 1975.

Mailer, Norman. *Genius and Lust: A Journey Through the Major Writings of HM.* New York: Grove Press, 1976.

Maisch, H. *Incest.* Trans. C. Bearne. New York: Stein and Day, 1972.

Malina, Judith. *The Diaries of Judith Malina, 1947–1957.* New York: Grove Press, 1984.

Malone, Hank. *Survival, Evasion, and Escape.* La Jolla, CA: Poets Press, 1985.

Mariani, Paul. *William Carlos Williams: A New World Naked.* New York: McGraw-Hill, 1981.

Marks, Ben. "Recollections: Portrait of a Diarist." *Angeles* (Mar. 1991): 50–59.

Martin, Jay. *Always Merry and Bright: The Life of HM.* Santa Barbara, CA: Capra Press, 1978.

———. "HM Speech." 21 Oct. 1986, University of Southern California. Twenty-five page typescript.

Martin, Lex, Jr. "Modern Version of Old Fable: Woman Loses Femininity When She Enters Man's World," *Chicago Sun* (17 Nov. 1946), "Book Week," 14.

Masson, Jeffrey Moussaieff. *The Assault on Truth: Freud's Suppression of the Seduction Theory.* New York: Farrar, Straus and Giroux, 1983.

Mathieu, Bertrand. *Betty Ryan, La Dame d'Andros.* Charleville-Mazieres: Musée-Bibliothèque Arthur Rimbaud, 1983.

———. "The Eurydicean Matrix: Symbolism, Rimbaud, and the Gnostic Outlook in the Writings of AN." Unpublished manuscript.

———. *Orpheus in Brooklyn: Orphism, Rimbaud, and HM.* The Hague: Mouton, 1976.

Maynard, John Arthur. *Venice West: The Beat Generation in Southern California.* New Brunswick: Rutgers University Press, 1991.

Meckstroth, Patricia. "AN's Struggle to Publish." Master's thesis, University of Chicago Library School, 1976.

Meiselman, Karin C. *Incest: A Psychological Study of Causes and Effects with Treatment Recommendations.* San Francisco: Jossey-Bass, 1986.

Merchant, Hoshang. "The Aesthetics of AN: Ariadne within the Echo Chamber." *Panjab University Research Bulletin* 17 (Apr. 1986): 29–39.

———. "AN's Texts of Pleasure: A Woman's Ta Erotika." Ph.D. diss., University of Panjab, 1982.

———. *In-Discretions: AN.* Calcutta: Writers Workshop, 1990.

Mesic, Penelope. "An Appealing Chapter in the Young Nin's Story." *Chicago Tribune Book World* (20 Aug. 1978): 2.

Metzger, Deena. "Insight, Intuition, Dreams . . ." *Los Angeles Free Press* (30 Jan. 1970): 34.

————. *The Woman Who Slept With Men to Take the War Out of Them, and Trees.* Culver City, CA: Peace Press, 1981.

Miles, Barry. *Ginsberg: A Biography.* New York: Simon and Schuster, 1989.

Miller, Alice. *Drama of the Gifted Child: How Narcissistic Parents Form and Deform the Emotional Lives of Their Talented Children.* Originally published as *Prisoners of Childhood.* Trans. Ruth Ward. New York: Basic Books, 1981.

————. *Thou Shalt Not Be Aware: Society's Betrayal of the Child.* Trans. Hildegarde and Hunter Hannum. New York: Farrar, Straus and Giroux, 1984.

Miller, Henry. *The Air-Conditioned Nightmare.* New York: New Directions, 1945.

————. "AN: 1903–1977." *Proceedings of the American Academy and Institute of Arts and Letters* 2, no. 28 (1978): 100–101.

————. "Between Freud and HM." *The Village Voice* 26 (26 May 1966): 5–6.

————. *Black Spring.* Paris: Obelisk, 1936; New York: Grove Press, 1963.

————. *Book of Friends; A Trilogy.* Santa Barbara, CA: Capra Press, 1987.

————. *A Devil in Paradise.* New York: New American Library, 1956.

————. "Un Etre Etoilique." *The Criterion* 17 (Oct. 1937): 33–52. Repr. in *The Cosmological Eye,* 357–64. Norfork, CT: New Directions, 1939; 1961.

————. *First Impressions of Greece.* Santa Barbara, CA: Capra Press, 1973.

————. *Hamlet Letters.* Ed. Michael Hargraves. Santa Barbara, CA: Capra Press, 1988.

————. *HM Miscellanea.* Berkeley, CA: Bern Porter, 1945.

————. *Letters of HM and Wallace Fowlie, 1943–1972.* New York: Grove Press, 1975.

————. *Letters to AN.* Ed. Gunther Stuhlmann. New York: G. P. Putnam's Sons, 1965.

————. *Letters to Emil.* Ed. George Wickes. New York: New Directions, 1989.

————. *Max and the White Phagocytes.* Paris: The Obelisk Press, 1938.

————. *Quiet Days in Clichy.* New York: Grove Press, 1965.

————. *Sunday after the War.* Norfolk: CT: New Directions, 1944. Includes his "Letter to William Bradley" and "Letter to AN Regarding One of Her Books."

————. *The World of Lawrence.* Eds. Evelyn J. Hinz and John J. Teunissen. Santa Barbara, CA: Capra Press, 1980.

Millett, Kate. *Sexual Politics.* Garden City, New York: Doubleday, 1970.

Moos, Einar. Film transcript of *Une Amitié Parisienne.* Paris, 1987.

Morin, Jeanne. *Le Journal Migratoire d'AN (1919–1920): Lecture Schizoanalytique.* Université de Sherbrooke, Canada, 1990.

Mudrick, Marvin. "Humanity is the Principle." *Hudson Review* 7 (Winter 1955): 610–19.

Murray, Colin. Review of *Seduction of the Minotaur. Time and Tide* (1 June 1961): 915.

Nichols, Elizabeth P. "New Books Appraised—Fiction." *Library Journal* 74 (1 Dec. 1949): 1818.

Norman, Dorothy. *Encounters: A Memoir.* San Diego, CA: Harcourt Brace Jovanovich, 1987.

Norse, Harold. *Memoirs of a Bastard Angel: A Fifty-Year Literary and Erotic Odyssey.* New York: William Morrow, 1989.

————. "Never Fuck with Karma." *Hustler* (Oct. 1976).

Novinger, Elizabeth Ann. "Neurosis and Transformation: A Study of Women's Roles in the Fiction of AN." Ph.D. diss., Florida State University, 1982.

Oates, Bob. "Poetry in Motion." *Los Angeles Times* (17 July 1988): Sports, 3.

Oates, Joyce Carol. "A Gigantic Plea for Understanding." *New York Times Book Review* (13 July 1980): 7, 24.

O'Shaughnessey, Lynn. "A Broken Trust." *Los Angeles Times* (10 Aug. 1992): E1.

Paine, Sylvia. *Beckett, Nabokov, Nin: Motives and Modernism.* Port Washington, New York: Kennikat, 1981.

Peck, Abe. *Uncovering the Sixties.* New York: Pantheon, 1985.

Peck, Ellen Margaret McKee. "Exploring the Feminine: A Study of Janet Lewis, Ellen Glasgow, AN, and Virginia Woolf." Ph.D. diss., Stanford University, 1974.

Pelensky, Olga Anatasia. *Isak Dinesen: The Life and Imagination of a Seducer.* Athens, OH: Ohio University Press, 1991.

Perlès, Alfred. "HM in Villa Seurat," *Homage to HM.* Paris: Handshake Press, 1980.

———. *My Friend HM: An Intimate Biography.* New York: John Day, 1956.

———. *Sentiments Limitrophes.* Paris: Union Gén)éale d'Editions, 1987.

Peters, J. J. "Children Who Are Victims of Sexual Assault and the Psychology of Offenders." *American Journal of Psychotherapy* 30 (1976): 398–401.

*A Photographic Supplement to the Diary of Anaïs Nin.* Preface by Anaïs Nin. New York: Harcourt Brace Jovanovich, 1974.

Pierpont, Claudia Roth. "Sex, Lies, and Thirty-Five Thousand Pages." *The New Yorker* (1 Mar. 1993): 74–90.

Pine, Richard. *The Dandy and the Herald: Manners and Morals from Brummell to Durrell.* London: Macmillan, 1988.

Porter, Darwin. *Venus.* New York: Arbor House, 1982.

Potts, Margaret Lee. "The Genesis and Evolution of the Creative Personality: A Rankian Analysis of the Diary of AN Volumes I–V." Ph.D. diss., University of Southern California, 1973.

Pyly, Michael. "The Curious Double Life of Ian Hugo." *The Scotsman* (27 Aug. 1970).

Rainer, Tristine. *The New Diary: How to Use a Journal for Self-Examination and Expanded Creativity.* Los Angeles: Tarcher, 1978.

Rank, Otto. *Art and Artist: Creative Urge and Personality Development.* Trans. Charles Francis Atkinson. New York: Knopf, 1932; New York: Agathon Press, 1975.

———. *The Don Juan Legend.* Trans. and ed. David G. Winter. Princeton, NJ: Princeton University Press, 1975.

———. *The Double: A Psychoanalytical Study.* Trans. and ed. Harry Tucker, Jr. London: Maresfield Library, 1989.

———. *The Incest Theme in Literature and Legend.* Trans. Gregory C. Richter. Baltimore: Johns Hopkins University Press, 1973.

Reeves, Thomas G. *A Question of Character: A Life of John Fitzgerald Kennedy.* New York: Free Press, 1991.

Rexroth, Kenneth. "An Interview with Kenneth Rexroth," *Conjunctions* 1 (Winter 1981–82): 64.

Rexroth, Kenneth, and James Laughlin. *KR and JL: Selected Letters.* Ed. Lee Bartlett. New York: Norton, 1991.

Richard-Allerdyce, Diane. "The Feminine Creativity of AN: A Lacanian View." Ph.D. diss., University of Florida, 1988.

Robitaille, Gerald. *La Pere Miller: essai indiscret sur HM.* Paris: Eric Losfeld, 1971.

Rogers, W. G. *Wise Men Fish Here: The Story of Frances Steloff and the Gotham Book Mart.* New York: Harcourt, Brace and World, 1965.

Rolo, Charles. "Pot-Pourri." *The Atlantic* 194 (Aug. 1954): 86.

Rosenbaum, Ron. "Back in the High Life." *Vanity Fair* (Apr. 1988): 132–44, 154.

Rosenfeld, Isaac. "Psychoanalysis as Literature." *The New Republic* 113 (17 Dec. 1945): 844–45.

Rosenfeld, Paul. "Refinements on a Journal: *Winter of Artifice* by AN." *The Nation* 155 (26 Sept. 1942): 276–77.

Ryan [Gordon], Betty. "Close-Up 2 (AN in Paris, 1935–1939)." Unpublished manuscript, 6 pp. 9 Feb. 1991.

Salber, Linde. *AN*. Hamburg, Germany: Rowohlt, 1992.

Scholar, Nancy. *AN*. Boston: Twayne, 1984.

Schweitzer, Lea. "A Response to AN's Review of *At a Journal Workshop*." *Under the Sign of Pisces* 7 (Winter 1976): 5–8.

Secunda, Victoria. *Women and Their Fathers: The Sexual and Romantic Impact of the First Man in Your Life*. New York: Delacorte, 1992.

"Sex and Psychotherapy." *Newsweek* (13 Apr. 1992): 53–57.

Shapiro, Karl. "The Charmed Circle of AN." *Book Week* (1 May 1966): 3.

Sheed, Wilfrid. "Gore's Gospel." *The New Yorker* (26 Oct. 1992): 130–34.

Shengold, Leonard. *Soul Murder: The Effects of Childhood Abuse and Deprivation*. New Haven, CT: Yale University Press, 1989.

Smith, Harrison. "Ladies in Turmoil." *Saturday Review* 29 (30 Nov. 1946): 13.

Smith-Rosenberg, Carroll. "The New Woman as Androgyne: Social Disorder and Gender Crises, 1870–1936." In *Disorderly Conduct: Visions of Gender in Victorian America*. Ed. Victoria Wilson. New York, Knopf, 1985.

Snyder, Robert, ed. *AN Observed: From a Film Portrait of a Woman as Artist*. Chicago: Swallow Press, 1976.

Sontag, Susan. "Afterlives: The Case of Machado de Assis." *The New Yorker* (7 May, 1990): 102–8.

Spencer, Sharon. "The Art of Ragpicking." *The Widening Circle* 1 (Summer 1973): 20–21.

———. *Collage of Dreams: The Writings of AN*. Chicago: Swallow Press, 1977. Rev. ed., New York: Harcourt Brace Jovanovich, 1981.

———. "Delivering the Woman Artist from the Silence of the Womb: Otto Rank's Influence on AN." *The Psychoanalytic Review* 69, no. 1 (Spring 1982): 111–29.

———. "Femininity and the Woman Writer: Doris Lessing's *The Golden Notebook* and *The Diary of AN*." *Women's Studies: An Interdisciplinary Journal* 1 (1973): 247–57.

———. "Henry's Gift." In *Homage to HM*. Ed. Jim Haynes. Paris: Handshake Editions, n.d.

———. *Space, Time and Structure in the Modern Novel*. New York: New York University Press, 1971.

———, ed. *Anais, Art and Artists, a Collection of Essays*. Greenwood, FL: Penkeville, 1986.

Steloff, Frances. "Gotham Book Mart: Memoirs." *Intellectual Digest* (Dec. 1977): 92.

———. "In Touch With Genius." *Journal of Modern Literature* 4 (Apr. 1975): 827–30.

Stern, Daniel. "The Novel of Her Life." *The Nation* 213 (29 Nov. 1971): 570–73.

Stone, Albert E. *Autobiographical Occasions and Original Acts: Versions of American Identity from Henry Adams to Nate Shaw*. Philadelphia: University of Pennsylvania Press, 1982.

Stone, Jerome. "Fiction Note: The Psyche of the Huntress." *Saturday Review* 37 (15 May 1954): 32.

Stone, Laurie. "AN: Is the Bloom off the Pose?" *The Village Voice* 21 (26 July 1976): 43–44.

———. "Becoming a Woman in Male America: Margaret Mead and AN." In *Autobiographical Occasions and Original Acts: Versions of American Identity from Henry Adams to Nate Shaw, 190–230.* Philadelphia: University of Pennsylvania Press, 1982.

Sukenick, Lynn. "The Diaries of AN." *Shenandoah* 17 (Spring 1976): 96–103.

———. "Sense and Sensibility in Women's Fiction: Studies in the Novels of George Eliot, Virginia Woolf, AN, and Doris Lessing." Ph.D. diss., City University of New York, 1974.

Taft, Jessie. *Otto Rank: A Biographical Study Based on Notebooks, Letters, Collected Writings, Therapeutic Achievements and Personal Association.* New York: Julian Press, 1952.

Telander, Rick. "Understanding AN." *Chicago Sun-Times* (19 Mar. 1972): Midwest Magazine, 16.

"Tribute for AN." *International College Newsletter* (Spring 1977): 1, 4.

Trilling, Diana. Review of *This Hunger. The Nation* 162 (26 Jan. 1946): 105–7.

Tytell, John. *Passionate Lives.* New York: Carol, 1991.

Vidal, Gore. *Live from Golgatha: The Gospel According to Gore Vidal.* New York: Random House, 1992.

———. "Taking a Grand Tour of AN's High Bohemia Via the Time Machine." *Los Angeles Times Book Review* (26 Sept. 1971), 1, 5, 23. Repr. as "The Fourth Diary of AN." In *Homage to Daniel Shays: Collected Essays, 1952–1972.* 403–9. New York: Random House, 1972.

———. *Two Sisters: A Memoir in the Form of a Novel.* Boston: Little, Brown, 1970.

Vidal, Gore, and Robert J. Stanton. *Views from a Window: Conversations with Gore Vidal.* Secaucus, NJ: Lyle Stuart, 1980.

Wagstaff, Christopher, ed. *Robert Duncan: Drawings and Decorated Books.* Exhibition catalog. Berkeley: University of California Press, 1992.

Walker, Alice. "AN: 1903–1977." *Ms.* 5 (Apr. 1977): 46.

Walker, John. "A 7-Minute Epic Caps His Career." *International Herald Tribune* (14 Sept. 1970).

Wallerstein, Judith. *Second Chances: Men, Women, and Children a Decade After Divorce.* New York: Ticknor and Fields, 1989.

Watts, Alan. *In My Own Way: An Autobiography 1915–1965.* New York: Random House, 1972.

West, Herbert Faulkner. *The Impecunious Amateur Looks Back: The Autobiography of a Bookman.* Hanover, NH: Westholm, 1966.

Wickes, George, ed. *Lawrence Durrell/Henry Miller: A Private Correspondence.* New York: E. P. Dutton, 1963.

Williams, William Carlos. "Men . . . Have No Tenderness: AN's 'Winter of Artifice.'" In James Laughlin, ed., *New Directions No. 7* 429–36. Norfolk, CT: New Directions, 1942.

———. *Patterson.* New York: New Directions, 1963.

Wilson, Edmund. "Books—Doubts and Dreams: *Dangling Man* and *Under a Glass Bell.*" *The New Yorker* 20 (1 Apr. 1944): 78–82.

———. "Books—Isherwood, Marquand, AN." *The New Yorker* 22 (10 Nov. 1945): 97–98, 101–2.

———. "Books—A Note on AN." *The New Yorker* 22 (16 Nov. 1946): 114.

———. *The Forties.* Ed. Leon Edel. New York: Farrar, Straus and Giroux, 1983.

Winnicott, D. W. *The Family and Individual Development.* London: Tavistock, 1965.

———. *The Maturation Processes and the Facilitating Environment: Studies in the Theory of Emotional Development.* London: Hogarth, 1965.

Winslow, Kathryn. *HM: Full of Life.* New York: St. Martin's Press, 1986.

Wolcott, James. "Life Among the Ninnies." *New York Review of Books* (26 June 1980): 21.

Wolfe, Bernard. *Memoirs of a Not Altogether Shy Pornographer.* Garden City, New York: Doubleday, 1972.

Young, Marguerite. "Marguerite Young on AN." *Voyages: A National Literary Magazine* 1 (Fall 1967): 63–67.

Zaller, Robert, ed. *A Casebook on AN.* New York: New American Library, 1974.

Zee, Nancy Scholar. "AN: Beyond the Mask." Ph.D. diss., Brown University, 1973.

Zinnes, Harriet. "AN's World Reissued." *Books Abroad* 37 (Summer 1963): 283–86.

# Index

(Short stories and novels of AN are indexed alphabetically under Nin, Anaïs—works, fiction; all other subentries are arranged in order of appearance in the text.)

Erskine, John (*continued*)
AN, 77, 85–86, 87, 120; affair with Lilith,
80, 83, 84, 85, 97, 98; sexual relationship
with AN, 85, 87, 89, 96, 97–98, 101–102;
in AN's writing, 102, 111; blurb for AN's
Lawrence book, 119–120
Erskine, Pauline, 69, 79, 80
Evans, Oliver, 359–360, 366, 370, 378, 382
*Eve*, 337, 338, 341, 352
*Experimental Review*, 230, 247

*Fair Sex*, 352
Fanchette, Jean, 338, 355, 405; article on
AN, 340–342; as publisher of *Two Cities*,
340–343, 345, 346, 356
*Female Eunuch, The* (Greer), 393
feminism, 8, 69, 369, 393, 394–395
Ferlinghetti, Lawrence, 301, 334, 343, 374
Ferrone, John, 398, 408
Field, Frances. *See* Robinson, Frances Fox
*Finnegans Wake* (Joyce), 94, 220, 225
Flanner, Janet, 92
*Four Poems* (Vail), 256
Fowlie, Wallace, 267, 268, 271, 303, 340
Fraenkel, Michael, 131, 143, 210; friendship
with Miller, 126, 127, 171; and publication
of AN's books, 186, 187, 189, 192–193
France, Anatole, 57, 59, 61, 167
Francis, Mako, 376
Frank, Waldo, 182
Franklin, Benjamin, V, 8, 382–383, 392, 402
Fredericks, Millicent, 234
Freud, Sigmund, 7, 12, 22, 67, 321, 322;
AN's reading of, 95, 96, 97; Oedipal theory,
124–125, 152; seduction theory, 151–152;
and Rank, 163–164; belief in occult, 195;
and homosexuality, 279
Friar, Kimon, 274, 282, 315
Friends of Shakespeare and Company (Paris),
212, 225
Fruman, Norman, 361
Fuller, R. Buckminster, 400

*Galahad* (Erskine), 69
Gamez, Tana de, 49, 50–51, 350–351
Gary, Romain, 334–335
Gascoyne, David, 203
Gavronsky, Serge, 342–343, 360
Geber, Nils-Hugo, 348
Geismar, Anne, 306, 310, 311
Geismar, Maxwell, 314, 324–325, 339; and
publication of AN's diaries, 5, 311, 319,
373, 380–381; assessment of AN's writing,
5, 311, 321, 395; on Rank, 180; friendship
with AN, 306, 310–311, 321; review of *A
Spy in the House of Love*, 321
Gemor Press, 254, 264, 265, 269
Gernreich; Rudi, 318, 378
Gide, André, 79, 138, 212

Gilbert, Stuart, 179, 193, 203, 205, 212, 348
Ginsberg, Allen, 315, 316, 329, 334, 363
Girodias, Maurice, 279
Glanville-Hicks, Peggy, 306–307, 314, 321,
395
Godoy, Armand, 82
Gold, Herbert, 263
*Gondola Eye, The* (film), 345
Gore, Nina, 276
Gotham Book Mart (New York), 225, 253,
281, 291, 361, 378
Gotlieb, Howard, 406
Goyen, William, 337, 369
Graham, Martha, 285, 311–312
Graves, Edward, 78
Greer, Germaine, 393
Guérin, Eugénie de, 36
Guggenheim, Hazel, 286, 287
Guggenheim, Peggy, 256
Guicciardi, Horace, 58–59, 62, 66–67, 78, 220
Guiler, Edith (sister of Hugo), 39, 42
Guiler, Ethel (sister of Hugo), 139, 161
Guiler, Hugh (father of Hugo), 41, 58, 78, 79
Guiler, Mrs. Hugh (mother of Hugo), 58, 78
Guiler, Hugh Parker ("Hugo"; also known as
Ian Hugo): courtship of AN, 39, 41–43, 44,
46–48, 49–50; banking career, 41, 53, 56,
63, 69, 72, 81, 204, 222, 247, 265, 330;
correspondence with AN, 49, 50, 110, 178;
financial successes, 69, 82; dancing lessons,
75, 309; father's death and, 78; financial
difficulties, 88, 157, 176, 360; admiration
for Miller, 104, 131; and June Miller, 105,
106–108; in psychoanalysis, 133–135, 142,
168, 171, 308, 330; and Artaud, 143, 148;
interest in astrology, 143, 157, 195; painting
lessons, 203; transfer to London, 204, 206,
215–216, 217; and Lawrence and Nancy
Durrell, 207, 208, 216; transfer to New
York, 222, 246–247; becomes Ian Hugo,
251, 261, 265; engravings by, 251–252,
253, 259, 261, 265, 266, 269; retirement
from banking, 265, 300; as filmmaker, 278,
280, 293, 300, 305, 306, 320, 330, 333,
348, 356, 363, 379, 383, 385, 397; as
stockbroker, 300, 345; Maxwell Geismar
and, 310–311; and Caresse Crosby, 349;
death of, 414
—marriage to AN, 76–77, 86, 222, 247, 265,
377, 411; in AN's fiction, 16, 83, 308;
wedding ceremony, 50–51, 52; vacations
together, 52, 56, 66, 69–70, 89–90, 191,
220, 221, 227, 294, 320, 324, 326, 338,
345, 348, 356, 385, 404; Rosa's disapproval
of, 52–53; Guiler family's disapproval of,
53, 70, 79; sexual relations, 53–54, 55, 59,
68, 73, 76, 96, 97, 98, 101, 102, 114, 115,
120; encouragement of AN's writing, 54,
55, 56, 68, 89, 95; in AN's diaries, 54, 55,